DEDICATION

For Jack, whose untimely passing deprived him of the pleasure of seeing his dedicated scholarship materialize in this wonderful edition. With thanks to the many individuals and institutions, both Japanese and American, who graciously introduced us to Japanese culture and history, beginning in 1968. Those introductions resulted in our enduring love and appreciation of Japan. Special thanks to Keiko Garrison, the Kyoto City Tourism Office, and the Japan National Tourism Organization for their help in obtaining additional photos for this book The authors would further like to acknowledge the Tuttle staff who helped to prepare this book notably Angie Ang, Bob Graham and Fajar Wisnu Hardono.

Published by Tuttle Publishing, an imprint of Periplus Editions (HK) Ltd

www.tuttlepublishing.com

Copyright © 2010 John H. Martin and Phyllis G. Martin

Library of Congress Cataloging-in-Publication Data

Martin, John H.
  Kyoto : 29 walks in Japan's ancient capital / written by John H. and Phyllis G. Martin. – 1st. bilingual ed.
      376 p. : col. ill., col. maps ; 21 cm.
  In English and Japanese.
  Includes bibliographical references and index.
  ISBN 978-4-8053-0918-6 (pbk.)
  1. Kyoto (Japan)–Guidebooks. 2. Walking–Japan–Kyoto–Guidebooks. 3. Historic buildings–Japan–Kyoto–Guidebooks. 4. Historic sites–Japan–Kyoto–Guidebooks. 5. Kyoto (Japan)–Buildings, structures, etc.–Guidebooks. I. Martin, Phyllis G. II. Title.
  DS897.K83M35 2010
  915.2'1864045–dc22
  2009048495

ISBN 978-4-8053-0918-6

Distributed by

North America, Latin America & Europe
Tuttle Publishing
364 Innovation Drive
North Clarendon, VT 05759-9436 USA
Tel: 1 (802) 773-8930
Fax: 1 (802) 773-6993
info@tuttlepublishing.com
www.tuttlepublishing.com

Japan
Tuttle Publishing
Yaekari Building, 3rd Floor
5-4-12 Osaki
Shinagawa-ku
Tokyo 141 0032
Tel: (81) 3 5437-0171
Fax: (81) 3 5437-0755
sales@tuttle.co.jp
www.tuttle.co.jp

Asia Pacific
Berkeley Books Pte Ltd
3 Kallang Sector #04-01
Singapore 349278
Tel: (65) 6741-2178
Fax: (65) 6741-2179
inquiries@periplus.com.sg
www.periplus.com

23 22 21 20 19
10 9 8 7 6 5 4

Printed in China   1908RR

Kyoto

29 Walks in Japan's Ancient Capital

JOHN H. MARTIN AND PHYLLIS G. MARTIN

TUTTLE Publishing

Tokyo | Rutland, Vermont | Singapore

CONTENTS

Left: *The graceful Golden Pavilion at Kinkaku-ji.*

INTRODUCTION

Kyoto and Its Heritage

If one were limited to visiting a single city in Japan, there is no question that Kyoto would be the preferred choice. As the ancient capital of Japan, from its inception in 794 it set the cultural tone for the nobility, the Imperial court and eventually the nation at large. It also welcomed the various Buddhist sects that were to develop in Japan and which were to affect the beliefs of commoners and courtiers alike. Politics being what they are, the Buddhist temples were at first kept at arm's length by having them built on the surrounding hills rather than on the plain in the city proper. The interference of Buddhist monks in the previous capital at Nara was not going to be tolerated by the Emperor and his court in their new location, and thus few temples could be found in central Kyoto in the capital's early days. Now, 1,300 years after the city was established, the temples, shrines, gardens and remaining palaces of the Emperor and his nobles, scattered throughout and around Kyoto, provide an ambience that few other cities can offer.

To experience the essence of Kyoto, one should walk its avenues and streets, its alleys and byways. Only in this way can one appreciate the spirit of the place—its quiet lanes and bustling main thoroughfares, and its juxtaposition of houses and shops, temples and shrines, gardens and industries. Such an approach may seem to offer difficulties since many cities in Japan are centuries old and have streets laid out in a winding and seemingly incoherent pattern. Unlike many cities in Japan, however, Kyoto has a very orderly city plan based on streets which intersect at right angles. This systematic, regular plan reflects the fascination of the founders of Kyoto with the ancient Chinese capital of Ch'ang-an (present-day Xian) whose orderly street plan it copied. Specific main streets as well as the major rivers further subdivided this plan so that the grid pattern of Kyoto streets makes it an easy city in which to roam. Armed with the tourist map provided at the Tourist Information Center and a small compass (if one's sense of direction is fallible), you are unlikely to get lost. (The Tourist Information Center is on Karasuma-dori, the street headed north alongside the lighthouse-like tower, opposite the north side of Kyoto Central Station and the outdoor bus station.)

Where did it all begin for Kyoto? When in 794 the Emperor Kammu planned his new capital at Heian-kyo, the early name for Kyoto, he provided it with an auspicious descriptive name, since Heian-kyo means "Capital of Peace and Tranquility." The new capital was to enjoy peace and tranquility in its early years, a status which, unhappily, had all too quickly evaporated at the previous seat of government in Nara, 30 miles (48 km) to the south. There, the great Emperor Shomu, who had developed the grandeur of Nara, had been followed on the throne by his daughter, a woman too easily influenced by the men in her life. Unfortunate in her judgment and in her reliance on those about her, one of her lovers had been her prime minister who eventually rose in revolt against her rule while another lover was a Buddhist priest who had

Chishaku-in, opposite Kyoto National Museum.

Right: *The forested Arashiyama mountain range on the outskirts of Kyoto.*

intentions of usurping her throne. At the same time, the temples of Nara, meant to engender piety and to protect the state, were all too often controlled by priests who preferred to dabble in politics rather than keep to their religious profession. In order to govern, as the Empress's successor discovered, an Emperor was forced to deal with unnecessary political intrigue and unseemly infighting within the court and the Buddhist hierarchy.

Thus the Emperor Kammu, in order to escape the pernicious priests and meddlers in Imperial affairs, moved his capital in 784 to Nagaoka, today a suburb of Kyoto. Then, when that location proved inauspicious, he decided to create the new capital of Heian-kyo on the site of present-day Kyoto. This new center of Japanese governance was to be ruled by the Emperor without the interference in political matters of the Buddhist clergy who had bedeviled the court in Nara. Thus, the Emperor Kammu decreed that Buddhist temples were not to be located within the city limits. While he was a pious ruler and not opposed to the Buddhist faith, he saw a need to separate church and state so that each could remain paramount within its own realm. As a result, the earliest temples in Kyoto (with one exception) were forced to develop outside the confines of the original capital; the hills about the city have thus been enriched with the Buddhist temples whose buildings, gardens, images and art treasures can still be enjoyed today by both local residents and foreign visitors.

The hills surrounding Kyoto were inevitably attractive to the nobles of the court as well as to emperors and princes. Thus mansions and palaces in the early Japanese *shoin* (palace) style were built on the outskirts of Kyoto. Many such edifices were to become temples upon the death of their owners, and although fires and wars have often destroyed such buildings, they have been rebuilt after each catastrophe, sometimes with a greater glory than previously. They remain to this day as reminders of an historic past as well as attractive sites for modern-day visitors.

A city composed of wood is prey to earthquakes, fires and floods—and to the destruction of war. Although some of the major sites in Kyoto have their roots in the ancient past, the present buildings are most often later reconstructions along traditional lines. The glory that was Kyoto in its "Golden Age" in the years between 800 and 1200 was to disappear in the next three centuries.

In particular, the later era know as Sengoku Jidai (The Age of the Country at War) in the 1400s and 1500s saw the virtual destruction of the city and its population. Two opposing Japanese armies were camped to the north and to the south of the city, Kyoto itself being the battlefield for a war which went on endlessly until both sides were exhausted and the city was devastated.

The clipped bush Yuseien Garden at Sanzen-in Temple in Ohara.

The return of peace under the generals Oda Nobunaga and Toyotomi Hideyoshi in the second half of the 16th century saw a gradual resurgence of life in Kyoto. When the pioneering Christian missionary Francis Xavier, one of the first Europeans to visit Kyoto, arrived in the city in 1551, he described it in a letter: "... formerly it had 18,000 houses.... Now, in fact, it is destroyed."

Xavier was simply reporting what a Japanese official had recorded in a more poetic way years previously when he described the capital as "... an empty field from which the evening skylark rises with a song and descends among tears."

Conditions had sunk to so deplorable an economic level in the mid-1500s that a contemporary document describes the Imperial Palace in terms which could well fit a peasant's hut. The Imperial income itself had declined to a point where the Emperor was reduced to selling the Imperial household treasures—as well as his autograph to anyone who would pay for it.

It was under the dictatorial but benevolent rule of Toyotomi Hideyoshi from 1582 to 1598 that Kyoto was rebuilt and began to prosper once more. With peace and the movement of many of the peasants from the countryside to the cities, the population of Kyoto was quickly restored. These newcomers soon became involved in commerce and the crafts, and within a few brief years a cultural and economic renaissance was under way. Temples and shrines were rebuilt, palaces and mansions of unparalleled splendor were erected, commerce flourished, and the citizens of Kyoto came to view their political ruler, Hideyoshi, almost as a god. The 35 years from the death of Nobunaga in 1581 (Hideyoshi's predecessor) to the death of Tokugawa Ieyasu (who succeeded Hideyoshi) mark the height of Kyoto's revival as well as the flourishing of the ostentatious Momoyama period of art.

Although Kyoto's glory shone less brightly once the capital of the Shoguns was moved to Edo (Tokyo) in the early 1600s, Kyoto remained the center of traditional culture for the nation as well as the home of the Emperor and his court. The city retained the aura of sophistication which had been its heritage, as well as the sensibility to beauty for which it had always been noted and which it never lost—a sensibility its brasher successor in Edo could never hope to achieve.

A manicured rock garden at Ryogen-in.

Even the departure of the Imperial court from Kyoto to Tokyo after 1868 has not dimmed the importance of the city. Its ability to retain the essence of Japanese culture is the main element for which Kyoto has always been valued, and the multifaceted culture of many centuries continues to flourish despite the sprawl of a modern, major world city beset with all the problems of the present century. Thus it is that millions of visitors continue to come to Kyoto each year to enjoy the city's traditions, its arts and crafts and the inspiration offered by its plethora of Buddhist temples and Shinto shrines, as well as its many private and public museums and its continually aesthetically satisfying gardens, palaces and villas.

There are various ways in which one can approach a city with treasures as vast and varied as those of Kyoto. One could search out its heritage chronologically from the earliest surviving buildings to its most modern structures. One could visit its religious edifices according to their affiliation—Zen temples, Shinto shrines and so forth—or one could concentrate on its palaces, its gardens, its literary associations or its museums. All are valid approaches.

Instead, in this guidebook, Kyoto's grid pattern of streets has been used as the basis of the approach since the city's fine transportation network permits one easily to explore the city segment by segment. (Those interested in specific sites can readily find them through the Contents or the Index.)

Ryoan-ji, Japan's most popular Zen garden, composed of gravel beds and moss-encircled rocks.

While the city spreads from the Higashi-yama mountains at its eastern perimeter to the mountains of Arashiyama and the Saga section to the west, it is easiest to divide the city into its central, eastern, western, northern and southern sectors in order to encompass the magnitude of the sites to be seen and make it easier for visitors to enjoy individual sites that can be visited. Thus each of these sectors is divided into "Tours" which can occupy a morning or an afternoon, and which can be left at any point to be returned to at another time if one wants a break. Directions are given from the bus stop nearest the site to be visited, and the map of bus routes on the Tourist Information Center map indicates the major bus routes in the city. Although these site visits are set up primarily for walking tours, occasionally a bus ride between sites is indicated for those who do not want a long walk. Naturally, taxis provide the easiest means of travel from within the city, and they can provide the most expeditious transportation to the various sites of interest. Thus the first part of the guide to Kyoto begins with the central portion, which lies to the east, and then the west of the Kamo-gawa (Kamo River—*gawa* means "river"). Each section begins with a brief introduction to the major sites in the area under consideration. The temples, shrines, palaces or villas which follow are then introduced, with directions for reaching the sites, the days and hours they are open to visitors, and whether a fee is charged for entry. The historical and cultural background of each site follows, and then

the present status of the site is described in detail. The festivals or ceremonies associated with the site complete the individual entries.

Although Kyoto was established in 794 when the Emperor Kammu moved the capital, first from Nara in 784 to Nagaoka (a suburb of Kyoto today) and then to Kyoto 10 years later, the city retains some vestiges of its early days. Its orderly street plan laid out on the plain within the encircling hills to the west, north and east, and its two main rivers, the Kamo-gawa to the east and the Katsura-gawa to the west, are enduring physical vestiges of those early years. Other enduring elements of the earlier city are of a more spiritual and cultural nature. These elements can be seen in the zest for life of Kyoto's residents as manifested in the city's festivals, the continuing artistic sophistication as represented in its crafts and arts, and the appreciation of its special architectural treasures which have been preserved or rebuilt after each disaster suffered by the capital and its inhabitants.

This book is organized into a series of 29 walking tours in and around Kyoto. Map 1 shows the location of the tours in Kyoto City; Map 2 shows the location of tours outside the city proper. The length of each walking tour varies, but each can be completed within a few hours, depending on how long one wishes to linger. All of the most popular sites are included, together with some spots that may be unfamiliar even to long-time residents. The first walking tour of Kyoto begins with one of the older sections of the city, a sector which retains the physical aspects of an earlier age.

Kyoto's Subway and Railway Network

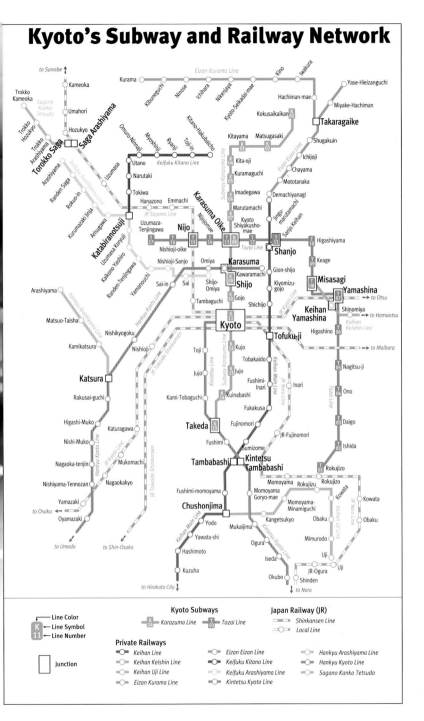

卍 *Torin-in*

SEE NIJŌ CASTLE AREA MAP PAGE 116

Chapter 1
CENTRAL
AND EASTERN
KYOTO

Prefectural
Gymnasium

Kyoto Brighton
Shimo-chōjamachi-dō

Aoibashi
Family Clinic

Shimodachiuri-dōri
Juttoku

NHK
New Kyoto
Marutamachi-dōri

Harvest Kyoto

Senbon-dōri

Nijō Castle
★ **9**
Nijojomae

Kokusai
ANA

Kamanza
Shinmachi-dōri

Oshikōji-dōri

Nishiōji-Oike   Tōzai Line
Oike-dōri

Nijō

Oike-dōri
Dental Clinic

Aneyakōji-dōri
Horikawa Inn

Oike-dōri

Yamanouchi

Nijōjinya
Sanjo-dōri

Sanjō-dōri

Rokkaku-dōri

Muromachi-dōri

Nishiōji
Sanjo

Onmae-dōri

Goin-dōri

Takoyakushi-dōri

Nishikikōji-dōri

Onishi
Seiemon
Museum

Takayakush

Sai-in
Den Shichi ®

Shijo-dōri
Ōmiya   Hankyu Kyoto Line

SAIIN

Sai-in

MIBU

Keifuku Arashiyama Line

Ōmiya
Ayanokōji-dōri

Mystays

Court Hotel
Kyoto-Shijō

Karasuma
Nikkō Princess

Bukkōji-dō

Mibudera Bukkōji-dō

Takatsuji-dōri
Manjuji-dōri

Matsubara-dōri

Municipal
Hospital

Matsubara-dōri

Kadai
Yuzen-en
Gallery

Takatsuji-dōri

Manjuji-dōri

Jusco

Gojo-dōri

SUJAKU

Kyoto
Research Park

Chudoji-dōri

Tōkyu

Yuzen Cultural Hall

10

Sumiya
Banquet
Cultural
Museum

Hanayamachi-
dōri
Shomen-dōri

Nishi-
Hongan-ji

Ryukoku
University

Higashi-
Hongan-ji

Shichijo-dōri

Central
Wholesale
Market

Crossroads Inn

Shichijō-dōri

8

Shin-Hankyu

Kyoto
Tower

UMEKOJI

SEE SHIMABARA MAP PAGE 138

Umekōji Park

Rihga Royal

Shiokōji-dōri

Steam
Locomotive
Museum

**KYOTO
STATION**

Hachijo-dōri

SEE HONGAN-JI AREA MAP PAGE 103
Hachijō-dōri

New Miyako

**KISSHŌIN-
SHINDEN**

Nishioji

KARAHASHI

Kanchi-in
College

To-ji
10

Kujō-dōri

Dai-ichi
Kyoto Teresa

SEE TO-JI TEMPLE MAP PAGE 132
Kujō-dōri

Kyoto
Minami
Kaikan

HIGASHI-

Kisshō-in
Tenmangu Shrine

Jujō-dōri

Jujō-dōri

KISSHŌIN

KAMITOBA

Walking Tour 1

Ancient Lanes to Kiyomizu Temple

In the years since World War II, Kyoto has changed greatly. The city of one-story traditional houses has seen modern buildings of extraordinary height rise in its midst. Travelers often come to Kyoto looking for a traditional Japanese city of low buildings and architecture of past centuries. Instead, they are amazed by the modern steel, glass and brick structures they find. Kyoto, as with every other city in the world, continues to grow and to change, for it cannot remain a museum frozen in time. Yet there is strong concern in Kyoto about the continuing danger to the city's historic nature and architectural heritage. There are ongoing attempts to preserve the best of the past in its temples and shrines as well as in its traditional housing. This initial walk therefore takes place in an area which has been designated as an historic section worthy of preservation, and it ends at one of the most venerable of Kyoto's temples, Kiyomizu-dera (Clear Water Temple). This walk accordingly offers a partial glimpse of the city as it existed prior to the modernization of Japan in the 20th century.

1 NINEN-ZAKA AND SANNEN-ZAKA

One could walk straight up sloping Kiyomizu-zaka from the bus stop to the temple, but a deviation two streets to the north along Higashi-oji-dori (the main north–south street)

Ninen-zaka, a pedestrian street lined with traditional shops and restaurants leading to Kiyomizu-dera.

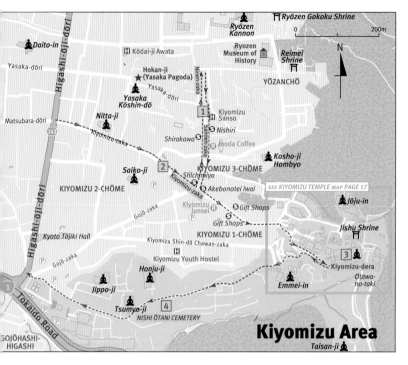

Kiyomizu Area

Taisan-ji

ffers a worthwhile diversion. Two streets
) the north, turn to the right on to Kodai
Minami Monzen-dori. At the second street
n the right, turn again to the right and climb
p the steps to Ninen-zaka (Two Year Slope)
) begin a walk into the past. This offers a
icture of the city of Kyoto as it once was.
ires have destroyed so much of old Kyoto
hrough the centuries that it is unusual to
nd an area that still provides the appear-
nce of a Japanese city before the modern
ge. Fortunately, Ninen-zaka and Sannen-
aka (Three Year Slope) offer just such a
ememberance of times past. Concerned over
he disappearance of the two-story shops
nd homes which were typical of Kyoto city
fe, the city government has created a few
historic preservation districts" in areas
vhich have remained comparatively un-
hanged. One such area encompasses
linen-zaka and Sannen-zaka.

For centuries pilgrims labored up Ninen-
aka and Sannen-zaka on their way to Kyo-
nizu Temple. (The strange names for these
treets have their basis in a superstition: to
tumble on Ninen-zaka brought two years
f misfortune, while a fall on Sannen-zaka

could result in three years of bad luck.) Here,
on these streets, the pilgrims found small
restaurants which offered food, inns which
provided a place to sleep and shops which
sold the Kiyomiza-yaki and the Awata-yaki
(*yaki* means "pottery") as souvenirs of a visit
to the temple, pottery which was made in the
stepped *noborigama* kilns that were formerly
ubiquitous on this hillside. Pilgrims still
climb these slopes, as do thousands of tourists. The narrow two-story wood and plaster
row houses one finds along the way once
covered all of Kyoto, and although frequently
destroyed by fire, they were always rebuilt in
the traditional architectural style with the
shop at the front and the family living quarters behind the sales area. Normally only 26
feet (7.9 m) wide, the buildings often extended as much as 131 feet (39.9 m) to the rear.
Some of them were two-story structures that
had narrow slatted windows at the front of
the second floor. Since it was forbidden for
commoners to look down upon passing *samurai* (warrior class) or *daimyo* (feudal lords),
the narrow, slatted windows could help to
hide the faces and eyes of curious merchant
families if they dared to peer in forbidden

fashion on their superiors passing beneath them. The great fire of 1864 destroyed 80 percent of Kyoto, and thus these buildings represent the latest rebuilding of the traditional cityscape prior to modern times.

Today's shops, with perhaps one or two exceptions, have modern storefronts and interiors. In the past, the shop consisted of a raised platform on which the merchant sat and perhaps even created the wares he sold. The would-be purchaser was always welcomed with a cup of tea so that a proper mood could be established before the merchant's wares were brought forth and displayed in front of the purchaser. Modern life seldom allows for such niceties, and thus the present shops are more oriented toward a contemporary display of chinaware or whatever is currently desired by the public. Ninen-zaka and Sannen-zaka are lined with old buildings which still serve as purveyors to the pilgrim and the tourist, although one must admit that tourists seem to be the main clients to whom the shopkeepers now appeal. But then, weren't pilgrims of past centuries souvenir seekers as well? For sale here are small Buddhas, iron lanterns, scarves–all the paraphernalia of an ephemeral trade which the visitor cannot resist. A few restaurants tempt the hungry with the variety of noodles such Japanese establishments offer, and, of course, the soft drinks of the modern age. One enterprising shopkeeper on Ninen-zaka even has a rickshaw in which one can be photographed or even transported, the latter, naturally, for an appropriate fee. A few rickshaws do still exist, but their day is past, and those which remain appear primarily at times of festivals.

Traditional Kiyomizu-yaki pottery is sold in shops along Kiyomizu-zaka.

② KIYOMIZU-ZAKA

Ninen-zaka bends gracefully, as a proper traditional Japanese street should, and ends in a short staircase which leads into Sannen-zaka. In turn, Sannen-zaka also ends in a steeper set of steps which lead up to Kiyomizu-zaka (Clear Water Slope). As has been the case for the past several centuries, pottery can be found for sale along both Ninen-zaka and Sannen-zaka, but you will noy encounter the full panoply of chinaware until you climb the steps at the southern end of Sannen-zaka and enter Kiyomizu-zaka, which leads uphill from Higashi-oji-dori to the Kiyomizu-dera Temple at the top of the street. In the last century, English-speaking visitors nicknamed Kiyomizu-zaka "Teapot Lane," a name it still

deserves. Here you can find shops which sell Kiyomizu-yaki (Kiyomizu pottery) and other chinaware. Souvenir shops line the street cheek by jowl. The street is always crowded with visitors heading to the temple, many in groups led by their banner-waving leader. It is always a street full of excitement and color during the daytime.

The making of porcelain was a craft and an art which began to flourish in Kyoto as a result of the incursions into Korea in 1592 and 1597 by Japanese troops under the command of Toyotomi Hideyoshi, the then civil and military ruler of Japan. The Koreans had learned the craft from the Chinese, and such products were appropriately summed up in one word in English-speaking countries as "chinaware." Among the prizes of war brought back to Japan in the 1590s were Korean ceramic craftsmen and artists, and a fascination with their work led in time to the development of fine Japanese porcelains. The cult of tea, which developed under Sen-no-Rikyu, with the patronage of Hideyoshi, in the late 1500s, also encouraged the development of the Japanese ceramic craft. Once there were 10 different schools or styles of pottery hereabouts; today only Kiyomizu-yaki remains–and it is no longer made in Kyoto but in Kyoto's outskirts due to the anti-pollution laws that have restricted industrial fires. Once the attractions (or distractions) of Kiyomizu-yaki have been experienced, the top of Kiyomizu-zaka is reached, and the entrance to the magnificent Kiyomizu-dera (Clear Water Temple) can be seen.

3 KIYOMIZU-DERA

Kiyomizu-dera (Clear Water Temple) is one of the oldest temples in Kyoto, its establishment even predating the founding of the city. The temple was created in 788, six years before the Emperor Kammu decided to move his capital to Kyoto. Legend has it that Enchin, a priest at a temple in Nara, had a vision that he would find a fountain of pure or clear water (*kiyo-mizu*) at which he could build a temple. At the Otawa-no-taki (the Sound of Feathers Waterfall) on the hillside where the Kiyomizu-dera now stands, he came upon Gyo-ei, a hermit residing at the Otawa Waterfall. To Enchin's surprise, the hermit announced that he had been awaiting Enchin's arrival, and now that the priest from Nara had arrived he could move on to a less settled area. He gave Enchin a log of sacred wood and instructed him to carve the log into an image of Kannon, the deity of mercy. With that, the hermit disappeared. Later Enchin found the hermit's sandals atop the mountain, leading him to the realization that he had been speaking with a manifestation of Kannon who had thereafter ascended from the mountain crest. Enchin carved the image of the 11-headed 1,000-armed Kannon, and he created a small, crude temple building to house the image–the beginning of Kiyomizu-dera.

Kannon was obviously pleased by Enchin's act and soon after another miraculous event occurred. Sakenoue Tamuramaro, the Emperor's leading general, went hunting for deer one day near the temple. Having shot a deer, he was immediately reproved by Enchin, who happened to come upon him with the dead animal, for, in the Buddhist faith, killing one of the Buddha's creatures is forbidden. The warrior, according to tradition, repented his action and as an act of contrition he had his house disassembled and given to Enchin for a proper temple building to house his Kannon image. Enchin's good fortune did not stop there. In 794, the Emperor had his palace buildings at his capital of Nagaoka (a Kyoto suburb today) disassembled prior to the move to his new capital at Kyoto. Deciding to erect an entirely new palace, he gave his Shishinden (Throne Hall building) to Tamuramaro as a gift in recognition of his military service to the nation. Tamuramaro, in turn, gave the huge structure to Enchin as a new main hall for his temple, since Tamuramaro had become

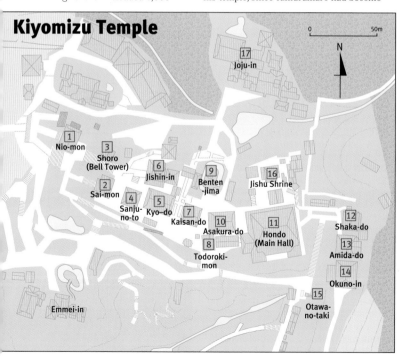

Kiyomizu Temple

0   50m

N

17 Joju-in

1 Nio-mon

3 Shoro (Bell Tower)

6 Jishin-in

9 Benten-jima

16 Jishu Shrine

2 Sai-mon

4 Sanju-no-to

5 Kyo-do

7 Kaisan-do

10 Asakura-do

11 Hondo (Main Hall)

12 Shaka-do

13 Amida-do

8 Todoroki-mon

14 Okuno-in

15 Otawa-no-taki

Emmei-in

a devotee of Kannon. That original building lasted until 1629 when it was destroyed by fire, and the main hall of the temple today is a reconstruction of what was originally an Imperial palace building. As such, it is one of the few major Buddhist temples with a cypress bark roof rather than the traditional tiled roof of such temples, a remembrance of its original condition as a portion of the Emperor's palace.

At the head of Kiyomizu-zaka lies the Kiyomizu-dera, which commands the top of this portion of the mountainside. On the left of the initial set of steps is a rare remainder of past times, the Uma-to-dome from the 1400–1550s, the Horse Stalls at which *samurai* and *daimyo* once left their horses when visiting the temple. By contrast, to the right of the steps leading into the temple grounds is a modern attraction, a 20th century solar clock. (The following entries are numbered so as to correspond with the numbered buildings on the accompanying map of Kiyomizu-dera.)

NIO-MON To the right of the Uma-to-dome horse stalls are steps which lead to the two-story Nio-mon (Gate of the Deva Kings) [1] with its cypress bark roof. Two Deva Kings (Nio) stand guard, as do two *koma-inu* (Korean lion-dogs), to protect the temple from the entry of evil forces. Alone of the many temple structures, this gateway escaped destruction in the 1478 conflagration. The 12 foot (3.6 m) tall Nio on the right has his mouth open to pronounce the Sanskrit "A" while the one on the left has his lips closed so as to pronounce the "Om" sound, these two sounds being the alpha and omega of Buddhist lore, symbolizing the all inclusiveness of Buddhist teachings.

SAI-MON A second flight of steps leads up to the Sai-mon (West Gateway) [2], another two-story gate whose large cypress-covered roof is held up by eight pillars. The gateway is elaborately carved and reflects the grandiose architectural taste of the Momoyama era in which it was created in 1607. The elephant heads decorating its end beams are said to be a detail brought back from Korea after the military incursions by Japan into that country in the 1590s. Two more Nio guardians stand on either side of the passageway through the gate as additional protectors of the temple. The Shoro (Bell Tower) [3] is to the left of the Sai-mon gate. Although the tower dates from 1596, its bell was cast in 1478.

SANJU-NO-TO The Sanju-no-to [4], the three-storied pagoda of 1633, rises behind the Sai-mon gate to the east, and is the tallest three-story pagoda in Japan. The pagoda was repainted in the traditional vermilion color in 1987 for the first time in a number of years, and this has made it stand out against the weathered brown color of the other buildings of the temple. The pride of early Buddhist temples was to have their structures enhanced by being painted with brilliant vermilion to reflect the grandeur of their Chinese architectural heritage.

KYO-DO A series of small temple buildings follow, buildings which usually are not open to the public. The first one, beyond the Sanju-no-to pagoda, is the Kyo-do (Sutra Storage Hall) [5], which holds the library of the sutras, the sacred Buddhist texts. The building is large enough to serve as well as a lecture hall for the monks, and it contains a Shaka Nyorai as its main image with a Monju, the Buddhist deity of wisdom, and a Fugen image, the Buddhist deity of virtue, on either side.

Sanju-no-to, the tallest three-story pagoda in Japan.

Near the entrance to Kiyomizu-dera, visitors sip water to purify themselves before entering the temple.

The ceiling of the Kyo-do is decorated with a painting of a coiled dragon. Behind it is the Jishiin-in (Temple of Mercy) [6], which is said to have been the favorite place of worship in the late 1500s of Toyotomi Hideyoshi, the military and civil ruler of Japan, and it retains some of his belongings.

KAISAN-DO The next building beyond the Kyo-do and to the right is the Kaisan-do (Founder's Hall) [7], also known as the Tamura-do in honor of the general who donated the Hondo (the main building of the temple) to Priest Enchin back in the 700s. The Kaisan-do holds four multicolored images: the first is of Gyo-ei, the hermit who was practicing austerities on the mountainside when Priest Enchin first appeared here; the second depicts Priest Enchin; the third represents Tamuramaro, and the fourth is of his wife Takako. These finely colored images, each 2.6 feet (76 cm) tall, are seated on multicolored platforms.

TODOROKI-MON After the Kaison-do you come to the Todoroki-mon or Chu-mon (Middle Gate) [8]. Temples traditionally have a main gateway followed by a middle gate before the Hondo (Main Hall) is reached. This 1633 middle gate has the name Todoroki-mon

(Gate Resounding to the Call of the Buddha's Teachings) from the fact that the religious chants of the priests should resound to the benefit of all believers. The gate is "protected" by two more Deva Kings who serve as guardians to the innermost areas of Kiyomizu-dera.

BENTEN-JIMA In the distance to the left is a small pond. In its center is a tiny island, the Benten-jima (Benten Island) [9], on which stands a shrine to the Shinto goddess Benten. Most Buddhist temples have one or more Shinto shrines attached to them to offer the protection of the native Shinto gods to the Buddhist deities. Japanese religion, except in the period from 1868 to 1945, has always been able to offer reverence to the original native gods as well as the Buddhist deities, the latter of whom first were accepted in Japan in the early 600s AD.

ASAKURA-DO Beyond the Middle Gate and to the left is the Asakura-do [10], a 1633 replacement for the original building destroyed by fire, which was a gift of Asakura Sadakaga (1473–1512), son of the Emperor Temmu. It has an 11-headed 1,000-armed Kannon with an image of Bishamon-ten and Jizo on either side. Ahead to the east is a stone with the traditional imprint of the Buddha's feet with an eight-spoked "Wheel of the True Law" imprinted on the heel. Custom decrees that by looking on such a memorial footprint one is forgiven of all one's sins. In the early years of Buddhism in India, images were not created of the Buddha and Bodhisattva. (A Bodhisattva is an individual who can achieve Nirvana but who chooses instead to remain active in this world to assist others toward the state of Nirvana. Thus a Bodhisattva serves as a living mediator between humans and ultimate reality.) In time, the influence of Hindu and Greek representations of their deities caused Buddhism to personify its sacred beings in human form. In the earliest centuries, however, before such iconography developed, the representation of the Buddha's footprints sufficed as reminders of the Way of the Buddha's Law.

One of the effects which the native religion of Shinto had upon Buddhism was the physical concern for purity at holy places and the need for individual purification before approaching the gods. Thus Buddhist temples, as with Shinto shrines, always have a water basin with a running fountain where one can purify one's hands (of deeds and actions) and one's mouth (of thoughts or spirit) before entering sacred ground. The Kiyomizu-dera fountain has been created in the form of a delightfully ferocious looking dragon which spews forth clear water instead of the traditional breath of flame. The basin which receives the dragon's stream is known as the "Owl Washing Basin" from the owl motif on the foundation stone beneath the basin.

Faith, myth and legend have a delightful way of becoming intertwined in all cultures, and Japan is no exception. The Japanese have always been attracted to tragic heroes as well as to their devoted followers, and none are better known to the people than Minamoto-no-Yoshitsune and Benkei, Yoshitsune's faithful companion in arms. In the late 1100s, Benkei was a monk of an unusual combative nature. Much given to uproarious conduct, he was a lover of duels, and he once vaingloriously swore to fight and to defeat 1,000 warriors and deprive them of their swords. Having conquered 999 such unfortunates, he chanced upon an armed 16-year-old boy, Yoshitsune, crossing the Gojo (Fourth Street) Bridge at the Kamo-gawa River below the Kiyomizu-dera. He challenged this easy mark, not knowing that the lad had been taught the art of swordsmanship by a *tengu*, a long-

nosed goblin learned in the arts of war. Since he wished to be fair to the young man, Benkei weighed himself down with iron *geta* (sandals) and a cumbersome sword. To his amazement, he was defeated by the youth. As a result, he pledged to become Yoshitsune's devoted companion, and thereafter he accompanied the handsome, courageous and able Yoshitsune in his many victorious battles and to his inevitable tragic end.

Benkei is remembered at the Kiyomizu-dera through the representations of his oversized *geta* and staff that stand just before the Hondo (Main Hall) of the temple. (The items are oversized since Benkei is said to have been almost 8 feet/2.4 m tall.) In the latter quarter of the 19th century, a blind

The Hondo of Kiyomizu-dera, built into the side of Mount Higashiyama, towers over the valley below.

blacksmith regained his sight after repeated prayers at the Kiyomizu-dera, and thus he created these versions in iron of Benkei's *geta* and staff as a thanksgiving offering to the temple for the return of his vision.

Another reminder of this legendary monk and his failure to win his 1,000th sword can be found at the Gojo (Fifth Street) Bridge at the Kamo River below the Kiyomizu-dera. A modern statue of Benkei has been placed at the western end of the bridge in a park in mid-traffic. Here, Benkei stands (in miniature), sword in hand, ready to take on all comers as they cross the Kamo-gawa River. He stands unchallenged today, no doubt because of the heavy traffic which creates a barrier no modern Kyoto pedestrian would ever defy.

HONDO The Hondo (Main Hall) [11] is the main attraction of Kiyomizu-dera, and it looms grandly beyond the Asakuro-do and the purification fountain. Its original structure before the 1629 fire was the Shishinden or Throne Hall of the Emperor Kammu, which was donated by Tamuramaro. The 190 foot (58 m) long by 88 foot (26.8 m) deep building of seven bays stands on the side of Mount Higashiyama and is supported by 139 pillars some 49 feet (15 m) tall, 59 feet (18 m) apart. Its huge hipped ridge roof, covered in *hinoki* (cypress) bark, rises 53 feet (16 m) high and is skirted with *moikoshi* (smaller and lower false roofs) on its east, west and north sides. These extra roofs provide covered open "corridors" on these three sides.

The Hondo's front (southern) veranda juts out by 25 feet (7.6 m) over the valley below, forming the large Butai (Dancing Stage) flanked by two wings, the roofed Gekuya (Orchestra). These two units are so-named since religious music and dance took place on this veranda. A fine view over a portion of the city of Kyoto and to the south can be obtained from the platform which sits in splendor high above the valley below the temple.

The interior of the Hondo has an Outer Sanctuary (Ge-jin) and an Inner Sanctuary (Nai-jin). The Outer Sanctuary is striking in its simplicity with its plain, massive unfinished columns and unfinished floor. Some 30 wooden tablets or paintings are hung high up on the walls, and they thus enrich the simple structure. These are votive gifts of tradesmen at the time of the 1633 rebuilding of the temple after its last disastrous fire. Among the most noted of these gifts are the four paintings of ships, three commissioned by the merchant-trading family of the Sumeyoshi and one by the Suminokura family, all from 1633–4. The Suminokura gift is particularly interesting since it shows a festival in rich colors on board a ship, and represented among its figures are European sailors and an African servant or slave. The painting stands 8.8 feet (2.6 m) tall by 11.8 feet (3.6 m) wide.

By contrast to the simplicity of the Outer Sanctuary, the Inner Sanctuary of the Hondo is of great splendor. At the center of the Naijin is a sunken stone-floored Innermost Sanctuary (Nai-nai-jin) where the sacred, hidden image is kept. The major gold leaf-covered images on public view stand behind vermilion wooden railings on a raised black lacquer platform, gold decorations hanging from the roof of the unit.

The primary image of the Hondo is the 1 1-headed 1,000-armed Kannon (Juichimen Senju Kannon), said to have been carved by Enchin in the 700s. It is a *hibutsu*, a hidden image, kept in a case, which is only brought forth every 33 years, its last appearance being in 2010. (The number 33 has religious significance since Kannon is said to have taken 33 vows to save mankind.) This 5 foot (1.5 m) image is unique in that two of its arms extend over its head, with the hands almost touching each other and seemingly supporting a tiny Buddha image at the apex. Each of the Kannon's 1,000 hands holds a different religious symbol.

To the right and left of the Kannon case are the Nijuhachibu-shu, the 28 supernatural followers of Kannon, each approximately 4.8 feet (1.4 m) tall. At each corner of the black lacquer platform stand the Shitenno, the Four Deva Kings, protecting all the images from evil. In a shrine at the east end is the carved image of Bishamon-ten while at the west end is the Jizo image; these and the Kannon are said to have been carved by Priest Enchin. Pictures of these three images hang at the end of the inner shrine so they can be seen even when their cases are closed.

NISHI-MUKI JIZO On leaving the Hondo and walking toward the hillside, the grand stairway leading down to the Otowa Waterfall should be bypassed at this time in order to visit the four small buildings which close the temple grounds on the east. The first of these is the minor "Westward Facing Jizo Shrine" (Nishi-muki Jizo) dedicated to the Bodhisattva who protects children, travelers and the dead. To the right of Jizo Shrine is the Shaka-do (Shaka Hall) [12] with a thatched roof. Within is a 3 foot (1 m) tall smiling image of the Shaka Buddha seated on a golden lotus flower. A nimbus appears behind his head. A magnificent lace-like aureole behind the full image is enriched with flying angels (*apsara*) with musical instruments. On either side of the Shaka stand a 13 inch (33 cm) tall Fugen and a Monju, the Buddhist deities of virtue and wisdom. Between the Shaka-do and its neighboring Amida-do to the right are some 180 small Jizo images under an open, roofed structure known as "The Hall of One Hundred Jizo" (Hyakutai Jizo). One folk tale holds that bereaved parents can view these images, and, if they find one which resembles their dead child, they can rest assured that the child is at peace.

AMIDA-DO The Amida-do [13] to the south of the Shaka-do has the traditional tiled roof of Buddhist temples. The building is divided into three sections: the first portion holds many *ihai*, memorial tablets to the dead; the middle section holds the Amida Nyorai image which is 6.3 feet (1.9 m) tall, its hands arranged in the *mudra* (the symbolic position of the hands) indicating contemplation. Amida is the Buddha of the Western Paradise, and the golden aureole behind his image has the traditional 1,000 Buddha figures in relief as well as a number of larger such images also in raised relief. It was here that the doctrine of the Nembutsu (Namu Amida Butsu, "Praise to the Buddha Amida") was proclaimed in 1188 by Priest Honen, thereby creating the cult of Amida and the Jodo sect of Buddhism. The repetition of this phrase insures one of being received by Amida in his Western Paradise after death. A special Nembutsu service takes place here five times a year.

OKUNO-IN The last building in this row is the thatched roofed Oku-no-in (the Inner Temple) [14]. This was the site of the original grass hut of Gyo-ei, the hermit whom Enchin came upon at this spot. Here Enchin created the rude hut which housed the three images he had carved of Kannon, Bishamon-ten and Jizo, and here later stood the house which Tamuramaro gave Enchin to replace the simple hut housing the sacred Kannon image. In front of the Okuno-in is a Butai, a dancing stage similar to but much smaller than the one in front of the Hondo (Main Hall). Behind the Okuno-in is the Nurete Kannon image, a figure standing in a water-filled basin. It is an act of purification and piety to dip water from the basin and pour it over the head of the Kannon.

OTAWA-NO-TAKI Below the Oku-no-in, at the foot of the grand staircase bypassed earlier, lies the Otawa-no-taki, the "Sound of Feathers Waterfall" [15]. Water falling down the three-part waterfall is said to have divine power which prevents illness, and thus many visitors will be seen drinking from long, wooden-handled metal cups which enable them to reach out and partake of the curative waters of the falls. The most devout of devotees of the temple can be seen at times, clad all in white, standing under the icy waters of the falls as an ascetic practice, even in the coldest of winter weather. The deity of these falls is Fudo-myo-o, a ferocious-looking deity who punishes evil doers. It is this Fudo, enshrined at the waterfall fount, whom the devotees worship as they toss coins into the basin before drinking the sacred waters.

JISHU SHRINE A most popular Shinto shrine exists right in the middle of the Kiyomizu-dera Buddhist temple, a not unusual situation prior to 1868 before the government forcibly separated the two religions, often through destructive physical separation. Somehow the Jishu Shrine [16] remained on the small hill

just behind the Hondo of the Kiyomizu-dera. As with many Shinto shrines, it has more than one god resident. In this case, it enshrines the tutelary Shinto god of the land on which the temple and shrine sit. It also enshrines the wayward brother, Susa-no-o, of the Emperor's supposed ancestress, Amaterasu-no-mikoto.

If that were not enough, the shrine also reverences Okuninushi-no-mikoto, and a statue of the god and a rabbit stand at the head of the steps leading up to this tightly packed set of Shinto buildings. The ancient *Kojiki*, the legendary account of Japanese history, tells of a deceitful rabbit which was punished by having its skin peeled from its body. Okuninushi is said to have taken pity on the rabbit, to have healed it and led it to reform its ways. Thus they are both honored here. More important, however, and particularly to young women, who can be found giggling at the shrine, is that the god of love and good marriages resides here.

The heart of the shrine are the Mekura-ishi (Blind Stones). These two stones are set some 60 feet (18 m) apart. If one walks from the first stone to the second with eyes shut, and arrives at the second stone (without opening the eyes while walking) and repeats the loved one's name continuously en route, success in love and marriage is guaranteed. The unsteady walker, it is presumed, had best seek another lover. There are other alternatives for the unsteady, however, since the shrine has a most successful business in the sale of charms which can guarantee success in love, luck in examinations, easy delivery in childbirth, good luck, long life, wisdom, good fortune with money—and, just to prove that the gods are up to date, the shrine also can make available charms for safety in traffic. Little wonder that it is a popular shrine.

JOJU-IN A visit to the Kiyomizu-dera between November 1st and November 10th provides a special delight. For then the garden of the Superior of the temple is open to the public. The Joju-in, the Superior's residence [17], can be reached by a path to the north of the main entrance to the Kiyomizu-dera. Originally a private temple for the Emperor Go-Kashiwabara (reigned 1500-26), it is noted for its exquisite garden usually attributed to two of Japan's most noted landscape gardeners—Soami (1472-1523) and Kobori Enshu (1579-1641).

The Joju-in (Superior's residence) at Kiyomizu-dera features a famous garden and pond.

The Superior's small garden on the edge of the Yuya-dani Valley seems much larger than when it is viewed from the veranda and rooms of the Joju-in's north-facing *shoin* (main room). This seeming spaciousness is derived from the device of "borrowed scenery" whereby the plantings in the garden seem to merge with the neighboring hillside as though all in view were part of the garden itself. The garden is created around a pond which has two islands in its midst. A large stone in the pond, the Eboshi-ishi (Eboshi Stone), is so-called from its resemblance to the formal hat (*eboshi*) worn by the nobility in the Heian period (798–1200); the angle of the stone suggests the head of a nobleman bowed in prayer. A water basin whose shape resembles the long sleeves of a young girl's *kimono* is called the Furisode or sleeve basin. This stone was donated to the temple by Toyotomi Hideyoshi in the 1590s. Noted as well are some of the garden's stone lanterns, particularly the one called *kagero* (Dragonfly) on the larger island.

DAIKU-DO Returning from the Joju-in toward the entrance to the temple, a series of 500 small stone Buddha images surrounded by ferns on a hillside are passed, the images having been placed about an 11-headed Kannon. Further toward the western end of the grounds is the Dai Kodo, the Great Lecture Hall, built in 1978 on the 1,200th anniversary of the founding of the temple.

The Taho Kaku (Tower of Treasures) of the Dai Kodo has a wing on either side, and the walls of the base of the tower hold a Buddha's footprint 13 feet (3.4 m) long while the walls surrounding the footprint have 4,076 images of the four major Buddhas. The 79 foot (24 m) walls about the area have an image of these four Buddhas inscribed on them: Taho Nyorai on the north wall, Shaka Nyorai on the south wall, Yakushi Nyorai on the east wall and Amida Nyorai on the west wall. The upper hall of the tower contains some of the ashes of the historic Buddha.

The walk down the hill to Higashi-oji-dori and the bus lines can be taken by the alternative street Kioymizu-michi which parallels Kiyomizu-zaka one street to the south. Partway down the hill is the Tojiki Kaikan, the Pottery Hall, where one has yet another chance to purchase Kiyomizu-yaki or other ceramic wares before leaving this center of traditional and contemporary pottery.

4 NISHI OTANI CEMETERY

At the foot of the hill at Higashi-oji-dori to the left lies the entry to the Nishi Otani Cemetery, one of the two oldest cemeteries in Kyoto. The small double bridge over the waterway has been nicknamed the "Spectacles Bridge" (Megan-bashi) since the reflection of its semi-circular arches in the water make for a complete circle and the circles and the structure of the bridge can be perceived as a pair of eye glasses. A cemetery may seem to be an unusual place to visit, but this mortuary for the abbots of the Nishi Hongan-ji Temple and the followers of the Jodo Shinshu sect of the great priest Shinran offers another aspect of Japanese life.

When Shinran died on November 28, 1262, his body was cremated, and eventually in 1694 a portion of his remains were moved from his original burial site to a hexagonal mausoleum at the Nishi Otani cemetery. (A portion of his ashes were also placed in the Higashi Otani cemetery of the Higashi Hongan-ji Temple, which is a branch of Shinran's faith.)

TAIKO-DO The path over the double bridge above the waterway leads to the main gate to the cemetery, and once past the gateway the Taiko-do (Drum Tower) is to the left. This two-story structure has been used as place of penance for refractory monks, and here they do penance by beating a drum (*taiko*). Behind the Taiko-do is the Shoro, the bell tower of the complex. Ahead is the Amida worship hall with its gilt image of Amida. To the south of the Amida-do are two structures: in the modern building to the southwest a Japanese-style lunch may be obtained, and here visitors may purchase flowers to place in the mortuary building. The building to the southeast of Amida-do contains the office responsible for receiving the ashes of deceased members of the sect.

HAIDEN Behind and to the left of the Amida-do is a two-story gateway, and beyond it is the Haiden (Oratory) which stands before Shinran's tomb. At the Haiden the ashes of the dead are ceremonially received by a priest in a brief religious service before committal to the Mortuary Hall. In 1966, the Muryoju-do (Hall of Immeasurable Bliss) was erected to the south of the Haiden. This modern concrete structure with a pebble finish is a columbarium for the ashes of members of the sect. There is a large chapel on the second floor for services, its entry wall enriched with a gold screen and a golden image of Amida. Across the open courtyard is the columbarium building where the ashes of the deceased are placed in compartments. To the right and left of Shinran's tombs, in an area not open to the public, are the graves of the abbots of the Nishi Hongan-ji Temple. Old trees about the area lend a dignity and serenity to the site.

GETTING THERE

Bus 18, 100, 206 or 207 can be taken from various points in Kyoto (including bus 100 or 206 from Kyoto Station) to Higashi-oji-dori and the Kiyomizu-michi bus stop, which lies between Gojo-dori (Fifth Street) and Shijo-dori (Fourth Street). On leaving the Nishi Otani Cemetery, you are back at Higashi-oji-dori. Here, the same buses or a taxi can be taken to your next destination within the city.

Kiyomizu-dera Temple is open from 6:00 a.m. to 6:00 p.m. although a number of the buildings within are closed after 4:00 p.m. There is an entry fee at the entrance to the main portion of the complex during the hours that all of the buildings are open. Many charming restaurants and shops can be found along Ninen-zaka and Sannen-zaka.

Walking Tour 2

SANJUSANGEN-DO AREA
The 1,001 Golden Kannon, the General and the Potter

1. **Sanjusangen-do** 三十三間堂
2. **Kyoto National Museum** 京都国立博物館
3. **Hoko-ji Temple** 方広寺
4. **Mimi-zuka** 耳塚
5. **Hokoku Shrine** 豊国神社
6. **Kawai Kanjiro Memorial House** 河井寛次郎記念館

Sanjusangen-do is one of the temples that all visitors to Kyoto wish to see, for its 1,001 golden images are a truly remarkable sight. These images are particularly unusual when one recalls the number of centuries in which they have been in place despite the many fires, earthquakes and even wars that Kyoto has suffered. While this walk begins with the spectacular golden Kannon images of the Sanjusangen-do, there are other fascinating sites virtually across the street as well as a few streets away, places which the average visitor too often misses. These other attractions are connected with Toyotomi Hideyoshi, who ruled Japan at the end of the 1500s and who brought prosperity back to the formerly war-ravaged city. In addition, the lovely house of one of the most distinguished potters of the 20th century, that of Kawai Kanjiro, is another site which few foreign visitors have heard of, and yet it offers an invitation into a well-to-do but traditional home right in the heart of Kyoto. It is a home of a man of taste and artistic ability, and the kilns in which he made his pottery are one of the unusual aspects of a visit to his home and workshop.

① SANJUSANGEN-DO
Of course, there is little doubt as to where to start this particular walk, since the Sanjusangen-do Temple with its golden

A fraction of the 1,001 golden images of Kannon in Sanjusangen-do.

Kannon images will always top any visitor's list of places which must be experienced. Sanjusangen-do is on the south side of Shichijo-dori at Yamato-oji-dori.

Sanjusangen-do is one of the most famous temples in Kyoto because of its large main image of the 1,000-armed Kannon as well as the 1,000 golden images which surround it. The temple's official name of Renge-o means "Lotus King," the name given to the Senju Kannon who was regarded as the lord of all the other forms of Kannon. (Kannon can appear in 33 different incarnations.) The name "Lotus King" was appropriate for this temple since here the devotion to Kannon has been carried to an extravagant level with its 1,001 images of Kannon, the god of mercy, each image standing on a golden lotus blossom. Renge-o-in (Sanjusangen-do) was created in 1164 at the request of the former Emperor Go-Shirakawa (1127–92), a devotee of Kannon, who wished to bring peace to the country by promoting the spread of Buddhism and its doctrines. The Emperor was assisted in the construction of the temple by Taira-no-Kiyomori (1118–81), the de facto civil ruler of Japan. The Taira leaders, as the actual political rulers of the state, identified themselves with the donation of the 28 gods whose images appear at the rear of the temple. These deities protect the Buddhist universe—as the Taira felt their clan protected and brought peace to Japan.

Historically, the temple sat amid the various Imperial villas that existed in this eastern area of Kyoto. It had many buildings, including a five-story pagoda in the southeastern section of the grounds, a Shinto shrine in the northwest area and an Amida hall, among other buildings. All these structures were destroyed in a fire in 1249. The temple was rebuilt at the order of the then Emperor Go-Fukakusa so as to appear just as it had been before the conflagration. However, only the Hondo (Main Hall) was reconstructed. Certain images had been saved from the fire, and

these included the head of the main Kannon image, 156 of the 1,000 smaller Kannon and the 28 followers of Kannon. The Main Hall was reconstructed between 1251 and 1253, and the leading artists of the day recreated the 1,001 images of Kannon, of which 125 of the smaller images are from the pre-fire temple. The temple was completed and re-dedicated in 1266.

Sanjusangen-do, as with most temples, has a tile-topped plastered wall about the borders of its grounds, and its Great South Gate (Nandai-mon) was rebuilt about 1590 in the elegant style of Momoyama times (1568–1603). On the eastern side of the property, the temple outer wall is broken by the restored vermilion To-mon (East Gate) and corridor in the Kamakura period (1185–1333) style, a mid-20th century restoration. A stone garden and a pond of the Kamakura period lie between the gate and its corridor and the Sanjusangen-do Hondo. The Hondo (Main Hall) is 390 feet (118 m) long by 54 feet (16.4 m) wide. The temple derives its common name from the fact that it has 33 (*san-ju-san* means 33) bays created by the 34 pillars that subdivide (and support) the

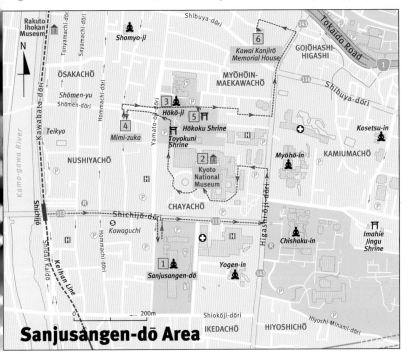

Sanjusàngen-dō Area

The graceful curving tiled roof of Sanjusangen-do.

gradually curving, tiled roof. (The word *do* in Sanjusangen-do means "hall.") Each bay has wooden shutter doors and behind these are movable *shoji* panels. The 33 bays symbolize the 33 incarnations into which Kannon can transform himself in his merciful acts of saving mankind from the miseries of human existence.

The central image of the Juichimen Senju Kannon (the 11-headed 1,000-armed Kannon) has 500 sculpted images of this deity arrayed on either side of him. The main image is an 11 foot (3.3 m) tall (including the pedestal) gilded Kannon seated on a lotus blossom. This Kannon, with eyes of crystal, was created in the *yosegi* style, that is, composed of many hollow wooden blocks that were put together and then roughly carved. Thereafter the image was finely carved, smoothened, lacquered and then covered with gold leaf. It was created between 1251 and 1254 by the most distinguished sculptor of Kamakura times, Tankei (1173–1256), the son of the sculptor Unkei (died 1223), when in his 82nd year. It and nine of the smaller Kannon images here are the only truly authenticated works by Tankei.

This central image, as with the 1,000 smaller images, has 11 small heads about the crown of its head. Although the Kannon has only 20 pairs of arms, since each of the 40 arms saves 25 worlds, figuratively 1,000 arms are represented. The image is seated on an octagonal lotus blossom pedestal with seven rows of petals. A large oval aureole behind it has small images of the 33 manifestations of Kannon amid an open-work pattern of clouds and sacred trees. The smaller images of Kannon (each about 65 inches/165 cm tall) were constructed by the same *yosegi* technique as described above. This permitted

several craftsmen to work on the same sculpture at one time, and the technique also created a lighter wooden image that was less likely to split. The images are grouped 500 on either side of the main Kannon, standing in 10 rows of 50 each. The images were created not only by Tankei (1173–1256) but by 70 other sculptors under his direction. The 1,001 images of Kannon symbolize the 33,033 ways in which mankind can be helped by this god of mercy (1,001 images multiplied by the 33 possible incarnations equals 33,033).

The gods of wind (Fujin) and thunder (Raijin) stand at either end and in front of the rows of 1,000 Kannon. The image of Fujin, the god of wind, stands 3.8 feet (1.1 m) tall and holds a large bag of wind over his shoulders. Raijin, the god of thunder, is 3.5 feet (1 m) tall and is surrounded from behind by a circlet of drums which he beats with his drum sticks, thereby causing thunder to roll. Both deities are of a ferocious mien, and both were actively feared and placated by the people in earlier times. Behind the 1,000 Kannon are the statues of the 28 followers (Nijuhachi bushu) of Kannon, Buddhist deities with human or animal heads who protect mankind. The Nijuhachi bushu were made during the Kamakura period (1185–1333) or later, and are approximately 5 feet (1.5 m) in height. The 28 images are the spirits of deified wisdom, beauty, prosperity, relief for the poor, etc., and are lined up in a row along the rear corridor of the temple. Additional images of the Nio, Fudo, Jizo and other Buddhist deities are also located in the rear of the building.

On leaving the Sanjusangen-do building, observe the platform under the eaves of the rear of the structure, for here takes place the annual ancient Hikizome Matsuri (First Shooting of the Year). The Hikizome (or Toshiya) Ceremony is held on the 15th of each January and represents the initial archery contest of the New Year. Since the arrows launched seemed to fly through the air one after another, the ceremony is also called Toshiya ("Passing Arrows"). These bow and arrow contests first began in 1606 on the west veranda of the temple, and they remained most popular among the *samurai* (warrior class) right through the Edo period (1603–1868). The archers had to shoot their arrows from a squatting position, aiming from the south end of the veranda to the target, 3 feet (1 m) in diameter, at the north end, 197 feet (59.1 m) away. (As a result, the pillars have had to be protected by metal coverings against stray arrows.) In former times, the contests began at 6:00 p.m. and continued for 24 hours. At age 22, the 1686 champion, Wasa Daihachiro, sent a record 8,233 arrows to the target at the north end of the veranda out of 13,053 that he had shot. Today, the contest on January 15th begins at 9:00 a.m., but it is only a modest repetition of the Toshiya of former times. In truth, it is no longer a real contest, but remains as a tradition worth retaining. As part of the tradition of this ceremony, a collection of bows and arrows is displayed on the south end of the interior of the hall.

2 KYOTO NATIONAL MUSEUM

Across Shichijo-dori from Sanjusangen-do is the Kyoto National Museum, and it is worth a visit since it presents an excellent picture of the arts of Kyoto's past. It perhaps is best saved for a rainy day (as with other museums) when one does not wish to be traipsing between outdoor temples and shrines.

The Kyoto National Museum was founded in 1875 as an Imperial museum, and in 1897 its original building was erected in the then current European style that can best be described as Victorian Neo-Renaissance. The museum was given to the city of Kyoto in 1924 and then was nationalized in 1952. In 1966, a modern addition (designed by Keiichi Morita) was opened. Originally planned as a museum for important items of artistic or historic merit from temples and shrines that the Meiji government took over, it has developed a substantial collection of its own—as well as borrowing from private collections and religious institutions when mounting special exhibitions. As one of the major holdings of artifacts and historical art of early Japan, the exhibits cover the period from pre-history through the Edo period (to 1868). In as much as the collections are extensive, many of the objects in the museum's holdings are rotated; thus it is not possible to indicate those items currently on view. The collections include art, religious objects, and items of archeological and historical interest. These include sculpture, paintings, ceramics and pottery, metal work, lacquer, toys, dolls of Japan, calligraphy, sutra scrolls, paintings, Buddhist images and costumes. Chinese works of art are represented as well since they had a major influence on Japanese art and tastes in the past. Special exhibitions are mounted in the spring and autumn in the original Meiji era building. Labels are in Japanese and in English, and a guidebook to the collections (in English) is available in the museum shop. The museum also contains research and photographic laboratories.

RECALLING TOYOTOMI HIDEYOSHI

When one leaves the Kyoto National Museum and exits on to Shichijo-dori, walk to the right (west) to the corner of Yamato-oji-dori (the next cross street) and turn to the right. On Yamato-oji-dori you are then about to encounter the end of Japan's medieval period and to become acquainted with the intriguing figure of Toyotomi Hideyoshi (1536–98), the military general and civil ruler of the late 1500s (he ruled from 1585 to 1598). Hideyoshi, who brought peace and prosperity back to a devastated Kyoto, was one of the major personalities in the history of Japan. He was honored by the citizens of Kyoto in particular, for Kyoto was a city that had suffered the depredations of war and fire and the privations of starvation and disease, all caused by the country's internecine wars of the previous 100 years. Hideyoshi's day in the sun was a comparatively brief but glorious one. By 1585 those who opposed him had been conquered and he ruled a pacified nation; by 1598 he was dead, leaving a memorable legacy that the thankful people of Kyoto could not forgot. These 14 years were important ones in Japan's history, and they are especially remembered as the glorious Momoyama period when art flourished, business and commercial enterprises revived and Japan was at peace.

Statue of a seated Hideyoshi at Hokoku Shrine.

Hideyoshi is recalled in many places in Kyoto, but in the portion of the city covered in this walk you will encounter some of the most memorable reminders of his life: Mimi-zuka, the mound which commemorates his brutal wars in Korea; the Hoko-ji, the site of the image of the Buddha that was meant, in a vainglorious moment, to outshine that of the Daibutsu (the Great Buddha image) of Nara and whose memorial bell, which was to herald an era of peace, led instead to the downfall of his son and the eradication of his line; and the Hokoku Shrine, the restored Shinto shrine to his spirit. It is best to begin with what remains of the Hoko-ji Temple.

3 HOKO-JI TEMPLE

The Hoko-ji Temple is on the east side of Yamato-oji-dori, one and a half streets from Shichijo-dori, just beyond the Hokoku Jinja (Hokoku Shrine) whose main entrance faces Shomen-dori, a street heading downhill to the west. The entrance to the Hokoku Jinja should be bypassed, for the Hoko-ji grounds begin at the end of the shrine property. Hoko-ji is open from 9:00 a.m. to 5:00 p.m. There is no entry fee.

The only historic remnant in the Hoko-ji, the one-time site of the Great Buddha of Kyoto, is its infamous temple bell. There is no charge to see it, but if you wish to strike the bell with its beam, the attendant may collect a small fee for this privilege. Although the history of the temple is fascinating, other than seeing the bell it is not worth entering the remaining buildings, which date from the 1970s after the latest fire to plague the temple. The Hoko-ji Temple was erected by Toyotomi Hideyoshi in part out of his own vanity and in part as a ploy to disarm all but the new warrior class (*samurai*), which officially came into being as a result of the codification of rank and status that Hideyoshi began and which the Tokugawa shoguns would formulate definitively after 1600. This "pious" act of creating the Hoko-ji Temple was hardly based on religious zeal. Determined to build a huge image of the Buddha that would outclass the Daibutsu (Great Buddha) of Nara, Hideyoshi boasted that his Great Buddha would be created in five years rather than the 20 years it had taken to build the Daibutsu of the Emperor Shomu in the 7th century. The temple grounds that held Hideyoshi's gigantic image and its hall covered an area 780 feet (237 m) from east to west by

822 feet (250 m) north to south. Hideyoshi's vassals (the *daimyo* or lords dependent upon him) were required to furnish the funds and the thousands of workers needed to bring this 160 foot tall (48.7 m) Buddha into being. Originally intended to be cast in bronze, difficulties with the casting led instead to the creation of the image in wood. This was then lacquered, 10,000 bags of oyster shells being ordered as part of the raw materials for this process. The Hondo (Main Hall), built in 1587 to house this gigantic image, stood 222 feet (67.6 m) by 330 feet (100.5 m) by 200 feet (61 m) high.

The creation of the Buddha image gave rise to a way of disarming the general populace. Many citizens had maintained their own weapons for defensive purposes or for use when pressed into military battles in the previous century of the Sengoku Jidai (the Age of the Country at War). The armed monks who had plagued the government before being crushed by Oda Nobunaga, Hideyoshi's predecessor, were also a target. Thus a government decree ordered the surrender of "any sword, short sword, bows, spears, firearms or other types of arms." The avowed purpose of this 1585 "Taiko's Sword Hunt" (as the campaign was known, Taiko (His Highness) being the title by which Hideyoshi was regarded by the public) was to melt down such metals in order to create the nails and bolts needed for the erection of the great hall to house the Buddha at the Hoko-ji. With the public deprived of arms, according to official pronouncements, the populace would have a double benefit: without arms, there would be less chance of death from armed conflict and, by giving their arms for the sake of the Buddha, the donor would be granted peace not only in this life but in the next world as well. In the long run, this not only removed the danger of uprisings against the ruling authorities, but emphasized the class distinction between soldiers and farmers and soldiers and merchants. It made the wearing of a sword a badge of rank, a privilege granted only to the *samurai*. The rigid stratification of society during the following 265 years of Tokugawa rule, after Hideyoshi's demise, was in process.

The Bukko-ji Temple, which stood on the site of Hideyoshi's projected Great Buddha image, was conveniently moved across the river in order to provide sufficient land for the gigantic undertaking. Canals were dug and a

Ioko-ji, home of the great bell of 1615.

new bridge was built, the Gojo-O-hashi, the Great Bridge of Fifth Street, to facilitate the delivery of materials to the site. The temple was completed in 1589, and 1,000 priests participated in the dedication ceremonies. Unhappily, the image was doomed to failure: in 1596, a great earthquake damaged much of the Kyoto area and the Great Buddha was destroyed. Two years later, Hideyoshi was dead. The question of Hideyoshi's successor lay open since his intended political heir, his son Hideyori, was only five years old. Ostensibly, the various lords who formed a regents' council had pledged to support Hideyoshi's son as the next political ruler when he came of age. Dissension among them, however, enabled Tokugawa Ieyasu to gain control of the government by 1603, both by guile and by force. Concerned to create a new ruling family, he determined to get rid of Hideyori in time. In order to weaken Hideyori financially as the years went by, Ieyasu encouraged him and his mother to melt 10 million gold coins from Hideyoshi's estate to obtain the needed funds for a gigantic image to replace the destroyed Great Buddha.

For Hideyori's political supporters, this rebuilding of the Great Buddha provided an opportunity to restore the family's flagging political influence. Thus the rebuilding began in 1603. Unfortunately, a fire in the nearly completed hall destroyed the work already done. Ieyasu convinced Hideyori and his mother once more that the project had to be completed, thereby further sapping the Toyotomi coffers. By 1609 the Buddha had been recreated (in wood), and by 1612 the temple was restored. This second hall was 272 feet (81.6 m) long by 167.5 feet (50.3 m) deep and rose 150 feet (45 m) into the air. Ninety-two pillars supported the roof over the 58.5 foot (7.6 meter) tall Buddha. In 1615, to mark the completion of the project, a huge bronze bell was cast and mounted in its own structure. It still stands, 14 feet (4.2 m) tall and 9 feet (2.7 m) in diameter; it is 9 inches (22.5 cm) thick and weighs 82 tons. On it, Hideyori had inscribed the words KOKKA ANKO ("Security and Peace in the Nation"). Ieyasu, looking for a pretext to undermine Hideyori, whom he found too handsome and too capable and thereby a political threat to his and his family's continued rule, had not only refused to contribute funds to the rebuilding of this popular memorial to Hideyoshi, but claimed that the second and fourth characters in the inscription on the bell could be read as "Ieyasu." Thus the intent, he claimed, was to place a curse upon him. In time, Ieyasu resorted to armed force, and in 1615 he besieged Hideyori in his castle in Osaka, a castle which Hideyori had inherited from his father. The Toyotomi family was exterminated, and one of the justifications used by Ieyasu for his treacherous and brutal course of action was the supposed threat that had appeared on the great bell at the Hoko-ji. Later, the head of Toyotomi Hideyori's seven-year-old son was displayed at the Sanjo (Third Street) Bridge in the same manner as were those of traitors and criminals.

The Hoko-ji Temple today is a rather nondescript complex. The 1609 Buddha and its hall, which were restored at vast expense by Hideyori and his mother, were destroyed by an earthquake in 1662, and the replacements of these were lost in a fire in 1798. The new image of 1843, which replaced the previous Buddha, was destroyed in a 1973 fire. Thus the existing halls of the temple are not very important since all that was of consequence has been consumed by the flames of the centuries. What alone remains of the original Hoko-ji is the great bell of 1615 in a belfry which was rebuilt in 1884. The offending characters of KOKKA ANKO were removed at Hideyori's order soon after the bell was completed because of Ieyasu's pretended offense at the curse he claimed to read into the characters. Today, one can have the experience of pulling the cord which sends the wooden beam of the belfry crashing against the side of the bell–either to sound the praise of Hideyoshi or to curse Ieyasu, as one is so inclined.

One other item of note remains from the 16th century temple: the huge stone walls along Yamato-oji-dori that served to hold the embankment on which the Hoko-ji Temple was built. These gigantic stones were gifts from Hideyoshi's *daimyo*, many of whom competed with each other to see if they could send an even larger stone from their fiefdom than their donors. The stones are still in place, today encompassing the grounds of both the Hoko-ji Temple and the Hokoku Shrine. The entrance to the present Hokoku Shrine at the head of Shomen-dori is approximately the entrance to the Great Buddha Hall of the past.

4 MIMI-ZUKA

Before leaving the Hoko-ji, note the Mimi-zuka mound, which was created in front of the Great Buddha Hall of the Hoko-ji. It reflects the obverse side of the honor given to Hideyoshi in his own day, for it is illustrative of the cruelty of wars waged by the warriors of that time as well as of later times. The Mimi-zuka mound is on Shomen-dori just west of where that street intersects with Yamato-oji-dori (west of the entrance to the Hokoku Shrine) and immediately to the west of the children's playground. Mimi-zuka is a mound in which the ears and noses of defeated Koreans were buried after the Korean wars of Hideyoshi in 1592 and 1597. The mound originally stood in front of the gateway to the Daibutsuden (Hall of the Great Buddha) of the Hoko-ji Temple, a hall which has now been replaced by the Hokoku Shrine in honor of Toyotomi Hideyoshi. The mound is a tall hill behind a fence and is topped by a very tall *sotoba* (a five-part memorial stone). In 1592, Toyotomi Hideyoshi determined that he would conquer China, a part of his dream of ruling all of East Asia. He sent a massive army into Korea, penetrating to Pyongyang and the Tumen River to the border of China. Ultimately forced by the Chinese to retreat to the south of Korea, his war was not a success; it merely resulted in many casualties on both sides as well as a continuing antagonism with Korea and China. In 1597, he launched a second attempt against Korea so as to reach

China, a land of whose vast dimensions he was not that knowledgeable. Harassment of his supply lines by Korean armored boats and the combined military forces of Korea and China proved overwhelming obstacles to his expansionist goals. His death in 1598 provided his successors with an excuse for a withdrawal from Korea, which lasted until the 19th and 20th centuries.

The custom of victorious armies to sever the heads of the defeated enemy for presentation to their commander as proof of victory proved logistically impractical during these overseas military adventures. Therefore, in 1592 the ears of the defeated enemy were cut off and shipped back to Kyoto in barrels of brine. They were buried in a mound, Mimi-zuka (Ear Mound), marked by five large circular stones in front of the gateway to the Daibutsuden (Hall of the Great Buddha) of the Hoko-ji Temple. Again, in November 1598 the ears and, this time, the noses of 38,000 victims of the Japanese forces in Korea were buried in Mimi-zuka. The noses were hung up by threes for inspection, for verification in Korea, and counted before they were pickled and shipped. According to some sources, the mound should be called Hana-zuka (Nose Mound) since it was noses rather than ears that were shipped and buried.

A moat 12 feet (3.6 m) broad was created about the mound, 720 feet (216 m) in circumference and 30 feet (9 m) high. On top was placed a five-story 21 foot (6.3 m) tall *sotoba* with a 15 foot (4.5 m) wide base. In earlier days, a bridge with railings crossed the moat from the north side. The mound and *sotoba* were built at Hideyoshi's orders, and on June 12, 1597, he had 300 priests chant a requiem prayer for the Korean dead. In former times, when Korean embassies came to the Court on official visits, they always worshipped at this mound.

5 HOKOKU SHRINE

The Mimi-zuka mound reflects the senseless military ardor of Hideyoshi, and today it remains, ironically, before the Hokoku Shrine, the Shinto memorial to Hideyoshi's enshrined spirit. The Hokoku Shrine is on Yamato-oji-dori where Shomen-dori meets Yamato-oji-dori, north of the Kyoto National Museum. There is no admission charge to the shrine. Its Treasury is open from 9:00 a.m. to 5:00 p.m.

The era of peace and a growing economy, after the devastation which had been visited on Kyoto by the century of civil war, endeared Hideyoshi to the public. His festival celebrations, though sometimes brash, also warmed the citizens of Kyoto to his rule. Thus, after his death, one of the popular songs sung by the people at his shrine summarized these feelings:

Who's that
Holding over 400 provinces
In the palm of his hand
And entertaining at a tea party?
It's His Highness [Taiko]
So mighty, so impressive.

When Hideyoshi gave a tea party, he savored the quiet essence of the tea ceremony as created by tea masters such as Sen-no-Rikyu. On the other hand, he could go to the extremes to which his nature inclined. His passion for tea reached such a height that when he held a tea party for the public at the Kitano Tenman-gu shrine in October of 1587, he invited "even those from China" to attend. One had only to bring a mat to sit on and a tea bowl. Some 5,000 people are said to have attended the "tea party."

On Hideyoshi's death, the Emperor Go-Yozei in 1599 ordered that a Shinto shrine to Hideyoshi's spirit, the Hokoku Jinja, be constructed at the foot of Amida-ga-mine (Mount Amida) to the east of Higashi-oji-dori, since in death Hideyoshi was seen as a *kami* (god).

The shrine became a gathering place for the people of Kyoto each year on the anniversary of Hideyoshi's death, a great festival being held in front of it. The festival was captured in a six-panel painting by Kano Naizen (owned by the shrine and on public view in its Treasury) in the early 1600s, documenting the admiration of the people for Hideyoshi. Such esteem for his predecessor concerned the new Shogun, Tokugawa Ieyasu. As a result, through the years Ieyasu did everything in his power to erase Hideyoshi's name. Gradually, the shrine and the burial place of Hideyoshi were eliminated by Ieyasu.

With the end of the Tokugawa era in 1868, however, the new Meiji government began the restoration of Hideyoshi's reputation together with the shrines connected with him. On April 9, 1875, the Prefecture of Kyoto received an Imperial Order to rebuild the shrine to Hideyoshi. A 10-year reconstruction program gradually restored the Hokoku Jinja to its previous glory—but on a major portion of the grounds of the Hoko-ji Temple instead of at its original site at the foot of Amide-ga-mine (Mount Amida) to the east of Higashi-oji-dori. Thus the Hoko-ji was reduced drastically from its original size and importance, part of the Meiji government's hostility to Buddhism and a policy of downgrading of Buddhist temples. The former Kara-mon (Chinese-style gateway), which once had stood before Hideyoshi's Fushimi Castle, was brought to the

The Heiden (Offertory) in front of the Honden (Main Hall) at Hokoku Shrine.

Hokoku Shrine in 1876 from its previous location, thus depriving the Konchi-in Buddhist subtemple of the Nanzen-ji Temple of one of its treasures.

To create the appropriate space that Meiji grandeur demanded for the restored Shinto shrine to Hideyoshi, some of the buildings of the Hoko-ji Temple were moved to the north, thereby restricting the temple to but a corner of its original site. By September 15, 1875 the shrine was in place and, in a great ceremony, Hideyoshi's spirit was transferred to the inner shrine building. Hideyoshi's cynicism in the creation of the Hoko-ji Temple, with its great Buddha, was now being equaled by that of the Meiji government in the re-creation of this Shinto shrine in order to reverse the disdain of Ieyasu for Hideyoshi. But its underlying motive was to show the new government's hatred of both the Tokugawa Shoguns and their 260 years of political rule of Japan and of Buddhism.

The Hokoku Shrine consists of a number of buildings and, as with most Shinto shrines, all but the Honden (Spirit Hall) and its enclosure are open to the public. A traditional *torii* stands at the entrance to the grounds, and beyond it a series of lanterns (in vermilion painted wood) are raised on posts leading to the Kara-mon (Chinese Gate). The gate faces west down Shomen-dori, and from it hangs the original tablet-name for the shrine, created by the Emperor Go-Yozei in 1599. The cypress bark roofed Kara-mon gateway is supported by six large wooden pillars. Relief carvings of cranes on the transoms enhance the doors of this gateway as do the two finely carved cranes under the front gable. So realistic are the carvings of the cranes by the noted 16th century sculptor Hidari Jingoro that it is said that he left them without eyes so that they would not fly away. In keeping with the ostentatious nature of the Momoyama style of Hideyoshi's day, the ornaments of the re-stored gate were gold-plated. Beyond the Kara-mon gate is the Honden, the sacred building where the spirit of Hideyoshi is enshrined, ensconced behind a fence which separates the sacred from the secular realm. A gilded statue of the seated Hideyoshi stands before the fenced inner area of the Hokoku Shrine. To the north of the main pathway is a smaller Shinto shrine with a series of small vermilion *torii* before its small shrine building. To the southeast of the main shrine is the Treasure House with items connected with

Hideyoshi and his times, including the folding screen mentioned above that depicts the seventh anniversary of Hideyoshi's death. In addition, swords, armor, iron lanterns and manuscripts of the 16th century, all with Hideyoshi associations, are on display.

6 KAWAI KANJIRO MEMORIAL HOUSE

In contrast to the late 19th century attempt to glorify Hideyoshi at the Hokoku Shrine, a short walk to the northeast of the shrine brings one to a simpler and more attractive site. Seldom can a visitor to Kyoto see the interior of a traditional Japanese house, but the Kawai Kanjiro Memorial House offers just such an opportunity. On leaving the Hokoku Shrine, a right turn brings you on to Yamato-oji-dori. Follow this street to the north for three blocks. At the third cross street, turn right and walk east for two blocks before turning left (north). Kawai Kanjiro house is midway on the east side of this street. The house is open from 10:00 a.m. to 4:30 p.m. except on Mondays. It is closed from August 10 to 20 and from December 24 to January 7. Entry fee for adults, children free.

Born in 1890, Kawai Kanjiro became a noted 20th century potter and master of ceramic craftsmanship. His growing interest in traditional pottery led him to be one of the founders of the Japan Folk Craft Museum in Tokyo and to bring attention to traditional Japanese folk crafts. Living in Kyoto, the center of traditional craftsmanship, he established a kiln at the rear of his house, and both his home and studio can be visited today. In 1937, his home was destroyed in a storm, and in rebuilding it and his work area he was inspired by traditional rural Japanese house architecture. The entrance to the house has a hall that would have been the area in which a farmer kept his animals. Here Kanjiro hung one of his wooden sculptures, an art form he took up in his later years. Beyond the entry hall is the reception room with a Korean-style wooden floor and an open hearth. A calligraphic inscription on the rear wall translates as "Folk Craft Study Collection," and display shelves that can be viewed from either side hold some of his treasured folk collections. The room beyond the reception room was the family dining area with a large table. Under the table is a *kotatsu*, the traditional brazier to provide warmth to those at the table. An image of the Buddha carved by a 17th century priest-folk artist sits upon the table.

The dining room of the Kawai Kanjiro Memorial House, built along traditional lines.

A traditional staircase with drawers beneath the steps leads to the upper sleeping quarter with its wooden floor and ceiling. Adjacent is a small room with a *tokonoma*, and on its wall is a calligraphic riddle whose answer is "tea." Here Kanjiro and friends could enjoy tea in a relaxed manner rather than with the formality called for by the traditional tea ceremony. The walls of this room, as with some of the other rooms, are decorated with the wooden masks that the artist began to make when in his seventies. Behind the rooms on the first floor, a gravel path set off by bamboo plants leads to Kanjiro's workshop and "Smoking Room" where the potter's twin kickwheel, stepped *noborigama* kilns and pieces of his ceramic ware are on display. The kilns were used by Kanjiro from 1919 until his death in 1966, and continued to be used by some of his followers until 1971 when new anti-pollution laws forced the closure of all wood-fired kilns in Kyoto. The Kawai Kanjiro house is a charming memorial to a famed potter, a house which illustrates how a prosperous artist tried to recapture the past in his daily life. It stands in sharp contrast to the golden images of the Sanjusangen-do and to Toyotomi Hideyoshi's dreams of glory.

GETTING THERE

Bus 206 or 208 from Kyoto Station to the Sanjusangen-do-mae bus stop on Shichijo-dori leaves you at the Kyoto National Museum, which is opposite the Sanjusangen-do Temple. Alternatively, bus16 or 202 or 207 to the Higashi-oji-dori/Shichijo-dori bus stop leaves you just north of the temple, and the temple is one street west on Shichijo-dori from this bus stop, just to the west of the Kyoto Park Hotel.

Sanjusangen-do is open from 8:00 a.m to 4:30 p.m. between March 16 and October 31 and from 9:00 a.m. to 4:00 p.m. between November 1 and March 15. Entry fee.

The Kyoto National Museum is entered from the Shichijo-dori side. It is open daily except on Mondays from 9:30 a.m. to 5:00 p.m. If a national holiday falls on a Monday, the museum remains open that Monday but is closed the next day. The museum is closed during the New Year holiday (from December 26 through January 3). Entry fee.

From the end of the tour at Kawai Kanjiro Memorial House, you can walk back (south) to the east–west street. A turn to the left (east) brings you to Higashi-oji-dori at the next corner. There take a taxi or bus 18, 202, 206 or 207 for a return to the center of the city or other destinations as desired.

Walking Tour 3

HIGASHIYAMA AREA

Higashiyama: The Widow's Temple, the Gion Cart Temple and the Great Chion-in

1. **Yasaka Pagoda** 八坂の塔
2. **Ryozen Historical Museum** 山歴史館
3. **Gokoku Shrine** 霊山護国神社
4. **Ryozen Kannon Temple** 霊山観音
5. **Kodai-ji Nunnery** 高台寺
6. **Daiun-in (Gion Cart) Temple** 大雲院
7. **Maruyama Park** 円山公園
8. **Chion-in Temple** 知恩院

To traverse the lanes between the temples and shrines and the romanticized story of the Taira Empress who alone survived the battle of Dan-no-ura in 1185 and who here took the tonsure to spend her final days as a nun in prayer for her lost child and family. The nearby Higashi Otani Cemetery, with its tomb to Priest Shinran, is a sacred spot to those millions who follow in the Jodo Shinshu faith of this great Buddhist religious reformer of the 1200s, who was persecuted for his faith. The close of the Japanese medieval period is also remembered by a site which again recalls the tempestuous relationship between Toyotomi Hideyoshi and Tokugawa Ieyasu (see Tour 2), for it contains the Kodai-ji Nunnery where Hideyoshi's widow, Kitano Mandokoro, spent her years after Hideyoshi's death. The modern age is not ignored, for the Ryozen Historical Museum is a monument to the heady days of the mid to late 19th century when the Tokugawa Shogun's government was losing power and the new Meiji era and modern Japan were being born. An aspect of the unhappy consequences of the militaristic spirit of that period is marked by the gigantic concrete Kannon image that arose after World War II in memory of and expiation for the millions who died in the two decades of Japan's Greater East Asia folly. Even more recently, the new Daiun-in Temple, with its

unusual pagoda in the shape of a huge Gion cart, has added a new element to the skyline at the foot of the Higashiyama hills, a temple which enriches the city with examples of the Buddhist murals of the Chinese caves of Dun Huang as well. There is also a lighter side to this area of Kyoto with its *ochaya* and *geisha* entertainment in the inns along the narrow streets between Higashi-oji-dori and Kita-mon-mae-dori, and with the opportunity to savor the non-alcoholic delights of *amazake*, once the beverage of Buddhist nuns, or to enjoy the restaurants about Maruyama Park. The tour then ends at the great Chion-in Temple, where priest Honen is buried and where the devotion to Amida and to Honen is celebrated with great reverence.

1 YASAKA PAGODA

We begin this tour at the small Hokan-ji Temple, the oldest temple in Kyoto, which is best known for its Yasaka Pagoda. It is most easily reached from the bus stop at Higashi-oji-dori and Kiyomizu-michi, the same bus stop used in Tour 1. Buses 202, 203, 206 or 207, which run along Higashi-oji-dori, serve the bus stop. After alighting from the bus, walk three streets north on Higashi-oji-dori and then turn right on to Yasaka-dori. A *torii* gate stands at the entrance to Yasaka-dori at Higashi-oji-dori, and that street, after a slight jog to the right and then the left, will lead you to the tall pagoda of the small Hokan-ji Temple. The temple grounds are open between 9:00 a.m. and 4:30 p.m. Entry fee.

The Yasaka Pagoda and its few tiny buildings are all that remain of the Hokan-ji Temple, said to have been established by a family named Yasaka-no-Miyatsuko, who had probably come to Japan from Korea and settled in this region in the 500s, some two centuries before Kyoto was created as a city.

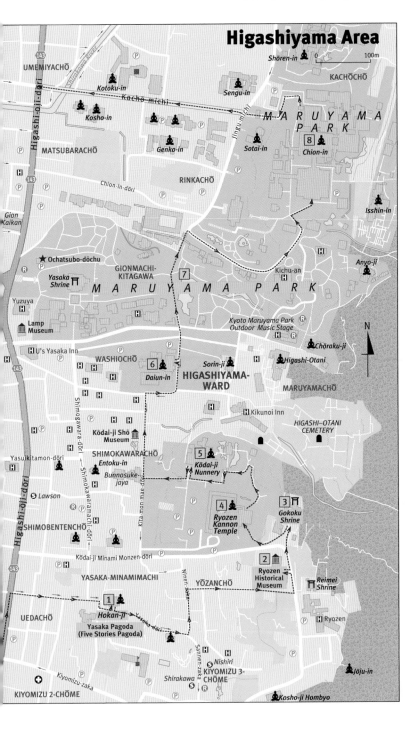

Higashiyama Area

Shōren-in

0   100m

KACHŌCHŌ

UMEMIYACHŌ

Kotoku-in

Kachō-michi

Sengu-in

Kosho-in

M A R U Y A M A

P A R K

MATSUBARACHŌ

Genko-in

Sotai-in

8

Chion-in

Chion-in-dōri

RINKACHŌ

Isshin-in

Gion
Kaikan

Ochatsubo-dōchu

GIONMACHI-
KITAGAWA

M A R U Y A M A

P A R K

Anyo-ji

Yasaka
Shrine

7

Kichu-an

Yuzuya

Kyoto Maruyama Park
Outdoor Music Stage

Lamp
Museum

Chōraku-ji

U's Yasaka Inn

WASHIOCHŌ

6

Daiun-in

Sorin-ji

Higashi-Otani

HIGASHIYAMA-
WARD

MARUYAMACHŌ

Shimogawara-dōri

Kōdai-ji Shō
Museum

SHIMOKAWARACHŌ

Entoku-in

Bunnosuke-
jaya

5

Kōdai-ji
Nunnery

HIGASHI–OTANI
CEMETERY

Yasukitamon-dōri

Kikunoi Inn

Lawson

Shimokawaramachi-dōri

4

Ryozen
Kannon
Temple

3

Gokoku
Shrine

SHIMOBENTENCHŌ

Kōdai-ji Minami Monzen-dōri

2

Ryozen
Historical
Museum

Ninen-zaka

YASAKA-MINAMIMACHI

YŌZANCHŌ

Reimei
Shrine

Ryozen

1

Hokan-ji

UEDACHŌ

Yasaka Pagoda
(Five Stories Pagoda)

Yasaka-dōri

Nishiri

Sannen-zaka

KIYOMIZU 3-
CHŌME

Jōju-in

Kiyomizu-zaka

Shirakawa

KIYOMIZU 2-CHŌME

Kosho-ji Hombyo

The five-story Yasaka Pagoda towers over the Higashiyama neighborhood.

Their religious life is thought to have centered around the Hokan-ji, which tradition says was created in 588 by Prince Shotoku, the founder of Buddhism in Japan. This claim is, no doubt, one of those pious but questionable traditions, since the prince would only have been 16 years old at that time. Nonetheless, the temple was to become one of the principal Buddhist temples of Kyoto in the early centuries of the city. Historically regarded as the symbol of Kyoto, those who conquered the city were always anxious to display their colors at the Yasaka Pagoda. Time, however, has taken its toll on the original temple buildings, and the pagoda was replaced in 1192 by Minamoto-no-Yoritomo, founder of the Kamakura Shogun's government. The temple was later destroyed once more by fire and, of the reconstruction by Shogun Ashikaga-no-Yoshinori in 1440, only this five-story pagoda remains, the oldest pagoda in Kyoto. It was restored in 1618 by the governor of Kyoto.

The Hokan-ji Temple precincts are entered on the south side. Today, the temple consists of the five-story pagoda of 1440 and a few small buildings to the north of the pagoda. Two of these units are memorial halls with the flaming jewel atop their pyramidal roofs. The unit on the west (left when facing them) is the Taisho-do (Memorial Hall) to Prince Shotoku, the supposed founder of the temple. The Taishi-do contains an appealing image of the 16-year-old prince, a favorite image that appears in many temples, of the young man praying for his father (Emperor Yomei) as the emperor lay on his deathbed. The small building to its right is the Yakushi-do, with its gilt image of the Buddha Yakushi, the Buddha of healing and medicine, with his staff in his left hand. To the right of the Yakushi-do is the small modern Treasure House, while to the east of the pagoda is a Shinto shrine. The five story Yasaka Pagoda is 126 feet (38 m) tall, and the interior walls, ceiling and columns of its base level are decorated with paintings, among which are images of Bodhisattvas on the walls. The interior of many pagodas have been decorated in this manner, and this is one of those rare examples which are available for viewing. In the center of the base level, on each side of the main pillar that supports the pagoda, are images of the four Nyorai Buddha: Hojo on the south, Amida on the west, Ashuka on the east and Shaka on the north. A large phoenix tops the spire of the pagoda.

EAST OF YASAKA PAGODA To the east of the Yasaka Pagoda are two sites which a century ago ranked among the most important in the city. Today, they are seldom visited and are mentioned here more as a curiosity. These are the Ryozen Rekishi-kan museum and the Gokoku Jinja shrine (a memorial to those who died in opposition to the Tokugawa Shoguns' rule that ended in 1868).

2 RYOZEN HISTORICAL MUSEUM

The Ryozen Rekishi-kan (Historical Museum) is located across the road from the Gokoku Shrine on Kodai-ji Minami Monzen-dori. It is open from 10:00 a.m. to 4:30 p.m. except on Mondays and the New Year holiday. Entry fee. The Ryozen Rekishi-kan is a museum depicting the history of the period on either side of 1868, the year in which the rule of Tokugawa Shoguns passed into history and the modernization of Japan under the name of the Meiji Emperor began. The displays consist of photographs, writings, armaments and other artifacts that relate the events of this epic period of change in Japanese political and cultural life. Special exhibitions on the Meiji era are also presented. In a sense, the museum replaces the memorial to the heroes of the Restoration, noted above, as time often effaces the public memory of men and events. As a specialized museum whose labels are in Japanese, few foreign visitors will patronize it,

but it is mentioned here for those interested in the period of drastic change in Japan after the 1860s.

3 GOKOKU SHRINE

The Gokoku Jinja, also known as the Kyoto Shrine, is to the east of the Yasaka Pagoda at the top of Kodai-ji Minami Monzen-dori,

4 RYOZEN KANNON TEMPLE

The Gokoku Shrine and the Ryozen Rekishi-kan (Historical Museum) represent the heady days of the 1870s when the new Meiji government came into power and Japanese nationalism began the flowering which would ultimately lead to disaster for much of the world in the mid-1900s and then to the defeat of Japan in 1945. The Ryozen Kannon Temple, just a short distance away, marks the regret most Japanese feel for the extremes to which nationalism took the nation in the decade and a half after 1930. The route to the Ryozen Kannon Temple heads back down Koda-ji Minami Monzen-dori to Kita-mon-mae, the first narrow street to the right. A turn on to this street brings the towering image of the concrete Ryozen Kannon figure into sight and then the entrance to the temple grounds. The temple is open from 9:00 a.m. to 5:00 p.m. Entry fee.

In 1955, a 79 foot (23.7 m) tall seated Kannon image in concrete was built by a transportation firm to honor the war dead of the Pacific War (World War II in the Pacific and Asia). It honors not only the Japanese who died in combat but the dead of the Allied forces who opposed Japan. When you pay the entry fee, you receive a lighted incense stick; this is to be placed in the large incense pot before the shrine where prayers may be said for the peaceful repose of the dead. A modest Nio-mon gate leads into the Ryozen Kannon grounds. Beyond the entryway, a reflecting pool is situated before a large roofed incense pot where you may place the lit incense stick and pray. Behind the incense pot is the Hondo, the main shrine building, topped by the huge Kannon image. On the ground floor is an altar, under the base of the gigantic 11-headed Kannon, the god of mercy, the main image of the memorial temple. In the northwest section of this level is an image of the recumbent Buddha as he appeared when he passed from this life upon achieving Nirvana. A 5 foot (1.5 m) tall Buddha on a lotus is in the southwest area. A staircase behind this portion of the building leads into the lower part of the

This large statue of Kannon honors the fallen Japanese and Allied soldiers of the Pacific War.

huge Kannon image where the altars have the figures of the zodiac year.

Behind this main structure is a Memorial Hall to the Japanese war dead with a file of names of all those who died in the years of the Japanese wars of the 1930s and 1940s. To the north of the main temple building is an 8 foot (2.4 meter) long memorial footprint of the Buddha, and west of that is a gold sphere under a roof. Beyond, to the north, is a garden. To the south of the main Kannon structure is a second Memorial Hall to the war dead of the Allied forces of the 1940–5 Pacific War. An altar (with English captions) and a file of the names of the Allied dead is maintained here. The altar contains soil from each of the military cemeteries in the Pacific. Just west of the Allied memorial, toward the entry gate, is a modern shrine of 1,000 Buddhas with an image of a Buddha with an infant in his arms. To the south of the Allied memorial is an open domed structure with an outdoor altar with benches where memorial services are held. This solemn and impressive contribution of a private citizen to the memory of the war dead is a fitting representation of the sorrow felt by the Japanese for the errors and disasters brought upon so many by the Japanese military rulers of the 1930s and 1940s.

which is one street to the north of the street in front of the entrance to the Yasaka Pagoda. Take Kodai-ji Minami Monzen-dori up the hill. At the top of the road, on the left as the road turns to the south, is the Gokoku Shrine. The shrine is open during daylight hours without charge. The is an old shrine meant to serve as the protector of the city and it differs little in appearance from other Shinto shrines. The buildings are behind a vermilion fence on the left as one mounts the hillside street to the shrine entrance. Within the grounds, beyond the entry *torii*, is the unpainted Heiden (Offertory), and beyond that is the Haiden (Oratory) and then the fenced Honden (Spirit Hall). As such, for the casual visitor it is of historical interest only. A century ago, when Shinto was being turned into the militaristic faith that served the military and the State, it held greater significance for the Japanese public than it now does. To the south of the Gokoku Shrine, a monument of major importance was raised in the late 19th century, a site now almost forgotten. This monument was dedicated to the heroes of the movement in the decade prior to 1868 who opposed the Tokugawa Shoguns and who helped to bring about the Meiji Restoration and the modernization of Japan. Here are buried a number of the heroes of that era, including Kido Koin, one of the leaders of Meiji times.

5 KODAI-JI NUNNERY

Adjacent to the Ryozen Kannon Temple and to its north is the Kodai-ji Nunnery, the retreat of Toyotomi Hideyoshi's widow when she became a nun after her husband's death in 1598. It represents, in a sense, the conclusion to the story of the hatred of Shogun Tokugawa Ieyasu, Hideyoshi's successor, for Hideyoshi and his family. When one leaves the Ryozen Kannon Temple, the entrance to the Kodai-ji Nunnery is on the south side of the Kodai-ji grounds. If the nunnery is approached from Kita-mon-mae-dori, beyond the entrance to the Ryozen Kannon Temple on that street, a path which turns to the right leads along the south side of Kodai-ji to its entry gate. Kodai-ji is a Zen temple of the Rinzai branch of Buddhism and is open daily from 9:00 a.m. to 4:30 p.m. Entry fee.

The fact that Kodai-ji is a nunnery adds another interesting element to the Hideyoshi–Ieyasu relationship as described in Tour 2 above. Kodai-ji was originally founded in 838,

but its renaissance as a Buddhist nunnery began after Hideyoshi's death in 1598. In 1605, Shogun Tokugawa Ieyasu granted this temple to Hideyoshi's widow, Kitano Mandokoro, when she became an *ama* (nun) to pray for the soul of her husband, and here she lived until shortly before her death. Ieyasu was more than generous in helping to create a magnificent nunnery for the widow, a political ploy to indicate his regard for the Toyotomi family—although his ultimate intent actually was to obliterate the family of Hideyoshi. The rebuilt temple was designed by two architects under Ieyasu's orders, and by 1604 all the temple structures had been erected. Sanko Joeki, the former abbot of Kennin-ji, was installed as its founding abbot. To further console Kitano Mandokoro, Ieyasu ordered that the So-mon Gate to Hideyoshi's castle in Fushimi, with its carvings of foxes and dragons by Hidari Jingoro, be moved to Kodai-ji in 1605, and this became the still extant Omotemon (Front Gate) to the nunnery. (The gate on the west side of the temple grounds is not open to the public; the front or main gate is on the southern side of the nunnery.) The Keisho-den was also moved from Fushimi to serve as Kitano Mandokoro's residence. This building was later turned into the Ko Hojo (the Abbot's small quarters), but in 1847 it burned to the ground along with the Dai Hojo (the Abbot's large quarters), the Kara-mon (Chinese gate) and other buildings. The temple is said to have been one of the most attractive temples in the luxurious Momoyama style in the late 16th and early 17th centuries.

Kitano Mandokoro, who had taken the religious name of Kodai-in, spared no expense in the enhancement of the Kodai-ji, but at best she had tragic years here as a nun. The Hoko-ji Temple and its Buddha were completed in 1612 in her husband's memory, and its great bell was dedicated in 1614. Ieyasu (as detailed under the entry on the Hoko-ji) interpreted the inscription on the bell as an offense against him, and in time he would destroy all the memorials to Hideyoshi. Then, in November of 1614, Ieyasu led his army against Hideyori (the son by Hideyoshi's favorite consort, Yodogimi) at Hideyori's Osaka Castle. A truce was arranged whereby the outer defensive walls were leveled and the moat was filled in. The following year, Ieyasu treacherously returned to the attack when he led 200,000 soldiers in the second battle against the castle (which Hideyori had

The dry landscape garden in front of the Hojo (Abbot's quarters) at Kodai-ji.

inherited as a five-year-old boy in 1598 at his father's death). Hideyori's 100,000 men were overwhelmed, and the Toyotomi family was annihilated. (Hideyori's small son, aged seven, was beheaded and his head posted on a bridge over the Kamo River in Kyoto, as were those of criminals or traitors. Hideyori's daughter, aged five, was sent to a nunnery in Kamakura for the rest of her life. (Alternative tales claim that Ieyasu permitted the Toyotomi family to escape by boat and that they were befriended by one of the *daimyo* for life—a not too likely story.)

Yodogimi, Hideyoshi's favorite concubine and the mother of Hideyori, died at the siege of Osaka Castle, reputedly by having one of her servants kill her so she would not fall into Ieyasu's hands. She died despite a plea to spare her life by Ono Harunage, who had rescued Ieyasu's granddaughter (who had been left as a hostage with Yodogimi) from the flames of Osaka Castle. After the siege of the castle and the death of its defenders, thousands of heads were placed on pikes lining the road from Fushimi to Kyoto as a warning to any prospective opponents of Shogun Tokugawa Ieyasu.

Kodai-ji continued to exist as a Buddhist temple after the death of Kitano Mandokoro. Sanko Joeki, abbot of the Kennin-ji Temple, had been appointed as founding priest at the nunnery, and Kodai-ji has remained as one of the largest and most important subtemples of Kennin-ji since that time. Kodai-ji was damaged by a number of fires in 1789 and then, ironically, in 1863, as tension increased between the incumbent Tokugawa Shogun and those who wished to restore the Emperor to power, the temple was damaged once more. The supporters of the Imperial cause, suspecting that one of their Tokugawa opponents had taken refuge in Kodai-ji, attacked the temple and set fire to some of the buildings. Thus today only a few of the temple's original 17th century structures still exist: the Omote-mon Gate, the So-mon Gate to the nunnery, the Kaisan-do (Founder's Hall), the Kangetsu-dai covered bridge and walkway, the Otama-ya (Sanctuary), and the Kurakasa-tei and the Shigure-tei (two small tea houses). A new Hojo (Abbot's quarters) was erected in 1913.

Kodai-ji is entered through the Omote-mon Gate on its southern side, and the path leads you to the left to the ticket booth. From there you proceed ahead and then to the right behind some temple buildings toward the Kangetsu-dai (Moon Viewing Platform) and the Kaisan-do (Founder's Hall). The Kang-etsu-dai is a roofed corridor or bridge that leads over the stream between the Garyu (Dragon) Pond and the Engetsu (Crescent Moon) Pond to the Kaisan-do (Founder's

Hall). It has a small four-pillared structure in its mid-length. In this center section, when the Kangetsu-dai was located at Hideyoshi's Fushimi Castle, Hideyoshi would sit to gaze at the moon. In the northern section of the ponds is an island in the shape of a turtle, while in the southern portion is a group of stones meant to resemble a crane, these two animals being the traditional symbols of longevity. Work on the ponds and garden was begun by the famous landscape designer Kobori Enshu in the 1620s, but the design was not perfected for another 65 years.

A path leads alongside the garden to the front walkway to the Kaisan-do, which was dedicated to the memory of Sanko Joeki, the founding priest of Kodai-ji. To create a memorial hall befitting her temple, Kitano Mandokoro commissioned the decorating of the pillars, walls and ceiling of the Kaisan-do by leading artists from the Kano and Tosa schools of painting. The ceiling of the inner room boasts not only a dragon by Kano Eitoku (1543–90) but also the ceiling from Kitano Mandokoro's carriage, while the ceiling of the front room contains a portion of the roof of the war junk created for use by Hideyoshi in his war against Korea and China. The inner shrine contains an image of Sanko Joeki, while the statues on either side of the steps are of Kinoshita Iesada and Unryo-in, Kitano Mandokoro's elder brother and younger sister. The four panels of the shrine in this hall are by the noted 15th century artist Kano Motonobu.

The Kangetsu-dai, the roofed corridor with its Moon Viewing Pavilion, which leads to the Kaisan-do from the west, is continued on the eastern side of the Kaisan-do. The corridor is named the Garyoro (Reclining Dragon Corridor) from the resemblance of its sloping roof to the back of a reclining dragon, the roof tiles having been laid in a manner that resembles the scales on the back of a dragon. (Only a short length at its far end may be entered.) If the Kaisan-do would appear to be overly decorated, it cannot match the Momoyama period splendor of the Otama-ya, the Spirit Hall or Mausoleum. A path leads from the central walkway of the Kaisan-do to the east and to the front gate of the Otama-ya, a building enclosed behind white walls. Built to the east of the Kaisan-do in 1606, it is particularly noted for its *tatamaki-e* (raised lacquer work), an early example of what has become known as the art of Kodai-ji-maki

(lacquer). Gold lacquer artistry reached a luxurious peak in the designs in this Spirit Hall, and the walls, furniture, cabinets, altar and altar dishes are all decorated in the Kodai-ji-maki-e technique.

The altar is truly a masterpiece of lacquer craft. Its central image of worship is that of Kannon. Instead of having the usual Bodhisattva images on either side of the main image, the Kannon in this memorial hall is flanked by two miniature shrines. The shrine on the left holds a wooden image of the seated Hideyoshi, the shrine case having designs in gold from Kitano Mandokoro's carriage. Hideyoshi's hat is the one sent to him by the Emperor of China. On the opposite side of the altar on the right is a wooden image of Kitano Mandokoro as a nun. The building is further embellished with paintings by Kano school artists and the classical "Thirty-six Poets" by Tosa Mitsunobu (1434–1525).

East of the main buildings and further up the hillside are two thatch-roofed tea houses, also from Fushimi Castle, connected by a thatch-roofed walkway. They bear the names of Shigure-tei (Shower of Rain) and Karakasa-tei (Umbrella). Shigure-tei was designed by Toyobo Sochin, a disciple of Sen-no-Rikyu, the great tea master and garden designer of the late 1500s. At the time of Hideyoshi's 1587 tea party at the Kitano Tenman-gu shrine, to which he invited everyone to be present, even "those from China," all the important tea masters designed tea houses which were exhibited at the tea party. Toyobo's tea house eventually found a permanent home at Kodai-ji Temple. The Karakasa-tei is so-named since, from the inside of the tea house, the poles or struts supporting the thatched roof radiate from a central point at the conical peak of the roof—thereby resembling the struts of an opened umbrella from the underside. The real name of the tea house is more romantic: Ankan-kutsa (Place of Idleness).

Northwest of the Kangetsu-dai are two small buildings, one of which is the Iho-an (Cottage of Lingering Fragrances). According to one account, it was the favorite tea ceremony house of a wealthy merchant and the courtesan Yoshino-tayu, a famed dancer and beauty who later married the merchant. Another account claims this to be an incense ceremony building, supposedly of Hideyoshi's time. Nearby is Entoku-in, a subtemple of Kodai-ji which was once the mansion of

The Iho-an tea ceremony house in the Kodai-ji Temple complex is noted for its large circular window.

Kinoshita Toshifusa, a nephew of Kitano Mandokoro. The Hojo (Abbot's Quarters), rebuilt in 1913, has a landscape painting on its *fusuma* that is thought to be by Tohaku Hasegawa, while the garden of the Hojo lies to its north, a Momoyama dry garden with magnificent rocks from Hideyoshi's Fushimi Castle. Among the treasures of the temple on display between November 1st and 10th each year are gold screens by Kano Motonobu (1476-1559), Kano Koi and Hasegawa Tohaku (1539-1610). Certain relics of Hideyoshi and Kitano Mandokoro remain as well, notably his writing box, her black lacquer "clothes horse" and a set of small dining trays and covered bowls, all originally from Fushimi Castle.

A lighter and less solemn aspect of a nun's life can be experienced across from the west side of Kodai-ji on Kita-mon-mae-dori at the Bunnosuke-jaya, one of the few remaining *amazake* shops that once flourished in this area. *Ama* are nuns, and Buddhist nuns are not supposed to consume alcohol. Thus the lees of *saké* (the solids left after pressing and filtering) were used to make a sweet, non-alcoholic beverage—one much favored by the nuns. Behind the building is a small shrine to Daikoku-ten, the god of wealth, said to have been brought to this spot by Kitano Mandokoro from Fushimi Castle since Daikoku-ten was Hideyoshi's patron deity.

Just north of this tea shop is a garden (now in private ownership) that can be seen from the tea house property. Designed by Kobori Enshu, it is a *karesansui* (dry landscape) garden in which Kobori used stones from Fushimi Castle after Ieyasu had it leveled in 1620, five years after Ieyasu had eliminated the last of the Toyotomi family.

The narrow lanes between Kodai-ji and Higashi-oji-dori once held the homes of Kyoto's well-to-do. The changes that occurred after World War II led to the abandonment of these villas by merchants who could no longer afford to maintain them. Now the villas have become inns and tea houses. It is an interesting area to wander about, particularly in the evening when the inns and tea houses along the narrow lanes come to life.

6 DAIUN-IN (GION CART) TEMPLE

Continuing to the north on Kita-mon-mae-dori from Kodai-ji and Bunnosuke-jaya, you cannot help but be reminded that the Yasaka (Gion) Shrine is not too far distant, for looming up ahead is what seems to be a gigantic Gion cart such as is pulled along the central streets of Kyoto every mid-July during the Gion Festival. The structure, however, is immense and obviously permanent. What you see is actually no cart: it is the huge and extraordinary pagoda of the Daiun-in Temple,

The Daiun-in Temple resembles a huge Gion cart.

a pagoda that was constructed in the shape of a gigantic multistory Gion Festival cart in concrete. Kita-mon-mae-dori comes to an end as you walk north, and you must take a right turn and then a left turn at the next street on the left. This places you before the entrance to the Daiun-in. (The temple is open from 9:00 a.m. to 4:30 p.m. Entry fee.)

The Daiun-in Temple buildings are 20th century and are an unusual addition to the Kyoto scene. The temple precincts are entered through the Administrative Building, with the large room to the right of the entry hall serving as a museum of the temple's treasures. As its focal point are a standing image of Amida with a seated monk to the right and the image of a medieval official to the left. The cases in the room display scrolls and other articles of a religious nature. A path from the entry building leads along a garden on the right to the entry to the pagoda. At the base of the pagoda is an altar with a seated image of Amida, hands in a contemplative position. Behind the image, an aureole holds small raised Buddha figures, which stand out from the traditional 1,000 Buddha images impressed in the aureole. A series of stairways from the entry hall lead up to the two outer platforms at the top of the pagoda, the walls and ceilings along the way covered with paintings depicting the Buddhist murals in the Dun Huang caves of western China. Explanations of the paintings are provided in both Japanese and English. The two outside platforms under the roof of the pagoda provide an excellent view over Kyoto on three sides, with the Higashiyama mountain range on the fourth side to the east.

⑦ MARUYAMA PARK

Leaving the Daiun-in and continuing north on the path, one comes to the beginning of Maruyama Park (Maruyama Koen) straight ahead and on the right. The rear portion of the Yasaka (Gion) Shrine (not to be confused with Yasaka Pagoda) is on the left. But first a digression is in order to a small temple at the beginning of the slope of Higashiyama range on the right, a temple associated with a much-loved romantic and tragic story.

CHORAKU-JI A road runs eastward along the south side of Maruyama Park in the direction of the mountains. At the end of this roadway lies a long stone stairway which leads to the Choraku-ji Temple. The temple is open from 9:00 a.m. to 5:00 p.m. Entry fee. Choraku-ji was built by priest Saicho (Dengyo Daishi), one of the two major Buddhist priests at the time of the founding of Kyoto in the 790s. The temple was created sometime between 782 and 806 by the Tendai sect, but it was rebuilt in the 14th century by Priest Ippen, who converted it to the Ji sect of Buddhism (see below). Successive emperors worshiped here, and thus the temple had a degree of prominence.

A minor temple today, Choraku-ji is best known for the most noted individual associated with it: Taira-no-Tokuko, better known as the former Empress Kenrei-mon-in. At the sea battle of Dan-no-ura between the Taira and Minamoto clans in 1185, she and her mother-in-law (who was holding Kenrei-mon-in's seven-year-old son, the Emperor Antoku) jumped into the sea with the child to end their lives when the battle was lost. The Empress had also flung herself into the sea to escape capture by the Minamoto forces, but she was saved from drowning by being dragged from the water by her long hair. Sent back to Kyoto, she lived in a small hut belonging to a poor priest, and at 29 she took the tonsure at Choraku-ji. As an added catastrophe after the deaths of her family and her degradation, an earthquake destroyed the miserable hut in which the former Empress had taken refuge. She was moved to the Jakko-in Temple in the Ohara region to a 10 square foot (1 sq m) retreat, and there she lived out her life in prayer.

Up the long stone stairway of this hillside site, the entrance to the Choraku-ji Temple leads to a further climb to the only early buildings that remain today: the Hondo (Main Hall), Shoro (Bell Tower), Kuri (Priests' Quarters)– and a modern Treasure House which completes the complex. The small Hondo has a double roof and, within, a black lacquer altar has a noted image of Priest Honen in its sometimes closed altar case. The Shoro is to the left (north) of the Hondo, and beyond it a little way further up the hillside is a charming dell. Here, a small open but roofed unit holds two Jizo images. Beyond it is a small waterfall descending from the hillside, and across the resulting rivulet is an equally small Shinto shrine to the deity of the temple land.

Adjacent to the shrine is the modern Treasury. Within it on the left wall is a picture of Kenreimon-in as a nun with Awa-no-Naishi, her faithful aide. The statues of seven priests once associated with the temple are ranged across the back of the building. In the row of priests, the end two are seated images while the third from the left is a monk in a Chinese-style chair. The middle image, carved by Kosho in 1420, is of Ippen Shonin, founder of the Ji sect of Buddhism, which was dedicated to the continuous repetition of the Nembutsu ("All Praise to Amida"). (Ippen chose as his Buddhist name a word which means "for one and for all," indicative of how the Nembutsu usage was making Buddhism a universal religion in Japan rather than just an aristocratic religion as it had first been.) The full-length statue of priest Ippen chanting the Nembutsu, with the small Amida images issuing from his lips as he walks on a pilgrimage, is stiff and angular, and it is nowhere as successful in portraying a walking devotee of Amida as is the image of Kuya in the Rokuhara-mitsu-ji Temple. Its sharply carved cheeks are reminiscent of the style of carving employed in *Noh* masks.

HIGASHI OTANI CEMETERY Returning down the path from the Choraku-ji, on the left hand side of the street is the entrance to the Higashi Otani mausoleum and cemetery. The grounds and temple are open from 9:00 a.m.

to 5:00 p.m. without charge. Established in 1671 as a mortuary chapel for the abbots of the Higashi Hongan-ji Temple in central Kyoto, Higashi Otani has become an important cemetery since a portion of the cremated ashes of Priest Shinran Shonin, the founder of the Jodo Shinshu sect of Buddhism, was reburied here in 1653. Followers of this sect often desire to have their cremated remains buried close to the ashes of the founder. A handsome gateway decorated with carvings of chrysanthemums and other flora provides an entrance to the grounds, and then a sloping path turns to the right. Ahead on the right is the roofed Purification Basin with an extended bronze dragon from whose mouth the water issues. Directly beyond this structure is a long temple building with a hall for funeral services. Across from these units is the small Hondo (Main Hall) with its altar figure of Amida sculpted in wood. A shrine on the right holds a portrait of Shinran and one of Prince Shotoku, while on the left are portraits of past abbots of the Higashi Hongan-ji Temple. Behind the Hondo are other temple buildings not open to the general public.

In front of the Hondo, a flight of steps to the east lead up to the forecourt before the massive Mausoleum of Shinran. A small roofed oratory stands before a richly ornamented Kara-mon (Chinese-style gate) to Shinran's tomb, a lattice-fenced wall stretching to the right and left of the gateway. Behind the gate is a plain granite wall which encompasses the Tomb of Shinran. Rectangular in shape, it is 30 feet (9 m) high with a circumference of 102 feet (30.6 m). The wall is crowned in front with a tiger-shaped stone, said to have been Shinran's favorite. Returning down the steps to the level of the Hondo, a short path to the left (south) passes the temple bell and through a gate. To the left, rising tier upon tier up the hillside, is the Higashi Hongan-ji Cemetery, crowded with thousands of tombstones. Part way up the hillside is a memorial building. On August 15th each year, the 20,000 graves are decorated with candles as a part of the service for the dead, whose souls return briefly to this world and then return to the netherworld at the end of the O-Bon period. The candle lighting ceremony begins at 6:00 p.m.

MARUYAMA PARK Returning to the north–south street from which the walk to the Choraku-ji Temple began, a right turn brings you back to Maruyama Park, which is bounded on the north by the grounds of the Chion-in Temple, by the mountains to the east, and by the Higashi Otani mausoleum grounds and the Choraku-ji Temple to the south. Maruyama Park is one of the larger public parks in Kyoto. In the past it was the site of several temples, but all were destroyed over time by fires. Within the park is the site of the former Sorin-ji Temple which was established by the great priest Saicho (Dengyo Daishi) in the latter part of the 8th century; its site is now marked only by the Yakushi-do shrine. The famed 12th century poet Saigyo lived here in a cell at the Sorin-ji at one time.

In 1871, the government turned the area into a public park, one of the first such public pleasure parks in the city. With the wooded Higashiyama mountains as a background on the east and the shrine and temples on its three other sides, it is an oasis away from the traffic and noise of the city streets. Two ponds, with a charming arched bridge over the stream between them, a water spout tossing a spray of water into the air, and the maples, willows, cherry trees and colorful bushes have made this a favorite area with Kyoto residents. With restaurants about it, the park has been a place for quiet relaxation and enjoyment for over a century. The center

of the park is noted for its hundreds of cherry trees, whose blossoms in early April provide an additional pleasure. In the past they were viewed in the evening by torchlight, and this tradition is still maintained, albeit modern illumination is now provided.

You might enjoy a pleasant rest in the park or some refreshments before returning to Higashi-oji-dori to the west of the park. Here, at the intersection with Shijo-dori, a number of bus lines or taxis are available to the various sections of the city or to the Chion-in, which lies just to the north of the park within walking distance.

8 CHION-IN TEMPLE

Chion-in lies at the foot of Awata-yama of the Higashiyama mountains in extensive grounds (35 acres/14.5 hectares). Chion-in is a very important temple in Buddhism, for it is the seat of the Superior of the Jodo (Amida) sect, with more than 7,000 subtemples throughout Japan as well as branch temples overseas. Thus it is well worth being described in detail. The sect was founded by priest Honen Shonin, for here he had his small hermitage, and here is his mausoleum, a sacred spot for believers. The temple compound includes 17 halls and five gates, and from 1619 to the

Maruyama Park is a favorite cherry blossom viewing site in early April.

The huge San-Mon Gate is the main entrance to the grounds of Chion-in Temple.

1870s it had an Imperial prince as its head until the Meiji government dissolved that relationship. In 1872, under pressure from the government in its anti-Buddhist campaign, the Shue-do (Assembly Hall) of the temple was used as the site of the Kyoto Exhibition, and it was here that Doshisha University, a Christian institution, had its initial meeting to found that missionary enterprise.

Priest Honen, the founder of the Jodo sect of Buddhism, was born in a small village in present-day Okayama City. When he was nine years old, his father was fatally wounded by an attacker, and his dying father implored his son not to seek revenge but to become a monk. Following his father's wishes, he studied at the Bodai-ji Temple near Okayama under a local priest who was also his uncle. Eventually, he moved to the monastery of Mount Hiei outside of Kyoto, where he was ordained into the priesthood in 1147. At 18 he left the monastery to wander as a hermit, seeking religious instruction from leading Buddhist priests throughout Japan. Settling in time in a hut in Kyoto, in 1175, when he was 43, he became convinced that salvation could come solely through the repetition of the Nembutsu (Namu Amida Butsu—"All Praise to the Amida Buddha"). In accepting this belief, he rejected the concept that one could

be saved through one's own efforts. As the "Age of Mappo" drew near, the Age of the Destruction of Buddha's Law, Honen became convinced that man could no longer attain salvation by himself; one could still gain admittance to Paradise, but only through exclusive reliance on Amida and his mercy.

As Honen taught this doctrine, and as his fame grew, he was asked to preach at the Imperial court, but he devoted himself instead to preaching primarily to the common man. In 1198, at 66, he put his ideas into writing and so he made his teachings available to later generations as well as for his own time. His very popularity engendered jealousy in other, more orthodox Buddhist theologians, and this envy plagued him during his life-time and was to trouble his sect even after his death. (In 1201, Shinran (1173-1262) became one of his disciples, and he was later to found a variant Jodo sect.) By 1204 Honen had 190 disciples, but in that year the temples at Mount Hiei struck out at his faith by having the court forbid the use of the Nembutsu as an exclusive means of salvation. Basically, these temples were concerned over the grow-ing popularity of Honen's teachings and the spread of his beliefs among the people. His enemies even reached into the Imperial court to attack him, and when one of his disciples,

Anraku, accepted two court ladies as nuns, his theological opponents influenced the former Emperor Go-Toba to order the execution of Anraku and another of Honen's priests in 1207. As a corollary action, the Emperor also exiled Honen from Kyoto in that same year, when Honen was 74–an opportunity to spread his doctrine beyond the capital. At 79 Honen was pardoned. He returned to Kyoto, and re-established his hermitage at the present site of Chion-in. The following year he undertook a religious fast, a pious act that closed his life with his death.

The persecution did not end with Honen's death, for his remains, and later his ashes, had to be secreted at various temples to escape the wrath of his theological opponents before the ashes came to rest in 1234 at the site of his former hermitage, the Chion-in Temple and the mausoleum for his ashes, a tomb which one of his disciples, Genchi, had erected in his honor. The new temple was destroyed by fire in 1431, but the greatest benefactor was Tokugawa Ieyasu, who had it rebuilt on three terraces–the Jo-dan, Chu-dan and Ge-dan (upper, middle and lower terraces). Another fire in 1633 burned all but the San-mon, Kyo-zo, Amida-do and Seishi-do, but Shogun Tokugawa Iemitsu had the temple restored over the next eight years.

SAN-MON GATE Today, the temple grounds beyond Higashi-oji-dori are entered primarily through the San-mon Gate on its western side at Jingu-dori. This huge gateway is at the top of a series of stone steps with large lanterns standing on either side of and in front of the steps. Built between 1617 and 1619 at the order of Shogun Tokugawa Hidetada (restored in 1989), it is a two-story structure with a tile roof. The massive gateway measures 90 feet (27.4 m) wide by 44 feet (13.4 m) deep, by 80 feet (24.4 m) tall. It is a gate with three portals, each with a set of huge double doors, and is one of the most impressive gateways in Japan. A huge tablet, 5 feet (1.5 m) by 8 feet (2.4 m), in the calligraphy of the Emperor Reigan (1663–87) reads "Kacho Zan" (Flower Summit Mount). The second floor of the gateway has a hall in Chinese style, and on a platform at the rear of the hall is an image of Shaka (Sakyamuni) as the main object of worship, with images of Zenzai-doji on his left and Suda-choja on his right. On each side of the main images are eight life-sized *rakan* (disciples of Shaka) by the sculptor Koyu. The interior of the hall is decorated with paintings of mythological animals, dragons, and geometrical designs in rich colors, while the ceiling is enlivened by a painting of a dragon and *apsara* (angels) in the clouds. From the balcony, one can look down the avenue in front of the gate with its cherry trees leading up to the temple–and to the city beyond.

MIE-DO (MEMORIAL HALL) Once past the San-mon Gate, the largest and most important building of the temple, the Mie-do (Main or Memorial Hall) is on the left. The hall was built in 1639 in the Momoyama style by order of Shogun Tokugawa Iemitsu to hold the image of Honen as its main object of reverence. The single-story 11 by 9 bay structure is 174 feet (53 m) long by 140 feet (42.7 m) deep, and it stands 94.5 feet (28.8 m) high. It is surrounded by corridors 11 feet (3.4 m) wide. Under the southwest corner of the roof is an oiled umbrella (*kasa*) which was left in place by the builders at the time of construction as a charm to protect the Mie-do against the forces of evil. Legend, and there is always one, claims that the umbrella flew from the

hands of a boy, the Shinto deity Inari in disguise, as the protector of the Chion-in to safeguard the temple against fires.

The front portion of the Mie-do interior is designed for worshippers, and this area, 34 feet (10.4 m) deep, is covered with 250 *tatami* mats in this 825 mat-sized hall. The attention of the worshippers is directed to the illuminated altar section to the north. Two rows of pillars divide the altar area into three parts, each with an image platform along its rear wall. The central or middle section holds an elaborate shrine in which, behind closed doors, is the seated image of Honen, said to have been carved by the founder of the sect as a self-portrait. Except on ceremonial occasions, the doors to this shrine are kept closed. The altar area is a contrast of black walls and golden pillars so that the golden central section, to which the worshippers' attention is directed, stands out in all of its richness.

The section to the right (east) of this middle area has various shrines, the main shrine holding the Amida image which Honen is said to have worshipped. Another shrine has the image of Zendo, the Chinese master of

Buddhism to whom the Nembutsu practice can be traced. The image has internal organs of brocade, a Chinese Buddhist influence that was meant to make the image a "living" being. This Kamakura period (1185–1333) image is a standing figure, its hands held in prayer, its mouth open. At one time the image had six small Amida figures issuing from its mouth—an indication that the priest was repeating the Nembutsu. Memorial tablets to past abbots are lodged here as well.

Additional shrines hold images of important priests, including that of Genchi, who, as one of Honen's leading disciples, established Chion-in on the site of Honen's hermitage, The section to the left (west) of the central area serves as a memorial to the early Tokugawa who benefited the temple: in a shrine case (*zushi*) on the left is an image of Ieyasu, the first Tokugawa Shogun, who not only rebuilt portions of the temple in the early 1600s but who had the remains of Shinran moved from this area and thus made physically more evident the division between Honen's form of Jodo Amida faith and that of his most famous disciple Shinran.

A group of resident monks stride across the courtyard of Chion-in Temple.

There are additional images, including that of Tokugawa Iemitsu, who ordered the rebuilding of the temple after its latest fire. Hanging in the hall is a large tablet in honor of Honen which reads "Mesho" (Brillant Illumination), a bit of an oddity since it was created at the request of the Emperor Meiji at a time when his government was doing its best to eliminate Buddhism from the Japanese scene. Overall, the shrine glitters with its decorations in gold and black: gilt metal lotuses in giant bronze vases stand 21 feet (6.4 m) tall, great pillars are encased in gold leaf, large ceremonial drums stand in the altar area, and even the door hardware is in the shape of animals. The awe-inspiring visual atmosphere lives up to the Mie-do's alternate name of Dai-den (Great Hall).

SHUE-DO (ASSEMBLY HALL) Corridors surround the Mie-do, as mentioned earlier, and, from the middle of the rear corridor, a 197 foot (60 m) long roofed bridge leads to the Shue-do, the Assembly Hall. The Shue-do, in turn, is connected to the Hojo, the Superior Abbot's Quarters. The corridor lying between the two buildings is the work of the famed craftsman Hidari Jingoro, and the corridor is noted for its *uguisubari* floor–a "bush warbler floor" that emits a sound when trod upon. The Sue-do was constructed in 1639 and is 78 feet (23.8 m) deep by 146 feet (44.5 m) long.

The hall serves a number of purposes: here the monks gather to form the religious processions which are an important part of ceremonial occasions; here religious services are held; and here monks chant the sutras. Some 48 drums are available for religious use by worshippers in this 360-mat hall, a hall so impressive that it has been known with some exaggeration as a "1,000-mat hall." Two altars are the focal point of the hall: the central shrine holds a bronze image of Amida with his hands in a contemplative *mudra* while on either side of him is Seishi on the left and Kannon on the right, all three the works of Eshin Sozu (942–1010); a secondary shrine has an Amida with a Monju in wood on his right in the guise of a robed Buddhist monk. A curiosity that is always pointed out is a huge wooden spoon (O-shakushi), 8.2 feet (2.5 m) long and weighing 66 pounds (30 kg), which is stored in the rafters of the front corridor of the Shue-do at its southeastern end as one moves toward the Dai Hojo.

At the southeast side of the Shue-do is a courtyard and a garden and from its south side there is an entrance both to the garden and to the Hojo (the Abbot's or Superior's Quarters); the garden contains a Bussoku-seki, a stone with the footprint of the Buddha inscribed upon it. A 1639 Kara-mon (Chinese gate) to the Superior's Quarters was created in the ostentatious Momoyama manner, but its doors are only opened for guests of the greatest importance.

THE HOJO (ABBOT'S QUARTERS) The Hojo is composed of two parts: the Dai Hojo and the Sho Hojo, the Greater and Lesser Abbot's Quarters. Particularly noted for its fine *fusuma* (sliding screens) by artists of the Kano school, it is a nine by six bay building with a *hinoki* (cypress) bark roof. Surrounded by corridors, the building is 120 feet (36.6 m) long by 87 feet (26.5 m) deep. The surrounding corridors open on to 11 rooms, which are divided by the *fusuma*. The Dai Hojo is more important than the Sho Hojo since it has a sanctuary for a Buddha image, and thus its screen paintings are richly and gorgeously painted in gold leaf while those of the Sho Hojo are more simple and are painted on plain rather than gilt paper.

The interior of the Dai Hojo is divided into two sections–a north and south set of rooms. The first room on the south side, the portion you enter from the corridor from the Sue-do, is the Matsu-no-ma (Pine Tree Room) by Kano Sadanobu (1596–1622). The Stork (or Crane) Room by Kano Naonobu (1607–50), the middle room on the south side, is so named from the painted storks and pines on a gold ground on the *fusuma*. The room is also known as the Butsu-no-ma since at its rear is an alcove with a standing Amida image on a platform. The third room faces both to the south and to the east, and is one of three rooms on the east side which, when brought together by the removal of the intervening *fusuma*, can become a large, formal Audience Hall for the one-time prince abbot.

The last room has a slightly raised platform (*jodan*) on which the abbot would sit. The room's decorations of plum and bamboo were undertaken by Kano Noanobu in cooperation with Kano Nobumasa. The *tokonoma* by Noanobu features a painting of a Chinese poet looking at a waterfall, and adjacent is a *chigaidana* (staggered shelf), both of which are on the north wall of the room. To the left

The garden of the Hojo (Abbot's Quarters).

of the *chigaidana* on the west wall are doors with red tassels which open to a small room to the rear, the tassels symbolizing the doors behind which guards would have been stationed were this a secular building.

The other rooms are also named for the paintings on their *fusuma*, and these rooms, facing to the north and west, are usually seen as one leaves the Sho Hojo at the end of the visit. The first room on the northeast side of the building is the Ura-jodan-no-ma (Behind the Upper Room or the Prince's Room), where the prince abbot took the tonsure on becoming the superior of the temple. It has a raised *tatami* platform as a seat for the prince abbot, and its *fusuma* are decorated with pine trees on gold.

The next room to the west is the Chrysanthemum Room (Kiku-no-ma), where the paintings of the sparrows by Kano Nobumasa are so life-like that it is said they appear to be flying out of the picture. The Heron Room (Sagi-no-ma), also by Nobumasa, is the third room on the north side, and its rear *fusuma* depict herons while the side *fusuma* show willow trees in winter.

Two rooms on the west side complete the building. The one in the northwest corner is the Willow Room (Yanagi-no-ma), where the trees are shown in winter. The last room in the southwest corner is the Plum Tree Room (Ume-no-ma), which also depicts a wintery

scene with the branches of willow and plum trees covered with snow. These two rooms were decorated by Kano Sadonobu. When going from the Dai Hojo to the Sho Hojo, there is a wooden door that has a faded painting of a cat, famed for the fact that the cat seems to be looking at the viewer no matter from what spot or angle it is regarded. Past the door, a covered bridge leads to the Sho Hojo.

SHO HOJO The Sho Hojo to the northeast is 79 feet (24 m) wide by 69 feet (20.7 m) deep, and is divided into six rooms by *fusuma* (sliding screens). All the rooms are surrounded by corridors encircling the exterior of the building. The first two rooms occupy the western side of the building, the white *fusuma* of the first room (Rante-no-ma) being decorated with blossoming trees while the second room, the Bird and Flower Room (Kacho-no-ma), by Nobumasa, has small pine trees on the *fusuma* with birds flying to the trees. The third room on the north side is an interior room, the Hermits' Room (Rakan-no-ma) with a grouping of 16 *rakan* (disciples of Shaka) in front of a building on its white *fusuma*, also the work of Nobumasa.

Turning the corner to the third (east) side of the building, one arrives at the double room which occupies the entire east side. This is the Audience Room (Jodan-no-ma), with its raised platform for the prince abbot's seat. The rear wall behind the platform has a *tokonoma* with mountains and pines under snow as well as a set of *chigaidana* (staggered shelves). The wall at the inner side of the platform has doors to a small inner room with large tassels while the outer wall has a built-in desk in *shoin* style. The ceiling above the platform has a raised, coffered ceiling. The adjacent room, facing the platform, has a Chinese scene with mountains, a lake and houses. Both rooms are by Naonobu and Sadanobu. Turning the corner to the fourth (south) side is an interior room, the Snow Covered Landscape Room (Sansui-no-ma), decorated by Sadanobu. The rear *fusuma* depicts mountains and a house while the *fusuma* on the right features a boat and a lake. The *fusuma* on the left side shows a mountain and a house. All the landscapes are executed in black and white.

A return is made to the Dai Hojo, passing by the 4th through the 11th rooms (as described above). Both the Dai Hojo and Sho Hojo open on to a garden designed by Kobori

Enshu in 1644. It includes a dwarf pine that was planted by Shogun Tokugawa Iemitsu himself. A little stone bridge that crosses a small gourd-shaped pond is also of note.

SEISHI-DO East of the Mie-do on the hillside is the Seishi-do. A long flight of stone steps leads up the hillside to the east from the Mie-do, and at the top of the steps and through a gate on the left is the Seishi-do on the site where Honen lived and died. Here, after Honen's death, his followers built the Kaisan-do (Founder's Hall), and here the carved wooden image of Honen stood until 1638, when it was moved to the present Mie-do. At that time, the image of the Bodhisattva Seishi was placed in the former Kaisan-do since this Bodhisattva is considered to be a previous incarnation of Honen. The Seishi-do was erected in 1530 and thus it is the oldest building of the Chion-in. It is in two parts, the front hall for worshippers and the back half holding the image of Seishi.

MAUSOLEUM A further flight of steps leads from the Seishi-do to the Mausoleum, which was erected in 1613. The original memorial tomb was created in 1234, but this reconstruction shows the style of the Momoyama period in which it was rebuilt. Two huge bronze lanterns stand before the mausoleum while a small Haiden (Worship Hall) is in front of a Kara-mon (Chinese-style) gate, then there is a grill, and finally the tomb of Honen. (The hillside above the mausoleum holds the general cemetery for the temple.)

AMIDA HALL (AMIDA-DO OR BUTSU-DEN) To the west of the Mie-do, and connected to it by a roofed corridor, is the Amida-do, the hall dedicated to Amida, the primary Buddha of the Chion-in. It is at a right angle from the Mie-do due to the terrain of the precinct. (This hall is just above the San-mon entry gate and the Re-to pagoda.) From the earliest period of Chion-in's history there has been a special building devoted to Amida, the original hall being constructed by Honen's disciples on the hill to the east near the site of Honen's hermitage. In 1710, it was moved to its present location, and then in 1912, on the 700th anniversary of Honen's death in 1212, a new Amida Hall was created through the gifts of the faithful. On the front of the hall is a tablet which reads "Otani-dera" (Otani Temple, so-called from the original

name of the area and the temple), which was inscribed and given as a gift by the Emperor Gonara (1526–57). The plaque was mounted on the earlier as well as the present building.

The double-tiled roof hall (a hall which represents the Pure Land of Amida) faces to the east so that the worshippers when praying to Amida are facing toward Amida's Western Paradise. The main object of veneration is a 9 foot (2.7 meter) tall gilt image of Amida. Inside this Amida image is a tiny Amida which was created by Priest Kwan-in and which Honen held to his bosom on his death bed. The gold and black contrast that is found in the Mie-do is further carried out in the highly decorated interior of the Amida-do. On the matted floor at the front of the worship area are drums for use during services.

RE-TO (MEMORIAL PAGODA) Just south of the Amida-do is the pagoda to the 7.5 million spirits. A two-story pagoda with vermilion wooden fabric and white walls, it holds an image of Amida on its main, raised floor. Beneath it is a charnel room that is connected with the Amida-do by an underground passageway.

KYO-ZO (SUTRA HALL) Southeast of the Mie-do toward the hillside is the two-story Kyo-zo (Sutra Hall) built by order of Tokugawa Hidetada in 1616. A mixture of Chinese and Japanese architectural elements, it is topped with a ball that caps the square, pyramidal tiled roof. The lower story of the Kyo-zo has an open "corridor" created by the freestanding pillars of the structure. The building contains the complete set of the Buddhist *Issai-kyo Sutra*, which was printed at the time of the Sung dynasty in China in the 12th century. The 5,600 volumes are in an octagonal revolving bookcase, which is so well constructed that it will turn upon the slightest touch. A common belief held that revolving the bookcase three times would grant merit to the individual turning the books, which in effect meant their complete reading. The lower shelf of the case has eight deities carved in wood as well as the statue of Fu Hsi and his two sons, P'u Chien and P'u Ch'eng. Fu Hsi was given credit for having invented the form of the revolving sutra case in China.

TAIHEI-TEI (PEACE HALL) Opposite the front of the Mie-do and to the right of the head of the steps of the San-mon entrance to the main temple grounds is the Taihei-tei, the Peace Hall. Rebuilt in concrete after a 1958 fire, the building serves as a rest hall, tea room and religious articles sales counter for the benefit of visitors. Within is a cauldron 11 feet (3.3 m) in diameter by 3.5 feet (1.1 m) in height that was cast in 1604 by the famous cauldron maker Onishi Yojiro. (Public restrooms are to the west of this building.)

DAI SHO OR SHORO (GREAT BELL) The temple bell, the largest bronze bell in Japan, lies to the southeast of the Taihei-tei on a rise of a number of steps. Cast in the 1630s, it stands 10.8 feet (3.3 m) high, is 9 feet (2.7 m) in diameter, 11.4 inches (28 cm) thick and weighs 74 tons. The wooden belfry in the Tenjikuyo (Indian) style was created in 1678. It takes 17 men to pull back the clapper in order to ring the bell. On the 19th and 25th of each month it booms forth in commemoration of the death of Honen on that day in April 1212. It is rung on special occasions as well, but each year between April 10th and 25th it sounds majestically in the annual celebration of Gyoki-e in memory of Honen. It is known throughout Japan, since on New Year's Eve it is tolled 108 times to ring out the 108 sins to which mankind is susceptible—an event that is televised throughout the nation.

HOMOTSU-KAN (TREASURY) The Treasury is a modern fireproof concrete building opposite the Mie-do. Among its many treasures are a noted 13th century painting (Raigo) in colors of Amida's descent from his paradise, surrounded by his 25 Bodhisattvas, to receive the souls of the dying.

There is also the Honen Shonin Eden from 1299–1301, a picture scroll by Tosa Yoshimitsu of Honen's life in 48 scrolls; and a standing statue of Zendo from the T'ang period (618–907) in China, who was one of the important figures in Jodo (Amida) beliefs in China. Legend holds that when Zendo said his prayers to Amida, a halo of light would issue from his mouth. There are, of course, numerous other treasures as well.

CHION-IN CEREMONIES
April 19–25–Gyoki-e: The most important service of the year is the Gyoki-e since it commemorates the death of Honen in 1212. There are daily processions and services by 200 priests dressed in rich brocades.

The bronze bell at Chion-in is the largest in Japan.

November 1–10–Viewing of the temple treasures: From 9:00 a.m. to 4:00 p.m. the temple treasures are on display in the Homotsukan (Treasury). Viewing fee.
December 31–Omisoke (Last Grand Day): At midnight the temple bell is tolled 108 times symbolizing the 108 sins to which mankind is liable. In a sense, this is a ceremony of absolution that permits believers to begin the new year afresh and free of sin.

GETTING THERE

The beginning of the tour at Yasaka Pagoda can be reached from the bus stop at Higashi-oji-dori and Kiyomizu-michi. Buses 202, 203, 206 or 207, which run along Higashi-oji-dori, serve the bus stop. This is the same bus stop used in Tour 1 and portions of this tour could be easily combined with parts of Tour 1.

Chion-in, perhaps the highlight of this tour, is open daily from 9:00 a.m. to 4:00 p.m. Free entry. However, the Hojo and Sho Hojo are only open in the autumn, for a modest fee. On leaving the temple, buses 11, 12, 18, 203, 206 and 207 stop at the Chion-in-mae bus stop on Higashi-oji-dori just to the west of the temple's San-mon Gate. These can take you to the south or the north of the city.

Walking Tour 4

KENNIN-JI AREA

The Six Realms of the Dead, the Dancing Saint and Zen Beginnings

1 **Chinko-ji Temple** 六道珍皇寺
2 **Rokuhara-mitsu-ji Temple** 六波羅蜜寺
3 **Ebisu Shrine** 京都ゑびす神社
4 **Kennin-ji Temple** 建仁寺
5 **Yasui Kompira Shrine** 安井金比羅宮

The contrast between the secular and the religious has always permeated Kyoto life and history. Kennin-ji, one of the earliest and most important of Kyoto's Zen monasteries, for example, is a next door neighbor to the Pleasure Quarters that have made the name Gion synonymous with the pursuits of the "floating world" of *kabuki* and of the *ochaya* (tea houses) where men can be well fed while being entertained by *geisha* (if they can afford such luxurious pleasures and have the proper introduction to the proprietress of the *ocha-ya*), as well as other delights both licit and illicit. This is the area to be explored on this and the next walk.

The Rokuhara district, which forms part of this tour, has its own major sites, such as Ebisu Shrine, whose festive occasions are thronged by businessmen and the general public in the hope of increasing their wealth. It has the Wakamiya Shrine just north of Gojo-dori (Fifth Street), which presides over the district itself as well as the great pottery fairs held annually on Gojo-dori. Here, too, is the Rokuhara-mitsu-ji Temple, which enshrines the magnificent, realistic image of that Saint of the Marketplace, Priest Kuya, portrayed as though still walking the streets of the city, beating his drum while repeating the Nembutsu ("Praise to Amida Buddha") that issues from the image's mouth in the form of tiny Amida figures.

The Rokuhara district where this walk begins was once the seat of the proud and powerful. Here, in the mid-1100s, the Taira

clan and their followers had their mansions and governmental offices—before Taira-no-Kiyomori made the mistake, after his forces had killed Minamoto-no-Yoshitomo, of permitting the Minamoto children to live if they were placed in monasteries to become monks. In time, they grew up and revolted against Taira rule, a revolt which in 1185 led not only to the burning of the palatial mansions of the Taira (and much of eastern Kyoto) but to the death of Kiyomori's family, his followers and his Imperial grandson. Here, after 1185, the

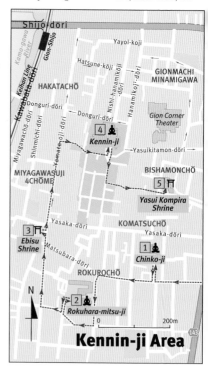

Kennin-ji Area

Visitors crowd the entrance to Chinko-ji, the "Six Realms of the Dead Temple."

Minamoto victors set up their Kyoto headquarters, so that the area remained the locus of political power in the city under the rule by the Minamoto Shoguns from Kamakura between 1185 and 1333.

There is the mysterious in this sector as well, for portions of the Rokuhara district were once the burial grounds for the common people, and here is supposed to be located the "Six Avenues" that lead to the other world, where the souls of the dead reside until called back for the brief O-Bon period each mid-summer by the bell of the Chinko-ji Temple. The Yasui Kompira Shrine in the district, while not mysterious in itself, has its mystery in that Kompira, the deity worshipped at the shrine, has never been truly identified, and confusion reigns as to his true identity—which in no way discourages those who pray to him for safety in travel.

It was at Kennin-ji that tea first became popular as a beverage that alerts but does not intoxicate. When Priest Eisai established the Kennin-ji monastery, he reintroduced tea as a beverage from China, a refreshment that had previously not received the welcome it was to engender from this time on. Tea moved eventually from the monastery into daily life, and special establishments were created for the enjoyment of the beverage. While the *ochaya* (Honorable Tea Houses) of the area serve a more potent beverage today, the origin of tea culture is still remembered not only in the formal tea ceremony but in the historical procession each spring to commemorate the bringing of the first, tender tea leaves to Kyoto from Uji each year for the benefit of the Shogun—a procession still celebrated as a remembrance of times past.

① CHINKO-JI TEMPLE

The Rokudo-mairi, the "Six Roads Pilgrimage," is the legendary road that links the world of the living and the world of the dead, or the spirit world. One old belief held that if you were to stand in the middle of this road while beating a gong and calling out the name of a deceased family member, the voice and sound would guide the ancestral spirit back to this world for the annual visit of such spirits to their former homes.

The Rokudo-mairi is thought to be near the Chinko-ji Temple, which is also known as the Rokudo-san, the "Six Realms of the Dead

Temple." The association of the temple with the road of legend can be attributed to the fact that the Toribeno Cemetery once extended from Kiyomizu-dera and the adjacent Nishi Otani mausoleum to the Rokuhara-mitsu-ji area, which lies north of Gojo-dori (Fifth Street) and between Higashi-oji-dori and the Kamo-gawa River to the west. This area was known as the "land of the dead," a place where the bodies of those who died without family were often abandoned, and a pilgrimage to Toribeno was a symbolic journey through Rokudo (Six Realms of the Dead). The small Rokudo-no-Tsuji square in front of Chinko-ji is said to stand at the beginning of the six avenues leading to the several levels of hell. This connection of the temple with the supposed avenue led to the custom among the poorer people of Kyoto of praying here for the souls of their deceased loved ones.

Chinko-ji is a small, rather nondescript temple which lies north of Matsubara-dori. Walk north from Matsubara-dori into the short street that leads to the small square formed by the Chinko-ji Temple buildings on the east, north and west sides. The buildings at Chinko-ji are only open occasionally, thus it is best to inquire at the Tourist Information Center downtown as to their times of admission.

In the middle, before the Hondo (Main Hall), is a modern, stylized *sotoba* (five-part memorial stone), 16 feet (4.5 m) tall, within a stone fence and with pine trees along its side. On the left (west) side of the square is a small shrine, and just beyond it to the north is a plastic-roofed area covering a large Jizo image with a stone lantern before it and a stone flower holder on either side. Around this central unit are some 200 smaller Jizo images or inscribed stones. (Images of Jizo are often placed in cemeteries or places associated with death since he is a protector of the dead.)

On the right side as one enters the square is a small *kura* (storage building) and then a building that houses those connected with the other world (see below). This right side of the entrance to the square was a favorite meeting place for the itinerant nuns who gathered here in the mid-summer Bon season, when the souls of the dead return to this world for a brief stay. Here they would solicit alms by exhibiting picture screens of hell to the people who gathered to pray for the souls of the deceased. (The "floating population" of Japan in the period after the 1500s, despite the attempts to control the movement of the populace by the Tokugawa government, consisted of pious monks and nuns and artists raising funds for their own benefit.)

The hall beyond the *kura* can be looked into from the outside even when it is not open. It is divided into two parts: the left section contains an image of Emma, the king of hell, with an attendant on either side. The right half of the building holds a statue of Ono-no-Takamura, a noted poet of the first half of the 800s, whose fame as a writer led many to believe that he was a messenger to and the secretary of the ruler of hell itself. He is accompanied by two emissaries from hell. At the north end of the square is the Hondo (Main Hall), which contains a statue of Yakushi, a particularly important Buddha for this area since it is believed that he is able to rescue the suffering from hell.

The temple bell, the Mukae-gane (Bell of Welcome) to the southeast of the Hondo, is rung during the Bon period in summer, and it is thought that its sound can be heard in the other world, the world of the dead. The sound ostensibly leads the spirits of that region back to earth. Priest Keishun is said to have had the bell created, and when he left for a three-year visit to China to study Buddhism, he had the bell buried. Curiosity overcame the priest left in charge of the temple, and he unearthed the bell and rang it in order to hear its pure sound. On his return to Japan, Keishun reprimanded the curious priest since, he claimed, he had heard the sound of the bell even in China.

☑ ROKUHARA-MITSU-JI TEMPLE

If Chinko-ji is connected with beliefs involving the dead, the nearby Rokuhara-mitsu-ji Temple is associated with the pious Priest Kuya, who was concerned to save the souls of individuals while they were still living and to assure them of a place in Amida's Western Paradise after death. The temple lies to the west and south of Matsubara-dori, the same street traversed to reach Chinko-ji. Coming from Higashi-oji-dori on Matsubara-dori, turn left at the fourth street on the left, which brings you to the temple on the west side of the street. (It is open from 8:00 a.m. to 5:00 p.m. There is an entry fee to the Treasure House but no fee to the temple itself.)

Rokuhara-mitsu-ji was established by Priest Kuya, the "Dancing Saint" or "Saint of the Marketplace," in 963, and the continued

A statue of Kannon in the courtyard of Rokuhara-mitsu-ji Temple.

existence of the temple is a testimony to the importance of this man who affected the lives of the common people during his own and later times.

Kuya Shonin (903-72), according to some accounts, was the son of the Emperor Daigo (reigned 897-930), a claim often made to give distinguished commoners a noble heritage. Whatever his lineage, whether noble or otherwise, he devoted his life to helping the common man, traveling from village to village, aiding and instructing the peasants in digging wells, building and repairing bridges and roads, and caring for the sick. A devotee of Amida, he spread the belief and faith in Amida as he traveled from town to town, chanting and singing the Nembutsu ("Praise to Amida Buddha") to folk tunes while he danced and beat upon his wooden food bowl to keep time. Clad in a thin deerskin, a bell about his neck so as to draw attention to his mission, his antler-headed staff in one hand, he danced the byways of villages and the streets of towns singing:

One never fails
To reach the Pure Land
If one calls,
Just once,
The name of Amida.

(This chanting dance is still performed at the Todai-ji Temple in Nara on May 2nd in honor of Emperor Shomu and at the Kuya-do Temple in Kyoto in mid-November in memory of Priest Kuya.)

Kuya came to Kyoto in 938, making his home in the marketplaces where he begged for food, a standard practice of Buddhist monks since the giving of alms by the faithful to monks is considered a religious duty. He sang and danced the praises of Amida, but he also attended the sick and the poor, making green tea from bamboo for them and offering them a little pickled plum with the tea while he intoned a Buddhist invocation. Many of the sick were healed under his care. The populace named him the "Saint of the Marketplace" or the "Nembutsu Saint"—just as villagers had named the wells he helped them dig as "Amida wells."

Kuya arrived at the great monastic center of Enryaku-ji on top of Mount Hiei to the northeast of Kyoto in 948, and there he was received into the monastery for study and monastic discipline. He was given the name of Kosho by the noted priest Ensho of Enryaku-ji. In 951, however, a plague settled upon Kyoto, and Kuya returned to the city and carved a large image of the 11-headed Kannon. He pulled this image on a cart through the streets of Kyoto, thereby, according to popular belief, helping to end the plague. Eventually he built a temple, Saiko-ji, on land given by the great Taira family (whose mansions lay in the district), and here he served as its head priest. Here, too, his image of Kannon was ensconced, and thus began the history of the Rokuhara-mitsu-ji. The temple was enlarged by his successors and, though tradition states that the present main hall of the temple is the original Seiko-ji Hondo, that original building was destroyed in a fire. The present hall and its Kannon image date from 1463.

As with other legends concerning noted figures in early Japanese history, it was recorded that, at his death, Kuya washed and put on clean clothes, lay down facing to the west, his eyes closed as he meditated. Thus he died, facing the Western Paradise where he would meet Amida. It is said that a heavenly perfume and music filled the air at the moment of his demise.

After Kuya's death, his disciples expanded Rokuhara-mitsu-ji, and it became a center of Tendai (Amida) Buddhism. During the ascendancy of the Taira clan (1140–83), the Taira and their followers had their mansions in this area, and the temple flourished under their patronage. Upon the fall of the Taira in 1183, when Minamoto Yoritomo attacked Kyoto and the Taira forces, the Taira set fire to each of their 20 mansions before fleeing the city. Some 4,000–5,000 houses of their retainers and of the general populace went up in flames, but the Main Hall of the temple was spared during the conflagration, which destroyed much of this portion of eastern Kyoto.

Fires have destroyed the temple buildings on numerous occasions since that time, and the Hondo of 1463 is the oldest part of the temple still standing. When Hideyoshi built his Great Buddha at Hoko-ji Temple in the 1590s, he generously repaired Rokuhara-mitsu-ji as well. A further restoration was carried out in 1969.

The one-story Hondo (Main Hall), of decorated vermilion posts and beams contrasting with white plaster walls and a dark-tiled roof, offers an attractive sight in the heart of a busy city district. Set before the steps leading into the Main Hall are a large incense pot and a perpetual flame. To the left of the steps is a box of stones from which the devout can build small stupas (pagodas), in accordance with the belief that the souls of dead children

wander at the border of the River Sai, condemned to pursue salvation by building towers of stone, which are kicked down by sadistic demons. Jizo, the guardian of children, drives away the demons. Thus the piling up of stones, such as at this temple, can help the souls of the children to Buddhist salvation.

Within the Hondo, the main image is an 11-headed Kannon with a Jizo on its left and a Yakushi Nyorai on its right. At the four corners of the altar stand the Shi-tenno (Four Deva Kings) on guard against the forces of evil. These guardians were carved by the great 13th century sculptor Unkei.

The main reason for visiting the Rokuhara-mitsu-ji is to see the statues preserved in its Treasury Building, a separate small, fireproof, ferro-concrete building to the southwest of the Hondo. It contains a number of notable statues of the 12th to 13th centuries. On either side of the interior entry of the building is a display of scrolls, the temple holding the written will of the great priest Kobo Daishi (Kukai) among other treasures. Against the left wall in the Treasury proper is a freestanding image of Emma, the unpleasant looking king of hell, with a scribe and attendants on either side. Against the right wall is an image of Yakushi Nyorai, the deity of healing, with a medicine pot in his left hand. He is flanked by life-sized Shi-tenno guardian images on his right and left. The major treasures of the temple are lined up along the rear wall of the building (some labels are in English), and they include a number of the finest portrait statues of the Kamakura period (1185–1333). The seated images are approximately 3 feet (90 cm) tall. From left to right, the statues are:

1. A seated statue of the sculptor Tankei, a rosary in his hand. This 1264 image is claimed to be a self-portrait.

2. A 12th century realistic seated image of Jizo by Unkei. This Jizo was originally the main object of worship in the Jurin-in of the Bodai-ji Temple near Hachijo-dori (Eighth Street), and it is thought that it was flanked by the figures of Unkei and Tankei, which still stand on either side of it today. As the Kei family temple, the Bodai-ji was created by Unkei near his workshop. The image, now darkened by time, was once painted in rich colors; traces of cut gold leaf patterns can still be seen on parts of the robe. The image has the extended ear lobes of a Buddhist prince,

pendant ear rings, crystal eyes and the third "eye" of knowledge in mid-forehead. A separately carved wooden necklace has been placed upon its chest. In its left hand it holds the magic jewel associated with Jizo.

3. A seated painted wooden image of the sculptor Unkei, a rosary in his hands. It is thought that this may also be a self-portrait.

4. A 13th century seated image of Taira-no-Kiyomori (1118–81) reading a sutra scroll is here realistically represented—but as a monk, a role beyond his moral capabilities. The sutra scroll is held in both his hands as he peruses it, and his sleeves flow in rich drapery from his arms.

5. A life-sized Jizo by the 11th century sculptor Jocho. The deity appears in the form of a young monk with long sleeves, a fly whisk of hair in his left hand. His empty right hand would once have held the mystic gem which Jizo normally holds. The eyes of the image are of glass. A fretwork aureole with small Buddhas stands behind the image.

6. The famed painted wood image of Priest Kuya by Kosho, the fourth of Unkei's sons, is preserved in the Treasury. Kuya is seen as the itinerant priest that he was in life: he is clothed in his short, shabby deerskin covering, his feet shod with straw sandals. A round gong hangs down his chest, supported from a harness around his neck. In his right hand he holds a T-shaped wooden hammer to beat the gong as he dances and sings the praises of Amida, and in his left hand he holds his wooden staff with its antler top. From his mouth, on a wire, issues a row of six tiny Amida images, symbolizing Kuya's constant repetition of the Nembutsu in praise of Amida. These six images represent the six characters of the spoken Nembutsu (*na-mu-a-mi-da-butsu*). Thus Kosho has, in a sense, carved the voice of Kuya as he chants the Nembutsu while on a pilgrimage.

A realistic portrait, down to the wrinkled and worn deerskin, the prominent Adam's apple of his neck, the veins in his arms and legs, and even the seams on the inside of his sleeves—all are portrayed in a life-like manner. Here, the "Saint of the People" is represented as he would have appeared to the people of his time. An innovative and original presentation, it was created in a novel and successful manner and represents the climax of Kamakura realism in sculpture.

7. An image of a member of the Taira era wearing an *eboshi* (nobleman's tall hat) on his head, a formal representation of a governmental figure of the middle ages.

8. A figure of Kobo Daishi (Kukai) seated on a Chinese chair, his shoes beneath the chair. This realistic but restrained portrait was created by Chokai, a disciple of the master sculptor Kaikei, between 1249 and 1256. In his right hand Kukai holds a rosary and in his left hand is a thunderbolt. This portrait sculpture is modeled after an image in the To-ji Temple created by Kosho, but it is a stiffer presentation of the great Buddhist priest.

3 EBISU SHRINE

The Rokuhara district has developed as a commercial center through the years, and thus it is only appropriate that a shrine to Ebisu, the Shinto patron of success in business, should be enshrined here. Thus we move from a saint, who was concerned with helping people to Amida's Western Paradise after death, to a deity whose concern is wealth in this life. (Ebisu Shrine is located west and then north of Matsubara-dori. After returning to Matsubara-dori, turn left and then make a right (north) turn on Yamato-oji-dori, the next through street. Ebisu Shrine is on the left hand side just ahead. The shrine is open during daylight hours without entry fee.)

Ebisu, the god of wealth, depicted at Ebisu Shrine.

Ebisu is one of the seven gods of good fortune, the only one of the seven to originate from Japan. He is the patron of business and merchants, thereby making him a very popular deity. A chubby fellow, he appears with a fishing line and a fish in his hand. His shrine in the Gion district is behind two *torii,* with the usual stone lanterns and the guardian *koma-inu* (lion-dogs) before the second *torii.* Shrine buildings line the left (south) side of the precincts, while a dragon fountain at the water purification basin is on the right. Straight ahead is the Heiden (Offertory), behind a wooden fence, on which is a large drum. The Honden (Main Building) enshrining the god spirit is behind the Heiden. To the left of the rear portion of the Honden is a life-sized statue of a white horse; white horses are often found at Shinto shrines since they are said to be favorites of the gods. Beyond is a formal gateway to the street on the west.

The Ebisu Shrine is most noted for its ceremonies, which occur throughout the year. The festival-loving Ebisu and his joyous ceremonies reflect one aspect of the Japanese temperament when it comes to religion: the acceptance of the life of this world and the pleasure that can be enjoyed while one is here. On the other hand, there is the contemplative aspect of the Japanese nature as well, and it can be realized at the Kennin-ji Zen monastery, just a short walk north along Yamato-oji-dori.

④ KENNIN-JI TEMPLE

As an active monastery, the interior of the monastic buildings of the Kennin-ji Temple and its subtemples are generally not open to the public, but they may be visited in the morning if permission is obtained in advance in writing from the temple office. Generally, permission is granted for morning visits if one's purpose is of a serious nature. (The temple Hondo, a few subtemples, and the temple Treasury are open to the public from November 1st to 10th from 9:00 a.m. to 4:00 p.m. The grounds are open to the public daily without charge.)

Kennin-ji was the first Zen temple established in Japan and, as such, it was the head temple for Zen monasteries in Kyoto for many years. The temple was begun by Priest Eisai in 1202 at the request of the Shogun, and it is here that Eisei (1141–1215) established the Rinzai sect of Zen Buddhism in Japan.

When he was 14 years old, Eisai went to the monastic community of Mount Hiei to enter the religious life. Here he studied the Tendai version of Buddhism. Achieving the goal of many Japanese monks, he journeyed to China, the source of Japanese Buddhism, in 1168 to study at Tendai monasteries. He made a second trip in 1187, not returning to Japan until 1191 when he settled at a temple in Kyushu, where he began to teach the doctrines of Zen Buddhism that he had encountered in China. With his belief that Zen would protect the state during Mappo (see below), his doctrines attracted the attention of Shogun Minamoto-no-Yoriie, and the Shogun invited him to Kyoto to head Kennin-ji and to establish the Rinzai sect of Bud-dhism there.

Chouontei Garden, nestled behind the main building at Kennin-ji, the oldest Zen temple in Kyoto.

In time, Eisai was to establish Zen monasteries in Kamakura as well, the seat of government of the Shoguns. At his death, Eisai was buried at Kennin-ji.

Eisai lived during Mappo (The Age of the Disappearance of the Buddhist Law), a degenerate period that was thought to have begun about 1050, a period in which men would realize the inability of man to understand Buddhist doctrine or belief. In those degenerate days, one could no longer depend on one's own mind or one's own efforts, nor could one call on Amida or on scripture or ceremonies for help. What was needed, according to Eisai, was an intuitive method of spiritual training in order to obtain a lofty transcendence over worldly care, a transcendence of the individu-

al that would permit the religious seeker to reach the fundamental unity that pervades all existence and the universe. The mental discipline involved in this method would develop a mind receptive to the basic truths of the universe, a mind which was under control and free from the fear of physical danger from without or passion from within. A mind under such control was worthy of an abbot–or a soldier, as the military of the Kamakura period (1192–1333) came to believe.

The encouragement of the growth of Zen monasteries was one aspect of the Shoguns' policy. In the case of Kennin-ji, its physical size was so huge that it was made a national project. Its construction was completed in 1205. Unfortunately, the growth of military

A painting of a dragon in the Chinese style by Kaihoku Yushu decorates a ceiling at Kennin-ji.

government would in time lead to war and the fall of the Kamakura government. Burned in 1256, rebuilt in 1257-9, the monastery was enriched by the Minamoto, the Hojo and the Ashikaga rulers in turn. At the height of its power, it had 53 subtemples. The wars of the Sengoku Jidai (Age of the Country at War) in the 15th and 16th centuries, particularly the Onin Wars of 1467-77, led to the virtual destruction of Kyoto. Kennin-ji was spared during this time, but in 1556, in another outbreak of fighting, the temple was almost completely destroyed.

Many of the present Kennin-ji buildings date from the 18th century or later. Only the Chokushi-mon (Imperial Messenger's Gate), also called the Yatate-mon (Arrow Gate) from the scars left upon it during the civil wars of the 15th and 16th centuries, remains from the early period of the temple's existence. This black gate at the southern edge of the temple precincts is said to have once been a portion of the nearby Rokuhara headquarters of the Taira clan.

In 1763, the restoration of the Kennin-ji Temple began in earnest, both through new construction and by moving of buildings that belonged to other temples to the Kennin-ji

site. The Butsu-den (Main Hall or Buddha Hall), originally at the Tofuku-ji Temple just south of the main area of Kyoto, was put in place in 1763 and was handsomely refurbished. What is now the Abbot's apartment (Hojo) originally was a temple building from the Ankoku-ji Temple in Hiroshima Prefecture, a structure built by the first Ashikaga Shogun, Takauji, in the 14th century. It was moved from Ankoku-ji in the 1590s. Near the south gate of the temple grounds is the Marishi-ten Shrine, which was built in 1327 by Seisetsu, a Chinese priest who is said to have brought the clay from China to create the image of Marishi (Queen of Heaven) with its white face and colorful clothes, and who is here riding upon seven golden boars. The shrine has always been a popular one among the *geisha* of the Gion district.

Among the most noted treasures of the monastery are the paintings of Kaihoku Yusho (1533-1615). In the late 1590s, a few years before his death, Priest Ekei, the abbot of the Ankoku-ji, moved to Kennin-ji and, with the financial help of Hideyoshi, he began the restoration of the fire- and storm-damaged Abbot's Quarters. In 1598, he had his artist friend Kaihoku Yusho create five sets of painted sliding doors (*fusuma*) for the Hojo. Yusho is noted for the directness and vitality of the straight line, which succeeds in simplifying technique–as would be expected in paintings for Zen monasteries. He painted landscapes and dragons at the Kennin-ji Temple, which holds his largest body of work. In 1934, a typhoon inflicted serious damage on the temple, and the paintings were remounted as 50 hanging scrolls. Done in the Chinese "impressionistic" style, the paintings present vistas of temple buildings with hints of trees and hills about the structures. They are now in various subtemples of the complex.

The Zenkyo-an subtemple in the grounds of the Kennin-ji was also restored in 1599 after the damage suffered by the main temple. Here, Yusho created a dozen panels of pine, bamboo and plum trees in black ink on a gold leaf ground, based on a theme in Chinese paintings. Other screens by Yusho are in Kanzen-ji (another subtemple), as is a pair of six-fold screens in the Reito-in in ink and light color. The subjects of the Reito-in screens are those of scholars talking or viewing the distant scene. Many of these paintings can be viewed during the November showing of the temple's treasures.

Kennin-ji is noted not only for the Zen faith which was here brought to Japan but also the monastery's connection with tea. Although Kobo Daishi (Kukai) introduced tea into Japan from China in the 800s, it did not become fashionable until it was reintroduced by Eisai. Eisai brought the plant and beverage to Japan for religious purposes, since it helped to keep monks alert during long nightly devotions. It also served as a mild medicine in certain illnesses. Eisai wrote a book about the value of tea, and a simple tea ceremony that began at Kennin-ji was later developed into the highly formal and stylized approach of Sen-no-Rikyu and others in the late 16th century and thereafter. Legend holds that Eisai's devotion to tea was supported by the young Shogun Sanetomo when Eisai weaned him from wine to tea drinking.

Each spring the Shogun required the tea dealers of Uji to present their first tea leaves in Kyoto, a crop that arrived packed in large ceramic jars. In memory of those times, a procession of tea jars is carried each year on May 2nd from Kennin-ji to Yasaka Shrine along Yamato-ojo-dori and then Shijo-dori.

5 YASUI KOMPIRA SHRINE

At the beginning of this walk, it was indicated that a mystery surrounded the Yasui Kompira Shrine, where this walk ends. Thus, perhaps, it is well to move from so serious an institution as Kennin-ji to a shrine that can insure one's well-being when traveling. The Yasui Kompira Shrine is between Higashi-oji-dori and Kennin-ji, to the west of the Yasaka Pagoda. The shrine can most easily be located by starting from the Higashiyama-Yasui bus stop (midway between the Kiyomizu-michi and the Shijo-dori stops) and then by walking to the west. Turn left at the first through street, and the second street on the left leads to the shrine. (The shrine is open during daylight hours. Its museum (Kompira-Ema-kan) is generally open from 10:00 a.m. to 4:00 p.m., but is closed on Mondays.)

Kompira is a deity about whose identification there is confusion. (Kompira originally was the Indian deity Kumhira, the crocodile god of the Ganges River in India.) Some say he is one of the various Shinto deities, while others claim he was an early Japanese emperor. Nonetheless, he is a being who is worshipped and who is found to be efficacious in answering prayers from his believers despite his anonymous nature.

In the 9th century, a temple to Kompira was erected in Shikoku, perhaps by Kukai (Kobo Daishi), and a number of similar temples sprang up in time all over Japan. In 1872, the Meiji government made the Shikoku Temple a Shinto shrine (as were other Kompira units) to Okuninushi-no-mikoto, god of Izumo, but it remains unclear as to who the deity is who resides there. Be that as it may, Kompira is a very popular deity who is invoked by travelers and seamen in times of need or in gratitude for past favors.

Down the narrow street from Higashi-oji-dori, you arrive at a shrine that is not unlike other Shinto shrines. The Heiden (Offertory) has racks to the north and south of its platform on which *ema* have been hung. *Ema* are prayer boards on which one writes a prayer or a wish. They usually bear a depiction of the deity or of a scene connected with the deity of the shrine. Thousands of *ema*, some of which are centuries old, are on view in the Shrine Museum. Some of these *ema* have traditional horse pictures, while others are of *sumo* wrestlers or boats, since Kompira is the seaman's patron. Painted on wood, some of these *ema* are by noted artists of the Edo period (1603–1868), when such pictures were given to shrines by devotees.

Beyond the Heiden to the west is the Honden (Spirit Hall) with its Kara (Chinese-style) roof. Additional ancillary buildings are on either side of the main shrine buildings, the museum being to the east (in front of the Heiden). A curious stone with a hole in its center is to the left of the Heiden. It is covered with *fude*, the name stickers that pilgrims usually affix to the gates of Buddhist temples, an indication to the deity that one has given reverence to him. Strangely enough, the shrine now has a Glass Gallery with objects of Art Nouveau glass.

GETTING THERE

Begin the tour at Chinko-ji. The remaining sites are nearby. To reach Chinko-ji, take bus 206 or 207, which travels north and south on Higashi-oji-dori, to the Kiyomizu-michi bus stop (the same stop as in Tour 1). From there, walk west on Matsubara-dori (the westward extension of Kiyomizu-michi) for one long block. Turn north to Chinko-ji, which lies at the end of this side street.

Walking Tour 5

GION AREA

The Gion Shrine, the Pleasure Quarters and the Floating World

☐1 **Yasaka Shrine (Gion Shrine)** 八坂神社
☐2 **The Pleasure Quarters**
　　花街 (祇園、先斗町、嶋原)
☐3 **Ichi-riki Ochaya** 一力茶屋
☐4 **Central Kyoto** 京都中心街 (寺町通)

The section of Kyoto bounded by Sanjo-dori (Third Street) and Shijo-dori (Fourth Street) on both sides of the Kamo-gawa (Kamo River) can truly be called Kyoto's "Pleasure Quarters." There are historic reasons for this, primarily because the section of the city to the east of the Kamo River encompasses the Gion district which, since the late 1500s, has been the *geisha* and *ochaya* (tea house) section, and here it was that *kabuki* also had its beginnings. Although the ranks of *geisha* have thinned in modern times, the *geisha* and the *ochaya* still have

their places here, and *kabuki* continues to delight its followers on the stage of the Minami-za (South Theater) in Gion.

The area to the west of the Kamo River offers a different type of pleasure, since the streets between Karasuma-dori on the west, the Kamo River on the east, Shijo-dori on the south and Oike-dori on the north form a shopper's paradise. Here, department stores and specialty shops can please the most avid of consumers, be they connoisseurs of the finest of crafts and of fashion or devotees of the latest in tourist ephemera.

Although modern commercialism abounds within this crowded enclave, traditional pleasures are not overlooked. Each year during July, this area enjoys the annual Gion Festival, when the great Gion carts are pulled by men in traditional attire in memory of the city's deliverance from a plague many centuries

The main two-story gateway (Ro-mon) leading to Yasaka Shrine.

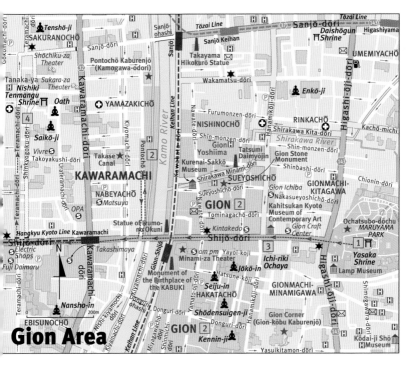

ago. That ceremony begins at the Yasaka Jinja (Yasaka Shrine), commonly called Gion Shrine, to the east of the river, and that is where this walk will also begin.

1 YASAKA SHRINE (GION SHRINE)

Yasaka Shrine (or Gion Shrine) is one of the most important Shinto shrines in Kyoto, and is much beloved by its citizens. The shrine is located near downtown at the intersection of Shijo-dori and Higashi-oji-dori. It is open at all times. No admission fee is charged.

As the shrine to the spirit of the *kami* (deity) who is honored at the great Gion Festival, Yasaka Shrine is the starting point for the festival procession that winds its way through the streets of Kyoto every July 17th. It is also a special center for worship on New Year's Day and on other traditional occasions.

Reputedly founded in 656 AD, before the creation of Kyoto as a city, the shrine is dedicated to the Shinto deities Susa-no-o-mikoto (the wayward brother of Amaterasu, the supposed progenitor of the Emperor's line), his spouse Inada-hime-no-mikoto and their five sons and three daughters. It became an important center of worship after Kyoto was

established as the capital of Japan in the 790s since epidemics were often rampant, and Susa-no-o was regarded as the Shinto god of medicine. An epidemic in 869 AD led to the origin of the Gion Festival, when thousands prayed to Susa-no-o for relief from the spread of the plague. The head priest of the shrine led a procession of citizens through the city as a supplication to the god and, when the plaque ended, this event became a popular festival that has continued ever since.

Under the movement known as Ryobu (Dual) Shinto, beginning in the 800s, an attempt was made by the Buddhist clergy to show that the Shinto deities (whom the mass of the people then still preferred to the Buddhist gods) were but temporary manifestations in Japan of the major Buddhas and Bodhisattva. Thus, an amalgamation of the two faiths developed, and most Shinto shrines came under the control of Buddhist monks. Even the architecture of many shrines (the Yasaka Shrine, for example) took on the style of Buddhist religious buildings. With the restoration of Imperial rule in 1868, Buddhism was forced to separate from Shinto, and Shinto shrines reverted to a non-Buddhist form–albeit certain practices and architectural styles of Buddhism were retained. Thus Yasaka Shrine became solely a Shinto shrine once more, although its Buddhist overtones remain in its architecture.

You approach the shrine from Shijo-dori by means of a brief set of steps that lead to the Ro-mon, the main two-story gateway of the Muromachi period (1497), with its vermilion posts and white walls. A Shinto guardian in each bay on the sides of the entryway stands sentinel against any evil influences that might impinge on these sacred grounds. Once beyond the entry gateway, an additional brief set of steps, guarded by stone *koma-inu* (Korean lion-dogs), leads to a *torii* and the main area of the shrine.

Within the shrine grounds there are a number of buildings, both large and small, dedicated to various Shinto *kami* (deities). The main portion of the shrine has a roofed purification water basin ahead on the right. To its left, in the center of the precinct, is the roofed Heiden (Offertory), while the important Honden (Spirit Hall) is further to the left. Beyond the Heiden to the right is the *kagura*, the roofed ceremonial stage for religious performances. On the northern edge of the

Worshippers bowing before the shingle-roofed Honden at Yasaka Shrine.

precincts are the storage buildings for the Gion Festival *mikoshi* (portable shrines). Most of the shrine buildings date from a 1654 reconstruction, and some of the *mikoshi* storage units are enhanced with paintings commissioned by worshippers of the shrine deities.

The Honden (Spirit Hall), the most important structure of the shrine, is a single-story building with a half-hipped and a half-gabled roof covered with thick wood shingles. This main structure is painted vermilion and is 69 feet (21 m) long by 57 feet (17 m) deep. Three long ropes are suspended from the front overhanging roof, with a metal pan-shaped bell at the top of the ropes. These ropes are pulled by worshippers to sound the bell so as to attract the attention of the shrine's *kami* before bowing with hands held in prayer. On the south side of the grounds, a second entrance to the shrine is through a 30 foot (9 m) tall stone *torii* from 1646, one of the largest such Shinto stone gateways in Japan. Beyond it, a large vermilion gate with Shinto protecting archers on each side of the entryway has gifts of matted casks of *saké* stacked to its rear.

The Yasaka Shrine is much frequented by the citizens of Kyoto, some wearing modern dress, others adorned in traditional *kimono*. One of the most charming sights is to see recently born infants (often held by proud grandmothers in formal, traditional attire) being brought for registration at the shrine– or children in formal *kimono* or *hakama* when they are brought to the shrine in November at the time of the Shichi-go-san (7–5–3) Festival for blessings by shrine attendants.

Although there are frequent fair days at the Yasaka Shrine, a number of festivals are outstanding, the New Year festival at the beginning of January and the Gion Festival in July in particular. Okera Mairi is the name of the New Year festival, and on New Year's Eve an herb called *okera* is burned in the lanterns at the shrine from 8:00 p.m. through to the dawn of New Year's Day. It was customary in the past to come to the shrine with a thin rope, which was then lit from the lanterns, or to obtain a few embers in a pot, which could then be taken home to light the cooking fire of the New Year (before modern kitchen stoves). If one lit one's cooking fire from the sacred shrine fire and cooked *zoni* (rice cake boiled with vegetables) on New Year's Day,

The annual Gion Festival features a colorful parade of floats and participants dressed in traditional attire.

health and happiness were bound to ensue throughout the New Year. Hopes for a good New Year can be further insured by attending the shrine on New Year's Day to pray. On this occasion, traditional dress is often worn by women, and *maiko* (apprentice geisha) attend in black *kimono* with a white pattern. *Maiko* also place ears of rice in their hair to mark this festive occasion.

On February 3–4, the Setsubun celebration marks the traditional end of the coldest part of winter. Beans are scattered in temples and shrines to drive out demons and to bring in good luck for the new season. The ceremony is celebrated at many temples, but at Yasaka Shrine an evening bonfire brings the bean scattering festivities to a close. Another festival, held on May 2, is the Chatsu Dochu ceremony: each spring prior to 1868, the Shogun required the tea dealers of Uji to present the first tea leaves of the year to his provisioners packed in large ceramic jars. In remembrance of this event, large tea jars are paraded from the Kennin-ji Temple along Yamato-oji-dori to Shijo-dori and thus to Yasaka Shrine by bearers in costumes of the past.

The Gion Festival is the most spectacular of the shrine events. The first ceremony to mark the festival begins on July 2, when the shrine *mikoshi* (portable shrines) are taken from their storage sheds and are blessed for the coming festival (11:30 a.m.). On July 10, the most important shrine *mikoshi* is carried to the Kamo River for a ceremonial cleansing and purification by the chief priest of the shrine. Afterwards, the *mikoshi* is carried back to the shrine on the shoulders of the young men who took it to the river (7:00 p.m. to 8:00 p.m.). On that same day, celebrants in traditional garb welcome three *mikoshi* of Yasaka Shrine as the Gion Festival season starts (5:00 p.m. to 9:00 p.m.). With lanterns on long poles, they accompany the *mikoshi* to City Hall, at the intersection of Oike-dori and Kawaramachi-dori, and there dance groups perform at 6:00 p.m. in front of the City Hall building. Thereafter, the procession returns to Yasaka Shrine.

From July 15 to 17 the main events of the Gion Festival occur. This great festival is celebrated by the people of Kyoto as well as by thousands of visitors who come to the city specially for the occasion. On July 15–16, the festival carts are stationed along Shijo-dori west of the Kamo River, where they may be viewed close up, and music and festivities occur each night. On the morning of July 17, the festival parade of many large and small floats takes place along Kawaramachi-dori and Oike-dori; stands along Oike-dori provide seats, which may be reserved in advance. This summer festival provides a colorful and intriguing time, both for its participants and those who observe the carts and the costumes of other centuries. Other festivals and ceremonies occur at the Yasaka Shrine throughout the year. These are listed in the monthly calendar distributed by hotels and the Kyoto Tourist Office.

2 THE PLEASURE QUARTERS

Leaving Yasaka Shrine from the main entrance at Higashi-ojo-dori, Shijo-dori lies straight ahead. This street is the main route for the next portion of this walk, some diversions to its north or south occurring along the way. The *geisha* districts of Gion are to the south of this street, while the *geisha* areas of Shimbashi are to the north.

Beginning in the late 1500s, with the revival of Kyoto life at the end of a century or more of wars, the original pleasure districts

Performers in the classical Japanese dance-drama kabuki wear elaborate costumes and make-up.

of Kyoto developed on either side of the Kamo River just below and above Shijo-dori. Today, the *geisha* quarters, *ochaya* (tea houses), restaurants and theaters are still located in these districts.

The Pleasure Quarters of Kyoto, in particular the Pontocho, Gion and Shimbashi areas, present aspects of Japanese life that deserve an adequate description. Since the activities of portions of these quarters are by their nature only quasi-public (language, expense and proper introduction barring most foreigners from the *ochaya* and the world of the *geisha*), and since the theater performances that offer a sampling of *geisha* talents and an introduction to the tea ceremony are restricted to certain times of the year, an introduction to the Pleasure Quarters follows.

The areas on either side of the Kamo River at Shijo-dori (as well as the dry areas of the river bed) became the center of the Pleasure Quarters of Kyoto from the late 1500s. With the prosperity that began under Hideyoshi in the 1580s, and which continued under the Tokugawa Shoguns, a new merchant class developed in Kyoto. Although the merchants were the lowest class of society as far as official policy was concerned, they were prosperous and had money to spend. Thus, the Shoguns permitted them some leeway in

behavior (other than was normally prescribed for their class) in the "licensed quarters," where they could find entertainment and pleasure of various kinds.

Four elements composed the divertissements of the Pleasure Quarters. There were the restaurants or tea houses on either side of the river—as well as on the dry river bed in the summer, where dining could take place—and many of these continue to serve the public today along the narrow stone-paved pathway of Pontocho and on the west bank of the Kamo River. There were the *ochaya*, in which the *geisha* and *maiko* (apprentice *geisha*) entertained the wealthier of Kyoto's pleasure seekers. There were, as well, the theaters for *kabuki*, *bunraku* (puppet plays), and other such forms of cultural entertainment. Lastly, there was the illicit trade of prostitutes (both female and male), of which the puritanical Shoguns did not approve but condoned, within limits, in recognition that certain activities could never be fully controlled by either Confucian precepts or governmental decrees.

KABUKI The art of *kabuki* had its beginnings here in the late 1590s when a young woman, in the service of the great Shinto shrine of Izumo on the Japan Sea, appeared

Maiko (apprentice geisha) stop for a chat in the Gion district.

THE ENIGMATIC GEISHA

Despite Kyoto's male-dominated associations, the women in Kyoto have always had a part to play in the pleasure quarters (aside from the activities of prostitutes, whom society neither recognized nor condoned but who continued to flourish). A group of entertainers known as *geisha* sprang up, women of talent who could dance, sing, play on traditional instruments, carry on witty conversations and, above all, please the male patrons of the *ochaya* in which they practiced their arts. The role of the *geisha* was an honorable one, the word itself implying a trained artist. *Geisha* were not prostitutes, as is sometimes supposed in the West, although they often became the lovers of well-to-do patrons who supported them, the cost of their costumes and grooming and their general upkeep being exceedingly expensive.)

Two areas became the center of the *ochaya* in which *geisha* entertained those who could afford an evening of their professional services of song and dance—as well as the delights of the palate as catered to by the *ochaya* owners. These *ochaya* developed both north and south of Shijo-dori—along Hanami-koji-dori on either side of Shijo and along the Shirokawa River to the north of Shijo. This latter came to be known as the Shimbashi (New Bridge) district, from a bridge across that narrow river. Both the Kamo and Shirakawa Rivers were much given to flooding; by 1670 an attempt was made to control the overflowing of these rivers, and they were contained within walls. This led to an increase in the land available for development. An improved and expanded pleasure district resulted to the east of the Kamo River, tea houses and theaters flourished, and from 1712 the *ochaya* of Gion were licensed by the government for *geisha* performances.

in Kyoto. A performer of sacred Shinto dances, Izumo-no-Okuni began to offer such dances in 1596 in an improvised "theater" on the dry bed of the Kamo in the Shijo-dori district. (A plaque on the west wall of the Minami-za Theater at Shijo-dori on the east side of the Kamo River commemorates Okuni's perfor-mances at this river bed location.) Okuni and her small group of female dancers performed the Nembutsu Odori, a religious dance that had its roots in the religious "dances" practiced by Priest Kuya (see Rokuhara-mitsu-ji in Tour 4) many years before. This religious observance had developed into a type of folk dance that, although it had roots in religious practice, had become a form of popular entertainment as well. (The O-Bon dances in many communities in Japan in August continue this tradition.)

In Okuni's hands, the Okuni Odori was able to blend folk, Shinto and Buddhist dance forms into a popular format that was soon imitated by other female performers. The popularity of her dances can be ascertained by the fact that Toyotomi Hideyoshi is said not only to have viewed them with pleasure, but that he rewarded Okuni with a coral necklace. From these religious dances, Okuni and her group soon branched out into a type of primitive theater of a farcical nature that came to be known as *kabuki*. Many of her skits (for they were not really plays in an artistic sense) were of an erotic nature, concerning the relationships of young men and prostitutes in bath houses and tea houses. (Some of her cohorts were well suited by inclination and experience to portray aspects of the seamier side of life with great realism.) These farcical skits eventually came to the attention and displeasure of the authorities, and by 1629 the Shogun had banned such female performances.

Accordingly, another form of *kabuki* developed, with young men (many of them very attractive late adolescents) as the actors. Much given to acrobatics and mock sword play, these young actors soon developed a following of their own—particularly among the *samurai* and Buddhist priests who vied for the young men's charms. These two social classes were not supposed to attend functions that were primarily licensed for the merchant class—the lowest form of society in Tokugawa times. But attend they did, and many of these attractive youths aroused a passion among their viewers (homosexuality being accepted by many *samurai* and priests.) In the fights that broke out among the members of the audience for the favor of particular actors, there was a breakdown of decorum that the Shogun could not permit. Thus, in 1652 "young men's *kabuki*" was banned—but not until after the death of Shogun Tokugawa Iemitsu (1604–51), who himself reputedly had a certain fondness for youthful actors.

Thereafter, *kabuki* was permitted to continue if the performers were adult males—and ostensibly less physically or emotionally attractive to the audience. Women's roles were taken by males (*onnegata*), a tradition

The Ichi-riki ochaya, a 300-year-old red walled wooden place of geisha entertainment.

which continues to this day. By the Genroku period (1658–1710), a full-fledged *kabuki* drama had developed, with plays being written by capable authors, such as Chikamatsu, and with stagecraft that was innovative and spectacular, with its revolving stages, trap doors and other theatrical devices.

③ ICHI-RIKI OCHAYA

The areas of Shimbashi (along the Shirakawa River to the north of Shijo-dori and Gion (south of Shijo-dori) are still the heart of the *geisha* quarter of Kyoto. While many of the two-story tea houses in these two districts appear to be very old, most of them were built after the great fire of 1864, which devastated this area of Kyoto. *Ochaya* are generally wooden two-story, architecturally traditional buildings with protruding rust-colored, latticed windows (*bengari goshi*) on the first floor and *sudare* (reed screens) for privacy flapping in the breeze on the second floor. A *noren* (short curtain over the entryway with the name of the establishment upon it), and *inaru yarai* ("dog screens," slatted and curved bamboo barriers that keep dogs and people at a proper distance from the first floor windows and walls of the building), provide a distinctive ambience to the scene.

Several entire streets in Shirakawa and Gion preserve these traditional buildings, thereby providing an idea of what Kyoto looked like in days gone by. Today in Gion, some 119 *ochaya* exist where an evening can be spent at a dinner with entertainment by *geisha* and *maiko*. In 1974, Kyoto placed the Gion and Shimbashi districts under special protection, and the areas were made into a Preservation District the following year. In 1976, architectural guidelines were set for seven distinct *ochaya* facades, and grants subsidized by the city have assisted in the maintenance of the facades of the buildings in these two Preservation Districts.

Of all these, the more than 300-year-old Ichi-riki *ochaya* on the corner of Shijo-dori and Hanamoi-koji-dori is the most noted. It is known not only for its traditional architecture and ambience, but as a locale where famous historic events have taken place.

Here, Oishi Yoshio (1659–1703) led a life of planned dissoluteness, giving himself over to the frivolous life of the Pleasure Quarters, seemingly drinking to excess—all to disguise his real intentions and thereby mislead the Shogun's spies who were observing him. Oishi was a *ronin*, a masterless *samurai* who no longer had a lord (*daimyo*) to report to. This was Oishi's state since his lord had fallen into disgrace and had been forced to commit *seppuku* (ceremonial suicide). Determined to avenge the unfair treatment of his master,

Oishi divorced his wife and entered into a life of debauchery to disguise his revengeful intentions. Eventually, Oishi and 46 other *ronin* had a rendezvous in Edo (Tokyo), killed their master's opponent, and were eventually forced by the Shogun to commit ceremonial suicide. All are buried with their master at a Tokyo temple. (Their story, *The 47 Ronin*, has become a classic in Japanese literature and *kabuki* as well.)

Some 150 years later, the Ichi-riki again became the center of intrigue. In the mid-19th century, in the latter days of the Tokugawa Shoguns' rule, some of the opponents of the Tokugawa government would gather at the Ichi-riki under the pretense of a few friends having an enjoyable evening at a *geisha* party. Their real goal, however, was the overthrow of the government. Their plotting, and that of others of like mind, came to fruition in 1868 when the last Shogun signed the papers at Nijo Castle dissolving the Shogun's government and ostensibly returning the Emperor to power.

Today, the Ichi-riki plays host to Japanese power figures of the business world rather than the political world, but its attraction as one of the prime *geisha* houses in Kyoto remains. Hanami-koji-dori, the street on which the Ichi-riki is located, is one of the best

A traditional ochaya (tea house), with slatted and curved bamboo barriers along its outer walls.

The narrow Pontocho pedestrian walkway.

preserved of the old Gion streets of *ochaya* and the traditional Pleasure Quarters of Kyoto. It is a delightful area architecturally as well as historically in which to saunter. Many of the *geisha* live along Hanami-koji-dori to the south of the Ichi-riki and, in the evening, at about 7:30, the *maiko* and *geisha* begin their walk to work at the *ochaya* that have requested their services for the evening, a delightful sight with their beautiful *kimono* and extravagant coiffures.

PONTOCHO AREA The area on both sides of the Kamo River thus became the center of entertainment in Kyoto, particularly after legal authorization for *geisha* entertainment was granted by the Shogun. Today, restaurants as well as *ochaya* can be found not only in the Gion-Shimbashi area on the east side of the Kamo River but along Pontocho, a very narrow pedestrian street on the west side of the Kamo River. The Pontocho pleasure quarter, once the red light district of Kyoto, lies between Sanjo-dori and Shijo-dori and is a particularly intriguing section due to its highly and colorfully illuminated signs along this street of restaurants. (Prostitution was abolished by law in 1958, but the area has

its modern "love hotels," as the type has been so aptly named, where rooms can be rented by the hour).

The Pontocho area consists of two narrow streets: one (Pontocho) is a pedestrian walkway rather than a normal street, a home to many expensive restaurants and bars, as well as that modern replacement for traditional *geisha* entertainment—hostess clubs. Pontocho is the street closest to and parallel to the Kamo River, and many of the restaurants in the old buildings along this stone-paved passageway overlook the river. Some of these establishments have *yuka*, wooden platforms on the river's edge on which you can dine and enjoy the cool breezes of the river. At night the illuminated signs hanging from each restaurant or bar on Pontocho provide a colorful and striking visual enrichment for this pleasure quarter. Pontocho's parallel companion street to the west is Kiyomachi-dori, with its more modern buildings along the Takase-gawa, the Takase Canal. At night, the canal's dark waters provide an interesting contrast to the colorful and sometimes garish illuminated signs of Kiyomachi-dori, which are reflected in the water.

Toward the Sanjo-dori (Third Street) end of Pontocho is the Pontocho Kaburenjo Theater. Each spring (April–May) and autumn (October–November) the theater offers the Kamogawa Odori (Kamo River Dances). This theatrical spectacle, which had its beginning in 1872, offers Kyo-mai (Kyoto or Capital Dances) performed in the traditional *geisha* manner. Demonstrations of the tea ceremony are also provided.

Returning to the eastern side of the Kamo River, there are three theaters that offer traditional entertainment. The Minami-za (South Theater) is the oldest theater in Kyoto and in Japan, having first opened its doors in the 17th century—although the present building dates from 1925 and was modernized in 1990. The home of traditional *kabuki* drama, the highlight of its season comes every December at its *kaomise* (Face Showing) performances. During this month, the most important stars of *kabuki* appear in scenes in which they can demonstrate their prowess as performers in this highly stylized and entertaining form of theater. (A stone monument on the west side of the Minami-za Theater marks the area where Izumo-no-Okuni first performed her nascent form of *kabuki*, this area once having been a part of the river before the river was walled as a protection against flooding and before the area of dry land was extended.)

About 165 feet (50 m) east of the Minami-za Theater on Shijo-dori is the Meyami Jizo Shrine with its front gate and red lanterns. It is believed that the Jizo of this shrine can cure eye diseases.

On a side street south of Shijo-dori, between Hanami-koji-dori and Higashi-oji-dori, are the Gion Kaburenjo Theater and Gion Corner. Each April and May the Miyako Odori (the Cherry Blossom Dance—Miyako is the old name for Kyoto, so this is really the "Capital Dance") is presented by *geisha* and *maiko*. In the adjacent Gion Corner is the Yasaka Kaikan, a small hall that seats some 250 people and is attached to the Gion Kaburenjo. From March 1st through November 29th, a sample of traditional Japanese arts is performed twice each evening for visitors to the city. Created by the Kyoto Visitors' Club in 1962, demonstrations of *geisha* dancing, ancient court music, *bunraku* (puppet theater), flower arrangement and tea ceremony are presented. An English language commentary is provided. In addition, *geisha* and *maiko* present performances of the Gion Odori at the Gion Kaikan north of Shijo-dori on Higashi-oji-dori, in October and December.

Window shopping along Teramachi Street.

Food stalls at the Nishiki Koji Market.

4 CENTRAL KYOTO

The streets spreading out from the Kamo River west to Karasuma-dori between Shijo-dori and Oike-dori embrace the main shopping center of Kyoto. Along Shijo-dori are a number of well-known Japanese department stores and many specialty shops, which are always thronged with browsers and would-be purchasers. Covered arcades on Kyogoku-dori and Shin Kyogoku-dori between Shijo-dori and Sanjo-dori and in Teramachi-dori between Shijo-dori and Oike-dori provide all-weather enticement to purchase anything from fine old prints to the most outrageous of cheap souvenirs.

Numerous movie houses and restaurants offer further entertainment to locals and tourists alike. The area is always crowded with tourist groups from the provinces as well as hundreds of students on school tours and local citizens.

TERAMACHI This area of Kyoto became a commercial center fairly late in the city's history. At the time of Hideyoshi (late 1500s), a protective wall (Odoi) was built along the eastern edge of the city where Karawamachi-dori now runs. Teramachi (Temple District), the name of this area, is so-called since, as Toyotomi Hideyoshi rebuilt Kyoto as "his" capital after 1583, he had many of the temples that were favored by the people relocated to two areas, one along Teramachi-dori in the center of Kyoto and the other at Teranouchi-dori in the north-central part of the city. Those along Teramachi were primarily of the Jodo sect of Buddhism, while the ones along Teranouchi were of the Nichiren persuasion. Both time and fires have seen to the dispersal of many of relocated temples, but some still remain in this area.

Among the temples in the Teramachi area, perhaps the most famous is Honno-ji, because

Kyoto's Kamo-gawa River in spring.

of its associations with Oda Nobunaga. Nobunaga was Hideyoshi's predecessor who ended virtually all the internecine wars of the 1500s. It was at Honno-ji that Nobunaga was trapped by a traitor and was forced to kill himself and his family, a deed which Hideyoshi later avenged. Today, it is an association in name only, since the original Honno-ji was located a few streets to the south and west (south of Rokkaku-dori and east of Aura-no-koji-dori) before it burned down, and thus the present temple complex is from post-Nobunaga times.

In the post-Meiji era (after 1868), Kawara-machi-dori was opened and became a street of shops between Oike-dori and Shijo-dori. In addition, Kyogoku-dori and Shin Kyogoku-dori were created after 1871 and became known as "Theater Street" by foreigners who came to Kyoto. It is still an entertainment area, although now with small shops, many specializing in tourist souvenirs of an ephemeral nature, and restaurants rather than theaters predominate. It is a thriving and often crowded area with bright lights, and is popular with Kyoto residents as well as Japanese school tour groups.

One of the interesting byways of central Kyoto is Nishiki-koji-dori, which houses the Nishi Koji Market (Brocade Alley Market). It is located one street north of Shijo-dori, and runs from Shin Kyogoku-dori (a *torii* gate stands at the entry to the street before the small Nishiki Tenmangu Shrine) to Takakura-dori near the Daimaru department store.

Since the middle ages, there has been a public market in central Kyoto. Virtually the entire city was destroyed in the Onin Wars of 1467 to 1477. The market was re-established in the late 1500s, however, when Hideyoshi replanned the city. There are about 150 food dealers along this 500 feet (150 m) long stone-paved street. Most of the shops remain open until early evening, and the street presents a fascinating aspect of everyday life. (Most shops close on Wednesday; fish stores are closed on Sundays.)

THE TOKAIDO ROAD This walk is a loop, returning to the Yasaka Shrine, and it thus next leads east on Sanjo-dori (Third Street), which runs through the arcaded streets mentioned above (and is itself arcaded for a short while) as it heads eastward toward the Kamo River and the Sanjo bridge. The Sanjo-bashi Bridge over the Kamo River was originally built at the order of Toyotomi Hideyoshi in 1589, and after 1600 it marked the beginning of the Tokaido Road (To-kaido means "Eastern Highway").

The Tokaido was a 320 mile (512 km) route with 53 relay stations between the Emperor's capital in Kyoto and the Shogun's headquarters in Edo (Tokyo). This link between Kyoto and Tokyo became a major commercial route between 1603 and 1868 as travel on Sanjo-dori headed east to the valley between Kyoto and Lake Biwa and the Tokaido Road. Its importance as a major highway diminished in the late 19th century with the coming of the railroad, and its eclipse was virtually completed when the new expressway to Kyoto entered the prefecture to the south of the city in the middle of the 20th century. The very first milestone of the route, from which all distances were measured, stood at the eastern end of the bridge, today a memento of a vanished era.

Later times have, of course, necessitated the replacement of Hideyoshi's bridge by a structure that can carry the heavy traffic of a mechanized age. Only the *giboshi*, the bronze ornaments atop the posts of the railings, go back to the 16th century, all gifts of the leading *daimyo* of those days. Some of the stone pillars at each end of the bridge are original as well, the other stones having been used for the famous stepping stones in the garden pond of the Heian Shrine when it was created at the end of the 19th century.

At the southeast corner of the Sanjo Bridge, amidst the confusion of overhead electrical wires, the tracks of the Keihan rail line to Otsu, the terminal for many buses and the underground railway station, is a statue of a *samurai* bowing toward the northwest. The statue commemorates Takayama Masayuke (1747–93), also known as Takayama Hiko-kuro, who came to Kyoto when he was 18 and there began to delve into the history of the nation. Takayama was astonished to discover that the Shoguns had usurped the power of the Emperor to control the country. (He did not realize how powerless the Emperor had been through most of the centuries of the existence of the Imperial line.) He therefore traveled through the various provinces in an attempt to revive the prestige of the Imperial house. On his return to Kyoto, he fell upon his knees at the Sanjo Bridge to bow toward the Emperor in his palace to the northwest, to manifest the esteem due the Imperial house, as he is still bowing in this monument. Eventually, he offered himself as a symbolic sacrifice to the Imperial cause by committing *hara-kiri* for the sake of Imperial rule—one of the first overt acts of challenge to the Shogun's supremacy. In his memory, a statue to this exemplar of fidelity to Imperial rule was erected at the corner of the Sanjo Bridge after the Meiji Restoration of 1868.

STREETS OF ANTIQUES Although antique and curio shops abound in various areas of Kyoto, several streets in the Gion/Shimbashi district are noted for a proliferation of such stores. Nawate-dori is one such street, a north–south street one street east of the Kamo River and running south from the transportation hub at Sanjo-dori. Parallel to it is Hanami-koji-dori to the east, and then two other streets which run from Nawate-dori to Higashi-oji-dori. These are Furomonzen-dori and Shinmonzen-dori, also a center for major antique shops. Furomonzen-dori is the second street from the transport square while Shinmonzen-dori is the next street south. The latter has the greatest concentration of such specialty shops.

In the shops of these streets the variety and splendor of Japanese arts and crafts can be obtained for a goodly price—since such antiquities are in great demand by connoisseurs of Japanese art. Among the treasures to be found here are screens (*byobu*), wood-block prints (*ukiyo-e*), chests (*tansu*), pearls, Imari porcelain ware, Kutani ware and other types of porcelain. Scrolls, wood carvings, *netsuke*, *Noh* masks, fans, *obi*, *kimono*, brocades, silk textiles, lacquerware, jade, silk embroideries, damascene-ware and Buddhist religious art are also for sale. The merchants of the area issue a brochure describing the stores of the district. This is available at hotels, at the Tourist Information Center downtown, as well as at member shops.

Moving further south on Nawate-dori, beyond Furomonzen-dori and Shinmonzen-dori, the fourth street on the left when coming from the Sanjo-dori area is Shirakawa-minami-dori, parallel to the narrow, canalized Shirakawa River. This section of the Shimbashi area, with its willow trees and old houses with their rolled-down blinds on the second floor, offers many of the other traditional *ochaya* that remain. As a center for the *geisha* quarters, it was loved by the poet Isamu Yoshii (1886–1960), and one of his poems has been inscribed on a stone in this area:

No matter what they say,
I love Gion.
Even in my sleep
The sound of water
Flows beneath my pillow.

On November 8 at 11 a.m., *geisha* and *maiko* perform a tea ceremony at the stone monument that records Isamu Yoshii's affection for Gion and its traditional delights—delights the *geisha* continue to maintain.

Continuing south to Shijo-dori, a turn to the left leads back to the Yasaka Shrine at Higashi-oji-dori where a bus or a taxi can be obtained at the conclusion of this walk.

GETTING THERE

This is a loop walk. The sites on the tour are all in central Kyoto or within easy walking distance from it. The tour starts and ends at Yasaka Shrine, which is situated at the intersection of Shijo-dori and Higashi-oji-dori. It can be reached by walking or by bus 206 or 207 to the Gion bus stop. The Gion area is pleasant to visit at any time, particularly during the cherry blossom season in April or at the time of the Gion Festival in July.

Walking Tour 6

HEIAN SHRINE AREA
Imperial Palaces, Art and Crafts Museums and Heian Shrine

1. **Shoren-in (Awata Palace)**
   青蓮院門跡（粟田御所）
2. **Okazaki Park Cultural Center**
   岡崎公園（文化芸術エリア）
3. **Murin-an Villa** 無鄰菴
4. **Heian Shrine** 平安神宮
5. **Kuro-dani (Black Ravine Temple)**
   金戒光明寺（黒谷）
6. **Chion-ji (Million Times Temple)** 知恩寺

Jingu-michi-dori, which is central to this walk, provides everything from museums to a zoo to a concert hall to a center for the martial arts. It also has a shrine and a temple, both of which once served as palaces. One would think that a temple was a temple while a palace was a palace, but this not always true in Kyoto. The Imperial Palace had a periodic propensity for being destroyed by fire and, from time to time, the Emperor and his court had to find temporary refuge while the palace was rebuilt. Such refuge could be found in a temple that was temporarily sequestered by the court, and, on more than one occasion, the Shoren-in Temple was so honored. As a result, the temple has enjoyed not only Imperial favor but has been modified to suit Imperial tastes and still preserves some of the splendor with which the court endowed it.

That portion of Jingu-michi-dori on which the Shoren-in (or Awata Palace as it is also known) is located leads north to the cultural center that has developed as Okazaki Park in the past 100 years. At the north end of this street, beyond a gigantic *torii* that crosses the road, is another palace, this one being a memorial to the Imperial Palace of early Kyoto rather than a residence for royalty. The Imperial Palace of the late 700s has long

since been destroyed by fire, and its original location was abandoned by the court centuries ago. At the end of the 1800s, on the occasion of the 1,100th anniversary of the founding of the capital at Kyoto, a portion of the original palace was reconstructed in two-thirds scale as a shrine to the Emperor Kammu who had established Kyoto as Japan's capital and who had the first Imperial palace built in the city. Thus, the Heian Shrine at the end of Jingu-michi-dori today provides an idea of what the early palace looked like and also serves as a shrine to the spirit of the first and the last Emperors to reside in Kyoto as the capital of the nation. More noteworthy than the building, however, is the lovely garden behind it and to its side. Between the temple/palace of the Shoren-in and the partially reconstructed palace of Heian times (794–1200) lies the Okazaki Cultural Center. Here one can find the museums of contemporary art, of the traditional arts and crafts, and of general art, as well as the one of the first public libraries in Japan. A cultural hall for musical events and additional private museums border the area as does the Hall of Martial Arts, a unit which was once part of the early palace and today continues the martial arts tradition still enjoyed by many Japanese. Even the Kyoto Zoo can be found in the Okazaki Park, and here occurs the annual fireman's display of his skills and derring-do at the beginning of each year.

1 SHOREN-IN (AWATA PALACE)
The Shoren-in (Awata Palace) is on Jingu-michi-dori, the street that runs south from the Heian Shrine to Maruyama Park. (Buses 11, 12, 18, 202, 203, 206 or 207 take you to the Chion-in-mae bus stop from which you walk east to Jingu-michi-dori (in front of Chion-in) and then turn left (north) to the Shoren-in.

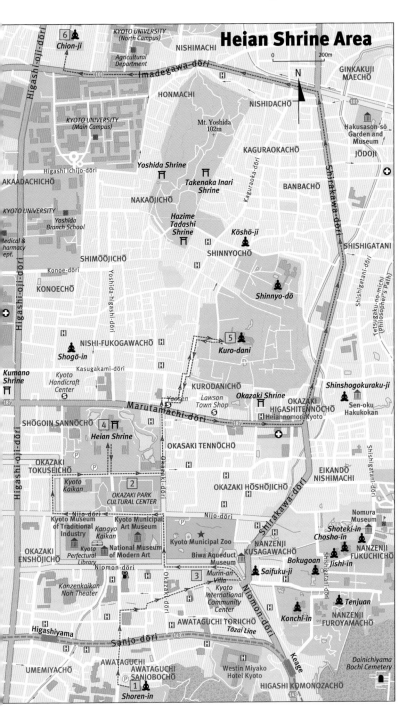

Heian Shrine Area

0   200m

N

6 Chion-ji

KYOTO UNIVERSITY
(North Campus)

NISHIMACHI

Agricultural
Department

Imadegawa-dōri

HONMACHI

NISHIDACHŌ

GINKAKUJI
MAECHŌ

KYOTO UNIVERSITY
(Main Campus)

Mt. Yoshida
102m

Hakusason-sō
Garden and
Museum

JŌDOJI

Higashi Ichijo-dōri

Yoshida Shrine

KAGURAOKACHŌ

AKAADACHICHŌ

Takenaka Inari
Shrine

BANBACHŌ

NAKAŌJICHŌ

KYOTO UNIVERSITY

Yoshida
Branch School

Hazime
Tadashi
Shrine

Kōshō-ji

SHISHIGATANI

Medical &
Pharmacy
Dept.

SHIMOŌJICHŌ

SHINNYOCHŌ

Konoe-dōri

KONOECHŌ

Yoshida-higashi-dōri

Shinnyo-dō

Tetsugaku-no-michi
(Philosopher's Path)

Shishigatani-dōri

NISHI-FUKOGAWACHŌ

5

Shogō-in

Kasugakami-dōri

Kuro-dani

Kumano
Shrine

Kyoto
Handicraft
Center

Yaosen

Lawson
Town Shop

KURODANICHŌ

Okazaki Shrine

Shinshogokuraku-ji

Sen-oku
Hakukokan

Marutamachi-dōri

OKAZAKI
HIGASHITENNŌCHŌ
Heiannomori Kyoto

SHŌGOIN SANNŌCHŌ

4 Heian Shrine

OKAZAKI TENNŌCHŌ

OKAZAKI
TOKUSEICHŌ

Kyoto
Kaikan

2

OKAZAKI PARK
CULTURAL CENTER

OKAZAKI HŌSHŌJICHŌ

EIKANDO
NISHIMACHI

Higashiyama-iriguchi-dōri

Nijo-dōri

Nomura
Museum

Kyoto Museum
of Traditional
Industry

Kangyo
Kaikan

Kyoto Municipal
Art Museum

Kyoto Municipal Zoo

NANZENJI
KUSAGAWACHŌ

Shoteki-in

Chosho-in

OKAZAKI
ENSHŌJICHŌ

Kyoto
Perfectural
Library

National Museum
of Modern Art

Biwa Aqueduct
Museum

Bokugoan

Saifuku-ji

NANZENJI
FUKUCHICHŌ

Jishi-in

Niomon-dōri

Okazaki-dōri

Kanzenkaikan
Noh Theater

3

Murin-an
Villa

Kyoto
International
Community
Center

Konchi-in

Tenjuan

NANZENJI
FUROYAMACHŌ

Higashiyama

Sanjo-dōri

AWATAGUCHI TORICHŌ
Tōzai Line

Keage

Dainichiyama
Bochi Cemetery

UMEMIYACHŌ

AWATAGUCHI

AWATAGUCHI
SANJOBOCHŌ

1

Shoren-in

Westin Miyako
Hotel Kyoto

HIGASHI KOMONOZACHŌ

A view of the Ko Gosho (Small Palace) from the garden at Shoren-in.

Alternatively, you can take bus 5 to the Jingo-michi-dori bus stop and then walk south on Jingu-michi-dori to the temple. The Shoren-in is open from 9:00 a.m. to 5:00 p.m.; it is closed on October 4th. Entry fee.

An exquisite former palace of the *monzeki* (Imperial) prince abbots, as well as the some-time residence of the Imperial ruler when the Imperial Palace burned, Shoren-in has a lovely Muromachi period (1334–1568) garden created about a pond. The site has been a Tendai sect temple for centuries and has had to serve as an Imperial palace as well from time to time. The temple had its beginnings as a city residence for Buddhist priests from the great Tendai monastery of Enryaku-ji on Mount Hiei. Priests from the Enryaku-ji often came to Kyoto in the 800s and thereafter to lecture, teach, hold memorial services for the dead or pray for the prosperity of individual aristocratic families as requested by these members of the nobility. Thus a need for housing for such priests on these occasions became a necessity and, as a result, the Juraku-in Temple was created at the site of the future Shoren-in to house the priests from the mountain monastery.

In 879, the Emperor Seiwa retired, and he built a detached palace, the Awata Palace, on the grounds of the Juraku-in, becoming a priest in the temple, a practice which was to become a normal procedure for many future retired emperors. The present Shoren-in temple was founded in 1144, and in 1153 the Emperor Toba ordered new buildings con-structed. Two years later, the Emperor's sev-enth son, Prince Kakukai (1134–81), became the head priest and second abbot of the Shoren-in. Thus began a tradition of being a *monzeki* temple, that is, a temple whose abbot was a member of the Imperial family. This heritage lasted until 1868 when the *monzeki* tradition was broken by the new Meiji govern-ment as part of its anti-Buddhist program. In 1868, the prince abbots returned to secular life, and the tie to the Imperial family ended.

KO GOSHO After paying the entry fee at the booth, walk to the entrance to the right and remove your shoes before proceeding along the corridors to the two main buildings or the garden viewing room, which also serves as a tea room. A roofed corridor to the left of the entryway leads to a second corridor on the right to the Ko Gosho (Small Palace), a lovely little building with a veranda on three sides. The corridor leading ahead from the entry brings you to the Shinden, the large palace.

The Ko Gosho was originally a portion of the Imperial Palace, and the present *tatami*-matted building was moved to this site beside the Ryushin Ike (Dragon's Heart Pond) at the request of Empress Go-Sakuramachi (1762–70) when the temple became her temporary palace. After her departure, the Ko Gosho served as the living quarters for the Imperial abbots. The Little Palace is separated into three *tatami*-matted rooms by its *fusuma* (sliding screens), and these are approached by way of a wood-floored veranda/corridor that can be separated from the rooms by movable *shoji* panels.

The Audience Room at the east end, nearest the pond, has a raised platform (*jodan*) on which the empress or prince abbot would be seated. Behind it is a *tokonoma* whose rear wall is decorated with flowers on a gold ground. To the right of the *tokonoma* are *chigaidana* (staggered shelves) with a painted tree as a background while birds are painted on the cupboard doors at the bottom of the *chigaidana*, the paintings being by Kano Motonobu (1476–1559). Two *fusuma* and two cedar doors separate this inner area of the Audience Room from the main portion of the *tatami*-matted building. These *fusuma* are decorated with a scene of women with children, while the two wooden doors display a painting of a cart with a bouquet (to the left) and a loom (on the right door). The middle room of the three rooms has a painting of a waterfall and a pine tree by Kano Motonobu while the third room has two cedar doors closing off the rear area, doors painted with birds and trees. The entire interior of the Ko Gosho can be closed off from its wood-floored verandas/corridors by *shoji* (thin paper-covered screens).

SHINDEN The original Shinden, the main palace structure, was built as a copy in miniature of an Imperial residence, even to the cherry tree on the left and the wild orange tree to the right in front of the building. Originally the forecourt, which holds these two ceremonial trees, was composed of white sand, but the shade from the huge camphor tree within the grounds has led to the sand being covered with cedar moss. Destroyed in the Onin War of the late 1400s, the Shinden was quickly reconstructed. Then, in the 17th century, the daughter of Hidetada, the second Tokugawa Shogun, became a consort of the Emperor Go-Mizu-no-o (reigned 1611–29),

An image of Amida found in the altar room of the Shinden, the palace's main structure.

and a palatial mansion was built for her at the Imperial Palace. When the structure was no longer used, portions of it were given to various temples, and the unit that came to Shoren-in replaced the Shinden. It became a palace in actuality in 1788 when the Empress Go-Sakuramachi moved here temporarily after the Imperial Palace burned in the Great Temmei Fire of that year. A subsequent fire in 1893 destroyed this building, and two years later the present structure was erected.

The present Shinden is enriched with the art of Tosa Mitsunobo (1434–1525) and Kano Eitoku (1543–90) among others. Mitsunobo painted the *fusuma* in the main entrance while Eitoku is represented in the Royal Messenger Room, both on the west side of the building. The three main rooms of the Shinden face south and have corridors on all sides, the north corridor being internal while the others are on the periphery of the building. You enter the Shinden today from the main entryway to the temple by means of the wood-floored corridor. The interior rooms are *tatami*-matted, and the first room you come to (the southeast room) is known as the Blue Fudo Room. It has *chigaidana* (staggered shelves) on the left third of the rear wall while the rest consists of a large *tokonoma* which has the painting of the blue Fudo, a Buddhist deity. The most impressive Heian period portrait of Fudo, the original painting (now in the Kyoto National Museum) is from the second half of the 11th century and is in color on silk. The Fudo has a blue body with a contrasting orange garment; red flames rise behind his blue body instead of from the normal *mandorla* (aureole). His left hand holds a sword while his right hand grasps a rope. Before him are his two attendants.

The middle room is the altar room, the rear section having *ihai* tablets to the memory of the prince abbots of the temple on either side of an Amida image. The third room is called the Pine Beach Room from the painting by Sumiyoshi Gukei of a beach and a pine tree on a gold ground. The cedar doors outside this room have quaint paintings of Gion Festival floats by the same artist. Behind these three rooms is the internal corridor previously mentioned and then a 10-mat room with a *kago* in it, a large closed palanquin with the Imperial chrysanthemum crest upon it. This heavy vehicle stands out against the background of the white *fusuma* on three sides of the room, with their paintings of storks among pine and cherry trees. A Kara-mon (Chinese-style gate) entryway to the Shinden is on this west side of the building, and it marks the end of a path from the large Kara-mon gateway in the external wall to the grounds, obviously a former entrance to the Shinden for its Imperial occupants and royal messengers.

The Shijoko-do is a small square building situated behind the Ko Gosho, with Zen-style cusped windows and a pyramidal tiled roof topped with a large flaming jewel such as is found on memorial buildings. This building is the heart of the temple since it holds an image of the Shijoko Buddha. Here, prayers were said for the welfare of the Imperial House and the nation. The roofed corridor that connects the main entranceway with the Ko Gosho and the Shinden leads to a large room from which you can view the Ko Gosho and the gardens. Tea may be obtained here, and a small counter sells guidebooks to the temple as well as small religious articles. The gardens of the Shoren-in are credited to Soami (1472–1523) and Kobori Enshu (1579–1647). Thought to have been created between 1443 and 1489, probably by Soami, the Ryushin Pond and Senshin Waterfall (a three-level stone waterfall that faces the "boat landing stone") were meant to be viewed from the Ko Gosho. A 13-tiered stone pagoda stands just beyond the pond while a small bridge crosses one end of the water.

The slope of the hill behind the pond is planted with Kirishima azaleas from the mountain of that name. The gardens were damaged in the 1893 fire and were reconstituted in 1909 by Ogawa Jihei. A path leads through the garden, around the lake and up the hillside, passing en route the Kobun-tei, a small building to the north of the pond. Created as a study for the abbot between 1764 and 1771, it has an altar as well as three places in which tea can be made. In the late 18th century, when the Empress Go-Sakuramachi was in residence at the temple, she used the building as a study. It has also has been used as a tea house.

The garden and pond are lovely at all times but they are particularly attractive in early April when the cherry blossoms cover the trees and again in autumn when the maples brighten the hillside with their gold and red leaves. While they are not part of the garden, the five huge old camphor trees of the Shoren in are notable. Four of these giants are just outside the temple walls while one is next to the Shinden. One of the four "outside" trees is at the entry gate—a gate that was formerly the kitchen gate but now serves as the main entrance to the temple grounds. The long roofed gate to the right of the present entry, above the wide stone steps, was the original entrance to the temple.

② OKAZAKI PARK CULTURAL CENTER

Leaving the Shoren-in and walking north on Jingu-michi-dori, the next cross street marks the Awata-guchi area, which has been a continuing entryway to Kyoto from the east, and here along Sanjo-dori lay the old Tokaido highway with its flow of traffic to Edo under the Tokugawa Shoguns. Until the end of the 20th century, much of this portion of Kyoto lay beyond the built-up part of the city, and the area was primarily noted for its temples to the east, north and south and for the famous swordsmiths who followed their craft in the vicinity.

In the 1870s, with the Meiji Restoration, the government levied restrictive laws against Buddhist temples and monasteries, and thus much temple land became available in this district for private or civic development. Many estates of wealthy or noble individuals came into being. By the turn of the century, the area north of Sanjo-dori also had its beginning as a cultural center when one of the first public libraries in Japan, the Kyoto Municipal Public Library, was begun in 1872. By 1894 Okazaki Park had been laid out north of

The two-story Murin-an Villa combines aspects of Western and Japanese architecture.

③ MURIN-AN VILLA

Before heading into the cultural center of Okazaki Park, it is worth turning east at Niomon-dori, one street north of Sanjo-dori, to visit one of the estates that came into being after 1868 when temple lands were confiscated by the Meiji government or when temples had to sell portions of their property to support themselves. Industrialists and government officials were able to obtain land in this area to which Kyoto was just spreading as a city, and one of these fortunate officials was Duke Aritomo Yamagata (1838–1922), who had been born into a *samurai* family and who here created his Murin-an Villa.

The Murin-an is north of Sanjo-dori and to the south of Niomon-dori just before Shirakawa-dori. Walk two streets east on Niomon-dori from its intersection with Jingo-michi-dori and then turn to the right. The entrance to the Murin-an garden is down the side street on the right. It is open from 9:00 a.m. to noon and from 1:00 p.m. to 4:00 p.m. It is closed on Mondays and the New Year holiday period. Entry fee.

In the late 1800s the Nanzen-ji temple sold off some of its land, a result of economic necessity under the punitive attitude toward Buddhist temples taken by the government. Some of the land was purchased by Yamagata, a Meiji statesman and Prime Minister from 1889 to 1891. The villa was begun in 1894, but its construction was interrupted by Yamagata's absence from Kyoto during the Sino-Japanese War. On his return, the villa was completed in 1896. The garden, finished in 1898, was designed by Yamagata and created with the assistance of Ogawa Jihei (1860–1932),

one of Kyoto's most famous garden designers; it is a comparatively modern one which varies from traditional garden planning guidelines by including unusual plants and an open lawn. The garden is in the shape of an elongated triangle about three-fourths of an acre (one-third of a hectare) in size, but it seems larger as it uses the device of borrowed scenery from the Higashiyama mountains visible in the distance. A stream runs through the gardens, its water coming from the nearby Lake Biwa through the Sosui Canal. Laid out on a slight slope, the water runs in three cascades into a pond and thence into the garden stream. A large rock is one of the important elements of the garden, so large that it had to be dragged into place by 20 oxen.

The villa is composed of three buildings, a traditional two-story main house and a two-story Western-style building. In the garden is a tea house modeled after an example of the Yabunouchi school of tea. As a Minister of State, Yamagata was involved not only in the Sino-Japanese War but in the Russo-Japanese War of 1905 as well. Just before that latter conflict, the Murin-an Conference was held on the second floor of the Western building of the villa. Here, an aggressive Japanese foreign policy was determined upon by Prime Minister Taro Katsura, Foreign Minister Jutaro Komura, Hirobumi Ito, who led the Seikyu-kai political party, and Yamagata, who was a military man. Yamagata died in 1922, and in 1941 the Murin-an was given to the city of Kyoto which maintains it as a cultural asset for the public. The tea house is available for hire for private and public use as are the Japanese-style rooms of the main house.

The spacious Okazaki Park is famous for its cherry blossoms in spring and its maple trees in autumn.

Sanjo-dori in conjunction with the Heian Shrine, commemorating the 1,100 years of Kyoto's life as a city, all but 25 of these years as the Imperial capital of the nation. The partial reconstruction of the original Daigokudan (Great Hall of State of the Imperial Palace) served also as a shrine to the first Emperor to reside in Kyoto as the capital. Nine years later, a portion of the adjacent area became the home of the first municipal zoo.

By 1933 a new note was added to the park when the Kyoto Municipal Art Museum was opened, and two years later the Butoku-den center for the traditional martial arts was brought to the west side of the Heian Shrine grounds. An exhibition hall had been developed as an addition to the growing complex, a multiuse unit, and as with all such multiuse buildings, its acoustics were not satisfactory for concerts. In 1960, a proper theater for musical and related events found a new home in the Kyoto Kaikan (Kyoto Hall).

By 1963 a Museum of Modern Art was added to the complex, joined in 1976 by the Traditional Industry Museum and the Nichizu Design Center. The area was further enriched by the locating of the Kanze School of Noh in the Kanze Kaikan on Niomon-dori, a school whose beginnings go back to the 1300s, and then the Fujii Art Museum settled here as well. In 1989 the Kyoto International Community Center made its appearance not too far from this cultural agglomeration, providing for diversified cultural offerings.

KYOTO INTERNATIONAL COMMUNITY CENTER (KYOTO KOKUSAI KORYU KAIKAN)

A short walk from the Murin-an brings one to the Kyoto International Community Center, where programs of interest are available to both local residents and visitors. As its name implies, it is meant to serve the growing international community in Kyoto and to provide educational and cultural activities on Japanese and international topics. A varied program is offered, and schedules of events may be obtained from the center. Activities are also listed in the English language tourist publications available in Kyoto. The building houses a library, meeting rooms, computer and video terminals and an intimate stage for dramatic productions, poetry readings, lectures, recitals and other educational and cultural activities.

Returning along Sanjo-dori or Niomon-dori to Jingu-michi-dori, a turn to the right on Jingu-michi-dori brings you to the Okazaki Park Cultural Center. Performances or exhibitions at the museums or halls below are listed in the English language newspapers and in the listing of events distributed by the Tourist Information Center and the City Tourist Office, available at most hotels and the Information Centers. Bus 5 or 32 will leave one at the Kyoto Kaikan Bijutsukan-mae bus stop for any of the places below.

OKAZAKI PARK (OKAZAKI KOEN) This park was opened in 1904 and consists of 21 acres (8.7 hectares) along the Sosui Canal that brings water to Kyoto from Lake Biwa on the other side of the Higashiyama mountain range. In the spring the cherry blossoms and in the fall the maple leaves of the trees in the park and in the zoo make the area a colorful and delightful place.

FUJII MUSEUM (FUJII SAISEKAI YURINKAN) The Fujii Museum is off Niomon-dori on the south side of the street before the entrance to Okazaki; the entry to the building is at the rear. The Fujii Museum is a private museum dedicated to Chinese art. It is open from noon to 3:00 p.m. on the first and third Sunday of each month, but it is closed in January and August. The museum will be opened upon a written request submitted a week in advance of the requested visit. No entry fee is charged but a contribution is welcomed.

The museum's holdings range from early bronzes through ceramics, paintings, jade, porcelains, furniture, costumes and other aspects of the art of China. Its paintings are primarily from the Ming and Ching eras. Some bronzes from India and early mirrors of Japanese provenance are held as well.

KANZE KAIKAN NOH THEATER The Kanze Kaikan hall, on the south side of Niomon-dori and west of Jingo-michi-dori, is a center for theater performances of traditional *Noh* and *Kyogen*. The Kanze School of Noh is one of five schools of *Noh* acting, and it was begun by Kan-ami (1333–84) and then developed by his son Ze-ami (1363–1443).

KYOTO MUNICIPAL ART MUSEUM (KYOTO-SHI BIJUTSUKAN) The Municipal Art Museum, opened in 1933, lies on the eastern side of Jingu-michi-dori, the north–south street in the middle of the Okazaki cultural area with the huge vermilion concrete *torii* across it. It is the first building on the east side of Jingu-michi-dori after Niomon-dori. The museum's holdings are primarily in the

19th (post-1868) and 20th century Japanese and Western paintings, sculpture and handicrafts. Aside from showing portions of its own collections, the halls are used for traveling or loan exhibitions as well as the work of local artists. It is open from 9:30 a.m. to 5:00 p.m. except on Mondays or from December 25 to January 3. The museum is open on Mondays when that day is a national holiday, but it is then closed the next day. Admission ranges from free to a charge of varying levels depending on the exhibition being shown.

KYOTO PREFECTUAL PUBLIC LIBRARY The Kyoto Public Library, opposite the Municipal Art Museum, was first opened in 1872 and, along with the Tokyo Public Library, is the oldest such institution in Japan. The monument in front of the library is of Gottfried Wagner, a German who was brought to Kyoto in 1878 to help in introducing new techniques in ceramic making and in the dyeing of fabrics.

KYOTO NATIONAL MUSEUM OF MODERN ART (KYOTO KOKURITSU KINDAI BIJUTSUKAN) Established in 1963 and rebuilt in 1986, the four-story museum designed by Fumihiko Maki is on the west side of Jingu-michi-dori just north of Niomon-dori. The museum has an extensive collection of contemporary Japanese prints, paintings, sculpture, ceramics, lacquer work and other crafts. It is particularly rich in the ceramic artistry of Kawai Kanjiro as well as works of Hamada Shoji.

In addition, the museum collects modern art from throughout the world, and its photographic collection, based on the Arnold Gilbert collection of Chicago from the late 19th century, is notable. The large and spacious halls of this modern building are used to mount major exhibitions from Japan and abroad. A small book counter and coffee shop are on the main floor. The museum is open from 9:30 a.m. to 4:30 p.m. (until 7:30 p.m. on Fridays) except for Monday and the New Year holiday. It is open on Monday if that day is a national holiday but then closed the next day. Entry fee.

KANGYO KAIKAN (PUBLIC EXHIBITION HALL) The Public Exhibition Hall, on Nijo-dori to the west of Jing-michi-dori, holds exhibitions of a commercial, educational or cultural nature.

KYOTO MUSEUM OF TRADITIONAL INDUSTRY AND THE NICHIZU DESIGN CENTER

The Museum of Traditional Industry, which opened in 1976, is located in Okazaki Park at Nijo-dori. The museum exhibits and offers demonstrations of the making of those traditional crafts for which Kyoto has always been famous. These include silk, bamboo, lacquer and paper works, ceramics, damascene, traditional dolls, cabinetry and Nishijin weaving on Jacquard looms. The crafts are available for purchase as well. A replica of an "eel house" or "bedrooms for eels," the traditional narrow Kyoto house, has been built on the lower level of the museum.

The museum building is a striking modern architectural structure with a curved lower level and a square upper part. The Nichizu Design Center on the third floor offers special exhibitions of a design nature. The museum is open from 9:00 a.m. to 5:00 p.m. It is closed on Mondays except on national holidays and from December 28 through January 3. Admission fee.

KYOTO KAIKAN (KYOTO HALL)

Kyoto Kaikan is a multipurpose building used for national and international meetings, for exhibitions, as a concert hall and a theater. Built in 1960 by architect Maekawa Kunio, a pupil of Le Corbusier, it contains two concert chambers and a large conference hall for 2,500 people. It is a center for musical performances for the city.

KYOTO MUNICIPAL ZOO

The zoo is the second largest in Japan after Tokyo's Ueno Zoo. Created in 1903, it lies behind the Kyoto Municipal Art Museum to the east of Jingu-michi-dori in Okazaki Park at the foot of the Higashiyama mountains. It is open from 9:00 a.m. to 4:00 p.m. Closed on Mondays. Its cherry trees in spring and maples in autumn provide a colorful backdrop to the zoo and the 700 animals within its spacious grounds. Entry fee.

BUTOKU-EN (MARTIAL VIRTUE HALL)

Built in 1935, the Center for the Traditional Martial Arts is located in the northwest corner of the Okazaki cultural complex. It serves as a school for fencing, *jujutsu* and archery every day except Sunday and holidays. The annual competition in these skills is held here from May 4th each year. The building is on the west side of the Heian Shrine.

4 HEIAN SHRINE

Heian Shrine (Heian Jingu), regarded as one of Kyoto's must-see sites, is located in the northern portion of the Okazaki cultural area. Kyoto had been the Imperial capital of Japan from 794 until the capital was moved in 1868 to Tokyo on the demise of the rule by the Tokugawa Shoguns and the beginning of the Meiji Restoration. The loss of the seat of government was a shock to the citizens of Kyoto as the city had been the Imperial and cultural center of the nation for over 1,000 years. The combination of the court and the great temples had enlivened and enriched the life of the city; now only the temples remained and they were under attack from a new government that was oriented to the Shinto faith and was anti-Buddhist. The court may have disappeared, but Kyoto's heritage could not be ignored. In 1892, to celebrate the 1,100th anniversary of the founding of the city, it was decided to re-erect a scaled-down version of the Daigoku-den, the Palace of the Hall of State, of the original capital of 794. Instead of creating the replica on the site of the initial palace in the north-central area of the city (north of Nijo Castle), it was decided to place the project in the Okazaki area.

The rebuilt smaller edition of the Hall of State was dedicated to the memory of the Emperor Kammu (736–805) who had created the city of Heian-kyo (Kyoto) in 794. Then, in 1940, under wartime nationalism, the Emperor Komei (reigned 1831–67), the father of the Emperor Meiji and the last emperor to reside permanently in Kyoto as the capital, was enshrined here also. Thus the spirits of these two emperors are in the Heian Jingu shrine Honden (Spirit Hall). The rebuilt Daigoku-den (Great Hall of State) burned in 1976 and was reconstructed three years later. The creation of a portion of the palace of Heian-kyo in 1895 was accomplished on a two-thirds scale of the original structure. Rebuilt were the Daigoku-den, the East and West Main Halls, the Ote-mon (Main Gate), the corridors connecting the Ote-mon and the Daigoku-den, and the Soryu and Byakko towers of the corridors. A purification water basin lies to the left front of the Ote-mon Gate outside of the grounds proper. A huge concrete *torii*, bearing the Imperial 16-petal chrysanthemum in gold, was added in 1929 a good distance down Jingu-mich-dori from the shrine. The *torii* stands 80 feet (24 m) high. The top rail is 111 feet (33.3 m) long.

Heian Shrine was built in 1895 to commemorate the 1,100th anniversary of the founding of Kyoto.

The shrine (and this is a Shinto shrine with a worship area at the innermost portion of the grounds) is entered through the Ote-mon, a two-story gate that is a replica of the main gate into the original palace grounds. This vermilion painted structure with a blue tile roof has corridors extending to the east and west and thence to the north toward the Daigoku-den. The East and West Main Halls stand before the north–south corridors just beyond the Ote-mon. The ground of the fore-court between the corridors, the gate and the Daigoku-den to the north is covered with a white sand. At the end of the north–south corridors are two towers in the Chinese style, the Soryu-ro (Blue Dragon) on the east (right) and the Byakko-ro (White Tiger) on the west. In front of the Ote-mon to the west is a roofed purification basin.

At the far end of the courtyard is the Daigoku-den, which was the main government hall where the emperor held official business of state. When the Daigoku-den burned in 1177, it was never replaced—until this scaled-down version was created. The present building is 110 feet (33 m) long, 40 feet (12 m) wide and 55 feet (15.5 m) high. As with the Ote-mon, the structure is vermilion

with a blue tile roof. Before the hall, to the east side of its front steps, is a cherry tree, while to the west is a citrus tree, two traditional plantings as existed in the early days of the palace.

The Honden (Spirit Hall), which holds the spirits of the two emperors, is behind the Daigoku-den. Its innermost sector is an unpainted structure of *hinoki* (cypress) wood, 27 feet (8.1 m) by 28 feet (98.4 m) (not open to the public). It is surrounded by a wooden fence. The Honden was constructed in traditional Shinto style with vermilion posts and beams, white plaster, green barred windows and a tiled roof. Before the Honden is the Haiden (Prayer Hall), where people facing the Honden can pray.

The entry to the magnificent garden (fee) is to the left when facing the Daigoku-den. The garden was, of course, designed by a modern landscape gardener, Ogawa Jihei, but he attempted to keep to the spirit of Heian gardens. The huge 323,000 square foot (29,000 sq m) garden is centered on a large pond, the Seihogai-ike, as would have been true 1,000 years ago. The first part of the garden is a stroll garden with many cherry trees and eventually a small pond. The path

A carp-filled pond in the garden at Heian Shrine.

then leads on to the Seiho Lake which is connected with the Soryu-ike (Pond of the Green Dragon) by the Garyu-kyo (Dragon Stepping Stones), which provide a "path" across the water. (These stones once formed the base to the Sanjo-dori Bridge from Hideyoshi's time. They became available when the bridge was modernized at the end of the 19th century.) A roofed bridge built about 1910, the Taihei-kaku (Bridge of Peace) in the Chinese style, crosses the lake. It is topped by a phoenix, and it bears a resemblance in style to both the Gold and Silver Pavilions. The garden is lovely in all seasons: in spring when the weeping cherry trees and azaleas are in bloom, in summer when the iris and water lilies provide a visual delight, in autumn when the color of the maples enriches the gardens, and in winter when snow blankets the buildings and garden. The cherry trees can be found in the south garden.

NORTH OF HEIAN SHRINE Continuing north beyond Okazaki Park, we come to the area in which Kyoto University has its various buildings and then several temples and shrines of note.

KYOTO UNIVERSITY Founded in 1869, Kyoto University became one of two new national universities created for a nation attempting to align its future with the Western world (the other was Tokyo University). Previously, Confucian ethics, Buddhist lore and Shinto beliefs provided the under-girding for much of Japanese culture and learning. After the appearance of the American "Black Ships," it became obvious not only that knowledge of scientific advances occurring in the West was essential for the development of Japanese industry, but that a knowledge of Western society, its history and its goals were needed as well if Japan were to become a part of a world on which for so many centuries it had turned its back. Such knowledge was to be imparted to the most able of young Japanese in Kyoto by its new university. Thus it made a major contribution to the modernization of Japan, as it still does today.

Kyoto University has continued to develop and to expand between the Kamo River and Yoshida Hill for more than a century. Today, it boasts of world-class academics as well as an international flavor. The university is spread through much of northeastern Kyoto, its center being between Marutamachi-dori (on the south) and Imadegawa-dori (on the north) between the Kamo River (on the west) and Yoshida-yama (on the east). Buses 31, 201 and 206 along Higashoji-oji-dori to any of the bus stops between Marutamachi-dori and Imadegawa-dori bring you to specific sections of the university. Buses 17, 35 and 203 along Imadegawa-dori also go by the university's major buildings.

5 KURO-DANI (BLACK RAVINE TEMPLE)

At the southern point of Yoshida Hill, Priest Honen built his small hermitage, which he named Kuro-dani (also known as the Konkai Komyo-ji) for the Black Ravine in which he had studied on Mount Hiei. Kuro-dani is where Priest Honen came to the conclusion that the Nembutsu was the only means to salvation in the world after this one. In 1175, it was here that he came when he found the Tendai faith of Mount Hiei, where he lived as a monk, not satisfying. Here, in this location beyond the influences of the monastery or the city, he lived in a simple hermitage, devoting himself to prayer and study and renouncing the world around him. In his studies, he read Genshin's (Enshin Sozu's) *Ojo Yoshu* based on a commentary by the Chinese monk Shantao (Shendo) and, in 1175, at the age of 43, he found the religious conviction and satisfaction that had hitherto eluded him.

The Mie-do (Founder's Hall) at Kuro-dani holds a seated wooden image of Honen, its founder.

According to temple legend, while seated on a rock, fervently praying, Honen perceived a trail of purple clouds in the west, the Western Paradise of Amida, just as he came to realize the truth of the doctrine of Jodo (the Pure Land of Amida)–that the repetition of the Nembutsu can alone bring salvation. One of the most precious relics at Kuro-dani is the "Purple Cloud Rock" on which Honen was sitting when he received insight: "Only repeat the name of Amida with all your heart, whether walking or standing still, whether sitting or lying. Never cease this practice, even for a moment. This is the practice which brings salvation without fail, for it is in accordance with the original vow of the Buddha."

That Purple Rock, the main gateway and the pagoda are the only objects to have survived a 1935 fire. What had been a simple retreat was to develop into a full monastery by the close of the 1200s. Fires have destroyed the buildings on various occasions, and thus the present structures are all recent ones. Located on a hillside, a flight of steps leads to the 1860 two-story gate with two side units for the staircases to the second floor.

The most important building is the Mie-do, (Founder's Hall), a bright, *tatami*-matted hall with *shoji* on three sides and a plain wooden interior with four gilded pillars about the central shrine area. The shrine has a seated image in wood of Honen holding a rosary, reputedly carved by him in 1207, and brought to Kuro-dani in 1609. Lovely bouquets of flowers are before the image of Honen.

To the south and east of the Mie-do is the Amida-do, with a seated gilded Amida image with a 1,000 Buddha aureole behind it, said to have been created by Genshin. The ceiling of the hall is covered with a painting of a dragon. On the rear of the wall behind the Amida is a painted Buddha image, while to the right side of the hall is a small case with the symbolic 1,000 small gilt Buddhas figures. The temple cemetery lies beyond the main complex of monastic buildings, with a three-story pagoda consecrated to Monju, the deity of wisdom.

The temple lies just to the northeast of the Heian Shrine and Okazaki Park. It is open from 9:00 a.m. to 4:30 p.m. There is an entry fee to the Mie-do.

SHINNYO-DO Just to the north of Kuro-dani is the Shinnyo-do, another Jodo temple that was begun in 992, although its buildings are from a 1693 rebuilding. It also has a two-story gateway with side stair structures and then a three-story pagoda. The Hondo has an Amida image credited to Ennin (Jikaku Daishi, 794–864) while a secondary building on the left of the Hondo is the Shoin, a study with paintings of a pine tree, of a crane in flight and of a peacock and peahen. A *tokonoma* and *chigaidana* enhance the room, which looks out upon a lovely small garden of sand, stones and moss, the bushes at its rear screening the neighboring cityscape– and with Mount Daimonji as part of a "borrowed" scenery for the garden. (There is a fee to enter the Shoin and garden.)

The main festivity of the temple occurs from November 5 to 15 to remember a *daimyo* in the Middle Ages who recited the Nembutsu for ten days and nights. An annual Ojuya service is held at which the Nembutsu is recited. Many thousands of worshippers are drawn to the temple at this time. The services run from 5:00 p.m to 7:00 p.m. and from 9:00 a.m. to 5:00 p.m. on the 15th. There is also a procession at 2:00 p.m. on the 15th as the monks and children parade through the temple grounds.

YOSHIDA SHRINE Yoshida Jinja (Yoshida Shrine) lies to the north of Shinnyo-do. If you are on foot, you can take a path between them. If arriving at the Yoshida Shrine directly, take bus 203 to the Hyakumanben bus stop on Higashi-oji-dori, then walk south on Higashi-oji-dori to Higashi Ichi-jo-dori (just behind Kyoto University) and turn left. The street ends at the entrance to the Yoshida Shrine at the foot of the hill on which the shrine is located. The shrine is open during daylight hours with no entry fee.

Yoshida Shrine was founded by Fujiwara-no-Yamakage in 859 as the tutelary shrine of the Fujiwaras, the family who were the rulers behind the throne from the 700s onward. As a result, the shrine also served as the tutelary shrine of the capital and a continuing link with the Fujiwara family, whose original shrine and homes were in the Yamashina area just to the east of Kyoto. The Yamashina Shrine and the Fujiwara residence were moved to Asuka (south of Nara) when that area became the first settled capital of Japan. The shrine was later moved to Nara by Fujiwara-no-Fuhito in the early 700s when that new Imperial capital was created. Thus, as the power behind the throne, the Fujiwaras took their family shrine with them each time they moved.

A large vermilion torii greets visitors to Yoshida Shrine.

According to legend, the original Fujiwara ancestral spirits came to the Kasuga Shrine in Nara from their original shrine in Yamashina riding on the back of a sacred deer, since deer were believed to be the messengers of the gods. When the ancestral spirits were moved to Kyoto, it is said that once again they arrived on the back of a deer, and thus deer have always been associated with the Yoshida Shrine as well as with the Kasuga Shrine in Nara.

The Yoshida family leaders were the hereditary priests of the shrine, and in the 14th century these descendents of an ancient clan of diviners created an intellectual system meant to prove that Shinto was the root of Buddhism—in contrast to the reverse claim that had been promulgated by Buddhist priests as Ryobu (Dual) Shinto developed. They enshrined all "eight million *kami* (god spirits)" at Yoshida Shrine so it would become the central shrine for the nation. These pretensions came to an end when the Meiji government came into power and attempted to reduce any influence by Buddhism in Japan—even the claim that Shinto preceded Buddhism. With the establishment of Kyoto University, the shrine at least became the guardian shrine of that institution, if not the nation at large.

Yoshida Shrine is at the eastern end of Higashi Ichi-jo-dori where Yoshida-yama (Yoshida Hill) rises sharply from the flat land, and here is a large vermilion *torii* and two stone lanterns A wide tree-lined path leads to a second vermilion *torii* and to the flight of steps up the hill to the shrine. A roofed purification water basin is at the left of the second *torii*, and north of it is a small shrine replete with *torii*, Heiden (Offertory) and Honden (Spirit House) behind a vermilion fence. Here also is a small *kura* (storage building).

At the top of the hillside stairway is a plateau on which stands the main buildings of the shrine, primarily on a north–south orientation. The first portion of the precincts, separated by a vermilion fence from the second part, has at its southern portion a small roped area for a ceremonial fire. To the right (east) is a bronze recumbent deer, a reminder of the messenger that brought the deities of the shrine here from Nara. A roofed open structure, which can serve as a stage, is on the left, oriented to the west, facing a shrine building. Ahead to the right is a similar open and roofed structure.

Beyond the vermilion fence, which is entered through a *torii* passageway, is the roofed Heiden (Offertory), then a ceremonial stage to the right and, on the east, a staircase ascending the hillside to another small shrine. On the west side are the shrine offices and counter for the purchase of religious materials. Ahead to the north are four thatched-roofed main units in which the spirits are enshrined. Two sand cones stand before them in the raked sand beyond the Offertory. Between the second and third shrines is a painted screen with a lion. Inside the fence to this inner quarter is a pond on the right whose stream runs past the fence to the west. The main hall, the Dai-josho Daigen-gu, built in 1484, is unusual in that it is octagonal in shape with a thatched hip-and-gable roof.

The shrine is a popular one with the local people, and on ceremonial occasions it also attracts a large crowd from beyond its area. In a crowded city, its location on Yoshida Hill provides a park-like space for a respite from the busy streets below. It is also a popular venue for various ceremonies.

6 CHION-JI (MILLION TIMES TEMPLE)

North of Kyoto University is the Chion-ji Temple (not to be confused with the Chion-in Temple, which was described in Tour 3). Chion-ji is also known as the Hyakumanben Temple, the "Million Times Temple." Founded by Honen as a Jodo temple dedicated to Amida, it received its nickname during the time of Emperor Go-Daigo when a terrible pestilence raged in Kyoto and decimated the population. The Emperor ordered Abbot Sen-a-Koen Shonin to do what he could to insure the Buddha would bring this scourge to an end. The abbot arranged for an extraordinary service in which the Nembutsu was repeated a million times within 17 days to implore the aid of Amida in ending the disease. A great rosary of 1,000 wooden beads was turned as part of the ceremony during the service. The prayers were evidently effective, for on the millionth repetition of the Nembutsu the plague came to an end. In honor of his efforts, the Emperor conferred on the abbot the title of Hyaku-manben Dai Nezu, and a huge, extra long *o-juzu* (Buddhist rosary) was given to the temple.

The temple has been the victim of many fires, and was finally and permanently located at its present site in 1662. In 1930, the Dai Nezu, the world's largest *o-juzu*, was donated

The interior of the main hall of Chion-ji (Million Times Temple) is draped with the world's largest rosary.

to the temple, and it encircles the interior of the Mie-do, the temple's main hall. The temple grounds are entered through the San-mon, the main gateway at Imadegawa-dori, or through the side gate at Higashi-oji-dori. When you enter the grounds through the San-mon, the temple nursery is on the right. Next you encounter the Shaka-do and the water purification basin and, next to it, a Busso-seki, a stone with the engraved footprint of the Buddha. On the left of the main entry path is the Amida-do, which holds a notable image of Amida, the torso of which is said to have been carved by Priest Ennin (Jikaku Daishi)–but whose head appeared of its own miraculous accord thereafter. Directly ahead lies the Mie-do, the Founder's Hall or

Main Hall, with gold plaques at its roof edge impressed with the Buddha's footprints.

The Shaka-do is the second building on the right. Before if stands the aforementioned footprint of the Buddha. Within, the main image is of the gilded seated Shaka, gold hangings enhancing the altar area. To the right at the rear is an image of Fudo (a Buddhist deity), while a guardian stands at the two rear extremities of the building. Behind the building are other structures for the administration of the temple.

The Mie-do (Founder's Hall) is at the north end of the compound. On its front veranda to the right sits an image of Binzuru, the disciple of Buddha who failed in keeping to the standards of the faith. In life he was a

the fronts of the beams are in the shape of lion's heads. The *ramma* (transoms) over the horizontal beams have been carved in the shape of colored storks, a number of other birds and cherry blossoms. To the left of the main altar is an image of Amida as well as a number of *ihai* (memorial tablets), while to the right is a one-story gilt pagoda and an image of Honen in a shrine case in the shape of a golden temple.

The huge Hyakumanben Dai Nezu (rosary) of 1,080 beads is thought to be the largest such rosary in the world. It was given to the temple in 1930 to commemorate the 1,250th anniversary of the death of the Chinese monk Shan-tao (Zendo), who is considered the originator of the beliefs of the Jodo sect of Buddhism. This huge rosary is looped in double strands about the interior of the Mie-do. It is 328 feet (100 m) in circumference and weighs 176 pounds (80 kg). On the 15th of each month, a special service that uses the Dai Nezu takes place.

Chion-ji is located opposite the campus of Kyoto University. Take bus 203 or 206 to the Hyakumanben bus stop. The temple is open from 10:00 a.m. to 4:00 p.m.

physician, and thus some of the faithful use him as a talisman for curing portions of their body by rubbing Binzuru followed by their afflicted area. The interior of the Mie-do is resplendent with its large gold canopy over gold and black lacquered altar furniture. Black and gold brocade covers the altar, while a red and gold brocade covers the furniture before the main image of Genchi Shonin, a disciple of Honen, a rosary in his hand, in the center of the hall. The image is enshrined in a gilt case in the shape of a temple. Two large pine trees in urns at the large altar table contrast with the golden hangings from the ceiling. The bracketing of the beams above the front altar area ends in the shape of a dragon's head to the east and west while

GETTING THERE

Heian Shrine is the highlight of this tour, and its gardens are not to be missed. The best time to visit is April, when its numerous cherry trees are in bloom. Take bus 5 or 32 to the Kyoto Kaikan Bijutsukan-mae bus stop. The shrine entrance is at the head of Jingu-michi-dori beyond the huge red *torii* that towers over that street. The shrine is open from 8:30 a.m. to 5:00 p.m. from April through October and from 8:30 a.m. to 4:30 p.m. from November through March. Entry to the main part of the grounds is without charge, but there is an entry fee for the gardens.

If you wish to end the tour at Heian Shrine or the adjacent Okazaki Park complex, transportation by bus 5 or 32 from the Kyoto Kaikan Bijutsukan-mae bus stop or buses on Higashi-oji-dori can be taken to various parts of the city. From the northern sector of the tour, three streets to the west of Imadegawa-dori is a terminal of the Keihan electric railway, where escalators take you to trains going south. Various buses are also available at the intersection of Imadegawa-dori and the rail terminal.

Walking Tour 7

NANZEN-JI AREA

The Backward-looking Amida and the Tiger Cub Zen Garden

1 **Zenrin-ji/Eikan-do Temple** 禅林寺/永観堂
2 **Nomura Museum** 野村美術館
3 **Nanzen-ji Temple** 南禅寺
4 **Nanzen-ji Subtemples** 南禅寺塔頭
5 **Lake Biwa Canal** 琵琶湖疏水

Two temples and a private museum may seem a scant number of sites to be described in a single chapter, but these three may be visited by themselves or they can be combined with the temples and shrines along the Philosopher's Walk in Tour 7. On the assumption that combining these sites might lead to too long a day, these two temples and a museum are described separately. Each of the two temples has a number of buildings within their grounds, and one of them is among the major Zen temples in Kyoto.

The Taho-to Pagoda at Zenrin-ji amidst foliage.

Of the three places, the Nomura Museum is a highly specialized collection primarily of Japanese *objets d'art* together with choice selections of Chinese art. The major site, however, is the Nanzen-ji Temple and its subtemples. Nanzen-ji is particularly noted for its San-mon gateway, its Sho Hojo (Abbot's Small Quarters) with its painted *fusuma*, and its Zen-style "tiger and cubs" garden as well as for the gardens of some of its subtemples.

A few of the Nanzen-ji subtemples serve vegetarian fare (*shojin*) or tofu, and these can be delightful places for lunch. The Zenrin-ji/Eikan-do temple is primarily known for its "Backward-looking Kannon" and the lovely story which accompanies it. As a temple with a number of buildings, the complex offers a number of rooms with interesting *fusuma* and, above all, the Kannon mentioned above.

1 ZENRIN-JI/EIKAN-DO TEMPLE

The Zenrin-ji/Eikan-do Temple was founded in 856 by Shinsho-sozu, a disciple of the great 8th century priest Kobo Daishi (Kukai). The site was originally the villa of Fujiwara-no-Kanyu, but Shinsho was able to obtain the villa as a gift from the Emperor and to turn it into a temple.

In 983, the temple was rebuilt on a new and larger scale by the monk Eikan, for whom the temple was later renamed in honor of his charitable and religious activities. Eikan also built a hospital (the Tonan-in) on the temple grounds in addition to rebuilding the temple. At the Tonan-in, the poor and homeless could be cared for. The hospital grounds extended from Awata-guchi (Sanjo-dori) to Shishigatani, an extensive range of land. In order to produce medicine for the poor, Eikan planted a plum orchard, called the Hidenbai, whose fruit could be used as the basis for medicines. Largely destroyed in the Onin War of 1467–77, the temple was rebuilt thereafter, and by the end of the 1500s most of the buildings had been restored. In the 1880s, Zenrin-ji/Eikan-do underwent a major restoration under the monk Shugyoku, who also recreated the hospital, reopened the Hinooka Mountain Pass and even made plans for a canal to bring the waters of Lake Biwa to Kyoto.

Set on the peaceful hillside at the base of the Higashiyama mountains, Zenrin-ji is located amidst pines and maples. A small pond, the Hojo-no-ike (Abbot's Pond), in the forepart of the temple grounds, is crossed by a graceful stone bridge before the temple is entered through the Chu-mon gateway. Another gateway, the seldom used Chokushi-mon (Imperial Messenger's Gate), is in the Kara-mon (Chinese) style with a heavy arched gable roof. Just inside this gate is a long, raised sand rectangle on whose surface the priests keep raked designs.

Remove your shoes at the ticket booth and then proceed along a planned pathway along the wooden corridors and the eventual stairs to the upper level of the temple precincts. The corridor (Garyuro–"Dragon Path"), with its many turns as it connects the various

buildings of the temple, was built without nails. The temple complex is based about two small courtyards and then a split staircase to the upper levels of the hillside structures.

The first building one passes on the left after the entrance is the Kakujudai which has a large *tatami*-matted room (as are all the rooms hereafter) with cusped windows. This building on the west and the next three units on the north, east and south form an enclosed courtyard around a garden with a running stream. (This first building is one of the large display areas for the temple treasures shown annually in November.)

The second building on the north side of this first courtyard garden is the Ko Hojo (the Abbot's Small Quarters) of five rooms. Some of the rooms of this and the other buildings that lie ahead have *fusuma* (sliding panels) worthy of mention. Most of these *fusuma* are covered with plain gold leaf, while a number have a gold ground with scenes of nature painted upon this gold base. The fourth room of the Ko Hojo varies from the other three since it has a *tokonoma* and a statue of a monk seated before a scroll which hangs behind him on the wall.

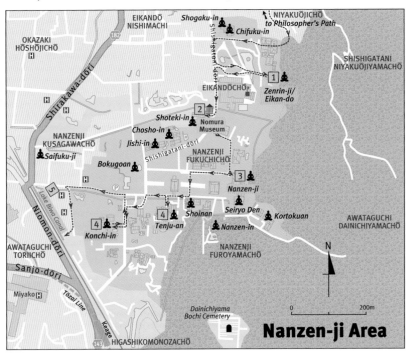

Nanzen-ji Area

The garden at the hillside Zenrin-ji/Eiken-do Temple is famous for its fall foliage.

The Juoso-den on the east side of the court-yard also has five rooms. The first holds the image of a monk (formerly gilded) seated on a Chinese chair with a scroll behind him. The *fusuma* of the second room have a hint of waves upon them, a Buddhist symbol of the impermanence of life. The third or middle room is an altar room with an Amida image seated on a lotus blossom, while a Fudo image on a lotus with an aureole with flaming edges stands behind Amida. The fourth room has white *fusuma* with abstract drawings symbolizing ocean waves, while the last room contains an image of a seated monk with a scroll behind depicting the temple layout.

The last building on the south side of this first courtyard is the Dai Hojo (the Abbot's Large Quarters), with rooms on three of its sides. The west side faces the Chokushi-mon gateway, with the raised sand garden and its raked decorations, and the center room on the west side has an altar with images of Amida, Seishi and Kannon. The second room on the third (or south) side of the Hojo (which faces on to the second courtyard) is a study for the abbot, and it has a set of *chigaidana* (staggered shelves) and a *tokonoma*. A portion of the south wall contains a writing shelf (desk) with *shoji*, and a raised platform has a Chinese chair without legs (the abbot's chair). The rear *fusuma* are decorated with paintings of trees, clouds and Chinese

figures against a gold ground, while the *fusuma* of the left wall depict mountains with a young man in Chinese garb in the center, a boat to the left and trees to the right.

A standing screen, 3 feet (1 m) tall, has the famous Amida Raigo (The Descent of Amida) of the temple. It depicts a golden Amida with a huge halo who is appearing over a hill. Seishi and Kannon, also in gold beside him, are standing on white clouds. At the bottom corners are small figures of the Guardians of the Four Directions, and in the center bottom are Bon-ten and Taishaku-ten. The picture is supposed to represent a vision which Eshin had on Mount Hiei, and it is a type of Amida Raigo painting that was particularly popular during the Kamakura period (1185–1333). It was not unusual for a dying person to grasp the cords that extended from the hands of Amida in such a picture (as was the case of the dying Fujiwara-no-Michinaga) so as to be certain to arrive in Amida's Western Paradise immediately upon death. This particular portrayal is considered to be one of the finest of its kind.

The corridor continues along the north side of this second courtyard, the east side of the corridor having a bell and public toilets behind it. The south side of the corridor runs along the north portion of the Dai-den (Great Hall), a large hall with six cusped windows. The front third of the building is for worshippers;

he rear portion encompasses the altar area. Two Shi-tenno at the extreme rear on the right and left protect the closed cases with the Dai-den's main Amida image, and the large altar s enriched by the gold hanging units before t. At the right front is an image of Binzuru, one of Buddha's disciples who fell from grace but who continued to follow the Buddha and to observe his teachings. (A physician in life, his image is reputed to be efficacious if one touches it and then touches the afflicted part of one's body.) The corridor leads around three sides of the Dai-den, and at the rear of the building it splits into two directions, both mounting a series of steps. Taking the right steps, you pass the Ihei-do with its memorial tablets and then at the top of some steps is the Amida-do (Amida Hall).

The Amida-do holds the statue of the famous Mikaeri-no-Amida, the "Backward-looking Amida" (Amida looking over his shoulder) of legendary account. It is recorded that at 4:00 p.m. on February 15, 1081, when Eikan was reciting the Nembutsu while walking around the image (the "walking or dancing Nembutsu" prayer), Amida came down from the altar to pray with him and to join him in the walking prayer. When Eikan stopped in amazement, Amida turned his head and over his shoulder said, "Eikan, os-oshi" (Eikan, you are slow!). To share this experience with others, Eikan had a 3 foot (1 m) tall Amida image carved with its head half turned to the right. The story and the image have become famous in Buddhist lore in Japan. Later, a statue of Eikan was placed behind and to the right of the Amida.

The Amida-do, with its coffered ceiling, has a colorful painted flower in each square of the ceiling; its columns have been covered with gold leaf (now tarnished), and painted decorations (faded) enhance the upper parts of the columns and ceiling beams while *ap-sara* (flying angels) decorate the ceiling. The Amida-do has a number of other wooden figures of Buddhist deities or noted monks in place, but the small "Backward-looking Amida" is its major image.

Returning to the point where the corridor splits into two, each with separate staircases, the steps can be taken to the north to the Kaisan-do (Founder's Hall), where the three founders of the temple are each seated on a Chinese-style chair. Beyond the Kaisan-do the roofed corridor ends, and you must put on slippers to continue up the hill on many steep

steps to the Taho-to Pagoda (closed). From this point, a limited view can be had of the whole of northern Kyoto across to the mountains in Arashiyama/Sagano.

2 NOMURA MUSEUM

From Zenrin-ji, you can continue on to the Nomura Museum and the Nanzen-ji temple. Walk south on the main road in front of the temple until you come to a high school. To the right across from the school is the Nomura Museum. The museum is open from 10:00 a.m. to 4:00 p.m. for the spring and autumn exhibitions. It is closed on Mondays and from June 10 to September 10 and from December 5 to March 10. Entry fee.

The Nomura Museum is a post-World War II museum which exhibits the private collection of Tokushichi Nomura, a financier who was responsible for the Daiwa Bank and Nomura Securities Company, among other enterprises. The collection of Japanese art within includes paintings and hanging scrolls, lacquerware, pottery, *Noh* masks, costumes, calligraphy and items concerned with the tea ceremony. The museum also holds Chinese ceramics. Only a limited number of objects are shown at any one time, and these are changed each month.

3 NANZEN-JI TEMPLE

The Nanzen-ji Temple is the next stop on this walk. Since you may wish to come to it directly, directions are given at the end of the chapter from the Nomura Museum or the Zenrin-ji/Eikan-do Temple as well as by bus from the heart of the city.

Nanzen-ji (South Temple of Enlightenment) belongs to the Rinzai school of Zen Buddhism and is located in a pine forest just below the Higashiyama mountains. As one of the major Zen temples in Kyoto, it shall be described here in some detail. Aside from its major buildings, the Nanzen-ji has 12 subtemples. At one time a very large compound, it is now reduced to some 27 acres (10.8 hectares) after having been forced to sell off much of its land in the 19th century. A number of the subtemples have notable gardens, but only a few of these are open to the public except through special permission. Fortunately, the three most important gardens are available for visitation. Two of the subtemples serve vegetarian lunches in their gardens.

The temple was originally a villa for a retired emperor rather than a religious site.

Emperor Kameyama, unhappy with his relationship with the Kamakura Shoguns, abdicated in 1274 at the age of 26 and built a retirement retreat, the Zenrinji-dono, at the eastern edge of the city. Beautiful gardens were laid out and two palaces were created, the Kami or Natsu-no-miya (Upper or Summer Palace) and the Shimo or Fuyu-no-miya (Lower or Winter Palace).

Problems plagued the villa on a continuing basis, and thus in 1290 the Emperor invited Priest Fumon of the Tofuku-ji Temple to rid the palace of a ghost which was troubling it. Fumon accomplished the task simply through *zazen* (seated meditation) without the intoning of any sutra. The Emperor was so impressed by this demonstration of the efficacy of Zen meditation that he rewarded Fumon by giving him a portion of the villa lands (the Shimo-no-miya) on which to create a temple. The Emperor continued to live at the upper palace (Kami-no-miya), studying Zen doctrines under Fumon, and he gave himself the title of Ho-o (Great Priest). Eventually, Fumon requested the second palace for his temple as well. His request was granted and Fumon began the creation of the Nanzen-in (now a subtemple of the Nanzen-ji temple). The construction of Nanzen-in was aided by the former Emperor, who personally helped to carry some of the dirt needed for its foundations. Nanzen-in today contains a statue of the Emperor as a priest, he having taken the tonsure in 1289. Thus was the Nanzen-in temple founded, the first unit of the Nanzen-ji complex which was to become the headquarters of the Zen-shu branch of the Rinzai school of Zen Buddhism.

In 1297, the Butsu-den (Buddha Hall) of Nanzen-ji was begun, and Zen flourished here to the great envy of the ever militant and parochial Tendai monks of Mount Hiei. Thus, in 1393, they raided the temple and put it to the torch. Fire again destroyed the rebuilt complex in 1447, and again the reconstructed temple was leveled during the Onin War in 1467. Toyotomi Hideyoshi rebuilt the temple in 1597, providing it with a new Butsu-den (Buddha Hall), and in 1611 the Emperor Go-Yozei gave it the Seiryo-den of the Imperial Palace which became the Dai Hojo (Abbot's Large Quarters), and Shogun Tokugawa Ieyasu granted it a building from Hideyoshi's Fushimi Castle for the Sho (or Ko) Hojo (Abbot's Small Quarters). Another gift was the Chokushi-mon Gate, which originally was the Nikka Gate of the Imperial Palace. The temple grounds were expanded in the Edo era (1616–1868) as Nanzen-ji enjoyed the Shoguns' favor, and it could boast of a total of 62 subtemples on grounds covering 114,819 *tsubo*. (A *tsubo* equals approximately six square feet.) Unhappily, the anti-Buddhist mood of the new Meiji government after 1868 reduced its grounds to 33,966 *tsubo*, leaving it with only nine subtemples. (Today, the complex is back to 12 subtemples.)

The esteem accorded Nanzen-ji can in part be credited to the fact that the most capable Rinzai Zen master has always been selected as its abbot. The temple continues to serve in the training in Zen practices, and monks come from throughout Japan to practice *zazen* (seated meditation).

The huge two-story San-mon or Tenka-no-Ryu-mon (Mountain Gate or Dragon Gate) provides an impressive entry to the grounds. One of the three largest gateways in Japan, it was first built in 1296 but was destroyed by fire in 1447. In 1626, Todo Takatora, one of Shogun Ieyasu's most trusted generals, had the San-mon rebuilt as a memorial to the warriors of both sides who had died a decade earlier in the battle in which Ieyasu's forces annihilated those of Toyotomi Hideyori (Hideyoshi's son) at Osaka Castle.

The gate, with its five openings between six huge upright columns, has a small building with arched windows in the Zen style on either side, the entrances to the steep stairways leading to the upper level of the gate. A railing runs around the narrow platform outside the second story of the gateway, from which a view of the city can be obtained. The gate is surmounted by a large roof with slightly turned-up corners and, as with many temple gateways, the sides of the gate openings are plastered with *senja fude*, stickers bearing the names of the devout who have placed them there. The higher the sticker is placed, the more likely is it to be noticed by the gods. As a result, an expandable/retractable walking stick and sticker-pasting rod was devised for use by pilgrims whose physical reach never satisfied their spiritual aspirations for divine notice.

The upper floor of the gateway is named Gohoro (Five Phoenixes). It contains a Buddha image, two Bodhisattva and 16 *arhat* (Buddhist hermits or holy men) as well as images of Tokugawa Ieyasu and Todo Takatora

A gable-roofed subtemple building of Nanzen-ji.

The painted ceiling is the work of Kano Tanyu and Tosa Tokuetsu, who decorated it with phoenixes (birds) and heavenly maidens.

The San-mon Gate has made its mark in literary history. There is a famous *kabuki* drama with a scene from the life of Ishikawa Goemon, who hid out (which is to say, he lived) in the upper level of the gateway to hide from the authorities. As a thief, he had killed in the course of his first robbery, and so became an outlaw. When he was 37, according to one story, he tried, unsuccessfully, to steal a Sung dynasty celadon "Plover Incense Burner" from Fushimi Castle. (This incense burner of Hideyoshi's was claimed to have the power of attracting plovers when its incense was burned.) Pursued and apprehended in 1585, he and his young son Ichiro were condemned to be boiled in oil in an iron kettle in the bed of the Kamo River. Ishikawa held his young son above his head during this ordeal before finally collapsing into the boiling oil with the child.

The Hatto or Butsu-den (Lecture Hall or Buddha Hall), dates from 1918 since it replaces one that burned in 1895. It has a Shaka image accompanied by Fugen and Monju on a very high altar with *ihai* (memorial tablets) before the main image. The ceiling is decorated with a painting of a dragon by Imao Keinen. The Dai Hojo (Abbot's Large Quarters), beyond the Buddha Hall, is composed of two joined buildings, the Dai Hojo and the Sho Hojo. The larger unit, the Dai Hojo, serves as the entry to these quarters.

The Dai Hojo was originally the Seiryo-den of the Imperial Palace, built for the then reigning Emperor by Hideyoshi in the 1590s. When Ieyasu came to power as the Shogun, he was intent on erasing Hideyoshi's name from history, and thus he gave the Emperor a new palace in 1611 to replace the one commissioned by Hideyoshi. As a result, the Dai Hojo, as a former palace building, is constructed in the traditional palace manner with a hipped and gabled roof covered with cypress bark instead of the usual tiled roof of Buddhist temple buildings. It is divided into eight rooms.

The entry hall has the ticket booth on the left where the fee for visiting the Dai and Sho Hojo is paid; the room on the right has a view of a small waterfall in the garden. From the entry hall, a passageway at the rear leads north past a series of four small rooms on the right. The paintings on the *fusuma* (sliding panels) in these rooms are by the artists of the Kano school of painting and were once part of the Imperial Palace. The first room has a *sozu* in the garden beyond it, a bamboo pipe that collects water until it becomes top heavy and then dumps the water with a thud—originally used to scare animals away from the garden crops or flowers. The second room consists of the public toilets. The third room has plain *fusuma* but the fourth room has waves painted on the *fusuma* on the left (all these rooms have plain *shoji* for their exterior wall). The last room has a *chigaidana* (staggered shelves), a *tokonoma* and a writing desk bay, the right wall having a painting of a dragon.

At the end of the passageway, turn left to the Sho Hojo, which originally was part of Hideyoshi's Fushimi Castle south of Kyoto. The Sho Hojo (Abbot's Small Quarters) is the most noted of the two buildings because of its dry garden and painted *fusuma*. The outside corridor on the south side of the Sho Hojo opens on to four rooms noted for painted *fusuma* on a gold ground of Chinese figures or scenes of nature.

The first room facing the garden is the Willow Room. This is followed by the Musk Room, with paintings by Kano Motonobu

Nyoshintei, the austere dry landscape garden adjacent to the Sho Hojo at Nanzen-ji.

(1476–1559). The room behind it is the Naritaka-no-ma (Sounding Waterfall Room), a small six-mat room with a *tokonoma* and *chigaidana*. An ornate painting picturing a large waterfall with Chinese beauties in an idealized landscape is in the *tokonoma*. The Emperor Go-Yozei (early 1600s) once resided in this room when the room was still part of the Imperial Palace.

Next to these two rooms is the Midday Room, with Kano Eitoku's (1543–90) paintings of the Niju-shiko, the "Twenty-four Examples of Filial Piety." This central room on the south side of the building facing the garden has a small altar room behind it, a Heian period (795–1200) Kannon image being the object of reverence. The West Room is the last of the four rooms on this side.

The beams in the Sho Hojo were carved by the noted wood master Hidari Jingoro (1594–1634). The Zen *karesansui* (dry landscape) garden of the Sho Hojo is said to be the work of Kobori Enshu (1579–1647) and is among the more noted of Japanese Zen gardens. Here, sand, bushes, trees and a few rocks constitute the garden. There are many interpretations of its symbolism: does it represent a tiger and her cubs crossing a river or does it present the symbol of the crane and turtle, traditional garden concepts of longevity? A tea house by Kobori Enshu (1577–1645) in the garden has paintings within by Hasegawa Tohaku (1539–1610). This latter building is not open to the public.

On turning the corner from the south side of the Sho Hojo to the west side, the first room is the Crane Room, where the *fusuma* exhibit the artistry of Kano Eitoku (1543–90). The three rooms that follow, also transported from the Fushimi Castle, are famous for their paintings of tigers in a bamboo grove, the Tora-no-ma (Tiger Rooms). Altogether there are 39 murals illustrating tigers, painted by Kano Tanyu (1602–74) on *fusuma* that were first covered with gold leaf. The rooms on this side of the Sho Hojo look out on a separate dry garden. The covered corridor turns from a northern direction to the east and continues to the north. A dry garden is to the right, and a pond, two tea houses and then a newer building for use by the priests are on the left.

Retracing your steps along this corridor back to the northern side of the Sho Hojo, you pass a series of small rooms each having multipanel painted screens (*byobu*) on display. At the end of the corridor, a *kago* is suspended from the ceiling (a *kago* is a traveling palanquin for those of the upper classes, carried on the shoulders of porters). As you turn the corner of the corridor, a larger room has a *tokonoma* and *chigaidana* with *fusuma* bearing scenes of a waterfall and of people in Chinese garb. One last room has Chinese-style furniture on display.

4 NANZEN-JI SUBTEMPLES

Twelve subtemples are in the Nanzen-ji complex, only a few of which are open to the general public on a continuing basis. These include Nanzen-in, Chosho-in, Tenju-an and Konchi-in.

NANZEN-IN The Nanzen-in subtemple is located to the south of the Dai Hojo and the Hatto (Lecture Hall) and past the brick aqueduct coming from the Sosui Canal carrying water from Lake Biwa. (The Nanzen-in is open from 8:30 a.m. to 5:00 p.m. Entry fee.) As mentioned earlier, the Nanzen-in was the first structure of the Nanzen-ji Temple to be built on the site of Emperor Kameyama's retirement palace. Destroyed in the Onin War, the deeply religious mother of Shogun Tsunayoshi had this subtemple rebuilt in 1703 along its original lines.

The grounds of the Nanzen-in subtemple are entered through the western side of the precincts, and the path leads along one side of the Hondo (Main Hall) toward the front of the building and the garden and stream which lie before it. The Hondo consists of a large *tatami*-matted main room with a shrine in the rear. Within the temple grounds is a small memorial building within a walled area, a flaming jewel topping the Chinese-style roof. A portion of the Emperor Kameyama's remains have been interred here, as has a statue of the Emperor in priestly garb.

The landscape garden, originally the most noteworthy element of the Nanzen-in, was purportedly designed by Muso Kokushi (1271–1346). However, the garden has been altered so often, most recently in Edo times (1615–1868), that little of its original design remains, other than remnants of its large heart-shaped pond and stroll garden. It is, nonetheless, an attractive garden with moss and cedar and maple trees about it. Tiny islands exist in the pond, one in the design of the ideogram *shin* or "heart." A hill rises sharply behind the pond and garden, a waterfall on the hill feeding the pond. Above, on top of the hill just alongside the top of the brick aqueduct, is the temple *shoro* (bell tower).

CHOSHO-IN The Chosho-in is a small subtemple (also called the Marishi-ten) north of the main gateway at Nanzen-ji that has an image of Marishi-ten (Queen of Heaven in Chinese and Japanese Buddhism) brought from China by Priest Seisetsu. The garden is at its loveliest when azaleas are in bloom. The Okutan restaurant within the Choshu-in serves fresh tofu to the public at lunch time; some 300 years of serving vegetarian fare have perfected this culinary form. Guests can dine inside or on a deck overlooking the garden or on another built out over the pond.

TENJU-AN The Tenju-an subtemple is to the south of the San-mon and across the path that leads to the Dai Hojo. (It is only open in the spring and autumn from 9:00 a.m. to 5:00 p.m. Entry fee.) It was established in the mid to late 1300s in honor of Priest Fumon, the founder of the Nanzen-ji, by Priest Kokan-shiren, the 15th Chief Priest of the Nanzen-ji. Destroyed in the Onin War of 1467–77, along with the other buildings of the temple, it was not re-established for 130 years until Hoso-kawa Yusai rebuilt the Tenju-an's Main Gate, Hondo (Main Hall) and Shoin (Study) in 1602, all of which are still standing.

The roof of the Hondo is wood-shingled, and in its principal room is a life-sized wooden statue of Fumon, while in one corner are the memorial tablets of the Hosokawa family. The year the building was erected, Hasegawa Tohaku painted the 32 *fusuma* of the main hall in various themes: a nobleman riding a donkey; Daruma, the priest who began Zen Buddhism in China; landscapes with pines and cranes, etc. The temple holds a self-portrait of Fumon as well as portraits of Hosokawa Yusai and his wife.

The gardens of the temple were originally created at the time the Tenju-an was built. The front garden of the Hondo has a geometrically designed footpath in white sand and moss, while its main sector is a raked gravel and rock garden enriched with moss and trees. The southern garden near the Shoin has two ponds separated by a peninsula reaching from the Shoin and joined by another peninsula from the far side of the lake. A waterfall before the trees in the background provides a backdrop to the pond. The garden was re-modeled in 1605 by priest Kozan Kyose at the time of the reconstruction of the temple, and it was again remodeled in the late 19th century; the island with a bridge connecting it to the shore is a Meiji period addition. A cemetery in the temple grounds includes the graves of Hosokawa Yusai (1534–1610) and his family and other noted Meiji individuals.

KONCHI-IN The Konchi-in subtemple is located in the southwest of the Nanzen-ji complex. (It is open from 8:30 a.m. to 5:00 p.m. Entry fee.) Originally an independent temple in northwest Kyoto, Konchi-in was moved to its present site in the late 14th or early 15th century and became affiliated with Nanzen-ji. Damaged in the Onin War of the 1460s, it was restored in 1600 by Ishin

5 LAKE BIWA CANAL

Leave the Nanzen-ji complex by the road on the south side of the huge main gateway and continue west to the highway. Turn left to the Lake Biwa Canal and Sanjo-dori street. The Lake Biwa Canal or Biwako Sosui (*sosui* means "canal") and incline can be observed between the intersection of Niomon-dori/Shirakawa-dori and the Keage stop of the Keihan Keishin rail line (east of the Miyako Hotel) as the incline comes from the southeast where it emerges from a mountain tunnel.

From the early days of Kyoto, thought had been given to the creation of a water link between Lake Biwa (to the east of Kyoto and beyond the Higashiyama mountains) and the city. A plan had been drafted by Taira-no-Kiyomori in the 12th century, and Toyotomi Hideyoshi found it of interest in the late 1500s as well. Its consummation, however, had to await the use of modern technology after the Meiji Restoration in the late 19th century. Work began in 1885 and the project was completed by 1904.

A canal 7 miles (11.2 km) long with a drop of 11 feet (3.3 m) was created from Lake Biwa (in the Mii-dera railway station area) to the western side of the Higashiyama mountains in Kyoto. At the Keage area in Kyoto (the eastern end of Sanjo-dori at the mountains), a rail incline of 1,820 feet (546 m) was created between the canal and the level of the Kyoto plain. Boats that had crossed the canal could be loaded on to steel trucks and lowered on the rails for the 118 foot (35.4 m) drop between the canal and the city. The water power generated by the drop was used by a hydro-electric plant near the bottom of the incline (at the eastern end of Niomon-dori) to generate power to haul the boats as well as for general use in the city. This was the first hydroelectric plant in Japan in 1891, and it still operates on a limited basis—and is now a museum as well. It made possible the use of the first electric trams in Kyoto from 1901 until the late 1960s when trams (electric street cars) were discontinued.

For a number of years the canal was used to transport both people and goods between the cities of Otsu and Kyoto, some 200 boats using the canal and carrying 157,000 passengers a year by the end of its first five years in operation. Part of the water that was brought to Kyoto in the canal was sent over a brick viaduct through the Nanzen-ji Temple grounds and then through pipes across the eastern part of the city, under

Cherry blossoms line a path over the Lake Biwa Canal.

the Kamo River, and to the Horikawa River for use in irrigation. Obviously, the advent of rail and automotive transportation in time brought an end to the use of the canal for transportation purposes, but the water from Lake Biwa still serves the city.

The Miyako Hotel is on the nearby hill if refreshments are desired, or a visit can be made to the Kyoto International Center (see Tour 6). Otherwise, transportation can be taken back to the heart of the city. A surface rail line runs from the corner of Shirakawa-dori to the Sanjo-dori terminal at the Kamo River and Sanjo-dori. Buses to all parts of the city can be boarded at this terminal. The Tozai subway line Keage station can also be taken. It is just south of the Nanzen-ji Temple grounds at Shirokawa-dori and Sanjo-dori, with connections to the north–south subway line at Karasuma-dori.

Suden, and the Hojo (see below) was moved here from Fushimi Castle. At one time it had a Kara-mon (Chinese-style) gate from Fushimi as well, but in the latter part of the 19th century this was moved to the rebuilt Hokoku Shrine (see Tour 2) in honor of Hideyoshi, an action undertaken, no doubt, as a spiteful removal since the new Meiji government did not approve of the favor which the Tokugawa Shoguns had shown to the Nanzen-ji.

The Hojo (Lecture or Main Hall) is a medium sized *shoin* in the Momoyama style with a hipped and gabled cypress roof. It has six rooms in a U-shaped layout with *fusuma* decorated with paintings of the Kano school. The center room is the altar room, with a large black lacquered altar and shrine. To the right are two rooms, the inner being the Chrysanthemum Room and the room before it the Crane Room. To the left of the altar or center room are two other rooms, the rear one with an elevated section (*jodan*) with *chigaidana* (staggered shelves) and a *tokonoma* decorated with a painting of a pine tree.

In front of the Hojo is a dry garden that was created by Kobori Enshu (1577–1647). It was commissioned by Ishin Suden, the priest who acted as the Tokugawa government representative on aid to temples and who was responsible for the restoration of Konchi-in, which he used as his administrative headquarters, in the early 1600s. Enshu was given the commission to design new gardens for the temple, including the *karesansui* (dry garden) in front of the Hojo. The background of this garden has an embankment planted with bushes and trees. Two groupings of rocks, one vertically laid out (to the right) and one created on a horizontal plane (to the left) represent the traditional crane and tortoise motif. The garden in front of the plantings changes from large stones to fine gravel to moss, and a contorted tree adds interest to the overall layout. The west end of the garden is closed by a memorial building in honor of Suden.

East of the Hojo is a garden built about a lotus pond with a crane and tortoise island, a two-slab stone bridge and a small Shinto shrine across from the pond. A path around the pond leads to a large ceremonial gateway, lined with lanterns, which leads to a *torii* and then a walled enclosure entered through an inner Kara-mon gate. Within the walls is a memorial to Shogun Tokugawa Ieyasu, a small Toshogu shrine which Ishin Suden built in 1628 following the instructions in Ieyasu's

will. It is a strange combination of a black lacquered Buddhist building in front and a yellow and vermilion painted Shinto building to the rear, with plaque cutouts of birds and animals in color about the building. The interior of the front portion has a painted dragon on the ceiling and pictures of the Shoguns across the beam before the altar area. Eight *arhat* (Buddhist hermits) are on either side of the front room while the inner room has the main image of Ieyasu. Behind the Main Hall is a noted tea house with eight windows.

GETTING THERE

Zenrin-ji/Eikan-do is located south of the Nyakuoji Shrine on the Philosopher's Path (see Tour 7), and can be visited as an extension of that walk. It is also approximately due east of Okazaki Park (see Tour 6). To get there directly, take bus 5 to the Eikan-do-mae bus stop and walk east to the temple, which is open from 9:00 a.m. to 5:00 p.m. or from 8:30 a.m. to 4:00 p.m. during winter months. Entry fee. The temple treasures are on view from November 1–30 annually from 9:00 a.m. to 4:00 p.m.

The Nanzen-ji Temple complex is located at the foothills of the Higashiyama chain of mountains at the eastern end of the extension of Niomon-dori, the street which runs along the southern perimeter of the Okazaki cultural area. Take bus 39 or 103 to the Keage bus stop (or the Tozai subway line to the Keage station) and then walk 400 yards north and east to the temple, or take bus 5 to the Eikan-do-mae bus stop and then walk east to the road to the Eikan-do and then south to the Nanzen-ji. If coming from Zenrin-ji/Eikan-do or the Nomura Museum, simply continue to the south on the street which runs in front of these.

The Nanzen-ji Temple grounds are always open, while the hours of the various buildings are 8:00 a.m. to 5:00 p.m. from May through October and from 9:00 a.m. to 5:00 p.m. from November to April. An entry fee is charged to the San-mon gateway and to the Hojo as well as to the subtemples mentioned above.

To return, you can take the Keihan railway surface train at Shirakawa-dori and Sanjo-dori back to the Keihan terminus at Sanjo-dori and the Kamo River (for various buses to the center of Kyoto) or the Tozai subway from Keage station. Restaurants can be found along Sanjo-dori or in the Miyako Hotel.

Walking Tour 8

HONGAN-JI AREA

A Temple of Momoyama Magnificence, a Temple Divided and an Abbot's Garden

1. **Kyoto Station** 京都駅
2. **Nishi Hongan-ji Temple** 西本願寺
3. **Higashi Hongan-ji Temple** 東本願寺
4. **Shosei-en** 渉成園
5. **Mibu-dera Temple** 壬生寺

Not far from Kyoto Station are temples and a garden that can attest to the faith of the believers in one of the largest of the Buddhist sects in Japan while at the same time exhibiting the richness of the art of the period in which the original structures were created. The Nishi Hongan-ji Temple is the older of the two temples and the one worth concentrating upon, for it exemplifies the structure of the temples of this sect and is also the site of

The glass and steel Kyoto Central Railway Station.

some of the most magnificent, ostentatious Momoyama period (1568–1615) examples of architecture and interior design. Its special rooms may only be seen by appointment, and thus it is essential that reservations be made upon arrival in Kyoto to assure a possible visit to these extravagantly decorated chambers.

Higashi Hongan-ji is the second temple of this sect, not too many streets removed from its elder companion temple, but it shall be touched upon only briefly since it lost many of its treasures in a late 19th century fire. However, it still retains its lovely garden a few streets to the east, a garden that exemplifies an earlier type of Japanese landscape and which is thus frequently used by filming crews when creating *samurai* dramas for television and the movie screen.

1 KYOTO STATION

It is easiest to start this walk from Kyoto Station. The Kyoto Central Railway Station is the place where most visitors first arrive in the former capital of Japan, whether they come by train or bus. The station itself can be somewhat of a shock to the first-time visitor, since its 15-story glass and steel structure is not what one would expect in the traditional center of Japan. Its creation in 1998 was a bone of contention for those devoted to traditional Kyoto–for it is as out of place as is the Kyoto Tower "lighthouse" that rises across from the station. What the station does prove, nonetheless, is that Kyoto is both a city of traditions as well as a modern city of the 21st century. The plaza on the north side of the station has many bus lines, local and long distance, as well as an underground shopping center, while the Central Post Office is on the western side of the plaza.

At 198 feet (60 m) tall and one-third of a mile (0.5 km) long, Kyoto Station soars over

the city, housed as it is in its huge modern structure. It is a rail station which has every-thing—offices, a hotel, restaurants, shops, a department store—and its various levels are connected by escalators and elevators reaching all of its 15 floors while foot bridges allow connection between various portions of the station complex. Its train platforms permit local and long distance travel, including the express Shinkansen (Bullet Train) and Kintetsu rail lines on its south side, while one of the city subway lines can be boarded on the lower level. The plaza on the north side of the station has many bus lines, local and long distance, as well as the Central Post Office on its western side, and beneath it is a continua-tion of the shopping area of the station.

Directly ahead from the plaza on the north-ern side of Kyoto Station is Kyoto Tower, the tallest structure in Kyoto, a monstrous light-house like structure whose only virtue some

say is that it can permit (for a fee) a bird's-eye view of the city from its observation floor above the city. At the eastern side of the building is the Kyoto branch of the National Tourist Office on Karasuma-dori, where maps, information, travel advice and even some reservation information can be obtained without charge.

From the station plaza area, turn west onto Shichijo-dori (Seventh Street) and pro-ceed to its intersection with Horikawa-dori. Turn right (north) on to Horikawa-dori and go three blocks to the southern side of the Nishi Hongan-ji Temple grounds on the west-ern side of the street. The entrance to the temple is in the middle of the long Horikawa side of the complex.

② NISHI HONGAN-JI TEMPLE

The Nishi Hongan-ji Temple is the headquar-ters of the Jodo Shinshu sect of Buddhism, which is based on the teachings of priest Shinran Shonin (1173–1262). Shinran had come under the influence of Priest Honen, who had simplified Buddhist doctrine to the repetition of the Nembutsu as being sufficient to bring one to Amida's Paradise, and Shinran was to develop this doctrine further. While Honen's doctrines seemed radical to the monks of his day, the teachings of Shinran, Honen's disciple, became even more radical.

As Shinran's faith developed, he conceived that Amida's promise of salvation to all (the "Primal Vow" which is what Hongan means—Amida's pledge to save all beings from suffering through faith in him) was sufficient in and of itself, and that the various practices that had developed in Buddhism were not essential. Thus he discarded the idea of celibacy for the Buddhist priesthood and was induced by Honen to marry, taking as his wife the daughter of Fujiwara-no-Kanezane, a leading member of the Imperial court. He abandoned other precepts such as that calling for the abstinence from eating meat.

From Shinran's teachings, his followers developed a new sect, the Jodo Shinshu branch of Buddhism—the "True Pure Land Sect"—as opposed to the Jodo-shu (the Pure Land Sect) of Honen. Shinran died in his 90th year in 1262, and although his followers and those of Honen continued to increase, both sects underwent years of persecution until, in 1591, Toyotomi Hideyoshi granted Jodo Shinshu 80 acres (32 ha) of land in central Kyoto where it finally found a permanent home. Jodo Shinshu spoke to the concerns of the farmers and the poor, and thus it continued to increase its membership.

Jodo Shinshu flourished in the years of peace that came with its establishment in Kyoto, but the religious sect was considered a possible threat by Tokugawa Ieyasu when he came to power in the early 1600s. Thus, in 1603, Ieyasu split the sect into two branches, the newer unit being located to the east of the original; the Nishi (West) Hongan-ji and the Higashi (East) Hongan-ji came into being as a result. Fire destroyed the Nishi Hongan-ji in 1617, and the new complex that arose from the ashes between 1630 and 1657 was embellished with some of the finest rooms from the former Fushimi Castle and Jurakudai Palace of Hideyoshi, granted to the temple by the Tokugawa Shogun in a continued attempt to obliterate Hideyoshi's name and physical remembrances in Kyoto. Then, in 1639, the temple opened Ryukoku University in Kyoto for scholarly study.

With the end of the rule by the Tokugawa Shoguns and the beginning of the Meiji period in 1868, Nishi Hongan-ji suffered persecution such as was levied by the newly militant Shinto-oriented Imperial government against all forms of Buddhism. Some of its land was seized, leaving but 27 of the original 80 acres granted by Hideyoshi. The Monshu (Head of the sect) struggled against government control of religion, and this created a new impetus for the religious growth of the sect. In 1872, the Monshu sent students abroad to investigate how other religions were faring, and new ideas and practices were brought back to enrich the faith. In 1888 a journal was begun in English to reach beyond Japan's shores, and in 1897 missionaries were sent overseas, particularly to Hawaii and the United States and eventually to South America and elsewhere. As the headquarters of the Hongan-ji school of the Jodo Shinshu sect, Nishi Hongan-ji became one of the largest and most wealthy of Kyoto temples. Today, the sect has more than 20,000 priests, 12 million believers worldwide and 10,500 temples. Its monks may marry and wear lay clothing if they so desire. The chanting of their services has been enriched by its contact with Western music and practices (witness the small organs in the Amida-do and Daishi-do), and its most solemn festivals are marked by high color in religious vestments and ceremonials. European customs have affected the life of the church, and it now supports Sunday schools, kindergartens, women's organizations and Scout groups as well as up-to-date schools, universities and language institutes, the latter being aimed at overseas mission work.

So much for the background to the sect, information which helps in understanding the importance of the Jodo Shinshu branch of Buddhism. A visit to the Nishi Hongan-ji begins by viewing the non-working but ornamental Kara-mon (Chinese-style) gate on the south side of the grounds on Shichijo-dori, an ornamental gate that stands before the luxurious Momoyama Audience Chamber of the Shoin. It is the most noted gateway of the temple and, as its name implies, it was done in the Chinese (Kara) style, a phrase which in Momoyama times (1568–1603) meant a flamboyance of architecture and decoration. It is so embellished with decoration that it has been called the Higureshi-no-mon, the "Sunset Gate" or "Day-long Gate" on the premise that you could spend so much time in admiration of it that dusk would overtake you before you realized it. With its gabled, over-arching roof, its black lacquered and colorful enameled sections, its gilded metal work, its carvings of Chinese lions frolicking on the panels of the doors of the gate, and its figures of dragons, tigers, peacocks and humans against a background of clouds, pine trees, peonies and bamboo, it is a splendid work of art.

The open-work carvings on the sides of the gate reflect events in Chinese history: Hsu-yu, the legendary Chinese hero, who is here washing from his ears the obscene suggestion from the Emperor that he accept a governmental position. Opposite stands a herdsman protesting Hsu-yu's action—since Hsu-yu is thereby polluting the water from which the herdsman's cattle must drink. The gate with its cypress bark roof supported by six pillars originated in Hideyoshi's Fushimi Castle as the Chokushi-mon (Imperial Messenger's Gate) before it was moved to Nishi Hongan-ji Temple in 1632.

There are two gates on the Horikawa-dori side of the temple grounds, the entry side to

the complex: the Sei-mon (West Gate), one of the finer gateways of Kyoto temples (rebuilt in 1645), and the Hondo-mon (Main Hall Gate). The former has a wall behind the opening, no doubt going back to the ancient belief that this could help prevent the entry of evil forces into the compound. (Unsightly wire netting about the gate has been erected in an attempt to deter the nesting by birds and the subsequent fouling of the gates by the flocks about the temple grounds.)

The Daishi-do or Goei-do (Founder's Hall), built in 1632, is the southernmost of the two main temple buildings, on the left side as one faces the complex, considered the more honorable position. The Amida-do (Hondo) is to its right to the north. Constructed in 1636, the Daishi-do is 189 feet (567 m) long by 147 feet (441 m) deep by 90 feet (270 m) tall, and it has a 477-mat main space. The sanctuary area (Ge-jin) has two large rooms on either side with gilt pillars and walls decorated with lotus flowers and leaves. The front of the sanctuary is completely decorated in gilt with gilt trellis folding doors. The gilt *ramma* (transoms) above the doors are enriched with carved flowers, which also are gilded. To the right and left of the trellised doors are two *fusama* (sliding panels), the right one

The main entrance of Nishi Hongan-ji Temple has an undulated Chinese-style gable on the front.

decorated with a painting of pines covered with snow and the left with bamboo trees and a tree with birds. A small organ sits to the far right of the worshippers' area.

In the center of the inner sanctuary (*naijin*) is the altar, with its 2 foot (60 cm) seated image of Shinran (1174–1268), a wooden image said to have been carved by Shinran himself when he was 71. After his death, the image was varnished, a portion of Shinran's ashes being mingled with the varnish. (The remainder of his ashes were divided between the Higashi Otani and the Nishi Otani burial grounds, where they were placed in special tombs.) As a result, this image is held in great esteem by Jodo Shinshu members.

On either side of this main altar are portraits of the abbots who succeeded Shinran. Above the center part of the sanctuary are two characters in gold on a dark background which read "Ken Shin" (The Truth Realized), an honorary title granted Shinran by Emperor Meiji (an anomaly since the Emperor's government was then persecuting Buddhist establishments). *The ramma* (transoms) above the doorway of the sanctuary are delicately carved and covered with gilt. In the side rooms to the left and right are two large old *kakemono* (hanging scrolls) with invocations to Amida in large gold characters on a blue background.

The Amida-do (or Hondo, Main Hall) is a building from 1760 which replaced its 1591 predecessor that had been destroyed by fire. It is 138 feet (41.4 m) long by 126 (37.8 m) feet wide and stands 78 feet (23.4 m) high. The central shrine, with slender gilt pillars and a design of the chrysanthemum flower and leaf, contains the wooden image of Amida Nyorai by an artist of the Kasuga school. Memorial tablets to Emperors and scroll portraits of several illustrious priests of the temple hang to the right and left of the Amida image. In the room to the left of the altar is a portrait of Prince Shotoku (573–621), while in the room to the right is a portrait of Honen (1133–1212). Additional portraits of great priests of India, China and Japan hang here: Nagarjuna, Vasubandhu, T'an Luan (Donran), Tao Ch'o (Doshaku), Shan-tao (Zendo) and Genshin.

The entire interior of the Amida-do is elaborately decorated, in particular the sliding screens with a gold background, on which are painted a peacock and a peahen perched on a peach tree with white blossoms, the work of an artist of the Kano school. Over the gilt carvings of peonies in the *ramma* are carvings of *apsara* (angels or heavenly maidens) in full relief.

Between the Hondo (Amida-do) and Horikawa-dori, to the north, is the Kyodo, the sutra library. This double-roofed structure was built in 1678 and contains a complete set of the Buddhist scriptures.

The Shoro (Bell Tower) is in the southeast area of the temple grounds next to the Soro pond. This 1620 Shoro contains the bell that had formerly been at the Koryu-ji Temple in Kyoto, and it has an inscription upon it by Fujiwara-no-Michinori (died 1159). In the north corner of the grounds is the Drum Tower, housing a pair of very old drums that once belonged to the Saidai-ji Temple in Nara. A large gingko tree behind the Hondo-mon gate was once thought to have been a protection against fire, for tradition holds that, in case of fire, the tree would emit sprays of water to quench the flames.

While the amount of gilding makes the public worship rooms of the temple outstanding, these pale in comparison to the richness of the other semi-public buildings and rooms granted to the temple by the Tokugawa Shogun in 1632. Not only was the marvelous Momoyama period (1568–1603) Kara-mon gate given to the temple, but many of the exquisite rooms that once formed a portion of Toyotomi Hideyoshi's Jurakudai Palace and his castle/residence at Fushimi were moved to the temple as well. These elements make the Nishi Hongan-ji one of the richest temples in Japan in architectural and interior design, for these rooms were decorated by the finest artistic masters of their time. The rooms are particularly rich in the paintings of the Kano school, a family of painters descended from Kano Masonobu (1434–1530), who came to Kyoto and initiated a family of artists who flourished in the 16th and 17th centuries.

DAI SHOIN COMPLEX The rooms of the Dai Shoin (Great State or Abbot's Apartments) are enriched with the work of various Kano artists, among them Eitoku, Hidenobu, Koi, Ryokei, Ryotaku and Tanyu. The work of Maruyama Okyo and Maruyama Ozui also enhance the rooms. These paintings lack the element of mystery or symbolism of Zen paintings; instead, they hark back to traditional scenes of a decorative nature from Chinese paintings, whose designs and subjects were

The Taiko-ro (Drum Tower) at Nishi Hongan-ji houses a pair of ancient drums brought from Nara.

appealing to the military rulers of the day.

The Dai Shoin complex is shown at specific times of the day (see the hours of entry in the Getting There section). The complex includes a large entrance hall with three rooms which lead to the Taimenjo (Hideyoshi's Audience Hall) and its garden, several private rooms called the Shiro-shoin, two *Noh* stages and the separate Hiunkaku (Floating Cloud Pavilion).

Many of the interior paintings were created after the buildings had been reassembled at Nishi Hongan-ji. However, they all exemplify the spirit of the Momoyama era of the late 1500s when the buildings were first erected.

The *Noh* stage south of the Dai Shoin was a gift from the Shogun in 1674. It once stood in Sumpu Castle in Shizuoka. The *Noh* stage in the courtyard north of the Shiro Shoin is the oldest *Noh* stage in Japan (1587), and was brought from Fushimi Castle. It was created with great simplicity, as befits the *Noh* tradition, rather than in the ornate style of the Momoyama period (1568–1603) when it was built. The *Noh* drama could be watched from the corridor of the Shiro Shoin. A *Noh* play is presented on this stage on the 21st of May each year in memory of Shinran.

DAI SHOIN ROOMS AND GARDEN The Dai Shoin (Abbot's Rooms) is entered from the south through a large entrance hall with a cypress roof and traditional curved Chinese gate. (Since tours of these special rooms are given in Japanese, the following descriptions will be of help to non-Japanese visitors.)

The Nami-no-ma (Wave Room) room is so-named from the ceiling panels and *fusuma* (sliding screens) decorated with paintings of waves. To the north of the Wave Room is the Tora-no-ma, the Old Tiger Room. This room is named after a set of paintings of tigers by Kano Eitoku that have, unfortunately, lost their brilliance and are not as readily discernible as they once were. ("Old" is used to distinguish this from another room with tiger paintings elsewhere in the complex.)

Between the Tiger and the Wave Rooms is the Taiko-no-ma (Drum Room), named after the original and extant painted drums in the ceiling panels. There is a small *tokonoma* that is covered with gold paper of a later date (as are the walls). This room was used by Hideyoshi to examine the heads of his defeated enemies. (Some claim that the red in the ceiling was painted with blood!) The *ramma* (transom) between the two rooms is a carved fretwork depicting grapes and squirrels.

To the south is a long porch leading to the Taimenjo (Audience Hall). The porch has a creaking *uguisubari* (nightingale) floor that announces anyone who is approaching the hall, a precaution historically against unwanted intruders. The Taimenjo, which also is known as the O-shoin, Kon-no-ma or Stork Room, was Hideyoshi's Council Hall, and it is the finest and largest of all the rooms in the Dai Shoin. Today, it is used by the abbot of Nishi Hongan-ji, who preaches here twice a month. Originally from Fushimi Castle, it is floored with 203 *tatami* mats, and it is approximately 395 square yards (316 sq m) in size. Having 45 pillars, it is divided into three sections, each succeeding unit at a slightly higher level than the previous one. The pillars at the north (far) end of the room are closer together than those at the front, giving the illusion that the room is longer than it actually is. The ceiling is a coffered one with painted decorations.

The lower section of the Audience Hall is the larger portion of the room. The walls and *fusuma* are decorated with pine and plum trees and cranes while the ceiling has birds and flowers, all by Kano Ryokei. A window in the shape of a ceremonial fan opens into the upper section to the north. The middle section is separated from the lower section by a floor plank and has painted murals on its western and northern (rear) walls. The north wall has a painting by Kano Tanyu of "The Four Aged Sages on Mount Shang," wise men who were summoned by Emperor Hui of the Han for consultation. The *fusuma* on the west wall has a painting of "The Queen Mother of the West," both obviously from Chinese history. Huge red tassels on two of the panels of the north wall indicate that the area beyond these doors housed guards who were always on duty for the protection of Hideyoshi when the chamber was part of his mansion.

At the northeast part of the room is the small raised area in which Hideyoshi sat when holding audiences. The north wall has a scene of the interview by the Emperor Wu Ti with a female wizard who is presenting the Emperor with the peaches of immortality, the painting being a backdrop to a set of staggered shelves (*chigaidana*). At the east side of this area, the *ramma* (transom) has carved flying storks, rushes and clouds, attributed to the noted artist Hidari Jingoro. This eastern portion of the upper section has all the elements of a *shoin* (study): a raised floor, a

writing shelf with *shoji* window screens and *chigaidana*. The *fusuma* have paintings by Kano Tanyu of children at play.

A long corridor runs along the eastern side of the Audience Hall, and, when the *fusuma* of the hall are rolled aside, the garden can be viewed. Even the ceiling of this corridor is painted, with pictures by Kaiho Yusetsu of books and a wisteria blossom frieze.

The *karesansui* dry rock garden is called Kokei (Tiger Glen) and was designed by Asagiri Shimanosuke. This dry rock garden has a "lake" of white sand, which is supplied with its "water" from a stone "waterfall." The traditional crane and turtle islands are connected to the rest of the garden by a single arched stone that forms a bridge. The garden differs from most such in that it uses sago palms, which were brought to Japan by the Portuguese. In the winter they have to be wrapped with straw to protect them from a colder climate than their normal habitat.

West of the Audience Hall, behind the *fusuma*, are the Sparrow Room, the Wild Goose Room and the Chrysanthemum Room. The Suzume-no-ma (Sparrow Room) at the southwest corner of the Dai Shoin is a lovely small room with *fusuma* and wall panels painted by Maruyama Ozui, featuring sparrows, bamboo branches and chrysanthemums on a gold ground. Ozui was most skillful in the use of gold and silver powder in his paintings. He also decorated the coffered ceiling with flowers. The cedar doors were decorated by Kano Ryokei with monkeys and flower baskets of peonies, wisteria, cherry and other blossoms on a cart.

The Gan-no-ma (Wild Geese Room) is similar in size to and north of the Sparrow Room (18 mats), and is named for the somewhat damaged wild geese painted by Kano Ryokei on a gold background. The *ramma* (transom) between this and the adjoining room is also carved with wild geese. Ryokei's paintings on the ceiling are of a species of clematis.

The last of the three rooms in a row on the western side of the Dai Shoin, the Kiku-no-ma (Chrysanthemum Room), was used as a waiting room for guests. This room has yellow and white chrysanthemums, several types of fences and autumn grasses on a gold ground as painted by Kaiho Yusetsu (1598–1677) on the *fusuma*; he also painted fans on the coffered ceiling. There are fans on the veranda as well, painted by Yusetsu and Kano Koi (died 1630). The cedar doors illustrate a cat asleep under peonies on one side and a willow tree and herons on the other side, both painted by Kano Ryotaku.

The Shiro Shoin (White Study) received its name since the newly installed planed wood had a light, natural look to the cypress timbers—which eventually darkened to the present color.

To the north of the Audience Hall are Hideyoshi's Apartments of State, which he used with his Cabinet. They consist of three rooms divided by *fusuma* panels: the Shimei-no-ma or Jodan-no-ma, the Nio-no-ma and the San-no-ma. The Shimei-no-ma or Ichi-no-ma (Purple or First Room) was probably Hideyoshi's private chamber, and it has the typical elements of an elegant *shoin* (study): a floor with two levels, a 10-mat upper level (Jodan-no-ma) with a *tokonoma* and *chigaidana* shelf arrangement and a writing shelf with an arched *shoji* window. The room is decorated with murals by Kano Koi and Kano Tanyu from legendary Chinese Imperial history concerning the exemplary Emperors Yao and Shun. Metal fastenings chased with designs of lions and peonies cover the nail heads on posts, the ceiling is coffered and the *ramma* are carved with peonies and phoenixes.

The Ni-no-ma (Second Room) is similar to the first, although it does not have the raised platform and *tokonoma* and shelf of the latter. It, too, was painted by Kano Koi and Kano Tanyu, again with murals of legendary accounts from Chinese history illustrating a Ming text of Confucius' admonitions as to Imperial behavior. The paneled ceiling is of the type normally found in noble residences.

The decorations of the San-no-ma (Third Room or Peacock Chamber) (cherry trees, peonies and peacocks) are by Kaiho Yusetsu. The *ramma* in all three rooms are attributed to Hidari Jingoro, those between the second and third rooms being of peonies and long-tailed fowl. This 18-mat room becomes a *Noh* stage when the *tatami* are removed, and the other two rooms become the audience area.

The Shozoku-no-ma (Costume or Dressing Room) is a small room behind the Shiro Shoin complete with a *tokonoma*, *chigaidana* shelves and a bell-shaped window. The rear wall is decorated with a hunting scene by Kaiho Yusetsu, while a mural of the historic fight between Atsumori and Naozane in 1184 is on another wall of the room.

KURO SHOIN The abbot's private chambers, built in 1657 and located in the Kuro Shoin to the north of the Dai Shoin, are not open to the public. These are rooms in which the abbot can hold private meetings or be at ease. It is less formal than the Dai Shoin and has the usual features of *shoin* architecture: a *tokonoma*, a built-in desk with a bell-shaped window, shelves and *shoji*. These rooms are called Kuro Shoin (Black Study Rooms) because the pillars and ceiling were darkened with black lacquer. The alcove walls and *fusuma* have ink paintings by Kano Tanyu (1602–76) of Chinese figures. The Kuro Shoin also has a tea room complex of two rooms. The ink paintings of mountain scenery in these rooms are by Kano Tansaku, a grandson of Kano Tanyu.

HIUNKAKU PAVILION (FLOATING CLOUD PAVILION) Hideyoshi had built his Jura-kudai Palace (Palace of Pleasures) in the northern part of Kyoto as an extravagant showplace. Within it, in 1587, he created his "Pavilion of Floating Clouds," a three-story structure with a tea room (Okujaku-tei), a bath room (Kokakudai) and a chamber for resting. The pavilion was removed to Fushimi Castle when Hideyoshi decided to destroy the Jurakudai, and later it was probably moved about 1615 to Nishi Hongan-ji when Fushimi Castle was demolished by order of the Toku-gawa Shogun.

At Nishi Hongan-ji, the Hiunkaku Pavilion was placed in the southeast corner of the temple grounds, in the middle of the Soro Pond. At one time the only approach to this pleasure pavilion was by boat to its "boat-docking room," with a sliding trap door to the steps from the first floor. Today, the Ryu-hai-kyo (Devil's Back Bridge), the longest single-stone bridge in Japan, connects it to the rest of the precinct. This pavilion, along with Ginkaku-ji (Silver Pavilion) and Kinkaku-ji (Gold Pavilion), is known as one of the "Three Pavilions of Japan." It is 84 feet (25.6 m) across the facade and 41 feet (12.5 m) deep. The pavilion is decorated in a subdued style given Hideyoshi's taste for the extravagant and flamboyant. On the first floor is an entrance hall and three rooms. In the central room is a painting of the "Eight Views of Lake Hsiao-Hsiang" in China by Kano Tanyu and Zensetsu Tokuriki (1591–1680). In a second room with three levels is "Willow Trees Under Snow" by Kano Eitoku.

Hiunkaku Pavilion at Nishi Hongan-ji stands in the middle of the Soro Pond.

The second floor has the Kasen-no-ma (Hall of Famous Poets) with the painting of the "36 Famous Poets," while the ceiling has paintings of grape vines and squirrels, both by Kano Sanraku (1559–1635); this room also has an elevated section of eight mats. The second floor has a veranda with a low railing on all sides. On the third floor is a painting of Mount Fuji by Kano Motonobu. This picture is sketched on gold ground, and you can only obtain a full view of the scene by kneeling before it. Unfortunately, it is now very faded. An adjacent caricature drawing of a grove of trees is thought to have been a *jeu d'esprit* by Hideyoshi himself. The third floor once provided a fine view of the Higashiyama mountains, but modern construction now interferes with the former view.

Kokakudai, the bathroom of the pavilion, is connected to the pavilion by a covered corridor. It contains paintings by Kano Eitoku (1543–90) in the upper room. Stairs lead down to a steam bath and to baths for hot and cold water. Adjacent to the pavilion is the Okujaku-tei, a tea house with a 3 1/3-mat main room, a washing/storage room for utensils and a corridor.

In the garden is the Kocho-tei, a rest house, and the Sei-ren-sha, a tea house. A pool called Shogetsu-sha and a spring called "Waking from Sleep Spring" in an area of plum trees also enrich the grounds.

③ HIGASHI HONGAN-JI TEMPLE

To proceed to Higashi Hongan-ji Temple, return south on Horikawa-dori to Shichijo-dori at the southern edge of Nishi Hongan-ji. Turning left (north) at Karasuma-dori at the east side of the Kyoto Tower Building (past the National Tourist Office) brings you to the southern edge of the Higashi Hongan-ji Temple. The main entrance is in mid-block on Karasuma-dori.

Higashi Hongan-ji is the headquarters of the Otani branch of Jodo Shinshu. (The Daishi-do and Amida-do are open from 9:00 a.m. to 4:30 p.m. No entry fee is charged.) The two branches of Jodo Shinshu at Nishi Hongan-ji and Higashi Hongan-ji have the same history until the 1600s; thus the pre-1600 background to Higashi Hongan-ji can be found under the description of Nishi Hongan-ji.

The division of the sect into two parts was a political ploy by Tokugawa Ieyasu after he came to power at the beginning of the 1600s. He needed only to look at the attitude of the sect in the period after 1550 to feel that the monks offered a potential threat to the peace of the realm. In the time of Oda Nobunaga, the head of the then unified Hongan-ji Temple and his older son fortified themselves in Osaka and withstood a siege by Nobunaga's forces. Therefore, when Hideyoshi succeeded Nobunaga in 1582, he bypassed Kosa, the

HIGASHI HONGAN-JI AREA

On leaving Nishi Hongan-ji, a walk to the north to the far end of the walled grounds brings you across the street from the interesting Costume Museum, which is located in an office building. The museum is on the fifth floor of the Izutsu Office Building at the corner of Horikawa-dori and Shin-hanaya-dori, across the street from the northeastern corner of the Nishi Hongan-ji Temple. (It is open from 9:00 a.m. to 5:00 p.m. except on Sundays and during changes of exhibitions. An entry fee is charged. The museum is about a 10 minute walk from Kyoto Station. Take bus 7, 28, or 78 to the bus stop at the north end of the Nishi Hongan-ji.)

The Costume Museum shows examples of Japanese costumes from the earliest of times to the present. Beautiful examples are handsomely mounted on appropriate mannequins in modern display cases. These costume exhibitions are changed two or three times a year. An English language pamphlet is available, and costumes are labeled in English as well as in Japanese. A souvenir/postcard counter is provided.

Across from the Nishi Hongan-ji lies Monzen-machi, the "District Outside the Temple Gates." A large gateway at the Horikawa-dori entry to a street that runs between the Nishi and Higashi Hongan-ji Temples marks the beginning of the district. Particularly at its western end, along and just off Horikawa-dori, are shops selling all those items connected with Buddhism, ranging from small rosaries to the large Butsudan chests for family altars within the home. Incense, candles, altar cloths and small gongs are among the numerous items that can be purchased. For centuries the area has been host to pilgrims to the temples as well as visitors to the city, and small *ryokan* (inns) can be found throughout the district.

head of the temple, and his older son by appointing another of Kosa's sons as abbot, and granted the sect land in Kyoto (the present Nishi Hongan-ji) for their headquarters.

Shogun Tokugawa Ieyasu, who succeeded Hideyoshi, used the device of "divide and conquer" when it came to Jodo Shinshu. He had a second temple built on a 30 acre (12 ha) site in central Kyoto for the son Hideyoshi had bypassed, thereby assuring a lack of unified action on the part of the sect. Thus the original temple became the Nishi (West) Hongan-ji while the new one became the Higashi (East) Hongan-ji.

Fires have plagued the Higashi Hongan-ji on four occasions, and the last, decisive fire in 1864 (caused by an attempt by Imperial adherents to overthrow the Tokugawa Shogun) wiped out all of the temple buildings. The disaster was brought on by the Daimyo of Choshu in his attempt to seize the Emperor in the struggle between the rising Imperial forces and the last Tokugawa Shogun. The temple buildings were rebuilt between 1879 and 1911; they were restored in 1984. Only the major buildings are open to the public—the Daishi-do (Founder's Hall) and the Hondo (or Amida-do). The remainder of the buildings are not open since their treasures were lost in the last fire. (It is possible to visit these other structures by request a day in advance through the Japan Travel Bureau, one's hotel or by application at the temple office.)

The rebuilding of the temple occurred at a less than propitious time since, after the restoration of Imperial power in 1868, Buddhism was severely slighted by the new Meiji government with its Shinto leanings. The fact that the temple was rebuilt through public appeals by the abbot indicates that Buddhist beliefs and practices could not easily be eradicated by a militant Shinto government. Not only did gifts of money flow in, but women cut their long hair and sent it to the temple as an offering to be made into ropes to pull the beams of the buildings into place during construction. Fifty-two such giant hawsers, the longest of which is 36 feet (10 m) long and 1.3 feet (30 cm) in circumference, weighing 2,334 pounds (1,050 kg), were created from these donations, and they are still on display in the corridor between the Daishi-do and the Amida-do.

The temple grounds are entered through a gate that is known by two names: the Hondo-mon (Main Hall Gate) or Amida-do-mon (Amida Hall Gate), a gateway which originally belonged to Hideyoshi's Fushimi Castle but was given to the temple by Shogun Ieyasu. The original gate was lost in the 1864 fire, and this identical replacement was built in 1909.

The Hondo (Main Hall) is an Amida-do, a hall of the Buddha Amida, the primary deity of the Jodo Shinshu sect. It is located in the southern part of the temple grounds. In front of the Hondo to the southeast is the Shoro, the temple belfry, the original having come from Hideyoshi's castle at Fushimi. Lost to fire, a duplicate was constructed in 1893. A gigantic bronze water vase in the shape of a lotus flower stands before the hall in a circular pond. The water flowing from it comes by means of a pipe from Lake Biwa, the same water being available in various places as fire protection for the temple. Two very large pairs of excellent bronze lanterns stand before the Hondo and the Daishi-do.

The Hondo/Amida-do is a 401-mat structure supported by 70 columns. It is 170 feet by 150 feet (50.9 by 45 m) and 90 feet (27 m) high, and is divided into two parts, the sanctuary and the place of worship. The sanctuary has three sections, the *nai-jin* or central sanctuary and the two *yoma* or side sanctuaries. The central portion holds the Shumidan, the altar which symbolizes Mount Sumeru, the central mountain in the Buddhist universe, with the image of Amida Nyorai by Anami Keikei (13th century) in a shrine. Behind, on the right, is an image of Prince Shotoku, while on the left is one of Priest Honen, founder of the original Jodo sect. An Imperial tablet by the Emperor Kameyama is hung to the right of the shrine. In the left sanctuary are

The outer wall of Higashi Hongan-ji Temple.

images of the Six Patriarchs of the Shin sect: Nagarjuna, Vasubandhu, T'an Luan (Donran), Taih'o (Doshaku), Shan-tao (Zendo) and Genshin. Golden-trellised folding doors separate the sanctuary from the worship area. This latter section has a *tatami*-matted floor for worshippers, and large gilt lamps are suspended from the ceiling. The Hondo and Daishi-do (Founder's Hall) are connected by a passageway in which, under glass, are displayed the ropes made from human hair that were employed in constructing the building.

The gateway at the street in front of the Daishi-do or Goei-do (Founder's Hall) is a two-story double-roofed structure. The plaque on the gate reads "Shin Shu Hon Byho" (Shin Sect Main Temple) in the handwriting of Prince Fushimi. The second floor holds images of Shaka with Maitreya and Amamda, carved by Rennyo Shonin. The ceiling has paintings by Seiho Takeuchi of celestial beings in flight. The gate, which was begun in 1907 and completed by 1911, is 100 feet (30 m) wide, 88 feet (26 m) long and 90 feet (27 m) tall. An interior stairway leads to the second floor (generally not open to the public).

The double-roofed 927-mat Daishi-do (Founder's Hall) is the largest wooden building in Kyoto and the second largest such building in Japan. It is 190 feet (57 m) long by 240 feet (72 m) wide and stands 125 feet (38 m) tall, and the structure is supported by 90 columns. It is connected with the Hondo by a covered bridge. The sanctuary is subdivided in the same manner as the Hondo, and the interior is lavishly decorated in gilt and metal work with gilt trellis doors between the sanctuary and the worshippers' area. Gilt chandeliers hang in the public area.

An image of Shinran, founder of Jodo Shinshu, and reputedly carved by him, is in the shrine in the center of the altar which, as in the Hondo, is mounted on a symbolic Mount Sumeru. The statue was given to Priest Jonenbo by Shinran as a parting gesture when Shinran left Shimosa province during the course of his exile. An image of the 22nd patriarch, Rennyo Shonin, is behind the altar, and on the left are images of successive patriarchs of the sect. Buddha's name appears on tablets on either side, and in the upper front of the central sanctuary is a tablet with the characters for "Ken Shin" (Truth Realized), the posthumous name given to Shinran by the Emperor Meiji. The calligraphy is in the Emperor's hand. The *ramma* above the gilt folding doors at the front of the sanctuary are carved with angels playing musical instruments. The worshippers' area is *tatami*-matted, and large golden lighting fixtures hang from the ceiling.

The Chrysanthemum Gate or Chokushi-mon (Imperial Messenger's Gate), slightly to the north of the Daishi-do at the street, derives its name from the two 16-petal Imperial chrysanthemum crests, one on each of its doors. The original gate came from Fushimi Castle, but it, too, was lost in the 1864 fire. In 1913 the new gate was dedicated, having been rebuilt in the style of the Momoyama period (1568–1603). The O-Shinden, to the north, is a ceremonial hall, but it and the other temple buildings are not generally open to the public except by prior request.

④ SHOSEI-EN

The abbots of Higashi Hongan-ji enjoyed a villa set within its own park grounds, a residence just a few streets from the temple. Although the major buildings of the villa have disappeared, the garden remains a delightful park. Shosei-en is located two streets east of Higashi Hongan-ji, one street north of Shichijo-dori and one street south of Rokujo-dori. It is bounded on its eastern side by Kawaramachi-dori. (It is between the two east–west streets Kamizuzuyamachi-dori and Shimsusuyamamachi-dori. The garden is open from 9:00 a.m. to 4:00 p.m. Entry fee.)

A former villa of the abbots of the Higashi Hongan-ji, the alternate name of Shosei-en–Kikoku-tei—comes from the Kikoku (quince) hedge that once surrounded it. Originally the site of a villa of Minamoto-no-Toru (822–95), Minister of the Left and a son of the Emperor Saga, in 1631 the grounds were given by Shogun Tokugawa Iemitsu to the 13th abbot, Sennyo, of Higashi Hongan-ji, and a portion of Hideyoshi's Fushimi Castle buildings were brought here. Completed in 1657, it had various buildings arrayed around the Ingetsu-ike, a pond originally supplied with salt water (from Osaka) monthly and where salt was made so as to imitate life on the seashore. These buildings were destroyed by fire in 1864 in a civil disturbance in an attempt to overthrow the Tokugawa Shogunate, the same fire which destroyed Higashi Hongan-ji.

The garden was, in part, designed by the noted poet and landscape designer Ishikawa Jozan (1583–1672) and in part by Kobori Enshu (1579–1647). It was renowned for its "Thirteen Beautiful Landscapes" which were featured in numerous *tanka* poems; unfortunately, many of these landscapes were destroyed in the same fire that demolished the villa. In the center of the garden is the pond Ingetsu-ike, with islands covered with large trees. To-no-shima (Tower Island), a small islet, has a nine-layer lantern that is believed to mark the tomb of Minamoto Toru, and to its east a smaller isle of stones.

The main island is approached from the west over an arched wooden bridge or by means of an arched stone bridge from the east; a covered bridge leads from the island to the north. On a hill on the island among trees is the Shukuen-tei, a two-mat tea house with ancillary small rooms, one of which holds a stove for the making of tea. The covered bridge that leads from the tea house island to the north has a moon viewing platform at its center.

The Sochinkyo, a small 2 1/2-mat tea room with an entry area, is at the edge of the pond to the southwest. On the east of the garden is a trellised wisteria vine, which was a gift of Emperor Go-Mizuno-o (reigned 1611–29). The Bokaku gate, a two-story gate with side stairways, leads to a family shrine with screens painted by Munakata Shiko (1905–77). To the north of the gateway is a grove of cherry trees and then two buildings connected with a bridge. To the east of these structures is an L-shaped building with a pond before it, and further to the east is the Tairetsuseki, a one-story building. Various other buildings lie beyond the Bokaku gate, the main villa buildings being behind a wall. The garden is a favorite place for use by the film industry in its creation of *samurai* dramas, since the grounds exhibit a "rural" setting such as often needed for the medieval soap operas favored by audiences in Japan.

On leaving the garden, a return to the plaza before the Kyoto Station offers various bus lines, the subway and taxis for transportation within or beyond the city. There, various bus lines can take one to the Mibu-dera Temple, which lies to the north and west of the gardens which have just been left.

⑤ MIBU-DERA TEMPLE

Mibu-dera is not a major temple, but it is noteworthy for its performances of *Kyogen*, light-hearted dramas which began in the 1300s. (The temple is located just below Shijo-dori (Fourth Street) to the east of

Senbon-dori and the San-in main line railway tracks. It can be reached by City buses 3, 11, 26, 27, 28 or 203 to the Shijo-Bujo bus stop, but a taxi would be the easiest way to get to the temple.)

One curiosity about Mibu-dera is that hundreds of small Jizo images line one of the paths of the temple grounds. These images once stood at street corners to offer protection to passerbys as they crossed streets in the city. When the streets were widened in modern times and the automobile age began, the Jizo images were removed to the Mibu-dera grounds–probably to offer them the needed protection from the motoring age.

Kyogen (comic dances in pantomime) are the main reason a visitor would come to the temple. These began when Priest Enkaku, in the early 1300s, had a vision in which Prince Shotoku, the early proponent of Buddhism in Japan, urged the priest to bring Buddhist doctrines to the mass of the people .These "plays" (for they are more like skits than serious plays) are performed at the stage of the Dai Nembutsu-do hall at the north end

Actors dressed as samurai relax between shots at Shosei-en, a favorite locale for historical dramas.

of the temple grounds next to the temple school. The north side of the school has a roof over a portion of its first floor, and seats for viewing the performances on the stage are in this roofed area.

The "plays" are meant to be didactic in nature since they emphasize the rewards for good actions and the punishments for evil acts. The action is accompanied by flutes, drums and gongs while the costumes of the amateur actors are gifts given as memorials by worshippers. Masks are worn, and some have become so valuable that they are now considered museum pieces and are no longer worn during the plays. The plays have some 25 to 30 characters, and there are more than 30 such plays. One of the more popular ones is one in which two men in the market place fight and end by hurling clay plates from the stage. Some four to five plays are presented each day during the February 3–4 and April 21–29 festivals, from 1:00 p.m. to 5:00 p.m. On the last day of each festival, the action goes on until 10:00 p.m.–and there is no charge to the audience. English plot summaries are available, but the slapstick nature of the action virtually speaks for itself.

One other festive occasion is worth attending, and it occurs on the second Sunday and Monday and the third Sunday of August. This is the Rokusai Nembutsu Odori, folk dances in attractive costumes to the accompaniment of gongs. As with *Kyogen*, the dances are meant to teach Buddhist doctrines. Ancient dances as well as some more recent comic pantomimes are included in the repertoire and there is no charge for the 8:00 p.m. performance.

TRADITIONAL CRAFT CENTERS As the capital of Japan from 784 to 1868, Kyoto attracted leading crafts people from all over the country to service the needs of the Imperial court as well as cultured *samurai*, wealthy merchants and the main schools of tea. It was thus a city of small workshops filled with artisans vying with each other to fulfill the needs of a demanding clientele.

There are two "cultural centers" in Kyoto devoted to explanations and demonstrations of the famous *yuzen* dyeing technique for fabrics, a method that was first perfected in Kyoto in the 17th century by the Kyoto painter Miyazaki Yuzen. See below for an explanation of *yuzen* dyeing. In addition, an embroidery museum is nearby.

An artist hand paints fan-shaped patterns on to a silk kimono using the yuzen dye method.

KYOTO YUZEN CULTURAL HALL (KYOTO YUZEN BUNKA KAIKAN)

The Yuzen Cultural Hall is a five-minute walk from the Nishi Kyogoku station of the Hankyu Railway. The hall is four streets east of the station (on the north side of the street) on Gojo-dori (Fifth Street). Bus 13 from the Kyoto Central Station or bus 32 from Shijo-Kawaramachi to the Nakanishi-Gojo bus stop will bring you close to the hall. (The hall is open from 9:00 a.m. to 4:00 p.m. daily except Monday; closed from December 29 to January 4. Entry fee.)

About the year 1700, Miyazaki Yuzen (who lived in the Gion district and to whom a statue has been erected at Chion-in) invented a method by which hand painting on silk (Tegaki Yuzen) could be employed to produce beautiful patterns on *kimono* material. The resulting fabrics were expensive and could only be afforded by the well-to-do. In 1876, with the introduction of chemical dyes and the invention of stencil dyeing (Katagami Yuzen) by Hirose Jisuke, the mass production of *yuzen-zome* became possible. At the Yuzen Cultural Hall, both traditional hand painting and stencil dyeing are demonstrated.

The first floor of the hall consists of displays, including a film of the process (in English), while the techniques of *yuzen* dyeing are demonstrated on the second and third floors. In the stencil technique, dyes are applied through the stencils, beginning with the lightest colors. Up to 20 stencils can be employed for a design. (The design on the stencil is made by perforating the paper with a needle) In the more traditional technique, the dyes are applied by hand with a brush. This is a more time-consuming and delicate technique, and thus the traditionally dyed fabrics are the most expensive. (A sales counter offers examples of *yuzen* dyed materials as well as printed information on the technique and its products.)

YUSEN MUSEUM (KODAI YUSEN-EN)

The Kodai Yuzen-en is one long street south of Shijo-dori on Takatsuji-dori, just east of Omiya-dori. It can be reached by means of the Hankyu underground rail line to the Omiya station or by bus 6, 206 or 207 to the Matsubara bus stop. (The building is open from 9:00 a.m. to 5:00 p.m daily. It is occasionally closed for seasonal *kimono* exhibitions. Closed from December 19 to January 5. Entry fee. Additional charge for green tea.)

EMBROIDERY MUSEUM (NIPPON SHISHU YAKATA)

At the Katsura River and Nishi-Gojo-dori (West Fifth Street) is a museum devoted to embroidery. Since it is off the normal bus routes, it is advisable to take a taxi to the location. (Open from 9:00 a.m. to 5:30 p.m. Entry fee.) Traditional embroidery is exhibited and its creation by hand and by machine is demonstrated. Special exhibitions of embroidered work are held periodically. A sale area is on site.

> ## GETTING THERE
>
> You can walk to Nishi Hongan-ji from Kyoto Station in about 10 minutes. Alternatively, bus 7, 28 or 78 can be taken from the plaza in front of Kyoto Station to the Nishi Hongan-ji-mae bus stop on Horikawa-dori in front of the temple. The temple buildings are open from 9:00 a.m. to 4:30 p.m. without charge. Tours of the magnificent Dai Shoin buildings occur at 10:00, 11:00, 1:30 and 2:30 on weekdays and at 10:00 and 11:00 on Saturdays from the temple office in the southwest quarter of the main compound. Requests for tours should generally be made at this office a week in advance of the date of the proposed visit. The tours are conducted in Japanese. There is no fee for these tours.

Walking Tour 9

NIJO CASTLE AREA
The Immovable Kannon and a Luxurious Castle

1 **Rokkaku-do Temple** 六角堂
2 **Nijo Jinya** 二条陣屋
3 **Shinsen-en Garden** 神泉苑
4 **Nijo Castle** 二条城

I In the heart of modern Kyoto is an ancient temple, naturally attributed to Prince Shotoku as is any very old temple. Rokkaku-do does date back at least to the 1200s, if not earlier, but it is the lovely pond and swans in the midst of tall buildings and its association with the Ikenobo Flower Arranging School that makes it of particular interest. The flower school developed from the temple, and today

the Ikenobo both literally and physically overshadows the temple from which it sprang. The Ikenobo Building is a modern skyscraper on Karasuma-dori. Its builders most sensitively created an open plaza and pool at ground level at its rear to complement the Rokkaku-do temple—and to return to it the pond which legend claims as the reason for its origin.

To the north of Rokkaku-do is the Museum of Kyoto, one of those delightful examples of early Japanese "modern" buildings in the Western architectural mode which were created at the end of the 19th century. Once the home of the Bank of Japan, it now houses an institute whose display rooms illustrate the

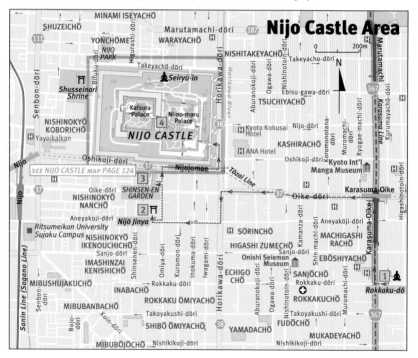

The Rokkaku-do Temple lies hidden away, enjoying a secluded setting amidst towering neighbors.

early history of Kyoto. Two other places in this part of Kyoto bring to mind the tales of medieval *samurai* and *ninja*. One is Nijo Jinya, a private home on the outside but a fortress within of secret passageways and disappearing staircases that would delight any aficionado of *samurai* derring-do.

The other is the impressive Nijo Castle of the Tokugawa Shoguns, more a fortified palace than a castle as such. The splendor and richness of the rooms of this World Heritage Site remain a showpiece almost 400 years after they were first conceived and constructed, and it is a sight that few visitors would want to miss.

1 ROKKAKU-DO TEMPLE

This tour begins with the Rokkaku-do Temple, which is situated east of Karasuma-dori on Rokkaku-dori, midway between Shijo-dori (Fourth Street) and Oike-dori. It is set back behind a tall modern building (the Ikenobo Headquarters) which is built in part on stilts so as to provide a plaza for the temple. (The Shijo station of the city subway or the Hankyu Electric Railway (here an underground line) are just south of Rokkaku-dori and the temple. Buses 5, 28, 59, 203, 205 and 207 stop at Karasuma-Shijo-dori. The temple is open from 9:00 a.m. to 5:00 p.m. No entry fee is charged.)

ROKKAKU-DO (CHOBO-JI) Chobo-ji is more often known by its alternative name of Rokkaku-do (Hexagonal Hall) because of its shape. It is claimed that the temple was founded by Prince Shotoku in 587, a somewhat unlikely date since the Prince would then have been but 15 years of age. In the prince's time, there was a pond where the temple now stands (the modern Ikenobo office building to the north and west of the temple has tried to re-create this pond in a contemporary manner). According to legend, the prince bathed in the pond when this was open countryside, first placing on the ground at the edge of the water the 2 inch (5 cm) tall gold Nyorin Kannon image he carried with him as a talisman. When he tried to pick up the Kannon on coming out of the water, it had become far too heavy to lift. That night Kannon appeared to the prince in a dream and informed he wished to remain at the pond. Thus, it is said, the prince built the temple to Kannon at this spot.

Another report states that when the Emperor Kammu laid out the plan for his new capital of Heian-kyo (Kyoto) in 794, almost 200 years later, the Rokkaku-do stood in the way of one of the projected main streets of the new city. The Emperor sent a messenger to explain the problem to the Kannon image in the temple. In response, a cloud enveloped the temple and moved it just far enough so as not to interfere with the new city street plan. The Heso-ishi (Belly Button Stone) on the temple grounds has often been referred to as the "navel" of Kyoto, since it is popularly supposed to be a base point used in the planning of the city layout and thus ostensibly marks the center of the city.

It was to this temple that Priest Shinran, the eventual founder of the Shin Jodo sect of Buddhism, is said to have made a retreat for 100 days as he sought a greater satisfaction within Buddhism than could be offered by the Tendai Buddhist teachings that he had grown up with and lived under at the Enryaku-ji monastery on Mount Hiei. At dawn on the 95th day of his retreat, Prince Shotoku (who was believed to be a reincarnation of Kannon) appeared to Shinran in a dream, suggesting that he consult with Priest Honen, the founder of the Jodo (Amida) Buddhist sect. This Shinran did, becoming one of Honen's disciples. (In time, Shinran instituted the new teachings that became the basis for the Jodo Shinshu sect; see the discussion under Nishi Hongan-ji.)

In the 15th century, the 12th abbot of the Rokkaku-do, Sankei Ikenobo, created a flower arrangement method (*ikebana*) in the Ike-no-bo (Priests' Lodging Beside the Pond) when preparing flowers to be placed before the temple's image of Kannon. The school of flower arranging that developed from his floral art was continued by a family who lived in a building behind the temple, and today the school continues to flourish in its headquarters in the tall modern building adjacent to the temple on the northwest.

The Rokkaku-do Temple lies hidden away behind the modern Ikenobo building on Karasuma-dori. Its entry is to the east of Karasuma-dori on Rokkaku-dori. Although overshadowed by its towering neighbor, the temple enjoys a delightful setting even in this crowded commercial center of Kyoto—through the courtesy and generosity of the Ikenobo building alongside it. Mindful of the ancient legend of the pond here in which Prince Shotoku bathed and at whose side he built the temple, the Ikenobo building has created a covered plaza (screened off from busy Karasuma-dori) in lieu of what might have been part of the building's ground floor. Here a pond has been recreated, partly within the Rokkaku-do precincts and partly under the open first floor of the Ikenobo structure.

Huge carp swim serenely around Rokkaku-do's contemporary pond.

The pond is filled with large *koi* (carp) of various colors—as well as being the home to a white swan and a black swan. Thus the pond provides a most pleasant setting for the temple.

The Rokkaku-do Temple building was rebuilt in 1876, and its Hondo (Main Hall) is hexagonal in shape. Above the Hondo proper is a second pyramidal roof topped with a large, gilt-bronze "jewel" of a memorial nature. This second roof not only covers the main temple building but offers a covered area in front of the temple as well. In front of this double-roofed structure, once you have passed the entry gate on Rokkaku-dori, are two large stone lanterns on either side of the path to the Hondo. To the left of the path is a life-sized bronze figure of Priest Shinran, a rosary in his left hand and his pilgrim's staff in his right hand as he makes his pilgrimage to the Rokkaku-do in search of religious understanding. To the right of the path is a roofed water basin for purification before entering the temple, the water issuing from the mouth of a bronze dragon.

The second roof over the temple provides a "porch" before the hexagonal Hondo, and hanging from this roof is a huge red paper lantern. Beneath and before the lantern is a large Chinese-style bronze incense pot on six legs, a holder for the incense sticks that worshippers light and place in the sand within the pot before praying. There is also a Chinese-style table under this front roofed area of the temple.

The front wall of the enclosed Hondo is open above a 3- foot (1 m) high wall that separates the worshipper from the inner sanctuary. The interior of this small Hondo is resplendent with gilt-covered pillars and a gilt rear wall. Two long pendant gilt units cascade from the interior ceiling. The altar table and adjacent religious furniture before the image area are in black lacquer with gold highlighting, and they stand out in contrast to the gilt of the area behind them. On either side of the interior stand triangular-shaped votive candle holders. Beyond the altar table, on the left, is an image of the two-year-old Prince Shotoku at his first prayers, and in the center of the rear portion of the Hondo is the main image of the temple, that of Kannon. A dark figure with multiple arms, the Kannon stands out against its gilt surroundings. It is obviously not the same Kannon of the Shotoku legend.

On the western side of the temple grounds, a covered shrine against the precinct wall holds the large Heso-ishi stone with water flowing over it and with a small Fudo image before it. On either side of the stone hang many colored *origami* paper cranes. To the north of this shrine are numerous images of the Buddha and other Buddhist beings sculpted on flat stones two feet tall, all set within the framework of a very small garden. Next comes a small structure with a Buddha image accompanied by guardian deities.

Beyond this is the modern Ikenobo building and the attractive contemporary pond. The pond, a reminder of the pool in which Prince Shotoku bathed, lies to the northwest and is partially behind the Hondo. A section of the pond flows under the open plaza of the first floor of the Ikenobo structure, huge carp and two swans enlivening the otherwise still waters. Directly behind the Hondo is a life-sized image of Kannon and then a small garden that lies in front of a one-story temple building with its white *shoji* panels.

In the northeast portion of the precinct is a memorial *sorinto* (the "umbrella" spire atop a pagoda). To the right of this and against the eastern wall of the temple grounds is a small memorial building with a flaming jewel on its rooftop, a symbol that it is a memorial to a Buddhist saint, in this case to Prince Shotoku. The main image within is of the 16-year-old Prince praying for his dying father, the Emperor Yomei, and above and behind the image is a figure of the two-year-old Shotoku, his hands clasped in his first prayer. Between the two images is a round mirror such as is usually seen in Shinto shrines. At the right rear is an image of the prince on horseback at the time of the late 6th century battle of Shigisan against the court officials who opposed Buddhism.

To the south of this memorial building is a seated, modern, many-armed Kannon with the traditional image of Amida on his crown. Two rows of attractive metal screens form an arc behind this Kannon, the modern screen being composed of the traditional 1,000 images of the Buddha. Further south is a vermilion-fenced area with two small Shinto shrines. The southernmost of these two shrines is composed of three units, each with a sacred mirror within, and over these three is a gabled roof in the Kara (Chinese) style. The intricate carving on the roof beams includes a figure of a man carrying rice sheaves as well as carved animals and birds. All of these small Shinto shrines have thatched roofs and are covered by an additional protective roof.

IKENOBO SOCIETY AND SCHOOL OF FLOWER ARRANGING The adjacent school of flower arrangement headquarters is on Karasuma-dori, just north of Rokkaku-dori, in a tall attractive modern building just around the corner from Rokkaku-do. The school teaches both classical and modern forms of flower arrangement, and has branches in other countries as well as in Japan. English is spoken at the school for those wishing to learn more about the Ikenobo Society. An exhibition is held at the Society's headquarters each November.

MUSEUM OF KYOTO Not far from the Ikenobo Society building is the Museum of Kyoto, formerly the Heian Museum, a classic brick Meiji period building. It houses a permanent exhibition devoted to the early years of Kyoto's existence and is worth a visit. (The museum is on Takakura-dori, two streets east of Karasuma-dori and just south of Oike-dori. It is thus one street north of the Ikenobo building and then two streets to the east. It is open from 10:00 a.m. to 6:00 p.m. but is closed on Mondays, national holidays and the New Year period. Entry fee.)

The museum, a branch of the Ministry of Education, is primarily an archeological research institute rather than a museum, but it does have public exhibits concerned with the past of the ancient capital. A very fine pamphlet in English gives a full description of the five major rooms/exhibits. The Paleological Association of Japan was created in 1951 and moved into this building in 1966. The three-story brick structure (whose bricks were imported from England) is typical of Meiji architecture (1868-1910) in the Western mode. At one time it housed a branch of the Bank of Japan.

The first room on exhibit is devoted to the prehistory of Japan through the Jomon and Yayoi periods. The second room focuses on Yamashiro province (Kyoto) before the establishment of Heian-kyo (Kyoto), while the third room shows the Heian capital from 794 to 1185. The Central Hall contains a restoration of an interior scene from the Seiryo-den (the living quarters of the Imperial Palace) of the Heian period. The fourth room contains exhibits related to the literature and life of the Heian period, while the fifth room is devoted to Lady Murasaki Shikibu and her classic novel, *The Tale of Genji*.

There is also a section on the film industry in Kyoto since many films have been made in the studios in western Kyoto. Thus, the collection consists of archeological finds, reproductions of Heian paintings and costumes and the scale model of the Seiryo-den. It is an interesting small display of aspects of Kyoto's early history.

2 NIJO JINYA

On leaving the museum, walk along Oike-dori (one street to the north of the museum) to the west, four streets past Horikawa-dori, and then turn left (south) to reach Nijo Jinya.

Nijo Jinya is one of those anomalies of history, a house that became an inn for *daimyo* (feudal lords) making their required courtesy call to the Shogun's Kyoto headquarters at Nijo Castle. It is an anomaly since this ancient building is the type in which Japanese television revels, with its soap operas of medieval swashbuckling sword play and intrigue—a house with secret passages, disappearing staircases, hidden rooms and trap doors—all the necessary props for *samurai* soap operas. A fascinating building still owned by descendents of its original creator, Nijo Jinya can be visited by appoint-

ment, but a translator is a necessary accompaniment for a full understanding of the secrets of the Nijo Jinya since the guide lectures in Japanese. (Nijo Jinya is situated on Omiya-dori, north of Anekoji-dori. Take bus 9, 12, 50, 52, 61, 62 or 63 to Horikawa-Oike or to the Tozai subway Nijo station and walk west four streets to Omiya-dori and south to the building in mid-street. Reservations must be made one day in advance. Tours are at 10:00 a.m., 11:00 a.m., 2:00 p.m. and 3:00 p.m., with a limit of 15 to a tour; no children under high school age. Not open on Wednesdays. Tours are in Japanese only. Entry fee.)

Ogawa Hiraemon, a former *daimyo* who became a rice merchant, built this private residence in the early 1600s just to the south of Nijo Castle and the Shinsen-en Garden, a house still owned by his descendents. Thirty years were spent in the construction of this Jinya, a fortified villa, given the uncertainties of the time after the death of Toyotomi Hideyoshi. Some of the *daimyo* who came to Kyoto on official business stayed with Ogawa, and his home gradually became an inn as well as a private residence. He built the house with such stability and so many safety features that it has survived the many catastrophes nature has inflicted on Kyoto. It even withstood the three-day Great Temmai Fire of 1788, when all else about it and the center of the city went up in flames. Its specially covered roof, windows with fireproof blinds that can drop into place, clay doors, complex water system of 12 interconnected wells—all these novel elements helped to protect it.

Nijo Jinya looks like a one-story building from the outside; inside it is a three-story structure. The building has some 11 downstairs rooms and 13 upstairs rooms, all heavily decorated. The building has a *Noh* hall and a tea ceremony room, and thus is a grand residence fit for a nobleman rather than a merchant. The building is a fortress within. It has all the elements which make for a Japanese TV spectacular with black-clothed *ninja* spies scaling walls, disappearing behind seemingly solid partitions and performing improbable feats in impossible situations.

There are hidden and disappearing staircases, hollow spaces in the ceilings and walls from which bodyguards could appear, walls constructed so as to allow for eavesdropping and *shoji* that cause the shadows of intruders to give them away without their realization. Secret tunnels under a garden pond, rope

ders—all the accouterments of mystery,
rigue, bravery and treachery are present.
nether these devices were ever needed or
ed is not the question. They exist, and they
e there to tickle the imagination of readers
Japanese stories or viewers of films of
dieval intrigue.

SHINSEN-EN GARDEN

contrast to the private fortress of Nijo Jinya
the nearby Shinsen-en (Sacred Spring
rden.) In the year 794, the Emperor Kammu
d his palace built in the north-central por-
n of Kyoto. Fires destroyed the complex on
ltiple occasions, and eventually the site was
andoned. Alone of all the magnificence that
ce enhanced this section of Kyoto, there
mains the small Shinsen-en, a tiny portion
the pleasure grounds once enjoyed by em-
rors and empresses, princes and princess-
and members of the courtier class.
Given to the To-ji Temple in recent centu-
s for a detached subtemple, the tiny garden
still a pleasant forepiece to the temple
ilding and restaurant that overlook the
nd, its vermilion bridges and small Shinto
rine. It is yet another place for quiet relax-
on in the heart of the commercial sector
the city. (The Shinsen-en lies just south of
jo Castle and on the north side of Oike-dori.
is three streets west of Horikawa-dori. Take
s 75 to the Shinsen-en-mae stop or take
s 9 or 12 or 50 or 52 or 61 or 62 or 63 to the
jo-jo-mae bus stop, or the Tozai subway to
e Nijo-jo station. The garden is open without
arge during daylight hours.)
All that remains of the impressive Imperial
lace that was built in 794 for the Emperor
mmu and his entourage is Shinsen-en
rden. When the palace was built, the
nperor decreed that a walled pleasure
rden be created to the south of it, and this
rden was some 33 acres (13.2 ha) in size.
extended from Nijo (Second Street) to
njo (Third Street). When the palace burned
1177 (it had burned down some 17 times
two centuries), the then Emperor moved
s residence to Kobe for a period of time,
d thus the tiny garden was abandoned.
In the 1600s, the Tokugawa government
ve permission to the To-ji Temple to build a
btemple on what remained of the site. The
rtheast corner of the original garden (about
e acre) was thus saved from further devel-
ment. A small Buddhist temple and three
ny Shinto shrines thus came into being.

When the Shinsen-en Garden existed in
the palmy days of the Heian court with the
full complement of its 33 acres (13.2 ha), all
the delights of the Heian period (794–1185)
aristocracy were practiced in this Chinese-
style park: there were Imperial boating parties; Chinese-style moon viewing and flower
viewing pavilions; the floating of wine cups
down the stream for the guests to pick up and
to compose an impromptu poem on a given
subject while imbibing. Pleasure pavilions in
vermilion lacquer dotted the park and were
even created at the edge of the pond to serve
for noble fishing expeditions.

It was said that dragons lived in the pond,
and at one period of drought in 824 even
Kobo Daishi (Kukai) prayed successfully to
the resident dragon for rain. The power of
Buddhism was thus proven effective—but the
composing of a poem by a noted poetess on
another occasion of drought also brought
relief. In reverse, there were times in the late
800s when the dragon had to be prayed to
for dry weather so as to preserve the crops
and prevent flooding. It is not surprising,
therefore, that the small island in the middle
of the pond has a shrine to the Dragon Queen.
No doubt the only real dragons, however, were
the dragon-headed boats used by courtiers.
The street leading to the west from the
Shinsen-en is called Oike-dori (Honorable
Pond Street), a reminder of the pond's more
auspicious days.

The garden has been restored in this
century to an approximation of its original
Chinese style, albeit at one-tenth of its earlier
size. The pond, called the Hojoju-ike, has an
island in the middle that is reached by a
stone bridge from the south and by a delightful arched vermilion bridge from the west. A
shrine to the Pious Woman Dragon Queen
(Zen-o-nyo-ryu-o) is on the island, as is a
stage for ceremonies or events of a religious
nature. An attractive large squat stone lantern
enhances the northeast section of the pond.

Since this garden was given to the To-ji
Temple, the Main Hall of the subtemple, the
Shinsen-den, contains an image of Kobo
Daishi. In 1963, a new north wall and gate
were erected, and the Hojo, a fairly large
building from To-ji, was placed next to the
Shinsen-den. There is a belfry in the northeast corner of the garden and a group of stone
Jizo images in the southeast area. On the
east bank of the pond is a shrine to the Shinto
goddess Benten, and there is an Inari shrine

An arched vermilion bridge crosses Shinsen-en's Hojoju Pond to the island in the middle.

with many *torii*, both shrines being quite small. A restaurant serving traditional Japanese food is located on the west side of the garden, and its sliding doors offer diners a charming view over the garden and the pond.

One of the garden's ceremonies should be noted: In late April or early May the *shinsen-en kyogen*, masked pantomime *Kyogen* plays, are presented in the garden from 1:30 p.m. to 6:00 p.m. on the first two days and from 1:30 p.m. to 10:00 p.m. on the last two days. There is no charge for viewing the *Kyogen* pantomime performances.

④ NIJO CASTLE

The centerpiece of this district is Nijo Castle (Nijo-jo), the luxurious palace of the Tokugawa Shoguns, meant to awe both the "Inside" and the "Outside" *daimyo* (lords) who came here to do obeisance to the Shoguns—after the delivery of the necessary expensive gifts. Five interconnected buildings, each of greater interior splendor and extravagance of decoration, recall the glory of the Tokugawa court. As Shoguns they were representatives of Imperial power, and their palace (since it is not really a defensible castle) has Imperial

period, but on the return of the capital to Kyoto, the original palace site was abandoned and a different location was occupied by the Imperial residence. In 1569, a mansion was built on a portion of the site of the original palace by Oda Nobunaga for Ashikaga Yoshi-aki, the last of the Ashikaga Shoguns. With the deposition of the Ashikaga in time by Nobunaga, the mansion became vacant, and in 1601, when Tokugawa Ieyasu became Shogun, he took over the land to build his Nijo Castle, ordering all the feudal "Outside Lords" of western Japan to undertake the construction of the castle at their expense. (They were the *daimyo* who sided against Ieyasu before his overwhelming victory at the Battle of Sekighara in 1603, which made him the secular ruler over Japan.) Ieyasu's administrative headquarters for Kyoto re-mained at Fushimi Castle south of Kyoto at this time, just as his permanent seat of gover-nance was established in Edo (Tokyo). Thus Nijo Castle served primarily as a showcase for Tokugawa power and wealth rather than as a residence.

The partially completed castle was first occupied by Ieyasu in March of 1603, and he did not return to it again until 1611 for a short stay. It was used again briefly in 1617 by his successor, and then in 1624–6 it was expand-ed and enriched with the completion of the Hon-maru and Ni-no-maru palace buildings and the *donjon* so as to serve as the locus in that latter year for an extravagant reception for the Emperor Go-Mizuno-o. In order to impress the court and the nobles, the five-story Tenshu Kaku tower of Fushimi Castle was moved to the Hon-maru area of the castle grounds, but this was destroyed by lightning in 1750.

The Ni-no-maru complex, completed at this time, is an excellent example of the *shoin* style carried to the extremes that un-limited wealth and little regard for austere beauty permitted. Elements that once marked the seriousness or austerity of Zen archi-tecture were here embellished with gold and precious metals. Here, various elements such as *tatami* flooring, painted *fusuma*, toko-noma alcoves and *chigaidana* shelves were borrowed from Zen temple architecture (as had happened at the Silver Pavilion earlier) and enhanced so as to become a part of secu-lar Japanese architecture.

Between 1624 and 1626 the finest artists were employed to create the most beautiful

stes and overtones. Historically important s a residence meant to impress all with the ower and wealth of the Tokugawa, it is re-membered as well as the locus for the surren-er of the Shogun's power to the 15-year-old Meiji Emperor by the last Tokugawa Shogun 1867. (The entrance to Nijo Castle is on orikawa-dori just to the north of Oike-dori.)

In Kyoto's earliest days, after the founding f the city in 794, the Imperial Palace grounds ncompassed a large area that included the ite of the later Nijo Castle. After a number of res, the palace was moved to Kobe for a brief secular building in Japan, and the overall supervision of the project came under the direction of Kobori Enshu (1579–1647). The loveliest elements of Fushimi Castle were relocated here and helped to enhance the overall decoration of Nijo-jo—truly a palace rather than a military stronghold. A special *Noh* theater was even built outside the O-Hiroma building of Ni-no-maru for performances during the Emperor's visit, as was a residential palace for the Emperor, structures which were removed thereafter.

Fire and the gradual removal of parts of the complex to other sites in time left only the Ni-no-maru comprising five buildings *in situ* along with the main East Gate and North Gate. (The five-story *donjon* was destroyed when hit by lightning in 1750, and then in 1788 the Hon-maru burned to the ground in the Temmai Fire.) Today, only the Second Building of the Ni-no-maru dates back to the earlier years of the castle, and much of the present structure reflects an 1855 restoration.

In 1863, Shogun Tokugawa Iemochi came from Edo (Tokyo) to the castle to consult with the Emperor, the first such visit in two centuries, an unheard of action during the previous 260 years. Here, he received the Emperor Komei's instructions to "expel the barbarian who were attempting to open Japan to international commerce. Unable to expel these foreigners who were infringing on Japan's sovereignty, and with the Shogun's authority collapsing, the last Tokugawa Shogun, Yoshinobu, here in Nijo Castle resigned his office in October 1867 in favor of the restoration of Imperial rule. In early 1868, an Extraordinary Council of State met in the presence of the new 15-year-old Emperor Meiji in the Grand Audience Hall of Nijo Castle to witness the Emperor abolish the Shogun's rule following the advice of his advisors. The castle became the temporary seat of the new Imperial government until it moved shortly thereafter to Edo, which was renamed Tokyo (Eastern Capital).

With the relocation of the capital to Tokyo, the castle was made available to the Kyoto prefectural government for offices. Many of the paintings of the castle were rolled up and stored between 1868 and 1883 while the castle was occupied by various local governmental offices. Unfortunately, some painted doors and metal work in the building were

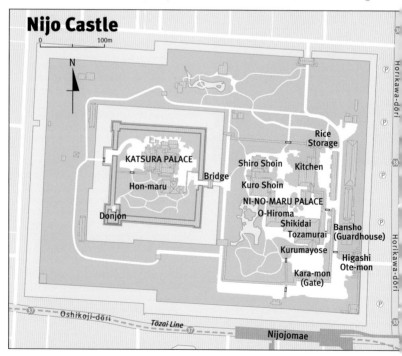

Nijo Castle

The corner turret, imposing stone wall and outer moat of Nijo Castle.

vandalized by local officials who, once the craze for Westernization began, had little appreciation of Japan's past. In July of 1884, the castle was returned to the Imperial family and was named an Imperial Detached Palace, and the restoration of its structure and interior finishing was begun.

At this time, the 16-petal chrysanthemum was now substituted for the Tokugawa crest of three hollyhock leaves that previously had proclaimed their ownership of the castle. In 1939, the historic complex was given to the City of Kyoto (and renamed Nijo Castle), which today preserves it and has opened it to the public since 1940.

In 1893, the mansion of Prince Katsura on the grounds of the Imperial Palace was removed to the site of the main keep of the original Nijo Castle, that area having been destroyed in the Great Temmai Fire of 1788. In 1928, at the enthronement of the Emperor Showa (Hirohito), the great banquet that formed part of the enthronement ceremony was held in this building. Then, in 1965, the Seiryu-en Garden was created to serve as a reception area for public functions of the city as well as being available to the public.

The castle grounds cover about 70 acres (28 ha), of which 78,580 square feet (7,722 sq m) are buildings. The grounds are surrounded by moats and by imposing stone walls with turrets at the southeast and southwest corners. The main entrance is through the iron-bound Higashi Ote-mon (Eastern Main Gate) on Horikawa-dori just north of Oike-dori, after entry tickets are purchased at the booth outside the castle walls. (In all, there are four gateways to the grounds.)

Within the castle's outer walls is the Bansho, the Guardhouse that regulated the entry of official visitors to the castle. Built in 1608, from 1634 to 1868 when the Shogun was in Edo the guardhouse was manned by 50 staff at a time. Today, the building has mannequins representing guards of the Tokugawa era as they would have appeared on duty in the past.

The Kara-mon (Chinese-style) or Shiyaku-mon Gate is the second gate traversed. This gate is a delight, with its imposing curved gabled roof of *hinoki* (cypress) bark and its carved wood and fine metal work. The outer panels of the gate have carved cranes, butterflies and flowers, while the inner panels offer

Chinese lions, tigers, and a dragon. Said to have been the work of Hidari Jingoro, it once stood at Hideyoshi's Fushimi Castle. In Hideyoshi's day, it held his paulownia crest, which was later replaced by the Tokugawa hollyhock leaves, and since the Imperial Restoration of 1868 it boasts the 16-petal Imperial chrysanthemum. Beyond the gate is a walled courtyard with pine trees, a court that leads to the five buildings of the Ni-no-maru.

NI-NO-MARU The courtyard before the Ni-no-maru complex ends at the Carriage Approach Gate (Mikuramayose), with its carvings of peonies and phoenixes enriched with color and gold, also attributed to Hidari Jingoro. The Mikuramayose (front porch or entryway) offers access to the Ni-no-maru, a series of five buildings with 33 rooms (and 800 *tatami* mats) connected with corridors, with the *uguisubari-no-roka* ("nightingale floors") that squeak when walked upon–a security measure to keep anyone from entering the inner areas of the castle buildings unnoticed. The ceilings of the connecting corridors between the buildings were originally quite plain, but after 1867 were painted. The Ni-no-maru is a Buke-fu Shoin, a *samurai* style residence with Momoyama period (1568–1615) decoration.

Status and rank were hierarchical and rigidly fixed in Tokugawa times, and the Ni-no-maru reflects such stratification through the height of its floors. Each of the five buildings, as one progresses through them, has a floor slightly higher than the previous one, and access was by rank: Imperial messengers were received at the lowest level (First Building); the Tozama, the "Outside Lords" of the realm, were greeted at the Third (and higher) Building, while the Fudai, the "Inside Lords," were received at the next higher Fourth Building. The last building, where the Shogun resided when at the castle, was at the highest level. Seating in the Audience Hall was hierarchical as well, the title and rank of each lord determined the seating arrangements in the hall. All the precautions necessary to protect the Shogun were taken: no swords were permitted within the Ni-no-maru, all doors between the five buildings were kept locked from the upper to the lower level, and doors with ornate tassels in the several rooms mark the location behind which guards were on duty at all times when visitors to the castle were present.

Within the buildings, all was luxurious. Each room was named for the mural-sized painted scenes on the *fusuma*, and the nails and bolts of construction were hidden behind elaborately chased and ornamented gold-plated copper covers. Each Audience Chamber had a raised portion where the Shogun sat when in attendance, and ornate carvings on the transoms at the ceiling between levels were crafted with different scenes on either side. Coffered ceilings were delicately painted, such ceilings indicating the importance of the room. The *fusuma* paintings were done by leading Kano school artists: Kano Sanraku (1559–1635), Kano Koi (1569–1636) and Koi's two pupils, the brothers Kano Tanyu (1602–74) and Kano Naonobu (1607–50).

The Carriage Approach Gate (Mikuramayose) to the Ni-no-maru complex at Nijo Castle.

FIRST BUILDING (TOZAMURAI) The largest of the five units, it is thought that this and the next two buildings were brought from Fushimi Castle in 1625, while the fourth and fifth buildings were constructed *in situ* in 1625. The entry room is the 24-mat Willow Room (Yanagi-no-ma), from its paintings of willows on a gold ground. Behind it is the Young Pine Room (Wakamatsu-no-ma), also of 24 mats, with young pines and cherry trees on the *fusuma*. Its coffered ceiling has painted grape vines. (The artist who did the paintings in these two rooms is not known.) The rooms were used by the Shogun's inspectors to verify the identity of visiting feudal lords. The next rooms to the west of the Willow Room along the corridor are the two-part

"Waiting Rooms" for *samurai* (Tozamurai-no-ma) of 40 mats and of 36 mats, also called the Tiger Rooms because of the *fusuma* paintings of tigers and bamboo on a gold ground. The tigers are not realistic, such animals being known only at second hand by the artists of the Kano school who depicted them. These rooms have coffered ceilings and *ramma* (transoms) of floral carvings. (All the rooms are surrounded by corridors, these corridors connecting the five buildings at their corners. All rooms, in a sense, are thus "inside rooms" since they are behind the corridors, although the *fusuma* could be opened to the corridors and the outside if so desired. Rooms at the rear of these chambers are seen on the return passage through the buildings.)

This decorative transom featuring colorful pea-cocks divides two of the Ni-no-maru's rooms.

SECOND BUILDING (SHIKIDAI) The gallery from the First Building leads to the west to the Second Building of four rooms, the most important of which is the south-facing Shikidai-no-ma (Room of Decorum and Salutations) of 45 mats. Just upon reaching this building there used to be a pair of cedar doors with a Korean-style lion whose eyes seem to stare at the viewer no matter where he/she stood. (These doors are now freestanding exhibits just beyond the Shikidai-no-ma.)

This building was used for the reception of *daimyo* (lords) by the Shogun's ministers, and here the ministers received those gifts which custom decreed had to be offered by the *daimyo* to the Shogun on an annual basis. The Shikidai-no-ma has *fusuma* featuring two large pine trees on a gold ground on its north wall while the lower portion of the *fusuma* shows geese in a rice field, flowers and bamboo trees. These paintings are by the then 25-year-old Kano Tanyu.

THIRD BUILDING (O-HIROMA) The third building, which has cedar doors at its entry-way with a painting of a goat and a pine tree branch, is the O-Hiroma (Grand Chamber or Audience Chamber), consisting of four rooms. The first room is the O-Hiroma-san-no-ma (Third Grand Chamber) which was a 40-mat

anteroom for visiting Tozama or "Outside Lords," those who became Tokugawa Ieyasu's vassals only after he had become the victor at the Battle of Sekigahara on October 21, 1600, when he won the overlordship of Japan. Its *fusuma* are decorated with a large pine tree by Kano Tanyu.

The *ramma* (transoms) by Hidari Jingoro are said to have come from Hideyoshi's Fushimi Castle, and, while one side of these open-work carvings might be carved with birds or animals, the reverse side usually features flowers. Each of the carved panels is made from one block of wood 14 inches (35 cm) thick. The nail heads in the wood-work of the room are covered with copper plated with gold, "the Nail Covers of Hanan-oshi shape," each one different in design and shape from all the others.

The Second and First Grand Chambers really form one unit, although they can be separated by *fusuma*. The Second Grand Chamber is on a lower level (for the *daimyo*) than is the raised inner room (specially for the Shogun). This is a 44-mat room with *fusuma* and wooden doors bearing paintings of a peacock in a pine tree, the carved ceiling being elaborately decorated with flower pat-terns on a dark blue and gold background. The carved open-work *ramma* (transom) between the room for the *daimyo* (Second Grand Chamber) and the Shogun's room (First Grand Chamber) of pine and peacocks is credited to Hidari Jingoro. Today, the room is peopled with mannequins representing the *daimyo* in attendance upon the Shogun, seated by rank, and decked in the costumes of the Edo period (1615–1868).

The First Grand Chamber in the northwest of the building is the upper portion (Jodan-no-ma) of the Grand Audience Hall (O-Hiroma). Large enough to accommodate 48 mats, it is where the Shogun sat on a raised platform so that he could overlook the *daimyo* in the room below him when holding an audience for these Outside Lords. Here, a Shogun sits, today in the form of a mannequin dressed in a Shogun's finery.

The *tokonoma* of this section is made from a single zelkova board 18 feet (5 m) long by 7 inches (18 cm) thick and 3 feet (1 m) wide. The rear *fusuma* are painted with a huge pine tree while the *chigaidana* shelf has a few slender bamboo and various flowers as a background. The doors of the east walls, behind which the guards were stationed, are decorated with beach scenes, and the large red tassels on the doors (Chodaiga-mae) always indicate the Musha-kakushi-no-ma (Bodyguards' Room) where guards were on alert duty, ready to act if needed to protect the Shogun. Thus the tassels on the sliding doors were both decoration and warning. The paintings in the room are by Kano Tanyu. The ceiling has elaborate designs against a gold ground similar to those of the previous room. All of this grandeur was meant to impress upon the Outside Lords the power, authority and wealth of the Shogun. (It was in this chamber, seated in the center of the room on October 14, 1867, that the 15th and last Tokugawa Shogun, Yoshinobu, returned the administrative power of government to the very young Emperor Meiji.)

FOURTH BUILDING (KURO SHOIN—BLACK CHAMBER)

The Fourth Building is a smaller but even more luxuriously decorated structure, for it was here that the Shogun granted audiences to the Inner Lords, those who had been his vassals before the battle of Sekigahara in 1600. The building comprises five rooms plus the inner guard room; four of the rooms form a square with the fifth being a wide hallway (used by visitors today on the return to the main entrance/exit). On the cedar wooden doors (*nuresagi-no-sugito*) at the entry to this building is the renowned painting of "Heron in the rain, perched on the edge of a boat" by Kano Naonobu (1607–50), the younger brother of Kano Tanyu.

The first room in this building is the Pine Beach Room (Hamamatsu-no-ma) of 35 mats. Here, the Inner Lords awaited their invitation into the Audience Chamber. Its northern and eastern upper walls depict a beach with pine trees painted by Mochizuki Guokusen, while its *fusuma* of pines and heron are by Kano Naonobu. The coffered ceiling has a phoenix pattern. The two rooms on the western side of the building comprise the Audience Chamber, and the northernmost half is the 24-mat room where the Shogun sat. The *tokonoma*, as in the previous Audience Chamber, is unusual in that it also has a long zelkova plank. The paintings in the *tokonoma*, by Kano Naonobu, are of a snow-covered pine tree with three birds in it. The *tokonoma* shelves offer examples of early cloisonné work. The walls and sliding doors of the *chigaidana* are painted with bamboos, while the eastern *fusuma*,

behind the doors where guards were located, have cherry blossoms with pheasants in a tree. A horizontal timber around the walls, about 7 feet (2 m) above the floor over the north and east walls, holds more than three dozen crests of the Tokugawa made of antique cloisonné and fine metal work. It is said that it was here that the last Tokugawa Shogun made the decision to resign authority to the Emperor. The lower room of 31 mats, where the Inner Lords sat, has paintings of birds and cherry blossoms over a rustic fence and a seashore picture. The coffered ceiling has a phoenix pattern.

FIFTH BUILDING (SHIRO SHOIN—WHITE CHAMBER OR OZA-NO-MA—HONORABLE SEAT ROOM)

The final section of the Ni-no-maru contains the private living quarters of the Shogun. Here, he was served only by women, trained in self-defense to protect the Shogun if need be, but even here there is an inside room for guards. The Shiro Shoin consists of four rooms (plus the inner guard space). The room in the northwest corner, the main Shiro Shoin of 15 mats with its *tokonoma*, is the most attractive and important room in the castle. This was the Shogun's personal room, and it had a raised floor (*jodan-no-ma*). The room preceding it, on a lower level of 18 mats, was used by his attendants. The *fusuma* of the White Rooms (Shiro Shoin) by Kano Koi are almost monochromatic scenes of Chinese mountains and rivers under snow. The coffered ceilings of black lacquered squares have flowers painted on them.

The room to the east of the lower room is the Sansui-no-ma (Mountain Water Room) of 18 mats. This was also for the attendants of the Shogun. The *fusuma* paintings continue the theme of the room to the north with its Chinese snow scenes. To the east of the Sansui-no-ma, in the southeast corner, is the Tonan-no-ma (Southeast Room) with cedar doors painted with flowers and with painted geese in the hallway corner. The last and innermost room is the northeast room, the Sleeping Sparrows Room (Nemuru Suzuma-no-ma), whose *fusuma* depict two sparrows asleep on snow-covered bamboo on a gold ground; the floral design on the coffered ceiling is on a brown ground.

From here you return to the main entry by means of corridors along the eastern side of the rooms of the four preceding buildings:

The rear of the Ni-no-maru seen from its garden.

FOURTH BUILDING (REAR ROOMS)

The first room in the northeast corner of the Fourth Building is a 28-mat room known as the Chrysanthemum Room (Kiku-no-ma) with embossed chrysanthemum flowers over a rustic fence by Kano Naonobu. The upper panels offer various kinds of fans while the ceiling has floral circles on a gold ground. The adjacent 66-mat hallway is called the Peony Room (Botan-no-ma) or the Waiting Room (Tamari-no-ma). Its *fusuma* and walls have peonies and white plum blossoms also by Kano Naonobu; it too has a coffered ceiling.

THIRD BUILDING (REAR ROOMS)

The first room at the rear of the Third Building is the Spear Room (Yari-no-ma) or the Taka-no-ma (Hawk Room) of 52 mats, which at one time held spears as part of the Shogun's armory. It is decorated with massive pines and hawks by Kano Tanyu. The last room of this unit is the Sago Palm Room (Sotetsu-no-ma) of 50 mats, which serves as a corridor. This room, which was badly damaged in the 1870s when the prefectural government had offices here, and the original paintings have been effaced. Plain gold paper replaces what had once been a noted portrayal of the fern-like sago palm.

SECOND BUILDING (REAR ROOMS)

The Elder Counselors' Rooms (Rochu-no-ma) consist of three rooms behind the main hall of the Second Building, and were used by the counselors for business purposes. The first room of 12 mats and second room of 14 mats have *fusuma* of a rice field after harvest, reeds, oak trees and geese in snow. The *fusuma* in the third room of 12 mats has herons on a snow-covered willow tree as well as cherry blossoms and long-tailed birds, reputedly painted by Kano Tanyu.

FIRST BUILDING (REAR ROOMS)

On turning the corner of the corridor, the Chokushi-no-ma (Imperial Messenger Waiting Room) of 76 mats is next, decorated with tigers and bamboo paintings. It was here that messengers from the Emperor were received by the Shogun or his emissaries. The two rooms on the north side of the First Building are the Chokushi-no-ma (Imperial Messengers Audience Hall) with an upper and lower level. The upper room (*jodan-no-ma*) of 21 mats has a raised platform of honor for the Imperial Messenger while the Shogun sat below him. The room has a *tokonoma* and a *chigaidana* decorated with maples in their autumn color, while the doors of the small closets above the *chigaidana* are ornamented with plum and cherry trees, globe flowers and mallows. The coffered ceiling is highly decorated.

The second room (Ni-no-ma) of 35 mats was for the Imperial Messenger and it has fir trees on a gold ground on its *fusuma* by Kano Sanraku. There is an interior room, the Fuyo-no-ma (Changeable Mallow Room) of 24 mats with peaches, flowers, a bamboo grove with sparrows and hydrangeas, among other paintings. It is also known as the Dark Room (Kuragari-no-ma) since it is an internal room; it has doors with painted peonies, bamboos, tigers, sheep, hares and geese. Most of the paintings, other than in the Fuya-no-ma, are by Kano Tanyu and his pupils.

GROUNDS OF THE NI-NO-MARU

To the north of the Ni-no-maru are two kitchens, one for the preparation of the Shogun's food and one for food for other occupants of the castle. A storage building for rice also remains intact. The many other buildings that were once on the grounds were either moved to other locations in Kyoto, razed or destroyed by fire.

The garden of the Ni-no-maru lie to the southwest of the O-Hiroma and Kuro Shoin.

The task of developing the gardens was given to Kobori Enshu (1579-1647) by Shogun Iemitsu in 1624, and this garden and a few temporary buildings were erected in honor of the 1626 visit to the palace by Emperor Go-Mizuno-o (1596-1680). The Gyoku Goten, a temporary palace connected to the Ni-no-maru, was created for the Emperor's residence, as was a *Noh* stage, and both were razed after his visit.

The garden is close to the moat of the original keep. According to tradition, this one acre garden was originally designed to avoid thoughts of the changing of seasons and the passing of time. No trees were to be planted, since they inevitably drop their leaves and give rise to thoughts of the transitory nature of life. (The present trees were planted at a much later time.) The garden is centered on a large pond, enhanced by water lilies, groupings of fine stones and plantings. Three islands, connected by four bridges of natural stone, lie within the waters: Horai (representing the Island of Eternal Happiness), the traditional Crane Isle (Tsuru-jima) on the left and Turtle Isle (Kame-jima) on the right, the latter two both symbolizing longevity.

In its original state, the pond was probably dry and the rocks and stones that composed it were gifts of great rarity from Tokugawa *daimyo*. Altered frequently through the centuries, the garden is now in Tsukeyama (Go-round Style), comprising rocks and ponds against a backdrop of pine, maple and other trees. The plantings have been arranged to permit for flowering or color throughout the year: January–February camellias, February–March apricot blossoms, April cherry and dogwood blossoms, May azaleas, June azaleas and cape jasmine, July–August Indian lilac, September–October bush clover, November maple, December fire thorn.

HON-MARU The original Hon-maru, consisting of a square-walled castle or main keep of five stories, was destroyed by lightning in 1750, and then the palace to house the Shogun and his retainers was destroyed by fire in 1788. Both units were originally from Hideyoshi's Fushimi Castle.

The present Hon-maru is surrounded by an inner moat and steep rock walls. It was the 1847 town villa of Prince Katsura, which stood on the grounds of the Imperial Palace, and it is the only existing building here in Imperial style. With the removal of the royal family to Tokyo after 1868, the villas on the palace grounds were removed, the Katsura Villa being relocated here in 1893 as a gift from Prince Katsura. At the time, it was thought that the Dowager Empress would reside in it, but she died before being able to occupy the mansion.

The Hon-maru Villa is entered through a bridge walkway over the inner moat. It is open only during the third weekend of November, from 9:30 a.m. to 3:30 p.m.

SEIRYU GARDEN The large Seiryu-en (Seiryu Garden) was constructed in 1965 for official receptions of city guests and for cultural events. Here, two tea houses are located, the Koun-tei and the Waraku-an. The garden has over 1,000 stones, of which 800 stones (plus one tea house) were originally part of the early 1600s residence of Ryoi Sumi-nokura (the merchant and engineer responsible for the Takagase Canal and the opening of the Oi River to navigation), which sat near the Takagase Canal in the Pontocho (Shijo-dori) area of Kyoto. The gardens are of both a traditional (in the western half) and a modern design with a lawn (eastern half), and they cover 177,610 square feet (16,500 sq m).

GETTING THERE

Nijo Castle, the highlight of this tour, is especially pleasant to visit in mid-April when the cherry blossoms are in bloom. In early June and again in early November an annual tea ceremony is held. From 9:30 a.m. to 3:00 p.m. tea masters serve tea ceremony to the public for a fee in the Seiryu-en Garden of the castle.

To reach Nijo Castle, take the Tozai subway line to Nijo-jo-mae station. Alternately, take bus 9, 12, 50, 52, 61 or 67 to the Nijo-mae bus stop. The castle is open from 8:45 a.m. to 4:00 p.m. (gates close at 5 p.m.) in summer and from 9:00 a.m. to 3:30 p.m. in winter, but it is closed on Mondays. If a national holiday falls on a Monday, the castle is open that day but then is closed the next day. It is also closed from December 26 to January 3 each year. Pay the entry fee at the ticket booth on Horikawa-dori, just outside the castle's main gate. At the conclusion of the tour, you can return to other sectors of the city by means of the Tozai subway or one of the many bus lines listed above.

Walking Tour 10

TO-JI TEMPLE AREA
The Esoteric Temple and the Shimabara Pleasure Quarter

⓵ **To-ji Temple** 東寺
⓶ **Shimabara** 嶋原

The hills to the north, east and west of Kyoto have provided a natural barrier about the city, but the way south has always been open toward Osaka and the Inland Sea. The original southern boundary of Heian-kyo (Kyoto) lay at Kujo-dori (Ninth Street) where the great Rajo-mon (Rasho-mon) gate provided a grand entrance to the city. The capital to the north of the gate was protected by the

placement of To-ji (East Temple) and Sai-ji (West Temple) to either side of the Rajo-mon. The temples may have offered the city spiritual protection, but for practical purposes they were no barriers to any armed foe.

This lack of protection in the area to the south of Kyoto was remedied at the end of the 1500s when Toyotomi Hideyoshi built his great Fushimi Castle a few miles below Kyoto to guard the city from the south (see Tour 27). In Hideyoshi's day, and even later, the area below Kujo-dori was still open countryside interspersed with a few shrines and

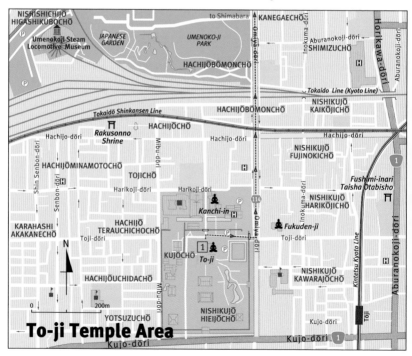

To-ji Temple Area

temples. In time, the Tokugawas were to dismantle Fushimi Castle, for under their strict rule there was little chance of revolt against the Shogun's government.

Then, in the late 19th century, the railroad came to Kyoto and, with its eventual realignment and the addition of the Kintetsu and the Shinkansen rail lines, Kyoto Central Station and the raised railroad tracks today form a new "barrier" at Hachijo-dori (Eighth Street). This new barrier, however, has been no more effective than the Sai-ji or the To-ji Temples were, and the sprawl of the modern city now spreads to the south, engulfing old temples and shrines in the growth of modern Kyoto.

THE SOUTHERN ENTRY TO HEIAN-KYO

When Kyoto was established in 794, there was one experience the Emperor Kammu had faced in the former capital of Nara that he did not wish to encounter again: the interference in governance of the nation by the Buddhist clergy. Thus he planned his new capital so that the Buddhist temples would be outside the city gates rather than within the capital itself. Of course, a city and its people needed the religious and supernatural protection which Buddhism could offer. Thus he designated a site to the east and to the west of the main city gate for two temples: To-ji (East Temple) and Sai-ji (West Temple).

Before too many years had passed, To-ji, at the order of the next Emperor, had come under the leadership of Priest Kukai (Kobo Daishi). Kukai (774–835) had brought Esoteric Buddhist doctrines from China, where he had studied the latest in Buddhist thought, and he proposed that the To-ji Temple should observe the Shingon rules of Buddhism, the better to protect the state and city. The temple was thus known as the Kyo-gokoku-ji (Temple for the Transmission of the Teachings to the King and for the Protection of the State). This purpose suited the needs of the Emperor and the court, and thus the To-ji flourished under Imperial patronage. Sai-ji, on the other hand, had no leadership such as Kukai offered at To-ji, and so the temple suffered. A fire in 990 damaged the temple buildings severely, and when the pagoda burned in 1233 (the sole structure of the temple still standing by that time), Sai-ji became merely a memory. A memorial stone to the west of Shichi-honmatsu-dori is all that remains to remember it.

The Rajo-mon (often called Rasho-mon), the main gateway of Heian-kyo, was built in 789 and stood about 115 feet (35 m) wide by 69 feet (21 m) tall. It declined with the years as well, serving as time went by as the city morgue and a hide-out for disreputable characters before it too passed into oblivion. Today, it is remembered primarily as the title and setting for Ryunosuke Akutagawa's short story and the award-winning movie by Akira Kurosawa. A stone monument next to a playground at the intersection of Kujo-dori and Senbon-dori, a few blocks west of To-ji, is the only reminder of the Rajo-mon Gate that was once traversed by aristocrats, priests, merchants and beggars entering the noble city of Heian-kyo.

To-ji Temple, however, lived and continues to flourish due to the efforts of Kukai, who rejuvenated the temple and turned it into a bastion of Shingon belief. Shingon has a mystic bent to it (it is related to Tantric Buddhism which had its strength in Tibet), and Kukai's To-ji Kodo (Lecture Hall) was filled with Buddhist images arranged in the pattern of a mystic mandala (picture). Today, To-ji is designated as a World Heritage Site.

① TO-JI TEMPLE

In 796, shortly after the founding of the new capital of Heian-kyo by the Emperor Kammu, the To-ji Temple was erected. Then, in 823, Emperor Saga (reigned 810–23), the successor to Emperor Kammu, appointed Priest Kukai as the Superior of To-ji. The Shingon doctrines of Buddhism that Kukai had brought to Japan provided a new emphasis for the Buddhism of his day. They held that anyone could attain Buddhahood after this life through faith and actions instead of having to wait until the end of the present cycle of time.

When Buddhism was first propagated in Japan, it was considered to be applicable only to the ruling classes, a situation that still prevailed at the founding of Heian-kyo at the end of the 8th century. Kukai, on the contrary, believed that Buddhahood was accessible to women as well as men, and to commoners and nobles alike. Thus he fashioned his approach to daily life with a concern for all levels of society. He did all he could to improve the condition of the average person. He opened a school for commoners, compiled the first dictionary in Japan in order to assist in the educational process, made medicines available to all, introduced new techniques in agriculture, improved roads and built bridges to assist farmers.

As Superior of To-ji, Kukai made the temple's Kodo (Lecture Hall) the center both of his beliefs and the visual realization of the mystic or magical significance of the mandala (a representation of the various Buddhist deities centered around the image of Dainichi Nyorai, the central Buddha) in paintings or tapestries. The physical alignment of the three-dimensional images that he placed in the Kodo reflected their arrangement in the painted representations of the Womb and Diamond Mandalas that he had brought back from China. For Kukai, art was a visible aspect of religion, and thus religious statues, paintings and manuscripts enriched the temple and monastery under his leadership. Here, in the Kodo, his seminary for Mikkyo (Esoteric) Buddhism was located. The Kodo, accordingly, was the most important building in this Shingon temple.

The layout of To-ji followed the pattern that had been employed in the construction of temples in Nara when it was the earlier capital of the nation. Buildings were aligned in a straight line from the Great South Gate (Nandai-mon or Minami-dai-mon) northward. Behind the gateway was the Kondo (Golden or Main Hall), followed by the Kodo (Lecture Hall) with the Jikido (Refectory) at the rear. Additional buildings to the left (from the southwest to the northwest) of the main structures included the Kancho-in (where priests were ordained as Masters of Tantric Buddhism) in the southwest portion of the compound, then the Kyaku-den (Guest House), and finally the Taishi-do or Mie-do (Founder's Hall), created after Kukai's death. The pagoda was erected to the east of the main axis of the temple, and a small Shinto shrine to protect the temple lands was placed to the west of the pagoda.

As with virtually all temples in the city, To-ji suffered destruction in the Onin Wars in the period 1467–77, and thus the present buildings are not the original ones. The temple's spacious gardens and three ponds remain, but the original size of the temple was four times its present size. Today, the temple is the headquarters of the To-ji branch of Shingon Buddhism, and it consists of a 24 acre (10 ha) area with walls and gates on all four sides. Although it is possible to enter the grounds of To-ji through any of its four gates,

the main entrance is through the Great South Gate (Nandai-mon). The original great gateway to the To-ji on its southern side was lost with time, earlier replacements were destroyed by fire, and then in 1894 the gate was replaced by the present eight-pillared Great South Gate which had formerly been the West Gate of Sanjusangen-do. The Rengei-mon Gate on the western side of the temple grounds was built in 1191 and is the temple's oldest structure.

To the east of the Great South Gate stands the temple pagoda, with three small ponds to its north. The tallest pagoda of any temple in Japan, it stands 187 feet (561 m) high in the southeast area of the temple compound. Originally constructed at Kukai's order, it has burned down five times since its construction in 826. The present structure was created in 1644 by Shogun Tokugawa Iemitsu, and it contains the Four Buddhas on the Shumidan (dais) and paintings of the Eight Great Bodhisattva whose images are represented on the wooden walls of the interior. This pagoda does not contain a relic of the Buddha (the original purpose of pagodas), but it stands as a symbol of the "Mandala of the Two Worlds" (discussed under the Kodo below).

Directly to the north of the Great South Gate is the Kondo, the Main Hall of To-ji. The Kondo was first erected in 796 at the inception of the temple. It burned down in 1486, and it was replaced about 1606 by the present structure with a double roof in the Irimoya (hipped and gabled roof) style. An extra small roof above the lower roof marks the main entry to the Kondo. It is the largest structure in the To-ji and one of the largest of the Momoyama period (1568–1603) buildings extant in Kyoto.

The main image in the faded vermilion and white interior of the Kondo is that of Yakushi Nyorai, the Buddha of healing or medicine. This 10 foot (3 m) tall image is a Muromachi period (1336–1568) copy of the original Heian statue that was lost to fire in the late 1400s. On either side are his attendants Gakko and Nikko, all three images with a gilt aureole behind them. Under the draperies of Yakushi are the 12 Godly Generals, attributed to the sculptor Kosho. Huge bronze urns with gilt lotuses stand on either side of these images. The altar table before the images is vermilion, while the altar furniture on the floor in front of the images and table are of a black lacquer.

The Kodo (Lecture Hall) is the most important building of the temple, rather than the

Kondo as is the usual case, for the images within this building conform to the Tantric pattern based on Mikkyo (Esoteric) Buddhist principles. (Such a pattern usually appears on mandalas, Buddhist pictures or representations of a perfect, enlightened universe.) With images of 21 major deities, the figures are of great importance since they provide a three-dimensional version of the pictorial mandalas in which Dainichi Nyorai is the central figure surrounded by other Buddhas in a circular pattern. These images served as the central focus of ceremonies meant to protect the state.

As called for in the Shingon sutra (sacred texts) and as seen in the mandalas, the central figure is the seated Dainichi Nyorai Buddha, 7 feet (2 m) tall, with the four Kongo-kai (Diamond World) or Supreme Buddhas (Ashuku, Hosho, Fuku and Amida) about him. The Diamond World symbolizes the wisdom of the Buddha which is as hard as a diamond and capable of crushing all illusions. To the west (left when facing the main images) are the Go-dai Myo-o (Five Radiant Kings or the Five Great Kings of Light) all from about 839; one of them, Daitokuji, is seated on a bull. All are centered upon a seated Fudo Myo-o with an upright sword in his left hand. Ferocious looking as they are, these kings are only ferocious in appearance in order to frighten away evil, the better to protect mankind—and their multiple arms and heads add to the mystic nature of their powers. The Five Great Kings and the Five Bodhisattvas were new concepts, brought back from T'ang China by Kukai, for they were not known to the Buddhism of Nara prior to the late 700s.

At the four corners of the complex stand the Shi-tenno, the four kings who protect the Buddha world from evil. Between the pairs of the Shi-tenno are Taishaku-ten on the west and Bon-ten on the east, both of painted wood. They show their Indian nature in that Bon-ten has four heads (one atop its main coiffure), four arms and is seated on a group of four geese. Taishaku-ten is seated upon a white elephant. (Neither of these Indian stylistic approaches with the unusual steeds were to be accepted in the Japanese iconography in the long run.) The images in the Kodo are said to have been commissioned by Kukai in 825, and tradition claims that Kukai carved these images, a rather doubtful possibility. While these statues are physical representations of the painted mandala that symbolically present the truths of the world, the

The Kondo and five-tiered pagoda are To-ji's most recognizable structures.

actual "Mandalas of the Two Worlds" that Kukai brought from China with him were so worn (from use) that by 821 they had disintegrated and had to be replaced by copies. The present copies in colors on silk were painted between 1688 and 1703.

The original refectory, the Jiki-do, was dated to the beginning of the temple in the 790s, but has burned down twice since then. The present structure was erected in 1930. Rather than a dining room, it has served as a place of study. Traditionally, the main image in this building is Bishamon-ten, protector of the north, with a pagoda in one hand and a spear in the other. The Jiki-do image originally stood in the Rajo-mon when that gate was the main entryway to the city, and the image served to protect the city which lay to its north. When the gate disintegrated, the image was brought to To-ji. This helmeted Bishamon-ten image from the 9th century is dressed in Chinese armor. The helmet has a phoenix at each of its four sides, representing the four directions from which it protects the city. The hall also holds a golden Kannon holding a bottle-shaped vase containing a lotus bud. To the left of the main image is a large mandala, while to the right is a scroll depicting a Myo-o. *Ihai* memorial tablets are to the far right and left.

The Kancho-in (Supreme Purification Hall) lies in the southwest corner of the temple grounds. It was originally built in 1069 after the pattern of Seiryu-ji Temple in China, at which Kukai had studied Mikkyo Buddhism. Destroyed by fire on several occasions, the present structure dates from 1634. The Kancho-in serves as the locus for the Kancho (or Kanjo) service, an initiation rite into the higher mysteries of Shingon Buddhism, at which time monks are granted the title of "Master of Esoteric Buddhism." The walls of the Kancho-in contain portraits of the eight great priests of Mikkyo Buddhism as well as Sanskrit characters. Since 1882, by Imperial order, prayers for the Emperor's health and national peace have taken place here.

The Mie-do or Taishi-do (Founder's Hall) is located to the west of the Kodo and Jiki-do, and is situated within its own walled precinct. The one-time site of Kukai's residence, the present building was constructed in 1380. Within is the painted wood seated image of Kukai created by Kosho in 1233. The image has his right hand holding a rosary in his lap while his left

Seirentei, a rustic tea house at Toji-in Temple.

hand holds a symbolic thunderbolt to his chest. His shoes are in front of him and a water jar is at his side. With a round and plump face, the image is a realistic, if symbolic, representation of Kukai which is enhanced by the skillfully carved drapery folds of his robe; it is not an actual likeness since it was created some 200 years after Kukai's death. It is thus an idealized portrait meant to serve as an inspiration to the worshippers viewing it, and it is so well composed that it became the model for later images of Kukai by other artists. Among other images in the Mie-do is a Fudo Myo-o, a deity who punishes evil doers, from about 850. A sword is upright in his right hand and a rope in his left hand, a pigtail hanging down his chest on the left. On the 21st of each month, the Mie-do is open to the public and it is thronged with worshippers who come to pray before the image of Kukai.

Originally, there were two *azekura*-style (log construction) Treasure Houses to the north and south of the temple buildings. One burned in 1000 and the other in 1127. All of the treasures which Kukai had brought back from China with him, including some of the ashes of Buddha, were said to be in these original treasuries. The surviving and later treasures which the temple accrued through the centuries are now kept in a fireproof concrete Treasury Building (Homotsu-kan) at the northern end of the temple precinct. Here, a portion of the temple's treasures are shown twice a year, from March 20 to May 25 and then from September 20 to November 25. (Open from 8:30 a.m. to 4:30 p.m. Entry fee.)

The treasures of To-ji include, among many other items, paintings of the patriarchs of the Shingon sect of Buddhism which Kukai brought back from China in 806; the Ryokai Mandala of the 9th century; manuscript letters in Kukai's hand as well as those written by the great Priest Saicho of the Tendai sect of Buddhism, a contemporary of Kukai; land records going back to 752, prior to Kukai's time; a huge Senju (1,000 arm) Kannon image of 877, the largest wooden statue in Japan; a Jizo from the Heian period (794– 1085); and a set of gilt-bronze Buddhist ritual implements of esoteric Buddhism from Tang China. The Treasury also holds the Kodo's three Shinto images from the 9th century, the oldest known Hachiman image in which the deity is represented as a seated Buddhist priest, and two Shinto goddesses. These are but a sampling of the treasures which are

Lanterns on the façade of one of the minor buildings of To-ji Temple.

shown on a rotating basis. Some of the finest sculptures still remain in the Kodo (Lecture Hall), arranged in the pattern of a mandala as planned by Kukai in the early 800s.

The To-ji holds many ceremonies throughout the year, but one event which occurs monthly is worthy of mention. Kukai died on the 21st of the month, and a memorial service is held in the Mie-do each month in front of his image on this day. In addition, one of the great outdoor fairs of Kyoto is held on this date monthly. Open-air stalls selling food, beverages, clothing, antiques, tools, kitchen items, dried seaweed and dried fish, ceramics, baskets, textiles—and anything else which you may desire—are available. Some 1,500 vendors, some of whose families have been selling at these monthly markets for centuries, set up their stalls.

NEARBY SITES

From the intricacies of Buddhist esotericism it is possible to move to areas of a lighter note. One of these is a museum of both model and life-sized railway trains while the other offers a view of the one-time secondary "Pleasure Quarter" of Kyoto. Leave To-ji though its east side to Omiya-dori and continue along Omiya-dori to the north and under the railroad overpass. Turn left on the second street on the left after the rail line and, after four streets, you will arrive at Senbon-dori.

THE STEAM LOCOMOTIVE PRESERVATION HALL

Across the street on the left, you will see the Steam Locomotive Preservation Hall, a railroad museum that was created at the edge of a portion of the rail yards to the west of Kyoto Central Station. Actual trains as well as model trains of Japan Rail rolling stock are on display. Not only are steam locomotives displayed, but they are operated at 11:00 a.m., 1:00 p.m. and 3:00 p.m. The place is a delight for train buffs. (The hall is open from 9:00 a.m. to 4:30 p.m. except on Mondays. When a public holiday falls on a Monday, the closing day is shifted to Tuesday for that week. Entry fee.)

The museum is adjacent to a lovely garden, Midori no Yakata, opened in 1994 to mark the city's 1,200th anniversary. Entry fee. The garden features a five-tiered pond and winding paths through a variety of plantings. The garden adjoins a public park, Inochi no Mori.

② SHIMABARA

Return to Omiya-dori where it intersects with Shichijo-dori (Seventh Street), walk north on Omiya-dori for one more street, and then turn west for four streets. This brings you to the Shimabara district. The Shimabara (Western Pleasure Quarter, as opposed to the Gion or Eastern Pleasure Quarter) was originally located between Gojo-dori (Fifth Street) and Shichijo-dori (Seventh Street), west of Omiya-dori, and extended to the present north–south right of way of the San-in main line railway. The Shimabara district still lies to the west of the Omiya-dori, although today its life as a pleasure quarter has come to an end.

In contrast to the To-ji, which is a center of piety and holds examples of exquisite art, the not too distant Shimabara quarter stands in apposition to religious life. In 1641, there were two "Pleasure Quarters" in the Shijo-dori (Fourth Street) area of Kyoto. The Toku-gawa Shogun, worried about their effect on the morals of its military followers or as a locus for disturbances by rowdy commoners, as well as their proximity to Nijo Castle and the heart of the city, ordered the westernmost of the two districts moved to the southwest, near the Tamba-guchi exit to the city.

Here, the relocated "Pleasure Quarter" became known as the Shimabara district, a name taken in defiance of the government since the Shogun had, with much trouble, only recently put down an insurrection in Kyushu at Shimabara. The new "licensed" district catered to all the pleasures, ranging from the theater to drink and the pleasures of the flesh. (It and the Yoshiwara district in Tokyo were the two major "red light" districts in Japan in the Edo era (1600–1868).) Shima-bara was a district crowded with brothels, and it flourished for three centuries until its "houses of pleasure" were closed in 1958 when the national government outlawed pros-titution and the "licensed" districts came to an end. Today, a rather run-down sector be-tween the Nishi Hongan-ji Temple to the east and the wholesale food markets (on the far side of the San-in rail line) on its western borders, it is primarily of historic interest.

Shimabara originally consisted of one street that ran through it from east to west while three streets ran north to south, there-by creating six blocks in the district, each of which had its own name. Set off by a 10 foot (3 m) wide moat beyond which an earthen wall separated the district from the rest of the city, it had but two entrances, the O-mon or Dai-mon (Great Gate), which still exists on its eastern side, the old houses beyond it giving a flavor of the one-time district, and a smaller gate on its western side. Within the walls, the main places of pleasure were divided into two parts: *ageya*, where men were entertained, and *okiya*, residences where the entertainers awaited a summons from the *ageya*.

In a hierarchical society, even the *demi-monde* had its social levels. At the top were the *tayu*, women who were educated and gifted in the arts, music, poetry and repartee. At a lower level were women with lesser tal-ents who could not command the higher class of clientele (or fees) who were attracted to the *tayu*, and those of lesser talents offered attractions more of a carnal nature. Thus Shimabara was a place of pleasure in every sense—from intellectual to alcoholic to sexual gratification for those with money. The area with its brothels flourished from 1641, when this pleasure quarter was removed from central Kyoto to this district, until 1958 when prostitution was outlawed. Its main *raison d'etre* having disappeared under a new moral-ity, the district declined, and today Shimabara has become a backwater of social history.

Two historic buildings in the Shimabara district still exist: the Sumiya, an *ageya* or place of entertainment, and the Wachigaiya, an *okiya* ("storehouse") or residence from which the women were summoned. The Sumiya (1670s, revamped in 1787) is a two-story wooden building, its *shoji*-screened windows protected by wooden grills. One of

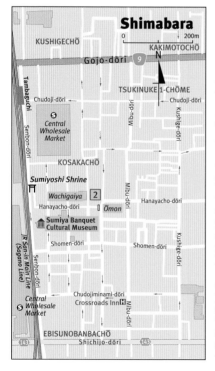

Shimabara

KUSHIGECHŌ

KAKIMOTOCHŌ

Gojo-dōri   9   N

0   200m

Tambaguchi

Chudoji-dōri

TSUKINUKE 1-CHŌME

Chudoji-dōri

Jōjō-mību

Kushige-dōri

Central Wholesale Market

Senbon-dōri

KOSAKACHŌ

Sumiyoshi Shrine

Wachigaiya   2

Hanayacho-dōri   *Ōmon*   Hanayacho-dōri

Mibu-dōri

Kushige-dōri

Sumiya Banquet Cultural Museum

Shomen-dōri   Shomen-dōri

JR San-in Main Line (Sagano Line)

Senbon-dōri

Chudojiminami-dōri

Central Wholesale Market   Crossroads Inn

Mibu-dōri

EBISUNOBANBACHŌ

Shichijo-dōri

A procession each April re-creates the era when Shimabara was a flourishing and popular district.

the more important buildings of the former pleasure quarter, it is today a private building available as an *ochaya*, a tea house, by private reservation for more sedate modern entertainment.

(In recent years, as the Sumiya Banquet Cultural Museum, it is open from 10:00 a.m. to 4:00 p.m., closed Mondays and from mid-December until the end of January. Entry fee.) The building has been preserved fairly closely to its original condition. The interior was richly decorated with finely painted *fusuma* (sliding screens), *ramma* (transoms) with cutout work in the form of hearts or fans, and some ceilings can even boast of painted fans. Transoms and *fusuma* that served as window screens and entry screens varied, giving each room its own very special character. You enter the front gate of the Sumiya into a courtyard with the entry alcove on the right. Ahead is the entrance to the kitchens. As in any proper villa, some of the rooms have a raised platform (*jodan*) and a built-in desk and even arched windows, *tokonoma* and *chigaidana* (staggered shelves), all of which show the influence of Zen architecture even in the pleasure quarter. One of the more sumptuous rooms on the upper floor has its decorative

elements inlaid with mother of pearl. In other words, the stylized ideal for aristocratic residences and tea houses was the model for these houses of pleasure.

The Wachigaiya, originally a residence for the *tayu* of Shimabara, has been greatly remodeled since it first appeared on a 1716 map, but it still exists as a building even if its interior no longer reflects the layout it once enjoyed. The Wachigaiya is now a private tea house that is open for guided tours and occasional events. (Inquiries can be made at the Tourist Information Office.)

Another aspect of the past also remains: the Kaburenjo Theater still exists in Shimabara since the theater was always an important part of the pleasure quarters

When a *tayu* was summoned to an *ageya*, she made her way regally through the streets on her high wooden *geta* (clogs), a richly decorated robe over her *kimono*, with its large *obi* worn in the front. Her fancy oiled umbrella (*kasa*) protected her elegant hairstyle, which was enhanced with hairpins and tortoiseshell combs. She was accompanied by a more simply dressed female attendant. The spectacle of Shimabara's past is partially revived in a festival held on the third Sunday of each April at the Josho-ji Temple, in which the Dochu (Procession of Tayu) is re-enacted. (The Josho-ji is in the northern Kyoto, not the Shimabara district. The ceremony takes place here since a noted *tayu* connected with the temple donated its main gateway and is buried here.)

GETTING THERE

To-ji Temple lies to the north of Kujo-dori (Ninth Street) and west of Omiya-dori, approximately a 10–15 minute walk southwest of Kyoto Station. Buses 19, 20 or 208 to To-ji-minami-mon-mae (the south gate on Kujo-dori) or 207 to To-ji-higashi-mon-mae (the east gate on Omiya-dori) go to the temple, which is open from 8:30 a.m. to 5:30 p.m. but 4:30 p.m. from September to March. Most of the grounds can be entered without charge but there is an entry fee to the area of the main buildings and a separate fee to the Treasury.

At the completion of this tour, a return to Omiya-dori, or to the intersection of Shichijo-dori and Omiya-dori, or to the intersection of Omiya-dori and Gojo-dori brings you to various bus lines for all parts of the city.

Walking Tour 11

TOFUKU-JI AREA
An Imperial Burial Ground and a Zen Monastary

1 **Sennyu-ji Temple** 泉涌寺
2 **Tofuku-ji Temple** 東福寺

As mentioned at the beginning of Tour 10, the hills to the north, east and west of Kyoto have provided a natural barrier about the city, but the way to the south has always been open toward Osaka and the Inland Sea. The original southern boundary of the city lay at Kujo-dori (9th Street) where the great Rasho-mon gate provided a grand entrance, the capital being protected by To-ji (East Temple) and Sai-ji (West Temple) to either side of the Rasho-mon. The temples may have offered the city spiritual protection, but they were little barrier to any armed foe. This lack of a barrier in the area to the south of the city was remedied at the end of the 1500s when Toyotomi Hideyoshi built his great Fushimi Castle to protect the city from the south (a replica, which is a semi-amusement park, now stands near its original location).

The area below Kujo-dori in Hideyoshi's day, and even later, was still open countryside interspersed with a few shrines and temples.

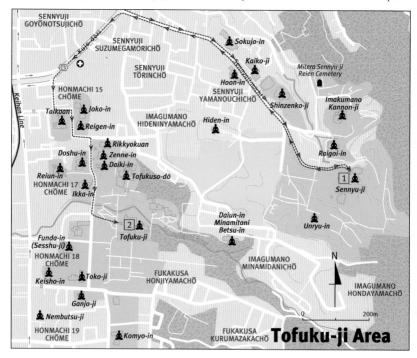

Tofuku-ji Area

In time, the Tokugawas dismantled Fushimi Castle, for under their strict rule there was little chance of revolt against the Shogun government–until the beginning of the breakdown and final dissolution of their rule in the mid-19th century. Then, in the late 19th century, the railroad came to Kyoto, and, with its eventual realignment and the addition of the Kintetsu and the Shinkansen rail lines, Kyoto Station and the raised railroad tracks today form a new "barrier" at Hachijo-dori (Eighth Street). This new "barrier," however, has been no more effective than the Sai-ji or the To-ji Temples were, and the modern city now spreads to the south of this "barrier" and even beyond Fushimi, engulfing old temples and shrines in the growth of the modern city of Kyoto.

The Rasho-mon gateway and the Sai-in Temple disappeared with time, and the ancient To-ji Temple alone remains. In the early middle ages, new temples appeared at the southern edge of Kyoto. The burial site of the Emperors was established at the Sennyu-ji Temple, just to the south and east of the original boundaries of the city, and then, with the coming of Zen Buddhism to Japan, the Tofuku-ji Temple also developed to the southeast as one of the great centers of Zen in Kyoto.

South of the Tofuku-ji, the ancient Shinto shrine to Inari continued to hold sway, ever growing in esteem and wealth and covering its portion of the eastern range of mountains with its thousands of vermilion *torii* gates. Other shrines came into being, the Jonan-gu and the Goko-no-miya, among them, which once served as palace sites for the Emperors. Even today Emperors inhabit the area, albeit in their graves in the Fushimi-Momoyama area, where the first and the last Emperors to reign in Kyoto–Kammu and Meiji–are now entombed.

Further to the south of Kyoto, villas of the aristocracy of Heian and later times were to be created along the Uji River toward the village of Uji, some of these becoming temples for the sake of the souls of their former owners after their demise. Most noted of the villas that became a temple is the Byodo-in, one of the loveliest of temples in the region, as well as the Hokai-ji, now hidden away in suburban reaches of Kyoto. The ancient Daigo-ji Temple and its allied Sambo-in up the Yamashina Valley were revived in time, and these two temples reflect not only the early years of religious settlement of the

Kyoto area but the splendor which Toyotomi Hideyoshi demanded for the garden he planned at the Sambo-in.

Thus the area to the south of Kyoto developed. If its former villas often became temples, its one-time palaces became shrines, and the religious life of Kyoto continued to be enriched both spiritually and artistically. These sites beyond the city proper are worthy of a few days of exploration. They run the gamut of an unusual Chinese-inspired monastic site in the Mampuku-ji, the striking "tunnel" of *torii* with which devotees of the Inari Shrine have covered the mountain behind that early shrine, to the Momoyama period inspired garden at the Sambo-in of more than 800 rocks, a garden which Toyotomi Hideyoshi is said to have designed. Less than 15 to 30 minutes away from central Kyoto, these areas are well served by the Keihan Electric Railway, Japan Rail, the Kintetsu Rail Line, and by buses from the heart of the city. They offer yet another sample of the amazing variety which Kyoto and its environs have to offer the visitor.

When Kyoto was established in 794, there was one experience the Emperor Kammu had faced in the former capital of Nara that he did not wish to encounter again: the interference in the governance of the nation by the Buddhist clergy. Thus he planned his new capital so that the Buddhist temples would be outside the city gates rather than within the capital itself. Two Buddhist temples, however, were permitted to be established at the southern entrance to the city: the Sai-ji (West Temple) and the To-ji (East Temple), a brief distance to either side of the Rasho-mon, the main entrance gate to Heian-kyo (Kyoto). The Sai-ji was ravaged by fire in time, and by the year 1200 it had ceased to exist; today a plaque marks its one-time location, the only reminder of its original existence. The Rasho-mon gateway declined with the years as well, serving as time went by as the city morgue before it also passed into oblivion and is remembered primarily by a marker and a 20th century movie of note.

The To-ji Temple, however, lives on due to the efforts of Kukai (Kobo Daishi, 774–835) who rejuvenated the temple and turned it into a bastion of Shingon Buddhist belief. The Shingon sect of Buddhism has a mystic bent to it (it is related to Tantric Buddhism, which had its strength in Tibet). Kukai's To-ji Lecture Hall (Kodo) was filled with Buddhist images arranged in the pattern of a mystic mandala. Shingon doctrines, according to Kukai, had the power to protect the state, and thus the temple gained the patronage of the Emperor despite the Imperial desire to keep Buddhism at a comfortable arm's length distance. The temple continues to flourish, and one of the more interesting times to visit it is on the 21st of each month when the monthly fair in honor of Kukai is held. Then the temple grounds are filled with stalls selling every conceivable type of goods from antiques to art objects, to textiles and food.

The Sennyu-ji Temple is the least known of the three temples in this section, partially due to its out-of-the-way location despite its being comparatively close to the center of Kyoto city. From 1242 until 1866 it was the burial place of most of the Imperial line, the last Emperor to be interred in its grounds being the Emperor Komei (reigned 1846–66), the father of the Emperor Meiji, who died just prior to the removal of the capital to Tokyo. The Tofuku-ji Temple, the third of the temples in this chapter, was one of early Zen temples and, despite damage by fire in the last century, it retains buildings and gardens of major interest. Its gardens are of particular note since they have all been designed within the 20th century, and they therefore provide a view of the direction of garden design in the post-classical era of Zen gardens.

To-ji is the most important of these three temples, but it was covered in Tour 9. Kukai not only established the To-ji as an important temple in the new capital of Kyoto, but he is credited with establishing many other temples as well, some of which he did, a number of which it is doubtful he could have created. He did have an association with the Sennyu-ji temple, but its importance is more concerned with the Imperial family than with this important priest of the 9th century. The Sennyu-ji Temple is 1 mile (1.6 km) southeast of the Sanjusangen-do Temple, to the south of the main line railway overpass on Higashi-oji-dori just before it bends to head into Kujo-dori; the fourth road on the left after the railroad leads to the Sennyu-ji Temple and the Imperial burial grounds.

1 SENNYU-JI TEMPLE

The Sennyu-ji Temple (also known as Mitera, the Imperial Temple) served as the mortuary temple for the Imperial family from the burial of Emperor Shijo in January 1242 to that of

Emperor Komei in December 1866, the last Imperial burial at this temple. (Komei's son, the Emperor Meiji, was buried in an overly ostentatious tomb on Momoyama hill just south of Fushimi. Komei's grandson, Emperor Taisho and great-grandson, Emperor Showa (Hirohito), are buried outside of Tokyo.)

HISTORY Kobo Daishi, the founder of the Shingon sect, built a simple hermitage at this site between 824 and 833. He called it Horin-ji (Temple of the Wheel of the Law). The temple that succeeded this small hermitage in 885 eventually fell into ruin, but was revived in 1218 by Priest Shunjo. The site lay in a hollow surrounded by pine-clad hills, and the name of the temple, Sennyu-ji (Water of the Bubbling Spring), derived from a spring that flowed under a cliff near the main hall of the complex and which was considered to have arisen miraculously. The Emperor Shijo (reigned 1232–42) had great respect for Priest Shunjo, who had studied Buddhism in China for 12 years and who became abbot at the Sennyu-ji after his return from China. Shunjo enforced the proper rules of Buddhist discipline for his monks, and he also became the founding patriarch of the Hokkyo Ritsu form of Buddhism. Although dedicated to the Ritsu sect, the temple served as a seminary for the study of the teachings of the Tendai, Shingon, Zen and Jodo schools of Buddhism as well. So impressed was Emperor Shijo by Shunjo's learning and sanctity, he directed that, upon his death, he (the Emperor) be interred at Shunjo's temple. Thus in 1242, with the Emperor's death, began the interment of 14 generations of Emperors over the next six centuries.

PRESENT STRUCTURES AND GROUNDS

On the road leading up to the Sennyu-ji Temple, you pass the Sokujo-in, a subtemple of Sennyu-ji. In it are an image of Amida and the 25 disciples of Amida, the latter originally having been at the Fushimi-dera at Momo-yama just south of here. All but three of the 25 disciples are original figures.

The entry gate to the 57 acres (22.8 ha) that surround the Sennyu-ji Temple at the base of Mount Tsukinowa originally was a gateway to the Imperial Palace, a gift from Oda Nobunaga (1534–82). The present temple buildings were erected in 1668, and the Imperial tombs and stone memorials lie behind the temple to the north of the Reimei-

The Shari-den (Hall of Sacred Ashes) at Sennyu-ji Temple was originally part of the Imperial Palace.

den (Hall of Spirits). To the right of the gate is the ticket booth and beyond that, further to the right, is the Kyozo (Sutra Storage Hall). The Kannon-do, to the left just beyond the entry gateway, has a Yohiki Kannon image, created in memory of and as a prayer for the soul of Yohiki (Yang Kuei Fei), the beautiful beloved of the 8th century Chinese Emperor Hsuen Tsang of the T'ang dynasty. It is said to have been commissioned by that Emperor, and was brought to Japan in 1225 by the Japanese priest Tankei. Whether it was commissioned by the Emperor, and whether it is the original life-like image of Yohiki, is open to debate since many art critics consider it to be an example of Song art (906–1127) of a later date. (Yang Kuei Fei was a cruel and deceitful individual, and she was strangled by order of the Emperor's army despite the Emperor's devotion to her.)

The path leading from the main gateway to the Butsu-den (Buddha or Main Hall) has at its end on the right a Bath House for the monks, while across from it on a slight hill is the Chinju Shrine, a Shinto shrine protecting the temple. To the right, before the Butsu-den, is the Sennyu-sui (Water of the Bubbling Spring) for which the temple was named, the original "miraculous" spring of the temple, which is now enclosed in a covered grotto.

The Butsu-den, the large building at the end of the main path from the entry gateway, is a fascinating building due to the intricate internal interlocking wooden structure of its roof. It has three images as the main objects of veneration instead of the normal single image. They are Shaka (in the center) with Miroku on his right and Amida on his left, each seated on a lotus blossom. The ceiling before the images has a painting of a dragon by Kano Sansetsu, a dragon image called Nakiru since the echo which results when you clap your hands creates a noise similar to the sound of a dragon's cry—according to those who have evidently experienced a dragon and his sound. The wooden wall behind the three images is painted on its reverse side with an image of Amida. On either side in the rear of the building is a large Chinese chair; in the left rear corner is a shrine case with three monks seated on Chinese chairs, while in the rear right corner is a shrine case with another three images in Chinese attire together with two guardians.

Behind the Butsu-den is the Shari-den (Hall of Sacred Ashes), which is not open to the public. The building was originally a structure of the Imperial Palace, and it was moved here to serve as the Shari-den in 1714. Beyond and to the southeast of the Shari-den is the Reimei-den (Hall of Souls) where are enshrined 130 memorial tablets for the emperors from the 38th Emperor (Tenchi), as well as Imperial consorts, princes and princesses. Before the Reimei-den is a Kara-mon, a Chinese gateway. To the rear of the Reimei-den, on higher ground beyond a fence, is the Tsukinowa-ryo, the tombs of the Imperial families from 1242 to 1866, and beyond the Imperial cemetery, is the Kaisan-do (Founder's Hall) dedicated to Priest Shunjo, the founder of the temple. Neither the grave-yard nor the Kaisan-do are open to the public. To the left of the Reimei-den is a closed area that has at its entry the Chokushi-mon (Imperial Messenger's Gate), which leads to the private Gozasho (Resting Hall for the Imperial Family.) The Honbo, the Abbot's Quarters, to the left of the Remei-den, was once part of the Imperial Palace at the begin-ning of the Meiji period (1868). It was a gift to the temple when the capital and palace were established in Tokyo after 1868.

An insignificant little wooden bridge, the Yume-no-uki-hashi (Floating Bridge of Dreams), lies between the Sennyu-ji and the neighboring Tofuku-ji Temple to the south and west. At the time of Imperial interments in the past, fruits and other perishable offerings to the dead Emperor were thrown into the stream beneath the bridge as the burial pro-cession moved slowly at midnight to the burial site. The chief treasure of the temple is a sup-posed tooth of the Buddha, said to have been brought from China by the third abbot. It is kept in a finely designed 14th to 16th century gilt metal reliquary in the shape of a pagoda about 3 feet (1 m) tall. The tooth is exceedingly large and probably came from a horse. It is exhibited on October 8th annually.

Each year, from April 15 to 17, the Nehan-e takes place. This is a ceremony in which the temple displays its Nehan-zu, a very large painting 26 by 52.5 feet (7.8 m by 15.8 m) showing the Buddha's death and achieving Nirvana. This largest representation of the death of the Buddha is a 16th century work by Abbot Meiyo. Its figures are life size and colorful. The painting contains the image of a cat, an unusual occurrence for such paintings since a cat often symbolizes unfaithfulness. According to legend, a cat was seated near the artist when he was painting the picture. Having painted the cat into the picture, the artist is reputed to have said to the cat, "So you want to enter Nirvana also?" At this the cat disappeared and was seen no more.

In addition, a *kakemono* of the 500 *rakan* (individuals who have achieved enlighten-ment while still living) by Cho Densu is on display and flower arrangements are also on view (9:00 a.m. to 4:30 p.m.).

2 TOFUKU-JI TEMPLE

The next temple in this tour is Tofuku-ji, a Zen temple, and thus one not associated with Kukai. Along with Daitoku-ji, Shokoku-ji, Kennin-ji, Tenryu-ji and Myoshin-ji, Tofuku-ji is one of the most important Zen Buddhist temples in Kyoto, and at one time it was the leading seat of Buddhism in the capital. This Rinzai sect temple was founded in 1236, but

San-mon Gate at Tofuku-ji Temple, the oldest Zen main gate in Japan and a National Treasure.

The Tsuten-kyo Bridge across the pond in front of the double-roofed San-mon Gate at Tofuku-ji.

most of the temple was destroyed by a fire in 1881, at which time it lost its 49 foot (14.7 m) tall Daibutsu (Great Buddha) image, which has not been replaced. Thus the present seven major buildings are replacements built primarily between 1911 and 1932. The temple is particularly noted for three of its gardens, two of which are 20th century creations.

HISTORY The Tofuku-ji Temple was created in 1236 by Michiie Fujiwara near the site of Fujiwara Michinaga's Hosho-ji Temple. The location was symbolic since it hearkened back to the great days 200 years previously of Fujiwara Michinaga's rule, and it was meant to serve as a continuing symbol of the importance of the Fujiwara family to stable governance in Japan. Even its name, Tofuku-ji, is symbolic since it represents a contraction of the names of the two great temples of Nara, the Todai-ji and the Kofuku-ji. The temple was 19 years in construction, and on its completion the first Superior of the temple was Ben-en (d. 1279). The Tofuku-ji proved to be a popular temple to various rulers, and it was added to by Shoguns Ashikaga Yoshimochi (1386–1428), Toyotomi Hideyoshi (1536–98) and Tokugawa Ieyasu (1542–1616).

PRESENT STRUCTURES AND GROUNDS
The Tofuku-ji Temple has three gates, the Chokushi-mon (Imperial Messenger's Gate) facing west, the Rokuhara-mon and the two-

story double-roofed San-mon, both facing to the south, with a rectangular pond with a bridge crossing it in front of the San-mon to the south. The temple buildings beyond the San-mon are all aligned on a north–south axis. The Chokushi-mon (Imperial Messenger's Gate) was a gift from the Emperor Kameyama in 1268, and it originally formed a part of the Imperial Palace. The Rokuhara-mon Gate had at one time been a gateway to the Rokuhara headquarters in Kyoto of the Kamakura military Shoguns (1185–1333). The San-mon is the most important as well as the most impressive of the three gates. Built about 1250 to 1275, it is a copy of the Nandai-mon Gate of the Todai-ji Temple in Nara. Fires in 1319, 1334 and 1336 seriously damaged the temple, and the gateway was among the structures that were destroyed. It was rebuilt by 1425, and was repaired under Toyotomi Hideyoshi in the 1590s. In 1969, the gate was disassembled and was reopened in 1978, having been completely refurbished.

Standing 72 feet (21.6 m) high, the San-mon Gate is a two-story structure. On the second level is a large hall with images carved by Jocho (d. 1057). The central image of the Buddha is a 16th century work by the monk Koei. The ceiling paintings of clouds and *apsara* (angels) are by Cho Densu (also known as Micho, 1352–1431), a temple monk who lived his entire life here, assisted by his student Kan Densu from China. The central

The checkerboard garden at Tofuku-ji's Hojo.

image of the Buddha is accompanied by 16 *arhat* (individuals who have achieved enlightenment in this existence), eight on each side of the Buddha. The framed tablet on the outside of the gate is in the calligraphy of Shogun Ashikaga Yoshimochi. An outside stairway that begins at a covered portico on the east and west sides of the gate leads to the second floor hall. This second floor of the gateway is only open to the public in November. (Entry fee.)

To the west of the San-mon gateway are two noted buildings, both concerned with cleanliness, an important element in Japanese culture. The smaller of the two buildings to the south is the Tosu (Lavatory), and to its north is the Yokushitsu (Steam Bath). Both buildings are from the early 15th century. The Yokushitsu could accommodate 350 monks at a time. These buildings can be viewed from the outside through their window openings.

To the northwest of the San-mon is the Zen-do, the Meditation Hall for the monks where they could sit in *zazen* (meditation), an important element in Zen training and worship. To the north of the San-mon is the Hondo (Main Hall), a 1932 reconstruction after the 1882 fire. Its main image is that of

Shaka and his two assistants, all three protected by four small Shi-tenno guardians. Its ceiling bears a huge dragon painted by the modern artist Domoto Insho. Here, on March 15th of each year the large painting "The Entry of the Buddha Sakyamuni into Nirvana" (39.5 by 59 feet) (12 by 18 m) is exhibited. East of the San-mon, a set of steps leads to the Shinto shrine that protects the temple. (The Hondo is open 9:00 a.m. to 4:30 p.m. Entry fee.)

The Hojo (Abbot's Quarters) and its gardens were destroyed in the 1881 fire. The Hojo was rebuilt in 1890, but the four gardens were not recreated until 1939 by Shigemori Mirei (1895–1975), and then they were laid out in a modern format, although designed in the spirit of Zen aesthetics. The South Garden in front of the Hojo (on the south) is composed of four rock groupings meant to symbolize the Horai, the Blessed Isles (from east to west: Eiju, Horai, Koryo and Hojo). These compositions are set in raked sand, this sea of sand being called Hakkai (Eight Rough Seas). In the right corner on the west are five moss-covered "sacred mountains." (The Hojo and gardens are open 9:00 a.m. to 4:30 p.m. Entry fee.)

The Hojo's Western Garden consists of moss and azalea bushes trimmed in a checkered pattern in imitation of a Chinese method of dividing the land. In the North Garden, north of the Hojo, facing the Tsuten Bridge and Sengyokuken Gorge, square-cut stones and moss make up the design of the garden, the small squares of stone being distributed in a loosely checkered manner. This garden overlooks the gorge of the Sengyokuken where the maple trees are a blaze of color in the autumn. The Eastern Garden has been created from five cylindrical stones in a moss setting so as to represent the main stars of the Big Dipper. These stones originally formed part of the base of temple buildings that no longer exist.

The grounds of Tofuku-ji are split by the Sengyokuken Gorge, which runs from east to west. Three bridges cross the ravine, the middle one being the Tsuten-kyo, the Bridge of Heaven. A covered bridge built on tall stilts to span the deep ravine, with a tiled roof and a lookout over the gorge, it is itself an attractive addition to the maple-clad sides of the ravine. (Fee to cross the bridge.) Across the Tsuten-kyo Bridge is the Kaisan-do (Founder's Hall) with a statue of Priest Ben-en, the first

Section of a stone garden at Tofuku-ji Temple.

Superior (Abbot) of the temple. A large roofed gateway provides an entrance to the Edo period (1616–1868) garden of the Kaisan-do. A stone path down the middle of the garden leads to the Founder's Hall and divides the garden in two. The western half of the garden consists of a fascinating raked sand dry garden in a precise checkerboard pattern. In one corner, the traditional crane and tortoise motif can be found in the use of moss, rocks, trimmed bushes and one tree; on the east side of the walk is a pond crossed by a stone bridge. Plantings close the vista on the east, and trimmed bushes and stones enrich the area about the pond.

Enshrined in the Ryugen-an is a wooden image of Mukan Fumon (Daimyo Kokushi), a monk who studied at the Tofuku-ji under Ben-en and who became the founder and the first Superior of the Nanzen-ji Temple in Kyoto. In Fumon's wood image, a wood and crystal reliquary was found in the shape of a rosewood *gorinto* (a small five-part stupa), with a crystal jar wrapped in brocade and containing a small rosary, a small sutra scroll and *shari* (a relic of a portion of the body of a Buddhist saint). These elements vested the image with the spirit of the individual represented. This naturalistic statue was created shortly after Fumon's death in 1291. (The Ryugen-an is usually open in the autumn; inquire at the Tourist Information Office in downtown Kyoto.)

The Funda-in (Sesshu-in), a subtemple of Tofuku-ji just to the west of the main grounds, was founded in 1321 by Sozan Jozin. Sesshu (1420–1506), the noted painter, stayed here on a visit to Kyoto. He was eventually asked to compose the garden of the Funda-in. Fire and lack of care in time ruined the garden, but in 1939 it was recreated by Shigemori Mirei using classical Japanese motifs. The garden is in two parts, one south of the Funda-in Hojo and the other to its east. The south garden employs the traditional crane and tortoise symbolism—two rock groupings in moss form "islands" in a sea of raked sand. The "island" on the west is the Tortoise Island while the second one to the east is the Crane Island. The eastern garden has a Chinese theme with the "Mountain of the Immortals" (Horai). (This garden is open 9:00 a.m. to 4:00 p.m. Entry fee.)

The Shokaku-an subtemple of the Tofuku-ji is also known as the Temple of Writing Brushes. The temple has a tomb for such brushes, and each year on November 23rd a memorial service is held for brushes, pencils and pens from all over Japan. A procession of hundreds of *yamabushi* (itinerant Buddhist priests) and a *chigo* (page boy) march to the temple. Many of the *yamabushi* carry large bamboo stalks in the shape of writing brushes. Thousands of used brushes, many brought by boys and girls, are hurled into a fire in the precincts of the temple. Prayers to Buddha are said by youngsters for the betterment of their ability in calligraphy and their studies. From 2:00 p.m.

GETTING THERE

Take bus 202 or 207 or 208 to the Sennyu-ji-michi bus stop. The temple is a long walk upgrade—a taxi would be helpful to the temple gate. The Sennyu-ji is a central temple of the Shingon sect of Buddhism and it is open from 9:00 a.m. to 4:30 p.m. daily. Entry fee.

Tofuku-ji Temple is located on the eastern side of Kyoto between Kujo-dori and Jujo-dori. The Tofuku-ji station of Japan Rail as well as the Keihan electric railway are the closest rail stations to the temple to the southeast of the station. Bus 6 or 16 from Shijo-Karasuma also serves the temple. The temple is 1 mile (1.6 km) southeast of Kyoto Station, and is open from 9:00 a.m. to 4:00 p.m. Entry fee.

A return to the center of Kyoto can be made by bus 6 or 16 from the main highway to the west of the temple grounds or by train from the Tofuku-ji station to the northwest of the temple.

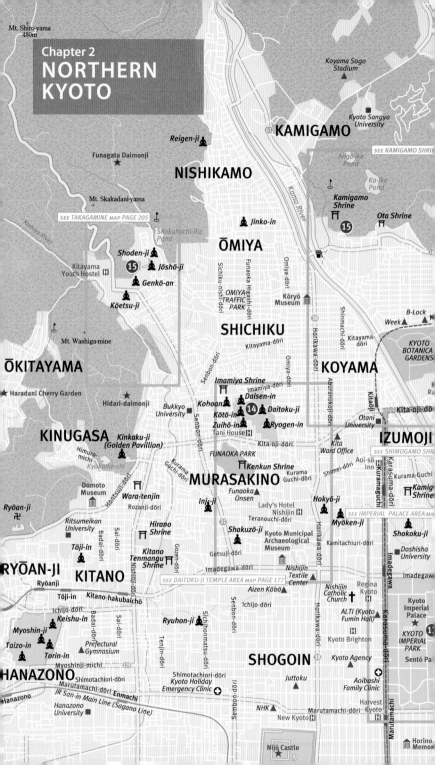

Mt. Shiro-yama
480m

Koyama Sogo
Stadium

Reigen-ji

Funagata Daimonji

KAMIGAMO

Kyoto Sangyo
University

Ango-ike
Pond

SEE KAMIGAMO SHRI

NISHIKAMO

Ko-ike
Pond

Mt. Skakadani-yama

Kamigamo
Shrine

SEE TAKAGAMINE map PAGE 205

Jinko-in

Ota Shrine

Shakuhachi-ike
Pond

ŌMIYA

Shoden-ji

Jōshō-ji

Kitayama
Youth Hostel

Genkō-an

Kōryō
Museum

B-Lock

Week

KYOTO
BOTANICA
GARDENS

Kōetsu-ji

OMIYA
TRAFFIC
PARK

Mt. Washiga-mine

ŌKITAYAMA

SHICHIKU

Kitayama-dōri

KOYAMA

Haradani Cherry Garden

Hidari-daimonji

Bukkyo
University

Imamiya Shrine

Imamiya-dōri

Kohoan

Daisen-in

Daitoku-ji

Kita-oji-dō

Kōtō-in

KINUGASA

Kinkaku-ji
(Golden Pavillion)

Zuihō-in

Ryogen-in

Tani House

Kita-oji-dōri

Otani
University

IZUMOJI

Himuro-
michi

Kyōkōike-chi

FUNAOKA PARK

Kita
Ward Office

SEE SHIMOGAMO SHR

Domoto
Museum

Kenkun Shrine

Aoi-sō
Inn

Kurama-Guchi

Ryōan-ji

Wara-tenjin

MURASAKINO

Kurama
Guchi-dōri

Shimei-dōri

Kamig
Shrine

Rozanji-dōri

Funaoka
Onsen

Hokyō-ji

Ritsumeikan
University

Hirano
Shrine

Inji-ji

Lady's Hotel
Nishijin

Myōken-ji

Shokoku-ji

Tōji-in

Teranouchi-dōri

Shakuzō-ji

Kyoto Municipal
Archaeological
Museum

Kamitachiuri-dōri

Doshisha
University

RYŌAN-JI

Ryōanji

KITANO

Kitano
Tenmangu
Shrine

Gotsuji-dōri

Imadegawa-dōri

Nishijin
Textile
Center

Imadegawa

Tōji-in

Kitano-hakubaichō

Aizen Kōbō

Nishijin
Catholic
Church

Regina
Kyoto

Kyoto
Imperial
Palace

Keishu-in

Ryuhon-ji

Ichijo-dōri

ALTI (Kyoto
Fumin Hall)

KYOTO
IMPERIAL
PARK

Myoshin-ji

Kyoto Brighton

Taizo-in

Prefectural
Gymnasium

Kyoto Agency

Sentō Pa

Torin-in

Myoshinji-michi

SHOGOIN

HANAZONO

Shimotachiori-dōri
Kyoto Holiday
Emergency Clinic

Juttoku

Aoibashi
Family Clinic

Harvest
Kyoto

Marutamachi-dōri Enmachi

JR San-in Main Line (Sagano Line)

NHK

Marutamachi-dōri

Hanazono
University

New Kyoto

Horino
Memo

Nijō Castle

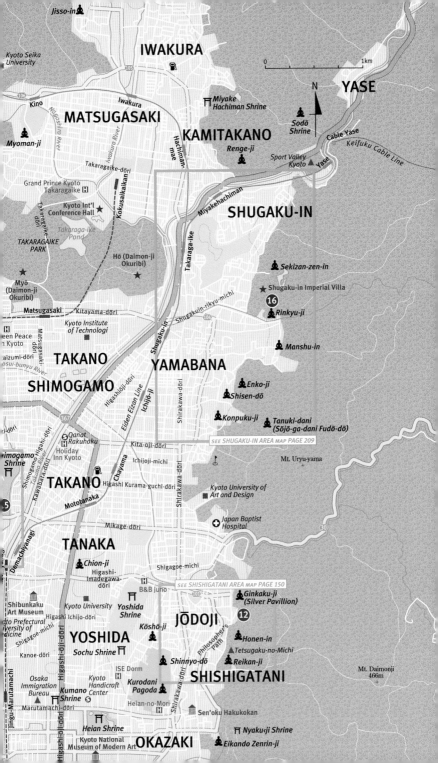

Jisso-in

Kyoto Seika University

IWAKURA

YASE

0   1km

N

Kino

Iwakura

105

MATSUGASAKI

Myoman-ji

Miyake Hachiman Shrine

KAMITAKANO

Hachiman-mae

Renge-ji

Sodō Shrine

Sport Valley Kyoto

Cable Yase

Yase

Keifuku Cable Line

Takaragaike-dōri

Grand Prince Kyoto Takaragaike

Kyoto Int'l Conference Hall

Kokusaikaikan

Miyakehachiman

SHUGAKU-IN

TAKARAGAIKE PARK

Takaraga-ike Pond

Takaragaike-dōri

Hō (Daimon-ji Okuribi)

Takaraga-ike

Sekizan-zen-in

Myō (Daimon-ji Okuribi)

Shugaku-in Imperial Villa

Matsugasaki

Kitayama-dōri

Kyoto Institute of Technologi

16

Rinkyu-ji

Shugakuin-rikyu-michi

Shugaku-in

104

Manshu-in

Green Peace in Kyoto

Matsugasaki-dōri

TAKANO

Takano-izumi-dōri

Takanosui-bunyu River

SHIMOGAMO

YAMABANA

Enko-ji

Shisen-dō

Higashijoji-dōri

Eizan Eizan Line

Ichijō-ji

Shirakawa-dōri

Konpuku-ji

Tanuki-dani (Sōjō-ga-dani Fudō-dō)

367

Qanat Rakuhoku

Kita-ōji-dōri

SEE SHUGAKU-IN AREA MAP PAGE 209

Shimogamo Shrine

Holiday Inn Kyoto

Ichijoji-michi

Mt. Uryu-yama

Shimogamo-Hirahi-dōri

Takano River

Kawabata-dōri

Chayama

Ichijoji-michi

TAKANO

Higashi Kurama-guchi-dōri

Mototanaka

30

Mikage-dōri

Kyoto University of Art and Design

5

Demachiyanagi

Japan Baptist Hospital

TANAKA

Chion-ji

Higashi-Imadegawa-dōri

Shigagoe-michi

Shibunkaku Art Museum

to Prefectural iversity of edicine

Kyoto University

Yoshida Shrine

B&B Juno

SEE SHISHIGATANI AREA MAP PAGE 150

Ginkaku-ji (Silver Pavillion)

12

101

Higashi Ichijo-dōri

Kōshō-ji

JŌDOJI

Honen-in

YOSHIDA

Sochu Shrine

Shinnyo-dō

Tetsugaku-no-Michi

Reikan-ji

Shigagoe-michi

ISE Dorm

Kanoe-dōri

Higashioji-dōri

Kyoto Handicraft Center

Kurodani Pagoda

SHISHIGATANI

Osaka Immigration Bureau

Kumano Shrine

Heian-no-Mori

Mt. Daimonji 466m

Marutamachi-dōri

Jingū-Marutamachi

Sen'oku Hakukokan

Heian Shrine

Nyakuji Shrine

Kyoto National Museum of Modern Art

OKAZAKI

Eikando Zenrin-ji

Walking Tour 12

SHISHIGATANI AREA
The Silver Pavilion and the Philosopher's Path

1. **Hakusason-so Villa** 白沙村荘
2. **Jodo-ji Temple** 浄土院
3. **Ginkaku-ji Temple (Silver Pavilion)** 銀閣寺
4. **The Philosopher's Path** 哲学の道
5. **Honen-in Temple** 法然院
6. **Anraku-ji Temple** 安楽寺

The Shishigatani area along the foot of the Higashiyama mountains in eastern Kyoto is one of the more delightful sections of the city, with a private garden of a traditional artist, the artistic retreat of a medieval Shogun, and its quiet and charming hillside temples. With the exception of the Ginkaku-ji Temple (Silver Pavilion), it is a section the tourist agencies usually overlook since it is not conducive to the easy herding of groups of tourists. Yet this portion of the city is a favorite one for the citizens of Kyoto and for knowledgeable visitors who have long enjoyed the Tetsugaku-no-michi (The Philosopher's Path), which borders a canal.

The Silver Pavilion at the beginning of this walk was a Shogun's toy, his palatial villa where he could ignore the vicissitudes of war,

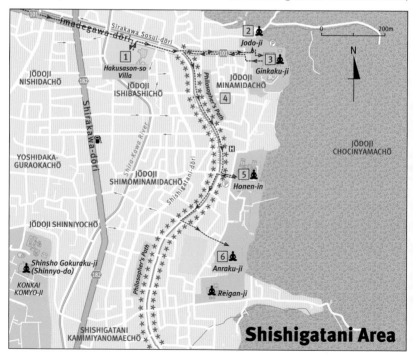

Shishigatani Area

The garden pond and tea house of Hakusason-so Villa, the former home of an artist.

starvation and famine that were rampant in Kyoto in his day. Here, in the northeast part of Kyoto, beyond the city itself, he and his friends could turn life into an art and create and enjoy new aesthetic pleasures despite the horrors of war around them.

The era was one of important cultural advances despite the dreadful conditions in Kyoto for the mass of people, and yet it was a period which set the standards for Japanese taste, creating those elements that are often regarded as purely Japanese, from the use of *shoji* and *tatami* to the development of the tea ceremony, *Noh* theater and other cultural elements. Influenced by the Chinese culture which Japanese Zen monks brought to Japan and to the court, the well-to-do created their paradise here on earth while the majority of the people had only the hope of a heavenly paradise through their devotions to Amida and entry into his Western Paradise after death. Thus it is somewhat ironic that the Philosopher's Path moves from the earthly glories of the Silver Pavilion to the humble temples of the Honen-in and the Anraku-ji, where the worship of Amida brought hope for the future at a time when life on earth was so bitter for those caught in the midst of famine, disease and war, with all of its misery.

Just outside the Silver Pavilion, along the canal of the Philosopher's Path, are several small restaurants where you can enjoy a simple lunch as you stroll from site to site.

Alternately, you might sit on a bench along the canal and enjoy an *o-bento* lunch purchased in advance. On the eastern side of the canal are the lovely Honen-in and Anraku-ji Temples, both with thatch-roofed gateways, that lead to a main hall where Amida is revered. Other temples, shrines and tombs enrich the walk, but it is the path itself and its environs that make the visit to the sites worthy of a full day's enjoyment in one of the lovelier corners of a fascinating city.

① HAKUSASON-SO VILLA

The walk begins at a handsome private garden at the far eastern end of Imadegawa-dori, just before the pathway to Ginkaku-ji (Silver Pavilion) at the Hakusason-so Villa. The villa and its gardens are on the right hand side of the street and are open from 10:00 a.m. to 5:00 p.m. Entry fee.

HAKUSASON-SO VILLA The painter Kansetsu Hashimoto (1883–1945) was one of those happy individuals whose artistic abilities were recognized in his day and who was able to create his own form of an earthly paradise near the pleasure palace of a one-time Shogun. The Hakusason-so, built in 1916, was his private villa, and here he not only had his residence but his studio as well. Kansetsu painted in the traditional style, and a small gallery behind the villa exhibits selections of his work on a rotating basis, as well as objects of Greek and Persian pottery, Chinese clay figures, Indian miniatures, Chinese and Japanese paintings and calligraphy, all of which he collected.

The villa is noted for its garden, a stroll garden created around a pond and a stream. A thatch-roofed gateway leads into the attractive garden and to a path along a meandering brook that empties into a pond, the main villa lying across the water. This building (Zonkoro) was Hashimoto's atelier. The pond and the path are encompassed by azaleas along with pine trees and a variety of bushes. Ferns and mosses cover much of the ground while colorful carp enliven the pond and stream. A stone slab bridge over the pond outlet, with large ornamental pine trees, stone lanterns and *sotoba* (five-part memorial stones), leads to a second section of the pond in front of a small viewing hut with a large "moon window." Across this second smaller pond is a tea house, the object of view from the hut opposite. The garden, which makes use of the "borrowed scenery" of Mount Daimonji, is at its best in the spring with its cherry blossoms and then again in the fall with the many colored hues of its maples.

Kansetsu was fascinated by ancient Japanese stone carvings, and thus in one area of the garden in a bamboo grove behind the villa are various small stone images. These stone mourners for the Buddha on his death were obtained from throughout Japan, and in the springtime they peer out from among flowering irises. A small seven-story stone pagoda and a small Hokyoin pagoda in the Indian style enhance the grounds. For a small fee, one can enjoy powdered green tea (*matcha*) and a traditional tea cake in a *tatami* room in the main villa, with a view across the pond.

② JODO-JI TEMPLE

On leaving the Hakusason-so, turn right along the extension of Imadegawa-dori toward the small Jodo-ji Temple, which lies in front of and to the left of the Silver Pavilion (Ginkaku-ji Temple) along with the previously mentioned restaurants on the right. Primarily for local worship and not a tourist attraction, Jodo-ji (Paradise Temple) today is an insignificant temple whose history, however, goes back to the early Heian period (795–1200). This Pure Land (Jodo) sect temple was once a large establishment in a village outside of Kyoto called Jodo-ji-mura. As was the case with many temples, in the 8th century it burned to the

ground. The next morning a blaze of light on the nearby hillside led the curious to the source of the brilliant glow, and there they found the Amida image of the temple, charred but intact. Ostensibly it had fled to safety on the hillside during the conflagration.

Legend has a way of involving great personages with individual temples or events, and in this case it is Kobo Daishi (Kukai) who is so honored. One of the numerous plagues to which Kyoto was susceptible was decimating the city in the early 800s. Kukai built a large "Dai" ideogram (Dai means "great"– in this case in reference to the Law of the Buddha) on the hillside where the Amida image of the Jodo-ji had taken sanctuary– and the great plague came to an end. From that time on, whenever plague or famine or other evil ensued, a great "Dai" would be raised on the hillside and burned.

So began the ceremony, still observed today, when a huge "Dai" is set on fire on nearby Nyoi-ga-take Mountain each mid-August to light the spirits of the deceased back to the other world at the end of the O-Bon Festival. The Jodo-ji still exists as a temple despite a later fire in 1449 and the seizure of much of its lands by Shogun Ashikaga Yoshi-masa when he built his Silver Pavilion pleasure palace on the temple grounds. In the rebuilt main hall of Jodo-ji, a large image of Kobo Daishi and the charred Amida image still have a place of honor. The Jodo-ji, however, is but a curious footnote to history, for the important site lies to the right of the small temple where the path from Imadegawa-dori ends at the entrance to the Silver Pavilion, the Ginkaku-ji Temple.

③ GINKAKU-JI TEMPLE (SILVER PAVILION)

Ginkaku-ji today belongs to the Shokoku school of the Rinzai Zen sect of Buddhism. While it is one of the more important tourist sites in Kyoto, it also serves as a temple.

Just prior to the start of the Onin War (1467–77) in which Kyoto would be laid waste in a senseless conflict in which the city itself was the battleground between opposing forces, Shogun Ashikaga Yoshimasa (1475-90) turned his back on the capital. In the northeast area of the plain on which Kyoto sits, beyond the confines of the city and Yoshida Hill and just below the Nyoi-ga-take Mountain, he decreed a pleasure palace of a simple and refined nature where he could enjoy its garden, tea, incense and the more esoteric

The elegant two-story Silver Pavilion, once the nursery of the arts, with a phoenix sculpture at its peak.

pleasures of this world. Symbolically, it faced to the east, away from the realities of the miseries the people of Kyoto would suffer during a decade of internecine fighting. That a temple, the Jodo-ji, stood in the way of his plans was of little concern. The temple was removed, leaving but a relic of the former religious center (see above).

Work on the villa, dedicated to the pleasures of the aesthetic senses, began in 1460. Work was interrupted by the Onin War, and was only resumed after Yoshimasa's retirement on June 27, 1480. Three years later, Yoshimasa took up residence at the Silver Pavilion, and building continued until his death at 56 in January 1490, by which time there were some 12 buildings and an exquisite garden in the complex. Upon his death, the palace became a Zen temple. The temple was named Jisho-ji (Mercy Shine Temple) after Yoshimasa's posthumous name.

The villa was so huge, some 30 times its present extent, that it was called Higashi-yama-dono (Eastern Hills Palace) rather than a villa. In time, fires destroyed all but two of the buildings, the Silver Pavilion (Ginkaku-ji) and the Togu-do (East Request Hall). Although restored in the 17th century, by the 1860s the complex had fallen into ruin once more and, as a 1890s guide book reported, "The Palace is so dilapidated as to be scarcely worth looking at, except from an antiquarian point of view." Fortunately, in the 20th century it has

been restored to its quiet but elegant beauty once more.

In Yoshimasa's time, the villa and its gardens were the cultural and aesthetic center of the nation. It was the nursery of the arts: noted painters enjoyed the Shogun's support, and here the art of the tea ceremony was brought to new heights. Banquets, moon viewing, incense parties, tea ceremony, flower viewing, poetry appreciation, all became high arts again as they had been in the times of Heian-kyo (795–1200). Yoshimasa himself summed up his feelings for the villa:

I love
My hut
At the foot of the Moon Awaiting Mountain
And the reflection
Of the sinking sky.

(The mountain behind the villa to the east is Tsukemachi-yama or Moon Awaiting Mountain.)

A rising stone path through a row of pine, cedar and maple trees leads from the city street and the small restaurants to the simple tile-roofed So-mon main gate of the Silver Pavilion. Once within the gateway, turn to the right and proceed along a path bordered by camellias and other bushes edged by a low stone wall, above which rises the unique tightly made bamboo fence of a rustic nature known as the Ginkaku-ji-gaki style of fencing.

At the end of this sand-covered pathway, a 90-degree turn to the left leads you to the ticket booth and the simple one-story tile-roofed gateway to the inner grounds of the temple. This tree-lined and fenced entrance corridor is but preliminary to the beauty which lies beyond the second gateway and the Kuri, the priests' large tile-roofed private living quarters.

Beyond the second gate, a diamond-shaped stone pathway set in sand, with raked sand and azalea bushes on either side, leads to the imposing heavily gabled curved-roof Kara-mon (Chinese) gateway of the first half of the 17th century. Beyond the gateway, a Zen-style arched (cusped) window offers a preview of the main Ginshaden Garden which lies ahead. The entry to the Ginshaden sand garden is through a small doorway in the garden wall to the right. This doorway opens on to the Ginshaden Garden with the Silver Pavilion building on the right and the Hondo (Main Hall) on the left. The path continues, leading you toward the Hondo (not open to the public) from which the sand garden can be viewed, a garden which will be described after the Hondo and Togu-do are viewed.

The original Hondo (Main Hall) was destroyed by fire and the present structure, with its cedar bark roof, dates from the second quarter of the 17th century. The building has four rooms, and a small altar at the rear of the *tatami*-matted central Buddha Room has an image of Sakyamuni (Shaka) as the object of veneration. In the front of the room is a cushioned seat and drums for use in worship.

Between the Hondo and the adjacent Togu-do is a small garden with a stone water basin in the so-called "Peasant" or "Priest's Robe" style, as well as a granite lantern of the Uzumasa type.

Built in 1487, the four-room thatch-roofed Togu-do is one of the two original buildings from Yoshimasa's day still standing. Yoshimasa is said to have used the front room of the Togu-do, the Butsu-no-ma (Buddha room) of eight mats and thus the largest of the rooms, as his residence. A wooden statue of Yoshimasa in a monk's robe is housed in this room, a statue that replaced two noted images of the Buddha and one of Kannon. Legend has it that Yoshimasa himself carved this blackened image which has crystal eyes.

Perhaps the most famous unit of the Togu-do is the room in the northeast of the building, the Dojin-sai (Friendly Abstinence), a

small 4 1/2-mat room which Yoshimasa used for tea ceremony; in a sense it is the proto-type of what has become the traditional tea-hut room. (The tea room is preceded by a four-mat room in the southeast corner where guests awaited permission to enter the tea room.) The tea room has a *tatami*-matted floor, a board ceiling, a built-out writing alcove, a *tokonoma* (an alcove in which a flower or perhaps a scroll is displayed), *chigaidana* (staggered shelves) and a fire "box" for tea making that is sunk in the center of the floor. Sliding waist-high wooden panels with *shoji* above enclose its outer walls. It was an intimate room meant for seating no more than four to five people at a time.

A two-room building to the north of the Togu-do, the Rosei-tei, was constructed for Yoshimasa as a pavilion for enjoying the pleasure of incense. The building had disappeared with time, but in 1895 an exact reconstruction of the original Rosei-tei was recreated.

The gardens of the Ginkaku-ji were planned by Soami, the most noted landscape designer of medieval times. He was also responsible for the design of the buildings. In two sections, one part of the garden is typical of the *karesansui* (dry garden) of sand while the other is a classical Japanese garden with a lake, stream and plantings. The first section of the garden, the *karesansui* garden, is encountered when one passes through the gateway from the Kuri (Priests' Quarters) garden into the Hondo area. This garden of 1¾ acres is the Ginshaden, the Sea of Silver Sand, composed of a 2 foot (6.1 cm) high plateau of sand raked in a pattern to suggest a sea in motion. The Ginshaden is so placed that when the moon appears over Tsukemachi-yama (Moon Awakening Mountain) to the east, the sand sea seems to ripple in the gleam of the silvery moonlight. This sand sea is often referred to as Sei-ko, West Lake, to draw a parallel between it and the famed West Lake near Hangchow, China, after whose shape it is designed.

Adjacent to the sand sea there rises the Kogetsu-dai, the Moon Viewing Platform. A large truncated cone of sand, this shaped hill has been described as a miniature Mount Fuji, as a moon viewing platform, or as a cone of sand designed to reflect and heighten the effect of moonlight on the Silvery Sand Sea. From the upper floor of the Silver Pavilion, it is said that the cone appears to be a silvery full moon reflected on the bosom of a silver

Kogetsu-dai, a truncated cone of white sand.

lake. Ginshaden and Kogetsu-dai are also seen as a combination of the sea and the mountains. Kogetsu-dai, "The Mound Facing the Moon," 6 feet (1.8 m) tall by 16 feet (4.8 m) in diameter, is reputed to be where Yoshimasa sat to gaze at the moon. (It is interesting, however, that these two sand units, which are so striking, were not mentioned before the Edo period (1615–1868)−and it is known that they occupy the site of buildings that burned to the ground.) Mounds of sand originally existed in dry gardens so that the paths and designs could be replenished as needed. Here, such a mound has become an aesthetic attraction with a life of its own.

The second part of the garden is of the classical Japanese type employing water, rocks and plantings. The rocks and stones come from all over Japan, as tribute or duty to the Shogun from his feudal lords. Each stone has a name and a recorded history. This is a stroll garden, for one needs to walk its paths to savor and to enjoy the changing views of water, trees, stones and plantings. Azaleas and moss complement the water and the rocks in the shade of large trees. Central to this garden, and adjacent to the Silver Pavilion, is its pond, Kinkyo-chi (Brocade Mirror Pond), with crane and turtle islands that are symbols for longevity. (Real turtles

nap in the sun on the islands.) The scene is enhanced by the Sengetsu-sei (Moon Watching Fountain), a tiny waterfall whose ripples in the water into which it falls are meant to "wash away" moonlight on the surface of the water. Every stone, as mentioned previously, has a name: one stone in the midst of the pond is known as "The Stone of Ecstatic Contemplation," while a small stone bridge (one of seven over the waterways) is "The Bridge of the Pillar of the Immortals." Each vista is meant to bring to mind a reference to one of the Chinese or Japanese literary classics.

A path leads past the Togetsu-do and Rosei-tei up the hillside to the spring whose sparkling waters served as the basis for the Shogun's early tea ceremony. The spring remains as the source of the water for the stream and pond in the garden. Naturally, each temple needs its Shinto shrine to appease the spirit of the land it occupies, and Ginkaku-ji has two such small shrines, the smaller in the northeast corner of the grounds and the larger one next to the Silver Pavilion.

The Silver Pavilion building, which despite its name was never given the intended coating of silver leaf, was Yoshimasa's attempt to create as perfect a retreat as his grandfather, Shogun Ashikaga Yoshimitsu, had created at the Gold Pavilion (Kinkaku-ji) (see Tour 14). A surprisingly small and simple building, it was designed to a different aesthetic than was observed by later, more ostentatious military rulers of Japan.

A rather plain wooden building of two stories, its lower floor is divided by *fusuma* (sliding panels) to provide for rooms of varying sizes as desired. The first floor is 22 by 18 feet (6.6 by 5.5 m) with sliding waist-high wooden doors with *shoji* above the lower wood portion for its exterior walls. Its interior has a flat board ceiling. The upper floor over the flaring roof of the first floor has three arched or bell-shaped windows in front and back, while the two sides have two such windows and a pair of paneled doors between them. This 18 square foot (1.6 sq m) upper level is surrounded by a railing about its narrow exterior "porch." The roof, which flares upward at its four corners, is surmounted by a gilt bronze phoenix bird.

The lower floor is named Shin-ku-dan (Empty Heart Hall), and features an enshrined image of Jizo, protector of children, and 1,000 small Jizo images. The upper floor,

The Philosopher's Path, a favorite walk in spring and fall, runs alongside a canal.

called Cho-on-kak (Tidal Sound Hall), has a gilt Kannon image reputed to have been created by Unkei (13th century). The interior is varnished with black lacquer against which the gilt image is resplendent. Because of the Kannon image, the building has also been known as the Kannon-den (Kannon Hall).

After you have viewed the Silver Pavilion building (unfortunately, only from the outside), take the path around the pavilion back toward the exit to the grounds.

4 THE PHILOSOPHER'S PATH

Back on the extension of Imadegawa-dori from which you entered the Silver Pavilion grounds, walk to the canal that passes under the street. Take the Philosopher's Path, which runs along the far (western) side of the canal, to the left (south). Away from the bustle of the city streets you can follow the narrow canal past interesting homes, shops and an occasional small restaurant. Quiet hillside temples offer a separate attraction of a pleasant nature, one of the most interesting being that of the Honen-in Temple.

The Philosopher's Path is so-named since it was once the locale of the daily walk of Kitaro Nishida, a Japanese philosopher (1870–1943). It runs along a canal from near the Ginkaku-ji for 1.3 miles (2.3 km) south toward the Zenrin-ji/Eikan-do Temple and thereafter along a city street to the Nanzen-ji Temple. The canal and its adjacent path are embowered with cherry blossoms in the early spring, and in the autumn the brilliant reds and vibrant yellows of the leaves of its various trees turn the area into a palette richer than that of any artist.

5 HONEN-IN TEMPLE

At the tenth small bridge over the waterway, leave the canal temporarily and turn to the hillside and the Honen-in Temple. Honen-in is on the beginning slope of the hillside along a north–south path through the woods. After crossing the bridge over the canal, walk to the north–south path beyond the canal, turn north (left) and enter the grounds of the Honen-in. (The temple grounds are open from 6:00 a.m. to 6:00 p.m. without charge.) The temple Hondo (Main Hall) is only open from April 1–7 and November 1–7, since its primary purpose is to serve as a training center for monks. Entry fee.

The Honen-in is dedicated to the memory of priest Honen (1133–1212), who had entered the Enryaku-ji monastery on Mount Hiei to the northeast of Kyoto at the age of 15, where he astonished the monks with his religious precocity. Moving to the site of the future Kurodani Temple in Kyoto (see Tour 6), in his solitary studies there he encountered the Jodo (Pure Land) doctrines in the *Ojo Yoshu* (Essentials for Salvation) written by Priest Genshin. Embracing these new doctrines, he rejected the Tendai teachings of the Enryaku-ji and became the popularizer of the repetition of the Nembutsu ("Praise to Amida Buddha") as the only means for eventual entrance into Amida's Pure Land. It is said that he would repeat the Nembutsu as many as 60,000 times a day.

In time, Honen and two disciples (Anraku and Juren) erected an image of Amida at the foot of the Nyoi-ga-take Mountain (the site of the present Honen-in) in order to perform services before this outdoor image three times a day as well as at night. For many years, the worship site only consisted of the roofed open-air Amida image, a sculpture which has been attributed to Genshin (942–1017). Not long after Honen's death in 1212, the roof over the Amida was destroyed by the monks of the Enryaku-ji temples of Mount Hiei, the enemies of Honen and his Jodo sect.

It was not until the Tokugawa Shoguns came to power in the early 17th century (and after the Enryaku-ji temples and their monks had been eliminated by Oda Nobunaga in the mid-1500s) that the present main hall (Hondo) was built in 1680. Under Shogun Tokugawa Ietsuna, rooms from Toyotomo Hideyoshi's Fushimi Castle were granted to the temple, and these were attached to the new Hondo. It has been the tradition of the temple for the monks to place 25 flowers on the floor before the Amida image in the Hondo every morning. These flowers symbolize the 25 Bodhisattvas who accompany Amida when he descends from his Western Paradise to receive the souls of the newly deceased. When the 4:00 a.m. bell is rung for morning services, fresh cut flowers are placed before the altar. (The bell is rung again at 4:00 p.m. for services.)

A great deal of the charm of the Honen-in comes from its location in the woods at the foot of Nyoi-ga-take Mountain, for it offers a quiet retreat away from the city's clamor. The walkway from the city to the temple grounds is lined with cedars, great camellias and bamboo. A simple gateway with a thatched roof and a gate of inset bamboo rods, reminiscent of a small Japanese country farmhouse, lies at the end of the path. Beyond the gateway, one descends eight broad stone steps into the grounds of the temple itself, and on either side of the path just within the compound lie two long rectangular sand mounds. Periodically, the monks rake the surface of the sand to create a new design on each unit, generally with designs symbolizing the seasons (on the left) or offering abstractions of a religious nature, often of a water nature symbolizing the Buddhist theme of impermanence (on the right). Toward the hillside beyond the sand mounds is a small building with bell-shaped windows, said to have served at one time as a bath house, which is used periodically today for special exhibitions. Further up the hillside, above the entry gate, is the temple Shoro (belfry).

Just beyond the sand mounds, a stone bridge crosses a stream which leads from a small pond. On the left is a small *kura* (a fireproof storage building) whose interior is open to view and which holds the temple sutras (sacred writings) on shelves along three of the walls. In the center of the *kura* is a shrine with an image of Amida and a case holding 1,000 tiny Amida images. To the right of the main Amida image is a figure of Bishamon-ten, with a pagoda in one hand and a staff in the other hand, the protector against evil, which always flows from the northeast. A companion figure on the other side of Amida has its hands clasped in prayer, and both images are colorfully dressed in Chinese-style clothes. Beyond and slightly to the southwest of the *kura* is a 13-tiered stone pagoda.

The main path from the entry gate crosses the aforementioned bridge, composed of flat stone slabs with a low stone balustrade. At the north end of this path is the Hondo (Main Hall) of the temple. The path diverges to the right and left when it reaches the Hondo, the left path leading to the building entrance. The right path makes a 90-degree turn to the north at the eastern end of the Hondo before ending at a wall. At the turn is a 12 foot (3.6 m) high *sotoba* (a five-part memorial stone), and at the end of the path on the hillside to the right and set into the hill is a shrine to Jizo. A Busso-seki, a stone with the imprinted footstep of the Buddha, is adjacent.

When the Hondo is open to the public, a corridor to the right of the entry leads to the

The simple gateway to the Honen-in Temple, set on a forested hillside along a path through woods.

Nai-jin (Inner Hall) of the Hondo. Here is the altar with its image of Amida, said to be by Genshin, its hands held in the contemplative *mudra*. At his side are the two Bodhisattva who accompany him, Seishi on the right and Kannon on the left, and at the side of the two attendants are additional images. Twenty-five flowers representing Amida's followers are reverently placed on the polished floor before Amida each morning. The Nai-jin is a 100-*tatami* matted hall with numerous "crab-shaped" drums for use during worship services. The Hondo has a double roof, bell-shaped windows and an arched ceiling to the main hall. On either side of the Hondo are internal courtyards, the one on the north being noted for its seven-color camellia tree. These courtyards separate and connect the Hondo with the other rooms of the complex.

On walking down the interior corridor on the north side of the Hondo, you come to the six rooms in the northeastern portion of the complex that came from the apartments of Hideyoshi's Fushimi Castle. These rooms formerly were part of Hideyoshi's Audience Hall, and they were granted to the temple by the Shogun Tokugawa Ietsuna shortly after the Hondo was re-erected in 1680. Outside, wooden verandas encircle the building with a private garden on the east of the apartments, separated from the public grounds by a stone,

earth and a hedge wall. In this garden is a pond in the shape of a reversed "C," with a stone bridge over one segment of the water. A stone lantern, a stone basin and a Shinto shrine complement bushes and moss that form the greenery of the garden before the woods of the forested hillside beyond.

The four small rooms at the southern end of these apartments each have *fusuma* (sliding screens) painted with modern abstract drawings in vivid colors. The two most important rooms of this complex are the two 10-mat rooms at the northern end of the apartments. These rooms are usually combined into one large room through the removal of the intervening *fusuma*. The *fusuma* panels of the rooms have paintings of pine and willow trees, flowers and birds on a gold ground by Kano Mitsunobu (1561–1608). The north end of the second room has a *tokonoma* with large white flowers on a gold ground on the rear of its wall while the adjacent *chigaidana* (staggered shelves) have painted scenes, and the cedar doors which end the inner *tatami*-matted corridor have a painting of a pine tree. The four smaller rooms to the south of these 10-mat rooms complete the Fushimi apartments.

On leaving the Fushimi apartments, the wood corridor leads west, past a number of rooms, of which three can be noted. One is

15-mat room with a black and white dragon that fills its rear *fusuma* and the *fusuma* on the two sides of the room. The second is a 30-mat room with a *tokonoma* and a large *chigaidana* on its north wall, which crosses the full building (east to west). During the April and November periods when these apartments are open to visitors, large screens from the temple's treasures are on view here. The third room is a 15-mat room. At the end of the corridor on the east side of these rooms is a 4½-mat tea room with a *tokonoma* with a view over the previously mentioned inner garden and pond. The ceiling of the room is quite low and forces one to bend (to bow or humble oneself) on entering the room.

The monks' large dining hall (refectory), with an image of Monju, is where temple treasures are shown during the period the temple is open to the public. Then a turn to the right leads to a two-story building whose upper floor of two small rooms with a view over Kyoto may be visited. On leaving the Honen-in grounds through its thatched-roof entry gateway, follow the Philosopher's Path to the south. Along the way on the left you will pass the temple graveyard in which the novelist Tanazaki Junichiro (1886-1963) is buried.

Mention has been made of Honen's two disciples who worshipped at the open-air shrine to Amida in the early days before the Honen-in existed as a formal set of buildings. These two men were to suffer the enmity engendered by Honen's enemies, and they are remembered at the Anraku-ji Temple, which lies to the south of Honen-in along a continuation of the path from the Honen-in on the east side of the canal. The Anraku-ji Temple grounds are open from 9:30 a.m. to 4:00 p.m. on Saturdays, Sundays and National Holidays in April and May, and during the second week of June, October and November. Entry fee.

When, in the late 12th century, Honen began to preach his doctrine that reliance on the Nembutsu was all that was needed for salvation, he was confronted with many opponents among the monks at Mount Hiei and the six Buddhist sects in Nara and within the court. Two of his disciples, Anraku (?-1207) and Juren (1169?-1207) were the most effective proselytizers of Honen's version of Buddhism. Unable to preach in the city without interference by their clerical enemies, they preached in the countryside at the foot of the Higashiyama mountain range at Shishigatani, where they created a small temple.

Two noble ladies, Matsumushi (Pine Beetle) and Suzumushi (Bell Cricket), of the Emperor Go-Toba's court (sources differ on their relationship to the Emperor) became enamored of the new teachings as preached by Anraku and Juren—or with the conveyors of the teachings, depending on which account one believes—and became nuns. The Emperor Go-Toba, furious at this seduction (real or imagined) of two of his court ladies, had Anraku and Juren seized.

Another interpretation of the events states that the court had become convinced by Honen's enemies (primarily on Mount Hiei) that the new doctrines preached by Anraku and Juren, of equal salvation for all people, were incompatible with the safety and security of the state. Thus, persecution of the new belief and its followers was ordered on the pretext that two court ladies had been led astray by the two priests and had entered the new faith without Imperial approval.

Given an opportunity to recant their belief in the Jodo tenets and in the Nembutsu, which they refused to do, the two priests were beheaded in the place of execution for criminals in the bed of the Kamo River at Rokujo-Kawara. Anraku asked permission to say the Nembutsu before his death, telling his executioners that after this recitation, on his 10th repetition of the name of Amida, they could execute him. He repeated the Nembutsu several hundred times and then Amida's name ten times. At that decisive moment of the tenth calling of Amida's name, and as the executioner acted, great purple clouds gathered from the west, the direction of Amida's Western Paradise to which Anraku was being welcomed by Amida and his Bodhisattvas.

The court ladies are reputed to have committed suicide. Honen himself was defrocked by order of the Emperor and exiled to Tosa for his teaching of the Nembutsu as the only way to salvation—an action which evidenced the power of Honen's monastic enemies within the court. For Honen, exile provided an opportunity to spread his truth in new realms. Evidently, time took its toll on the Emperor's conscience, for, when unpleasant dreams plagued various individuals and these dreams were reported to the court, they were interpreted as being caused by the Emperor's actions against Honen. After four years of exile, Honen was permitted to settle in Osaka. An oracle's interpretation of additional dreams in 1211 led the Emperor to permit Honen to return to Kyoto, where the aged priest settled in Otani (at what was later to become the Chion-in Temple) in a small hermitage. It is said that on his return from exile in 1212, Honen created the temple of Anraku-ji in honor of his slain disciples and their two converts at the place where the priests had preached.

6 ANRAKU-JI TEMPLE

The small temple of Anraku-ji in the verdant foothills of the Higashiyama Mountains is a branch of the Nishi-yama Zenrin-ji school of Jodo Buddhism. Its Hondo (Main Hall) was erected about 1581, the original hall having been destroyed by fire. Stone steps lead to a simple thatched gateway at the entry. Within the temple precincts, a narrow path bordered by azaleas, camellias, maples, pines and moss leads to the hillside; the main buildings of the temple are hidden away in the greenery to the left. A life-sized image of Jizo stands to the west of the Hondo while a 13-tiered stone pagoda rises on an azalea-covered hillock. Near the center of the temple grounds, a path on the right diverges from the main path. Following the right arm of the path at the crossing, you come to the graves of Anraku and Juren fenced with a low stone fence in a 1904 restoration. Straight ahead on the main path to the east, toward the mountainside and up two flights of steps, lie the graves of the

two court ladies, Suzumushi and Matsu-mushi. Their graves were marked with a low stone fence when they were restored in 1897.

The Hondo (Main Hall) lies at the end of the left arm of the transverse path. As can be expected, the central image in the rear section of the Hondo is of Amida with Seishi and Kannon to his left and right. It is claimed that these images, which predate the temple, are the tenth century work of Priest Genshin (942–1017). An ancient Jizo image, together with two very large gilt hangings above the images, complete the altar figures.

A shrine on the left has images of Honen and his noted disciple Shinran together with a Kannon figure. The Honen image (said to have been carved by Honen himself) stands in a small shrine in the shape of a temple, covered with hundreds of Namu Amida Butsu inscriptions on paper. In a shrine to the right, framed with a colorful brocade, are images of Matsumushi on the left and Suzumushi on the right, with Anraku and Juren behind and above them on the left and right respectively.

To the east of the Hondo, and connected to it by a covered walkway, is a *tatami*-matted *shoin* (residential building) of two rooms (often joined into one room) for special use. Additional temple buildings for the staff of the temple are adjacent. Two small Shinto shrines near the Hondo offer the protection of the local *kami* to the temple.

The Hondo at Anraku-ji Temple, which is located on a hillside outside the spa town of Bessho.

DAIMON-JI Leaving Anraku-ji and crossing the first bridge over the canal, return to the Philosopher's Path along the west bank of the canal to continue a pleasant walk south along the waterway. The Nyoi-ga-take Mountain lies to the east; here on its top, the impressive Daimonji fire celebration takes place each August. We have already met with the legend of the apparition of Amida surrounded by a blaze of light which was seen on this mountain in the 800s.

The bonfire which Priest Kukai lit in the 800s as a protection against the plague finds a counterpart today on each August 16th when a huge "Dai" (meaning "great") ideogram composed of large bundles of pine branches is created on a clearing 1,500 feet (460 m) up on Nyoi-ga-take (or Daimonji-yama as it is also known) above the Zenrin-ji/Eikan-do Temple.

At 8:00 p.m. the ideogram is set on fire, and four other enormous fires are lit at 10 minute intervals on hills across the valley. The other four ideograms include the Myoho (Supreme Law of the Buddha), the Funagata (boat-shaped), the Torii-gata (*torii* or gate-shaped) and the Hidari-Daimonji (left-handed Daimonji). Since five mountains are involved, the festival is also known as the Gozan Okuribi Festival (Five Mountains Fires Which Return the Souls of the Deceased). This brings to a close the O-Bon Festival, when the spirits of the dead, which have returned to their homes on August 12th for a brief visit, are now ready to return to the other world. This great flaming illumination is intended to guide the spirits back to that other world at the end of the festival.

SEN-OKU HAKKO-KAN Continuing south on the path which runs before the Anraku-ji, a bridge on the right over the canal leads one back to the Philosopher's Path on the west side of the canal. Take this path to the next major cross street to the west (to the right). The Sen-oku Hakko-kan Museum is one street to the west and then to the north. The museum is open from 10:00 a.m. to 4:00 p.m. but is closed on Sundays, Mondays and national holidays as well as during July and August and from December through February. Entry fee.

The Sen-oku Hakko-kan Museum consists of two modern buildings, one for its permanent collections and one for changing exhibitions. The latter are generally shown from March 1 to June 30 and then from September 1 to November 30. The permanent collection is composed of items from the Sumitomo Collection (the Sumitomo family land is opposite the museum). The collection was begun by Kichizaemon Sumitomo, and he collected ancient Chinese bronzes for over 30 years until his death in 1926. In recent years, the Sumitomo family created the museum and a foundation for its continued support so that the public could view the collection. Aside from the bronzes of the Chinese Shang and Zhou periods (16th century BCE to 221 BCE), Chinese paintings, musical instruments and calligraphy are included in the museum holdings. The bronzes include mirrors, bells, Buddhist images and wine and food vessels. Approximately 600 bronzes are shown at any one time in the four exhibition rooms of the permanent collections building. An English language brochure is available in the museum.

On leaving the museum, you can either continue to the Zenrin-ji/Eikan-do and the Nanzen-ji Temples (in the next walking tour) by following the north–south street just to the east of the museum to the south, or you can take the street in front of the museum to the west to the north–south Shirakawa-dori. Here bus 5, 203 or 204 or a taxi can be taken.

GETTING THERE

You can walk the Philosopher's Path in either direction, north or south, but many prefer to start at its northern end with the Silver Pavilion and then to explore the quiet Honen-in and Anraku-ji Temples along bypaths adjacent to the canal. (If you are energetic, the walk can be continued to the Nanzen-ji Temple with its noted Zen gardens. See Tour 7 below.) The optimal times to visit are in April when the cherry trees are in bloom and in fall when the red maples and other trees provide a beautiful canopy.

Ginkaku-ji is open from 8:30 a.m. to 5:00 p.m. from March 15 to November 30 and from 9:00 a.m. to 4:30 p.m. from December 1 to March 14. Entry fee. To reach the Ginkaku-ji area at the nothern end of the Philosopher's Path, take bus 5, 203 or 204 to the Ginkaku-ji-michi bus stop and walk to the east from Shirakawa-dori on the extension of Imadagawa-dori.

Walking Tour 13

KYOTO'S IMPERIAL PALACE

The Old Imperial Palace and a Museum of Gold and Silver Pavilion Treasures

1. **Original Imperial Palace** 御所
2. **Kyoto Imperial Palace** 京都御所
3. **Shodaibu-no-ma** 諸大夫の間
4. **Sento Palace** 仙洞御所
5. **Omiya Palace** 大宮御所
6. **Shokoku-ji Temple** 相国寺

Kyoto Gosho, the former Imperial Palace, was once the center of Kyoto, serving both as the Emperor's residence and the seat of governance for all of Japan. It was relocated to what is now Kyoto Gyoen National Garden (also called Kyoto Imperial Park) after the fires of the 1200s. A tour of the palace should not be missed, even though the buildings date only from the mid-19th century after reconstruction following the last decimating fire. Within the palace's walled enclosure is the resurrected splendor of another age. Its halls, its painted *fusuma* and its gardens all recall the glory of Heian times (794–1200). Once the most sacred of area of the capital, accessible only to those of noble rank, today it may be visited by foreign tourists on application to the Imperial Household Agency office in the northwest sector of the garden grounds.

Kyoto Gyoen is a large green tract bound by Teramachi-dori on the east, Karasuma-dori on the west, Marutamachi-dori on the south and Imadegawa-dori on the north. Within its grounds, to the southeast of Kyoto Gosho, are two other former imperial residences, Sento Gosho (Sento Palace) and Omiya Gosho (Omiya Palace.)

1 ORIGINAL IMPERIAL PALACE

The Original Imperial Palace was located in the north-central portion of Heian-kyo (Kyoto). Today, the Daigoku-den stone marker is all that is left as a reminder of the location of the original palace. The marker stands between Sembon-dori on the east and Rokken-machi-dori on the west, north of Marutamachi-dori and about 1 mile (1.6 km) southeast of Kitano Shrine. The stone marker indicates the site of the Dai Dairi (Great Inner Enclosure) of the Imperial Palace of Heian times (795–1188).

The Original Imperial Palace, built in 794, encompassed the entire north-central area of the city of Heian-kyo (Kyoto), extending from Ichijo-dori (First Street) in the north to Nijo-dori (Second Street) to the south between Higashi Omiya-dori (East Palace Street) on the east and Nishi Omiya-dori (West Palace Street) on the west. It measured 4,600 feet (1,380 m) from north to south and 3,800 feet (1,140 m) from east to west, some 300 acres (120 ha) in all. The walls of the "Ninefold Enclosure," as it was known, with their five white bands denoting Imperial status, were pierced by 12 gates, and the grounds included not only the Imperial Residence (Shishin-den or Imperial Living Quarters) and the Imperial Sleeping Quarters (Seiryo-den) but various governmental offices (Hassho-in), including the Daigoku-den (Great Hall of State) and the various Departments of State.

Fire destroyed the palace buildings on numerous occasions and, after the 1177 fire, the then Emperor moved his residence to Kobe. When the Imperial court returned to Kyoto, the palace was relocated in the area of the Tsuchi-mikado, the present palace grounds which had previously served as a temporary residence when the main palace was destroyed by fire or earthquake.

The city itself had never developed its western half, and thus the new palace was

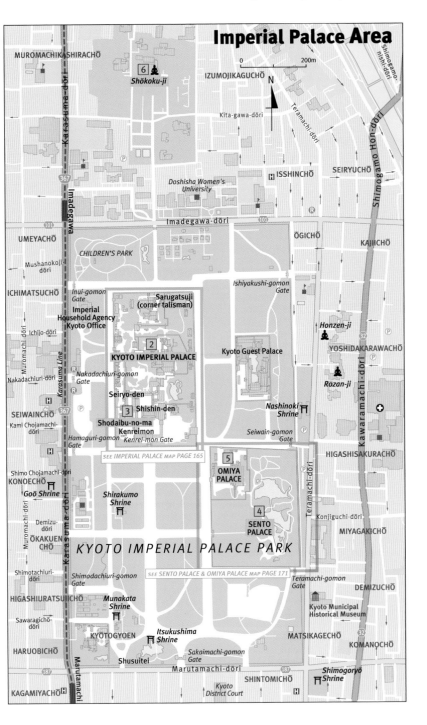

Imperial Palace Area

MUROMACHIKASHIRACHŌ

Shimogamo-nishi-dōri

6 ♨
Shōkoku-ji

IZUMOJIKAGUCHŌ

0   200m

N

Kita-gawa-dōri

Teramachi-dōri

SEIRYUCHŌ

H ISSHINCHŌ

Shimogamo Hon-dōri

Doshisha Women's University

ŌGICHŌ

KAJIICHŌ

Imadegawa-dōri

367
Imadegawa

Karasuma-dōri

101

101

UMEYACHŌ

CHILDREN'S PARK

Mushanokoji-dōri

ICHIMATSUCHŌ

Karasuma Line

Inui-gomon Gate

Imperial Household Agency Kyoto Office

Sarugatsuji (corner talisman)

Ishiyakushi-gomon Gate

Honzen-ji

YOSHIDAKARAWACHŌ

Ichijō-dōri

2
KYOTO IMPERIAL PALACE

Kyoto Guest Palace

♨
Rozan-ji

32

Muromachi-dōri

Nakadachiuri-dōri

R
Nakadachiuri-gomon Gate

P

Seiryo-den

SEIWAINCHŌ

H

3 Shishin-den

Nashinoki Shrine

H

Kami Chojamachi-dōri

Shodaibu-no-ma
Kenreimon

HIGASHISAKURACHŌ

O

Hamaguri-gomon Gate

Kenrei-mon Gate

Seiwain-gomon Gate

P

SEE IMPERIAL PALACE MAP PAGE 165

Shimo Chojamachi-dōri

KONOECHŌ

H

5
OMIYA PALACE

Teramachi-dōri

Goō Shrine

Shirakumo Shrine

H

4
SENTO PALACE

Konjiguchi-dōri

Muromachi-dōri

Demizu-dōri

ŌKAKUEN CHŌ

KYOTO IMPERIAL PALACE PARK

MIYAGAKICHŌ

Shimotachiuri-dōri

Shimodachiuri-gomon Gate

SEE SENTO PALACE & OMIYA PALACE MAP PAGE 171

Teramachi-gomon Gate

DEMIZUCHŌ

HIGASHIURATSUJICHŌ

Munakata Shrine

Kyoto Municipal Historical Museum

Sawaragichō-dōri

H

Itsukushima Shrine

32

HARUOBICHŌ

KYŌTOGYOEN

H

MATSIKAGECHŌ

KOMANOCHŌ

Shusuitei

Sakaimachi-gomon Gate

187

187

Shimogoryō Shrine

H

Marutamachi-dōri

SHINTOMICHŌ

Marutamachi

KAGAMIYACHŌ

H

Kyoto District Court

H

located to the east to occupy a more central location in the city as it had actually developed. What today is Senbon-dori was, in Heian times, the location of the 2½ mile (4 km) long central grand willow-lined Suzaku-ojo (Red Sparrow Boulevard), 250 feet (75 m) wide, which extended from the Rajo-mon gate on the southern edge of the city right to the Imperial Palace, dividing the city into its Sakyo (eastern or left) and Ukyo (western or right) sectors.

The original city of Heian-kyo (Capital of Peace and Tranquility) was a rectangle 3.5 miles (5.6 km) from north to south and 2.5 miles (4 km) from east to west. There were eight north–south streets, varying from 80 to 170 feet (24 to 51 m) in width, parallel to the main Suzaku-oji, and nine wide avenues running from east to west. Surrounded by a stone wall 6 feet (1.8 m) high with a 9 foot (2.7 m) ditch on either side, the city was divided into 400 sectors called *cho*, which were further subdivided into 32 residential plots, each 50 by 100 feet (15 by 30 m). Six canalized streams ran through the city from north to south. With 40,000 houses and a population that soon reached 100,000, it was second in size only to Constantinople and Cordova in the West in the 9th and 10th centuries.

Work on the city was begun in March of 793 after the Emperor Kammu had sent a delegation of priests to inform the local Shinto deities (*kami*) of his intention to build the new capital and to request their favor. In addition, a clay figure of a warrior was buried fully armed on the height of the mountain (Shogun-zaka) to the east of the new capital to protect and to give warning of impending attack, should Heian-kyo ever be threatened. By October of 794 the Emperor had moved into his new palace, which eventually had 30 pavilions; however, the city continued under construction for 13 more years, development being hampered by insufficient funds.

The Emperor wished his new capital to outshine all other capitals (notably that of China) in its cultural attainments. He was named Principal of the new university, an appropriate honor since he was a student of Chinese civilization, which underlaid all Japanese learning. His son, Emperor Saga, in time was to enhance the life of the court by introducing elaborate Chinese dress and etiquette into court life. The luxurious life of the nobles had its negative side, however, in that the nobility had to be given tax-free lands to support their ceremonial ways, a situation which in time was to cause acute financial problems for the Imperial government.

Unlike Chinese administration, education in Japan was not intended to select the most capable of individuals for positions of administration within government. In Japan, rank, family and nobility were foremost in selecting those who could attend the university and who would later govern. In time, the luxurious and effete nature of court society led to an aristocratic class that was not concerned nor involved with the real problems of the nation. After 1185 a more hardy group would shoulder aside the court from power; reign the Emperor might, but he and his court were peripheral in time to real governance and actual rule.

By the time the Kamakura government took power in 1185, the Dai Dairi had burned some 14 times in its 400 years of existence. The original site, now remembered only by the Daigoku-den marker, was abandoned, and the palace was moved to its present location. By 1228 fire had destroyed all the original buildings of the city, and by 1600, of the 260 feudal houses that had been built, only a dozen or so remained intact. A city of wood and thatch had always prone to catastrophe.

Known as Heian-kyo (City of Peace and Tranquility) during Heian times (794–1185), the city was called Miyako (Capital) after the year 1200. After 1870 it was renamed once more as Kyoto (Capital)–although Tokyo ("Eastern Capital") became the actual seat of governance once the palace and governmental offices were established there.

The present site of the palace was originally the location of homes of the nobility, much of the ground belonging to the Fujiwara family. Fujiwara-no-Kunitsuna owned an historic mansion on the property, the Tsuchimikado Higashi-no-toin, a complex that was repeatedly used by the Emperors as a temporary residence when their palace was destroyed by fire or earthquake. By 1308 the present location of the Imperial Palace had come under Imperial ownership, and in 1336 Emperor Komyo made the site the official Imperial palace, a status it held until 1868 when the capital and Imperial residence were moved to Tokyo.

Some 28 emperors resided here for 531 years, despite the fact that the palace burned down more than a dozen times. After the depredations of the Onin War (1467–77) and

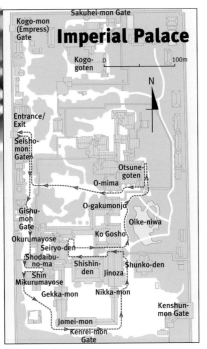

the Sengaku Jidai (Century of Civil Wars), the palace was repaired and rebuilt by the conquering general Nobunaga, then by Hideyoshi, and subsequently by Tokugawa Ieyasu. A fire destroyed the palace in 1788, and it was rebuilt on its present site in 1790 by Matsudaira Sadenobu on the basis of ancient palace structures. Burned again in 1854, it was rebuilt by 1856 in the traditional style of early Kyoto.

② KYOTO IMPERIAL PALACE

The 18 buildings of Kyoto Gosho, the Imperial Palace, joined by covered corridors and separated by Japanese-style gardens, stand in the north-central part of Kyoto Gyoen (Kyoto Imperial Park) grounds on 27 acres (10.8 ha) out of the 220 acre (88 ha) park. At one time this area was a "Court Town," surrounded by the outer palace walls and with the residences of the noble families around the palace. After the Meiji Restoration of 1868 and the removal of the Imperial court to Tokyo, the noble residences either moved or taken down, Prince Katsura's mansion being moved as a gift to the Nijo Castle in 1898 to replace the buildings that were destroyed by fire in the Hon-maru area of that castle.

The walls about Kyoto Gyoen (the Imperial Park) that surround the Imperial Palace grounds are pierced by 12 small gates from the surrounding avenues: one to the south, five on the east, four on the west and two on the north. The grounds of the Imperial Park (outside the grounds of the Old Palace itself) are planted with pines, maples, oak, birch and gingko trees. Some of the gardens once belonged to the mansions of noble court families, the Kujo, the Konoe and the Saionji prior to 1869. To the northern side of the palace, for example, stood the mansion of the Nakayama family, the family into which the Emperor Meiji was born on November 3, 1852. The Sachi-no-I (Well of Divine Help) in which the future emperor was first bathed lies in this area, and it is covered with a gabled lid and enclosed with iron bars.

The buildings of Kyoto Gosho are surrounded by high plastered walls 750 feet (225 m) long to the east and west and 1,500 feet (450 m) long to the north and south. These brown plastered walls (*tsuiji*), with five white stripes that denote Imperial status, are surmounted by a tiled roof. About the perimeter of the walls is a narrow channel in which fresh water from Lake Biwa constantly runs. At the northeast corner of the walls, the corner is inverted to make it a "non-wall," and there is also a small carving under the tiles of a monkey (reputedly created by Hidori Jingoro) called the Sarugi-tsuiji, both of which serve as a protection against the evil which comes from the northeast. The adjacent minor gate, the Kimon, is sometimes referred to as the "Devil's Gate" since it faces the northeast, the direction from which trouble flows. The walled Imperial Palace grounds (within the walled Imperial Park) have four main gates: the Kenrei-mon Gate to the south, a gate only used by the Emperor and opened twice a year for viewing by the public; the Kenshun-mon to the east, formerly used by Ministers of State and later by the Empress and the Empress Dowager; the Gishu-mon on the west (originally used by Imperial princes and nobles); and the Sakuhei-mon on the north (for Imperial consorts and court ladies). North of the Gishu-mon is the Seisho-mon, for the lowest court ranks; today, it is the visitors' entrance from which tours begin. There are 14 smaller gates for use in emergencies.

Having cleared a time for a visit to the palace from the Imperial Household Agency, the grounds of the palace precincts are

The Okuramayose entrance to the Shodaibu-no-ma waiting room for imperial visitors.

③ SHODAIBU-NO-MA

The first place the guide brings each group to is the Okuramayose (Carriage Porch), which was the original entryway for the Emperor. Beyond is the Shodaibu-no-ma (Room of Dignitaries), which consists of three rooms where nobles awaited entrance into the palace. These rooms are arranged according to rank. As you face the south side of the building, the room on the left, the Sakura-no-ma (Cherry Blossom Room) has,

naturally, *fusuma* decorated with cherry trees by Hara Zaisho. This room is for those of the lowest rank. The middle room is the Stork or Crane Room, decorated by Kano Eigaku. The *tatami* mats of these first two rooms are bound with a plain brown binding. The third room, to the right, is the Tora-no-ma (Tiger Room), which was reserved for those of highest noble rank. Its *tatami* are bound with silver ribbon with a flower pattern. The *fusuma* of this third room with its tigers were painted by Kishi Gantai.

entered through the Seisho-mon Gate where a guard examines the entry passes. You are then escorted past *kura* (small storage buildings) on the west and past the Gishu-mon Gate to approach the first of the 18 palace buildings, which are all linked by covered corridors or galleries.

SEIRYO-DEN From the Shodaibu-no-ma, the tour passes the Shin Mikuramayose (New Carriage Porch), built in 1915 for the Emperor Taisho. Since by 1915 the Emperor would arrive at the palace by automobile, a new palace entrance was needed to accommodate a different type of vehicle than the traditional carriage pulled by oxen. This entry porch is in traditional style on the outside but within it is modern with glass windows and carpeted floors. This entrance is reserved for the Emperor, Empress and Crown Prince.

Formerly, the Shenka-den, a sanctuary to hold the sacred mirror, stood here, but this building was granted to and moved to the Kashiwara Shrine to the south of Nara when the tomb to the Emperor Jimmu was created in the late 19th century under the influence of the rabid nationalism of the day.

The New Carriage Porch leads to the Seiryo-den (Serene and Cool Chamber), so-named for the stream of water that runs under its steps; between the porch and the Seiryo-den is the Hagi-no-tsuba (Bush Clover Court). In the original palace, the Seiryo-den was the Imperial residence hall where the Emperor lived, but in time its function changed and it became a ceremonial hall. This 69 foot (26 m) long by 52 foot (15.6 m) wide 1850s reconstruction adheres closely to the original Seiryo-den. The structure is in the Shinden-zukuri style, the style of sleeping quarters or residences from the period between 794 and 1192. Made of Japanese cypress, it also has a cypress bark roof. Double-hinged doors and heavy hinged shutters suspended from the roof (which are held open by iron rods that hang from the roof) are noticeable elements of early court architecture. Within the 10-room hall (which can be made into one large room through the removal of its *fusuma* or the silk curtains/screens/bamboo blinds that were used to create "rooms") is the Naruita, a board at the entryway that emits a noise when trod upon, thus serving as an alarm to alert the guards.

The main room (Moya) in the center of the building contains the Micho-dai, the throne on which the Emperor sat on ceremonial occasions. It is covered with a silk canopy with hangings of red, white and black. To the right and left of the throne area are two stands meant to hold the Imperial regalia on state occasions. Protective animals stand on either side of the throne as guardians against evil, the left hand one being a *koma-inu* dog while the right hand one is a *shishi* (lion). To the left of the Moya is the Ishibai-dan, a dirt area which was "cemented" with white lime. Here, the Emperor would stand, making symbolic contact with the earth when worshipping his ancestors. The area was covered with sand before the Emperor stepped upon it, since white sand was thought capable of canceling evil forces. A screen in strong colors depicting the four seasons is adjacent to this sacred sector.

The *fusuma* in the hall are by Tosa Mitsukiyo, with a Chinese or Japanese poem to accompany each picture; these Tosa school paintings are appropriate since the Tosa school took their subjects from Japanese history rather than that of China as did the Kano school of painters. The 16-petal Imperial chrysanthemum symbol is ubiquitous in the decorations of this hall. It was in the Seiryo-den that the Emperor performed the Shi-hohai (Worship of the Four Quarters) on New Year's Day.

To the north of the central room was the Yon-no-otodo, the Imperial sleeping quarters of several rooms: the Fujitsubo, the Kami-itsubone, the Hagi-no-to and the Koki-den for the Emperor's consorts. A two-mat "closet," surrounded by screens depicting the Chinese emperors enclosed the Emperor's sleeping area. The western portion of the Seiryo-den has five small rooms: the O-chozu-no-ma (the Emperor's Morning Purification Room), the O-yudono-no-ma (the Emperor's Bath Room), the Asagarei-no-ma (the Emperor's Dining Room), the Daiban-dokoro (a room for ceremonial meals) and the Oni-no-ma for the Emperor's ladies-in-waiting.

A corridor leads from the Seiryo-den to the Shishin-den, and at the corner of the corridor is a glassed screen that lists the annual court events and ceremonies. Wooden stairs also lead from the Seiryo-den into the To-tei, the East Yard, which is covered with white sand. In the yard in front of the Seiryo-den are two bamboo trees behind small wooden fencing, the Kara-take or Kan-chiku (Han Chinese bamboo) and the Kure-take or Go-chiku (Wu Chinese bamboo) named after the two ancient Chinese kingdoms of Han and Wu.

SHISHIN-DEN The Shishin-den (Ceremonial Hall), also known as the Nan-den (Southern Palace Hall) or the Purple Imperial Residence Hall, is a one-story structure that is a faithful copy of the original 8th century building, which was influenced by Chinese architectural styles. Here, the most important court ceremonies took place, including the New Year Audience and Coronations. Visitors today approach the building from the south, and the courtyard and the Shishin-den are viewed through the tile-roofed triple gateway, the Jomei-mon Gate, opened only for enthronements. The courtyard is walled by the tile-roofed Kairo, a double corridor of vermilion posts with gates on the south, west and east sides. The compound within these walled and roofed corridors is covered with raked white sand, meant to reflect the light of the sun and the moon into the palace hall. Appropriately, the west gate is named the Gekka-mon (Moon Gate) and the east gate is the Nikka-mon (Sun Gate).

Within a fence before the steps leading into the Shishin-den are a cherry tree (Sakon-no-sakura) and a citrus tree (Ukon-no-tachibana), derived from the names of the Imperial archers and horsemen, bodyguards who once stood guard on either side of the palace entry. (The Sakon (left) and Ukon (right) bodyguards were originally chosen from among the sons of the Regent or Chief Advisor to the Emperor, and they were organized in two bodies of archers and horsemen). The steps leading into the Shishin-den are 18 in number, corresponding to the 18 noble ranks within the court hierarchy. (In Chinese lore, the number nine was an

The Shishin-den (Ceremonial Hall) as seen through the vermilion columns of the Jomei-mon Gate.

auspicious number; by doubling this sum, a greater auspicious state was achieved). These steps, with white-painted ends, have easy risers to facilitate the carrying of the Imperial palanquin into the palace buildings. The side steps to the Shishin-den retain the number nine by limiting these steps to this number. The Shishin-den is 108 feet long by 74 feet deep (32.4 by 22.2 m). The eaves project by 20 feet (6 m), thereby creating a corridor about the structure. Above the front staircase hangs a tablet with Shishin-den in calligraphy. As with the Seiryo-den, the shutters, which are hinged from the top, are hung in their open state by rods from the eaves. The steep palace roof is of cypress bark 40 layers deep, some 12 inches (31 cm) thick.

Within, in the center of the hall, is the 1915 Imperial throne (Takamikura) created for the enthronement of the Emperor Taisho. It is in the shape of an octagonal Imperial palanquin, painted in black lacquer and surmounted by a golden phoenix 5.7 feet (1.5 m) tall with eight smaller golden phoenixes at the points of the octagonal roof. The silken curtains about the throne are renewed every spring and autumn. Behind the throne is a nine-panel screen, the Kensei-no-shoji (Sliding Screens of the 32 Chinese Sages), a copy of the original screens of the year 888 by Kose-no-Kanaoka. These copies were by Hiroyuki Sumiyoshi in the second half of the 18th century, the rear of these sliding panels being painted with peacocks and peonies. The Empress's throne is to the right and to the rear of the Emperor's throne and is 10 percent smaller.

To the east of the Shishin-den is the Jin-noza, a building with a board floor in which affairs of state would be discussed. Further to the east, to the east of the Kairo (corridor), is the Shunko-den or Kashiko-dokoro, a sanctuary where the Imperial mirror (one of the three Imperial treasures) was held at the time of the 1915 enthronement. Within are three rooms: the Ge-jin (Outer Room), Nai-jin (Inner Room) and Nai-nai-jin (Innermost Room)–where the sacred mirror was kept during the enthronement period.

KO GOSHO The Ko Gosho (Little Palace), comprising three large rooms, is connected to the Shishin-den by a corridor. This building is a 1958 replacement since in August of 1954 fireworks set off in the Kamo River landed on the thatched roof of the Ko Gosho and burned it down. The building faces to the east, toward the palace pond and garden, and its three rooms of 18 mats each were used for audiences and receptions. The innermost room is the Jodan-no-ma, the room with the raised platform for the Emperor or Crown Prince. The *fusuma* have scenes of the four seasons and the annual events of court life painted in brilliant colors, with broad blue stripes representing clouds at the bottom and top of each scene. Northwest of the Ko Gosho is a *kemari* (ancient football) field.

OIKE-NIWA The Oike-niwa (Pond Garden), a lovely landscaped stroll garden to the east of the Ko Gosho, was created by Kobori Enshu (1579–1647), as reconstructed in the late Edo period (19th century). It is centered on a large

pond fed by a waterfall containing a sandbar, stepping stones, bridges, small islands and a boat dock. In the foreground is a beach formed of small black stones, while a stone bridge leads across a portion of the waterway. The black stones were gifts from the Daimyo of Odawara and were taken from a beach near Mount Fuji; each came wrapped in silk. This attractive garden, designed by Emperor Go-mizu-no-o and Kobori Enshu, was the one Emperor Meiji always remembered after his move to Tokyo. The water actually comes from Lake Biwa via an underground aqueduct, and it eventually flows to the Kamo River.

O-GAKUMONJO A corridor leads from the Ko-gosho to the O-Gakumonjo (Imperial Hall of Studies), a six-room structure in the *shinden-zukuri* style. Here the emperor received instruction from his tutors, and the halls were used for the cultivation of poetry and music as well. There are three Audience Chambers (*gedan*, *chudan* and *jodan*), which face to the east and the garden. These are

A stone bridge crosses the pond of the Oike-niwa, a beautifully landscaped stroll garden.

decorated with pictures of 18 Chinese scholars by Hara Zaisho and with scenes of birds and flowers of the four seasons. These rooms are each of 12.5 mats and have coffered ceilings and *ramma* (transoms) between the individual rooms. The other three rooms are the Kari-no-ma (Wild Geese Room), with painted *fusuma* by Renzan Gantokan, the Yamabuke-no-ma (Japanese Globe Flower Room) by Maruyama Okyu, and the Kiku-no-ma (Chrysanthemum Room) with paintings by Okamoto Sukehiko. The coffered ceilings are richly decorated. It was in this building that the monthly poetry party was held, Imperial lectures were offered and the New Year's rite of reading took place.

OTSUNE-GOTEN When the Seiryo-den was held to be no longer proper for the Emperor's residence, the Otsune-goten (the Everyday Palace), 74 feet by 95 feet (22.2 by 28.5 m), was built to accommodate the private chambers of the Emperor. This building is not open to the public. Among its 11 rooms, laid with a total of 673 *tatami*, is the Moshi-no-kuchi (Herald's Entrance) of 30 mats, its *fusuma* decorated with pine trees and monkeys. This room was for official business, which was conducted through the court ladies and not with the Emperor directly. The Kenji-no-ma is the largest and most attractive of the rooms,

its *fusuma* bearing Chinese Court scenes on a gold ground by members of the Kano school of painters, and it was where the Imperial regalia would be kept. The three-room Audience Chamber had a raised platform in its innermost room (Jodan-no-ma).

There are four rooms in the southern portion of the building for the daily life of the Emperor. The two-room O-kazashiki is where the Emperor received instruction in the composing of *tanka*, the Ichi-no-ma (First Room), was a sitting room, the Ni-no-ma (Second Room) was for meeting with other members of the Imperial family, and then there were four more rooms clustered about the 18-mat sleeping chamber, whose *fusuma* were decorated with bamboo and tigers. Matted corridors surrounded these rooms. An annex, the O-mima (August Three Rooms) was where informal audiences took place, these rooms being decorated by the Tosa school of painters with scenes from the ancient Japanese court. Here, *Noh* performances could be given on a *Noh* stage under a separate roof of its own. In addition, Buddhist ceremonies took place in the O-mima.

ADDITIONAL BUILDINGS There are several additional structures, primarily for the Empress, the Empress Dowager and the Princesses. The Kogo-goten was the living

The 11-room Otsune-goten accommodated the Emperor's private chambers.

Sento Palace and Omiya Palace

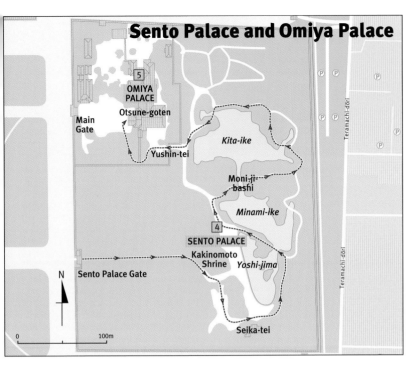

OMIYA
PALACE

5

Main
Gate

Otsune-goten

Yushin-tei

Kita-ike

Teramachi-dōri

P P P

P P

P

P

Moni-ji-
bashi

Minami-ike

4

SENTO PALACE

Kakinomoto
Shrine

Yoshi-jima

Teramachi-dōri

N

Sento Palace Gate

Seika-tei

0   100m

quarters for the Empress and was connected with the Otsune-goten by a long corridor. The Jishin-den (Earthquake Hall) was for use by the Emperor in times of seismic disturbances, and the O-Suzumisho (Pure Cool Hall), with a stream running under it, was for the Emperor's summer evenings. A tea pavilion, the Chosetsu, and the O-hana-goten, a section for the Crown Prince (where the Emperor Meiji lived before coming to the throne), are also in this area. This inner complex once held the three-room Kenji-no-ma, where the Imperial sword and jewel were kept. The Higyo-sha quarters for the Emperor's second wife was also in this area, known also by the name of Fujitsubu (Wisteria Yard). The palace kitchens stood in the large open space on the west as one leaves the palace complex, an area now covered with azaleas, moss and pines. These buildings were removed as a protection against fire at a later date after the court shifted to Tokyo.

(After the death of Emperor Hirohito, his son did not ascend the throne from the Imperial Palace in Kyoto but had his coronation in Tokyo, thereby ending a tradition of 1,000 years or more.)

4 SENTO PALACE

Separate from the Imperial Palace is the Sento Gosho, the retired Emperor's villa, to the southeast of the main Imperial Palace complex. (Permission to visit the Sento Gosho must be obtained at the Imperial Household Agency in the northwest corner of Kyoto Gyoen and, generally, must be applied for two days in advance of the date you wish to visit the Sento Gosho grounds, although in April, May, October and November it is best to apply five days in advance. Tours begin at 11:00 a.m. and at 1:30 p.m. for those over 20 years of age. The Sento Gosho is not open on Saturday afternoons, Sundays, public holidays and

The wall surrounding the Sento Gosho garden.

The glory of the Sento Palace is its stroll garden.

from December 25 to January 5. Tours are conducted in Japanese only. Be certain to ascertain where the tour begins when making reservations since the Sento Palace is a good walk from the Imperial Household Agency.)

Work on the Sento Palace was begun by the Tokugawa Shogun in 1627 as a retreat for the Emperor Go-Mizuno-o who had as one of his consorts Kazuko, the daughter of Shogun Tokugawa Hidetada. Under the direction of Kobori Enshu, the villa and its lovely stroll garden in 18 acres (7.2 ha) around two lakes encompassing 2.4 acres (1 ha) were completed a few years later. In the meantime, the Emperor, discouraged by the interference of the Shogun in his life, suddenly abdicated in 1629 in favor of his minor daughter, the first Empress in many centuries.

Destroyed by fire on various occasions, the Sento Palace was not rebuilt after the 1854 fire. Today, the 9 acre (3.6 ha) landscaped garden, the glory of the Sento Palace, is all that remains. Lakes, waterfalls, inlets, bridges, tea ceremony rooms, stones and huge trees make the Sento Palace Park a lovely stroll garden. To the southeast of the Imperial Palace buildings and close to Teramachi-dori, the larger of the two lakes has two islands reached by stone bridges, one of which is roofed over with wisteria. The groves of maple and cherry trees in the park have created a small forest in the heart of the city. Originally, a wall separated the Sento Gosho garden from that of the Omiya Gosho of the Empress, but this was removed in the mid-1700s and additional stroll paths were added to the garden.

On the grounds of the Sento Palace, the Dai-josai (Grand Thanksgiving Festival) was traditionally performed by the Emperor at the time of his enthronement (until the 1990 enthronement in Tokyo). Two temporary structures, the Yuki and Suki Palaces, were where the Emperor, in an overnight ceremony, offered prayers and sacred food to the Imperial ancestress (Amaterasu) and the gods and goddesses of heaven and earth, the most important ceremony of an Emperor's entire reign.

5 OMIYA PALACE

Adjoining the Sento Gosho was the Omiya Gosho. The Omiya Palace was the home of the Dowager Empress, and she moved here after her husband's retirement or death. Constructed in 1643 by the Shogun for the Empress Tofukumon-in, the consort of the Emperor Go-Mizuno-o and fifth daughter of the Shogun Tokugawa Hidetada, she resided here after Go-Mizuno-o had abdicated. (He spent many of his long years of abdication visiting his detached palaces, particularly the Shugaku-in of which he was most fond, and he avoided the Sento Palace built for him by his father-in-law, the Shogun.) Connected to the Sento Palace by a covered walkway, the Omiya Palace also burned in the 1854 fire. Today, a reconstruction of the palace stands on its original site, and is available to Imperial family members or special guests when visiting Kyoto. The Omiya Palace is not open to the public, but you may visit the extensive garden.

The Omiya Palace was rebuilt in 1867 for the Empress Dowager Eisho, the widow of Emperor Komei and mother of Emperor Meiji. Once separated by a wall from the gardens of the Sento Palace, the two gardens now form one unit, with the North Pond and its swift Male Waterfall overhung with trees and its Female Waterfall with its more gentle flow of water. The Maple Bridge crosses the channel which connects the North and South Ponds. The islands of the South Pond once held pleasure pavilions but all are now gone. Two tea pavilions exist in the southern portion of the garden, the Seika-tei and the Yushin-tei, the latter moved here from the mansion of the Duke of Konoe in 1884.

6 SHOKOKU-JI TEMPLE

The Shokoku-ji Temple lies to the north of Doshisha University, one street north of Imadegawa-dori and to the east of Karasuma-dori. While the temple grounds are open to the public, the monastic buildings are closed to general visitors except from November 1st through the 10th when the Hondo, the Hatto, the Kaisan-do and the Zuishun-in subtemple are open. However, the temple's interesting Jotenkaku Museum is open daily from 10:00 a.m. to 4:30 p.m. except when exhibitions are being changed. There is an entry fee to the museum and to the other buildings when they are open.

Shokoku-ji ranks as the second of the five Rinzai Zen temples in Kyoto, and the construction of its seven great buildings was begun in 1383 and completed in 1392 by Shogun Ashikaga Yoshimitsu at the request of Emperor Go-Kameyama. Yoshimitsu favored the Zen sect of Buddhism, and this temple was to serve as the Muromachi Bakufu headquarters of the government that he had established 14 years earlier. In fact, the temple was built near the eastern portion of the Hana-no-Gosho, Yoshimitsu's palace and the adjacent site of the Muromachi Bakufu government. The fact that it took 10 years to build the temple gives some idea of the sumptuousness of its parts in its day. As its first Superior, the noted priest Muso Kokushi was named its honorary abbot. During the Muromachi period (1336–1568), it was a prominent headquarters for Zen scholarship. Its priests became advisors to the government, and ties between the temple and the Ashikaga rulers were very close.

The 15th century proved disastrous for the temple, for all of its buildings were destroyed in a 1425 fire. Restored by 1466, they were destroyed once more in 1467 in the Onin War. Ironically, that war started at the Tenkai-bashi (Heavenly World Bridge) near the temple, and the temple grounds were used as a military camp during the ensuing years of strife.

The Hatto (Lecture Hall) at Shokoku-ji.

One hundred years were to pass before the temple was rebuilt. Toyotomi Hideyori built the Hatto or Dharma (Lecture Hall) in 1605, and then Tokugawa Ieyasu had the San-mon (Main Gate) built. Fire once more afflicted the temple in the Great Temmai Fire of 1788, and all that remains of its full complement of pre-1788 buildings and 21 subtemples is the Hatto. In 1807, other buildings were constructed, using portions of the old Gosho of the Imperial Palace. However, the original Butsu-den (Buddha Hall) and San-mon (Main Gate) were never rebuilt.

Today, the Shokoku-ji has 100 subtemples under it. Among these are the Kinkaku-ji (Gold Pavilion) and the Ginkaku-ji (Silver Pavilion). The main temple buildings today sit in a 216 acre (86.4 ha) compound. The temple grounds are entered from a street that runs through the Doshisha University campus, the temple obviously having lost some of its property under the Meiji government. The small enclosed central gate leads to a plain arched bridge which crosses the temple pond and then to the central portion of the complex where the San-mon Gate once stood. A roadway on either side of this central section is bordered by subtemples.

The Hatto (Lecture Hall), the only early building extant, is 87 feet (26 m) long by 66 feet (20.1 m) wide, and it is the oldest existing Hatto in Japan; it has a double roof and faces south. Within is the original graceful image of Shaka (Sakayamuni), with Ananda (his favorite disciple) on his right and Kasho (Mahakasyapa), foremost of those who kept the monastic rules), on his left, all three seated on a platform some 7 feet (2 m) off the floor. The ceiling of the Hatto is decorated with a painting of a dragon, as is traditional in Zen lecture halls. On the west side of the hall are benches for the monks, while at the rear left is a large drum behind a fence, and next to it are figures of three abbots and a monk, the latter seated on a Chinese chair. A temple bell hangs at the rear right center, while at the far right are images of Shoguns and Emma, the king of hell. Between and before these are a tripartite Chinese screen and a Chinese chair for the abbot. Along the right (east) wall is another drum and then two sections with *ihai* memorial tablets.

The Hojo (Abbot's Quarters) is not open to the public, but has some excellent painted *fusuma*, including one of many bamboo by the Zen priest Gyokurin.

An archery exhibition at the Rozan-ji Temple where Lady Murasaki wrote "The Tale of Genji."

NEARBY SITES

To the west of the Imperial Palace along Teranouchi-dori are a few locations of minor interest. One is the Rozan-ji Temple, which is reputed to be the site of the villa of Lady Murasaki, author of *The Tale of Genji*. Today, a garden in her memory has been created in the temple grounds. There are two minor museums as well: the Kitamura Bijutsukan, which holds a private collection of tea ceremony items, is open to the public from 10:00 a.m. to 4:00 p.m. from March through June and September through November, and the Kyoto Rekishi Shityokan, which is devoted to the history of the city of Kyoto. It is open in the morning, primarily on weekdays.

Just to the north of the Old Imperial Palace and at Imadegawa-dori/ Karasuma-dori is Doshisha University, founded in 1875 at a meeting in the Shue-do of Chion-in Temple by Joseph Mishima and Kakuna Yamamoto in cooperation with the American Board of Foreign Missions. After 1897 it severed its connection with its American sponsors, but its New England-style Amherst House is a reminder of the close ties between American Protestantism and what began as a girls' school, a training school for nurses and a hospital. From its simple beginnings, the school thrived, and today it is a full-fledged co-educational university with a rich offering of courses. (The university, and the two sites which follow can be reached by way of the Imadegawa subway station or by buses 51, 59, 201 or 203 to the intersection of Imadegawa-dori and Karasuma-dori.)

Just to the east of the above intersection, on Imadegawa-dori, is the Reizei Mansion in a walled enclave. The Reizei family is descended from Fujiwara-no-Nagaie (1005–64). A later family member, Fujiwara-no-Teika, was the compiler of the *Shinkokinshu*, an anthology of Japanese poetry, in 1205. He inspired various other noted families of poets in his day and later. Of the noted poetic families of the past, the Reizei alone remains, and their mansion is the repository of this historic family's collections.

The Butsu-den (Buddha Hall) is to the west of the Hojo, and it contains six rooms. The first is a 24-mat room with *fusuma* on two sides depicting bamboo on a gold ground, which were painted by Gyokurin. The 42-mat middle room on the south side has a Kannon painstakingly drawn with Chinese characters from the Kannon sutra. The landscape in black ink on white by Zaichi Hara on the *fusuma* is of Mount Fudara in China. Next is a 24-mat room with *fusuma* painted by Shunkei Imei, the 115th abbot, of plum trees on a gold ground. The northwest room has scenes of elegant Chinese cultural life by Zaicho Hara. The rear middle room features paintings on the *fusuma* of cherry blossoms on Mount Yoshino, *fusuma* which were originally in the Imperial Palace. The last room on the northeast contains paintings by Zaicho Haera of legendary hermits of China. Thus the interior of the building has paintings ranging from the "trick" Kannon one composed of Chinese characters to landscapes in various media.

The Kaisan-do (Founder's Hall) is to the east of the Hatto behind a wall. Its large hall has a landscape scene on its western *fusuma*, and along its rear wall are images of National Teacher Abbot Fumyo and three other past abbots. The middle of the rear wall has an alcove in which an image of the founding abbot, Muso Kokushi, is located. Next comes the commemorative *ihai* to past abbots. The east wall is divided into two parts, the first section holding images of the three shoguns who were major contributors to the temple, while the last is of Ashikaga Yoshimitsu. Many notable people, including Ashikaga shoguns, are buried in the grounds, primarily at the Jisho-an. The most famous individuals are Ashikaga Shogun Yoshimasa (1435–90), who built the Silver Pavilion, and Fujiwara Seika (1561–1619), a noted Chinese scholar.

The Zuiho-in is the only subtemple of the Shokoku-ji open to the public, and then only in November. Its main hall has five rooms, the second with a dragon on its rear *fusuma*, while the next is decorated with mountain scenery. The third is an altar room with an image of the Buddha and his disciples against gold *fusuma* decorated with a peacock and hen. The last and largest room has a *tokono-ma* and a *chigaidana*. At the rear of the hall is the delightful interior garden, with its two ponds crossed by a stone bridge and then a garden and its waterfall. The return to the main hall, after crossing the bridge, is to a secondary building that is connected with the main hall by a long corridor.

The Jotenkaku Museum is the most important part of the temple complex since it is both open to the public throughout the year and holds the treasures of a number of the Shokoku-ji's subtemples, including the Golden (Kinkaku-ji) and Silver (Ginkaku-ji) Pavilions. Some of these treasures are seen in rotating exhibits. The museum was created in 1984 on the 600th anniversary of the founding of the head temple. It is a modern fireproof building with an exhibition hall, grand hall, library, tea ceremony room and storage areas for the treasures of Shokoku-ji and its allied temples. The tea ceremony room, Muchu-an, was created from some of the old timbers salvaged from the Golden Pavilion after its 1950 fire, and is available for tea ceremony. The Grand Hall is used for lectures, study, training and Zen meditation. A special showing of temple treasures occurs from October 5 to December 20 annually. Entry fee. The museum has a fine collection of art from the 9th century on, its strength lying in the period after the 13th century. Special exhibitions are held in spring and autumn for a period of two months each. It is appropriate that the temple has a museum since Shogun Yoshimitsu established a painting academy at the temple, where Sesshu and Kano Masonobu, among others, studied.

GETTING THERE

The Old Imperial Palace is in the grounds of Kyoto Goen in north-central Kyoto and it can be reached via subway by taking the Karasuma line to Marutamachi station. Alternately, it can be reached by bus 2, 30, 32, 36, 47, 204 or 206 to the intersection of Imadegawa-dori and Karasuma-dori. Application for admission to the palace grounds must be made to the Imperial Household Agency office, which is in the Kyoto Gyoen grounds to the south of Imadegawa-dori and just east of Karusama-dori. The office is open from 9:00 a.m. to noon and from 1:00 p.m. to 4:00 p.m. weekdays. Passports are generally requested.

The palace tours (usually but not always in English) take place at 10:00 a.m. and 2:00 p.m. on weekdays and on Saturdays in April, May, October and November. Tours of the grounds of the former Sento Palace are at 11:00 a.m. and 3:00 p.m. (Japanese language only). Tours are not given on Sundays, public holidays or between December 25 and January 5. It is best to request admission for a date other than the day the request is made—although it is sometimes possible to join the next tour if you arrive at the Agency office at least 20 minutes in advance of the tour time. Tours of the Old Imperial Palace begin at the Seisho-mon Gate to the grounds in the middle of the west side of the palace walls, recognizable by the guard house and the group awaiting entry. You should be at the gate at least 15 minutes in advance of the beginning of the tour. The palace is open to the general Japanese public without reservations one week in April and one week in October—a good time to avoid due to the crush of crowds.

Walking Tour 14

DAITOKU-JI TEMPLE AREA

A Weaver's Paradise, a Nunnery of Dolls and Daitoku-Ji Zen Temple

The northernmost portion of central Kyoto can lay claim to several sites of interest, but foremost in importance is the great Daitoku-ji Zen temple with its many subtemples, each with an interesting or more varied garden than its neighbor. Here, the art of the tea ceremony was perfected, and here is buried that most important tea master, Sen-no-Rikyu, whose exquisite taste set the standard for all tea masters thereafter.

Daitoku-ji has so many important subdivisions that much of this tour is devoted to these temples. Of Daitoku-ji's 22 subtemples, only a few are open to the public, and some of them may only be visited at the beginning of November. Nevertheless, they are important enough that an effort should be made to visit whenever they are open to the general public. (The dates are given below for when each of them is open.) However, the seven main structures of the Daitoku-ji proper are of note, and the most famous garden of all the subtemples, that of the Daisen-in, may be visited throughout the year. Primarily a center of Zen learning and meditation, those subtemples not open to the public are intent upon keeping to their religious ways and thus have not allowed themselves to become tourist attractions.

Wars can be disruptive not only to religious life but also to crafts and to trade. But, strangely enough, war can sometimes lead to changes and improvements in these fields. So it was with the craft of weaving in the late 1400s. Luxurious fabrics had been much in demand by the Imperial court to grace their elegant and non-productive lives. The aesthetic pleasures of fine clothing came to an end, however, as a result of the Onin Wars of the late 1400s, and even the weavers themselves were lost to Kyoto for a number of years. When they returned from their self-imposed exile, they settled in what had been the "Western Army Camp" (Nishijin) area of Kyoto, and there, with new techniques learned in Osaka in the 1470s, the weaving craft revived and became famed for both its practical materials and for its rich brocades.

1 NISHIJIN TEXTILE CENTER

While there will be some walking in this tour, public transportation (or taxis) will come in handy, for the distances to be covered are fairly considerable, more than normally followed in this guidebook. The first location to be visited is the Nishijin Textile Center. (Take bus 9 or 12 along Horikawa-dori to the bus stop at the intersection of Horikawa-dori and Imadegawa-dori—in fact, these two bus lines can be used to reach the other sites on this tour. If coming from the subway to the Imadegawa station, take bus 59 or 203 along Imadegawa-dori to

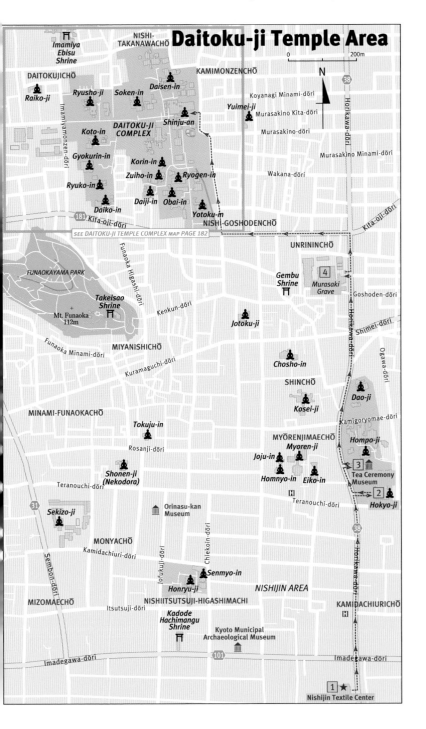

Daitoku-ji Temple Area

NISHI-TAKANAWACHŌ

Imamiya Ebisu Shrine

DAITOKUJICHŌ

Raiko-ji

Ryusho-ji   Soken-in

Daisen-in

KAMIMONZENCHŌ

0   200m

N

38

Koyanagi Minami-dōri

Yuimei-ji

Murasakino Kita-dōri

Shinju-an

DAITOKU-JI COMPLEX

Murasakino-dōri

Koto-in

Murasakino Minami-dōri

Gyokurin-in

Korin-in

Murasaki Minami-dōri

Wakana-dōri

Zuiho-in   Ryogen-in

Ryuko-in

Daiji-in   Obai-in

Daiko-in

181 Kita-oji-dōri

SEE DAITOKU-JI TEMPLE COMPLEX MAP PAGE 182

Yotoku-m

NISHI-GOSHODENCHŌ

UNRININCHŌ

FUNAOKAYAMA PARK

Funabka Higashi-dōri

Gembu Shrine

4

Murasaki Grave

Goshoden-dōri

Takeisao Shrine

Mt. Funaoka 112m

Kenkun-dōri

Shimei-dōri

Jotoku-ji

Funaoka Minami-dōri

MIYANISHICHŌ

Kuramaguchi-dōri

Chosho-in

Ogawa-dōri

SHINCHŌ

Dao-ji

MINAMI-FUNAOKACHŌ

Tokuju-in

Kosei-ji

Kamigoryomae-dōri

Hompo-ji

Rosanji-dōri

MYŌRENJIMAECHŌ

Myoren-ji

Shonen-ji (Nekodora)

Joju-in

Homnyo-in   Eiko-in

3 Tea Ceremony Museum

31

Teranouchi-dōri

Sekizo-ji

Orinasu-kan Museum

H

Teranouchi-dōri

2

38

Hokyo-ji

MONYACHŌ

Kamidachiuri-dōri

Jofukuji-dōri

Chiekoin-dōri

Sembon-dōri

Senmyo-in

NISHIJIN AREA

Honryu-ji

MIZOMAECHŌ

NISHIITSUTSUJI-HIGASHIMACHI

Itsutsuji-dōri

Kadode Hachimangu Shrine

KAMIDACHIURICHŌ

H

Kyoto Municipal Archaeological Museum

Imadegawa-dōri

101

Imadegawa-dōri

1 ★

Nishijin Textile Center

the intersection with Horikawa-dori to the modern Nishijin Textile Center, which is on the west side of Horikawa-dori just to the south of Imadegawa-dori. The center is open daily from 9:00 a.m. to 5:00 p.m. without charge. *Kimono* shows (for groups only) take place between 10:00 a.m. and 4:00 p.m. There is a fee for the *kimono* show.)

The Nishijin area is a fairly large and somewhat amorphous one. It spreads from just south of the Daitoku-ji Temple (Kita-oji-dori) down to Imadegawa-dori and from the Kitano Tenman-gu Shrine area to Horikawa-dori. This area received its name from the wars of the 15th century, which laid waste this area as well as virtually all of Kyoto. Nishijin means "Western Army Camp," for that was what was here in the late 1400s. When the Onin War ended, and as peace was restored to Kyoto, this area began to revive as a place of work and residence, and it was here that the weavers resettled. The weavers had moved to Sakai (the port of old Osaka) and to Yamaguchi during the wars of the 15th century, and there they learned some new (to them) Chinese techniques of weaving.

Traditional weaving of silk on a loom in the Nishijin sector of Kyoto.

Additional immigrants from the mainland who came to Japan as a result of Hideyoshi's Korean incursions in the late 1500s also added not only new techniques in weaving but the secret of making gold thread. These improved techniques helped Kyoto weavers to develop more luxurious materials for their major customers—much of their income coming from the woven silk goods they supplied to the Imperial court and aristocracy.

The weaving of silk in Kyoto was a tradition that began even before the city was established. Among the early settlers in the region was the Hata family, who brought the techniques of weaving silk from the Chinese mainland when they emigrated to Japan in the 300s. Weaving thus became a major source of income in the new capital when it came into being in the 800s, and this craft continued to flourish until the Onin War. Revival came slowly at first after the war, and, when it did come, the Nishijin weavers organized themselves into a guild. When they obtained the monopoly for weaving, their future seemed assured, and by the early 1700s there were some 5,000 weavers working in the private homes of the Nishijin.

All was not smooth sailing, however, for the fire of 1730 destroyed many of the houses and looms in the district, some 3,000 looms

reputedly having been lost. In the 1830s, moreover, the government, in one of its anti-luxury moods, prohibited silk weaving altogether. The move of the capital and the court to Tokyo in 1868 might have adversely affected Nishijin production, but the relocation was offset by the new technology that began to come from the West, the importation of Jacquard looms leading to a mechanization of and an increase in production of hand-loomed cloth.

Since the 1980s, the outlook for Nishijin has diminished. Young people have other alternatives than to become weavers, the import of inexpensive woven goods from factories in newly industrialized countries has posed a serious threat, and the diversification of weaving to other areas of Japan, which began at the time of the Onin War, inexorably continues. Although 3,000 looms were in use in the area in the 1980s, whether the Nishijin area will remain a textile center is an open question.

A center for display and sales of Nishijin products began in 1925 with the opening of the Textile Museum. In 1976, the new Nishijin Textile Center was opened. On the first floor of the center are displays, an information enter, and a restaurant. On the second floor you can see Jacquard and hand-operated looms in action and visit a sales area. On the third floor are exhibits of old Nishijin weaving and *kimono*.

There is another building devoted to the craft of Nishijin weaving, the Orinasu-kan, which has displays of Nishijin artistry and offers the chance to participate in weaving itself. It lies to the west of Horikawa-dori and between Imadegawa-dori and Teranouchi-dori in what had once been a weaving factory. It is best to take a taxi to the location since it is in a built-up area of the Nishijin quarter and not easy to find.

On leaving the Nishijin Textile Center, the route continues by bus or on foot north along Horikawi-dori for two streets (on the east side of Horikawa-dori). Then turn east into Aburakoji-dori to another Kyoto traditional craft center at the Raku Bijutsukan (Raku Museum). (The Raku Museum is open from 10:00 a.m. to 4:00 p.m., but is closed on Mondays and on national holidays as well as from August 11 to September 8 and from December 17 to January 7. Entry fee.) The museum was opened in 1977 to exhibit the low-fired *raku* ware (*raku yaki*) that had been created by the masters of the Raku family since the latter part of the 1500s by Chojiro 1516–92), its originator, at the special request of the tea master Sen-no-Rikyu.

According to legend, Chojiro used clay from Hideyoshi's Jurakudai Palace grounds, and his work was so good that Hideyoshi gave him a seal with the character *raku* to be impressed on his bowls. His tea bowls had a soft texture to the touch and kept the tea warmer than had stoneware. Thus, the museum contains selections of *raku yaki* as well as documentation from the Raku family archives. Two exhibitions are presented each year of a small number of choice objects, exhibitions worth seeing for those interested in Japanese ceramics. The exhibition labels and brochures are in English. The early *raku yaki* tradition has been continued by the family and the artistry and craftsmanship of their wares continues to be exceptional.

2 HOKYO-JI (DOLL TEMPLE)

Three streets to the north of Imadegawa-dori on Teranouchi-dori, one street east of Horikawa-dori, is the Hokyo-ji Rinzai Zen nunnery (open from 9:00 a.m. to 4:00 p.m. daily. Entry fee.) This nunnery was founded in 1360, and although it has *fusuma* and religious images of interest, the real reason to visit this temple occurs twice a year when it puts its collection of dolls on display. As a result, it has always had the nickname of Ningyo-dera or "Doll Temple."

In the past, this nunnery was the recipient of dolls from the Imperial court, in particular dolls from the Emperor Komei's era (1845–66). The temple has another more sentimental appeal, for in the last days of the rule of the Tokugawa Shoguns, the Imperial Princess

Display of traditional dolls and accoutrements at Hokyo-ji (Doll Temple).

Kazu-no-miya was forced to marry a Tokugawa Shogun for political reasons, despite the fact that she had been engaged to a prince when she was six years old. She used to play in the temple during her childhood, and the temple is a remembrance of her happy early years before her later contractual marriage.

The best time to visit the temple is at the twice-a-year doll display from mid-February to mid-March, at the time of the traditional Hina Matsuri (Dolls' Festival). The exhibit is also mounted in mid-October to late-November. You enter the temple from its Teranouchi-dori entry gate. After paying the entry fee, turn right past a display case of traditional costumes. A corridor runs along the moss garden on the south side of the Hondo (Main Hall), and then you come to rooms that display dolls and *bunraku* puppets. A turn to the left to another corridor leads to the Shinden, with a garden on the left, and eventually one comes to a room with life-sized figures of children and men in traditional costumes as well as other rooms of mannequins in traditional garb. A corridor leading back to the entry has cases with displays of Japanese and foreign dolls. Games such as *sugoraku* (played with dice) and *tosan* (a fan-throwing game) are shown. Thus, the Doll Temple offers a view into the clothing and toys of an earlier era.

3 TEA CEREMONY MUSEUM

The cult of the tea ceremony developed in the late 1500s and thereafter, and one cannot speak of the tea ceremony in Japan without making reference to Sen-no-Rikyu, one of the most noted figures in artistic realms in Japan. A master of flower arranging and the master of the solemn preparation of tea in the formal tea ceremony, he was an advisor to Oda Nobunaga and Toyotomi Hideyoshi in the last quarter of the 16th century. The rules he laid down for the tea ceremony still hold true today, and this quiet appreciation of the art of serving tea, with its concomitant appreciation of the fine ceramics involved in the ceremony, are still widely taught.

A favorite of Hideyoshi, Sen fell from favor in his 71st year. The reasons for his fall have never been known, but speculation ranges from his refusal to permit Hideyoshi to marry his beautiful young daughter to the fact that he had a representation of himself carved as an image of the Buddha and placed in the San-mon of the Daitoku-ji Temple, an action which is said to have enraged Hideyoshi.

Guests being served tea by a tea master.

At any rate, in 1591 Sen was ordered to commit *seppuku*, an act which Hideyoshi is said to have regretted thereafter. Sen committed suicide as ordered, and his remains were buried in the grounds of the Juko-in of the Daitoku-ji, the place of his death and the future site of the graves of his family in the centuries to come. Sen's family carried on the leadership in the area of tea ceremony, establishing a school in the early 17th century on land donated by the Empress Tofukumon. Sen's grandson, Sen-no-Sotan (1578–1658), divided the house of Sen and its property among his three sons, thereby creating the three branches of the family: the Omote (Front) Senke founded by son Soso, the Ura (Rear) Senke founded by son Shoshitsu, and the Mushanokoji Senke founded by son Soshu. The family traditions have been maintained since the 16th century, and members of the Sen family each devote six months in training at Daitoku-ji.

The three branches of the Sen family still retain leadership in tea ceremony matters, and the Ura Senke Foundation has been established to teach the art of tea ceremony (*cha-no-yu*) and to present exhibitions of related materials, such as ceramics, writings and related tea ceremony materials. Branches of the school of tea have been set up overseas by the education section of the organization. The Chado Research Center has a library for the academic study of tea ceremony and a gallery which mounts small exhibitions (9:30 a.m. to 4:30 p.m., closed on Mondays) It also offers demonstrations of *cha-no-yu* (tea ceremony) weekly at its headquarters.

The gardens of the Ura and Omote Senke are noted for their various tea houses. (The Ura Senke gardens may only be visited by advance permission, the Omote Senke is not generally open to the public). Tea ceremony gardens and their paths (*roji*) are quite simple, the emphasis being on the garden as a preliminary to the ceremony. Thus the garden should not draw attention to itself but serve as a form of contemplative preparation as one walks to the tea house. Stepping stones in the path were an innovation in the early years to avoid the mud of a path in inclement weather, and stone lanterns, as well, were set along the path in order to light the way to the tea house for an evening tea ceremony.

Among the Ura Senke tea houses are the Konnichi-an (created by Shoan's son Sotan in the late 1600s), Yu-in, Kanun-tei, Mushiki-ken, Totsutotu-sai, Hosen-sai and Taityu-ken. The Omote Senke has the Fushin-an, Angetsu-tei, and Tenetsu-do.

The Fushin-an was built for Toyotomi Hideyoshi by Sen-no-Rikyu when Hideyoshi created his Jurakudai (Palace of Pleasures) in Kyoto in 1596. When Hideyoshi destroyed the Jurakudai Palace, he is said to have given the Fushin-an to Sen as a gift. This story is probably apocryphal, since Hideyoshi ordered Sen to commit *seppuku* a few years before the Jurakudai was dismantled. The history of this tea house is not clear, but it is thought that Hideyoshi had the Fushin-an destroyed when Sen died. In the 1600s, Sen's grandson Shoan recreated the tea house, but it and its successors were destroyed by fire on several occasions. Last reconstructed in 1923, it is a 3¾-mat room entered through a low door (so one must assume a humble position when creeping in). The waiting bench under an exterior roof is one of the few remaining elements retained from early tea house style. Within is a sword rack and *tokonoma*, details retained from the design of the original structure. The sense of *wabi*, the cultivation of the simple and quiet, were hallmarks of Sen-no-Rikyu's approach to the tea ceremony, and his descendents have maintained that same spirit for over 400 years.

4 **LADY MURASAKI'S GRAVE**

Continue north along Horikawa-dori to the intersection with Kita-oji-dori. (Bus 9 or 12 or 204 or 205 or 206 goes through that crossroads to the bus stop.) Some 320 feet (100 m) south of Kita-oji-dori, on the west side of Horikawa-dori, there is a factory behind its wall. At a small opening between two of the factory buildings is a lane which goes back to a cul-de-sac. Here the graves of Murasaki Shikibu and Ono Takamura are located.

It is unfortunate that the grave of one of Japan's greatest writers, Lady Murasaki, who wrote so charmingly of the splendor of the Imperial court during the Heian period, and who described her times and surroundings so artfully and with such grace, should find her last resting place in so unlikely a location. Of course, one must remember that in her time this present portion of Kyoto lay in the countryside beyond the city of the late 900s. When Japan began its industrial expansion after 1870, insufficient thought was too often given to aspects of the nation's traditional heritage, and thus important historic or artistic sites were often neglected or lost.

Finally, in the spring of 1989, the grave of one of the most gifted writers in literary history (and the adjoining grave of another early author) were given the respectful treatment they deserve. New walls have been erected about the enclave, low granite fences have been placed before the graves, and the moss-covered mounds have been topped with new small *sotoba*. Lady Murasaki's grave is the larger of the two and is on the western side of the enclosure. Facing her grave on the south is a very large memorial stone inscribed in Japanese and English, which you can read in the accompanying photo.

A memorial stone next to the grave of Lady Murasaki Shikibu.

5 DAITOKU-JI TEMPLE

Return to Horikawa-dori and turn left (north) to Kita-oji-dori, where you make another left and walk for a few streets to the temples of Daitoku-ji in north-central Kyoto to the north of Kita-oji-dori and to the east of Senbon-dori.

Daitoku-ji is a Rinzai Zen monastery with 22 subtemples in its precincts. It is one of the most important monastery complexes in Kyoto and is also the largest Zen temple in the city, encompassing some 35 acres (14 ha) of north-central Kyoto. (At one time it embraced 100 acres/40 ha.) Seven of its 22 subtemples are open to the public: the Daisen-in, Hoshun-in, Koto-in, Ryogen-in, Zuiho-in, Obai-in and Sangen-in. Additional temples, as well as the Daitoku-ji Hojo, are open during the first 10 days of November. The monasteries contain some of the finest Zen gardens in Kyoto, and their treasures, shown each October or November, are of a rich and varied nature. The buildings are all representative of Zen architecture and the cultural influences of the Muromachi period (1336–1568) when Zen influenced the court and the military. As a result, the tombs of some of the most noted military leaders and Zen priests of the 15th to the 17th centuries can be found here.

The Daitoku-ji monastery complex was (and still is) a place for the serious study or practice of Zen contemplation, and thus for monks it has been a place of privileged residence for learning and meditative discipline of a Zen nature. The purpose of the complex remains a serious religious one, and although the precincts are heavily frequented by visitors, the majority of its 22 subtemples do not welcome the outside world and the distractions that could endanger the peace and purposes of a Buddhist monastery.

The Daitoku-ji temples provide classic examples of the Zen monastic building. Cloistered behind their own walls, independent of each other, each with its own history, they pursue their discipline tranquilly in their own manner, yet they remain bound together by meditative ideals and aesthetic tastes that have influenced all of Japanese life and culture, from gardening to the tea ceremony. Their gardens range from the simple to the elaborate, their paintings reflect the work of the major artists of their time, and their tea houses are reminders that here Sen-no-Rikyu perfected the tea ceremony before his ceremonial suicide (*seppuku*) at the order of Toyotomi Hideyoshi.

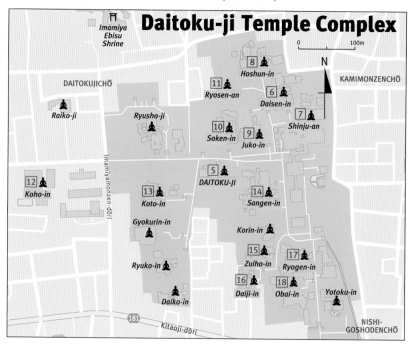

Daitoku-ji Temple Complex

The site of Daitoku-ji once held an Imperial villa during the Heian period (795–1185) in those years before the temple was established. Daitoku-ji (Temple of Great Virtue) was created by the Emperor Go-Daigo (1287–1335) from 1319 to 1324, and he appointed Priest Myocho (1232–1337), better known as Daito Kokushi, as its Superior, the first of many famous priests associated with the temple, often men who were noted artists and aesthetes. Myocho had converted both the Emperor Go-Daigo and his predecessor, the Emperor Hanazono, to his sect of Zen Buddhism, and thus Imperial support led to the growth of the monastery.

In 1333, Daitoku-ji was named the court temple for worship. A fire in 1453 seriously damaged it, and then in 1468 the Onin War led to its total destruction. Its Superior, Ikkyu-osho (1394–1481), took refuge in Izumo province along with the temple treasures. Restoration began in 1474 with court sponsorship, but primarily with the financial backing of merchants from Osaka under Priest Ikkyu, and most of the major buildings were completed by 1479. Ikkyu was said to be the son of the Emperor Go-Komatsu and a concubine, and he was renowned as a literary man, a poet and a painter as well as being a priest– and an eccentric.

The importance of the temple increased in the 16th century as Zen appealed to the victorious military, and these generals began to build the subtemples that today cluster in their walled compounds about the early Daitoku-ji complex. They built these as prayer places for their ancestors or for their own eventual resting place. The funeral services for one of the most noted 15th century generals, Oda Nobunaga, were held here on his death in 1582, his ceremonies being conducted by his successor, Toyotomi Hideyoshi. Thereafter, there was a further influx of the military who created or supported subtemples, of which in 1661–73 there were 24 in number. The Tokugawa Shoguns favored the temple between 1606 and 1868 but, in reaction after 1868, many of the subtemples suffered from the anti-Buddhist actions of the Imperial government, and the grounds of the temple compound were accordingly decreased. In the post-1945 era, Daitoku-ji has flourished once more.

From Kita-oji-dori, a pine tree-lined path leads from the South Gate into the temple grounds, passing various subtemples behind their walled enclosures, en route to the Chokushi-mon (Imperial Messenger's Gate). The South Gate is the symbolically more important entry, and the buildings along the street of its north–south axis are impressive in size. Once you begin to move along the subtemple paths beyond this major street, which is wide in order to accommodate temple processions on religious occasions, the pathways are not as broad nor as straight.

The Daitoku-ji *garan* or temple courtyard is the center of the parent temple, and here you should start your tour. The *garan* traditionally includes seven major buildings, and Daitoku-ji conforms to the Zen variation of the Buddhist *garan*. These seven elements are described below, and thereafter a number of the individual subtemples of note.

The Daitoku-ji *garan* begins at the end of the path mentioned in the paragraph above. (If you are arriving at the temple by taxi, the taxi driver will probably stop at the eastern side of the temple grounds, leaving you at the beginning of the *garan*.) The *garan* begins with the Chokushi-mon (Imperial Messenger's Gate), a gate that was originally the South Gate of the Imperial Palace in Kyoto, the palace built by Hideyoshi for the Emperor in the 1590s. This 1599 Kara-mon (Chinese-style) gate with a cypress bark roof was moved to Daitoku-ji in the 1640s, a gift from the Empress Meisho, to serve as the temple main entrance. Today, entry is barred except on the unlikely occasion when a messenger might be received from the court. Between the lintels of the portal are fine carvings representing bamboo, pine, plum, peony and birds.

SAN-MON In theory, Zen monasteries were built on the tops of hills, and thus the main gate to the temple is usually called the San-mon (Mountain Gate) even when, as here, the terrain is rather flat. Here, the San-mon is directly behind the Chokushi-mon. This Mountain Gate was originally built as a one-story gate at the time of the 1479 restoration of the temple by Superior Ikkyu, from income earned from the sale of a handwritten copy of *The Tale of Genji* that was owned by the temple. The San-mon is a five-bay gate with three portals. In 1589, Sen-no-Rikyu (1522–91), the famed tea master and priest, added the second floor. The stairways to the upper floors of the gate are external ones on either side of the gateway.

The upper floor of the San-mon (a closed area) is the location of a number of images. Shaka (Sakyamuni) is the main image with Anan and Kayo (Kasho), his two most important disciples, on either side. These statues were created in the Chinese style. The 16 *rakan* or *arhat* (individuals who have attained Nirvana while still in this world) in this hall are war booty brought back from Korea by Kiyomasa Kato in the 1590s and presented to the Daitoku-ji Temple.

Another significant treasure in the San-mon is a statue of the Buddha in the image of Sen-no-Rikyu, said to have been self-sculpted by Sen himself. Hideyoshi is reputed to have been enraged at the placement of this statue in the temple, not only at Sen's hubris in creating a Buddha in his own image but by the fact that when Hideyoshi passed through the gate he was walking below a representation of Sen. The image was saved only when permission was granted to remove it to the residence of Ikeda Teruma, the Daimyo of Bizen. It was returned to its original position in 1888 by a descendent, the Marquis Ikeda. The ceiling of the lower floor has a sepia drawing of a dragon in a circle and other painted decorations by Hasegawa Tohaku (1539–1610). Such ceiling dragons are a characteristic of Zen lecture halls and at times of other Zen monastic structures as well.

BUTSU-DEN The Butsu-den (Buddha Hall), a Chinese-style building with a tiled roof and arched windows in the Zen style, is situated just behind the San-mon Gate, thereby continuing the north–south alignment of the major buildings. It is 57 feet (17 m) by 54 feet (16 m) in size. Rebuilt in 1665, it contains a wooden image on a raised platform of Sakyamuni seated on the traditional lotus blossom. His disciples Anan and Kayo are on either side. Additional images from the 1540s in the rear include one of the temple's first Superiors, Daito Kokushi.

Tablets before the Sakyamuni image memorialize Emperor Go-Daigo, the founder of the temple, as well as the first two Superiors. There are faded paintings of *apsara* (heavenly angels) and clouds on the ceiling by Kano Motonobu (1477–1559) and a dragon and clouds on the *fusuma* (sliding screens) by Kaiho Yusho (1533–1615). The exterior and interior of the building are of undecorated wood but the pillars behind the dais are decorated with polychrome designs.

HATTO Directly behind and connected to the Butsu-den is the plain wooden double-roofed seven by six bay Hatto (Lecture Hall) of 1636, which replaced earlier lecture halls consumed by fires. On the third centennial of the founding of the temple, this Chinese-style building was re-erected by the feudal lord of Odawara Castle, Inaba Masanori. The traditional Zen lecture hall dragon on the ceiling is the work of Kano Tanyu (1602–74).

As a monastery rather than a public temple, the Hatto lecture hall is the location for instruction of the monks, and the lecture throne of the abbot holds the place of honor in the rear center of the building. Behind the Hatto and connected to it is the Kuri (the Priests' Quarters), originally the 1479 Abbot's Chamber (Hojo). Rebuilt in 1636 from the former Hojo, it now serves as the residence for priests.

The garden adjoining the Hojo (Abbot's Quarters), composed of three rock groupings and raked gravel.

HOJO To the north and east of the Kuri, and connected to it, is the Hojo (or Honbo), the Abbot's Quarters. The respect of former Emperors for the temple can be ascertained from the tablet which hangs in the Buddhist Service Room of the Hojo: the tablet with the Emperor Go-Daigo's inscription in six Chinese characters, dated August 24, 1323, reads "The Kingdom's Peerless Temple of the Zen Sect." The building is the administrative center for the Rinzai sect of Zen Buddhism and handles the affairs of all the branch temples of Daitoku-ji throughout Japan.

The formal (and seldom used) entrance to the garden of the Hojo (and thus to the Hojo proper) is through the Kara-mon (Chinese Gate) also known as the Higurashi-mon (Day Long Gate), a gate so beautiful that one can spend the day observing it. Originally one of the gateways of a castle which belonged to

Hideyoshi, it is richly carved with the work of Hidari Jingoro (1594–1634). The carvings on the front and rear are of birds; on the sides are pine branches with a peacock. A four-legged gate with a large curved gable on the front, it has a cypress bark roof. Elaborate metal fittings decorate the wood.

The 17th century garden beyond the Kara-mon gateway is a typical Zen garden with rocks and bushes symbolizing mountains from which a waterfall, composed of two large rocks, flows into a stone "stream" and thence into the flat raked gravel representing the sea. The garden has two conical sand piles in it, a device in Hojo gardens of this era, which were used to spread sand before individuals of importance, since white sand can overcome evil influences.

On the east of the Hojo is a second garden said to have been designed by Kobori Enshu but probably the work of Priest Tengu in 1636. It also is a walled *karesansui* (dry garden) with a line of small rocks and foliage at the base of a hedge shaped into two levels. Originally the garden used the technique of "borrowed scenery," whereby a distant row of pines beyond the double-hedge border led the eyes beyond the garden to the Higashi-yama mountain range (Mount Hiei) to the east. Modern utility wires and buildings have negated this intent.

The original Hojo was a donated house that had belonged to a Tendai priest who was converted to the Rinzai Zen doctrines by Daito Kokushi. It was destroyed in the Onin War, and Ikkyu built a new Hojo with the financial assistance of an Osaka merchant. In 1636, the present Hojo was erected to the north and east of the original building, since a larger Hojo was needed for an expanding monastery—as well as a larger Hatto (Lecture Hall) to hold more monks. The new Hatto took the space of the pre-1636 Hojo. The present Hojo of 1636 has eight rooms. The paintings in *sumi-e* ink on its *fusuma* (white heron, a countryman and his performing monkey, and sepia scenes of the four seasons) are by Kano Tanyu. The four front rooms are 24 mats apiece; the two middle rooms each have an altar alcove to their rear that holds an image of Shaka in the west room while a statue of Daito Kokushi (the temple's first Superior) and a small pagoda with bits of hair of Emperor Hanazono are in the east room.

Other buildings on the east side of the Chokushi-mon/Hatto complex include, from south to north, a 1622 bath house (no longer in use), the 1636 Kyozo (Sutra Storehouse) with a revolving bookcase and a statue of its Chinese inventor (Fu Daishi), and the Shoro (Bell Tower). In the path leading west from the complex is the Drum Tower, located before the Juko-in and Soku-in. As with most temples, Daitoku-ji has public ceremonies periodically throughout the year.

Clustered about the main buildings of the Daitoku-ji are a number of subtemples that are centers for individual religious practice. These subtemples usually have a number of small rooms connected by corridors which open on to small gardens, a garden being an essential element as it provides a place for quiet meditation. Some temples and their gardens are world famous (for example, the Daisen-in) while others have escaped the attention of all but the cognoscenti.

6 DAISEN-IN TEMPLE

We begin with the most noted of the sub-temples, the Daisen-in (Great Hermit Temple) which lies to the rear of the Daitoku-ji Hojo. The path on the west side of the Hojo leads to a second path to the right that runs behind the Hojo. The entry to the Daisen-in is on the north (left) side of this second path. (The temple is open from 9:00 a.m. to 5:00 p.m. in summer, and from 9:00 a.m. to 4:00 p.m. in winter. Entry fee; extra fee for green tea.)

The stone and sand garden of the Daisen-in is one of the most noted dry gardens in Japan. As a result, the temple has become a tourist mecca, which can lead to noise and over-crowding—the antithesis of Zen ambience. The garden is worth seeing, nonetheless. Daisen-in was founded in 1509 with Kogaku Shuko (1465–1548) as the first abbot, and his tomb is in the temple's precincts. The temple buildings consist of three structures: the Kyaku-den (Reception Hall), Kuri (Priests' Quarters) and Hondo or Hojo (Main Hall).

The south-facing Hondo (surrounded on three sides by its famed garden) is divided into three parts. The "West Rooms" consist of two rooms of six and 12 mats. The *fusuma* in the first room on the west, which depict mountains, pine trees, birds and flowers by a waterfall, were painted by Kano Motonobu (1477–1554) on eight screens. The second room from the west holds an image in a *zushi* (case) of a standing Kannon holding the wish-fulfilling jewel. The "Central Room" has a statue of the founder, Kogaku Shugo, as its main image. The *fusuma* have landscape paintings of the four seasons in ink on 16 screens by Soami (1472–1523). Finally, the "East Rooms" consist of two rooms of six and 12 mats. The room closest to the Central Room holds an image of a priest wearing glasses, while a Buddha image is in a *zushi* to his left and *ihai* are to his right. The last room has a *tokonoma* and freestanding shelves at its rear, and its *fusuma* depict agricultural scenes in sepia on eight screens by Kano Utanosuke (1513–75). (The original *fusuma* of these Daisen-in rooms are in the Kyoto National Museum, and thus these are copies.)

The noted garden of the Daisen-in appears on the three sides of the Hondo/Hojo, done in the *karesansui* (dry garden) style, attributed to Soami but more likely conceived by Kogaku Shuko, the founder of this subtemple. (In his diary, the founder of the temple records his collecting the rocks in 1509 and supervising the construction of the garden.) This type of Zen garden is thought to have been inspired indirectly by the pen-and-ink Song landscape paintings of the 960–1279 period in China. The garden covers approximately 120 square yards (100 sq m) and was created in 1512–13.

The garden on the east side of the Hondo is the most important one. This garden, only 12 feet (3.3 m) wide by 47 feet (14 m) long, was created by Shuko around a boat-shaped rock that once belonged to the Shogun Ashikaga Yoshimasa (1435–98). Rocks and shrubs at the beginning of the garden suggest mountains from which a narrow stone "stream" begins its course to the sea. Crane and tortoise islands (the traditional longevity symbols) line the course of the stream as it widens into a river of sand. A wall with a bell-shaped window (a later addition) divides the flow in mid-course, and in front of it the boat-shaped rock "floats" in the raked gravel river.

Toward the end of the east side (front) of the Hondo, the stream passes under a portion of the building to emerge into the south garden, a plain garden of sand that symbolizes the "sea," two small sand cones rising in it. In the far corner of this south garden is a sal tree, the tree under which the Buddha expired and achieved Nirvana. There are many interpretations of the significance or meaning of the garden: the ship of life headed to the

The famous walled karesansui (dry landscape garden) of the Daisen-in Temple.

ocean of rebirth or Nirvana is one of the more popular interpretations. No matter what its meaning, the garden is a fascinating one through which the passage of a stream moves from the north side of the Hojo to the east side, from the mountains of stone to the sea of sand in front of the main building. A cup of green tea is served by the monks for a small fee, so that you can sit and contemplate the garden if it is not too crowded and noisy at the time of your visit.

7 SHINJU-AN TEMPLE

A second subtemple is the Shinju-an, which is to the east of the Daisen-in along the path that runs in front of this temple. The path on the west side of the main buildings of Daitoku-ji should be taken to the path that crosses it at the rear of this complex. A right turn leads you past the entry to Daisen-in and to the entrance to Shinju-an at the end of the path. (This subtemple is open only by special permission and occasionally from November 1 to November 10. Entry fee when open. It is best to check with the Tourist Information Center downtown in advance as to whether the temple is open at the time of inquiry.)

The Shinju-an (Old Abbot's Lodge) was founded in 1429 by Ikkyu as a young monk. It later served as his residence; Ikkuy eventually became the somewhat eccentric Superior of the Daitoku-ji prior to the building's destruction during the Onin War of 1467–77. (His eccentricity can be attested to by one of his sayings that brothels were more conducive to meditation than temples.) Ikkyu was responsible for the rebuilding of Daitoku-ji Temple after its destruction, as well as for the reconstruction of the Shinju-an, which was rebuilt in 1490 as his residence. The building had *fusuma* by Jasoku (a pupil of Ikkyu) in black and white. It was noted for the strictness of its Zen training—as can be observed by the nature of one of its *shoji*, which is only a framework with no covering, thereby permitting the winter snow and winds to enter the meditating monk's room. The structure was rebuilt in 1638 by Goto Masukatsu.

In the reconstructed Shinju-an, the residential study (*shoin*), named the Tsuen-in, was once the women's dressing room of the Imperial Palace, and was a gift of Emperor Ogimachi in the 16th century. A statue of Ikkyu and a tablet with his writing are on display. (Another seated painted wood image of Ikkyu exists in the Shuon-an, a rod in his right hand and a black cape-like covering over his head, with decorations on the edge of the carved robe. Standing 33 inches (84 cm) tall, it was created right after his death and bears traces of his own implanted hair on the head, eyebrows, upper lip and chin. Such implantation was done to inject Ikkyu's spirit into the image.) The *fusuma* in the building are the work of Hasegawa Tohaku (1539–1610) and they consist of 12 black ink *sumi-e* paintings. The work of Soga Disoku (died 1483) is represented by 29 *sumi-e* landscape paintings, while the artistry of Soami (died 1525), Kano Motonobu (1476–1554) and Kano Eitoku (1543–90) also enhance the temple. Tohaku's paintings are of Chinese Zen priests at their enlightenment.

The Tei-gyoku-ken, a tea room, was designed and rebuilt in 1638 by the noted 17th century tea master Kanemori Sowa (1584–1656). The temple has three gardens, the most famous being the Zen garden named from the pattern of its 15 stones. The tiny but artistically conceived garden was designed by the tea master Murata Shuko (1422–1502), the first tea master in Japan and a student of Ikkyu, and his tomb is in the temple precinct. Here, too, are the tombs of Kwanze Kiyotsugu (known as Kan'ami, 1333–84) and his son Motokiyo (known as Seami, 1363–1443), famous exponents of the *Noh* theater.

8 HOSHUN-IN TEMPLE

The Hoshun-in, the next subtemple, is open to visitors. It is adjacent to and to the west of the Daisen-in at the end of the pathway that runs along the western edge of the Daitoku-ji Hojo. (It is open from 8:00 a.m. to 5:00 p.m. in summer and from 8:00 a.m. to 4:00 p.m. in winter. Entry fee. The subtemple's Treasure House is open from November 1 to November 10 from 9:00 a.m. to 4:00 p.m. Entry fee.)

Hoshun-in was founded in 1608 by the wife of Maeda Toshie (the Maeda family held the lordship of Kanazawa), and the family tombs lie within the temple's grounds. Toshie had served Oda Nobunaga as a general and then his successor Hideyoshi. It is to Toshie whom Hideyoshi, on his deathbed, entrusted his young son Hideyori. Toshie tried to combat the ambitious Tokugawa Ieyasu, who was determined to obtain control of the government after Hideyoshi's death, but Toshie's own death in 1599 thwarted these attempts to stop Ieyasu from taking over the government—and eliminating Hideyoshi's family.

Hoshun-in is entered along a path that leads to a bell-shaped window which looks out on to the main dry garden. The path turns to the right at the window and proceeds along the side of the garden to the main building. The Hojo has five rooms, the first two being of 10 mats with *fusuma* of a pale blue with white flowers on silvery-white plants at the rear. The middle room is the altar room, with its Buddhist image set in the rear alcove. The last two rooms also have pale blue *fusuma*, the one on the left of the fifth room depicting an ancient cherry tree in flower. The building and its rooms are a Meiji period (1868–1910) restoration after a fire.

The corridor that runs along the front of the Hojo now turns to the right along a side garden (the gardens are attributed to Kobori Enshu), and at its end is an arched bridge leading to the Donko Kaku, a two-story pavilion that resembles Ginkaku-ji (Silver Pavilion) in eastern Kyoto. The Donko Kaku, created in 1617, sits beyond the pond over which a bridge leads.

9 JUKO-IN TEMPLE

The Juko-in, the next subtemple of interest, was founded in 1566 by Miyoshi Yoshitsuga as a memorial to his father, Myoshi Chokie. The name of the temple was taken from the father's posthumous name. It is most noted for its connection with Sen-no-Rikyu (1520–91), the great tea master and landscape artist of the 1500s, and his family. This subtemple is located to the west of the Daitoku-ji Hojo on the path running to the west. The entrance is in the wall on the right before one comes to the Drum Tower. (The temple is only open to the public from 9:00 a.m. to 4:00 p.m. from November 1 to November 10. Entry fee.)

Shorei Sokin, the 107th chief abbot of Daitoku-ji, served as Juko-in's first abbot, and one of his disciples was Sen-no-Rikyu, who here received instruction in the doctrines of Zen Buddhism. As a result, Juko-in became the family temple of the descendents of Sen, who later created the three famous schools of tea ceremony (see above.). The Juko-in is most renowned for its 3½-mat tea room, the Kanin-seki, where Sen-no-Rikyu probably committed suicide in 1591 at the command of his former patron, Hideyoshi. Hideyoshi had turned against Sen, for reasons unknown. The tombs of Sen-no-Rikyu and successive generations of the Sen family are in the temple precincts.

The grounds of the Juko-in are entered through its front gate and along a path which then turns right, a bell-shaped window in the wall at the end of the walk looking into the front garden. At the window, the path turns to the right to the entry area to the Hojo, the temple's main building, the main garden lying before the Hojo. The painted *fusuma* in the main hall of the Hojo, considered among the finest surviving 16th century large-scale works of art, are by Kano Shoei and his son Kano Eitoku, and were created in 1566 in the Momoyama style of ink painting on a light gold-dust background.

In the 12-mat east room, the paintings are "The Eight Views of the Hsiao and the Hsiang Rivers" in China, attributed to Kano Shoei. The central room, with its polished lacquered floor, has the theme of "The Four Seasons," and has an image of a seated monk in the altar recess at the rear of the room. The 12-mat west room has the painting of "The Four Accomplishments," Chinese genre scenes of people and a landscape; the paintings in the central and the west rooms are by Kano Eitoku in black ink on a slight gold ground. The room behind the west room opens to both the north and the west sides of the Hojo. It is an 8-mat room with paintings on its *fusuma* on the south wall of monkeys in trees and on rocks; figures of people are on the east wall. The northeast (rear) room is also an 8-mat room with a *tokonoma* on its west wall while landscape scenes appear on its *fusuma*.

Before the Hojo is a *karesansui* (dry garden) composed of moss, gravel and stones complemented by a pine tree and a camellia tree. The garden is divided into three island groups, the two toward the middle joined by a ponderous stone bridge that forms the point of central interest. A dense carpet of moss covers much of the garden, while the "dry" components of this garden are meant to give the impression of flowing water.

The Kenin-seki tea room lies to the rear and to the right of the Hojo. Designed by Sen-no-Rikyu, it reflects the simplicity of design he favored for the art of the tea ceremony. It is traditionally said to be the room in which Sen held his last tea ceremony before his death. This very small room consists of three mats: one for the tea master and two for his guests. The *nijiriguchi* ("wriggling-in" entry) is the small opening in the left wall, so designed that visitors would have to bow and humble themselves while entering the tea room.

10 SOKEN-IN TEMPLE

The next subtemple of interest, the Soken-in, is adjacent to the Juko-in to the west and just beyond the Daitoku-ji's Drum Tower. It is where Hideyoshi held funeral services for his predecessor, Oda Nobunaga (1534–82), the military ruler of Japan. Here are buried Oda and two of his sons, Nobutada and Nobukatsu. Hideyoshi's mother, Omandokoro, is also buried at the Soken-in. The temple is not open to the public.

11 RYOSEN-AN TEMPLE

The Ryosen-an is to the west of the Hoshun-in and north of the Soken-in. It is not open to the public except by permission. The original Ryosen-an Temple was founded in the 1490s by Yoho Sojo (1430–1512), but in the early Meiji period (1868–1910) the temple was destroyed. After World War II, Ruth Fuller Saseki, an American, became a nun at Daitoku-ji and then abbess of the Jokei temple. She and Sokeian Sosaseki restored the Ryosen-an and created the First Zen Institute of America in Japan in its precincts. The institute translates Chinese and Japanese writings on Zen and does research on Zen teachings, as well as providing a research center and a place for the practice of meditation by non-Japanese.

12 KOHO-AN TEMPLE

The Koho-an subtemple is known primarily for its tea room garden by Kobori Enshu. It lies to the west of Juko-in Temple at the intersection of the third lane on the left when going west along the path in front of Juko-in. (Open to the public only during the autumn season (early November); special permission needed at other times. Entry fee.)

The original Koho-an was built in 1612 by Kobori Enshu and it was later rebuilt by Abbot Kankai. The temple has a Hondo (Main Hall), Butsu-den (Buddha Hall) and Shoin (Writing Hall). It was destroyed in a fire in the late 1700s, but was rebuilt to its original plans by Matsudaira Fumai, the Daimyo of Matsue. You enter the Koho-an grounds along a path that leads to the main building by way of the front path on the right. (A Kara-mon gateway at a second path also leads through the garden to the building.) Enter the Hondo through the first path and proceed to the first room, where you leave your shoes before walking past the second room, which has a bell at its roof.

The south garden next to the main building at Koto-in is composed mainly of maple trees and moss.

The third room is a corner room facing both east and south to the garden. This 10-mat room has *fusuma* with a gold ground with pines and bamboo paintings. (The walls and *fusuma* in the Hondo are decorated with black and white landscapes by Kano Tanyu and Kano Tanshin while those in the Buddha Hall are paintings on a gold ground by Masonori.) On its south side it faces the plain clay garden fenced with a low hedge and with a grouping of rocks at its west end. The middle room on the south side is the altar room, the altar itself being at the rear of the room in an alcove. Paintings of cherry trees are on the *fusuma* on the right, while a pine is on the left *fusuma* and a waterfall is on the rear left *fusuma*. The last room on the south is a 12-mat room with pines painted on the left and rear *fusuma* and bamboo and cherry trees on the right walls.

On the west side is the Bosen Tea Ceremony Room, a famed tea room in the *shoin* style. A large paper *shoji* mounted below the level of the ceiling on its western side restricts the view to a horizontal area, such as one would have from a boat window. (The name of the temple translates as Ko (solitary or alone), Ho (a thatched roof on a peasant boat), and An (a retreat or hermitage), thus "Hermitage of the Solitary Vessel.") The half *shoji* forces you to a seated position in order to see Kobori Enshu's garden, which has a stone basin, a stone lantern in a graveled

garden (representing the sea) with a moss garden (the distant land) and bushes (hills) beyond. The corridor leads from the tea room back to the entry room, past an open area with the well and wash room for the monks. The temple is unusual in that it has seven tea rooms as well as a garden designed by Kobori Enshu. The portion of the garden facing the *shoin* represents "The Eight Famous Views of Lake Biwa." In the southwest corner of its grounds are the tombs of Kobori Enshu and the Kobori family. Among the temple treasures is the Kizaemon tea bowl, a Korean Ido bowl said to have a curse upon it which afflicts its owners with boils. The last owners, the Matsudaira family of Matsue, placed it at the temple as a surety for their own good health.

13 KOTO-IN TEMPLE

The Koto-in is just beyond the Soken-in and is noted for one of its tea rooms, its association with Sen-no-Rikyu and the story concerning the wife of the founder of this subtemple. Koto-in (High Paulownia Temple) lies beyond the Soken-in. The path in front of the Soken-in (walking westward) comes to an intersecting path; a left turn here brings you to Koto-in, the first temple on the west side of the north-south path. (It is open from 9:00 a.m. to 5:00 p.m. Entry fee. The Treasure House is open from November 1 to November 7 from 8:00 a.m. to 5:00 p.m. Entry fee.)

In 1601, Hosokawa Tadaoki (1563–1645) was one of the leading military men (and one of the few to survive the bloody wars of the 16th century) whose career spanned the years of rule by Oda Nobunaga, Toyotomi Hideyoshi and Tokugawa Ieyasu. Tadaoki, a man of intellectual attainments and taste, established the Koto-in in memory of his father. In 1619, he devoted himself to the study of Zen doctrine under Priest Seigan (1588–1661) of Daitoku-ji, and he became a Buddhist priest with the name of Sansai. The *shoin* of the Koto-in, once the residence of Sen-no-Rikyu, was moved here by Tadoki, one of Sen's most distinguished disciples.

The main gate of the Koto-in Hondo leads to a path which turns on to a second, moss-bordered long stone path shaded by maple trees. A second gate leads to a bell-shaped window giving a view of the garden beyond as the path turns to lead to the south-facing Hondo. The present building was erected in the early 1900s to replace the original which was burned in the anti-Buddhist campaign of the Meiji era. At the ticket entry to the main building, the corridor to the left leads to the Hondo or Hojo (Main Hall), which faces on to the temple garden to the south. On the east side, an 8-mat room is followed by a 10-mat room, both with plain *fusuma*. As you turn the corner of the second room, you come to the main room of the Hondo, which opens at its rear to the altar room, with its tripartite division. In the right unit are two images of Shaka and one of Daruma (Chinese founder of Zen in the early 500s) and memorial tablets to past abbots. The central unit has a statue of Hosokawa Gyokuho, the founding abbot of the Koto-in and an uncle of Tadaoki, whom he appointed as the first priest of the temple. An image of Kannon is in a gold leaf *zushi* (shrine), with the four protecting Shi-tenno guardians painted on the shrine doors. The left unit has a statue of Tadaoki as well as the memorial tablets of the Hosokawa family.

The Hondo's west rooms include the 8-mat tea room called Horai (Blessed Isles), which has a wash basin hollowed from a stone brought from the Korean Imperial Palace during Hideyoshi's Korean wars of the 1590s, as well as a 10-mat room. A *tokonoma* and a *shoin* bay window desk are on the west wall, while a plaque on the east wall has the name "Horai" inscribed upon it. A *nijiriguchi*, the "wriggling-in" entrance to a tea house, on the west wall, may have originated with Tadaoki.

To the right of the ticket entry is the Ihoku-ken, which dates to the end of the 16th century, and it is said that Sen-no-Rikyu once lived here. The *fusuma* here were painted by Kano Yasunobu (1616–85), and the gold screen is the work of Itti Tekigenshi. To the north is a six-mat room, again with *fusuma* by Yasunobu. Attached to it is the Shoko-ken tea room, reputed to be one of the tea houses from Hideyoshi's extravagant tea party in 1588 at the Kitano Tenman-gu Shrine. Designed by Sen-Rikyu (Sansai) himself, it is believed to be the only authentic example still standing. The timbers of the tea room retain the natural condition of the trees instead of having been made into finished timber.

The garden south of the Hondo has a maple grove over a cleared ground, and at one side are the tombs of the Hosokawa family. Hosokawa Tadaoki's grave is marked by the stone lantern given to him by his tea master, Sen-no-Rikyu. Tadaoki's wife Tama is buried here also. She was the daughter of one of Oda Nobunaga's generals who turned against him and caused his death. She suffered banishment for a period of time, despite her innocence and her marriage to Tadaoki. During that banishment she was baptized and became a devout Catholic and assumed the name of Gracia. On the death of Hideyoshi, her husband sided with Tokugawa Ieyasu in the ensuing struggle to gain control of Japan. During that war in the year 1600, in danger of falling into the hands of one of the warlords opposed to Ieyasu (and therefore her husband's enemy), she followed her husband's order that she be killed rather than fall hostage to the enemy.

The early Kabuki dancers Nagoya Samzaburo and Izumo-no-Okuni (the originator of *kabuki*) are buried in adjacent graves. The temple is noted for the beauty of its maple trees that provide a colorful backdrop for the garden in the autumn, but more important are its many treasures of Chinese paintings by the Song painter Li Tang and numerous art objects of Chinese and Japanese provenance.

14 SANGEN-IN TEMPLE

The next subtemple, the Sangen-in, lies to the west of the main Daitoku-ji complex, opposite Daitoku-ji's Hatto. (It is open from 8:30 a.m. to 5:00 p.m. in the summer and from 8:30 to 4:00 p.m. in the winter.) A 1589 temple founded by Mitsunari Ishide, Asada Yukinaga and Tadamasa Mori of the western

The garden at Zuiho-in is a skillful combination of rocks and raked gravel, here covered with snow.

provinces of Japan, the Sangen-in has a noted *fusuma* of tigers and monkeys by Hara Zaichu. Its eight-windowed tea room, named Koan, is a fine example of the Oribe style of tea house. Sotan, Sen-no-Rikyu's grandson, is said to have trained here. The temple is also noted for its attractive garden.

15 ZUIHO-IN TEMPLE

The Zuiho-in is the third temple to the south after Sangen-in; it is opposite the Chokushi-mon Gate of Daitoku-ji. (It is open from 9:00 a.m. to 5:30 p.m. in summer and from 9:00 a.m. to 5:00 p.m. in winter. Entry fee.) The Zuiho-in was dedicated in 1546 by Sorin Otomo (1530–89), the son of an important Kyushu feudal lord, after he had come under the influence of the teachings of Tetsushu, the 91st patriarch of Daitoku-ji. In 1578, at the age of 48, however, Otomo became a zealous Christian and was baptized by a Jesuit priest under the new name of Francisco. As the overlord of his area of Kyushu, Otomo offered a safe harbor for Portuguese ships that had begun to arrive in Japan. Otomo's motives were mercenary, to gain riches and to pay for the interminable wars he waged against other feudal lords, despite his ostensi-

bly having first become a Buddhist monk and later a "devout" Christian. Coming under the influence of Francis Xavier, he permitted Xavier to evangelize in his domains, and he established orphanages, hospitals, churches and a seminary in his lands. Under his new religious guise, his wars became "crusades" during which he killed numerous Buddhist monks and nuns and destroyed Buddhist temples and shrines. In 1582, he was one of three Christian lords who sent a goodwill mission to Rome, which did not return for eight years, by which time Otomo was dead.

Bamboo groves and palm trees fringe the entrance to the temple grounds along a path leading to the Hondo (Main Hall.) The Hondo has three rooms which face the Garden of the Blissful Mountain (Zuiho-tei). A steeply raked dry garden, representing the waves of the sea, leads the eye to a series of large stones that culminate in an upright stone representing a mountain, the moss and bushes behind these representing land. The first room of the main hall is a 12-mat room with scenes of mountains on the *fusuma* on its three sides. The middle room is the altar room, with its altar alcove at the rear with the founder seated with a rod in his hand. The three sides of this room are decorated with mountain scenes. The third room is also a 12-mat room, with wild mountain scenery and a hut on its *fu-suma*. Turning to the right at the end of the front of the main hall, a tea room is located across from the Garden of the Tea Room. To the rear of the main hall is the modern Garden of the Cross, ostensibly a Christian garden dedicated to Otomo in this Buddhist monastery, albeit obviously a modern inter-pretation with little connection to the original gardens. To its right rear is a three-mat tea room with a tea preparation room; a *kura* (store room) stands behind these two rooms. A modern abstract garden of gravel with a square stone basin, a stone lantern and rush-es lies to the east of the main hall. This gar-den was created for the temple by Shigemori Mirei in 1961.

16 DAIJI-IN TEMPLE

The Daiji-in is next to the Zuiho-in Temple. The temple has a restaurant, the Izusen, which serves *shojin ryori*, Zen vegetarian meals, in red lacquered bowls in the shape of a priest's begging bow. On the edge of the garden leading to the Daiji-in is the "grave" of the writing brush of Lady Murasaki Shikibu, the author of *The Tale of Genji*.

17 RYOGEN-IN TEMPLE

The Ryogen-in Temple is just to the south of the Chokushi-mon Gate of Daitoku-ji on the west side of the street that leads to the gate-way. (It is open from 8:00 a.m. to 5:00 p.m. in summer but closes at 4:00 p.m. in winter. Entry fee.) The temple is the headquarters of the Minami school of Daitoku-ji Zen Buddhism.

Founded in 1502 by Priest Tokei Soboku, the Ryogen-in can boast of having five gar-dens ranging from the oldest garden of the Daitoku-ji temples, the Ryogin-tei (a moss garden) to the smallest garden in Japan, the Totekiku (a rock and gravel garden). The Omote-mon (Front Gate), Kara-mon (Chinese Gate) and Hojo (Abbot's Quarters) are the oldest surviving structures of their type in the Daitoku-ji complex, and they are typical of traditional Zen architecture.

You enter the Ryogen-in grounds through the Omote-mon gateway, turn to the right and on the left is the entry to the temple build-ings. Within the complex, the buildings to the immediate north (right) constitute the Kuri (Priests' Living Quarters). These rooms

The narrow dry Kodatei Garden at Ryogen-in.

are not open to the public. The interior corri-dor from the entryway which leads one into the complex is known as "The Passage of the Tea Room." To the left of the corridor is a small waiting room that looks out upon the Kodatei Garden. This narrow dry garden is composed of raked gravel with two stones from Hideyoshi's Jurakudai Palace at either end. These stones are referred to as "A" and "Un," the alpha and omega of Buddhism.

The room that looks out on this narrow garden holds two of the temple's treasures in exhibit cases: the Go-ban, the *go* board on which Toyotomi Hideyoshi and Tokugawa Ieyasu played *go*, and the Tanegashima, the oldest gun in Japan (1583). The west wall of this room has a *tokonoma*. The corridor leads on to the Hojo, the oldest extant meditation hall in Japan. The veranda about the Hojo is a wide one, and at its start it widens to serve as a passageway to the well that is located south of the corridor. The Hojo was the resi-dence, meditation hall and lecture room for the abbot, as well as serving the monks. It consists of seven rooms, three of them facing the Isshiden Garden. This garden originally had a tree that was more than 700 years old when it died in 1980. After its removal, the garden was recreated in the 13th century spirit of its creator, Soami, and it is now a Horai-style (Blessed Isles) garden. Its heavily raked gravel represents the sea, while the central rock represents Mount Horai. Two stones in the northwest corner represent a Crane Island while the moss mound stands for Tortoise Island, the two islands both being symbols of longevity.

The first of the three rooms facing the garden is the Rei-no-ma, a waiting room for those wishing to see the abbot. The *fusuma* on the rear and left walls are by Toshun, done in the Muromachi period (1336–1568), and they depict Chinese hermits in the mountains. On the floor are round raffia mats on which visitors sit while awaiting an audience with the abbot. The second room is where the abbot preaches to and debates theological points with the monks of the temple. The *fusuma* on the right and the rear right walls portray a dragon, while the *fusuma* on the left portray the sea; these paintings were done in the Edo period (1603–1868). The recessed altar area to the rear of the room holds a golden Shaka Nyorai, which was sculpted in 1250 by Gyoshin.

The third room is the Dana-no-ma, a room in which temple patrons can meet with the abbot for talks over tea. Its rear *fusuma* depict mountains, trees and birds, while the right *fusuma* has a painting of a large old tree. The wooden veranda continues around the corner from the front to the side of the Hojo. At its side is the Kaisoku-san garden with the separate Kaisan-do (Founder's Hall) in the northwest corner of the temple precincts.

The rear portion of the Hojo has four rooms, the westernmost room being the Jokan or Hokabu where the abbot keeps his robes and his iron begging bowl. Next to it is a tiny room (behind the altar of the preaching room), the Minzo, in which the abbot can sleep. In 1964, it was rebuilt and used for the storage of books and used clothing. Beyond it to the east is a two-mat room for sitting in meditation or for brief naps. The final room is the Gekan or Shoin-no-ma, an eight-mat reception room.

To the rear of the Hojo is the Ryogen-tei garden, a moss garden created by Soami in the Shumisan style. The moss represents the sea while the stone stands for Mount Shumisan, the mountain which in Buddhism is at the core of the universe. On the east side of the Hojo is the Totekiko Garden, which

boasts of being the smallest dry stone garden in Japan. The stones are surrounded by circles of rippling sand as occurs when an object is thrown into the water. Among the treasures of the temple are a Buddha image from 1250 as well as the previously mentioned *go* board on which Hideyoshi and Tokugawa Ieyasu played, and the Tanegashima, one of the oldest models of a European gun in Japan.

18 OBAI-IN TEMPLE

The Obai-in is next to the Ryogen-in to the south. (It is open from 9:00 a.m. to 5:00 p.m. Entry fee. The Treasure House is open from November 1 to November 10 from 9:00 a.m. to 4:00 p.m. Entry fee.) The Obai-in Temple was originally founded and built in 1588 by Kobayakawa Takakaya (1532–96) at the order of Hideyoshi; a tea pavilion by the monk Soshuku from 1563 stood here previously. The temple has a set of 16 panels on the west wall of the central room of the Kyaku-den (Reception Hall) by Unkobu Togai (1547–1618) on the theme of "The Seven Sages of the Wei Period" (in China, AD 220–420) as well as a superb landscape painting.

On leaving the Daitoku-ji at the end of a visit, you might notice, just to the north of the east gate, a shop that sells stones of all sizes and shapes meant for gardens. The prices are exceedingly high, since these stones are collectors' items. Japanese landscape architects and gardeners are very seriously selective as to shape, size, color and texture in choosing the appropriate stones for the proper place in a garden, and thus price is no obstacle in the creation of a fine garden.

NEARBY SHRINES

From the seriousness of Zen meditation, a diversion can be made on foot to a nearby park and its hilltop to the southwest of Daitoku-ji, for here, after many centuries of delay, the spirit of Oda Nobunaga, the military leader of the mid-16th century, was finally enshrined. The Kenkun Shrine to Oda Nobunaga is in Funaoka Park in north-central Kyoto. (It can be reached by buses 1, 12, 61, 204, 205 or 206 to the Kenkun Jinja-mae bus stop on Kita-oji-dori midway between Daitoku-ji bus stop and Senbon-dori. Imamiya-dori, the street with a large *torii* (on its north side) that intersects with Kita-oji-dori, leads southward to a path in Funaoka Park that climbs to the shrine. The shrine is open during daylight hours without charge.)

Oda Nobunaga (1534–82) helped to re-unify Japan after a century of civil wars, and the Emperor was particularly grateful to him for not only bringing peace to a large portion of the nation but for his support of the imperial house as well. On Nobunaga's death by treachery in 1582, he was succeeded by Toyotomi Hideyoshi who successfully petitioned the court for a site on Funaoka-yama for a shrine to Nobunaga. Although approval was granted, no shrine was built for the next 300 years, even though Nobunaga had been entered into the Shinto pantheon. Finally, in 1875, after the restoration of Imperial rule, a site was chosen in the Funaoka Park, and between 1880 and 1910 a Heiden (Offertory), a Honden (for Nobunaga's spirit), and a Shamu-sho (Shrine Office) were erected on the hill. Nobunaga's oldest son, Oda Nobutado (1557–82), who committed *seppuku* in Nijo Castle along with 90 of his followers when they realized they would be defeated by his father's assassin and his forces, is also enshrined here. An annual festival takes place at the shrine on October 19 each year, the Funaoka Matsuri. A parade of boys in medieval armor portray Oda Nobunaga's soldiers as they marched into Kyoto in 1568 to take control of the government.

IMAMIYA EBISU SHRINE Not too far from Kenkun Shrine is a much more popular destination, the Imamiya Ebisu Shrine. The Imamiya Shrine is to the northwest of Daitoku-ji. (It can be reached by bus 46 or 66 to the Imamiya Jinja-mae bus stop or bus 1, 12, 61, 204, 205 or 206 to the Kenkun Jinja-mae bus stop on Kita-oji-dori and then by walking north through the large *torii* over Imamiya-dori to the shrine. The shrine is open during daylight hours.)

The shrine was created in 994 on Funaoka-yama to the southwest of the present Daitoku-ji Temple, but it was moved to its present location in the year 1000. It began as a shrine dedicated to the god of pestilence in April of 1154 during a severe plague, and since plagues periodically assailed the city, the ceremonies to offer praise to Susa-no-o, the Shinto god of disease and health, have continued since that time to ward off illness. Thus the shrine still holds ceremonies, derived from those of centuries ago, to stave off disease.

The shrine is entered through a two-story vermilion gateway with a small building to either side. Straight ahead is a triangular area with pine and maple trees, while to the right is the water purification basin and a well. To the left is the raised Ema-do, which holds the shrines *ema* (religious plaques with donor's wishes inscribed). In the center of the grounds is the Heiden (Offertory) with the fenced Honden (Spirit Hall) area beyond a Kara-mon gateway. To the right of the two inner shrine buildings is a raised stage. Additional shrines are to the side of the center area.

The shrine is particularly popular for its many festivals and ceremonies, among which is the Yasurai Matsuri on the second Sunday in April. In earlier times, epidemics seemed endemic in Kyoto with the coming of spring, and the belief arose that the falling of the petals of spring flowers was the cause of the illnesses that plagued the people. Thus ceremonies were held to pacify the spirits of fallen flowers. The ceremony began in the 8th century after an epidemic, and it became formalized after an April 1154 plague when people prayed to Susa-no-o to pacify him so the plague would end. Today, crowds of devotees still circle the shrine beating on drums and gongs and chanting the phrase "Fasuri-bana yo" (Flowers Rest in Peace!). Costumes are *de rigeur*: dancers in black and red wigs (representing black- and red-haired demons who were thought to bring the plague) are part of the chanting procession, their parasols enhanced with flowers. On October 14th, the Imamiya-sha Shinko-sai Festival sees a noon procession of armored warriors, page boys and court ladies accompanying the shrine *mikoshi* through the area.

GETTING THERE

To reach Daitoku-ji and its subtemples directly, take bus 1, 12, 61, 204, 205 or 206 to the Daitoku-ji-mae bus stop. Alternately, take the subway to Kita-oji station, then walk a few streets to the west to the temple entrance. In general, the various subtemples accepting visitors are open from 8:00 a.m. to 5:00 p.m. in summer and from 8:00 a.m. to 4:00 p.m. in winter. There is an entry fee to the individual subtemples.

You can return to central Kyoto by taking one of the various buses that run along Kita-oji-dori or by walking east on that street to Kita-oji subway station.

Walking Tour 15

SHIMOGAMO AND KAMIGAMO SHRINES
The Thunder God's Shrines and an Artists' Village

1. **Shimogamo Shrine** 下鴨神社
2. **Kyoto Botanical Gardens** 府立植物園
3. **Kamigamo Shrine** 上賀茂神社
4. **Koetsu-ji Temple** 光悦寺
5. **Genko-an Temple** 源光庵
6. **Josho-ji Temple** 常照寺

The Shimogamo and Kamigamo Shrines (Lower and Upper Kamo) are two of the oldest Shinto shrines in Kyoto, predating the creation of the capital of Heian-kyo in 794. Both are involved with early Shinto mythology, and both are important as sites of ceremonies, and both are important as sites of ceremonies, and both are important as sites of ceremonies, the latter of which particularly enlivens the Kyoto year with its magnificent costumed procession reminiscent of Heian times. Situated in the triangle of two of the three major rivers which course through the city (the Kamo and Takano Rivers), this triangle also contains the Kyoto Botanical Gardens, the Kyoto Prefectural Library and Museum, the Shakamachi district with its Nishimura Villa just to the east of the Kamigamo Shrine, the Ota Shrine and Azekura Village.

To the west of the Kamo shrines and to the north of the Daitoku-ji Temple complex and the Imamiya Ebisu Shrine lies what, until comparatively recent years, was sparsely settled countryside. Here can be found the Shozan Kimono Design complex with its *kimono* studio, restaurants, pool and park-like area, as well as modern boutiques in the Kitayama area. Further north is the Koetsu-ji Temple, the one-time artists' colony begun by Hon'ami Koetsu (1557–1637), an artists' village which spawned what became known as the Rimpa school of art, created in the 17th century. Here are the tea arbors which enriched the artists' village and the Nichiren Temple which served them.

Nearby is Josho-ji, endowed with a gateway by Yoshino Tayu (as well as serving as the temple of her burial), a temple whose springtime procession of costumed *tayu* (the most sophisticated level of *geisha*) commemorates the life and death of the famed Shimabara courtesan of Koetsu's time. Between Koetsu-ji and Josho-ji is Genko-an, another temple whose Hondo retains the blood-stained ceiling that came the from Fushimi Castle. There, a number of the defeated warriors of Tokugawa Ieyasu paid with their lives in a

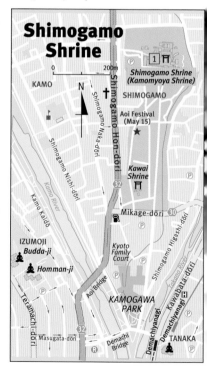

The striking vermilion two-story main gate to Shimogamo Shrine.

mass suicide at the beginning of the 1600s, prior to Ieyasu's ultimately successful military action that put the Tokugawa Shoguns in power for more than two centuries. A surfeit of riches in the area is further enhanced a little further to the north by Shoden-ji with its noted *karesansui* (dry landscape) garden.

1 SHIMOGAMO SHRINE

We begin with Shimogamo Shrine, which has protected the northeast portion of the Kyoto area since even before the founding of the present city. The shrine is in its own park in the triangle between the confluence of the Kamo and Takano Rivers in north-central Kyoto and to the east of the Shimogamo-hon-dori street. The shrine is open from 9:00 a.m. to 5:00 p.m. There is no entry charge.

The Shimogamo (Lower Kamo) Shrine and the Kamigamo (Upper Kamo) Shrine are two halves of the same shrine, both dedicated to Raijin, the god of thunder. The Shimogamo is the ancestral shrine of the Kamo family, early settlers in this area from Korea. There is no telling how far back in history this district served as the center of religious activity. Prayers were said here between the two rivers from very early times in periods of flood or drought before any shrine structure existed. The spirits of the river, of the waters and of the mountains (from which the waters came) were the deities worshipped.

As with the early history of so many sacred areas, the stories of the deities and how or why they came to be revered is not totally clear. Legend recounts that the deity of the Shimogamo Shrine was Tama-yori-hime, (*hime* meaning "princess"). Tama was walking by the river one day when she came upon a red arrow with duck feathers floating in the river. She took the arrow home (one version says she put it under her pillow and the arrow soon changed into the god Oyamakui in the shape of a handsome young man) and soon it was found that she was pregnant. Her family wished to know who the father of the child was and they could not believe her story that no man was involved with her pregnancy. When the child was old enough, the grand-parents tried to ascertain who the child's father was through a magical ritual. They assembled all the people and gave the child a cup of wine and instructed him to take it to his father. The child immediately ran into their house and placed the cup before the red arrow, which his mother had stuck in the thatch of the roof. Thereupon the child transformed himself into a thunderbolt and ascended into heaven with his mother. Thus, the shrine is connected with Raijin, the god of thunder, the divine son of Tama-yori-hime.

As to when the shrine buildings were erected depends upon the source believed. One tradition claims that Emperor Kammei

Costumed players re-enacting the ancient game of Kemare Hajime (kick ball) at Shimogamo Shrine.

(540–71) had the shrine built more than two centuries before Kyoto was founded. Other traditions credit Emperor Temmu in 677 as the founder, while another identifies the 8th century as its time of origin. If the last date is valid, then another belief can be true that Emperor Kammu (founder of Kyoto in 794) did homage to the gods of the shrine on the founding of his new capital. At any rate, the shrine is dedicated to Ho-no-Ikazuchi-no-mikoto, god of the mountains, and his daughter Tama-yori-no-hime-no-mikoto, goddess of the rivers, both of whom were the protectors of the province of Yamashiro (the province around early Kyoto). Since both the Shimogamo and the Kamigamo Shrines are also dedicated to Raijin, the god of thunder, you can see the coming together of a number of traditions.

As with many Shinto shrines, the main hall of the shrine was rebuilt every 20 years. Between 1036 and 1322, records show that this tradition was upheld every two decades, but thereafter the rebuilding took place at irregular intervals. The present main hall was last reconstructed in 1629 and again in 1863.

Shimogamo Shrine lies at the end of an extensive wooded park, the Tadasuno-mori. At the entrance to the shrine on its southern side is a tall vermilion *torii* with a vermilion fence extending east and west. A path leads straight ahead toward the vermilion two-story main gate, from which an unpainted fence stretches east and west. Just before this gateway, on the left, are two small shrines. A *torii* fronts one, and the other stands before three *sakaki* trees. Two of these trees have leaned against one another and so have grown together, thereby providing a symbol from which custom has produced a place of worship; these trees have been visited through the years by women who wish to live in the same harmony with their husbands as seen in these conjoined trees. As objects of reverence, the two trees have been encircled by a rope with the folded white paper talisman (*shimenawa*) which denotes the sacred.

In the center of the precincts is the Heiden (Offertory), 24 feet (7 m) by 18 feet (5.5 m), a raised and roofed platform that stands in a line with the entrance gate, and the Honden (Spirit Shrine) to the north. To the left of the

Heiden, in the southwest corner of the precinct, is a small offertory platform before a small vermilion fenced shrine. To the east of the Heiden is the Hosodono, a roofed platform for the musicians who play for performances of the sacred Azuma-mai dance. On the building to the east of the Hosodono is a long painted picture of Emperor Komei's procession (including the Imperial cart pulled by oxen) when he visited the shrine in 1863, a great event at that time since it indicated that the Emperor could break his seclusion to take part in secular or political events. This marked a part of the beginning of the end of the Tokugawa Shogun rule, which culminated in 1868 with the return to ostensible political power by the young Emperor Meiji.

The Mitarashi-gawa (River of Lustration) that flows through the eastern portion of the precincts in a walled canal (and under the Hosodono), is crossed beyond the Hosodono by a flat bridge, and beyond that is a vermilion arched bridge that is only used on ceremonial occasions. Beyond the arched bridge are steps that lead down to the stream on either side. A bridge and Shinto shrine with a thatched roof over it, the stream running beneath the structure, mark the point at which the Mitarashi-gawa enters the shrine grounds. This area and its "pond" are used for ceremonial rites of purification.

To the north of the Heiden is the fenced-in Inner Shrine area, the fence being solid below and slatted above. Two gateways pierce the fence, the major gate being in line with the Heiden. A screen a little way beyond the gate prevents a direct view of the Inner Shrine–and can serve to deflect the forces of evil that may impinge on the area. Behind this screen are two small thatched unpainted shrines. Three more such shrines are to the left while two more are to the right, defining, in a sense, an inner courtyard. The Innermost Shrine to the north of this "courtyard" is protected by a latticed fence across the width of the innermost sacred (and non-public) area, a gateway in the center opening into the innermost section. Again, a screen deflects both the view and the forces of evil. Behind this screen on either side are the two central Honden (Spirit Shrines), each with a 3 (1 m) foot tall seated lion at either end of the veranda, the one on the left with its mouth closed while the one on the right has its mouth open. To the left of these Inner Shrine units is a *kura* (storage building).

An Imperial procession during the Aoi Matsuri.

A variety of ceremonies and festivals are held at the shrine throughout the year. For example, on January 4, Kemari Hajime (Heian period kick ball) is held by players in costumes of the 700–1200 period. Players form a circle and kick the ball from one to another until one player misses. On the first Sunday of May, Yabusama, an archery contest is held in which arrows are shot at a target by young men on horseback dressed in medieval garb.

On May 15, the biggest festival of the year, the Aoi Matsuri (Hollyhock Festival) takes place. An Imperial messenger in an ox cart, his suite and some 300 courtiers start from the Old Imperial Palace at 10:00 a.m. and arrive at the Shimogamo Shrine at 11:40 for ceremonies. They leave at 2:00 p.m. and arrive back at the Kamigamo Shrine at 3:30. In Heian times, hollyhocks were thought to ward off thunderstorms and earthquakes. Thus these leaves are worn on headgear, are on the carts and are offered to the gods as well. Reserved seats can be obtained at the Imperial Palace at the start of the procession.

On August 7, the Nagoshi-no-Shinji (Ceremony to end summer heat) is held.

According to the traditional calendar, August 6 marks the end of summer. People float doll-shaped talismans in the pond for good luck–shamanistic images which receive the guilt of those who contribute to the ceremony. At night, in the center of the Mitarashi Pond, some five *igushi* (sacred sticks) are placed. At 7:00 p.m. young boys in loin cloths jump into the pond to retrieve one of the sticks. Possession of such talismans was thought to help in avoiding illness and the plague.

2 KYOTO BOTANICAL GARDENS

Beyond the Shimogamo shrine to the north-west are the Kyoto Botanical Gardens. They offer another restful location in a busy city. The Botanical Gardens are on the east bank of the Kamo River (approximately opposite the Kita-oji station of the city subway) with Kitayama-dori as its northern border. The intersection of the Kamo River and Kitayama-dori is five streets north of the Kita-oji subway stop–and the gardens are across the bridge. Bus 4 stops on Kitayama-dori in the center of the northern side of the gardens. The Kita-yama station of the city subway is at the northeastern part of the gardens on Kitayama-dori. The gardens are open from 9:00 a.m. to 4:00 p.m. daily. There is an entry fee to the gardens and an additional fee to the greenhouses.

Kyoto's Botanical Gardens were opened in 1923 to celebrate the enthronement of Emperor Taisho. They include a Memorial Hall to the Emperor, a library and several green-houses containing more than 3,000 plants. In early April, the cherry blossoms can be enjoyed, and on April 9 the Kamo-gawa Chamise celebration of springtime, a tea ceremony held on the banks of the Kamo River at the gardens, takes place.

Another cultural entity in the Kitayama-dori area is the Kyoto Prefectural Library and Museum at the corner of Kitayama-dori and Shimogamo-naka-dori. (The Prefectural Library and Museum can be reached by bus 4 to the Sogo Shiryokan-mae bus stop or by subway to the Kitayama station of the city subway line. It is open from 9:00 a.m. to 4:30 p.m. There is a fee for viewing the exhibits. The museum is closed on Sundays and na-tional holidays and between exhibitions. The library is closed on national holidays and the 20th of each month.) Kyoto's heritage of crafts has here been provided a public and academic home, where craft objects can be displayed in an exhibition hall and the literature on such crafts can be studied in the library. Folk arts and industrial arts are exhibited from the museum's own collection or through special loan exhibitions. The permanent col-lection contains works in ceramics, bamboo, lacquer, dyed materials, paintings, clothing and various other folk crafts. Listings of current exhibits can be obtained from the Tourist Information Center and in the monthly city events guides.

In 1995, to celebrate the 1,200th anniver-sary of the founding of the city, the new Kyoto Concert Hall designed by Arata Isozaki was created alongside of the Botanical Gardens to house the Kyoto Symphony Orchestra and to become the venue for classical music. The concert hall has a main hall of 1,833 seats and an ensemble hall of 500 seats, and it has a fascinating spiral ramp in its lobby ascend-ing to the upper levels of the hall. The acous-tics of the halls, happily, are excellent. Then, from the 1990s, the Kitayama-dori section has attracted young shoppers since it has become home to many boutiques, some of them in the most modern of architectural constructions.

3 KAMIGAMO SHRINE

To the northwest of the Prefectural Library is the Kamigamo Shrine, the companion of the Shimogamo Shrine to its southwest. As with the Shimogamo, the Kamigamo Shrine predates the founding of the city. It lies in the north-central part of Kyoto, just before the mountains to the north. It is at the far northern end of Horikawa-dori and across the Kamo River.

As noted above, the Kamigamo and Shimogamo are two halves of the same shrine, and both are dedicated to Raijin, the god of thunder and rain, the divine son of the deity Tama-yori-hime-no-mikoto. The shrine was founded by the Kamo clan in the early 500s as a protection against the clans from the north. With the settlement of the capital in 794 in Kyoto, Emperor Kammu designated the deities of the Kamigamo and Shimogamo Shrines as the protectors of the city on its northern border. As indicated under the Shimogamo entry, Emperor Temmu is cred-ited with building the shrine in 677, although alternative traditions credit Kammu with its physical origin.

Right: *Kamigamo, companion to Shimogamo Shri*

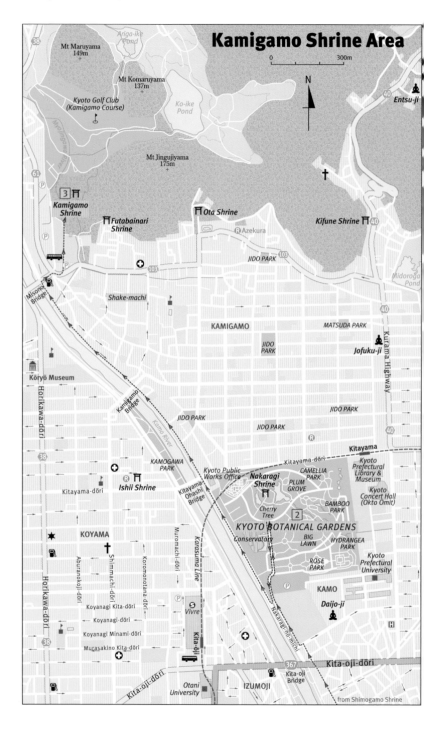

Kamigamo Shrine Area

0   300m

N

Ariga-ike Pond

Mt Maruyama
149m

Mt Komaruyama
137m

Kyoto Golf Club
(Kamigamo Course)

Ko-ike Pond

Entsu-ji

Mt Jingujiyama
175m

61

Kamigamo Shrine

3

Futabainari Shrine

Ota Shrine

Kifune Shrine

40

Azekura

Midoroga Pond

JIDO PARK

103

Misono Bridge

Shake-machi

KAMIGAMO

MATSUDA PARK

JIDO PARK

Jofuku-ji

Kurama Highway

Kōryō Museum

Horikawa-dōri

38

Kamigamo Bridge

Kamo River

JIDO PARK

JIDO PARK

JIDO PARK

40

Kitayama

KAMOGAWA PARK

Kitayama-dōri

Kyoto Public Works Office

Nakaragi Shrine

CAMELLIA PARK

PLUM GROVE

Kyoto Prefectural Library & Museum

Kyoto Concert Hall (Okto Omit)

Ishii Shrine

Kitayama-dōri

Kitayama-Ohashi Bridge

Cherry Tree

2

BAMBOO PARK

KYOTO BOTANICAL GARDENS

Conservatory

BIG LAWN

HYDRANGEA PARK

Kyoto Prefectural University

KOYAMA

Aburanokoji-dōri

Shinmachi-dōri

Koromonotana-dōri

Muromachi-dōri

Karasuma Line

ROSE PARK

KAMO

Daijo-ji

H

Koyanagi Kita-dōri

Vivre

Koyanagi-dōri

Koyanagi Minami-dōri

Murasakino Kita-dōri

Nakaragi-no-michi

Horikawa-dōri

38

Kita-oji-dōri

Otani University

IZUMOJI

367

Kita-oji Bridge

Kita-oji-dōri

from Shimogamo Shrine

An arched bridge over the small Omonoi River leads to the Main Gate of Kamigamo Shrine.

Regardless of when it was founded, Kamigamo has long been an Imperial shrine, and in its 17 centuries of existence, Emperors have come to the shrine on 96 occasions to pray. Before the Emperor Meiji, Emperors visited the shrine at 16-year intervals, the last such visitation being in 1863.

Until the year 1212, an unmarried daughter from the Imperial family resided here as a representative of the Emperor. With time, 22 secondary shrines developed within the precincts of the Kamigamo Shrine, and the present buildings date from the 1600s to the 1800s, each copying the style of its original structure. Even a town, Shake-machi, grew up to the south and east of the Kamigamo, comprising 275 houses belonging to families serving the shrine.

A large vermilion *torii* and fence mark the entrance to the shrine grounds, and a path with a green expanse of lawn on either side beyond the *torii* leads to a second *torii* and fence. From the second *torii*, the Honden (Spirit Hall or Main Sanctuary) and Mount Kataoka and the Jingu-ji Mountains come into view. Between the two *torii* and to the left is a thatch-roofed *Noh* stage. A stable for the sacred white horse is also situated on the left. To the far right, the Myojin River, which flows through the grounds, is crossed by an arched bridge. Beyond the second *torii*, the ground is covered with white sand, meant to impart an impression of purity and serenity.

In the midst of this sand "lake" sits the thatched-roof Heiden (Offertory) constructed in the Nagare architectural style. Before it are two 3 foot (1 m) tall conical mounds of sand, the Tata-suna (Sand Hillocks). The sand of these cones was sprinkled on the path before visiting nobility walked along it in order to purify the path. This protected visitors against "unlucky directions." "Purifying sand" was also scattered at the northeast gate (Demon's Gate) as protection against the forces of evil that always flow from the northeast.

To the right and before the Heiden is a ceremonial dance stage, and to the right and beyond the Heiden is a roofed unit covering the sand floor beneath it, a place for the musicians for sacred dances. The small Omoni River flows behind this area and is crossed by the Tame Bridge. The bridge leads to the thatch-roofed vermilion and white two-story gate, with east and west red and white corridors stretching from it. In times past, the Master of Religious Rites and the Kamo Vestal Virgin purified themselves with the waters of this stream. Behind this two-story gate are the Honden (Spirit Hall or Main Sanctuary) and the Gonden (Temporary Spirit Hall), both rebuilt the last time in the 1860s. Each of these shrines, which hold the symbol of the deity, are three-bay buildings with thatched roofs. Behind the Shrine, in the distance, is the cone-shaped Koyama (Sacred Hill), and

A miko (shrine maiden) strolls in front of the Heiden and Tata-suna sand hillocks at Kamigamo Shrine.

on its peak is a huge rock to which, tradition relates, the deity Wake-ikazuchi-no-mikoto descended in mythological times. The hill is considered a sacred area and is regarded therefore as a "Forbidden Area."

A variety of ceremonies and festivals are held at the shrine throughout the year, including the Aoi Matsuri, described above under the entry for the Shimogamo Shrine.

NEARBY SITES

Shake-machi just outside the Kamigamo Shrine on its southern edge along an east-west street is the Shake-machi district of northern Kyoto. This street has an irrigation channel running alongside the roadway on its southern side. Along the south side of the channel are the walls that enclose what were once the homes of the Shinto priests of the Kamigamo Shrine and their families. Small bridges span the channel to the doorways in the walls leading to the houses beyond. One of these homes, the Nishimura House, has now become a museum that is open to the public for a fee. (The house can be recognized from the sign at the entry to the wall (in Japanese) which indicates the entry fee.) Just one of several historic houses of the district, it has a lovely garden that is worth visiting.

AZEKURA VILLAGE Azekura Village is a post-1950 development in northern Kyoto. Its description as a "village" is a little grandiose. Yet it is a "Museum of Kyoto Dyeing and Weaving" by its own definition. To visit, follow the channel before the houses in the Shake-machi district as it gradually narrows to become a ditch, and it then turns to the southeast just before a huge camphor tree at the roadside. Follow the east-west street beyond the tree, turn left at the first narrow street to the north, and turn right (east) at the end of the street.

Azekura Village is a complex which includes the Sekizo-no-niwa, a garden of stone statues; the Suifu-kaku (Green Wind Pavilion), an artistic tea house; Azakura, a large restored 18th century *saké* warehouse that houses the Kyoto Minzoku Shiryo-kan, a museum of folk arts which displays utensils of the common people prior to the Tokugawa period; Hida Takashiya, the house of a village leader in the 19th century in which traditional weaving on looms is demonstrated; and the Kyoto Senshoku Bunka-kan, a museum of dyeing and weaving, showing modern Japanese textiles and related informational materials. An English language brochure is available. A restaurant is located in the main building. (Open from 9:00 a.m. to 5:00 p.m. except on Mondays. Entry fee. However, check beforehand since the buildings and grounds are sometimes rented out for private parties and therefore are closed to the public.)

On leaving the Azekura complex, you can return to the Kamigamo Shrine for a bus back to the Kita-oji subway station so as to continue this tour by bus from that terminal or by taxi.

4 KOETSU-JI TEMPLE

The Koetsu-ji Temple is located north of Kyoto in the foothills of the mountains of Takagamine. At one time the Takagamine area was considered far distant from Kyoto, and it was therefore just the right location for a village of artists of like religious persuasion. Thus it was here, at the location of the present day Koetsu-ji Temple, that Hon'ami Koetsu settled, followed by others of his artistic friends. The Koetsu-ji is located at the foothills of the mountains in Takagamine to the northwest of Daitoku-ji. (Take bus 6 to the Genko-an-mae bus stop and then walk briefly to the northwest along the roadway; or take bus 1 to the Gentaku-mae bus stop; this latter bus can also be taken from the Kita-oji station of the city subway. The temple is open from 8:00 a.m. to 5:00 p.m. Entry fee.)

Koetsu-ji is a temple of the Nichiren sect and is located at the site of the one-time country village that was begun by Hon'ami Koetsu (1558–1637), the painter, potter, lacquerer, landscape gardener, tea ceremony devotee and calligrapher, on land granted to him by Tokugawa Ieyasu in 1615. Here Koetsu created a village for his friends of the Nichiren persuasion, artists who shared his varied interests and many abilities. Offered an opportunity to move to Edo to Ieyasu's court, he turned down the Shogun's invitation, preferring instead to enjoy his retirement in the hills of Kyoto, a city of many cultivated and cultured individuals.

A map of Takagamine during Koetsu's day shows 55 houses belonging to Koetsu's artist friends as well as four Nichiren temples in the colony. Koetsu's relatives held a high position in the Buddhist Hokke sect (Nichiren) which was second only to Zen in popularity in Koetsu's time. The colony lasted 61 years, and it had among its residents or associated artists Tawaraya Sotatsu, Ogata Kanzan and Ogata Korin, among other noted craftsmen, artists and intellectuals who became known as the Rimpa school of art. They created the

Kamigata style, whose elegance became a hallmark of the culture of the townsmen of Kyoto and Osaka.

A narrow path between trees leads from the street into the grounds of the Koetsu-ji Temple, passing on the left the Shoro (Bell Tower) with an unusual thatched roof. At the end of the path is a building on the left (the Treasury) with a ticket office to the grounds on its right side. A bridge crosses from the second floor of the building, over the path, connecting the temple's Hondo (Main Hall) with the Treasury/Office building. The path then meanders through the grounds, with its five tea arbors based on designs by Koetsu. Tall cryptomeria trees stand out on Mount Takagamine ahead.

The Daikyo-an (Great Emptiness Hut) and its garden with its noted bamboo fence are all attributed to Koetsu. Here he retired at the age of 76 and here he is buried. The Hokke sect turned his tea hut site into a temple for the repose of his soul, and the temple retains Koetsu's favorite tea bowl and his portrait. On the grounds are a number of graves where Koetsu and his friends are interred. Within

Takagamine

the complex, a stone is also dedicated by the Koetsu Association to the American Charles Freer (who is also remembered by the Freer Gallery of Asian Art in Washington, DC) for his discovery of Koetsu's tomb, as well as his contributions to the appreciation of Japanese art. The Treasury Building contains some of Koetsu's works as well as of his followers.

5 GENKO-AN TEMPLE

There are a number of tea houses in this part of Kyoto with lovely views of the mountains, views that are particularly glorious when the maple leaves color in November. Also striking are the tall, straight cryptomeria trees on the hills about the area. Just down the road from Koetsu's "village" are two small temples of interest, the Genko-an and the Josho-ji. (Take bus 6 to the Genko-an-mae bus stop. The temple is open from 9:00 a.m. to 5:00 p.m. Entry fee.)

Genko-an was founded in 1346 as a Rinzai Zen temple by Tetsu-o, the first priest of Daitoku-ji. In 1694, however, Manzan Dohaku, a Zen priest of the Soto sect of Zen, became the priest of the temple, and since that time it has been a Soto Zen temple. The temple buildings are approached from the roadway through a garden with a gate with two *shoji*-covered round windows. The main building lies to the right, with its kitchen, living areas and temple rooms. At its end is a room with a *tokonoma*, a *shoin* desk and a window that looks out upon the temple's lovely garden.

The Hondo (Main Hall) of the temple, 69 feet (21 m) by 43 feet (13 m), is to the left of the above building. It was built by Seika-Koji, a carpenter, in 1694, and is dedicated to Sakyamuni and his two leading disciples, Anan and Kasho. To the rear of the building is an extension, the O-do, with a wooden image of priest Manzan Dohaku, under which are his bones. The Reishi Kannon image is in the western (left) portion of the main hall, an image that was favored by Emperor Gosai (reigned 1654–63) and is prayed to for good fortune. On the right side are two large windows, one round and the other square. The round one is called Satori-nomado, symbolizing Zen and religious awakening. The square window is called Mayoi-no-mada, symbolizing the afflictions of life: living, growing old, being ill and dying. Both windows look out upon the lovely garden behind the main hall.

The ceiling (Chi-tenno or Blood Ceiling) of the main hall is noted as it was brought from Hideyoshi's Fushimi Castle just to the south of Kyoto. It is composed of boards that once

The Honami-an tea house, one of five, in an idyllic setting at Koetsu-ji Temple.

A tokonoma and a lovely view of the garden enhance the main building of the Genko-an.

formed the floor of a portion of the castle in which 1,200 defenders committed suicide upon the surrender of Fushimi Castle in 1600, when Tokugawa Ieyasu's defending general lost the castle due to treachery from within. (This was prior to Ieyasu's final victory against his enemies at Sekigahara.) It is claimed that the blood-stained boards were installed here to soothe the souls of the warriors who had died.

6 JOSHO-JI TEMPLE

A second temple, just down the road and around the corner to the east of Genko-an, is the Josho-ji. It can be reached by bus 6 to the Genko-an-mae bus stop or by bus 1 to the Gentaku-mae bus stop from the Kita-oji station of the city subway. The temple is open from 9:00 a.m. to 5:00 p.m. Entry fee.

Josho-ji was founded in 1616 by Abbot Nikken, a distinguished Edo scholar, and was built by Koetsu's son close to the artists' village and the retirement retreat of his father. A Red Gate before the temple was a gift in honor of Koetsu by his friend, the famous Shimabara *geisha* Yoshino Tayu. She was a courtesan of the highest rank as well as a follower of both Koetsu and Abbot Nikken, and she is also remembered for her love affair with the essayist Haiya Jokei (1610–91),

a friend of Koetsu. She is buried in the temple cemetery. Her fame is remembered in a memorial service on the third Sunday of April, when a procession of *tayu* and their assistants progress through the temple grounds, and a tea ceremony supervised by various tea masters is held.

GETTING THERE

All of the sites on this tour are in northeastern Kyoto or, in some cases, beyond the city limits. Many are not within walking distance to one another, but they can all be visited in a single day via public transport. See the individual entries for directions to the minor destinations. To reach Shimogamo Shrine, take bus 1, 4, 14, 24, 54 or 205 to the Shimogamo Jinja-mae bus stop. The shrine is open from 9:00 a.m. to 5:00 p.m. For Kamigamo Shrine, bus 6, 16 and 46 can take you to the Kamigamo Jingu-mae bus stop. Alternately, from the Kita-oji subway station, bus 2 or 3 will take you to the Kamigamo Misono-bashi bus stop, from which you cross the river and then walk one street to the east to the shrine. Bus 9 also goes to the Kamigamo Misono-bashi stop. The shrine is open during daylight hours without charge.

Walking Tour 16

SHUGAKU-IN IMPERIAL VILLA AREA
A Poet's Retreat and the Villa of Ascetic Delights

1. **Basho-an and Konpuku-ji Temple**
   金福寺、芭蕉庵
2. **Shisen-do** 詩仙堂
3. **Shugaku-in Villa** 修学院離宮
4. **Renge-ji Temple** 蓮華寺

This tour encompasses a variety of sites, ranging from one of the two Imperial Detached Villas in the city to temples that are particularly noted for their exquisite gardens. Until well into the 20th century, much of northeast Kyoto lay beyond the city boundaries, and here in the valley, with Mount Hiei and the Higashiyama mountain range on the east and the Takano River on the west, was a rural area as yet undisturbed by the busy life of the ancient capital.

This valley is today served by buses and the trains of the Keifuku Eizan Railway Line, which starts from its Demachi Yanagi southern terminal just to the north of Imadegawa-dori. Developed in the form of a "Y," the railway reaches out to Yase in its eastern branch, where it meets the modern funicular and cable car to Mount Hiei and then the road to Ohara further up the valley. In its western branch, its ultimate terminal is Kurama, with the Yuki Shrine and Kurama-dera Temple.

Two other idyllic retreats and a small temple along the Keifuku line are visited today primarily for their gardens. The Shisen-do Villa, the retirement retreat of a noted 17th century poet and landscape artist, still remains a perfect retirement sanctuary set in a delightful garden. Not far away is the rebuilt Basho-an, where the noted *haiku* poet Matsuo Basho briefly took up a passing residence in the 17th century as he made his peripatetic way about Kyoto and elsewhere in Japan. The most noted of the gardens in the region, however, is that of the Shugaku-in Detached Villa,

the Villa of Ascetic Delight, particularly its upper level, with its magnificent view over a man-made lake and the northern range of mountains encircling Kyoto. Where the rail line diverges to the east at Takaraga-ike, the Renge-ji Temple, virtually hidden away behind houses on the route to Yase, secludes its lovely small pond and garden, so that it comes as a total surprise when one comes upon the small temple buildings against the hillside.

1 BASHO-AN AND KONPUKU-JI TEMPLE
There are two names that appear constantly throughout much of Japan—Priest Ennin, who was concerned with converting Japan to Buddhism, and Basho, the itinerant poet (itinerant in that he loved to travel) and who often stayed at the homes of his many friends. Basho has been one of the most quoted and imitated of Japanese poets, and remembrances of him can be found in various places since he often rambled about the countryside of Japan. He stayed with a friend not only in the Arashiyama district at the Rokushisha, but he is remembered for a visit to a very small dwelling, Basho-an, in the eastern hills of Kyoto as well.

Basho-an is on the grounds of Konpuku-ji in the northeastern sector of Kyoto. (Take bus 5 to the Ichijo-kinokoto bus stop on Shirakawa-dori where it intersects with the eastern extension of Kita-oji-dori. Go north three streets on Shirakawa-dori, and then turn right and take the street to the east uphill. Konpuku-ji and Basho-an are to the right, just below a temple at the head of this eastbound street. A narrow stone stairway leads to Konpuku-ji. It is easiest to take the Keifukuku Eizan train from the Demachi Yanagi station to the Ichi-jo station and then to take a taxi. Konpuku-ji is open from 9:00 a.m. to 4:00 p.m. Entry fee.)

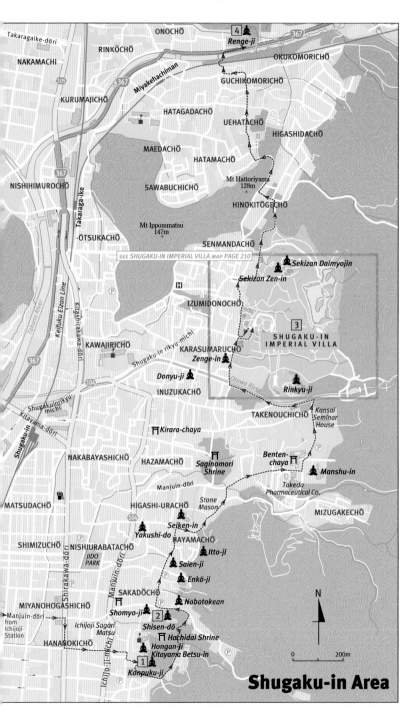

Takaragaike-dōri

ONOCHŌ

4 *Renge-ji*

367

NAKAMACHI

RINKŌCHŌ

OKUKOMORICHŌ

Miyakehachiman

367

GUCHIKOMORICHŌ

105

KURUMAJICHŌ

HATAGADACHŌ

UEHATACHŌ

HIGASHIDACHŌ

MAEDACHŌ

HATAMACHŌ

NISHIHIMUROCHŌ

367

SAWABUCHICHŌ

Mt Hattoriyama
128m

HINOKITŌGECHŌ

-ŌTSUKACHŌ

Mt Ippommatsu
147m

SENMANDACHŌ

SEE SHUGAKU-IN IMPERIAL VILLA map PAGE 210

Sekizan Daimyojin

Sekizan Zen-in

IZUMIDONOCHŌ

3

SHUGAKU-IN
IMPERIAL VILLA

KAWAJIRICHŌ

Shugaku-in rikyu-michi

KARASUMARUCHŌ

Zenge-in

367

104

Donyu-ji

INUZUKACHŌ

Otowa River

Shugakuinrikyu
michi

Rinkyu-ji

Kitayama-dōri

TAKENOUCHICHŌ

Kansai
Seminar
House

Shugaku-in

Kirara-chaya

NAKABAYASHICHŌ

HAZAMACHŌ

*Saginomori
Shrine*

*Benten-
chaya*

Manshu-in

Manjuin-dōri

Takeda
Pharmaceutical Co.

MATSUDACHŌ

Stone
Mason

MIZUGAKECHŌ

HIGASHI-URACHŌ

104

Seiken-in

SHIMIZUCHŌ

NISHJIURABATACHŌ

Yakushi-do

HAYAMACHŌ

Itto-ji

JIDO
PARK

Saien-ji

Enkō-ji

SAKADŌCHŌ

Nobotokean

MIYANOHOGASHICHŌ

Shomyo-ji

2

Manjuin-dōri
from
Ichijoji
Station

Ichijoji Sagari
Matsu

Shisen-dō

HANANOKICHŌ

Hachidai Shrine

*Hongan-ji
Kitayama Betsu-in*

N

1

Konpuku-ji

0   200m

Shugaku-in Area

The Konpuku-ji Temple was created between 858 and 874 by Priest Jikaku. In time it was destroyed, but was rebuilt in the 17th century by Priest Tesshu, a Zen monk. The temple had little claim to fame until about 1670, when the famous *haiku* poet Matsuo Basho spent some nights in a small building at the temple while roaming the northern area of Kyoto and composing his poems. Priest Tesshu was so proud of Basho's brief stay that he named the building in which the poet had lived the "Basho-an." In the 1760s, Yosa Buson (1716–83), one of Basho's successors as a noted *haiku* writer, searched for the location of Basho-an without success. Finally, local women and children led him to the now dilapidated structure in 1776. With the cooperation of the Konpuku-ji, he was joined by his disciples in reconstructing the Basho-an.

Buson had studied painting in Edo from the age of 11, an art form in the Chinese style that he would spend many years perfecting, fame not coming until he was 53. Perfecting his art of writing *haiku* poetry as well as painting, his economic situation during the last 15 years of his life was most secure, and it was at this time that he undertook the rebuilding of Basho-an, halfway up the hillside on which Konpuku-ji is sited. When he died at 68, his disciples established his tomb on the hillside above Basho-an. A number of these followers were later buried near their master. In recent years, the disciples of 20th century poet Aoki Getto gathered with him at the Basho-an to recite poems and to drink *saké*. After his death, Getto was interred on the hillside along with the earlier poets.

Basho-an sits on the hillside above the Kyaku-den (Reception Hall) of the small Konpuku-ji, a hillside terraced with rounded azalea bushes and a raked gravel dry garden at its base in front of the Kyaku-den. The thatched roof of Basho-an stands out on the hillside above the terraced bushes. A rustic path of stone steps leads up the hillside to the two-room cottage, consisting of a tea room with a room to the rear. Behind the building is a large stone inscribed with some of Basho's verses, and beside the house is a well that Basho is said to have used. A path leads up the tree-clothed hillside to the tomb of Buson, which is surrounded by the graves of his poetic followers Gekkei, Gekkyo and Tairo, among others. From the grave sites a

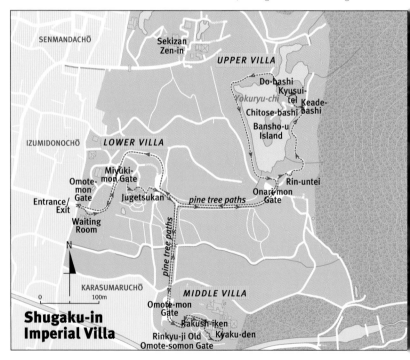

A serene view from the tatami-matted Poet's Room at Shisen-do of clipped azaleas and raked gravel.

view of northern Kyoto can be seen. Each year on November 12, the anniversary of Basho's death, a memorial service is held at noon in his honor. A wooden image of the poet is displayed, and after the service people compose *haiku* poems in Basho's memory.

2 SHISEN-DO

Not too far away, one of the loveliest gardens and attractive early houses in Kyoto remains as a reminder of another poet of the 17th century, a one-time warrior turned literati. The Shisen-do of Ishikawa Jozan is a delightful place to visit. Today, the house is the residence of a Zen monk, for it has come into the possession of the Soto Zen sect. It remains a charming home even though now as a temple its official name is Jozan-ji.

Shisen-do is east of Shirakawa-dori, the main north–south street in northeastern Kyoto. (Bus 5 from the Kyoto Central Station or from Shijo-Karasuma to Ichijo-ji, or the Keifuku railway from the Demachi Yanagi station to Ichijo-ji station brings you near the Shisen-do. If the train is used, after leaving the station on the east side, walk one street south to Ichijo-ji-dori and then turn left and walk up the hillside. Shisen-do is at the top of this part of the city, at the beginning of the forested area of the mountain. If using the

bus, get off at Ichijo-ji-dori and proceed up the hillside. The temple is open from 9:00 a.m. to 5:00 p.m. It is closed on May 23. Entry fee.)

Ishikawa Jozan (1583–1672) was one of Tokugawa Ieyasu's warriors, having served Ieyasu as a personal attendant from the age of 16. At the siege of Osaka Castle (1615), which led to the extinction of Toyotomi Hideyoshi's family, Ishikawa distinguished himself by the fury of his attack, during which he killed a number of the castle defenders. However, he had violated the military code, since Ieyasu's personal staff were not meant to become involved in battle. Passed over in the post-battle rewards, at 32 he abandoned the military life in favor of the study of Chinese classics and to work as a landscape architect.

To support himself and his aged mother, he became a tutor in the household of Asano Nagakira, the Daimyo of Hiroshima. On his mother's death, he moved to Kyoto where, in 1641, at the age of 58, he began the construction of the rural retreat in which he would reside for the next 30 years. On the slopes of the Higashiyama mountain range, in a wooded area, he built a scholar's comfortable hermitage, his Poet Hermit's Hall (Shisen-do), and its lovely garden. Shisen-do (Hall of the 36 Poets) was an appropriate name for his retreat, since he decorated his study with the portraits of the 36 most important Chinese poets. After his death in 1672, his retreat eventually came under Buddhist supervision, and a Shingon priest was assigned to the scholar's residence. In time it was decided that a Zen nun or a Zen priest should have the residency of Shisen-do, and to this day the hermitage belongs to the Soto sect of Zen Buddhism.

The simple, very plain entryway to Shisendo belies the beauty which lies beyond the rustic bamboo fence and stone stairway leading from the street to the house and garden within. The path, lined by bamboos, leads to an inner gate with a white patterned sand garden before the house–the pattern in the sand is made by means of a sweep by a common broom. The interior of the house today consists of a Buddhist worship room with an altar, a main room, a study and a priest's living quarters. On the upper level, a small "moon viewing room" with a rectangular window and a round window looks out over the lovely garden.

A room with a rush ceiling in the northeast corner of the house, the Shisen-no-ma or Poets' Room, is adorned above the *shoji* panels with the portraits of 36 famous poets (*shisen*) of China, all painted by Kano Tanyu (1602–74). Each portrait bears a poem to the individual poet from the brush of Ishikawa. A *tokonoma* and *chigaidana* are on the south wall of this *tatami*-matted room; a hollow, polished base of a tree stump 1 foot (30 cm) high is in the middle of the room. A huge old sazanqua tree is in the eastern corner of the house, offering its flowers in winter time. Seated on the *tatami*, with the exterior sliding panels removed, you can look out over the garden, with its white raked sand set off by the green of the clipped, rounded azalea bushes (representing islands in the sea of sand) and the tree-covered hillside.

In the spring, the colorful azalea blooms provide a unique beauty to the garden, as do the blossoms of wisteria in the summer and the crimson shades of maple leaves in the autumn. A man-made waterfall drops into a stream that meanders through the garden. At one point, the water is channeled into a *sozu*, a bamboo tube that is so arranged that when the tube is filled, the weight of the water within tips the tube to release the water. As the heavy tube tips, its end hits a stone, thereby making a hollow sound–meant to frighten wild animals from a garden or a farmer's field. The garden has been extended to the west since Jozan's day, and it provides an additional lovely area to the original garden. On May 25th each year a celebration in honor of Ishikawa Jozan is held, and personal items belonging to him are on view for three days from 9:00 a.m.

Two other sites adjacent to Shisen-do are of interest. The Kyoto Folkcraft Museum (Kyoto Minzoku-kan) is located across from Shisen-do. (It is open from 9:00 a.m. to 5:00 p.m. Entry fee). The museum is composed of a private collection of folk items, including ceramics, paintings, *sumi-e* drawings, old sign boards and other items of bygone Kyoto working-class life. Weaving classes are given, although the instruction is in Japanese only. Also adjacent to the Shisen-do is the Nobotoke-an, with a group of five tea houses in different styles. (These may be seen between 11:00 a.m. and 4:00 p.m. The entry fee includes the serving of tea.)

③ SHUGAKU-IN VILLA

The site of Shugaku-in Villa (Villa of Ascetic Delight) originally held a Tendai temple of that same name to the deity Fudo-myo-o before the year 1000. The temple was destroyed in the 1467–77 Onin War, but the village that had sprung up about it retained the name. Its later fame resulted from the desire by the Emperor Go-Mizuno-o in the mid-1600s to build a detached villa, which he located at the site of the original Shugaku-in Temple. Emperor Go-Mizuno-o (1596–1680) reigned from 1611 to 1629. It was a period of difficult relations between the Imperial house and the Tokugawa Shoguns, who had only recently come to power and who were clamping an iron dictatorship on the nation. Striving not only for power but honor, Shogun Hidetada forced the Emperor to marry his daughter so she could be one of the Imperial consorts. Relationships between the Emperor and Hidetada's successor, Iemitsu, were not agreeable either. In 1629, Go-Mizuno-o shocked the Shogun by abdicating in favor of his 8-year-old daughter (the first Empress on the throne since the mid-700s), and he became a Zen monk under the name of Enjo. (Imperial monks did not always follow the simplicity expected of non-royal monks, and thus a palace, a villa and even consorts were not unheard of.)

The former Emperor wished to build a detached palace, aside from the Sento Palace that the Tokugawas had built for him on the grounds of the Imperial Palace. Relationships between the two sides improved immeasurably once Go-Mizuno-o was off the throne, and thus the Shogun funded the project of a new pleasure palace for the former emperor. Go-Mizuno-o sent his agents, without success, to seek a likely site for a country villa. Then, on a visit to his eldest daughter, who had become a nun at Ensho-ji at the foot of Mount Hiei, he became fascinated with the possibilities of the site of her temple for his desired villa. Accordingly, Ensho-ji and his nun daughter were relocated to the Nara area.

The site the former Emperor chose covered 69 acres (28 ha). It sat high on the hillside, commanding a spectacular view of the area to the north and west of Kyoto, overlooking the valley and mountains. The new villa was built 30 years after the construction of the Katsura Villa. The two villas are in marked contrast. Katsura occupies a flat piece of land, and although its gardens are lovely the emphasis is on its buildings or its man-made scenery. At Shugaku-in, conversely, it was the natural scenery that was important, and the structures that were erected were fragile and meant to fit into the landscape.

The new Shugaku-in consisted of three levels, each with its own tea house, and these levels were referred to as the Shimo-no-Ochaya (Lower Tea House), Naka-no-Ochaya (Middle Tea House) and Kami-no-Ochaya (Upper Tea House). The tea houses were built among rice paddies with narrow connecting paths and, prior to 1868 when fences were erected, each level had a view beyond its own area. (The difference in levels between the lower and upper villa comes to 131 feet (39 m). By 1659 construction of the Lower and Upper Villas was completed; the Middle Villa did not come into being until later.

The Shugaku-in Villa was a favorite of Go-Mizuno-o, and he visited twice a year, staying at the villa (often with a large entourage) some 70 times in the course of the remainder of his life. His new villa was meant to be a rural retreat, and it was never considered a permanent residence. In time, with the death of his consort, the Empress Tofuku-mon-in, a portion of her palace was transferred to the Middle Villa area for Go-Mizuno-o's 11th daughter, Princess Ake. After the Emperor's death, the princess became a nun to pray for her father's soul, and the Middle Villa became the Rinkyu-ji Temple.

A gravel pathway leads through Shugaku-in's verdant lower garden.

Shugaku-in was abandoned some time after Go-Mizuno-o's death in 1680. It was restored in 1716 for former Emperor Reigen, the last of Go-Mizuno-o's children, who used it from 1721 to 1732 before it was abandoned once more on his demise. In 1822 to 1826 it was restored again for the Emperor Kokaku, but with his death in 1841 it fell into neglect. Repairs began in 1883 after the advent of the Meiji Restoration, and the paths between the three levels were widened and planted with evergreens. The Middle Villa was made a part of the entire complex since the temple units were no longer in use, and additional fields were purchased. These fields were turned into farmland to preserve the view.

The public is now admitted to the Shugaku-in grounds, but reservations have to be made at the Imperial Household Agency office in the Imperial Palace grounds (south of Imadagawa-dori and east of Karasuma-dori in the northwestern portion of the palace grounds.) Visitors gather at the waiting room outside the grounds, and at the appointed time the one-hour tour begins. The guide lectures in Japanese only. Thus a copy of the description below would be helpful while on the tour.

The Chitose Bashi Bridge connects two of the islands in Shugaku-in's Yokoryu-chi Pond.

SHIMA-NO-OCHAYA (Lower Teahouse) The tour begins with the approach to the Omote-mon, the front gate to the grounds where polished log pillars support the doors of polished bamboo. A small door within the larger door is used by ordinary visitors, the small-ness of the door forcing you to bow and humble yourself before entering the Lower Villa grounds. A path of fine pebbles leads to the Miyuki-mon, the gate for the Emperor. This west-facing gateway, which is only used by the Emperor, has a simple roof of shingled bark; a wood fence extends from it on either side. Other visitors enter through a side gate on the north side, and from there they move to the Chu-mon (Middle Gate). From the Chu-mon, a path of coarse white sand leads into the inner garden, passing a unit with a door-way of white *shoji* en route. The path continues over a stone bridge and island. Two stone lanterns along the path beside the pond are noted: the Lantern of Sleeve Shape or, by its other name, the Lantern of the Alligator's

Mouth. The second is at the ramp to the front garden of the Jugetsukan (Felicitous Moon Viewing Chamber). It is known as the Korean Lantern.

The Jugstsukan is the main building on the lower level and it served as the Imperial Chamber for the former Emperor. The building has seven rooms of 15, 12, 10 1/2, 6, 5, 4 1/2 and 1 1/2 mats. First is a 15-mat room with a raised portion (*jodan*) of three mats on which the Emperor sat. There are two alcoves, a standard *tokonoma* besides a set of staggered *chigaidana* shelves, and an alcove as long as the *jodan* or raised platform for the Emperor. The *chigaidana* has cupboards at its base with pictures of cranes and orchids by Hara Zaichu, while the *fusuma* have the painting of "The Three Laughters on Hui-hsi Bridge" by Kishi Ganku (1749-1832).

Next is a 12-mat room with a wide window on the west side. At its rear are a 4 1/2-mat anteroom and a 10 1/2-mat entrance room. Third is a 6-mat room and next to it is a 5-mat room facing the pond with a view of the Lantern of Sleeve Shape. It is thought that this room was used by the Empress Consort. The Jugetsukan is surrounded by its garden. The front garden, designed by Go-Mizuno-o, is surrounded by maple trees and has a stream that empties into the pond below the house.

NAKA-NO-OCHAYA (Middle Teahouse or Villa) You leave the Lower Villa through its East (or Back) Gate and pass into a wide area with a lovely view of the distant mountains. You then proceed along an alley of pine trees which forks, the left path leading to the Upper Villa and the right path to the Middle Villa. Prior to 1890 these paths were narrow tracks through the rice fields, but they were widened and seedlings of Japanese red pines were planted at their margins.

The right pine alley leads directly to the front gate of the Middle Villa, a bamboo gate in a bamboo fence. From this entryway the path leads to the Chu-mon (Middle Gate) with its shingled gable roof. En route, a gate with a tiled gabled roof was the entrance to the Rinkyu-ji Temple. As noted above, when the Middle Villa was created, the Rakushi-ken was its only building, built as a residence for Go-Mizuno-o's 11th daughter, Princess Ake, but in 1682, on the death of the former Empress Tofuku-mon-in, the Kyaku-den (Guest or Reception Hall) was created from the Empress's Okesho-no-ma (Dressing Room), which was brought here. The ornate Kyaku-den is set on a higher level than the simpler Rakushi-ken.

The Middle Villa covers about half of the site of Rinkyu-ji. The temple is on the left, while the two buildings in the center belong to the villa, the larger one being the Kyaku-den (Reception Hall) and the smaller one the Rakushi-ken (House of Bliss). (The temple buildings are not open to the public.)

The six-room Rakushi-ken was created in 1668 for Princess Ake as her palace, and the inscription in calligraphy by the Emperor provides its name. She continued to live in it when she became a nun after her father's death in 1680, and it remained the abbess's quarters until the temple she created was disestablished in 1868. The first room is six mats in size, with Kano Tanshin's painting of "Cherry Blossoms at Mount Yoshino" in an alcove. The second room of eight mats is the Tatsuta-no-ma (Tatsuta Room), from a paint-

ing of the Tatsuta River and its famous red maples, also by Kano Tanshin (1653–1718).

The villa faces to the south, with a veranda overlooking the pond and garden and a stream that flows into the pond. The garden has a lawn and a *kasamatsu* (umbrella pine), a low horizontally spreading trained pine that is only 2 feet (60 cm) tall. The garden also has a lantern called the "Christian Lantern" since the image carved upon it is said by some to be an image of the Virgin Mary, while two lines on the pedestal are said to be separated lines of a Christian cross.

The Kyaku-den is the larger and more ornate of the two buildings in the Middle Villa, as it contains the Okesho-den (Dressing Room) of the deceased Empress. (Since she was the daughter of Tokugawa Hidetada, whom her mother had to marry for political reasons, her Tokugawa crest appears in this building.) The Kyaku-den has a hipped and gabled thatched roof, an outer corridor of wood and an inner *tatami*-matted corridor on the south and west sides.

Its central room, the former Okesho-no-ma, is a 12 1/2-mat room that looks out upon the garden and is the most ornate of all the rooms in the villa. At its rear are a *tokonoma* and a *chigaidana*. The back wall of the *tokonoma* has its upper reaches sprinkled with gold dust in the shape of clouds, and below this are gold-painted silk squares that have been applied in a checkerboard pattern. The base has three rows of diamond shapes in blue and gold. The *chigaidana* shelves are known as "The Shelves of Mist," with poems from 1658 by nobles on the topic of "The Eight Views of Shugaku-in" pasted on its rear wall on a gold ground. These views also appear in the room as murals to accompany the poems. The cupboards below the *chigaidana* shelves have paintings of small scenes attributed to Priest Yuzen.

To the east of the Okesho-no-ma is a 10-mat room with painted lakeside landscape scenes in the four seasons by Kano Hidenobu (1775–1828) on all four sides. The nail heads are covered with metal bamboo leaves, while the door pulls are in the shape of a long-tailed rooster. In the corners of the ceiling are rings thought to have held mosquito netting, implying that the room was a sleeping chamber. Wooden sliding doors in the corridors depict the *yama* and *hoko* carts of the Gion Festival, painted by Sumiyoshi Gukei (1631–1705); other doors have carp swimming. The carp later had nets painted over them by Maru-yama Okyo (1733–95), since it was claimed that the fish escaped at night to swim with their peers in the pond in the garden below. Behind the Okesho-no-ma are two other rooms, a San-no-ma (Third Room) of 10 mats and the Butsu-no-ma (Buddha or Altar Room). The rear of the altar room has an empty altar shelf while the cupboards at the base bear paintings of fans depicting the four seasons.

Rinkyu-ji, as noted above, was disestablished in 1868, and its buildings were added to those of the Middle Villa. In 1872, however, the temple was recreated, and the buildings that had been a part of the secular Middle Villa were returned to their role as temple units. The temple is not open to the public and thus its Shoin (Study), its Kaisan-do (Founder's Hall) with a seated image of its founder nun Princess Ake, and its Hondo (Main Hall) are not shown. The temple has a landscape garden with a pond, a slender waterfall and a hill with an arbor.

KAMI-NO-OCHAYA (Upper Villa) The path between the pines leads from the Naka-no-Ochaya (Middle Villa) to the Kami-no-Ochaya (Upper Villa). To the left, a hill covered with bushes can be seen–the dam that was built to create the lake of the upper level. The hill consists of four tiers of stone walls, which are hidden by 40 varieties of tall hedges. The top of the dam is covered with clipped shrubs. The path ends at the gate to the Kami-no-Ochaya, the Onari-mon, and within you climb a set of narrow steps that lead upward between walls of thick clipped hedges. The wall of hedges blocks your view while you are mounting the steps, so that arrival at the top suddenly permits a magnificent view of the lake and the distant mountains.

At the top of the steps is the Rin-untei (Pavilion Next to the Clouds), a small two-room summer house recreated in 1824 after the design of the original building. The building is at the highest point of the grounds and it offers a magnificent panorama of the villa's pond, the valley and the hills about northern and western Kyoto. The distant hills provide a prime example of the use of "borrowed scenery" in a garden.

The Rin-untei has no permanent walls, just sliding *shoji* screens. A wooden veranda goes around the front of the 6-mat and 3-mat rooms. To the east is the wooden floored Senshi-dai (Poem Washing Porch) near a waterfall–probably used for improving one's poetic statement while listening to the sound of the falling water. There is a good view of the Odaki (Male Waterfall) from here, 24 feet (7 m) high, and the nearby small "Lantern for a Waterfall." Below is the smaller Medaki (Female Waterfall).

The 2 1/2 acre (1 ha) Yokuryu-chi (Pond Where the Dragon Bathes), is a pond created for pleasure boating as well as for the view. Peninsulas, coves, inlets and islands add to its attractiveness, the islands connected with the shore and with each other by bridges. The Chitose Bashi (Bridge of a Thousand Years) connects two of the islands. It has a Chinese pyramidal roof over its eastern pier with a phoenix on top, while the western pier has a hipped roof and benches under it. (Legend claims that the provincial governor who gave the bridge to the Imperial family was ordered by the Shogun to commit suicide since his gift was too ostentatious.) The bridge at one end rests on Bansho-u Island (Myriad Pines Landing), which has an arbor topped with a phoenix in the act of flying with a twig in its mouth. There is a boat landing and a small pavilion connected with a visit by the Emperor Meiji.

Another island has the Kyusui-tei summer house, which was also restored (as was the Rin-untei) in 1824. The building is basically a single 18-mat room with an L-shaped *jodan* (raised platform) for Imperial visitors. A small opening into an adjacent small room provides a "humble" entry for tea ceremony. This 6 foot (1.8 m) square room with a wooden floor serves as a service corner and sink for the tea ceremony preparation.

The Kaede-bashi (Maple Bridge) and Do-bashi (Earth Bridge) cross to the island, and from the island you can walk to the Momiji-dani (Maple Valley) and then to a boat house. A small island called Miho-ga-shima (Miho Island) is named for its supposed resemblance to the Miho-no-matsubara (Pine Beach in Miho) near Shizuoka. The path around the pond leads back to the Rin-untei pavilion and gate and the paths leading back to the exit of the villa grounds. (A mountain path, Kirara-zake, starts behind the Shugaku-in and leads up to Mount Hiei along a stream edged with cedar trees. In former times it was the path that Imperial messengers used in going between the court and the Enryaku-ji temples.)

4 RENGE-JI TEMPLE

One last site can be visited in this northeastern part of Kyoto, and that is the small Renge-ji Temple which has a pleasant small garden. Renge-ji is to the north and east of the Takaraga-ike Park and pond. (Take the Keifuku railway (Yase line) train to the Miyake Hachiman station, cross the bridge over the Takano River and turn right to walk to the temple entrance. Alternatively, take bus 17 or 18 to the Miyake-Hachiman-cho bus stop and walk to the right. (The temple is difficult to find since its small entryway lies between buildings, which hide the fact that the temple is behind them. Often it is best to take a taxi since drivers know where the temple is located. This Tendai temple is open from 9:00 a.m. to 5:00 p.m. Entry fee.)

The original Renge-ji was a Jodo sect temple located close to present-day Kyoto Station. As with most temples in the city, it was burned and completely destroyed in the Onin War of 1467–77, and it was not rebuilt until 1662. At that time it was recreated as a Tendai sect temple at its present location. The temple was fortunate in that it was patronized by men of learning, and among those who assisted in its rebuilding were Ishikawa Jozan (of the Shisen-do Villa), the painter Kano Tanyu, the Confucian priest Kinoshita Junan and the Zen priest Ingen.

Enter Renge-ji through the narrow space between two buildings facing the busy highway to Yase and Ohara. Behind these buildings you come to the entrance gateway to the temple. To the right is a thatch-roofed Shoro (Bell Tower), which is unusual in that the tower is enclosed. Next along the path, again on the right, is a granite *torii*, and at the far end of the narrow path is a Shinto shrine. Just beyond the granite *torii* is a roofed well. On the left side of the main path is a roofed structure holding a Jizo image, with many smaller but similar images on either side.

The entrance ticket to the Renge-ji is purchased in the temple entry hall. Behind the ticket booth is a corridor that leads past an altar room with an Amida image accompanied by Seishi on the left and Kannon on the right. The corridor then turns to the left, enclosing a large *tatami*-matted room from which the garden can be viewed. At the far end of the room are a *chigaidana* on the left, a *tokonoma* in the middle and two cedar doors on the right.

Renge-ji is noted for its small Edo period (1603–1868) stroll garden, which primarily consists of a pond fed by the waters of the Mount Hiei range (from the Takano River). The pond backs to the hillside and is surrounded by clipped azalea bushes, rocks and moss among surrounding maples and ginko trees, which are particularly beautiful in the autumn as they change color. Of particular note are the Renge-ji-style lantern with its tall rounded top, the "Turtle Rock" in the pond with an azalea bush growing out of it, and the traditional Turtle Island with its companion Crane Island. The main island with the lantern is connected to the rest of the garden by a flat stone bridge. The Hondo (Main Hall) lies to the right of and beyond the Shoin, with its entrance on the side of the building away from the pond. At its interior rear is a closed case, a golden Amida image standing to the left of the case. The ceiling of the Hondo has a painted dragon upon it, the work of Priest Kocho Nishimura, a leading scholar on Buddhist sculpture and an honorary professor at the Tokyo University of Fine Arts and Music. The dragon is a post-World War II painting.

GETTING THERE

The highlight of this tour is a visit to the Shugaku-in Detached Palace or villa, which you may visit only by prior reservation. Shugaku-in and the other sites mentioned in this tour are in northeast Kyoto at the foot of the Higashiyama mountains. (To reach Shugaku-in directly, take bus 5, 31, 36 or 65 to the Shugaku-in Rikyu-michi bus stop. From there, walk uphill (east) for 15 minutes to the palace entryway. Alternatively, take the Keifuku Eizan railway line from its Demachi Yanagi terminus to the Shugaku-in-mae station, and walk eastward approximately 20 minutes to the palace entry. Permission to tour Shugaku-in must be obtained in advance from the Imperial Household Agency office on the grounds of the Imperial Palace in Kyoto (see Tour 12). Tours are given in Japanese on weekdays and Saturday mornings at 9:00 a.m., 11:00 a.m., 1:30 p.m. and 3:00 p.m. There is no charge for the tour. Not open from December 25 through January 5. A return to Kyoto may be made either by bus, taxi or the Keifuku rail line described above.

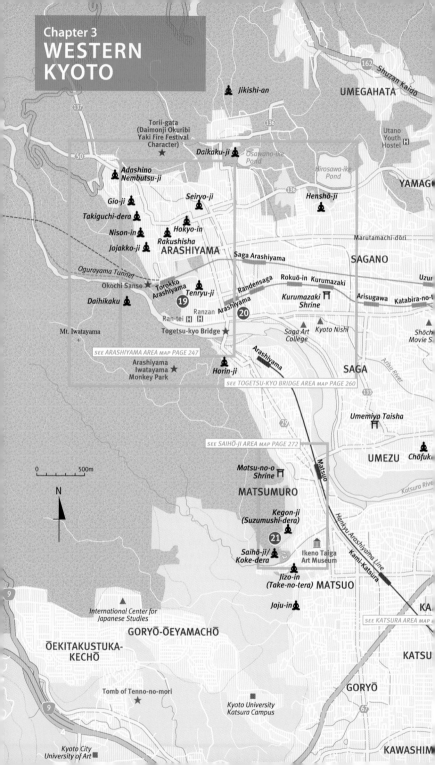

Jikishi-an

UMEGAHATA

162 Shuzan Kaido

137

136

Utano Youth Hostel

Torii-gata (Daimonji Okuribi Yaki Fire Festival Character)

Daikaku-ji

Osawano-ike Pond

Hirosawa-ike Pond

YAMAG

50

Adashino Nembutsu-ji

Henshō-ji

Gio-ji

Seiryo-ji

Takiguchi-dera

Nison-in

Hokyo-in

Rakushisha

Jojakko-ji

ARASHIYAMA

Saga Arashiyama

Marutamachi-dōri

SAGANO

Ogurayama Tunnel

Okochi Sanso

Torokko Arashiyama

Tenryu-ji

Randensaga

Rokuō-in

Kurumazaki

Uzur

19

Kurumazaki Shrine

Arisugawa

Katabira-no-t

Daihikaku

Ranzan

Arashiyama

20

Ran-tei

Mt. Iwatayama

Togetsu-kyo Bridge

Saga Art College

Kyoto Nishi

Shōch

Movie S

SEE ARASHIYAMA AREA MAP PAGE 247

Arashiyama Iwatayama Monkey Park

Horin-ji

SAGA

Arashiyama

Arisu River

133

SEE TOGETSU-KYO BRIDGE AREA MAP PAGE 260

29

Umemiya Taisha

SEE SAIHŌ-JI AREA MAP PAGE 272

Matsu-no-o Shrine

Matsuo

UMEZU

Chōfuk

Katsura Rive

MATSUMURO

Kegon-ji (Suzumushi-dera)

21

Saihō-ji/ Koke-dera

Ikeno Taiga Art Museum

Hankyu Arashiyama Line

Kami-Katsura

9

Jizo-in (Take-no-tera)

MATSUO

KA

International Center for Japanese Studies

Joju-in

SEE KATSURA AREA MAP

GORYŌ-ŌEYAMACHŌ

ŌEKITAKUSTUKA-KECHŌ

KATSU

Tomb of Tenno-no-mori

9

Kyoto University Katsura Campus

67

GORYŌ

Kyoto City University of Art

KAWASHIM

0   500m

N

Walking Tour 17

KINKAKU-JI AND RYOAN-JI

Benevolent Temples, a Model Palace and a Pavilion of Delight

1. **Ninna-ji and Omuro Palace** 仁和寺・御室
2. **Ryoan-ji Temple** 龍安寺
3. **Toji-in Temple** 等持院
4. **Kinkaku-ji Temple** 金閣寺

In the north-central portion of Kyoto, along Kita-oji-dori at the foot of Kitayama (North Mountain), is a crescent of noteworthy temples. At the southwestern end of the group is the Ninna-ji Temple, a World Heritage Site, which preserves not only its temple buildings but also houses the restored complex of what once was the Omuro Imperial Palace. The palace consists of a series of buildings interconnected by roofed wooden corridors which look out upon charming gardens and bring into reality exactly what one would anticipate Imperial palaces of early Kyoto to have been like.

A little further to the east are two more famous (popular and crowded) temples: Ryoan-ji and Kinkaku-ji. The former is noted, of course, for its mesmerizing dry garden of 15 stones adrift in a sea of sand within a walled courtyard, but it also can claim a series of Imperial tombs on the hillside behind it as well as a pond and a rest house where tofu and tea are served. Further to the east is the Domoto Museum and finally Kinkaku-ji, the Golden Pavilion, famed for its dazzling gold-clad pleasure villa of Shogun Ashikaga Yoshimitsu, floating over its surrounding pond. Turned into a temple after his death, nothing original remains; even the Golden Pavilion itself is a 1955 reconstruction after its destruction by a fire started by a deranged monk in 1950. Just south of these sites is Toji-in, the last resting place of former Shoguns amidst a lovely garden, and a repository of images of former rulers whose images were defaced in the turbulent years before the Meiji Restoration of the 1860s era.

1 NINNA-JI AND OMURO PALACE

Ninna-ji (Temple of Benevolent Harmony) and its lovely Omuro Palace is the best place to start this tour. The temple is open from 9:00 a.m. to 5:00 p.m. in summer and from 9:00 a.m. to 4:00 p.m. in winter. Entry to the temple is free; there is a fee to the Omuro Palace complex.

In 886, Emperor Koko ordered the construction of the Omuro Gosho (Omuro Palace), but he died shortly thereafter before the palace was finished. His son, Emperor Uda, ascended the throne when he was 21, and in 888 he completed the palace as a temple, the Ninna-ji, since his father had wished it to become a temple after his death. Then in 901, when he was 33, Emperor Uda abdicated in favor of his son Daigo, and Uda became the Superior of the Ninna-ji. Here, he reigned as ex-Emperor and monk emperor from the Suzaku-in of the Ninna-ji. He was the first emperor to become a monk in Heian times, and he started the Monzeki tradition whereby members of the Imperial family became the superior of major temples. From his death in 931 until 1868, the first or the second son of the Emperor became the Superior of the Ninna-ji for the next 30 generations. (Uda was also the first emperor to be buried behind the Ryoan-ji Temple.)

Although his son Daigo was succeeded by another of Uda's sons, Suzaku, Uda continued to rule behind the scenes. He gathered about him the associates of Sugawara-no-Michinaga, a group of those who were delighted with Chinese learning and art. Thus Ninna-ji became an artistic center since Uda claimed that he had abdicated in order to dedicate himself to his artistic interests. Prior to the Onin War (1467–77), Ninna-ji had 60 subtemples on its grounds, but the temple was destroyed during that war in 1467, and

it was not until more than 100 years had
passed that it was rebuilt with the assistance
of the Emperor Go-Mizuno-o and the Tokugawa Shogun in the 1630s. Among the buildings of the reconstructed temple, the Amida
Hall was created from the Shishin-den of the
Imperial Palace, which Hideyoshi had built
for the Emperor in the late 1590s, while the
Mie-do was once the palace Seiryo-den.
(These two buildings are described in Tour
13, "Kyoto Imperial Palace.")

In 1887, fire again struck the temple, and
25 of its buildings were destroyed. Only two
tea houses, the Hito-tei and the Ryokaku-tei,
survived in the Omuro Palace area. Reconstruction began at the turn of the century,
and by 1915 the Omuro Palace had been recreated in the Heian period (794–1200) style,
albeit following the building plan of the 16th
and 17th century buildings since the earlier
pattern was not known. Today, Ninna-ji is
visited both as a temple and for its noted
reconstructed Omuro Palace as well as in the
spring for its cherry trees, which have short,
thick trunks and multi-petal blossoms that
appear from mid to late April.

TEMPLE ENTRANCE The grounds of the
temple are entered by steps to the rebuilt
(1630s) San-mon (Mountain Gate), a two-story
structure with a heavy tile roof. On either
side of the three-portal entryway stand the
huge 11 foot (3.3 m) tall Kongo Rikishi (Nio),
guardian deities of the temple entrance. Two
protective *koma-inu* (stone lion-dogs) stand
in the gateway. Within the precincts of the
temple, to the left of the main path which
stretches from the San-mon Gate north to the
Chu-mon Gate, is the reconstructed Omuro
Palace, the two historic tea houses and the
palace gardens behind walls. To the right of
this main path is the Omuro Kaikan (Omuro
Hall), the 1935 Reiho-kan (Treasury), the
Omuro Flower Arranging School and the
priests' apartments.

Beyond the San-mon, a graveled courtyard
with walls and gateways on either side leads
to the steps of the one-story vermilion Chu-
mon (Central Gate). A Deva king stands guard
on either side of the passage through the
gate: on the left is Bishamon-ten with a small
stupa in his right hand and a rod in his left
hand, while on the right is Zocho-ten with a
vajra (symbolic thunderbolt) in his left hand
and a rod in his right hand. Both have wheel-
shaped halos behind their heads, and each

*One of the huge Kongo Rikishi deities that guard
the entrance to Ninna-ji.*

has two small figures before him. To the right
of and beyond the Chu-mon is the graceful
five-story pagoda, 108 feet (32.4 m) tall and
18 feet (5.4 m) square. It was erected in 1637
with the assistance of Shogun Iemitsu. To
the right of it is the Kusho Myojin, the Shinto
shrine which protects the temple, consisting
of three thatch-roofed one-story buildings
behind a solid wooden fence.

HONDO Directly behind the Chu-mon at
the rear of this inner compound is the Hondo
(Main Hall), formerly the Shishin-den (Ceremonial Hall) of the Imperial Palace, moved
here in 1676. Within, the main image is that of
a gilt Amida with Seishi and Kannon on either
side, each with a gold aureole. To the right of
the Hondo is the Kyodo (Sutra Storehouse).

MIE-DO In the northwest corner, to the left
of the Hondo, is the Mie-do (Founder's Hall)
in its own walled enclosure with a flaming
jewel atop its pyramidal cypress roof, symbolizing its memorial purpose. The hall was
made from the wood of the Seiryo-den of the
Imperial Palace and later, through a gift of
Shogun Iemitsu, of wood from the Palace
Nan-den. The image within, behind a small
mirror, is that of Kobo Daishi (Kukai) with an
elaborate arrangement of altar tables and gold
brocade decoration before it. To the right of

Kinkaku-ji and Ryōan-ji Area

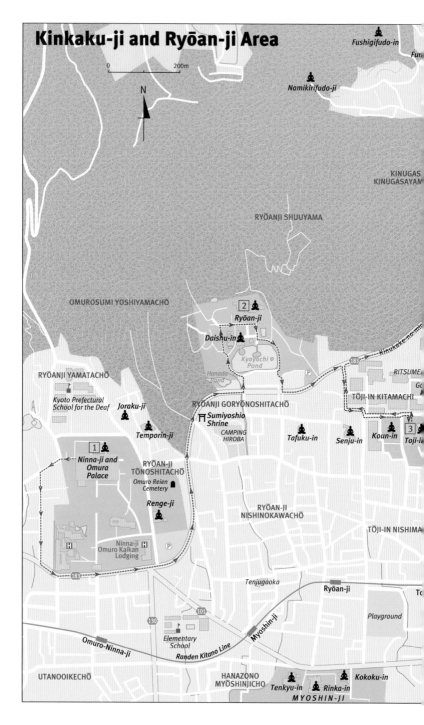

0   200m

N

Fushigifudo-in

Fur

Namikirifudo-ji

KINUGAS
KINUGASAYAM

RYŌANJI SHUUYAMA

OMUROSUMI YOSHIYAMACHŌ

2 Ryōan-ji

Daishu-in

Kyoyochi Pond

Hanada Pond

Kinukake-no-mi

183

RITSUME

Go

RYŌANJI YAMATACHŌ

Kyoto Prefectural
School for the Deaf

Joraku-ji

RYŌANJI GORYŌNOSHITACHŌ

Sumiyoshio
Shrine

CAMPING
HIROBA

TŌJI-IN KITAMACHI

Tafuku-in

Senju-in

Koun-in

3

Toji-i

Temporin-ji

1 Ninna-ji and
Omura
Palace

RYŌAN-JI
TŌNOSHITACHŌ

Omuro Reien
Cemetery

Renge-ji

RYŌAN-JI
NISHINOKAWACHŌ

TŌJI-IN NISHIMA

H

Ninna-ji
Omuro Kaikan
Lodging

H

P

183

Tenjugaoka

Ryōan-ji

To

Playground

Omuro-Ninna-ji

130

101

Elementary
School

Randen Kitano Line

Myoshin-ji

UTANOOIKECHŌ

HANAZONO
MYŌSHINJICHO

Tenkyu-in

Rinka-in

Kokoku-in

MYOSHIN-JI

the Mie-do is the very small Fudo-myo-do hall with an image of Fudo. Long bamboo dippers are available for the pouring of water over the Fudo deity as an act of worship. South of the Mie-do is the Kannon-do, with an image of Kannon, and south of that is the famous Ninna-ji cherry tree grove.

OMURO PALACE Returning to the entry courtyard behind the San-mon: to the west of this entry courtyard is the reconstructed Omuro Palace. First rebuilt in 1630, the Tsune Goten of the Imperial Palace was relocated here to replace the Omuro Gosho, which had been destroyed in the Onin War. Destroyed once more by fire in the late 1800s, it was rebuilt in the style of the Heian period (794–1200) *shinden* (palace) form of architecture. The entry to the palace complex is through a gate in the wall just beyond the San-mon. (The large Chokushi-mon (Imperial Messenger's Gate) in the middle of the walled area is a ceremonial gate and not a passageway.) In the entry courtyard of the palace precincts is a magnificent horizontally trained pine tree that serves as the focal point for this area. The huge entryway into the palace buildings has a gabled roof in the Chinese style, and all of the structures that make up the palace are interconnected with covered passageways, each offering views from differing perspectives on to the gardens of the palace. The first covered corridor leads from the entry building to the Shiro Shoin.

SHIRO SHOIN The Shiro Shoin (White Study), which looks out on a raked gravel garden and the Chokushi-mon gateway, is the first building beyond the entryway. It formerly served as an informal meeting hall for the Monzeki prince. Divided into three rooms and viewed from the veranda before it, its *fusuma* (sliding screens) were painted by Seihan Fukunaga in the years after its 1914 reconstruction. The *fusuma* of the three walls of the first room have paintings of cranes and pines in the snow; the second room has cranes on the left, a huge pine tree in the center, and on the *fusuma* of the right wall are waves breaking over large rocks. In the third room, the *fusuma* on the left wall is decorated with squirrels and small flowers beneath a pine tree; two *tokonoma*, a *chigaidana* shelf and two very large scrolls are on the center wall, while the *fusuma* of the right wall has another painting of two large pine trees.

SHINDEN Corridors connect the Shiro Shoin with the cedar bark thatch-roofed Shinden, the very large Main Residence. The veranda around the Shinden first takes you along the south side of the building, the side looking on to the raked sand garden and the Chokushi-mon Gate, as does the Shiro Shoin. At the entry to the Shinden are two wood panels with attractive paintings on the dark brown natural wood. One panel is of a pine covered with snow, while the second shows birds in flight; when you turn the corner, this latter panel has white and yellow chrysanthemums on its reverse side. The room behind this veranda is backed by half wood half *shoji* screens.

Continuing to the east veranda and to the north side of the Shinden, you have a full view of the lovely garden on to which the three rooms of the north side face. In front is a raked sand garden, and rising beyond it is the hillside with its plantings, ponds, rocks, a waterfall spilling into a pond, its two tea houses, the Hito-tei to the right and the Ryokaku-tei to the far left beyond the Remeiden, and a distant view of the pagoda rising above the trees.

This northern side of the Shinden is divided into three rooms. The rear wall of the first room is composed of half *fusuma* of painted flowers on a gold base, as is the left wall. The right wall has a colorful scene of men of the Heian court on horseback, with a lake to the right and mountains to the left. The second room has a scene of the Arashiyama Boat Festival on the *fusuma* on the left, while the right *fusuma* depict a Heian procession through the countryside. The third room has a *chigaidana* and *tokonoma* on the right wall, and the background of the *tokonoma* has a scene of hills and trees. The rear wall is made up of four doors with a painting of peacocks on a tree, while the left wall has a huge tree in white bloom. This 1914 reconstruction of the Shinden had the *fusuma* paintings done by Suekichi Kameoka while the paintings of "The Four Seasons" are by Zuisen Hara. The richly decorated building was originally used for formal meetings and ceremonies.

KURO SHOIN The next range of corridors leads to the Kuro Shoin (Black Study), the hall used for formal meetings by the Monzeki. It has *fusuma* painted by Insho Domoto, and its six rooms, arranged in three rooms back to back, are separated by *fusuma* on the north and south sides. To the north of the Kuro

Shoin, connected by a roofed corridor, is the Remei-den, which was built in memory of Emperor Uda, who completed the temple and was its first Superior. Memorials to the Monzeki and Imperial family are within; an altar with small tables is arranged before an Amida trio, while 30 books in Kukai's handwriting have traditionally been kept in this memorial building. The decorations of the hall were done by Suekichi Kameoka in 1914.

REIHO-KAN The temple Reiho-kan (Treasure House) lies in the courtyard to the east of the main courtyard between the San-mon and Chu-mon gateways. (It is open from the 1st to 3rd Sundays in October from 9:00 a.m. to 5:00 p.m.) The treasury includes images of Amida, Bodhisattvas and Shi-tenno guardians; scrolls in the hand of Kobo Daishi (Kukai); Chinese and Japanese furniture; textiles; and musical instruments among other treasures. The temple also holds a statue of the young Prince Siddartha by Inchi from 1252, whose figure is in the style of images of Prince Shotoku, although the draperies are in the Sung style; a symbol in the shape of the corona of the moon on his chest is a sign of absolute purity. The collection is worth seeing during the short period each year when the Treasure House is open. To the rear of the precinct in which the Reiho-kan is located is the Omuro Kaikan (Omuro Hall) for various religious and secular purposes of the temple and the sect. The Omuro School of Flower Arranging is in the temple precincts also, and information concerning the school can be obtained from the temple office.

Behind the northwest corner of the temple is the Omuro 88 Temple Pilgrimage, an approximately 2 mile (3 km) long wooded walking path that models in miniature the pilgrimage route in Shikoku followed by devout Buddhists. The first "temple" is denoted by a sign and the rest by small stone markers.

2 RYOAN-JI TEMPLE

Ryoan-ji (Temple of the Peaceful Dragon) is located ½ mile (¼ km) to the northeast of Ninna-ji along Kitasuji-dori. Taxis or buses are available if you do not wish to walk. The temple is open from 8:00 a.m. to 5:00 p.m. between March 1 and November 30, and from 8:30 a.m. to 4:30 p.m. from December 1 to the end of February. Entry fee.

This very popular Rinzai Zen temple is primarily noted for its stone and sand garden, for which there are numerous interpretations, all equally valid or not, as the viewer wishes to believe. It is best to see the temple in the early morning before the hordes of visitors appear, or at the end of the day when they have gone on to other sites or back to their

The Remei-den is a memorial to Emperor Uda, who completed Ninna-ji and was its first Superior.

The world famous sand and stone garden of Ryoan-ji reveals the stunning simplicity of Zen principles.

hotels. The temple site was originally the Heian period (794–1185) estate of a branch of the Fujiwara family who ruled the country under the Emperor. It also served on occasion as the home of a retired Emperor, and then it became a temple, the Tokudai-ji. Hosokawa Katsumoto (1430–73) created his estate on the ruins of the Tokudai-ji Temple, but in 1473 he died in the ongoing Onin War, leaving his 120 acre (48 ha) estate to become a temple, the Ryoan-ji. The original buildings were destroyed in the Onin War (1467–77), which left most of Kyoto in ashes. Reconstructed in 1499, it burned again in 1790. In the rebuilding of 1800 not all of its many structures were recreated.

The temple's present renown has made it an inevitable tourist destination, so that the calm of the stone garden, which is claimed to help in meditation, is frequently broken by the amplified descriptions of guides leading groups of Japanese tourists. Its present popularity is all the more remarkable since, until 1930, little attention was paid to its dry garden, a garden that today is one of the most popular tourist sites in Kyoto.

OUTER GROUNDS The precincts of the temple, in front of its main building and its walled enclave, have as their focus the 12th century Kyoyochi-ike (Mirror Shaped Pond), with its two small islands. The larger island is Benten-jima, with a small causeway and bridge that leads to a shrine to Benten, the Shinto goddess of good guck (the only female among the seven gods of good luck). The smaller island is named Fushidora-jima (Hiding Tiger Isle). Surrounding the pond are cherry, pine, iris and camellias brought from Korea.

To the west of Benten-jima is the Daishu-in (Big Pearl) Temple and then the Seigen-in, a resting and refreshment place for tofu, vegetarian fare and tea. For many years prior to the 10th century, Mandarin ducks (Oshidori) made the pond their home, and thus Ryoan-ji was also known as the Mandarin Duck Temple (Oshidori-dera). The water that creates the pond arises around two rocks in the southern part of the Kyoyochi-ike Pond, and the stroll garden around the pond was created in the late 1100s. It is usually visited after one leaves the Ryoan-ji buildings.

area to the Altar Room itself, a small area which extends beyond the rear of the Hojo. The Altar Room has a dragon ceiling painted by Cho Densu (1352–1431), while the altar has an image of Shaka as its primary object of veneration. To Shaka's left is an image of Monju, an image of Hosokawa Katsumoto and the *ihai* (memorial tablet) to Giten, first abbot of the temple. To the right of Shaka are images of Fugen, Abbot Giten and Abbot Chuko. Before the Shaka image are *ihai* for the Hosokawa family and prayer tablets for the current emperor.

Of the other rooms in the Hojo, the 20-mat front room on the west has *fusuma* of the Diamond Mountains of Korea in winter, while the companion east room has *fusuma* of the same mountains in summer. The 12½-mat rear east room has *fusuma* painted with scenes of the same mountain range in spring. These *fusuma* paintings are modern, having been created in the 1950s by Kakuo Satsuke.

To the west of the Hojo is a moss garden, and behind it is a garden and small pond with the oft-duplicated design of the Tsuku-bai, a round stone basin in the shape of a pierced coin in which to wash one's hands, The Tsuku-bai was a gift of Tokugawa-no-Mitsukuni (1628–1700), the compiler of *The Great History of Japan*.

KURI One enters Ryoan-ji by a broad flight of steps to the Kuri (Priests' Quarters) with its Kara-mon (Chinese style) entryway. The Kuri is the major building of the temple, the temple's many other buildings not having been rebuilt in the 1800 reconstruction. A small bell under the eaves is used for the call to services. To the rear of the Kuri is the Zoroku-an, the Tortoise Arbor Tea Room (not open to the public); Zoroku means "tortoise," the symbol of Genbu, the protecting deity of the north. The tea room is in the early 17th century style that was favored by Kishuza, a tea master of that time.

HOJO The Kuri is attached to the Hojo (Superior's Quarters) of 1797 by a wide corridor. The Hojo consists of six rooms (three rooms back to back), each opening on to a veranda, the Altar Room being the rear center room of these connected chambers. The center room to the front has side *fusuma* of dragons ascending and descending, while at the rear is a painted tree composed so as to resemble a dragon. Behind this front room is a second room that serves as a preliminary

RYOAN-JI GARDEN The flat sand and stone garden of Ryoan-ji is one of the noted gardens of the world, and it is interpreted in as many ways as there are visitors. The garden was little regarded until the 1930s, and, although it is supposedly a dry garden to be contemplated, contemplation is often difficult given the hordes of visitors who surge on to the veranda of the Hojo to view the stones.

The Tsuku-bai stone basin is used for washing one's hands prior to a tea ceremony.

The garden, created at the end of the 15th century, consists of 15 stones on a flat sand bed, a number symbolizing wholeness or completeness since the Buddhist world consists of seven continents and eight oceans. These 15 stones (only 14 of which can be seen at any one time no matter the angle of viewing) are in groups of 5, 2, 3, 2, 3 on a base of raked sand, which is raked daily in a fixed pattern. Some moss about the base of the stones provides the only greenery in the garden. This 50 by 102 feet (15 by 31 m) *kare-sansui* (dry garden) is attributed to Soami (1472–1523) by some authorities, while others claim it is by an unknown designer. It was restored in 1499 and was later endowed by two Tokugawa Shoguns, Ieyasu and Iemitsu.

Originally, the garden was open to the Kyoyo-chi Pond below it, but in the 17th century it was enclosed by the present wall. This earthen wall, composed of clay boiled in oil, surrounds the garden on three sides, while the temple Hojo forms a fourth side. The varied color of the wall is caused by the seepage of oil from the clay. Prior to the construction of the enclosing wall, the emphasis of the garden was not so much on the stones as on the vista beyond–an intent that has obviously been altered.

What is the significance of the garden? No one knows, but theories abound, all promulgated with great authority by those explaining their version of the symbolism of the stones. Perhaps the motto on the Tsuku-bai, the carved stone water basin, best sums it up: "The knowledge that is given is sufficient," or, "I learn only to be contented." For Zen, learning or knowledge is sufficient unto itself and is not for "use" in a popular sense.

IMPERIAL TOMBS The path from the entry/exit of the Ryoan-ji buildings leads to the landscaped garden, the Notkotso-do crypt and the Seigen-in refreshment pavilion alongside the Kyoyochi Pond. A path and steps at the west side of the pond, before the temple, lead through the Imperial gate to an area of tombs that lie behind (north of and above) Ryoan-ji, on the hillside to its rear. Directly behind the Hojo on an extension of this path are the Hosokawa and Imperial tombs, and across the path are the graves of Emperor Go-Suzaku (1009–45) and his sons, Emperor Go-Sanjo (1034–76) and Go-Reizei (1025–68). Beyond these are the tombs of Emperors Horikawa (reigned 1086–1107) and Ichijo

(986–1011), while the first emperor to be buried here was Emperor Uda in 931. All these Imperial graves were "enhanced" in the later 19th century by the Meiji government in their efforts to raise the Emperors to divinities. A view of Kyoto can be had from this higher ground.

INSHO-DOMOTO MUSEUM OF FINE ART
The Domoto Art Museum lies between Ryoan-ji and Kinkaku-ji on Kitasuji-dori, and thus can be visited on the way to the Golden Pavilion. (The museum is open from 10:00 a.m. to 5:00 p.m. but the entry is closed at 4:30. The museum is closed on Mondays and the New Year holidays as well as from March 25 to 31 and from September 25 to 31. Bus 59 takes you to the museum stop. Entry fee.)

Domoto Insho (1891–1975) was a versatile artist who created paintings, ceramics, stained glass and tapestries. In his early years he painted in a traditional Japanese style, but his later work shows French influence. The museum is devoted solely to his work. The white museum building, with purple and gold trim, mounts two main exhibitions a year, from April to September and from October to March.

③ TOJI-IN TEMPLE
Just to the south of Ryoan-ji Temple is Toji-in, which was founded in 1341 by Ashikaga Takauji (1305–58), the first of the Ashikaga Shoguns. (It was originally named Kitatoji-ji at the time of its founding.) The previous Kamakura military government, which governed Japan from 1192 to 1333, had ruled from Kamakura and had thus separated actual governance from the seat of the Imperial reign. It was Takauji's decision to return the seat of government to Kyoto once more, the better to oversee and control the throne. Thus began the Muromachi period (1336–1568), named for the section of Kyoto in which the Ashikaga Shoguns established their rule next to the Shokoku-ji Zen Temple and the present-day Doshisha University. Takauji commissioned Muso Kokushi to design a family temple for the Ashikaga, and Toji-in Temple was the result, with Muso being named its first abbot. He was also responsible for the design of the temple garden and pond. Here, for the next 200 years, many Ashikaga Shoguns were to be memorialized, and here would be placed images of most of the 15 Ashikaga Shoguns.

A view of the Hondo (Main Hall) across the Lotus Pond at Toji-in Temple.

The temple was burned on several occasions, the 1467–77 Onin War being particularly disastrous, but it was rebuilt in 1606. Added to in later years, the present buildings date to an 1818 restoration. In the 19th century, an anti-Ashikaga feeling developed among many Japanese, partially as a reaction against the ruling Tokugawa Shoguns who could not be opposed openly and who had, in a sense, shunted the Emperor aside as had the Ashikaga before them. In April 1863, a group of 20 *samurai* pro-Imperial partisans, raided the temple, decapitated three of the Shogun images (Takauji, Yoshimitsu and Yoshiakira), and planted their wooden heads in the Kamo River, the treatment usually accorded traitors. Six of the assailants (those most responsible for the act) were eventually decapitated, while the others were jailed temporarily. While the six *samurai* permanently lost their heads, those of the wooden images of the Shoguns were restored. The temple suffered under the 1868 Meiji Restoration of Imperial rule, and that year the

temple treasury was looted and many of the temple records were burned. As late as 1887, almost 20 years after the restoration of Imperial rule, people would pay ¥5 for the privilege of beating the image of Ashikaga Yoshimitsu (founder of the Golden Pavilion) in Toji-in. Happily, the temple and its garden are today restored and preserved.

HONDO You must remove your shoes on entering the Hondo (Main Hall) and replace them with the temple's slippers. The entry ticket is obtained from the counter directly ahead. Beyond the ticket area to the right and then again to the left is a large *tatami*-matted hall which faces on to the lovely garden that is the pride of the temple. Here one can sit and contemplate the beauty of the garden. Directly ahead on the right of the ticket counter, at the end wall, is a large painted image of Daruma, the Chinese founder of Zen (the temple was created as a Zen temple). The room behind this painting contains various artifacts: a suit of medieval armor, temple roof tiles, etc.

Behind this artifact room, to the east, is the main worship area, a Buddha image in the rear center of the room with many *ihai* (memorial tablets) to the souls of the dead on either side of the image. To the south of the veranda (which surrounds the building) is a *karesansui* (dry garden) of sand, rocks and moss with pines and maples offering a backdrop of greenery.

ASHIKAGA MEMORIAL BUILDING An arched bridge leads from the east veranda of the Hondo to the Ashikaga Memorial Building. Here, in the front two rooms are the statues of all the Ashikaga Shoguns except the fifth and the tenth. The *fusuma* were painted by Kano Sanraku (1559–1635) in India ink; they represent "The 24 Paragons of Filial Piety." The images of the Ashikaga Shoguns include the figures of Yoshimitsu (1358–1408, third Shogun and creator of the Golden Pavilion); Yoshimasa (1435-1490, eighth Shogun and creator of the Silver Pavilion); Yoshikatsu (seventh Shogun who died at the age of 10); Yoshiharu (13th Shogun, a short, unpleasant looking individual); and Yoshiaka (15th and last Ashikaga Shogun). The images are considered to be fairly realistic, the wearing of the moustache and short, pointed beard being customary.

In the middle chamber there is a row of Shoguns on either side of the passageway; the third (last) figure on the left is the seated Ashikaga Takauji (1305–58), the first Ashikaga Shogun, seen here as a lacquered figure in a Chinese or court robe and wearing the tall black ceremonial hat (*eboshi*) with a wand (*shaku*) of authority in his hand. Opposite him is a figure of Tokugawa Ieyasu (1542–1616), first Shogun of the Tokugawa line. The third and innermost room has an image of Jizo, the patron of the Ashikaga, attributed to Saicho (Dengyo Daishi, 767–822).

GARDENS From the Main Hall, a path is taken to the garden to the north of the building, a garden by Muso Kokushi that has been highly praised. Constructed in two parts, the eastern section is called Shinji-chi or Heart Shaped Pond (the pond being in the shape of the character *shin*, or "heart"), while the western section is the Fuyo-chi or Lotus Pond.

The gardens have an informal nature to them with a stream wandering through the area and a stone bridge leading to the traditional Horai "Island of the Blessed" from Chinese mythology. At one time Mount Kinugasa to the north provided borrowed scenery; today, unfortunately, the modern buildings of Ritsumeikan University hide the mountain and in no way enhance the distant view.

On a slight rise to the north of the Lotus Pond stands the thatched-roof tea house named Seiren-tei (Pavilion of Pure Ripples), a rustic structure planned by Ashikaga Yoshimasa, the eighth Shogun. In the spring, red, white and pink camellia blossoms enliven the garden while in the autumn the yellows and reds of the leaves of the trees create a colorful palette. A memorial stone to Ashikaga Takauji on the south side of the pond marks the site of his grave.

KYOTO MUSEUM FOR WORLD PEACE
At Ritsumeikan University, just above Toji-in, is the Kyoto Museum for World Peace, an exhibit in one hall that covers the story of the Japanese war exploits in East Asia in the period since Meiji militarism began Japan's descent into armed intervention against other nations, and which ended with atomic bombs being dropped on Hiroshima and Nagasaki. The story of the projected dropping of an atomic bomb on Kyoto is also covered. (Open 9:30 to 4:30, except on Mondays.)

4 KINKAKU-JI TEMPLE

A little further along Kitasuji-dori to the northeast brings you to Kinkaku-ji, the Golden Pavilion. Kinkaku-ji is at the foot of Mount Kinagusa. (The temple is open from 9:00 a.m. to 5:30 p.m. in summer and from 9:00 a.m. to 5:00 p.m. between October and March. Entry fee.)

Originally the mountain villa of Saionji Kintsune (1171–1242), the grounds included the Saion-ji Temple and his Kita-yamadai Villa with its 45 foot (14 m) waterfall. In time, the temple and villa fell into ruin, and the 4.5 acre (1.8 ha) site was eventually obtained by Shogun Ashikaga Yoshimitsu (1358–1408). In the manner of emperors, for Yoshimitsu was not shy in his pretensions, he retired at age 38, turning the role of Shogun over to his 9-year-old son Yoshimochi. As with retired emperors, he remained the power behind the throne, and he used his mountainside retreat, which he began in 1397, as a place from which his political power could be employed.

Here, in 1408, he entertained Emperor Go-Komatsu with a boating party, an occasion of the greatest display of ostentation in as much as it was the first time an emperor had deigned to stay at a villa of one who was not of noble status. Here, too, he held a reception for the ambassadors from China, for Yoshimitsu was captivated by the aesthetics of that great country.

Kinkaku-ji, the Golden Pavilion (originally called the Shari-den or Relic Hall), and the pond in front of it were designed to evoke the image of the Seven Treasure Pond found in Buddhist Paradise scenes. The pond was originally filled with flowering lotus plants, the symbol of the pure flower of truth of Buddhism rising from the mud of this world.

This retirement retreat was rather impressive, since it contained 13 buildings, among them an eight-gabled Shishin-den hall that resembled the same building in the Imperial Palace (replete with a throne at its center for this former Shogun), with eight dragons in gold lacquer on its roof; a Hall of the Court of Nobles; a Pavilion of the Mirror of Heaven; a Hall of the Confessor of the Doctrine; a North Gazing Hall (toward the hills); a Snow Viewing Arbor; a Relic Hall; a Hall of the Waters; a Hall of Fragrant Virtues; a Lesser Hall; a Jizo Hall; and, of course, the Golden Pavilion. All but the last of these buildings have disappeared with time.

After Yoshimitsu's death, following the instructions in his will his pleasure palace became the Rokuon-ji (Deer Park Temple) of the Rinzai sect of Buddhism, and the noted priest Muso Kokushi was invited to become the founding abbot. Despite the vicissitudes of war, earthquakes and fires, the Golden Pavilion, the heart of Yoshimitsu's complex, survived until 1950 when a deranged monk set it on fire. It was rebuilt in 1955 as an exact replica of the original pavilion, and it has been regilded since its reconstruction.

The grounds of the Kinkaku-ji are entered through the So-mon Gate and down a tree-lined path to an area before a yellow wall and the Chu-mon (Middle Gate). To the left of this entry path is the Shoro (Belfry), while to the right of the path is a large boat-shaped stone. A large camellia bush in the garden before the Kuri (Priests' Quarters) was planted by the Emperor Go-mizuno-o himself. The Hondo (Main Hall) of the Rokuon-ji Temple, rebuilt in the early 1600s at the order of Emperor Go-mizuno-o, and the Kuri (Priests' Quarters) lie to the right of the entry path. (These halls are generally not open to the public.)

HONDO The main image in the Hondo is a seated Sho Kannon (a gift of Emperor Go-mizuno-o), attributed to Jocho (11th century), with Bon-ten and Taishaku-ten on either side. To the right is a statue of Muso Kokushi, the first abbot of the temple, while to the left is a statue of Yoshimitsu in priestly garb. The *fusuma* in the hall bear sepia drawings by Kano Tanyu (1602–74), and the main hall also has paintings by Mincho (1352–1431) and Kano Tsunenobu (1631–1713). In addition, there is a portrait of Yoshitsune with an inscription by his son.

DAI SHOIN The Dai Shoin (Large Study) to the rear of the Hondo, which extends toward the Golden Pavilion and its pond, has *fusuma* decorated by Sumiyoshi Hiromichi (1599–1670) and Ito Jakakuchu (1716–1800). A noteworthy pine, named the "Land Boat Pine" from its boat-like shape, is in the north garden opposite the Golden Pavilion. At the end of the entry path, the Chu-mon or Kara-mon (Chinese style) gateway leads to the pavilion.

GOLDEN PAVILION The renewal of contact with Sung China brought many new artistic influences to bear on Japanese life, and Yoshimitsu surrounded himself with cultural advisors (since he had a major concern for the aesthetic aspects of life) who had been to China. As a result, the Golden Pavilion, the jewel in his retirement retreat, shows the influence of Sung architectural style. The three-story pavilion is 33 by 42 feet (10 by 13 m) in area and 42 feet (13 m) high, topped by a 3.7 foot (1.1 m) bronze phoenix with outspread wings, a 1955 reproduction of the original.

The first floor of the pavilion, the Ho-sui-in, was used as a reception hall where Yoshimitsu welcomed his guests. It contained an altar in the middle with the central image of Amida by An-ami, a Kannon by Unkei and a Seishi by Tankei. In addition, there were wooden images of Yoshimitsu, Muso Kokushi and Daruma and many Jizo. This floor is in the Heian period (794–1200) Shinden-zukuri architectural style, the style of early palace buildings. The Tsuridono platform juts out from the side of the pavilion into the pond, providing a dock for the boating parties that arrived in ornate Chinese-style boats which had been created on Yoshimitsu's orders.

The second floor of the pavilion, the Cho-on-do (Wave Roaring Hall), was created in the Bukko-zukuri style, the architectural style

The beauty of the Golden Pavilion is enhanced by the pond and stroll garden in which it is situated.

of a *samurai* house of the Kamakura period (1185–1333). This level was reserved for Yoshimitsu's private meetings with special guests, and here he held discussions of affairs of the day or of matters of an artistic nature. It had paintings by Kano Masanobu (1453–90), a central altar by a Sho Kannon by Eshin, with Shi-tenno images on the right and left.

The third floor, the Kyu Kyo Cho (Firmament Top), 23 by 23 feet (7 by 7 m), with a ceiling made of one piece of camphor wood, served as a private retreat for ceremonial tea drinking and contemplation with Yoshimitsu's most intimate friends. It is in the Sung-inspired Chinese (Kara-yao) or Zen temple style with its bell-shaped windows. It held a Jodo-style Amida and 25 Bodhisattvas.

The exterior of the first floor of the pavilion is of unpainted wood, while the two upper floors are lacquered and then covered with gold foil. (The replacement of the foil in 1987 under a general reconstruction program cost $5 million.) At one time, the pavilion was probably on an island attached to the shore by means of a bridge. The carp-filled pond before the pavilion, Kagami-ike (Mirror Pond), covers 1.7 acres (0.7 ha) and has numerous islands within it, some with noted (and named) stones. These islands represent the nine mountains and the eight oceans of the Buddhist creation story.

Behind the pavilion and up a short flight of stone steps is a small shrine, the Shin-un, to the god of the temple grounds, and then a spring, the Ginkasen, which supplied the water for Yoshimitsu's tea ceremony. The

1884. An old stone lantern, a stone basin and a stool before the building came from the former Ashikaga-Muromachi period (1336–1568) Hana-no-Gosho (Flower Palace). This simple tea house has a crooked post of rare wood from the Nandin tree setting off its *tokonoma*, and the shelves are of lespedeza wood. To the rear of the tea house is the post-1868 rebuilt Kyohoky-ro, where Yoshimitsu carried out state business.

FUDO-DO The path eventually leads through a moss garden to the Fudo-do, a small temple to Fudo-Myo-o with a stone image of Fudo and his attendants. The bushes about this tiny temple are covered with twisted strips of paper "fortunes" obtained from an adjacent fortune-telling machine.

(The mountain behind the Kinkaku-ji, Mount Kinugasa (Silk Hat Mountain), is reputedly so-named since one hot July day the former Emperor Uda ordered it spread with white silk so that his eyes could enjoy a cool, wintry sensation.)

Ryu-mon-baku, a small waterfall, has a large stone, the "Carp Stone," standing before it, to suggest the way carp can ascend a waterfall on the way to their spawning grounds. A noted style of bamboo fencing named for the pavilion, the Kinkaku-ji fence, leads up the hillside to the Kokei-bashi, a small stone bridge over an artificial valley and a pond that has a small island with a modest stone pagoda on it (with four Buddhas cut into the four sides of the stone base), dedicated to the White Dragon who controls the water supply.

SEKKA-TEI Stone steps up a winding path lead to the thatched-roof Sekka-tei, a small tea ceremony house built in honor of a visit by Emperor Go-Mizuno-o in the 1600s. Although destroyed in an 1874 fire, it was recreated in

GETTING THERE

Several of the sites on this tour, particularly Kinkaku-ji and Ryoan-ji, are among the most popular tourist destinations in Kyoto. They can all be reached easily by bus from central Kyoto, and are within walking distance from each other.

All the sites on this tour are located in the northwest-central portion of Kyoto. Ninna-ji can be reached by means of bus 26, 28 or 59, which stop outside the temple grounds at the Omuro-Ninna-ji bus stop. It can also be reached from the Omuro station of the Kitano line of the Keifuku electric railway. The temple is north of the station. Ryoan-ji, which is located between Ninna-ji and Kinkaku-ji, can be reached directly by bus 59 to the Ryoan-ji-mae bus stop. Alternatively, if coming from downtown, the subway can be taken to the Imadegawa station, and then bus 59 can be taken to the Ryoan-ji-mae bus stop. Kinkaku-ji can be reached by means of bus 12, 59, 204 or 205 to the Kinkaku-ji-michi bus stop or bus 50 to the Kinkaku-ji-mae stop. A return to the center of the city can be made by bus back at Kita-oji-dori (which runs in front of the Ninna-ji Temple) on bus 26, 28 or 59 to the Kita-oji subway station, and thus back to the heart of Kyoto.

Walking Tour 18

MYOSHIN-JI AREA

A Cheerful and Restless Spirit, a Contemplative Bodhisattva and Samurai Movies

1. **Sembon Shaka-do Temple**
千本釈迦堂（大報恩寺）
2. **Kitano Tenman-gu Shrine** 北野天満宮
3. **Myoshin-ji Temple** 妙心寺
4. **Koryu-ji Temple** 広隆寺
5. **Toei Uzumasa Eigamura** 東映太秦映画村

The central sector of Kyoto has not only the Imperial Palace and Nishijin, but to its west are shrines and temples of note. One, the Sembon Shaka-do Temple, is well known for its magnificent collection of Buddhist images in its handsome Treasury building (Reiho-kan), but is perhaps more remembered for the wife of its architect than for its treasured images. The temple has a memorial to Okame of the smiling face, whose humorous papier-maché representation in a popular mask is seen at festivals throughout Japan and whose quick mind saved her architect husband from a serious architectural *faux pas* during the construction of the Sembon Shaka-do. This memorial to a smiling spirit exists not too far from the Kitano Tenman-gu Shrine, which was created to appease the supposed unhappy and restless spirit of Sugawara-no-Michizane, a 10th century poet and statesman. The rendezvous of students for centuries, the Kitano Shrine is still patronized by those aspiring to success in intellectual endeavors, for Michizane, among other attributes, is now regarded as a Shinto spirit who can assist students and is the patron spirit for scholars as well. Even the non-literary flock to the Kitano Shrine each month, for here is held one of the great monthly fairs of Kyoto, where everything from antiques to food to knickknacks can be purchased on the shrine's monthly festive occasion.

Not too far away is the great Myoshin-ji Temple complex, with its many subdivisions. As with many of these complex units, only a few of the temples are open to the public, and those are the ones which will be described in this chapter. Next is Koryu-ji, furthest to the west of central Kyoto, dedicated to the memory of the ever-revered Prince Shotoku, the official proponent of Buddhism in early Japan. The temple was originally founded in the

A seated Chinese sage and his two small assistants in the Reiho-kan (Treasury) of Sembon-Shaka-do.

620s on the death of the Prince, and it is a mecca for those interested in early Buddhist artistry, for its attractive Treasury contains finely crafted images from the 600s on, including the famed statue of the contemplative Miroku, which was created in Korea.

The Toei Eigamura is a movie studio where films have been made for many years and where television soap operas originate today. The Toei Film Village is a filming complex that recreates everything from medieval Japanese times, with swashbuckling *samurai* epics and black-masked *ninja* to Edo period (1603–1868) Japan with its political intrigues. To the delight of adolescents (and adults), you can see films being made or be photographed in a cityscape of an old Edo (Tokyo) that no longer exists in reality.

1 SEMBON SHAKA-DO TEMPLE

A bus or taxi to Imadegawa-dori to the west brings you to the Sembon Shaka-do Temple. (The Sembon Shaka-do Temple is 400 yards (366 m) northeast of the Kitano Tenman-gu Shrine. Bus 52 or 203 on Imadegawa-dori from the Imadegawa subway station west to the Kamishichiken bus stop on Imadegwawa-dori. A sign with an arrow on the north side of Imadegawa-dori at the Kamishichiken bus stop points north to Sembon Shaka-do (in

English). The main entrance to the temple grounds is on Shichihonmachi-dori. The temple buildings are open from 9:00 a.m. to 5:00 p.m. Entry fee.)

According to tradition, the Sembon Shaka-do (Daihoon-ji) was founded by Emperor Yomei (reigned 586–87), a fairly unlikely event since the Emperor only accepted Buddhism on his deathbed, and the first Buddhist temples (the Shitenno-ji in Osaka and the Hoko-ji in Asuka) were built a few years later. The present Hondo (Main Hall) was built in 1227, and it is miraculous that the temple survived the Onin War (1467–77), which destroyed so much around it.

The architect of the Hondo was Nagai Takatsugi who, unfortunately, miscalculated the measurements for the main pillars and came up with posts too short. It was his wife Okame's suggestion which saved his reputation: she proposed adding brackets to the top of the posts to reach the correct height. This was done, but Okame died before she could see the success of her proposal. When the last beams were put into place, the workmen, in her honor, placed a mask of her round plump cheerful face on the ridge pole in praise of her. Thus the cult of Okame began and spread throughout Japan, and she became the deity of good luck, the granter of desires and the patroness of business prosperity. As a mask, her round face has red cheeks and small round eyebrows. In her honor, a statue of Okame sits to the right of the Hondo when one faces that building.

HONDO The main gate to the Sembon Shaka-do is on its south side, and a path leads past minor buildings to the Hondo. To the right, before reaching the Hondo, is the statue of the round-cheeked Okame, while to the left is the temple office and ticket booth where you pay the entry fee to the modern Treasury, which is behind the Hondo. The Hondo was originally created in the Shinden-zukuri style with a thatched roof; the roof was tiled in 1670, but in recent times it has been returned to its earlier thatched status. The central image on the main altar of the Hondo, in a closed case (opened for public viewing on August 8 each year), is that of Shaka Nyorai. Created in wood by Gyokai, the senior apprentice to the noted artist Kaikei, this 13th century image is 36 inches (90 cm) tall and covered with gold leaf. It is seated on a lotus and has an elaborate aureole of fine fret work with small Buddha images standing behind it. This Shaka is the only surviving work by Gyokai. The four pillars about the Shaka image case are decorated with colorful but fading images, and two poles stand at either side of the Shaka image case, each topped by round fanlike units with an image of Okame's face. Facing the veranda on the east is a corridor lined with cases with representations of Okame in all sizes and shapes, and at the rear of the corridor is a large wooden image of Okame.

REIHO-KAN The fairly compact precincts of the temple include a number of buildings, the most important being the Reiho-kan, one of the finest treasure houses in Kyoto, both for its building interior and its treasures. A 1973 fireproof concrete building, it has interior walls and ceiling of attractive wood, and its magnificent sculptures are arranged around three of its walls. On the left wall are an early Buddha image, the Shi-tenno guardians, a Jizo, a seated Dainichi with a large crown and the standing painted wood Ju Dai Deshi (Ten Great Disciples) made by Kaikei in 1218. These portraits of real individuals once stood about the Shaka image in the Hondo. At the rear center is a "Birthday Buddha" in bronze, a figure of the newborn Buddha with one hand pointing to heaven and one to the earth to indicate his sovereignty over both realms; a Heian period (794–1185) Senju (1,000 arm) Kannon; a Kamakura period (1185–1333) Jizo; and a set of a seated Chinese sage and his two small assistants. On the right side are six magnificent representations of Kannon, the deity of mercy, by Jokei II, dated 1224. The images average 7 feet (2 m) in height, and these exquisite unpainted wood figures are each backed by a full-length aureole of curved and delicately carved (fretted) wood. They show the influence of the fullness of Sung Chinese sculpture. Next to these are a Senju Kannon of the Heian period and two huge wooden frames, some 20 feet (6 m) tall, each of which once held an immense drum. One is decorated with carved peacocks while the other has carved dragons. On the fourth (entry) wall are two gigantic wheels of a court cart once used by Ashikaga Yoshimitsu (1358–1408), the creator of the Golden Pavilion (Kinkaku-ji).

Each year on February 3 the temple hosts the Okame Setsubun Festival. Okame is considered to be a patron of business and prosperity and thus this is a very popular festival. Well-known citizens of Kyoto, wearing Okame masks, scatter beans from the temple Hondo to drive out evil.

2 KITANO TENMAN-GU SHRINE

After visiting Sembon Shaka-do, take the street on the southern perimeter of the temple to the right (west) for a few blocks to the Kitano Tenman-gu Shrine. (This shrine is just north of Imadegawa-dori and east of Nishi-oji-dori. The grounds are open during daylight hours. No entry fee is charged except for entrance to the Treasury.)

The Kitano Tenman-gu Shrine is dedicated to Sugawara-no-Michizane (845–903), a poet and statesman who was an advisor to Emperor Uda and then to his son, Emperor Daigo. Michizane became the victim of a court intrigue, was disgraced and then banished to Kyushu in 901, dying shortly thereafter in exile. His death was followed by tremendous storms, disastrous floods, epidemics and even the death of the Minister of the Left, Fujiwara-no-Tokehira, who had had Michizane exiled, who died in a 909 epidemic. Again in 930 Kyoto suffered a series of calamitous storms, floods and then droughts and epidemics. The palace was hit by lightning and then the

Emperor Daigo fell ill and died. Finally, in 942, a dream was interpreted and brought to the attention of the court, and the interpretation held that the series of disasters inflicted on Kyoto was the result of Michizane's unhappy spirit, and that respite could only be had if the Tenjin Shrine (to the god of thunder) was rededicated to Michizane.

Michizane's spirit was therefore identified with that of the god of thunder, and in 947 a shrine was dedicated to him (at an existing shrine to the god of thunder) in order to bring relief to Kyoto. The shrine was also planted with many apricot (Japanese plum) trees, Michizane's favorite tree. In 959, a Fujiwara descendent, no doubt as a form of insurance, had the shrine enlarged. Meantime, to further allay Michizane's supposed angry spirit, his rank as Minister of the Right was restored. When problems still continued, he was elevated posthumously to the rank of Minister of the Left, and, finally, in desperation, the court raised him posthumously to the Prime Ministership. From 1004 on, visits were even made to the shrine by various emperors.

Through the years, the shrine gained in popularity, particularly since Michizane was also recognized as the patron of literature, of scholars and of students. In this present century of universal education in Japan, the shrine is heavily frequented by students in need of spiritual or supernatural assistance at examination time.

It was at the Kitano Shrine in October 1587 that Toyotomi Hideyoshi held his famous tea party, to which he invited everyone to attend, "even those from China." One had only to bring a mat to sit on and a tea cup. (In remembrance of this occasion, the Ocha Tsubo Hoken-sai (Tea Festival) is held every November 26.) In 1607, Toyotomi Hideyori (Hideyoshi's son) had the shrine rebuilt to include three gates, a Honden (Main Hall) and a Heiden (Offertory), their roofs covered with cypress shingles. The shrine was further surrounded by a grove of apricot (plum) trees, Michizane's favorite tree, as noted above. (On February 25 each year, a festival is held in honor of the blooming of the trees.)

MAIN BUILDINGS The shrine's southern entrance at Imadegawa-dori is marked by a huge granite *torii*, preceded by Korean *koma-inu* (lion-dogs) on either side. Small Shinto shrines and stone lanterns line the path through two more *torii* before coming to the main wooden gateway. Along the way are stone oxen, gifts of devotees of the shrine, in memory of the ox day in the old zodiac calendar, since on that day (June 9, 847) the

The Gate of the Three Luminaries at Kitano Tenman-gu has carvings of the sun, moon and stars.

shrine was first founded. The shrine precincts are behind a wooden fence which is pierced by a plain wooden two-story Nan-mon (South Gate), which is touched with gold and has colorful Shinto guardians on either side of the entryway. The Chu-mon (Central or Middle Gate) is also called the San-ko-no-mon or "Gate of the Three Luminaries," from the carvings of the sun, moon and stars on its beams (now largely effaced). The tablet over the entryway reads "Tenman-gu" in the calligraphy of the Emperor Go-Sai-in.

Beyond the gate are the main buildings of the temple: the Ema-do, the Treasure House, the Heiden (Offertory) and the Honden (Main Shrine). Directly beyond the gate to the right is the purification water fountain, while a small log treasury building is further to the right. On the left is the Ema-do with its votive paintings donated by devotees, a large wooden building raised on pillars.

The inner portion of the shrine precincts is enclosed by buildings and fences to form an inner courtyard, a path down its center lined with lanterns and a pair of bronze bulls and then a pair of *koma-inu* (lion-dogs). The unit on the right side of the courtyard offers religious goods for sale, while on the left side there is a unit for the placement of prayer candles. The roofed Heiden (Offertory) is on the north side of the square, and between the Heiden and the Honden (Spirit Hall) is an area paved with stone, so small that the two buildings are almost touching.

The Honden is decorated with carvings of birds and flowers on the lintel, attributed to the famed carver Hidari Jingoro. Before the oratory is a small fenced-in apricot tree, a duplicate of the one which supposedly once stood here and was so moved by Michizane's poem, written at the time of his exile, that the tree is reputed to have flown to Kyushu to be with him. Behind the Honden is the Jinushi-no-Yashiro, the Shinto shrine of the god of the temple grounds, said to date from 836, together with numerous other small shrines. East of the central courtyard is the *Kagura* (sacred dance) stage and the storage building in which the shrine *mikoshi* (festival god carts) are kept. The temple grove of apricot trees is noted, particularly for the trees' early spring bloom. The largest number of apricot trees is along the Kamiya-gawa stream on the western side of the grounds.

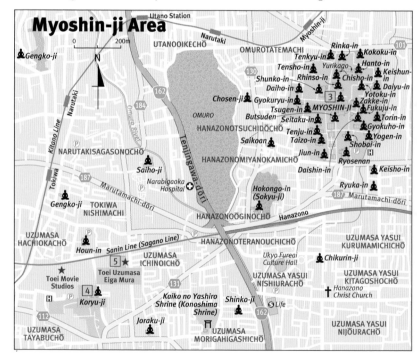

The two-story San-mon Gate to Myoshin-ji still has the arrow holes used during the Onin War.

The Homotsu-den (Treasure House) is open on the 25th of each month unless it is raining. (In summer, the treasury hours are 10:00 a.m. to 6:00 p.m. while in winter they are from 10:00 a.m. to 4:30 p.m. Entry fee.) The treasures of the shrine include paintings, sculpture, lacquer work, *ema*, court costumes, scrolls, screens, sutras and examples of calligraphy. The 13th century *Kitano Tenjin Engi* (Legend of the Kitano Shrine), which traces Michizane's life, is one of the temple's more famous holdings.

FESTIVALS The Kitano Shrine is noted for its many festivals, which include a festival and religious service to honor Sugawara Michizane on the 25th of each month. As part of the day's events, stalls are set up along the path leading into the shrine where food, used goods, antiques and various products are sold. It is a festive and popular occasion each month. Another highlight is the Baika-sai (Plum/Apricot Blossom Festival, held on February 25. The Japanese apricot is also referred to as a plum, thus both names are

used in reference to the tree and fruit. An open-air tea ceremony and memorial rites for Sugawarano-Michizane are held under the blossoms of his favorite tree. Offerings of rice wrapped in mulberry bark paper and decorated with plum blossoms are offered to the gods of the shrine. On October 1–4 of each year is the Zuiki Matsuri, a festival of gratitude to the gods for a good harvest. Events are held during these days and stalls sell food and goods each night.

3 MYOSHIN-JI TEMPLE

From the Kitano Tenman-gu Shrine, return to Imadegawa-dori and follow it to the main north–south street, Nishi-oji-dori. Cross the street to the terminal of the Keifuku electric railway, whose trolleys lead to the remaining sites of this tour, the first of which is the Myoshin-ji Zen temple, which can be reached from the Myoshin-ji station of the Keifuku line. The grounds of the Myoshin-ji are always open, but the individual subtemples have varying hours–see "Getting There" for details. The main buildings of the temple

(Butsu-den, Hatto, etc.) are open from 9:00 a.m. to 4:00 p.m. There is a fee for a tour of the Hatto and the Bath House as well as separate fees to some subtemples.

Myoshin-ji is one of the six major Zen temples of Kyoto, the other five being Daitoku-ji, Nanzen-ji, Tenryu-ji, Shokoku-ji and Tofuku-ji. It is the headquarters of the Myoshin-ji school of Rinzai Zen Buddhism. The temple grounds were originally the villa of Kiyowara Natsune (782–837), and it later became the retirement villa of Emperor Hanazono (1297–1348). In 1318, the villa became the Myoshin-ji Temple when the Emperor presented it to Priest E-gen (Kanzan Kokushi), who built the temple and became its first abbot. More than 40 sub-temple buildings were eventually clustered about the central temple buildings, many of these subtemples built by military leaders. The buildings were destroyed during the Onin War (1467–77), and thus a number of the present structures were erected after 1480. The temple benefited from the patronage of the powerful Hosokawa family after the Onin War, and was later assisted by Hideyoshi and the Tokugawa Shoguns, who financed the rebuilding of many of the 47 subtemples. Unlike Daitoku-ji, Myoshin-ji was not enamored of the worldly arts such as the tea ceremony and landscape gardening, for it maintained a simpler, stricter approach to religion. This does not negate its holdings of numerous treasures, but it was less "worldly" than its fellow major Zen temples.

The Myoshin-ji sect includes some 3,500 temples throughout Japan. Within the precincts of the temple, aside from the main temple buildings, there are 47 subtemples, only a few of which are open to the public, most notably the Taizo-in. The Garan (the seven main structures of the temple) will be found within the temple grounds, and the directions (see "Getting There") are given from the South Gate, which lies before the San-mon Gate, and then the descriptions move north within the structure.

The San-mon is a two-story gate which was restored in 1559. It is 49 feet (15 m) long by 26 feet (8 m) wide and it stands 53 feet (16 m) high. Its second floor has as it images the 16 *arhat,* and its ceiling is enriched with a painted dragon, various heavenly beings and other fabled creatures, all painted by Kano Genzaemon. Between the gate and the Butsu-den (Buddha Hall) stood four old pine trees—a symbolic representation of the four branches of Rinzai Zen Buddhism. The gateway retains the holes from arrows from battles of the Onin War. The Butsu-den is directly behind (north of) the San-mon Gate. It is a square (53 feet/17 m) double-roofed structure with a floor paved with bricks. Its main image, high up against its north wall, is of Sakyamuni accompanied by his attendants Kasho (Mahakasyapa) and Ananda, all by Kakusei. Above the main image in the roof structure, an elephant head protrudes to the east and west while lion heads protrude to the south from the major beam ends.

HATTO The Hatto, north of the Buddha Hall, is meant to serve the monks of the temple and is not a public place of worship, since this is a Zen temple for monks. It can hold up to 1,000 priests. Here, Buddhist rituals are performed and sermons are given by the temple master. The hall was rebuilt in 1657 and is 82 feet (25 m) long by 66 feet (20 m) wide and stands 66 feet (20 m) high. The floor is covered with plain tiles. The ceiling has a painted dragon in a circle (Unryu-zu, "Dragon in the Cloud") created by Kano Tanyu (1602–74). According to temple history, Tanyu meditated for three years as to the type of dragon to be created, and he then spent five years executing the painting on the ceiling. The dragon covers an area of 42 feet (13 m) in diameter. Considered the finest dragon of any temple in Kyoto, the dragon's eye seems to follow you no matter where you stand in the hall. As you look at the dragon from the western side of the interior of the building, the dragon appears to be descending, and then as you move south, then east, then north, it seems to ascend.

Three sides of the hall have raised *tatami* platforms, and the pillars before these are decorated with multicolored hangings. The colors are arranged in a series, with the highest ecclesiastical color followed by the next lower ranking color: purple, green, yellow, red and white. A raised platform on the north side is the place for the abbot's seat, a large Chinese-style chair, from which he lectures. In the western corner of the platform stands a tall pine tree and before it hang huge red lanterns. Benches are placed in the middle of the hall, and in the northeast corner is a bell in a small belfry, the oldest dated bell (698) in Japan. The bell is said to have been cast in Fukuoka in Kyushu, and it is mentioned in the *Essays in Idleness* by Yoshida Kenko in the

Elaborate tiles decorate the roof of one of the 47 subtemples in the Myoshin-ji Temple complex.

1300s. The building is not airtight; large spaces exist between the boards, an indication of the privation of monks in winter.

OTHER BUILDINGS The Kyo-do (Sutra Hall) contains a huge octagonal revolving bookcase, the sides of the case being carved by Chu-en, with colored Buddhist figures amidst rocks. Seated in a chair is the image of Fu Daishi, the reputed inventor of the revolving bookcase meant to hold the 6,771 volumes of sutras. There are 6,166 volumes in the Kyo-do. These are said to have taken 12 priests eight years to copy and were completed in May 1673.) The Yokushitsu (Bath House), which was built by the uncle of Akechi Mutsuhuide, the assassin of Oda Nobunaga, lies to the southeast of the Hatto. Its most noted unit is the steam room in which monks could sit in meditation.

Within the complex of buildings, the Hojo is the official residence of the temple abbot, although it is no longer used for this purpose. It was rebuilt in 1654 and it is 98 feet (30 m) long by 66 feet (20 m) wide and it stands 49 feet (15 m) high. The front of the building is divided into three rooms and these are decorated with *sumi-e* scenes of mountains, temples and people by Kano Tanyu. The main image in the Hojo is that of Amida, a statue created more than 1,000 years ago. The garden before the Hojo has two pine trees and cone-shaped sand hills, such hills being customary in Zen Hojo gardens.

The Kuri (Priests' Quarters—not open to the public) are attached to the Hojo by the Great Corridor. Rebuilt in 1653, this building is 59 feet (18 m) long by 76 feet (23 m) deep and 46 feet (14 m) high. It contains kitchens, a refectory in which 500 tables can be set up, a Buddha altar, the Council Chamber and the Provost's office. The Ko Hojo (Abbot's Small Quarters—not open to the public) contains the Abbot's apartments and is connected to the Hojo to the east. Its garden is on the site of Emperor Hanazono's original villa, which became the first building of the temple.

The Gyokuho-in or Hanazono Palace (not open to the public), is where Emperor Hanazono is said to have studied Buddhism under the founder of the temple, E-gan. Rebuilt in 1656, it is adjacent to the Ko Hojo. It holds a wooden image of the Emperor in priest's robes and it contains *fusuma* by Kano Tanyu. Four lovely panels in the sanctuary, representing the four seasons, are inlaid with mother-of-pearl and are claimed to have been brought back from Korea by Hideyoshi at the end of his 1592 war in Korea. They are said to have belonged to a sitting room of the Emperor Yuan-tsung of the T'ang dynasty in China. A small two-story bronze shrine in front of the Sanctuary is inscribed with seven characters which read "Glory to the Kannon Bosatsu," reputedly inlaid by a daughter of former Emperor Go-Mizunu-no-o with the Emperor's nails(!).

The Kaisan-do (Founders' Hall), to the east of the Gyokuho-in, is the oldest building in Myoshin-ji, dating to 1528. The interior of the structure is all in black, from its tiles to its pillars to the lacquered altar. On the altar in an innermost shrine is a wooden image of the founder E-gan. The image is constantly attended by a priest as though it were the living founder himself. Inscriptions in calligraphy on boards before the shrine are by the Emperors Hanazono, Go-Tsuchi, Go-Kashirobara and Meiji. A tiny Nehan-do on the altar is a bronze piece portraying the death of the Buddha and his achieving Nirvana.

The Ojikicho (Bell Tower), rebuilt in 1978, is to the west of the Hojo. The bell within is claimed to be the oldest known bell in Japan, and, according to temple legend, it was used by Prince Shotoku (who died in 622) to set the chromatic semitone of the Shi-tenno-ji Temple in Osaka, since it has the Huang tone of Chinese music. In this account, the bell was cast in 578, a date too early in Japanese history for this type of bell. The adjacent Semmondo-jo is the monastery where monks are trained. Begging and service are their main tasks, and they live by the Zen rule of "a day without work is a day without food." Zen discipline is strict for the temple monks, and creature comforts are disdained since the goal of a monk's life is enlightenment, not material rewards or comfort. Aside from this training unit for monks, the temple runs a high school and a college with 2,000 students. The latter are training to be monks or priests.

SUBTEMPLES OF MYOSHIN-JI TEMPLE

Three of the subtemples of the Myoshin-ji are open to the public throughout the year: Daishin-in (9:00 a.m. to 4:00 p.m.), Keishun-in (8:00 a.m. to 5:00 p.m.) and Taizo-in (9:00 a.m. to 5:00 p.m.). Of these, the most important is the Taizo-in, which lies to the west of Myoshin-ji's Hatto and the Butsu-den.

TAIZO-IN The Taizo-in is one of the oldest subtemples, having been founded in 1404 by Hatano Shigemichi, a Daimyo of Izumo, who was converted to Zen by the third Superior of the temple, Muin Shonin. The Hojo of the Taizo-in was built in the 17th century (earlier buildings were destroyed in the Onin War), and among its treasures are the painting "Catching a Catfish with a Gourd" by Josetsu, a Chinese painter who came to Japan in 1370 and who is considered the founder of the *sumi-e* (black on white) painting technique in Japan. (The original is in the Kyoto National Museum and thus this painting in the temple is a copy.) The painting was commissioned by Ashikaga Yoshimitsu and is based on the *koan* (a Zen riddle) of trying to pin down a slippery catfish with a gourd. Among other treasures are the "Four Sages of Mount Shang" by Kano Sanroku and letters by Emperors Hanazono and Go-Nara.

The temple is most noted for its gardens. On the west side of the Hojo is a *karesansui* (dry garden), perhaps by Kano Motonobu (1475–1559), who at one time lived at this subtemple. Within this garden, a "waterfall" falls into a pond with islands (including the traditional crane and turtle islands), capes and bridges; this dry garden is surrounded by a bamboo grove and rocks of varying sizes. Among the present gardens is the modern Yoko-in Garden, designed by Nakane Kinsaku, which is closer to a stroll garden than the traditional Zen garden. Four miniature landscapes have been created in this one garden, and the water of the "Dragon King Falls" comes through a series of red azaleas and two smaller falls as the water flows into the Gourd Pond. The "dragon" is a huge stone rearing up behind the falls. A particularly pleasant view of the falls and pond can be seen from the wisteria garden. The Yang Garden, in contrast, is set against a background of Japanese cedars, with seven ancient rocks standing in a sea of sand. The Yin Garden is based on a fan design created in black sand with eight rocks and a weeping cherry tree against a back drop of green shrubbery with low moss about the rocks.

OTHER SUBTEMPLES The Keishun-in subtemple is open from 8:00 a.m. to 5:00 p.m. in summer and from 9:00 a.m. to 5:00 p.m. in winter. Built about 1632, it is noted for its *karesansui* (dry garden), tea garden and stroll garden. Its Soan-style tea house is in the northeast corner of the grounds, an unusual element for a Myoshin-ji subtemple. The Daishin-in was founded in 1492 by the Hosokawa family and it is open from 9:00 a.m. to 4:00 p.m. It too has a modern garden created by Nakane Kinsaku.

Reiun-in lies northwest of the Hatto and opposite the Hojo, and has so many paintings by Kano Motanobu that it has been called "The Motanobu Temple." His paintings portray scenes of the countryside with trees, birds, flowers and historic individuals from Chinese history. These are now mounted as 49 *kakemono*. The Goko-no-ma (Imperial Visit Room) was added to the main building about 1543 on the occasion of an Imperial visit, and is one of the oldest *shoin*-style buildings extant. The garden beyond this room was created at the same time as the Goko-no-ma. The temple is sometimes open to the public in early November.

Tenkyu-in subtemple was built for Lady Tenkyu-in in 1631. The temple is noted for its painted *fusuma* in its Hojo in color on a gold ground by Kano Sanraku (1559–1635) and his son Kano Sansetsu (1590–1651). The *fusuma* divide the interior space of the temple building into three rooms. Particularly important is the eight-panel "Plum Tree and Pheasant" in the southwest room of the Hojo, a painting of an old plum tree in bloom and an old willow with drooping leaves. The *fusuma* of the middle room show bamboo and a group of tigers, while the third room offers morning glories, lilies and chrysanthemums, among other flowers.

Rinka-in subtemple has a sculpture of Toyotomi Hideyoshi's young son, who died in early childhood. The image was once in the Shoun-in before this was destroyed by Tokugawa Ieyasu in order to make space for his Chishaku-in Temple. The child is shown as though in a boat. (This temple is seldom open to the public.) Shunko-in has a bell with a clapper, obviously a relic from one of the European Namban Christian churches of the mid to late 1500s in Kyoto before the outlawing of Christianity. It is inscribed "IHS 1557" on three sides and has been displayed in the National Museum in Tokyo.

4 KORYU-JI TEMPLE

Return to the Keifuku rail line to visit Koryu-ji, which was created in memory of Prince Shotoku, and then on to Toei Uzumasa Eigamura, the Toei Film Studio. At the seventh stop, Katabira-no-suji station, transfer to a train headed back east on the adjacent tracks. The next station is Uzumasa station, the stop for Koryu-ji and Toei Eigamura. (The Koryu-ji Temple is located across the street from Uzumasa station of the Keifuku railway. The main gate of the temple is 300 feet (100 m) to the west of the station. The temple is open from 9:00 a.m. to 5:00 p.m. daily (9:00 a.m. to 4:30 p.m. from December to February) but is closed over the New Year holiday. Entry fee.)

Although Koryu-ji Temple is reputed to have been founded by Prince Shotoku in the year 603, it was probably originally founded on the banks of the Katsura River by the Hata clan soon after their arrival in the 4th century from Silla, Korea. In 622, it was relocated to its present site by Hata-no-Kawakatsu for the peaceful repose of Prince Shotoku's soul, since the prince had died the previous year.

The Hata family had originally come from China via Korea, bringing with them the advanced technologies of the mainland (silk culture, weaving, agriculture and distilling), which were to flourish in Japan and in Kyoto, in particular. (The Shinto shrine behind the Koryu-ji Temple honors the *kami* (Shinto deity) of weaving and the silk cocoon. A different rendering of "Hata" in ideograms can mean "loom.") The Hata were responsible for the creation of other temples within the city as well, and it has been suggested that their offer of land to the Emperor Kammu in the late 700s was the determining point in the Emperor's decision to relocate the capital.

The Koryu-ji Temple precincts are entered through the large gateway at the southern side of the temple grounds. On either side of this gate, in the niches to the right and left, are huge images in wood of Nio, Buddhist protecting deities. The first building on the right within the temple compound is the Kodo (Lecture Hall), which was originally built in 836 but burned down in 1150 and was reconstructed in 1165 as a seven-bay structure. It is thus the second oldest building in Kyoto. Its wide altar area holds its main images, a triad of ancient pieces, including a seated Amida flanked by a Kokuzo Kannon in wood from the 800s and an image of a seated Jizo in wood from 868. Jizo holds the mystic jewel in his left hand while his right hand is outstretched. An 11 foot (3.3 m) tall Fukukenjaku Kannon in wood from the late 8th century is to the right and behind the altar area, while a Senju Kannon (1000-arm Kannon) from the 9th century is to the left and rear of the altar area.

Behind the Kodo is the Taishi-do or Memorial Hall to Prince Shotoku, built in 1720, with two huge stone lanterns in front. Its main image is that of the prince at the

A sea serpent emerges from a pool to entertain visitors to Toei Uzumasa Eigamura movie village.

age of 33, a reputed self-portrait created by Shotoku in the year 606. In this representation of the prince, according to tradition, the image was originally clothed in the prince's garments, these clothes being replaced by the court as they disintegrated with age. The image now wears a yellow robe, a skirt and a crown. In the northwest portion of the grounds is the octagonal Keigu-in or Hakkaku-do of 1251, a one-story building with a cypress bark roof, each side measuring 7.5 feet (2.3 m). It contains a statue of Prince Shotoku at the age of 16. It also holds an early Nyorin Kannon presented by the King of Paekche (Korea) as well as an Amida Nyorai.

Behind the Tashi-do is the 1982 Reiho-kan, the New Treasury Building. (The Old Treasury Building is to the left.) This new fireproof building is lined with wood in its interior and provides a spacious and attractive center for one of the greatest collections of early Japanese Buddhist sculpture, its prize being the wooden Miroku Bodhisattva dating from the Asuka period (552–645). This priceless image was given to the temple in 623 by the kingdom of Silla (Korea) at the earlier request of Prince Shotoku. It is similar to the image in the Chugu-ji Nunnery south of Nara. Both images show the influence of Korean art of that day. Seated with its right leg crossed over its left leg, its left hand delicately held

before its face, it has an enigmatic smile as it contemplates Buddhist truths with its eyes closed. Created from one piece of wood, it is one of the most important sculptures in Japan.

Opposite the Miroku, on the south wall, are a standing Fukukenjaku Kannon in wood (12 feet/3.6 m tall) from the 600s, a seated wood Senju (1,000-arm) Kannon from 1012 and a standing Senju Kannon in wood from the 800s. A seated Jizo image in wood from 868, a circlet behind his head, holds the magic jewel in his left hand while his right hand is extended. Among the many other treasures are a 13th century Shotoku seated in a Chinese chair with a censer in his hands, an 8th century wood Bishamon-ten and a 10th century image of Hata-no-Kawakatsu and his wife. The painted surface on the last two images is still quite evident. In addition, there are some 50 or more images and small treasures, including an 11th century Zao Gongen in polychrome wood in a dynamic pose, brandishing a trident and balancing himself on his left leg preparatory to taking offensive action.

The most noted festival at Koryu-ji is the annual October 12th Ushi Matsuri. A priest dressed as Mandara, an Indian god, rides to the temple altar on an ox. He is accompanied by four priests representing the Shi-tenno or Four Deva Kings. He then intones a sacred sutra from an Indian archaic text.

5 TOEI UZUMASA EIGAMURA

Leaving the main entry gate of Koryu-ji, turn left and then follow the road north. This will bring you to the entryway to the Toei Movie Village. (The Toei Uzumasa Eigamura film studio lies to the north of the Uzumasa station of the Keifuku Arashiyama rail line. The street headed north, one street east of the station, leads to the studio, which is just before the San-in main line railway right of way. The studio is open from April to November from 9:00 a.m. to 5:00 p.m. and from December to March from 10:00 a.m. to 4:00 p.m. It is closed from December 21 to January 3. Entry fee.)

Toei Uzumasa Eigamura is a portion of the "back set" of the Japanese "Hollywood"—in as much as Kyoto was the birthplace of the Japanese film industry and this studio is still an active filming center today, albeit primarily for television. The 7 acre (2.8 ha) area contains not only the sets used in filming the "*samurai* swashbuckler" tales so dear to Japanese audiences, but it maintains sets representing aspects of the Meiji era (1868–1910) of Japanese history. Here are full-scale replicas of old streets of medieval Japan, the arched Nihonbashi Bridge of ancient Edo (the Tokyo of the Shoguns), the domains of *samurai* and *geisha* entertainers—altogether some 20 or more sets, both indoor and outdoor, that are in continuous use by film makers. Actors in costumes of the feudal times add "reality" to these false-fronted buildings as they wander the streets of the past, including Edo's famed Yoshiwara "red light" district.

A modern-day samurai relaxes between filming at Toei Uzumasa Eigamura.

An entertainment world in its own right, the center is equipped with everything from restaurants and souvenir counters to a dinosaur-like monster who rears its head from a pond to the delight of both youngsters and their elders. Special halls exhibit the history of Japanese film making. An Animation Studio, where special effects techniques are described, location studios for period scenes, and miniatures of settings of the past (castles, bridges, etc. of medieval or feudal Japan) all create a series of diversions for visitors of any age. Visitors are free to move around and observe the film making.

GETTING THERE

The major stops on this tour, including the Myoshin-ji and Koryu-ji Temples, can be reached by the Keifuku line trolley, which departs westward from a terminal at the intersection of Shijo-dori and Omiya-dori. The Keifuku rail terminal can be reached from downtown via bus 11, 28, 203, 205 or 207, which travel along Shijo-dori. Alternately, the Hankyu railway runs underground under Shijo-dori and has a station across from the Keifuku rail terminal. Myoshin-ji can be reached from the Myoshin-ji station of the Keifuku line. A street just behind the station leads to the north gate (Myoshin-ji Kita-mon) of the temple.

Alternatively, take the Japan Railway Sagano line from Kyoto station to Hanazono station. The street outside the station leads northeast to the southern entry gate to the temple. Bus 63 to the temple leaves you at the Myoshin-ji-mae (in front of Myoshin-ji) bus stop at the southern gateway to the temple. The grounds of Myoshin-ji are open at all times, but the individual subtemples have varying hours. The main buildings of the temple are open from 9:00 a.m. to 4:00 p.m.

A return to the center of town can be made by taking the Keifuku line trolley back east to its terminus. From there, take one of the buses mentioned above southward on Shijo-dori, or walk to the east to Karasuma-dori for the city subway.

Walking Tour 19

ARASHIYAMA AREA

From the Field of the Dead to the Temple of the Golden Dragon

1. **Adashino Nembutsu-ji Temple**
   あだしの念仏寺
2. **Gio-ji Temple** 祇王寺
3. **Takiguchi-dera Temple** 滝口寺
4. **Nison-in Temple** 二尊院
5. **Rakushisha Hut** 落柿舎
6. **Jojakko-in Temple** 常寂光寺
7. **Okochi Sanso Villa** 大河内山荘
8. **Tenryu-ji Temple** 天竜寺

A full day's outing often takes Kyoto residents to the western part of the city to walk the path that slopes from the Adashino Nembutsu-ji Temple down to the Katsura/Oi River at Arashiyama. The path, which lies along the foot of the mountains that border the city on its western edge, offers a variety of interesting diversions, ranging from an impressive cemetery to the unknown thousands of dead of past centuries who died unnoticed and uncared for, to a shrine connected with Prince Genji, the Shining Prince of *The Tale of Genji*, to the Zen temple built to allay the wrathful and revengeful spirit of the Emperor Go-Daigo. If romance and history are not enough, the path is interspersed with a sufficient number of restaurants and souvenir stands to satisfy any pilgrim or consumer.

It is best to start the walk at the northern end of this "Path of History" at the Adashino Nembutsu-ji Temple, with its dome-shaped Indian-style stupa and its memorial stones to some 8,000 unknown former residents of Kyoto. Along the way are the one-time retreats for victims of blighted love, such as the Gio-ji Temple, where thwarted love would eventually be chronicled in the ever-popular tale of love suicides. There is a contrast of homes as well, from the simple Rakushisha hut where the poet Basho came for a brief

visit to enjoy his host's hospitality, to the lush Okochi Sanso Villa of a former Japanese screen hero of the silent films. Among the temples there is Tenryu-ji, with its lovely pond and garden adjacent to the park along the Oi River, where colorful ceremonies take place at various times throughout the year. This fascinating area is always a pleasure in which to stroll in spring at cherry blossom time or in autumn when the colorful leaves of its trees provide an umbrella and a carpet of color. At such times, of course, all of Kyoto seems to be on hand, and so it is best to visit these locations on other than national holidays or weekends in these seasons.

1 **ADASHINO NEMBUTSU-JI TEMPLE**
We begin at the Adashino Nembutsu-ji, a temple to the unknown dead of past centuries which is located in the northwest section of Kyoto in the Toriimoto area. The temple, it is claimed, was founded by Priest Kukai (Kobo Daishi, 774–835) in the 9th century. It is said that prior to Kukai's time the bodies of those who were without family or friends had been left at this site unburied; thus Kukai dedicated a temple for the repose of the souls of these unfortunates. (Adashino means "Place of Sadness"). In the 12th century, Priest Honen (1133–1211) lived at the temple, and thus it became a center for the repetition of the Nembutsu ("Praise to the Buddha Amida") around which Honen centered his faith. As a result, the temple received its name as the place of worship at Adashino for the invocation through the Nembutsu of the name of Amida, and it became a locus for learning and worship for Honen's followers as the Pure Land (Jodo) sect developed from his teachings.

A path from the narrow main roadway leads up to the ticket booth at the entryway and within the temple grounds a path runs

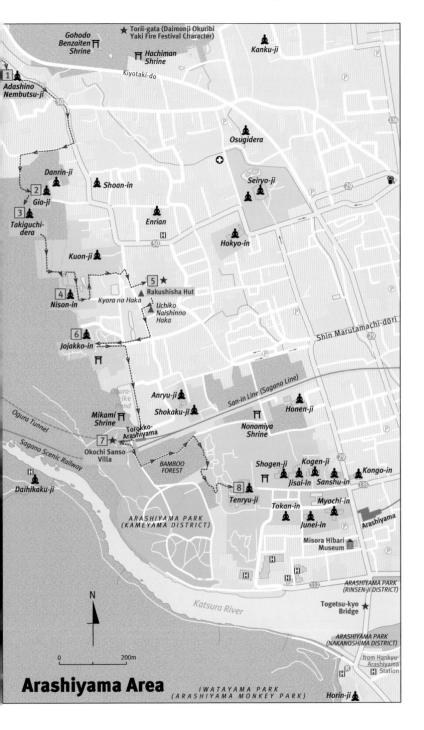

★ Torii-gata (Daimonji Okuribi Yaki Fire Festival Character)

Gohodo Benzaiten Shrine

⛩ Hachiman Shrine

Kanku-ji

Kiyotaki-do

1 Adashino Nembutsu-ji

Osugidera

Danrin-ji

Shoan-in

Seiryo-ji

2 Gio-ji

Enrian

Hokyo-in

3 Takiguchi-dera

Kuon-ji

5 ★ Rakushisha Hut

4 Nison-in

Kyora no Haka

Uchiko Naishinno Haka

6 Jojakko-in

Shin Marutamachi-dōri

Ogura-ike Pond

Anryu-ji

San-in Line (Sagano Line)

Honen-ji

Mikami Shrine

Shokaku-ji

Ogura Tunnel

Torokko-Arashiyama

Nonomiya Shrine

Sagano Scenic Railway

7 ★ Okochi Sanso Villa

BAMBOO FOREST

Shogen-ji

Kogen-ji

Jisai-in

Sanshu-in

Kongo-in

Daihikaku-ji

8 Tenryu-ji

Tokan-in

Myochi-in

Junei-in

Misora Hibari Museum

Arashiyama

ARASHIYAMA PARK (KAMEYAMA DISTRICT)

ARASHIYAMA PARK (RINSEN-JI DISTRICT)

N

Katsura River

Togetsu-kyo Bridge

ARASHIYAMA PARK (NAKANOSHIMA DISTRICT)

from Hankyu-Arashiyama Station

0   200m

Arashiyama Area

IWATAYAMA PARK (ARASHIYAMA MONKEY PARK)

Horin-ji

between a low walled area, with the graves on the right and the round, Indian-style stupa to the distant left. In the graveyard, around which you walk in order to reach the few small temple buildings, are some 8,000 small stone Buddha images commemorating the dead from 794 to 1868. In earlier times, only the nobility had gravestones and, obviously, there was not one cemetery alone that served as the final resting place for the ashes of the ruling classes. These 14th to 16th century images of the Buddha, which here serve as memorial grave stones, were found in bamboo groves all around the Adashino area, and about a hundred years ago they were gathered and placed here. The stone Buddhas are arranged in rows centered about a *sotoba* (memorial stone) and a Buddha image. It appears that these images in stone facing the *sotoba* and Buddha are in Amida's Western Paradise listening to Amida preach. A low stone wall surrounds the graves, and its entry is opposite the temple buildings through a small gateway in which hangs the graveyard bell. The bell has images of Amida in raised relief, and a flowery band encircles the bottom (the mouth) of the bell. Within the graveyard is a plinth with a seated image of Amida, a small 13-tiered *sotoba* before him, and an incense urn before the *sotoba*. (The temple requests that photographs not be taken of the graveyard and its stones.)

The temple buildings consist of the small Hondo (Main Hall), the Kuri (Priests' Quarters), both built in 1712, and a modern hall, all of which are opposite the gateway to the graveyard. The principal image at the rear of the Hondo is a gilded Amida by Tankei (1173–1256) with Amida's assistants, Seishi on his right and Kannon on his left. On either side before the Amida are other images, some in *zushi* (image cases). The black and gold hangings about the gilt Amida create an impressive interior to this hall.

To the right of this structure is the four-bay Kuri. A small one-bay Yakushi-do with a thatched roof (to the right when facing the gateway into the graveyard) contains images concerned with the next life: in the center is the figure of the Buddha Yakushi, a medicine pot in his left hand and a staff in his right hand; he is the deity who can heal illnesses in this life and who provides respite in the next life for the miseries one endures in this existence. The wall on the left has an image of Jizo, the protector and savior of children and the guardian of the dead, with infants before him, while the wall on the right has a painting of Emma, the king of hell, overseeing the unfortunate ones who are being pushed into the flames. Thus a foretaste of the life to come, as seen on the walls of this small building, can serve as a hope or a warning to worshippers who come here.

A field of roughly carved stone Buddha statues honoring the dead at Adashino Nembutsu-ji Temple.

Behind the Hondo, to the left, is a small thatch-roofed wall-less Jizo shrine that holds another image of Jizo, dedicated to the repose of the souls of unborn children (either through miscarriage or abortion). A recumbent image of a baby is on the right. A path beyond the Jizo image leads up through a lovely bamboo forest. On the far side of the graveyard is a scaled-down domed Indian-style stupa building such as was created in Sanchi, India, in the 1st century as a receptacle for relics of Gautama Buddha—the early form of a pagoda before it was changed into the "high-rise" unit that became the style in China and then later in Japan.

The Adashino Nembutsu-ji is noted for its annual O-Bon Memorial Ceremony, which occurs on the evenings of August 23rd and 24th. More than 1,000 lighted candles are offered to the Buddha images in the graveyard for the repose of the spirits of the unknown dead who are memorialized here. The memorial service begins at 6:00 p.m. Reservations for this service must be requested in writing to the temple in June. Then, on the night of the full moon in late September/October a Moon Viewing Ceremony occurs at the temple at 6:00 p.m. and later during that evening.

SOME SMALLER ARASHIYAMA SITES

On leaving the grounds of the temple, follow the path southward toward Arashiyama. The small and charming Gio-ji Temple, some 5 minutes down the path, is the next site of interest. (All of the sites listed hereafter lie along the path leading south from the Adashino Nembutsu-ji. Directions are also given for each site as though you were coming here directly for the first time by bus.)

2 GIO-JI TEMPLE

Gio-ji Temple is situated at the foothills of Mount Ogura between Adashino Nembutsu-ji to the north and the Nison-in Temple to the south. (Bus 62 or 72 to Toriimoto leaves you at a path going south to the Adashino Nembutsu-ji and so further south to the Gio-ji, while bus 11 or 28 leaves you at the Sagako-mae bus stop, from which you walk west to the path along the foothills and so north to the Nison-in and then further north to the Gio-ji, which is set far back along a path from the road, being the second temple on the right side of this recessed path. Gio-ji is open from 9:00 a.m. to 5:00 p.m. It is closed for the New Year holiday. Entry fee.)

Since marriages among the upper and ruling classes in Heian and Kamakura times (and later) were arranged for political or other non-amorous reasons, extramarital affairs were not unusual, particularly among those of the court or governing circles. Taira-no-Kiyomori (1118–81), the leading minister of his day, was no exception to the rule, but his attention span where his courtesans were concerned seemed to be of a somewhat limited duration. Attracted to a young dancer of great beauty and skill by the name of Gio, he made her his lover. Unfortunately for Gio, she introduced young Hotoke Gozen to Kiyomori, and Kiyomori was soon more attracted to this even younger dancer. Abandoned by Kiyomori, before leaving his mansion Gio wrote a poem on the *shoji* of her room as to the ephemeral nature of love. She then retreated to a temple at the foot of Mount Ogura in the Sagano area of western Kyoto along with her mother and sister to dedicate her life to prayer as a Buddhist *ama* (nun). Kiyomori's attention was soon ensnared by a third young lady, and Hotoke Gozen, at 17 years of age, also found herself displaced. By chance she came upon Gio's poem on the *shoji*, and thus she too retreated to a life of prayer at the same temple as her predecessor, joining 21-year-old Gio as a Buddhist nun. On Kiyomori's eventual death, his two former lovers raised a memorial stone to him on their hillside retreat, and, when they died, their remains were laid to rest next to Kiyomori's memorial.

One of the loveliest sites in western Kyoto is the tiny Gio-ji Temple, which consists of a small thatch-roofed building (reconstructed in Meiji times, 1868–1912) set in a lovely moss-covered garden amidst maple and bamboo trees. A simple thatch-roofed gate gives entry to the grounds and to the path which circles the moss garden of the small temple building. Off to the north is a bamboo forest. The path through the garden is marked by a cord barrier to keep people off the delicate moss carpet under the shade of the trees. In this moss garden before the temple building, water issues from a bamboo pipe in front of the small structure, and it then runs as a serpentine rivulet through the moss before disappearing underground. The little thatched temple building, looking like a small farmhouse, has but two rooms. The remnant of the early Ojo-in Temple, as described in *The Tales of Heike*, the entrance to the building is on its south side. You enter a small room with a *tokonoma* on the east side and a cabinet with arched openings on the west side. This latter unit is the altar area of this tiny temple, and behind each arched opening is an image. Of the six images, the central one is a small statue of Dainichi Nyorai, a copy of the one in Chuson-ji Temple in Hirai-zumi in northern Honshu. On either side of it are images of Kiyomori, Gio, her mother, her sister and Hotoke Gozen. The second or inner room has a large round "moon" window in its north side overlooking the bamboo forest. The window is covered by a square white paper *shoji*, the bamboo lattice on the outside of the window casting a patterned shadow on the *shoji*, presenting an attractive design element in the contrast of the round window with its translucent paper and the shadow of the lattice work on the *shoji*. On leaving the building, a path leads to the small graveyard with the graves of the two courte-sans and the memorial stone to Kiyomori.

3 TAKIGUCHI-DERA TEMPLE

Another temple whose fame is connected with blighted love, Takiguchi-dera is on the same path on which Gio-ji is situated, except that it is further up the hill. (The same directions for getting to Gio-ji apply for the Takiguchi-dera temple. It is open from 9:00 a.m. to 4:00 p.m. Entry fee.)

A minor temple of the Tendai sect, the temple was founded in the mid-9th century. It is famous not so much for its architecture or site as for a romantic tragedy ending in a suicide, the type of story which the Japanese love. Takiguchi Nyudo, one of Taira-no-Kiyomori's officers (the same Kiyomori of the Gio-ji tale) fell in love with Yokobue, a lady-in-waiting to the daughter of Kiyomori, the Empress Kenrei-mon-in (of the tragic tale of the Battle of Dan-no-Ura and the Jakko-in Nunnery in Ohara). Yokobue, unfortunately, was a lady whose court standing was beneath Takiguchi's rank, and due to the opposition to their marriage he became a monk and sequestered himself in this hillside temple. Yokobue eventually discovered his retreat, but her visit was rejected by her former lover. In despair, according to one account, she wrote a farewell poem and then committed suicide. Another version says that Yokobue became a nun and died of grief over her unre-quited love. Legend recounts that Takiguchi redoubled his prayers in atonement for his lover's death and for the repose of her soul.

The small path which leads up the hill to the Takiguchi-dera ends at a tiny ticket booth and then the path becomes a flight of steps held in place by short lengths of bamboo as the steps mount through the forest. Behind the ticket booth is a huge memorial slab and a group of *sotoba* commemorating the sad tale of the lovers connected with this temple. Although the upward path diverges into two separate routes, they come back together at the top of the brief climb.

At the head of the steps, on a small level area before the hill rises further, sits the sole building of the temple, the Hondo, looking (as with the Gio-ji) more like an attractive thatch-roofed farmhouse than a temple struc-ture. Set in a sand garden with shrubs, the building has a veranda on its south and east sides. Within the building, the rear wall has a set of *chigaidana* shelves (shelves of an alter-nate arrangement) and then two small seated images of a nun with her hands in prayer and of a monk, images of the ill-fated lovers. The north end of this very simple structure has *fusuma*, each painted in sepia with sketches of trees in the lower portion of the panels.

A path to the south leads into the bamboo forest to a small memorial shrine building, and then circles along the edge of a cliff (a viewing platform once hung over the edge of the cliff), and then back to the clearing, pass-ing a 20 foot (6 m) tall stone pagoda. Attractive as the site of the Takiguchi-dera is, it is greatly enhanced in the autumn when the maple trees of the hillside offer a brilliant display of color.

4 NISON-IN TEMPLE

Five minutes further south along the path to Arashiyama is the Nison-in (Temple of the Two Buddhas). The Nison-in is at the foot of Ogura-yama (Mount Ogura), and it can be reached by bus 11 or 28 to the Sagako-mae bus stop and then on foot along a road to the west to the narrow street which runs along the foothills of the mountain. The Nison-in lies to the north along this street. It can also be reached on foot along the same street from the north by taking bus 62 or 72 to Toriimoto and then walking south. This Tendai temple is open from 9:00 a.m. to 5:00 p.m. Entry fee.)

The Nison-in was originally founded in 841 by Priest Ennin (Jikaku Daishi), a student of Priest Saicho who created the Tendai sect of Buddhism at Mount Hiei under the patronage f Emperor Saga in the early 800s. Its name f Nison refers to its two (*ni*) images, that of 1e Shaka and the Amida main images in 1e Hondo. At this temple Fujiwara-no-Teika 1160–1242) compiled two classics of Japa-ese literature, the anthology *One Hundred 'oems By One Hundred Authors* as well as 1e important *Shin Kokin Waka-shi* (A New .nthology of Ancient and Modern Poets).

At the wish of Emperor Kameyama (died 304), a portion of the temple grounds, the an Tei Ryo (Cemetery of the Three Empe-ors), was set aside for Imperial graves, and 1e ashes of the Emperors Kameyama, Go-,aga (reigned 1242–46) and Tsuchi-mikado reigned 1198–1210) were buried here. The 2mple was one of the Four Auspicious Tem->les of the former capital, and it was respon-ible for administering Imperial Buddhist eremonies.

During the time of the persecution of 'riest Honen (who lived from 1133 to 1212), he founder of the Jodo sect and proponent of he repetition of the Nembutsu as the primary neans of salvation, Honen had to seek refuge n western Kyoto at the nearby Adashino Nembutsu-ji. It is not surprising that the Nison-in also became a residence for Honen or a time and then developed into a well-.nown center for his teachings. The temple :ontains a portrait of the priest sitting cross-egged. (Legend recounts Honen's displeasure vith the portrait since it showed him seated n an undignified manner: thus he is sup->osed to have recomposed the completed >ortrait to its present more dignified depic-ion through mental persuasion, thereby :orrecting the painted position of his legs.) he temple was noted as well for its breadth >f Buddhist views since the tenets of the 'endai, Ritsu, Hosso and Jodo sects have >een co-jointly taught here.

As with most temples, fires have proved lisastrous to the Nison-in, and thus the >resent Hondo dates from the 1504 to 1531 >eriod. Its main gate was formerly the Yakui-non (Yakui Gate) of the Fushimi Castle of 'oyotomi Hideyoshi, the 16th century military ind civil ruler of Japan. It was moved here in 1613 by the prosperous engineer and mer-:hant Suminokura Ryoi. The Nison-in is set >ack quite a distance from its entryway at he main road since it is a hillside temple on :he side of Mount Ogura. A ticket booth at the nain entry has a refreshment pavilion oppo-site it, and then the broad path from these two structures heads west to the steps lead-ing up the hill to the temple buildings.

At the top of the steps the path turns to the left and then to the right to the Kara-mon (Chinese-style) gateway with its modern copper "thatch" roof. Beyond the gate, the Hondo (Main Hall) lies ahead to the left, its entry area for the removal of shoes on the left. A narrow veranda is on the south and east (front) sides, a *kago* (palanquin carried on the shoulders of men) being suspended from the roof of the south veranda.

The Hondo is divided into three rooms. The *fusuma* (sliding panels) in the first room (the south room) depict Chinese scenes: a man in a Chinese robe coming up the hill with his aides behind him, a woman in a chair on a veranda, a woman in a palace and a sage walking, while the wall to the right has a blossoming tree that overlooks the sea and the rocks. In the rear of this section are *ihai* (memorial tablets) to the dead.

The middle room, as with the other two rooms, is divided into an outer and an inner area. In the inner area is the altar with the two Buddhas, Shaka who enlightens individu-als during this life, and Amida who saves them in the next life, each standing on a lotus with a full-flamed *mandorla* (aureole) behind them. A Jizo stands to the front and north of the two images. An altar and chair for the presiding priest during religious services is centered in the outer area. The *fusuma* in this room show a snow-covered hillside with trees on the left; on the right is a painted view of a hillside above the seas with mountains in the distance.

The third room has a memorial tablet in its interior portion, while the outer area holds a freestanding screen with a painting of peonies in a basket on a lacquered cart. (Such screens are sometimes changed and another may be in place.) The *fusuma* depict chrysanthemums and the red leaves of the maple trees in autumn, while the panels between the inner and outer rooms show Chinese men in a boat. On the right are paintings of the five founders of the Pure Land sect of Buddhism.

A small one by two bay building to the north of the Hondo is a Memorial Building with *ihai*, and to its north is a small shrine building with a phoenix on top. A sacred mirror stands before the closed image case, while a figure of the deity Fudo is to the right. Steps lead up the hill from the northern side

Rakushisha, the rustic cottage of the poet Mukai Kyorai, a disciple of the haiku poet Matsuo Basho.

of this building, and then to the north is the Shoro, the temple bell, all these buildings aligned on a flat area on the side of the hill. Aside from the Imperial (and other graves) on the hillside, the Shigure-tei (Drizzle Rain Arbor) of the poet Fujiwara Teika is within the temple grounds, while the tea house, Misono-tei, holds several famous paintings by Kano Eitoku (1543–90). The Nison-in is particularly noted for the beauty of the color of its maples in the autumn.

5 RAKUSHISHA HUT

From the splendor of a temple enriched by emperors and the last resting place of three former monarchs, walk five minutes southward along the path to Arashiyama to Rakushisha, a lowly hut associated with one of Japan's best loved poets. The hut lies along a path to the left (east) of the main path we have been following, and to the north of the Tenryu-ji Temple. (Take city bus 28 to the Sagako-mae bus stop and then walk north to the second cross street on the left where a left turn (west) toward the Ogura-yama foothills brings you to the Rakushisha cottage. It is open from 9:00 a.m. to 5:00 p.m. but is closed for the New Year holiday. Entry fee.)

Rakushisha was the cottage of poet Mukai Kyorai (1651–1704). In itself, this simple little house would probably be of little interest, but

Kyorai was one of the ten disciples of Matsuo Basho, the famed *haiku* poet, and Basho visited Kyorai at this house in 1689, 1691 and 1694; in 1691, he remained there as a guest from April 18th to May 5th. Kyorai's fame derives as well in that he was the poet who, after Basho's death, continued to write in the style Basho practiced and taught.

The cottage received its name from the 40 persimmon trees in Kyorai's garden. Loaded with fruit that Kyorai had sold in advance of the harvest, an overnight storm wiped out the crop and plunged Kyorai into debt. Instead of despair, Kyorai experienced enlightenment from this occurrence, and thus he named the cottage Rakushisha, "Cottage of the Fallen Persimmons."

The cottage itself is but a simple thatched building, a straw raincoat hanging on an outside wall, a small kitchen with its primitive cooking stove, and a garden comprising the establishment. Various large stones in the garden have *haiku* verse cut into them from Basho's final *haiku* in the *Saga Nikki*, the diary written at the time of his stay at this cottage. There is a stone monument at the back of the garden dedicated to all *haiku* poets, past and present. About 100 yards (90 m) north of the cottage is a simple stone in the Kogen-ji graveyard with the name "Kyorai" on it, marking the grave of the poet.

6 JOJAKKO-IN TEMPLE

Returning west to the path we have been following to the south, after a five minute walk the small Jojakko-in Temple is on the right, up the side of the hill. The temple lies along the path at the foot of the mountains between the Nison-in and the Tenryu-ji temples. (Take city bus 28 to the Sagako-mae bus stop just to the north of the tracks of the Japan Railways Saga line. Then take the first street on the left toward the mountain, and where it turns north, take the second street to the hillside. The entrance to Jojakko-in should be before you. The temple is open from 9:00 a.m. to 5:00 p.m. daily.)

During the late Momoyama and throughout almost all of the Edo period (1568–1868), the Fuju-Fuse (literally "Neither give nor receive") sect of Nichiren Buddhism, founded in 1595 by the monk Nichio (1565–1630) in Bizen, was in trouble. Nichio himself was banished to Tamba in 1595 by the displeased civil ruler Toyotomi Hideyoshi. Then, in 1600, he was further banished to Tsushima Island in the Japan Sea between Japan and Korea before being pardoned in 1612 by Shogun Tokugawa Ieyasu. He thereafter spent the last 18 years of his life in Kyoto.

This radical branch of the Nichiren sect would have nothing to do with non-believers of its precepts, and this led to persecution by the government. The sect was finally interdicted in 1614 along with Christianity by the Tokugawa Shogun, and it was not permitted to function again until 1876. Jojakko-in, as one of the temples of the sect, was originally begun by the priest Nittei with the aid of the important 16th to 17th century engineer Suminokura Ryoi (see Tour 2). The temple served as a refuge for the Fuju-Fuse priest Nichisada.

A thatched-roof Nio-mon gate with a Nio guardian (one of the Deva kings who protect temples against evil) on either side of the passageway leads to three sets of steep steps that mount the hillside to the small level on which the temple is sited. On this level, to the left of the central steps, is a Shinto shrine with a *torii* gate, a Heiden (Offertory) and a Honden (Spirit Hall). At the top of the central steps is the Myomi-do (Main Hall) with two other structures beyond at the head of the second northernmost set of steps. Between and behind the Myomi-do and its Shinto shrine, another set of steps continues up the hillside to the two-story Edo period (1603–

1868) Taho-to Pagoda, the pagoda serving as a symbol of the Lotus sutra, the Buddhist text primary to Nichiren beliefs. The hillside about and above the pagoda is thickly forested. The most noted thing about the Jojakko-in is the view from the temple grounds, where you can see all of Kyoto to the north, east and south, ranging from Mount Hiei in the north to as far south as South Kyoto.

7 OKOCHI SANSO VILLA

Further south, yet another five minute walk, lies Okochi Sanso Villa, the lavish architecturally traditional Japanese home of Danjiro Okochi, a famous silent screen star of *samurai* movies. It lies amidst a bamboo forest on the side of Ogura-yama. The villa itself sits in a 5 acre (2 ha) area with an extensive view from the upper garden across northern Kyoto to Mount Hiei and the Higashiyama range of hills. Closer at hand is Narabi-ga-oka, a hill associated with the famous 14th century essayist Yoshida Kenko, author of *Essays in Idleness*. (The Okochi Sanso Villa and gardens is 15 minutes on foot from the terminus of the Keifuku Arashiyama railway or the Nonomiya stop for bus 28. The uphill path, which parallels the south side of the San-in line of Japan Rail, leads to the villa entry at about the point at which the railway tunnels under Mount Ogura. Open from 9:00 a.m. to 5:00 p.m. Entry fee.)

The hillside on which the Okochi Sanso Villa is sited has two flat sections, the lower area set with tables and benches where tea and cakes or *kaiseki* lunches or dinners may be purchased. The upper level contains the one-time actor's traditional-style home.

Beyond Okochi's villa, a stroll garden leads up the hill to traditional tea houses on the property, and at the top of the hill there is a magnificent view of the narrow gorge of the Hozu River as it descends toward Arashiyama and the Togetsu-kyo Bridge. The villa and its grounds are a most pleasant place to visit, and the view of the Hozu River gorge, with the small boats making their way from the Hozu Rapids to Arashiyama, is a delightful sight for locals and visitors.

NONOMIYA SHRINE Descending the hill on which the villa exists, a noted small Shinto shrine lies 10 minutes away, between Okochi Sanso and the Tenryu-ji Temple to which this walk leads. Heading east from the villa, paralleling the San-in railway tracks, you come to

Okochi Sanso Villa, the traditional home of the famous silent screen samurai actor Danjiro Okochi.

the Nonomiya Shrine one street below the railway. (The shrine lies to the west of the Nonomiya stop of city bus 28 on the main north–south street which runs from the Togetsu-kyo Bridge through Arashiyama– the bus stop is at the last street just before the tracks of the San-in line of Japan Rail; alternatively, the shrine is a 15 minute walk from the Keifuku Arashiyama railway terminus. The shrine is open during daylight hours without fee.)

The Nonomiya Shrine is a very small shrine set amidst bamboo and maple trees to the north of Tenryu-ji Temple. Surrounded by a vermilion fence, enter the shrine through a black *torii* with a double crossbar. The Honden (Spirit House) is just beyond it. Additional small shrines are to the right and left of the main shrine. Not noted for either its architecture or setting, the importance of this small rustic shrine derives from literary factors alone since it played a part in Lady Murasaki's *The Tale of Genji*.

In the story, Genji followed the Lady Rokujo to the Nonomiya Shrine when she accompanied her daughter there for the daughter's year-long purification rites before the daughter represented the Emperor at Ise Shrine. Here, Genji and Lady Rukujo spent an amorous night together just a few days before

the two women left for Ise and Lady Rukujo and Genji had to part. Years later, Lady Rokujo became a mythic figure in the *Noh* play *Nonomiya*, in which she does a ghost dance, recounting to a traveling priest her humiliation caused by Genji's legal wife at the Kamigamo Shrine festival. She then disappears beyond the Nonomiya Shrine *torii*, freed by this confession from the curse of jealousy that has kept her vengeful spirit alive for so long.

An interesting annual ceremony (which occurs at many Shinto shrines in June) can be observed at the Nonomiya Shrine on June 30th. This is the Nagoshi-no-harigoshi, a purification ceremony. Individuals who walk through a large miscanthus ring supposedly will be protected against summer illnesses. If you are present on this occasion, you may wish to seek the protection offered by passing through the ring.

8 TENRYU-JI TEMPLE

The most important temple in the Arashiyama/Sagano area today is Tenryu-ji (Heavenly Dragon Temple). It lies just off the main north–south street which takes you from the Nonomiya Shrine southward. (Tenryu-ji is but two minutes northwest of the Keifuku Arashiyama railway terminus

Arashiyama. Turn right on the main street on leaving the station and go two streets north. On the left is the entrance to the temple grounds. Bus 28 also stops in front of the station area. The temple is open from 8:30 a.m. to 5:00 p.m. There are two separate fees: one for entry into the temple buildings and another for entry into the gardens, both paid at the ticket booth.)

HISTORY Tenryu-ji is on the site of an early temple and of later Imperial residences. The land at one time held the palace of a Heian prince, later the residence of the Emperor Go-aga (1270), and then the palace of Emperor Kameyama (died 1304). This latter Imperial villa occupied 4 square miles (10.4 sq km) of property, and here Kameyama's grandson, the future Emperor Go-Daigo (reigned 1319–8), grew up and was educated.

Go-Daigo was determined to be a ruler in fact rather than just another figurehead emperor, and in the power struggle against the Kamakura Shogun which ensued, he was deposed and exiled. Escaping exile, he won back the throne with the help of Ashikaga Takauji and other *daimyo* (feudal lords). Takauji was not happy with the rewards given to him by the Emperor (he really wished to be the Shogun and to revive the governmental situation which had existed under the Kamakura Bakufu–but with himself as civil ruler or dictator), and thus he rose in revolt,

defeated the Emperor's forces and compelled Go-Daigo to flee to the mountains of Yoshino, where the Emperor set up his court. Takauji enthroned a new emperor in Kyoto, and thus began the 62 year split between the Northern and Southern Courts and the concomitant continual warfare. When Go-Daigo died in Yoshino in 1338, he died holding the Lotus Sutra in his left hand and the Imperial sword in his right hand–a certain sign that his unhappy spirit would seek revenge for the troubles thrust upon him by Ashikaga Takauji.

After the Emperor's death, Muso Kokushi, a leading Zen priest of the day, had a dream in which he saw Go-Daigo rising from the Oi River in Arashiyama in the form of a golden dragon, obviously a vision caused by the Emperor's vengeful spirit. (In Chinese lore, a golden dragon was a symbol of the Emperor.) The priest therefore advised Takauji to build a temple in honor of the Emperor on the grounds of Go-Daigo's childhood home.

In 1339, to allay the Emperor's revengeful spirit, Takauji ordered the creation of the Tenryu-ji (Heavenly Dragon Temple) in Go-Daigo's honor, and Takauji himself even helped to carry earth and stones in the initial creation of the complex. Muso Kokushi was made the Superior (abbot) of the temple on its completion five years later, and it is said that during the construction the Shogun sent him to China to obtain the proper fittings for the temple.

Tenryu-ji's garden was one of the first to use the "borrowed scenery" of distant mountains in its design.

A view of the Sogen-chi (Enlightened Heart) Pond from the Hojo (Abbot's Quarters) at Tenryu-ji.

Tenryu-ji prospered, and in time it had 150 subtemples on its grounds, stretching almost as far as the Koryu-ji Temple in the Uzumasa district of Kyoto. Tenryu-ji was a Zen temple, and the Zen monks had close ties to Song China from which came Zen doctrine, and thus Muso Kokushi was an appropriate envoy for the Shogun to send to China. Shogun Takauji later granted the temple the right to send two "Red Seal" trading ships a year to China, and the temple was thus enriched since it farmed out its shipping business to merchants for a fee. All ships to China came to be known as "Tenryu-ji bune" (Tenryu-ji ships), and the trade continued in force for 36 years and then continued intermittently for another 120 years, enriching the temple financially as well as endowing the nation with art and learning from China.

Fire destroyed the Tenryu-ji buildings on eight occasions through the centuries, the last great fire in 1864 leaving little of the temple's former magnificence. The present buildings date from 1899, but the temple's glory is still the garden created by Muso Kokushi, the only remaining element that can be traced back to the early days of the temple. Of the Tenryu-ji's 150 subtemples in the past, 13 remain today, of which nine are within the temple precincts. Tenryu-ji was ranked by Shogun Takauji as the first among the five Zen temples of Kyoto, and it remains one of the eight chief temples and the head-quarters of the Tenryu-ji school of Rinzai Zen Buddhism.

ENTRANCE The temple is approached by one of two lanes which stand on either side of the earlier gateway (closed) with its un-used central pathway and stone bridge over a pond. A number of subtemples lie to the north of the northernmost of the two entry lanes and, although their interiors are generally not open to the public, you may enter and admire their front gardens.

At the end of the northern path, past the subtemples, are the Hojo (Abbot's Quarters) and Hondo (Main Hall). The temple is entered by way of an architecturally typical Zen-style building, in this case the one-time kitchen of the monastery. Within the entry hall, a large brooding pictorial representation of Bodhidharma, the Chinese founder of the Ch'an or Zen sect, dominates the hall beyond the ticket booth; here are the racks for visitors' shoes since shoes are not permitted within the building. The monastic wash room to the left, once open to the sky and with primitive plumbing, has now been modernized, depriving the monks of the hardships of their priestly predecessors.

MAJOR BUILDINGS The Hojo (Abbot's Quarters), which lies to the rear of the entry hall, contains four large simple *tatami*-matted rooms, which can be subdivided into smaller rooms by plain *fusuma* screens. The *shoji* of the quarters open on to the lovely garden and the Sogen Pond to the rear. At the east end of the rooms are two *tokonoma*, one with an image of Bodhidharma and the other with an abstract painting.

The Hondo (Main Hall) on the left of the entry holds the rooms for worship. The altar room, in Zen fashion, has a dragon painted on its ceiling, and a statue of Sakyamuni with a Monju and Fugen image at his sides is on a raised altar platform. The pillars and balustrades before the platform are painted vermilion. On either side of the images are *ihai* memorial tablets of past abbots. The *tatami*-matted end rooms can be used as one large room through the entire building or can be subdivided into two rooms. One such room contains portraits of previous abbots, while the north room has a *tokonoma* with a picture of the Red Fudo.

A covered corridor leads from the Hojo to the Taho-to-den, and contains a memorial tablet and a seated image of the Emperor Go-Daigo. The Taho-to-den is said to have been erected in part as a copy of the small palace building in which Go-Daigo lived in great simplicity in exile in Yoshino. A lectern stands in the front part of the small building, and the room's *fusuma* depict lions and tigers and a peony tree on a white ground. This memorial building to Emperor Go-Daigo was meant to allay his supposed vengeful spirit.

GARDEN The garden and its Sogen-chi Pond lie to the west of the temple buildings against the side of the hills of Kameyama. Laid out by Muso Kokushi (1271–1346) at the founding of Tenryu-ji, it is the only original element of the temple that has survived. The pond is shaped in the form of the ideographic character *kokoro* ("Enlightened Heart"). The principle features of the garden include a grouping of seven rocks (in the Chinese Song fashion) at the rear of the pond as well as a "dry" Dragon Waterfall (Ryumon-no-taki) with a dragon stone rising before it. This is a Heian-style (800–1200) pond with Song features, the landscape plan having been suggested from a Chinese painting of Mount Horai, the Buddhist Paradise.

The garden was the first one to make use of the device of "borrowed scenery"–using the Arashiyama and Kameyama hills (to the south and to the west) as a backdrop so as to provide a vista which extends the concept of the garden. It also offered a new approach to garden viewing–from a static position– since the garden can best be appreciated when seated on the *tatami* of the Hojo, the Abbot's Quarters.

The tombs of the Emperors Kameyama and Daigo II are behind the temple in Kameyama Park, where in the 13th century Emperor Kameyama had cherry trees transplanted from Yoshino. The sight of the cherry blossoms is a lovely one in early April.

OI RIVER AREA This tour has taken us south along a path at the base of Ogura-yama (the Ogura mountain range) from Toriimoto in the north to the Oi River and Arashiyama (Stormy Mountain), a hill which lies just south of the Oi River which courses through a narrow valley between Ogura-yama and Arashiyama. (The Oi River enjoys a change of name, as it is also known as the Hozu River to the west of the Arashiyama area or, as it runs through Kyoto, the Katsura River.)

The river at Arashiyama (the name of the mountain has become associated with the area on the north bank of the river as well as the mountain proper on the south bank) has always been a favorite pleasure spot. In the early days of Heian-kyo (Kyoto), the court and its nobles disported themselves along and on the river. Today, it is the average citizen of Kyoto who comes here to enjoy the scenery, the temples and the restaurants of the area.

The hills about the river are covered with pines and cherry trees (blooming in early April), and maples that paint the hills in brilliant colors in the autumn. In July and August, on moonless nights, cormorant fishing is carried out by fishermen in boats with baskets of fire at their prow in order to attract the fish. The fishermen's cormorants, who have been trained to disgorge the fish they catch, provide an interesting evening from 7:30 to 9:30 from July 1st to August 31st.

The garden at Tenryu-ji is one of the most attractive in Kyoto, particularly during the autumn and spring

On August 16th the Manto Nagashi (Floating Lanterns Festival) takes place. People gather on the Togetsu-kyo Bridge over the Katsura/Oi River to offer prayers and then to place paper lanterns with a lit candle afloat on the river, symbolizing the return of ancestral spirits to the other world. While the banks of the river in Arashiyama are delightful at all times, the autumn colors of the leaves on the hills are outstanding in early November.

The Togetsu-kyo Bashi (Togetsu-kyo Bridge), the "Moon Crossing Bridge" from an ancient poetic allusion to the moon crossing the sky, has existed at this spot for centuries, the present structure being a 1934 steel version which follows the design of an earlier wooden bridge at this location. On its south side are not only the Horin-ji and Daikaku-ji

Temples but Iwatayama Park, where monkeys roam freely. (These are discussed in the next tour.) On both sides of the river are restaurants. Boats may also be rented for pleasure on the water.

On the north side of the river is Kameyama Park. Just before its entrance, at the river, is a memorial stone commemorating Chou En-lai, the Chinese communist minister of state in the mid-20th century, who wrote a poem about this lovely site. Nakanoshima Park lies at the southern side of the Togetsu-kyo Bridge. Just to the south of the Keifuku railway Arashiyama station is the Rinsen-ji Temple, where Muso Kokushi, founding abbot of Tenryu-ji and other noted temples, is believed to be buried.

Two other minor but interesting sites can be found just before the last stations on the

June 30th the Nagoshi-no-Harai service to purify individuals of sins that may have accumulated during the past six month takes place. If you pass through a miscanthus ring that is set up on the shrine grounds and eat *minazuki* (a rice pudding sweet) and red beans, you can then face the torrid and humid summer months with equanimity. The service takes place at 6:00 p.m. The shrine is open during daylight hours without charge.

The second station from the end of the line is Rukuo-in. Here there is a small Zen temple with a lovely *karesansui* (dry garden) which uses Mount Arashiyama as borrowed scenery. The Rukuo-in nunnery was founded in the 13th century by nun Chisen, but it eventually fell into ruin. Princess Daijo became a nun in the 17th century and revived the nunnery, and it remained a *monzeki* temple (a temple headed by a member of the Imperial family) until the Meiji Restoration. It is popularly known as the "Bamboo Palace," and has excellent *fusuma* and a fine doll collection. (Open from 9:00 a.m. to 5:00 p.m. Entry fee.)

The Arashiyama area before the railway station and the Kameyama Park along the river offer numerous small restaurants where you may enjoy lunch or dinner. This area is often enjoyed by area citizens, particularly on weekends and national holidays. It is also known for its colorful and picturesque ceremonies, and thus crowds of Kyoto residents flock here on holidays, crowding the streets and the restaurants.

Keifuku railway line. The third station before the Arashiyama terminal is Kuramazaki station. Just to its south is Kuramazaki Shrine, from which the Mifune Matsuri Festival takes place on the third weekend in May.

In Heian days, the Emperor and his courtiers often disported themselves in boats on the Katsura River in Arashiyama. In remembrance of this, "courtiers" leave in procession from Kuramazaki Shrine for Nakanoshima Park on the banks of the river. At 2:00 p.m. they float down the river in decorated boats. The two largest boats have bowsprits of a phoenix and a dragon, and "court" musicians play traditional music as they float by. Tea ceremony is held on one of the boats.

Then on June 30th, the Natsugo-e Barai month-long festival begins at the shrine. On

GETTING THERE

The Adashino Nembutsu-ji Temple, where this tour begins, can be reached by Kyoto bus 62 or 72 to the Toriimoto bus stop, from which you can follow other strollers down a side path on the other side of the highway to the underpass beneath the road to a lane which in a few minutes leads to the temple, which is open from 9:00 a.m. to 5:00 p.m. Entry fee. Further exploration of the Sagano-Arashiyama area may be made as described in the tour that follows. If you have explored sufficiently for one day, you may return to the center of Kyoto by train on the Keifuku railway from the Arashiyama station or by bus 28. Hardy visitors to the area may wish to continue with the next tour, since it begins in the area of the Togetsu-kyo Bridge.

Walking Tour 20

TOGETSU-KYO BRIDGE AREA
The Hozu Rapids, the Worried Buddha and a One-time Imperial Palace

[1] **Hozu Rapids Ride** 保津川下り
[2] **Daihikaku-ji Temple** 大悲閣千光寺
[3] **Horin-ji Temple** 法輪寺
[4] **Seiryo-ji Temple** 清涼寺
[5] **Daikaku-ji Temple** 大覚寺

This tour picks up where the previous tour ended, albeit they are separate entities. Thus this walk begins on the north bank of the Katsura/Oi River outside of the Keifuku Arashiyama railway station or at the stop for bus 28 from Kyoto. If you walk south and cross the river over the Togetsu-kyo Bridge, there is a path to the right (west) that parallels the river on its southern bank. Here, the boats which come down the rapids of the Hozu River (the name for the narrow upstream section of the Katsura/Oi River west of the bridge) have their terminus, and here also other boats can be rented for an outing on the river.

If you follow the path to the west along the river bank, you will pass the uphill path which leads to the Iwatayama Monkey Park where monkeys roam freely. Further along the path the river bends, and suddenly you are away

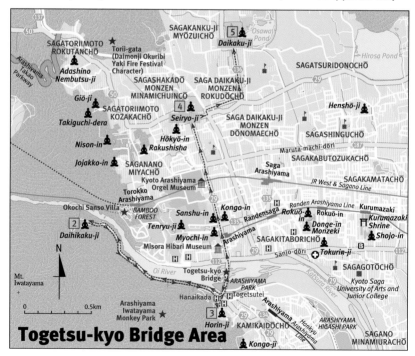

Togetsu-kyo Bridge Area

A flat-bottomed tourist boat headed for the Hozu Rapids.

from the populous area of Kyoto as you enter the narrow river valley with its many rocks in the stream, some of which Suminokura Ryoi (1155–1614) was responsible for clearing in order to make the Hozu River navigable at the beginning of the 1600s. The narrowing river is bordered by the rising hills, and the wildness of the area envelops you. Eventually, at an inn, the path rises sharply toward the Daihikaku-ji, the temple which Suminokura Ryoi erected in memory of the workers who died in the arduous task of making the Hozu River suitable for the transport of goods by boats from Kameoka and the west. The temple is not always open, but the riverside path is worth walking since it offers a feeling for the rugged quality of the gorge to the west.

1 HOZU RAPIDS RIDE

The trip through the Hozu Rapids is a voyage the more intrepid may wish to take down the Hozu River from Kameoka to Arashiyama. The Hozu River was an impassible waterway for transportation until Suminokura Ryoi, a noted engineer of his times, cleared the river of obstructions and made it navigable in 1606. What was originally created for commercial purposes serves today mainly for pleasure in the shooting of the Hozu Rapids in flat-bottomed boats.

Kameoka, a former castle town of 69,000 people, where the boat trip begins, can be reached on the San-in line of Japan Rail from Kyoto Station. It is 14 miles (22 km) west of Kyoto. From the Saga station in Sagano-Arashiyama to Kameoka, the rail route follows the course of the Hozu River on a level well above the river itself, passing through seven tunnels along the way. From the Kameoka station to the Hozu beach is less than 1/2 mile (3/4 km) to the boats at the Hozu Bridge. (It is also possible to take a bus from the Kyoto Station to Kameoka.) The boats employed to shoot the rapids are flat-bottomed and are 35 feet (10 m) long, 6 feet (1.8 m) wide, and 3 feet (1.8 m) deep. Each boat seats 10 to 15 people and is manned by men who pole the boat through the rapids.

The river is not too interesting until the rapids begin at Miyanoshita, where there is the small Shinto shrine, the Uketa Myojin, on the hillside on the left. The river winds eastward between the deep valleys and gorges of the Atago mountains on the north (left) and the Arashiyama mountain range on the south. The channel is narrowed by large rocks at Kaniginose, creating a huge flow of water. At Koayu-no-taki, the river is towered over by a sheer rock wall, and at Takase there are numerous rapids to test the boatmen's skill.

Shishi-ga-kuchi (Lion's Mouth) is a turbulent area, as is Nagase. The river makes a sharp bend from the north at Byobu-iwa, and then at Ochai the Kiyotakii River enters the Hozu, creating a whirlpool around a large rock in the center of the stream. The river narrows at Oze, causing waves as the boat passes by. On the hillside on the right is Daihikaku-ji, the temple built by Suminokura Ryoi in memory of the workmen who died in creating the navigable passage from Kameoka to Arashiyama. The 10 mile (16 km) trip takes 60 to 90 minutes. The boats operate between mid-March and the end of November on a regular schedule of approximately six boats a day.

2 DAIHIKAKU-JI TEMPLE

The Daihikaku-ji Temple, built by Suminokura Ryoi, can be visited on foot from the Togetsu-Kyo-bashi Bridge as described at the beginning of this tour. Daihikaku-ji is on the south side of the Oi (Hozu) River at Mount Arashiyama. Following the path to the west along the riverside, you pass a waterfall (Tonase-no-taki) and come to a pool (Chidori-ga-fuchi). From here, 1/2 mile (3/4 km) from the bridge, a steep path leads above an inn to the temple.

Suminokura Ryoi was both an engineer and a merchant of note, a man of great talents who became very wealthy during the era of Toyotomi Hideyoshi and Tokugawa Ieyasu. In 1603, under Ieyasu's direction, he built a large ship for trading with southeast Asia, and on the successful completion of this task, he was commissioned to make the Oi River into a navigable stream by turning it into a canal. Thereafter he cleared the rapids of the Hozu River as well so as open it to navigation. When Toyotomi Hideyori (Hideyoshi's son) and his mother funded the rebuilding of Hideyoshi's Daibutsu image and temple in Kyoto (destroyed by a major earthquake), the materials for the construction were brought down this waterway. In 1611, Ryoi made the Kamo River in the center of Kyoto navigable through the construction of the Takase-gawa canal along the western bank of the Kamo River.

Ryoi at one time lived on the hillside of Arashiyama with a fine view of the river and Kyoto in the distance. Concerned for the workers who had died during his river clearing projects, he built Daihikaku-ji in their honor. This minor temple holds an image of a 1,000-arm Kannon as well as a seated wood image of Suminokura Ryoi. Although the temple is not an important one today, it is a reminder of the difficulties faced when making rivers navigable for trade in the time of the Tokugawa shoguns.

NEARBY SITES

Back at the Togetsu-kyo-bashi Bridge, the road south leads after 1/2 mile (3/4 km) to the Horin-ji Temple, noted for its many ceremonies and a mecca for young students. A steep path on the right climbs to the temple on the western side of the narrow highway from the bridge. (The temple is open from 9:00 a.m. to 4:00 p.m. No entry charge.)

3 HORIN-JI TEMPLE

Horin-ji, it is claimed, dates from 713 and is very popular with Kyoto citizens. Its Hondo contains an image of Kokuzo, the Bodhisattva of wisdom, and is thus sometimes known by the name of that deity. Children aged 13 are taken by their parents to pray to Kokuzo for wisdom and for success in school. Kokuzo offers a variety of protections as he is also the patron of sewing, needles and entertainment.

Although approached by an impressive flight of stone steps, the temple and its grounds are not particularly attractive. The steps can be lit at night by the row of red wooden lanterns on posts, lanterns made in the style normally associated with Shinto shrines. At the plateau on top of the steps is a pair of large lanterns, an image of a goat to the far right and a religious symbol of a wheel on a post to the left. Horin-ji means "Temple of the Wheel of the Law," and thus a turning wheel is mounted on a post as a symbol of the Buddhist concept to which the temple was founded. To the left is a two-story red pagoda with white and green coloring.

The main temple building, the Hondo, with its image of Kokuzo, lies directly ahead, the few steps leading to the level of the Hondo having an image of a bull on the left and a lion on the right. Other than the pagoda and the animal images, the grounds and buildings are not particularly outstanding. The temple is, however, noted for its festivals and ceremonies, and among these are occasions honoring 13 year olds, those in the entertainment arts, those involved in the craft of lacquerware, as well as memorial services for worn-out needles and for equally well-worn dolls. One ceremony on September 9th remembers Kikujido, the Chrysanthemum Child, who obtained eternal youth by drinking chrysanthemum dew. On September 15th,

The Hondo of Horin-ji, situated in picturesque Arashiyama.

following the Buddhist precept that all forms of life are sacred, caged birds and fish are released on the banks of the Hozu River to the chanting of sutras. On October 14th, prayers and services are offered for worn-out dolls, which individuals bring to the temple.

KYOTO ARASHIYAMA MUSEUM Returning to the Togetsu-kyo-bashi Bridge and crossing to the north side of the river, nearby is the Kyoto Arashiyama Museum, a direct contrast to the many temples of the area since it is concerned with military affairs. The museum is located to the north of the Oi River (and of Sanjo-dori) to the east of the Togetsu-kyo-bashi Bridge (It is open from 9:00 a.m. to 4:30 p.m. Entry fee).

The museum contains ancient military armor and weapons that were originally collected by a private individual, Shindo Tateaki. Swords, lacquerware, possessions of General Oda Nobunaga of the 16th century and of Tokugawa Ieyasu of the 17th century, Meiji period (1868–1912) uniforms as well as paintings of war subjects make up the museum holdings. Objects from World War II are maintained in an outdoor area. This display includes a Zero fighter plane, a rarity since such items were ordered destroyed after the 1945 surrender. This one was found in a lake where it had crashed.

4 **SEIRYO-JI TEMPLE**

Returning to the main north–south street and heading north from the Togetsu-kyo-bashi Bridge, there are numerous small restaurants where you can rest and have lunch. Ahead lie the other two main temples in the area, Seiryo-ji and Daikaku-ji. A walk straight ahead to the north on the main road will bring you after some 20 minutes (or bus 28 can be used) to the Seiryo-ji (Saga Shaka-do) Temple. (Seiryo-ji is at the head of the street which runs from the Togetsu-kyo-bashi Bridge over the Oi River in Arashiyama and past the Arashiyama terminus of the Keifuku Arashiyama railway. The temple is open from 9:00 a.m. to 4:00 p.m. Entry fee.)

HISTORY Seiryo-ji came into being because of a wish that Priest Chonen of the Todai-ji Temple in Nara once had. Chonen had gone to China to study Buddhism at its Chinese source, and he envisioned the creation of a temple for an image of the historic Buddha that he wished to bring back to Japan. In China he had obtained a sandalwood image of Shaka (Sakyamuni), said to have been carved in India by Bishu-katsuma, a noted Hindu sculptor.

As with so many early tales, there are a variety of accounts of the creation of the statue. One story claims that it was carved from life by the sculptor when the Buddha was only 37 years old. Another account states that it is a copy of the first image of the Buddha, one that had been made at the request of King Udayana of India. Yet another version has the sculptor reaching heaven through mystical means to see the Buddha and to memorize his lineaments before returning to earth to create the statue. Modern art critics, who perhaps are more scientific and less romantic or gullible, say that the image was carved by an unskilled craftsman in China in Song times. Be that as it may, tradition claims that the sculpture was brought across the Himalayas to China, where it was worshipped for many years before Chonen brought it to Japan in 987.

The Shaka image was made in a manner not followed in Japan. The log from which it is created was first split lengthwise and shaped so that the two parts fit together smoothly. Then the inside portion of each half was hollowed out and the two shells mated for the finished image. The hollow space was a place for holy substances (or the internal organs which were made for it). This hollowing of the image also was done to prevent the eventual cracking inherent in solid images of wood.

On his return to Japan, Priest Chonen settled in the Sagano region west of Kyoto near Mount Atago, the highest peak in Kyoto. He chose the spot since the five peaks of Atago reminded him of the five peaks of Mount Wu Tai in China, the seat of much of Buddhist learning. The statue of Shaka was eventually installed in a building created for the sacred image, but this did not occur in his lifetime. (Chonen is said to have declared that a proper shrine would be built for the Shaka image, even if it took his second or third incarnation to bring about the structure the statue deserved.)

The Seiryo-ji Temple stands on the site of a villa of Minamoto-no-Toru (822–95), Minister of the Left and son of Emperor Saga, who turned his estate into a temple. A Hondo (Main Hall) had been built there in 945 (before Chonen's return to Japan) by order of an Imperial princess, and a Buddha image was placed in it. When Priest Chonen's Shaka image from China was installed in the eventual Seiryo-ji that came into being, it attracted the devotion of many worshippers, and the temple acquired the name of Saga Shaka-do from the hall in which the image was kept. In 1218, the temple was damaged in a fire, and it was repaired by the noted sculptor

Kaikei. The Hondo burned again in the late 17th century, and the present Hondo is a 1701 rebuilding. The Shaka image has survived these various conflagrations. In the Kamakura period (1185–1333) many copies were made of the Shaka, reputedly due to a rumor that the worried Buddha image had decided to return to China because of its distaste for the wars that ushered in the Kamakura era. One of the most noted of these is the one created by Zenkei, which is in the Hondo of the Saidai-ji Temple in Nara.

ENTRANCE The main entry to the temple is on the south side of the grounds, a tripartite two-story gate with a Nio guardian on either side of the opening. To the left of the gate, within the rather barren precincts, is the temple gift shop, and further west is a two-story pagoda with a small memorial hall behind it. To the north of these is the Shoro (temple bell). To the right of the gate is a small *torii* and Shinto shrine to protect the complex. A pond lies between the shrine and the Kyudo (Sutra Hall) on the right.

SUTRA HALL The Sutra Hall, with a flaming jewel atop its roof, has in its doorway a seated wooden image of Fu Daishi, the inventor of the revolving sutra (scripture) case within the building. He is accompanied by his two sons on either side, each of the images being painted in bright colors. Within the hall there are images of the four Shi-tenno guardian kings, one in each of the four corners of the structure, and the round posts and beams of the building are all heavily decorated in color. In the center of the hall is the huge revolving sutra case in vermilion, black and blue. The turning of the case equals a number of readings of the sutra and is considered an efficacious act, which one can do for a small fee.

SHAKA-DO The Shaka-do or Main Hall holds an ornate gilt shrine in its center in which the 5.3 foot (1.6 m) statue of Sakyamuni resides. The image is only exhibited on April 9th (the Buddha's birthday) and on April 19th, the occasion for the cleansing of Buddhist images. In 1953, silk objects shaped like human internal organs were found in the statue. It is said that they were created by nuns in China in order to create a living image of the Buddha when the image was still in that country. The shrine, with its painted carvings in which the image is kept, was a gift of the mother of Shogun Tokugawa Iemitsu in the mid-17th century. To the right and left are images of Monju and Fugen.

In some ways the Shaka-do is a bit of a museum, since the cases along its side walls display many objects connected with the history of the temple. The "internal organs" of the Shaka image are on display with notes about them in Japanese. There is a statue of the new-born Buddha standing in a bowl for the April water ceremony, and there are scrolls, some of painted scenes. A chest on a carrier, a *kago*, a Buddha in its own case and a pagoda in a case are among the other items shown.

In the far rear of the building are a 10 foot (3 m) tall revolving prayer unit and *ihai* in cases and on pedestals, while on the right (east) side of the building is an altar with an image of the seated Priest Chonen who brought the Shaka image from China. In addition, there is a scroll with an image of Prince Shotoku, religious vestments, a brilliantly colored mural, gold inlaid altar furniture, brushes, *Noh* masks, a *Noh* halberd and numerous other objects. Behind the altar is a Chinese carving of an image of the Buddha. The number of objects is overwhelming.

Behind the Shaka-do a corridor leads to a *tatami*-matted building with a long room, a *tokonoma* in its left rear section with a scroll of the Buddha hanging in it. Directly behind the Shaka-do is a Memorial Hall, while a pond to the west behind the Shaka-do has a 13-tiered pagoda on an island.

TREASURY BUILDING To the rear of the Sutra Hall and to the east of the Shaka-do is Seiryo-ji's modern fireproof two-story Treasury Building. (The Treasury is open from March 15 to June 1 and from October 1 to November 30. Entry fee.) The first floor is divided into two rooms, the initial rooms having images on either side of the central walkway. On the left is a seated Amida Buddha in the contemplative mood with an aureole behind it and Kannon and Seishi on either side. On the right is an image of Manjusuri seated on a lotus atop an elephant and another Manjusuri seated on a blue and green lion with a sword in his right hand and a scroll in his left hand. On the floor besides these images are gold crowns. The figures are dated to the 10th century.

The inner room contains, on the left, four Shi-tenno of the 10th century, a three-story stone pagoda and a delicate standing Buddha

with a handsome aureole. To the right are images of seven *rakan* (enlightened hermit monks) and a life-sized Bishamon-ten, a small pagoda held on his open hand. The stairs to the second floor are at the rear right of this hall, and the second floor displays both written and pictorial scrolls and a sixfold standing screen. In addition, there are numerous small articles ranging from brass ewers to items found within the Shaka image: cloth "internal organs" (a second set), coins, a bead necklace, crystal bead fragments, fragments of a small blue vase and a glass vial.

5 **DAIKAKU-JI TEMPLE**
On leaving the Seiryo-ji, walk four streets to the east and then turn left (north) to reach the Daikaku-ji Temple, the "Temple of the Great Science." Daikaku-ji lies in the northeast area of the Sagano district of western Kyoto. (This Shingon temple is open from 9:00 a.m. to 4:30 p.m. Entry fee.)

HISTORY The Emperor Saga (785–842) built a villa, the Saga-in, for himself after his abdication in 823. He had a *shinden*-style palace or villa constructed on a 100 acre (40 ha) plot next to the Osawa-ike, a garden pond he had planned in imitation of Lake Tungting in China. He lived in this palace for his last 20 years, enjoying the range of mountains to the north, Osawa Pond to the east and an open vista to the south, and savoring scholarship, poetry and his gardens, for he was a scholar and a poet. He was noted for his flower arrangements. The Saga school of Ikebana, which developed from a combination of the Seika style, the Moribana style and the Heika style, still flourishes here. The 15 acre (6 ha) Palace Garden is the oldest Imperial garden in Japan.

In 876, Emperor Junno turned the villa into a Shingon temple, and in many ways it is similar to the Ninna-ji Temple, since both were Imperial palaces consisting of a cluster of separate buildings connected by roofed corridors. As a result, its nature as a palace strikes one at first glance, since it does not have the normal temple ground plan. The buildings meander, with gardens interspersed among the various structures.

The complex obviously had its appeal to later emperors who retired here, most notably Kameyama (in 1276) and Go-Uda (in 1288). Daikaku-ji was a *monzeki* temple, with an Imperial prince as its abbot, from the time

Emperor Gouda entered the priesthood here in 1306 until the Meiji Restoration in 1868. A series of events which would shape future Japanese government and the Imperial family originated in this palace. The first of these occurred when Emperor Go-Saga (reigned 1242–6) abdicated to the villa as an abbot in 1246, giving the throne to his eldest son, Emperor Go-Fukakasa. However, he later forced this son from the throne in favor of his favorite (and younger) son Kameyama. After Go-Saga's death, his two sons disagreed, and a compromise was created whereby the descendents of the two would rule alternately upon the death of the reigning emperor.

In the 1330s, however, Emperor Go-Daigo's problems with Ashikaga Takauji led to war and the division of the kingdom into the Northern and Southern Courts for the next 62 years. In October of 1392, peace between the two courts was agreed upon in one of the rooms of Daikaku-ji, but Shogun Ashikaga Yoshimitsu tricked the ruling emperor of the Southern Kingdom, Go-Kameyama, into returning the Imperial regalia and reuniting the courts with the understanding that the alternate rule would thereafter be observed; the agreement was never honored. Go-Kameyama eventually retired to Daikaku-ji in bitter disappointment.

TEMPLE BUILDINGS Past the entry gateway, a series of trained pine trees on the right extend their long branches along the garden path. At the end of the path is the First Building with its Shomen-genkan, the front entry hall. This first room is decorated with a painting of a large pine tree and the red leaves of an autumn maple on a gold ground on three of the walls—a rather garish scene. A blue jar sits on the *tatami* before the *fusuma*. The inner room beyond the entry hall today consists of the sales shop and refreshment room. Here you put on slippers before continuing along the roofed wooden corridors between and around the various temple buildings.

The Second Building is the nine by five bay Shinden (main residence), a gift to the Daikaku-ji from Emperor Go-Mizuno-o-in the mid-1600s of the Shinden from the palace of his consort, Empress Tofuku-mon-in. In traditional Imperial palace style, a wild orange tree is planted to the right of the courtyard before the building while a plum tree is to the left. Within the Shinden, the *fusuma* of the first room are decorated with tree peonies and red plum trees, the work of Kano Sanraku (1559–1635). The rear *fusuma* in the second room are decorated with pine trees and storks while those on the left wall

The entrance to Shikidai, the Eighth Building at Daikaku-ji Temple.

feature storks, willow and flowering trees. The *fusuma* on the right wall have very faded foliage. A room to the rear of these two rooms, behind closed *fusuma*, is decorated with cranes and bamboo by Kano Tanyu (1602–1704).

The Sei-shinden (West Shinden) or Kyahu-den (Reception Hall) is the Third Building, a six-room *shoin*-style structure with a cypress bark roof. Originally, this contained the throne room of Emperor Gouda (reigned 1274–87), with *fusuma* painted in gold lacquer of phoenix, paulownia and bamboo. The main room has an altar area with a lantern in place of an image at its rear and with a closed case on either side of this area. It has plain *shoji* on three sides. The additional rooms in the building are the Scenery Room, the Hawk Room, the Snow Room, the Bamboo Room and the Maple Room, the latter two having painted flowers and animals on the lower panels, attributed to Ogata Korin (1661–1716). To the south of the Kyaku-den in the garden is a very large flower stand for flower arrangements in the style of the Saga-mibu Ikebana School.

The Fourth Building is quite a small building compared with the others. It has an altar with a seated monk with *ihai* on either side. Before the image is a small altar table with a small stupa and censer and brass cups.

The Fifth Building, before Osawa Pond, is the Shingon sect provisional Hondo (Main Hall), with five Godai-Myo-o images attributed to Kukai (Kobo Daishi), probably from the 12th century (c. 1176), possibly by Unkei. Ranging around 20 inches (50 cm) in height, these Fudo-Myo-o images (Gundari Myo-o, Kongoyasha, Gousanzo Myo-o, Gundari Myo-o and Daitoku Myo-o) are in cases in the rear of the large *tatami*-matted room. The many low tables in the room are used by worshippers for the copying of sutras. The modern concrete Treasury lies behind Building Four. The temple treasures of paintings and the will of Emperor Gouda are kept here.

The small many-sided Shingyo-den, a separate concrete treasury with the sacred flaming jewel on top, is the next building. It was created because of a disaster that occurred during the years the complex was used as the villa of its founder. Disease was rampant at this time in Japan, and Priest Kukai convinced Emperor Saga that an offering of *shakyo* (a simultaneous writing in calligraphy of the Hannya Shingyo sutra while reciting it) to the Buddha would end the plague besetting the country. The Emperor followed the advice offered and the plague subsequently came to an end. The Emperor's handwritten copy of the sutra is enshrined in this structure.

The Eighth Building (Shikidai) has three rooms, the first with *fusuma* depicting bamboo on a gold ground, the second with birds and trees done in black and white, and the third room with scenery also in the *sumi-e* ink technique. The Ninth (last) Building is a modest vermilion worship hall with a small Buddha image and a *zushi* (case) to the right containing the image of a monk.

OSAWA POND Adjacent to Daikaku-ji on the east is Osawa Pond, 23,900 square yards (20 sq m) in area, created through the construction of a dam. It had two islands and a group of rocks (now submerged) between the islands, symbolizing boats in search of treasure while at anchor on their way to Mount Horai, the Buddhist paradise. From dragon-shaped boats, the Emperor Saga here held moon viewing parties, particularly under the autumn moon, while in winter snow viewing parties were enjoyed. (Originally only 3 feet (1 m) deep, for the safety of boating parties, during the Kamakura period (1192–1333) the pond was deepened to 13 feet (4 m) so as to serve as a reservoir for the irrigation of adjacent rice paddies.) At the northern edge of the pond are numerous stone Buddha images from the Heian period (794–1200) as well as a vermilion two-story pagoda.

Jikishi-an Temple to the north of the pond is a haven for women disappointed in love. Many have written of their problems in the "Books of Reminiscences" at the temple–a form of therapy. (More than 2,000 of these notebooks have been filled.) Some of the women stayed on to become nuns.

GETTING THERE

The walk starts next to the Katsura/Oi River outside of the Keifuku Arashiyama railway station or at the stop for bus 28 from Kyoto. If you wish to go on the Hozu River boat ride, take the Japan Railways San-in line from Kyoto Station to Kameoka. At the end of the walk, take bus 28 from the Daikaku-ji or Seiryo-ji Temples back to central Kyoto.

Walking Tour 21

KATSURA IMPERIAL VILLA AREA

The Saké Shrine, the Moss Garden Temple and Katsura Imperial Villa

1. **Matsu-no-o Shrine** 松尾大社
2. **Saiho-ji/Koke-dera (Moss Temple)** 西芳寺/苔寺
3. **Katsura Imperial Villa** 桂離宮

The southwestern portion of Kyoto has three sites that are worth visiting, although entry to two of them is somewhat restricted. The site without entry restrictions is the Matsu-no-o Shrine, whose full program of 60 annual festivals makes it an intriguing place to visit. The other two sites, the Katsura Imperial Villa and the Saiho-ji Temple, each

require advanced reservations prior to a visit. While obtaining such reservations is not an insuperable barrier, it does call for planning well before the proposed visit in the case of the Katsura Imperial Villa and the willingness to partake in a religious ceremony in the case of Saiho-ji.

The area of southwest Kyoto, to the south of the Oi River in Arashiyama, where these three sites are located, has a history which predates the settlement of Kyoto as the ancient capital of Japan. Here, at the western edge of central to southern Kyoto, the

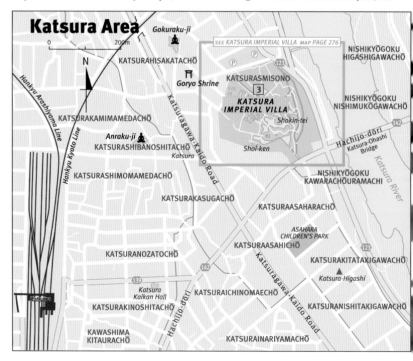

present-day Muko City was the site of the capital of Japan under the name of Nagaoka for the decade 784–94, after the Emperor Kammu had abandoned Nara as his capital. Bad luck, or evil spirits as it was claimed at that time, plagued the location, and it was eventually thought best to look for a new site for the seat of government. Thus, in 794, Heian-kyo, the early name of the present city of Kyoto, was begun to the northeast of Nagaoka. Today, an historical marker alone indicates the site of Nagaoka, which for 10 years was the Imperial capital of Japan.

The Matsu-no-o Shrine is remarkable as it has eight more festivals than there are weeks in the year, and thus is a popular location for visitors as well as for Kyoto citizens. Originally a shrine to the deities concerned with the growing of rice and the making of saké, the shrine has broadened its scope through the centuries so that now its festivals serve the needs of a modern society as well as the farmer and the brewer.

Further south lies the Saiho-ji or Koke-dera (Moss Temple), so named for its lovely moss-covered garden. Popularity was endangering the temple gardens, and thus restrictive requirements now govern who and how many may visit the temple at any one time. Reservations must be made in advance for a visit, a healthy entry fee must be paid and attendance at a lengthy religious service (in Japanese) precedes any visit to the grounds. To all purposes, therefore, admission to the garden is very restrictive.

The most noted site in this western portion of central to south Kyoto, however, is the Katsura Imperial Villa, a brief taxi ride from the Katsura station of the Hankyu rail line. Reservations must be made in advance at the Imperial Household Agency on the grounds of the Old Imperial Palace in Kyoto; generally such reservations must be made at least a week in advance of the proposed date of visit (you must present your passport at the Agency office). At popular tourist times, an even earlier request for a reservation is advisable. The villa is noted for its gardens, its tea houses and its *shoin* palace architecture, and a visit is one of the highlights of anyone's stay in Kyoto.

1 MATSU-NO-O SHRINE

This tour begins at the Matsu-no-o Shrine. The shrines lies at the foot of Matsuo-yama (Matsuo Hill) in western Kyoto.

HISTORY One of the oldest shrines in the Kyoto area, the Matsu-no-o Shrine existed before Heian-kyo (Kyoto) was created in 794. It was built by the Hata family, who originally came from Korea in the 400s. They were the purveyors of technological understanding needed by the less advanced Japanese of those times, bringing knowledge of the draining of marsh lands, of sericulture, weaving, distilling and other skills. Both this shrine and the Koryu-ji Temple in Kyoto were created by the Hata clan, and the Matsuo-no-o Shrine claims that it and the Hata family were responsible for influencing the Emperor Kammu in his decision to move the capital of the country to Heian-kyo.

The shrine is dedicated to Oyamakui-no-kami and his consort, and they, it is believed, offer special protection to *saké* brewers. (Oyamakui is said to have been the progenitor of the deity of the Kamigamo Shrine, Wake-ikazuchi-no-mikoto, a tale of a somewhat virgin birth that is related in the description of the Shimogamo Shrine.)

In 701, Hata-no-Imikitori, a descendent of the early Hata clan, moved the deity Ichiki-shima-hime-no-kami, the mountain god of Matsuo-yama, from the hillside to the new shrine he had commissioned. An additional Shinto god, Wake-ikazuchi, the son of the original shrine deity Oyamakui, was also enshrined to become not only the protector of the Imperial Palace in Kyoto but the protecting deity of Yamashiro (Kyoto Prefecture) and Omi and Tamba Provinces. In recognition of the protection offered the palace, these deities were granted Senior Grade of the First Court Rank by Emperor Kammu. They were also decorated with the Great Order of the Chrysanthemum, honors for which they were no doubt grateful! With time, the shrine deities became the patrons of other trades: the raising of rice as well as of *saké* making, and then of miso and soy sauce production as well as the making of vinegar. They protect building and construction, spinning, weaving, dyeing, giving birth and, in more recent times, have taken the responsibility for traffic safety. With such a diversification of responsibilities, the shrine's popularity with merchants, farmers, producers and the common people flourished, and numerous festivals further increased its appeal.

The Honden (Spirit or Main Hall) of the shrine was rebuilt in Muromachi times (in 1542) when the wealth of the shrine was

The double-arm vermilion torii decorated with a shimenawa rope at the entrance to Matsu-no-o Shrine.

increased by the manors it held in more than ten places in Japan. In the Edo period (1603–1868), the shrine was offered grants by the government, and great expanses of mountain and forest holdings in the Arashiyama area and in northwest Kyoto enriched the shrine and led to the construction of many of the present buildings. In 1871, it was made a First Class Government Shrine governing over 1,300 provincial shrines.

PRESENT STRUCTURES AND GROUNDS

To the west of the Matsuo railway station, a large stone *torii* indicates the roadway that leads to the shrine. At the end of this road, a double-arm vermilion *torii* decorated with a *shimenawa* (a thick twisted straw rope) marks the beginning of the shrine precincts. To the right is a pond with upright stones in the water and a waterfall at the far back.

At the end of the path from the vermilion *torii*, a series of stone lanterns stand before the steps to the two-story gateway, a Shinto guardian in the niche on either side of the passageway. The guardian on the left is dressed in red while the one on the right is in black, each having black and white checkered trousers. These protectors are themselves protected by modern wire mesh to keep the birds from fouling them. The mesh also serves another purpose since visitors can write their name, age and prayer or wish

on a wooden rice paddle (purchased at the shrine sales counter), which serve as *ema* (prayer boards). Visitors then leave these in the wire mesh so the deities can grant their wish. In time, these *ema* are taken down and ceremonially burned to help the wishes come true–and to free the mesh for more paddles and wishes or prayers.

Further on, beyond the gateway on the right, is the Purification Basin with water issuing from a fountain in the shape of a turtle. Ahead to the left is the shrine office and the sales counter where the rice paddle *ema*, other traditional *ema* forms, pamphlets on Shinto, special *obi* to insure safe pregnancies and other religious items are for sale. To the far left of this area is a roofed structure that protects the casks of *saké* donated by worshippers. Directly ahead of the gateway is the cedar bark thatch-roofed Heiden (Offertory), which can also serve as a *Noh* stage during festivals. It often bears straw-wrapped casks of *saké* given as gifts to the shrine deities by devotees of the shrine and its gods.

Beyond the Heiden, within the non-public fenced area, is the 1397 Honden (rebuilt in 1542) where the deities are enshrined. The fence about this inner area has a closed Karamon (Chinese-style) gateway, and in front of the gate is an offering box for coins for the support of the shrine. A heavy cord, which is attached to an overhead bell, can be pulled

as to obtain the deities' attention when
e wishes to pray. Within the closed gateway,
cedar bark thatch-roofed corridor leads to
eps that mount to the cedar bark thatch-
ofed Honden in which the main shrine
irit resides. On the platform before the
onden, in front of the doors to the shrine,
a protective silver *koma-inu* (lion-dog) on
e left, while on the right is a gold one. The
rk wood and white walls of the Honden
e enlivened by gold fittings beneath the
eep curving sweep of the roof with its
und gold Imperial chrysanthemums at
e end of the ridge pole.

To the left of the fenced-in Honden, with-
an enclosed area, are additional small
rines to various deities, while on the far
ght of the compound is a set of modern
uildings for shrine functions. To the right
the Honden, the Kamenoi-no-mizu (Turtle
ream) descends from its mountain source,
e Kame-no-I (Tortoise Well). The purity of
water served early *saké* makers, and the
ream was noted as a source of health and
ell-being. An interesting modern stone-
rraced watercourse lies before the build-
gs at the base of the Turtle Stream.

The Shrine Treasury has three carved
ooden images of the main deities of the
rine. Created in the Heian period (794–
85), they are the oldest Shinto images in
pan. Of painted wood, almost 3 feet (1 m)
l, it is currently thought that they were
rved between 859 and 876 (the original
ages are now in the Kyoto National Museum
r safekeeping.) In addition, the shrine holds
ceremonial articles and more than 4,000
rly writings. Although festivals and cere-
onies at Shinto shrines originally followed
e cycle of the agricultural year and the lunar
lendar, most festivals now occur on week-
ds so as to better serve a modern public
d to a five or six day work week. Of the 60
so festivals at this shrine, two festivals,
wever, follow a specific date on the calendar
ther than being held on weekends: these
e the New Year and Setsubun ceremonies.
mong the major festivals are the following:

ATSU-NO-O SHRINE FESTIVALS

nuary 1–Hatsu Mode: The year's first visit
Shinto shrines to pray for good luck in the
suing year. At the Matsu-no-o there is a
dditional New Year's *saké* tasting.

ril 12–Nakatori (Water Drawing): *Saké*
akers offer gifts to the deities since the

water from the shrine spring was favored in
early times for *saké* making.

April 24–Shino-sai: A festival dedicated to
the patron deity of *saké*. At 10:00 a.m. six
mikoshi, on the shoulders of young men,
move out from the shrine in a procession.
The group is led by youngsters who hold up
masks of the deity on sacred poles. The *mikoshi* are taken to the bank of the opposite side
of the Katsura River where they rest until the
end of the celebratory period on May 15th.

May 17–Kanko-sai: At 5:00 p.m. the six
mikoshi are borne back to the shrine on the
shoulders of young men and on carts. The
group is led by "courtiers" who wear costumes of the past and have hollyhock leaves
on their heads.

May 21–Matsuo Taisha Shinko-sai: A parade
in ancient costumes takes place along the
Katsura River, a tradition carried out for the
past 1,000 years.

Third Sunday in July–Onda-sai: A rice
planting ceremony in which the rice seedlings are planted in the shrine's paddy by
three young women in traditional attire.
These seedlings serve as protection for the
area rice crop against insect that might harm
them. People offer summer vegetables to the
shrine deities as part of the ceremony.

First Sunday in September Hassaku-sai
(a good harvest festival): This event was formerly celebrated on August 1st under the
lunar calendar. *Sumo* matches are offered to
the gods to keep them happy so the harvest
will be a good one. After 5:00 p.m. some
1,000 paper lanterns are lit.

November 15–Shichi-Go-San Festival:
Children aged three (boys and girls), five
(sons) and seven (daughters) are taken to the
shrine for blessings. Children are presented
with "thousand year" candy since these
sweets should help to guarantee a long life.

IKENO TAIGA ART MUSEUM Not too far
from the Matsu-no-o shrine is the Ikeno
Taiga Art Museum (Ikeno Taiga Bijutsukan),
approximately a 1/2 mile (3/4 km) mile south
on the main north–south road in front of
the Matsu-no-o Shrine. (The Ikeno Taiga
Museum is just before the Saiho-ji or Koke-
dera Temple. Take bus 63 or 73 to the Koke-
dera bus stop and walk to the west. The
museum is on the left hand side. The museum is open from 9:30 a.m. to 5:30 p.m.;
closed on Wednesdays and national holidays.
Entry fee.)

The museum, in a Western-style building, shows some four dozen works by the painter Ikeno Taiga (1723–76) at any one time, thus illustrating both his ink paintings and calligraphy. The painter ran a fan shop in Kyoto, having begun painting fans as a child to help to support his mother. Thus he was an independent artist who did not have to satisfy any but his own tastes. Influenced by the southern Chinese style of painting made popular at the Mampuku-ji Temple near Uji by its Chinese Zen priests, he experimented freely in his artistry. He brought a more emotive style to his painting than many of the academic artists who had been influenced by traditional Chinese art, and he is known as a master of the "literary school" of painting employing spontaneous, impressionistic brush strokes.

2 SAIHO-JI /KOKE-DERA (MOSS TEMPLE)

Beyond the Ikeno Taiga Museum is the Saiho-ji Temple. The popularity of the Saiho-ji (Temple of Western Fragrance) moss garden became its own enemy. To protect the fragile ecology of the garden and to return the temple to its primary purpose as a religious institution, in July of 1977 the temple's governing authority restricted admittance. It is still possible to see the gardens under certain conditions: you must request permission in writing to visit the temple and its gardens well in advance (7–30 days) of the date of visit. A self-addressed, stamped return envelope must be included with the request. The request must state your name, address, age, occupation and the date of your desired visit. (No one under 18 years old may apply.) A rather high entry fee must be tendered, and the visit requires attendance at a lengthy religious service where sutras are chanted or copied or where one sits in *zazen* contemplation. Naturally, all services are in Japanese. (You reach the Saiho-ji or Koke-dera (Moss Temple), its other popular name, on bus 63 from Sanjo-Keihan or by bus 73 from Kyoto Station to the Koke-dera bus stop and then walk west to the temple entrance.)

HISTORY A temple was originally created at the Saiho-ji location in 731 by priest Gyoki, ostensibly on the site of a villa that was reputed to have belonged to Prince Shotoku. The temple was rebuilt in 1339 by Muso Kokushi, who also laid out its famed moss garden on the remains of an older Jodo (Amida sect) temple. As with other temples, the many buildings of the Saiho-ji Temple were destroyed in the Onin War (1467–77).

Today, the comparatively recent Kaisan-do (Founder's Hall) and two tea houses remain in existence from the earlier period. The Shonan-tei, the older of the two tea houses, is said to be of Momoyama construction (1568–1603). In earlier years the temple belonged to the Jodo (Pure Land) sect of Buddhism, and its garden was a Paradise Garden representing the beauty of the life to come in Amida's Western Paradise. In 1339, Fujiwara-no-Chikahide requested Muso Kokushi to convert the temple from the Jodo to the Zen sect and Muso kept the same name for the temple by altering one of the written characters of the name so that its meaning came out as the "Temple of Western Fragrance" instead of the "Temple of the Western Paradise." New buildings and pavilions in the Chinese Zen style were constructed, and the design of the garden was altered. The hillside was dotted with temple buildings and small halls now all gone. Much of the garden has been changed as well, the *karesansui* (dry garden) alone retaining its original design.

Saiho-ji Area

0   200m

N

ARASHIYAMA
MIYANOMAECHO

1   *Matsu-no-o Shrine*

MATSUMUROOIAGECHO

Tsukiyomi Shrine

MATSUMURONAKAMIZOCHO

MATSUMUROYAMAZOECHO

MATSUMUROJIKECHO
Kegon-ji   Ikeno Taiga Art Museum

2   *Saiho-ji (Koke-dera)*   *Genchu-in*

MATSUOIDOCHO

YAMADAKITANOCHO

MATSUOJINGATANICHO

Matsuo

Hankyu Arashiyama Line

Saihoji River

The central building in this pre-Onin War period was the Shari-den (Reliquary Hall), a splendid two-story building whose lower floor was known as the Ruri-den (Lapis Lazuli Hall). The second floor held a relic of Gautama enshrined in a miniature crystal pagoda. The hall stood on the west side of the pond, a location later copied by the Gold and Silver Pavilions. The placement of the building beyond the pond hearkened back to the Buddhist vision of Paradise in which lovely pavilions seem to float above the water across a vista filled with lotus blossoms on the bosom of the pond.

PRESENT STRUCTURES AND GROUNDS

The 4.5 acre (1.8 ha) grounds are thickly covered with trees. The attendant shade plus the moist clay soil in a humid atmosphere have provided a fertile base for the growth of moss, and up to 40 varieties are represented throughout the garden.

The small Kojokan Gate, with its rough stone steps and tiled roof, divides the garden into two parts: the Lower Garden about the Golden Pond, and the Karesansui Garden, the dry landscape upper garden with its dry cascade. The latter is considered the first example of a "dry" garden of stone and sand. The pond in the lower garden is in the form of the Chinese ideogram for *kokoro* (heart/spirit). Within the pond (which is large enough that its ideogrammatic design is not easily recognized) are several islands joined by bridges.

The Momoyama Shoan-tei tea house is beside the pond, repaired by and lived in by Shoan, a son of Sen-no-Rikyu, after Sen's suicide. This is the only pre-Meiji building on the grounds today. A Japanese-style arbor with a plaque inscribed with poems enriches this lower garden, as does the path about the pond to create a stroll garden with its changing views. A bamboo forest is crossed before arriving at the Kojokan Gate, the dry garden and Shito-an, a tea house. The dry "cascade" of stones and the horizontal grouping of the rocks, rather than a vertical grouping in the Chinese style, gave new directions to Japanese landscape design. (Adjacent to it is a memorial building to Muso Kokushi.) With time, the rocks have developed a patina of lichen and moss while the carpet of moss beneath the trees has deepened to form a heavy cushion of green and yellow.

The months of May and June see the gardens at their best, the reds of the azaleas blooming early in this period and then the rains of June bringing a vividness to the color of the moss. In July, the lotuses in the pond blossom, and in the autumn the scarlet tones of the maple leaves add a new dimension to the garden.

③ KATSURA IMPERIAL VILLA

The highlight of a visit to southwest Kyoto, of course, is the opportunity to visit the Katsura Imperial Villa. The villa is described in detail below since the guide within the Katsura grounds often lectures only in Japanese, and thus the significance of areas of the buildings and grounds can be lost if you do not understand the language. The descriptions below follow the path the guide uses while lecturing.

Katsura Imperial Villa is located to the west of the Katsura River opposite the western end of Hachijo-dori and 3 miles (4.8 km) due west of Kyoto Station. It can be reached by taxi in 20 minutes from Kyoto Station or by means of the Hankyu railway from its underground stations on Shijo-dori to the Katsura station (by a local rather than an express train). The villa is a 10 minute walk from Katsura station, but it is easiest to take a taxi from the west side of the station since the route is not a straight line. Admission to the villa is by advance reservation only. Such reservations must be made at the Imperial Household Agency on the grounds of the old Imperial Palace in Kyoto. A permit is issued on the presentation of a passport. Since the villa is a popular site, and since admission is restricted to a small number of people at any one time, you must be prepared to make reservations (depending upon the time of year) a few days to weeks in advance of the day of your proposed visit. Tours of the villa grounds (the main *shoin* buildings are seen only from the outside) are conducted at 10:00 a.m. and 2:00 p.m. promptly, and only for those over 20 years of age. The villa is closed on Saturday afternoons, Sundays, public holidays and from December 25 to January 5. Tours are conducted in groups, the guide speaking in Japanese unless the group is composed primarily of foreigners.

HISTORY The site of Katsura Imperial Villa has been an aristocratic pleasure retreat since the early years of Heian-kyo (Kyoto). It is reputed to have been the location in the 900s of the pleasure villa of Fujiwara-no-Michinaga, the leading minister of government, and it is

The Shoin buildings of Katsura Imperial Villa comprise four staggered, interconnected structures.

thought that some of the scenes of *The Tale of Genji* took place in this area.

As the Katsura Imperial Villa of today, the *shoin* buildings and garden date to the early to mid-1600s. In the 1580s and 1590s, Toyotomi Hideyoshi as Kampaku (the secular ruler of Japan acting in the name of the Emperor) had fathered no successor. Due to his generosity to the Imperial family, he was permitted to "adopt" Kosamaru (Prince Toshihito, 1579-1629), the younger adolescent brother of the Emperor Go-Yozei. When Hideyoshi's chief wife, Yodogimi, gave birth to a son, the adoption was voided at the prince's suggestion, and Prince Toshihito thus began the Hachijo-no-miya branch of the Imperial family. A man of wit and intelligence, he developed an interest in art and in the classical literature of China and Japan, interests which influenced the gradual development of the Katsura Imperial Villa.

With the financial patronage of Hideyoshi, Prince Toshihito began a country retreat at Katsura, no doubt a simple rustic tea house at first. The pond, which once had been the centerpiece for a Heian-style summer mansion, had degenerated into a muddy morass. The original pond was gradually enlarged, the dirt from its development forming some of the "hills" and enhancing the terrain of the grounds of the villa-to-be. The traditional account of the creation of the villa claims that the noted landscape designer Kobori Enshu (1579-1647) began the villa with the financial assistance that Hideyoshi offered to the project. (This is a rather doubtful claim, since Enshu would have been far too young to be hired as a designer at this time.) According

to the legend, Enshu made three demands of Hideyoshi: that no expense be spared in the creation of the garden, that no time limit be set for its completion, and that Hideyoshi not view the project until after it was completed. (In fact, Hideyoshi died in 1598 before the project was well under way.) In reality, if Enshu were involved in the project at all, it was probably at a much later phase of the development of the villa and its grounds, and then probably only as a consultant.

The first structure of importance at the villa was the Ko Shoin (alternatively translated as the Old Shoin or Old Palace or Old Study). What began as a retreat noted for its simplicity gradually was expanded and elaborated into a villa of a simple but refined elegance in which small decorative elements of the *sukiya* style ("aristocratic refinement"– as opposed to the garish vulgarisms of the Tosho-gu Shrine at Nikko of Tokugawa Ieyasu at the same time) brought a restrained grandeur to the complex.

The start of construction of the Ko Shoin, according to some documents, can be dated to June 18, 1621. The Ko Shoin faced the pond, then smaller than it was eventually to become, and the prince began his garden. This became one of the first examples of a "stroll garden" in which a path encircling a lake was so laid out that varied views of the terrain were presented as the visitor moved along the path.

In all, the grounds of the villa cover 14 acres (5.6 ha). Toshihito died in 1629 when his son Prince Toshitada (1619-62) was only 11 years old. The villa and its grounds fell into decay, but a change for the better occurred in 1642 when Prince Toshitada married Maeda

Fuhima, the daughter of the leader of the wealthy Maeda clan. With the funds made available by his father-in-law, the prince added to the villa and perfected the grounds. As with his father, he had the intelligence, wit and a love of classical literature, all of which inspired his design of the improved retreat. Enamored of *The Tale of Genji*, he endeavored to recreate the ambience of Heian times at his villa, and elements of the landscape are meant to bring to mind the atmosphere and the scenery of early aristocratic Kyoto. He had rocks and trees arranged to reflect the landscape described in the literature of the era of the 800s–1200s, the days of glory of the old aristocratic court.

Toshitada enlarged the pond and improved the villa's garden, and he extended the Ko Shoin building as well. He added the Chu Shoin (Middle Shoin) to the original structure, and finally the Shin Goten (New Palace) in honor of an anticipated visit in 1633 by his cousin, Emperor Go Mizuno-o and his consort, Empress Tofuku-mon-in. This latter building was connected to the Chu Shoin by the Gakki-no-ma (Musical Instrument Room).

Each of the buildings was joined to the previous structure by its roof, the buildings being placed in a staggered fashion so as to provide for a maximum of fresh air and for unobstructed views of the garden and pond. The zigzag pattern which resulted has been poetically described as a "flock of geese in formation." Unfortunately, Toshitada died the year before the Emperor was to visit the Shin Goten and the villa. Toshitada left no heir, and thus Go-Mizuno-o-o's son, Prince Yasuhito, was chosen, by adoption, to continue the Hachijo-no-miya line. The Emperor, in 1663, visited what had now become his son's villa. The ensuing generations of the Hachijo line all died young and without heirs, and it was not until the next century that an inheritor (by adoption) lived long enough to leave his mark on the complex by unifying the villa and its garden. The 8th in the Hachijo line adopted the name "Katsura" as the family name, but with the death of the 11th in the line without heirs in 1881, the line became extinct.

In September 1883, the villa was taken over by the Imperial Household Agency and made into a Detached Imperial Palace (Rikyu). (The Katsura town residence, which stood to the north of the Imperial Palace buildings within the Old Imperial Palace grounds, was moved at the end of the 19th century to the Nijo Castle where it continues to exist today as an example of the Hachijo-no-miya Katsura taste in city architecture.)

PRESENT STRUCTURES AND GROUNDS

The Katsura Imperial Villa was restored in the 1980s after being closed to the public for a lengthy period of time. The Shoin were dismantled and repaired, the gardens were restored and a new Visitors' Center was created where those with reservations gather at the beginning of each tour of the gardens. The villa is noted for its gardens, its tea houses and for its Shoin buildings: a collection of a pond, 7 buildings, 8 water basins, 16 bridges and 25 lanterns.

The entry to the complex is on the northern side of the property, the villa being hidden within its wooded grounds and separated from the Katsura River by its forested rim. The perimeter of the grounds is surrounded by the Katsura-gaki, a live bamboo hedge whose branches are braided to create a living wall. This hedge leads to the Omote-mon (Front Gate) of polished upright bamboo, a gate that is only opened for the Imperial family or state guests. Visitors enter through the service entrance, which is bordered by the Hozaki, a fence of bamboo uprights with twigs woven between them to form a wall.

Some 164 feet (50 m) south of the Omote-mon is the Miyuki-mon (Imperial Gate), created in 1662 by Prince Toshitada for the visit of former Emperor Go-Mizuno-o. A simple gateway of bamboo, it has a heavy miscanthus thatch roof. Next to this gate is a large flat square granite stone on which the Imperial palanquin would come to rest.

From here, at a 90-degree turn, its occupant would walk along the blue-black pebbled Miyuki-michi (Imperial Way) between square-shaped hedges on either side of the lane toward the Ko Shoin. Some 98 feet (29 m) along the Miyuki-michi, a path to the left leads to Momiji-yama (Maple Hill) and the Momiji stables, both to the right of this new path, while on the left is the Sosetsu-yama (Sago Palm Hill). Continuing along the Miyuki-michi path, a small inlet on the right has the O-funaya (Boat House) for the pleasure boat once used on the villa lake. At the end of the Miyuki-michi, an earthen bridge leads to the miscanthus thatched Chu-mon (Central Gate) beyond which is the Shoin. Just before the gate, a peninsula jutting into the lake has its tip blocked by the Suminoe Pine

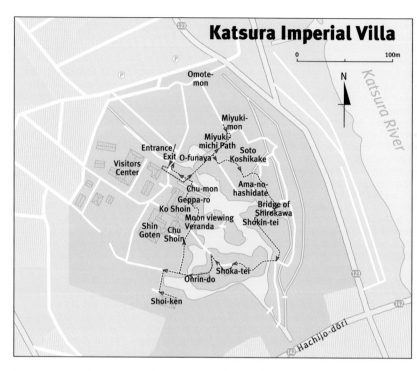

Katsura Imperial Villa

0   100m

N

Katsura River

Omote-mon

Miyuki-mon

Miyuki-michi Path

Entrance/Exit

Visitors Center

O-funaya

Soto Koshikake

Chu-mon

Ama-no-hashidate

Geppa-ro

Ko Shoin

Bridge of Shirokawa

Shin Goten

Moon viewing Veranda

Shokin-tei

Chu Shoin

Shoka-tei

Ohrin-do

Shoi-ken

Hachijo-dori

known as the Byobu-no-matsu (Pine Tree as a Screen), a pine meant to give but a glimpse of the lake, which will be better seen from an appropriate later viewpoint.

A large stone stands before the entry to Prince Toshito's 1610 Ko Shoin, thereby giving the 4-mat entry the name of Mikoshi-yose (Palanquin Porch), although the palanquin would have been left at the Imperial gate rather than coming to this stone unit. Adjoining this entry room is the 10-mat Yari-no-ma (Sword or Spear Room) with a rack at the ceiling to hold the weapons that visitors had to deposit here. The walls are papered with the Imperial formal crest as well as the paulownia crest. Behind the Yari-no-ma, to the south, is the 10-mat Irori-no-ma (Hearth Room) with its hearth; paintings on its cedar doors by Kano Eikei (1662–1702) feature a rooster resting on a basket and drum. It and the Sword Room are typical of buildings in the *buke-zukuri* (warrior house) style of architecture of the *samurai* class.

On the left, adjacent to the Sword Room with its four cedar doors painted with tigers, bamboo, reeds, herons, pine trees and storks by Kano Eitoku (1543–90), are the very plain

Ni-no-ma (Second Room) and the Ichi-no-ma (First Room) for the reception of guests. The Ichi-no-ma has a *tokonoma* as long as a *tatami* mat while the 15-mat Ni-no-ma is the largest room in all the Shoin. In front of these two rooms is the Hiro-en, a wide veranda from which the lake can be viewed when the external white *shoji* panels are set aside. From the Ni-no-ma there is a bamboo-floored platform of 12 feet square (1 sq m) extending from the Shoin, a platform called the Tsuki-mi-dai (Moon Viewing Platform) for the enjoyment of the evening view of the moon reflected in the water of the lake.

Behind the Irori-no-ma is the Chu Shoin (Middle Palace), which was added to the original Ko Shoin. The Chu Shoin and the Shin Goten (New Palace), built by Prince Toshitada after 1642 and 1662 respectively, are a step higher than the Ko Shoin. Since the land drops away in this area, these structures are raised on posts, the walls of the lower floor being of alternating white plaster and bamboo lath. The 6 foot (1.8 m) height above the ground of the two buildings removes them from the danger of flooding as well as providing for the circulation of air in the summer.

The Chu Shoin is an extension to the Ko Shoin. Its 10-mat San-no-ma (Third Room) is joined to the Irori-no-ma (Hearth Room) of the Ko Shoin. This San-no-ma is also known as the Sansui-no-ma (Landscape Room) as well as the Yuki-no-ma (Snow Room) because of its landscape scene by Kano Yasunobu 1616–85) of birds and pheasants in the snow. The Ni-no-ma (Second Room) has the painting of "The Seven Chinese Sages of the Bamboo Grove" by Kano Naonobu (1607–50) on its *fusuma*. The last room, the 6-mat Ichi-no-ma (First Room), was a sitting room for the later princes, and it has a landscape painting by Kano Tanyu (1602–74) that has been noted for its portrayal of crows. The room seems larger than it is due to its large two-mat *tokonoma* and its *chigaidana*.

A corridor, the Gakki-no-ma (Music Instrument Room) leads from the Chu Shoin to the Shin Goten (New Palace), and its four cedar doors have handles by Kacho in the shape of a broad-brimmed hat, while the paintings on the doors by Kaihoku Yusho (1533–1615) depict herons on a willow tree, reeds and geese. The 3-mat Gakki-no-ma has an alcove to hold a *koto* (Japanese stringed instrument).

To the south of the Gakki-no-ma is a broad lawn on which *kemari* (Heian period football), archery and horsemanship could be viewed from the veranda of the Gakki-no-ma. Beneath the eaves of the buildings is a shallow ditch filled with gravel to receive the rain pouring from the roof in inclement weather, thereby preventing the muddying of the building walls or the lawn.

The Shin Goten (New Palace) is also called the Miyuki-no-ma (Imperial Visit Room) since it was here that Emperor Go-Mizuno-o stayed at the time of his 1662 visit, the structure reputedly having been constructed specially for this visit. From the exterior, the New Palace appears to be a simple, almost rustic structure, but the interior enhances this simplicity by its rich details of rare woods and elaborately wrought door handles and nail covers. The first half of the corridor (or veranda) before the main rooms is wood-floored before the exterior shoji but *tatami*-matted for half of the corridor width before the inner rooms.

At the entrance to the New Palace are cedar doors with a painting by Kano Eitoku (1543–90) of a long-tailed bird in a tree. The door handles are noted since they are each in the shape of a pail with the flowers of the

Checkered pattern in the tokonoma of Shokin-tei.

four seasons: cherry and wisteria for spring, hibiscus for summer, chrysanthemums for autumn and camellias and plum for winter. These decorative door pulls are a relic of Ashikaga times (1333–1568), having been created then by Goto Yujo (1435–1512). The metal coverings of the nail heads are in the shape of narcissus, the flowers being of silver while the leaves are of gold, all by Kacho.

On the west side of the corridor/veranda is the 9-mat Ichi-no-ma (First Room), with a raised *jodan* (platform) of three mats for the Emperor with *chigaidana* shelves and a reading desk. The Katsura-dana shelves of the *chigaidana* are composed of various imported woods and are known as one of the three famed shelves in Japan, the other two being the Kasumi-dana (Mist Shelves) of the Shugaku-in Villa and the Daigo-dana of the Daigo-ji Temple in southeastern Kyoto. The coffered ceiling is of *keyaki* wood, and a large *shoji*-covered window adjoins the *chigaidana*, its upper section being in a comb shape while the wood of the reading shelf in the window is of mulberry. The door pulls are in the shape of the Chinese character for "moon."

The inner rooms of the New Palace were for the Emperor and his consort. These include the 9-mat Gyoshin-no-ma (Sleeping Room) behind the Ichi-no-ma, containing a triangular shelf for the Imperial sword and seal, the 3-mat Emon-no-ma (Robing Room), with three separate clothing shelves (cupboards), the 6-mat Haizen-no-ma (Service Room) and the 4 1/2-mat Keshon-no-ma (Dressing Room), whose rear shelves are back to back with the Katsura-dana shelves of the *chigaidana* in the adjacent room. This room later served as a sitting room for the princes' consort. Behind these rooms are the bamboo-

The Shokin-tei tea house at the Katsura Villa.

floored Ochozu-no-ma (Washing Room), with a well in its center, the Kewaya (toilet) with *tatami* flooring and place for a flower vase, and the Oyudono (Bath Room) with a wide-boarded floor and a bathtub.

The garden of the villa is noted not only for its variety and beauty but for being one of the earliest known stroll gardens and the model for all such gardens that followed. Such stroll gardens were meant to have a path that circles a body of water, and the path was to be so constructed that only one aspect of its various views could be seen at any one time. The details of the landscape were thus more important than the whole.

The path at the Katsura Imperial Villa was so devised so as to obscure the view of the lake or of a particular sector until such time as it could suddenly burst upon view. To this end, the stone path was not a smooth one, the stones being placed so that you had to concentrate on the placement of your feet so as not to stumble—thereby keeping you from looking at the distant view. At the appropriate location, the path would become smooth so that you no longer watched your feet—and thus you could suddenly take in the full beauty the designer had created to please the eye, the spirit and the mind. The details of the garden were thus meant to impress the intellect as well as the emotions, for specific elements of rocks, trees and hills were planned so as to recall scenes from *The Tale of Genji* and other classical landscapes of Chinese and Japanese literature.

The tour of the villa garden begins from the Myuki-michi (Imperial Way) and moves clockwise about the lake. At the start, the path, which diverges to the left from the Miyuki-michi, has the Momiji-yama (Maple Hill) on the right and the Sosetsu-yama (Sago

Palm Hill) to the left; these palms were said to have been a gift of the Satsuma clan of Kyushu since they are not normally indigenous to the Kyoto area. The path leads on to the Soto Koshikake, a roofed bench where guests who were invited to the tea ceremony in the Shokin-tei could await their call to the tea house. This simple gabled-roof rest stop has a miscanthus thatched roof; to the left are a small privy and a square stone wash basin called the Nijumagata (Double Measure Wash Basin) with a stone lantern behind it.

When you leave the Soto Koshikake, the lake and the Shokin-tei on its other side come into view. You cross the narrow waterway bringing water from the upper reaches of the Katsura River. The drop in the terrain in the garden creates a very small waterfall called the Tsutsumi-no-taki (Tabor Waterfall) since the sound of the falling water brings to mind the sound of a small drum. Two small islands connected by a stone bridge jut out into a "bay" in the lake, a section called Ama-no-hashidate, named for the scenic spot on the Japan Sea coast. The cape is formed by small flat black stones which reach out into the pond, a stone lantern at the tip of the peninsula representing a lighthouse.

Across from this peninsula, following the shoreline, the path leads to an 18 by 3 foot (5.4 by 1 m) long single granite slab, the Bridge of Shirokawa, a gift of Kato Kiyomasa (1562–1611), which spans the waterway to the Shokin-tei. Adjacent, on the near side of the bridge, is the Nagare-chozu (Washing Place in a Stream), a few stones at the edge of the bridge providing a place to wash one's hands before continuing to the Shokin-tei.

The Shokin-tei (Pine Lute Pavilion) is a tea arbor or tea hut on one of the higher man-made hills in the villa garden. It is oriented so that on its north, east and west sides it faces the lake. Its name is derived from the Chinese character for pine (*sho*), lute (*kin*) and arbor or pavilion (*tei*) in reference to the music of the pine trees as the wind moves through their needles. In the hut's eastern gable is the small name plate of Shokin-tei from the brush of Emperor Go-Yozei, the brother of Prince Toshihito. The roof of the hut is of miscanthus thatch extended sufficiently low so as to protect those in the hut against the glare of the mid-summer sun. The tea house has six rooms: the Ichi-no-ma (First Room), Ni-no-ma (Second Room), Cha-shitsu (Tea Room), two Tsugi-no-ma (Reserve

Rooms) and a Mizuya (Washing Room). The Cha-shitsu alone has a partially shingled and partially tiled roof.

The 11-mat Ichi-no-ma is the largest of the Shokin-tei rooms, and it looks out upon the lake and Ama-no-hashidate. To the front is a low open hearth with a plate rack behind it, 11 *tatami* mats in an L shape surrounding the hearth. The hearth serves a double purpose as a place not only to heat tea but as a source of warmth in winter time for viewing the lake and Ama-no-hashidate under snow. The most striking element in the Ichi-no-ma is the *tokonoma* and *fusuma* with a large blue and white checkerboard design. The 6-mat Ni-no-ma (Second Room) extends beyond the first room and features a *tokonoma* and *chigaidana*. Behind the Ni-no-ma is the 8-windowed Cha-shitsu (Tea Room), with a woven grass ceiling, a crooked post for its *tokonoma* (a form much desired for a *tokonoma*) and a small hearth inserted in the 3 1/2-mat floor.

To the west of the Shokin-tei, at the water's edge, is a long stone which served as a landing place for the pleasure boat used on the lake. The path from the Shokin-tei proceeds to an earthen bridge leading to a larger island behind which is the Hotaru-dani (Firefly Valley), so-named from the many fireflies to be found here in summer. In mid-island at the highest point is the Shoka-tei (Arbor for the Admiring of Flowers), a resting pavilion with four elevated mats in a U shape that could serve as benches, a hearth for warmth and a spherical stone basin outside for washing one's hands. The Shoka-tei was designed to resemble a countryside tea stall, even to the cloth hangings along the outside to keep the sunlight from the eyes of those resting within.

At the west end of the island is the Onrindo, a tiled-roof pavilion in the Buddhist style. Built by Prince Yoshitada to enshrine the *ihai* memorial tablet to his father, Prince Yoshihito, it came to hold the memorial tablets of the Hachi-no-miya family. These *ihai* have now been moved to the Shokoku-ji Temple in central Kyoto, to the north of the Imperial Palace, and the former Katsura city mansion on the palace grounds.

An earthen bridge connects the island with the mainland, and around a "bay" to the south is the Shoi-ken (Pavilion of Laughing Thoughts), a 6-room tea house with six round windows above the entry *fusuma*. A 4-mat Entrance Room (Kuchi-no-ma) leads to the 6-mat Ni-no-ma (Second Room). The portion of the wall below the exterior *shoji* of the Ni-no-ma ma is covered with cross-striped T'ang velveteen. To the right of the Ni-no-ma is the San-no-ma (Third Room), with a long hearth, a sideboard and tea utensils. To the left of the Ni-no-ma is the Ichi-no-ma (First Room), with a *tokonoma* and a study desk at the *shoji*-covered window. A spacious kitchen completes the layout. The arrow-shaped bronze door catches in the building were part of Hideyoshi's spoils from his Korean expedition of the early 1590s.

The path now follows the lake, passing below the Shoin, and ends at the Geppa-ro (Pavilion of the Moon and Waves), a 3-room tea cottage for moon viewing. It has a dirt-floored *doma* (service area) with a hearth, a stove, shelves, a closet and a sideboard. A faded painting of a foreign boat with Chinese and Japanese on board, from the Sumiyoshi Shrine, graces the wall of the *doma*. The inner portion of the roof of the Geppa-ro is open to the exposed bamboo rafters and the reed thatch so as to resemble a country cottage. Only the Ichi-no-ma (First Room) has a ceiling. This room also has a *tokonoma* and *tsukeshoin* (a built-in writing desk). The Naka-no-ma (Middle Room) is to the right of the Ichi-no-ma and looks out upon the lake and the Shokin-tei and the garden. The *fusuma* paintings of the Geppa-ro are by Kobori Enshu (1579–1647).

The tour ends at the Geppa-ro. You exit the grounds past the Palanquin Entry of the Ko Shoin to the Miyuki-michi (Imperial Way) path to the gate at the entrance to the villa.

GETTING THERE

To reach the beginning of the tour at the Matsu-no-o Shrine, take the local Hankyu railway train from Shijo-dori, changing trains at Katsura station for the Arashiyama line. The shrine lies to the west of the second stop from there, Matsuo station. Alternatively, take bus 28, 29, 63 or 73 to the Matsuo-taisha-mae bus stop or bus 3, 67 or 71 to Matsuo-bashi (Matsuo Bridge). The shrine lies to the west of these bus stops, and it is open during daylight hours without charge. The tour ends at Katsura Imperial Villa. Taxis usually wait outside the villa grounds for a return to Katsura station for the journey back to the heart of Kyoto.

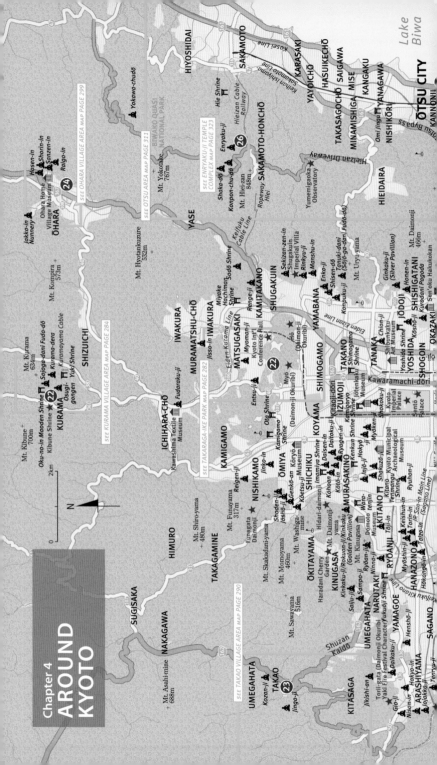

Walking Tour 22

KURAMA VILLAGE AREA

A Small Imperial Retreat and a Fire Festival

1. **Takaraga-ike Park Area** 宝ケ池公園周辺
2. **Entsu-ji Temple** 円通寺
3. **Myoman-ji Temple** 妙満寺
4. **Kibune Shrine** 貴船神社
5. **Kurama-dera Temple** 鞍馬寺
6. **Yuki Shrine** 由岐神社

Tour 16 in part covered those sites of interest to the immediate north of the junction of the Kamo and Takano Rivers. In this tour, we travel to sites further to the north. Some lie beyond the traditional city limits, into the countryside to the north of Kyoto. As one moves north of Kitayama-dori, beyond the junction of the aforementioned rivers, the foothills of the mountains that surround Kyoto to the north begin their ascent, and the sites which follow are to the north of these foothills.

Immediately to the north of the eastern portion of Kitayama-dori is Takaraga-ike Park with its pond (*ike*), and beyond the pond is the International Conference Hall. Here are held the many academic, business and trade conferences and exhibitions that have made Kyoto an international conference center. To the west of the Conference Hall is the Entsu-ji Temple, once one of the small delightful villas that Emperor Go-Mizuno-o enjoyed in his long 17th century retirement before abandoning it for his Shugaku-in Villa. Turned into a temple, Entsu-ji retains a noted garden with its bor-rowed scenery of the eastern mountains of Kyoto. To its north is the rather peripatetic Myoman-ji Temple, which has been located in various places in Kyoto.

Finally, toward the end of the Keifuku Eizan railway line, is Kibune Shrine, and then to the rail terminus in Kurama, the home of the Yuki Shrine and the Kurama-dera Temple on Mount Kurama. Here, the annual autumn festival at night, with its loin-clad young men carrying flaming torches and *mikoshi* (port-able shrines) up the hillside to the Yuki Shrine, is a highlight of the temple's annual festivities.

1 TAKARAGA-IKE PARK AREA
The Takaraga-ike Park and pond is the place to start an exploration of a portion of the area to the north of Kyoto itself. (The park can be reached from the station at the northern end of the subway line or by bus 17 from the

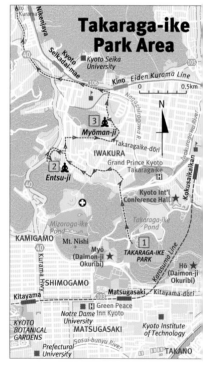

Once an Imperial villa, Entsu-ji Temple is a wonderful place to enjoy the changing of the seasons.

Keihan Sanjo station or bus 72 from the Shijo-Karasuma bus stop to the International Conference Hall and the park.)

The area in which Takaraga-ike Park is located originally lay beyond the limits of the city of Kyoto. Between 1751 and 1763, a pond was created in the woods to the north of Kyoto's foothills in order to serve as a reservoir for irrigation. In 1949, a park was planned for the area about the pond, a boon for a city that has little in the way of open or park areas. It was the 1960s before the park was constructed, and, with the completion of the original 1961 "Paradise for Children" playground (for children accompanied by parents), the development of this oasis began. In 1970, a Sports Square with tennis and rugby grounds was added, while in 1971 an Iris Garden was created. In 1974, the "Forest of Rest" came into being, followed by the "Forest of Cherry Trees" in 1977, and then the Western-style Square Lawn in 1978. In all, the park consists of 316 acres (126 ha). The pond is 1 mile (1.6 km) in circumference, and row boats can be rented. Thus the park and pond provide a pleasant escape from Kyoto's urban center.

On the banks of Takaraga-ike Pond is the Kyoto International Conference Hall (Kokuritsu Kyoto Kokusai Kaikan), a bustling place throughout the year with its many conferences and exhibitions. (The hall is open from 9:30 a.m. to 4:30 p.m., closing at 4:00 p.m. from December through March. It is closed on the third Saturday of the month and from December 27 to January 4. Entry fee.)

Opened in 1966 but not fully completed until 1973, the hall was designed by architect Sachio Otani. It combines the traditional and the contemporary in its design. Made of reinforced concrete, it is in the *gassho zukuri* architectural style, which reflects the steep roofs of traditional farmhouses in the Japanese mountains of central and northern Japan or, in a more popular description, hands held in prayer. Starkly modern, it sits to the north of Takaraga-ike Pond, with a backdrop of the hills which surround Kyoto in its northern reaches.

The 300,000 square foot (28,000 sq m) Kyoto International Conference Hall is a six-story structure containing four main halls. It can seat 2,000, and provides simultaneous translation in six languages. A separate tea ceremony house with a cypress bark roof, the Hosho-an, was designed by Shoshitsu Sen of the Ura Senke tea group.

To the west of the conference hall is the Kyoto Takaraga-ike Prince Hotel, a circular building designed by Togo Murano, which also boasts a separate traditional tea house. Its circular design offers an interesting contrast to the triangular shape of the conference hall, and it provides not only accommodations but restaurants and cafes for the public.

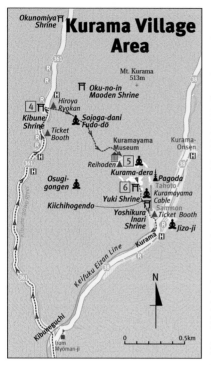

2 ENTSU-JI TEMPLE

By contrast, the Entsu-ji Temple, once an Imperial residence, offers a less bustling and much more rural ambience. (The temple is located 1 mile (1.6 km) southeast of the Kinomachi station of the Keifuku electric railway. Take bus 48 from this station to the Entsu-ji-michi bus stop and then walk to first north and then west. This same bus will take you from downtown Kyoto to the Entsu-ji-michi bus stop. A taxi from the end of the City subway line, however, provides the most direct route to the temple. The temple is open from 10:00 a.m. to 4:00 p.m. Entry fee. Photography is not permitted, and you are usually asked to check in your camera at the ticket desk.)

The site of Entsu-ji Temple was originally an Imperial villa, the Hataeda Goten, created by Emperor Go-Mizuno-o (1596–1680) with a view of Mount Hiei; its *karesansui* (dry garden) is attributed to the Emperor. The Hataeda Goten villa was a simple house where the Emperor could enjoy the changing of the seasons, free from the cares and intrigue of the capital. With the completion of Shugaku-in as an Imperial villa, the small mansion in the little village of Hataeda was no longer in use. It is claimed that the Emperor gave the house to the aristocratic Konoe family, and some accounts say that they turned it into a nunnery called the Entsu-ji. Emperor Reigen (reigned 1663–83) was the last of Go-Mizuno-o's children to reign, and it is said that he enjoyed the villa. Its Shoin was a 1678 gift from the Imperial Palace, and some sources hold that Emperor Reigen later converted the villa into a Buddhist nunnery for his foster mother. The many buildings and artistic treasures of the temple decreased in number with time, but an 11th century image of Kannon attributed to Jocho is still there. The main hall of the temple, the Hondo, faces the garden and Mount Hiei, and its adjacent altar room has the image of Kannon as well as photographs of Emperor Meiji and his consort.

The Karesansui Garden (dry garden) is the reason the Entsu-ji is noted today, having been restored after World War II from a Kobori Enshu design. A moss and stone garden of 40 moss-covered rocks enclosed on three sides by a low hedge of azaleas and sasanqua trees, it makes use of the distant Mount Hiei as "borrowed scenery"; adjacent trees are kept clipped so that the mountain is not obscured by their foliage. The simple dry garden and its borrowed view have made it one of the gardens favored by those interested in the effect of Zen on Japanese garden design.

3 MYOMAN-JI TEMPLE

To the north of Entsu-ji is Myoman-ji, a temple virtually unknown to foreigners but of interest both because of aspects of its architecture and for the legend that concerns its reputed one-time bell. (Take bus 48 from the Entsu-ji-michi bus stop to the temple, which lies to the south of the Kinomachi station of the Keifuku Eizan railway line. Take the road south from the station (or bus 48 which begins on the north side of the tracks) to the intersection with the main north–south highway that the road eventually meets. At the triangle where the two roads join is the Myoman-ji Temple on the west side of the road. The temple is open from 9:00 a.m. to 4:00 p.m. A contribution at the Hojo entrance is welcomed if one wishes to visit the temple garden.)

The temple was begun in the 13th century by the monk Nichiju, and it became a seat of one branch of the Nichiren Buddhist sect. Its

The entrance to the ancient Kibune Shrine, established before the city of Kyoto itself.

4 KIBUNE SHRINE

According to legend, and no self-respecting shrine or temple can exist without an appropriate legend, the mother of Emperor Jimmu (the mythological first Emperor of Japan) took a yellow boat (Ki-fune) up the Kamo River to its source and had a Shinto shrine built there to the god of the waters, a deity who could provide the area to the south with a sufficient flow for irrigation or who could cause floods. This is a pleasant attempt to explain the name of the shrine (Kibune or Kifune). The fact that the Emperor Jimmu is a legendary emperor does not add to the versimilitude of the account.

The Kibune Shrine is an ancient one since it is known to have existed even before Kyoto was settled in the 790s. The god enshrined here is Take Okami, and people came in times of drought to pray for rain. Since this spot is the source of the Kamo River, a white horse was sacrificed to the deity in times of flood to assuage his wrath, and a black horse was offered in time of drought as a plea for rain. It was here that the beloved priest of Kyoto, Priest Kuya, in the early centuries of the city's existence, came upon a deer that had been killed by a warrior—a deer whose skin he wore as a simple garment thereafter and whose antlers surmounted Kuya's staff. The shrine is similar to other Shinto shrines in its layout of *torii,* Heiden (Offertory), Honden (Spirit Hall) and smaller spirit structures.

The shrine holds a number of ceremonies or festivals throughout the year. The most important of these is the Kibune Matsuri on June 2, which begins with prayers for a good rice crop and is followed by a procession of young men carrying the shrine's portable *mikoshi* to the inner shrine. The ceremony is in honor of the god of water.

chief claim to fame was its bell, said to be the original of the Dojo-ji Bell (stolen by the temple monks from the Dojo-ji Temple in the Kii Peninsula), which is celebrated in the *kabuki* play of that name. (According to the legend, a woman disappointed in love for a priest of the temple turned herself into a snake and wrapped herself about a temple bell, under which the priest was hiding from his too persistent former lover. The heat of the snake's coils turned the bell into a furnace that killed the priest. The woman, once more in human form, is said to have drowned herself thereafter.) Naturally, the Dojo-ji Temple on the Kii Peninsula, which lost its bell, offers an annual celebration in the bell's honor.

A Nichiren temple that has had several locations, Myoman-ji now seems established at its present site in northern Kyoto. Cross an arched bridge over a small pond and a stream en route to the main gateway, which pierces the wall surrounding the temple grounds. Within the walls, a roofed Shoro (bell tower) lies to the left, while a roofed water basin, whose water issues from the mouth of a bronze dragon, is on the right. Ahead to the left is a walled enclosure with two gateways, behind which private buildings of the temple are located.

Beyond this enclosure lies a very tall square tower in the style of an Indian or South Asian stupa. At the four corners of the platform on which the stupa sits are smaller squat stupas. A roofed incense pot stands before the entryway to the tower, and within is a seated golden Buddha with his hands in the *mudra* of contemplation. Paintings of two Bodhisattvas are on the wall to either side of the image, while a painted leaf design is on the wall behind the Buddha as well as behind the painted Bodhisattvas. The stupa and its interior are rarities in Kyoto.

The Hondo (Main Hall) rises at the end of the main path. It is entered by means of a wide flight of steps. Within is an elaborate gold on black lacquer altar area, with gold hangings on the pillars about the seated Buddha image. On the right side of the path, after you pass the purification basin, two gates lead into the Hojo, one a Kara-mon (Chinese-style) gateway. The simpler gate is the one visitors use, and it leads into what was once the monastic kitchen area. A right turn down a passageway and then to the left leads to a room from which the walled monastic garden may be viewed. This *karesansui* (dry landscape garden) has raked gravel about its outer edges. In the foreground is a "dry" pond of dark small stones and a pine tree whose two trained extended branches enhance the background of large rocks and a small hill. A squat lantern lies at the rear as does a stone lantern on a stone pedestal to the left, all composing an attractive traditional dry garden. A pathway from the purification basin leads to a modern multipurpose building for use in temple activities.

Return to the Kinomachi railway station to take a train in the direction away from Kyoto to Kurama as well as to the Kibune Shrine.

KURAMA VILLAGE

Continuing to the end of the Keifuku rail line beyond Kibune-guchi, the train comes to its terminus at the village of Kurama, where you can walk through the town to the Yuki Shrine and then to the Kurama-dera Temple. (The temple is open from 9:30 a.m. to 4:00 p.m. except on Mondays and from December 25 to January 10. Entry fee.)

Even before Kyoto was thought of as a capital of Japan, the Kurama area had its historical moment in the limelight when the Emperor Temmu, fleeing in 683 from Prince Otomo, reached this place on a "saddled horse" which he left tied here. Thus, the name "Kurama" (Saddled Horse) is said to have come into being. In the non-historical realm, temple tradition claims that 6 million years ago, Mao-son, the great spirit of the earth who conquers evil, descended from the planet Venus to save mankind. Since then, his spirit has been resident at Kurama, where he governs the evolution of mankind and all living beings.

Returning to more historical claims, in 770, Gantei, a pupil of the Chinese monk Ganjin of Toshodai-ji in Nara, received spiritual emanations from Mao-son, having been led to Kurama by a white horse. He was enlightened as well by the spirit of Bishamon-ten, the protector of the northern quarter of the Buddhist heaven and the spirit of the sun, a deity of the Kurama-dera Temple.

In Chinese lore, which was accepted by the early Japanese, evil flows from the northeast, and thus, when Kyoto was first established, it was well that there was a Buddhist temple to the north of the city to protect the capital against these forces of evil. The existing Kurama-dera Temple, which offered such protection, had been founded, as stated above, by priest Gantei in 770. The place he chose, halfway up the Kurama Mountain, truly needed the mitigating effect of his temple in the 770s since the area was reputed to be a haven for evil spirits and robbers. In 796, again according to temple lore, the man in charge of temple construction saw a vision of the Senju (1,000-arm) Kannon, who is also considered to be the spirit of the moon. Thus, this deity was added to those to be worshipped. Mao-son, Bishamon-ten and Kannon form a triad called Sonten or Supreme Deity, the symbols of power, light and love for the Kurama-Kokyo sect. Therefore, at Kurama, Sonten is worshipped as the "creator of the universe and all living things which can arise in man's heart."

The marvelous was not unusual in these hills, if tradition is to be believed. The famous first Superior of the temple, Kanshin-Osho, once overpowered two snakes through incantations. He offered to spare their lives if they would bring a perennial spring of water to his temple—and a well of water immediately sprang up, a spring which still flows next to the Hondo (Main Hall) of the temple. In the

100s, again according to legend, *tengu* (goblins) still dwelt in the nearby hills. These beings were half human half goblin with red faces, long noses and a pair of wings. One of them is responsible in part for the events in the Minamoto-Taira feud of the 12th century.

Minamoto-no-Yoshitomo had taken the wrong side in a battle with Taira-no-Kiyomori, then de facto ruler of Japan. Yoshitomo was killed after the battle, and his three young sons were spared by Kiyomori on their mother's pledge that they would become monks. Yoshitsune, the youngest, was only a few months old when the pledge was made, and he was placed in Kurama-dera under the care of a wise monk. When he was 11, he learned of the heroic military deeds of his father and became determined to follow in his footsteps. According to legend, he developed great skill in swordsmanship under the training given him by a *tengu* in a valley northwest of Kurama-dera. In 1174, at 16, he left the temple to begin his military career. Eventually, he was to be responsible for the defeat of the Taira at Dan-no-ura in 1185–and to go down in Japanese history, legend, theater and literature as the high spirited, handsome, intelligent but tragic hero who was dead by 31.

5 KURAMA-DERA TEMPLE

Formerly a Tendai temple, Kurama-dera is now the headquarters of the Kurama-Kokyo sect founded in 1949. The buildings of the temple lie along steep mountain paths, on a plateau, and demand arduous uphill climbs.

Kurama-dera suffered the usual vicissitudes brought on by periodic fires. In 1872, all the buildings had to be reconstructed, and in 1945 a fire destroyed the Hondo (Main Hall) again. The present Hondo is a 1971 replacement. Although the grandeur of the temple has been lost to flames, ceremonies have continued the fame of the temple despite the disappearance of its ancient halls and treasures.

The temple is reached by passing through the Yuki Shrine, which lies on the hillside between the town of Kurama and the Kurama-dera Temple. The temple being further up the mountain, walkers must traverse the shrine before reaching the temple. A steep and winding path, the Tsuzura-zaka, makes its way 2/3 of a mile (1 km) uphill past Kurama-dera's Nio-mon Gate and over stone steps toward a level area on which the Hondo (Main Hall) sits. A cable railway also climbs partway up this hill, but if you use it, you will miss the shrine.

The main gate leading to Kurama-dera Temple, located on wooded slopes above Kurama town.

6 YUKI SHRINE

Up the hillside path beyond the Nio-mon Gate of the temple, you come to Yuki Shrine, built in 940 near the base of Mount Kurama to protect the temple and to honor the deities of the area. In 940, legend relates, the shrine god was brought here from the Imperial Palace in Kyoto by boys "carrying flaming trees" from the mountain. In honor of this occasion, on October 22nd of each year, young men carry flaming torches through the streets of Kurama in a nighttime procession in which the god of the shrine is carried in a portable *mikoshi* shrine, the *mikoshi* bearers first ritually cleansing themselves in the icy cold waters of the mountain stream. A set of steep steps leads from the hillside path to the shrine's Haiden (Oratory), which also serves as a gateway, the steps rising right through the middle of the structure.

Behind the Haiden is a huge tree circled with a sacred rope and paper *gohei* which define a living organism worthy of reverence. More steep steps follow before you reach the Honden, which holds the spirit of the shrine. Two lion images stand before the Honden as well as a small iron pagoda behind the lion on the right. To the left is a storage building in which the shrine *mikoshi* is kept.

Along the way are the Kawakami Jizo-do and then a monument (*sotoba*) to Yoshitsune, situated at the site of the Tokobo Temple in which he spent his first ten years. The path continues to wind its way steeply up the mountainside toward the small unpainted Chu-mon (Central Gate) of Kurama-dera, and then many steps lead to its Tenporin-do. This structure has two floors, each accessible separately from the rising hillside path. The lower portion has benches where you can consume the food sold on this level (*soba*, crackers, buns, etc.). The upper, primary level holds a huge seated golden Amida image with a gold wall behind it. The steps beyond the Tenporin-do lead to a plateau on which some of the major temple buildings are located; there is a fine view from the edge of the plateau. (En route to the Tenporin-do from the Chu-mon, a secondary path joins the main path. It comes from the top funicular station and the Taho-to Pagoda.)

In the center of the plateau above the Tenporin-do is the concrete Hondo (Main Hall) or Sonten. Before it are two very large bronze lanterns and then two seated lion/tiger statues. This 1971 Main Hall replaces its predecessor, which was destroyed by fire, and is entered from its sides. Within, on either side are sales counters (candles, devotional items, etc.) The main portion of the temple is separated from the public area by a wooden trellised wall. The inner area contains the trinity of Mao-son, Bishamon-ten and Senju Kannon. An additional Sho Kannon image by Jokei (1226), a realistically carved image, has been so well sculpted that its vestments seem as though they are actual garments. On the left in a small hall is an image of a *tengu* in remembrance of Minamoto Yoshitsune's training in swordsmanship by one of these creatures.

To the right of the temple's main hall is the small Akai-goho-zenjin Shrine building. Its front has shelves of plastic buckets filled with water (for use in case of fire), and within is the Shinto shrine that sits atop the miraculous well whose creation was described above.

To the left of the Hondo, at the edge of the plateau, is the Honbo, the temple offices and lecture hall, and from it a corridor leads toward the center of the plateau, terminating in a stage for religious performances. Because the Honbo is built on the side of the hill, it appears to be a one-story building from the plateau side, but a glance over the railings shows it to be a four-story building, three of its floors below the level of the Hondo area. Associated with the Honbo is the Shinden, which is used as a building for the copying of sacred texts (sutras).

Continue to ascend the mountain from the plateau. Above the Hondo lies the Shoro (belfry), then a stone monument to two Meiji period (1868–1912) poets, husband and wife, Tekkan and Akiko Yosano. The Reiho-den (Treasure House, open from 9:00 a.m. to 4:30 p.m.) is next along the path on another brief

level area. This three-story building has a natural science hall on its first floor devoted to the flora, fauna and geography of the area. An Exhibition Hall, the Yosano Memorial Hall and storage areas are on the second and third floors, and among the temple treasures on view are images of the Heian and Kamakura period (794–1333). Included is the noted Bishamonten image, which does not carry the usual pagoda in his left hand but instead uses that hand to shade his eyes as he scans the horizon to detect any dangers that might threaten Kyoto. Across the path is the attractive and simple Tohakutei, Akiki Yosano's study.

The path, now grown more primitive, continues steeply uphill, passing Iki-sugi-o-mizu the spring where in temple tradition Yoshitsune slaked his thirst. Toward the top of the path is the Se-kurabe Ishi, a stone against which Yoshitsune measured his height when he was 16, just before leaving the monastery for his life as a warrior. A path to the left, the Kinone-michi, leads to an area where the exposed intertwining roots of cedar trees are an interesting natural phenomena. Further along the main path is the Osugi Gongen, an ancient cedar tree which the temple states is the incarnation of Mao-son. Beyond this, you come to the Yoshitsune Shrine, the purported place where he learned the art of swordsmanship from a *tengu* (goblin). Beyond the Sojo-ga-dani Fudo-do (Sogo Valley Fudo Hall) with a Fudo image. The last structure on the mountain, and one of the most important, is the small Okuno-in-Mao-den, the Inner Temple. Here, Mao-son is said to have descended from Venus to earth.

From the Sojo-dani (Sojo valley–Sojo being the most exalted rank for a Buddhist priest) a path leads down to Kibune and its shrine, 1 mile (1.6 km) below in 15 minutes of walking. (For those concerned with distances on this journey, it is 1,000 feet/300 m from the Nio-mon Gate to the Yuki Shrine, and another 3,000 feet/900 m from there to the Main Hall. From the Main Hall to the Okuno-in is 2,600 feet/800 m and then 2,000 feet/ 600 m to the Kibune Shrine. From Kibune to the Kibune-guchi railway station is another 6,600 feet/2,000 m).

Although there are numerous ceremonies throughout the year at the temple, the most important one is held on October 22nd. It is a time when people pour out of Kyoto to Kurama a time when transportation and food services can be overextended–so if you decide to atten

Young men carry giant flaming torches and miko-shi enclosing the shrine spirits during the annual Kurama-no-Hi Matsuri Festival at the Yuki Shrine.

the Kurama-no-Hi Matsuri Festival at the Yuki Shrine, be aware of the popularity of the event. The festival commemorates the bringing of the god to the shrine in 940, and a re-enactment of that event takes place. (An alternative account states that the occasion commemorates a 10th century event when the Emperor Sujaku led a parade of torches in Kyoto as a prayer for peace and prosperity.)

At 6:00 p.m. residents along the Kurama Kaido (Kurama Highway) leading to the temple and shrine light torches some 50 feet (15 m) apart in front of their houses. Children carrying small torches and shouting *sairei sairyo* eventually gather at the gate to the entrance to the Yuki Shrine. Young men, none older than 25, clothed only in white loin cloths, carry 17 foot (5 m) tall *taimatsu* (pine torches) on their shoulders as they parade through town and up a slope to the rhythm of drums, chants and hand clapping. Two huge gilded and lacquered *mikoshi*, the shrine palanquins with the spirit of the deities inside, are carried in the procession, young women holding on to the ropes to keep the *mikoshi* balanced as it is carried on the shoulders of some 40 young men. It is traditionally believed, on the girls' part, that this will lead to easier childbirth for them in time. When the two *mikoshi* reach the stone steps of the San-mon Gate, two young men balance themselves on the tip of the carrying bars,

facing upwards in a rite called *choppen*, which is the highlight of the festivities.

(According to Fosco Maraini in his *Meeting With Japan*, this was initially an initiation or coming-of-age festival when the young men wore no loin cloths, and at the end of the ceremony they were picked up, tilted backwards and carried down the slope, their legs held apart for a public demonstration of their sexual maturity. A youth who had not taken part in the festival was not eligible to marry.)

When the last torch burns out, a priest cuts the rope across the entrance to the shrine and there is a scramble to find a good spot to watch the rites, which are then performed by the shrine attendants. Thereafter the ceremony is over. (Trains run until 12:30 a.m. for a very crowded return to Kyoto.) A return can be made from the Kurama station to Kyoto to the Demachi Yanagi terminus of the rail line. There the underground rail line along the east bank of the Kamo River or one of the bus lines that pass before the terminus can be taken to locations in Kyoto.

GETTING THERE

Kurama is 12 miles (19.3 km) north of Kyoto on Mount Kurama. It can be reached by means of the Keifuku electric railway in 35 minutes from the Demachi Yanagi railway station (Kurama line) to Kurama station, which is the last stop on the line. Bus 32 from Keihan Sanjo also goes to Kurama.

If you wish to visit both Kurama-dera and Kibune Shrine in one day, it is best to go to Kurama first and then to walk from there to Kibune. From the Main Hall of Kurama-dera, it is approximately a 25 minute walk to Kibune Shrine—or 50 or more minutes between the Kurama railway station and Kibune via Kurama-dera. (It is a long climb to the Main Hall of Kurama-dera and then to the point where you begin the descent to the Kibune valley, and it should only be undertaken if you are fit.) In any case, it would be wise to carry lunch, although there are a number of country inns in Kibune itself, some of which put dining platforms over the river in the summer.

Kibune Shrine can be reached directly by getting off at the Kibune-guchi station on the Kurama line. Bus 32 to Kibune-guchi from Keihan Sanjo offers an alternate route. In either case, it is a 30 minute uphill walk to the shrine.

Walking Tour 23

TAKAO VILLAGE AREA
The Fire Deity, a Troublesome Priest and a Derisive Scroll

1. **Atago Shrine** 愛宕神社
2. **Jingo-ji Temple** 神護寺
3. **Kozan-ji Temple** 高山寺

The high mountain ranges and the deep narrow valleys northwest of Kyoto provide the attractions of nature away from the urban sprawl of modern Kyoto, particularly in the spring blossom season and in the autumn when the leaves of the maple trees are dyed their various colorful hues. There are two approaches to the mountain ranges, one from the old valley road that leaves Kyoto to the northwest of the Ninna-ji Temple, and the other by the Arashiyama-Takano Parkway toll road. Of the two, the parkway is the more scenic as it twists and turns through the mountains with distant vistas of the hills on either side of the road. At rest stops it is possible to look at the river and the small boats making their way through the rocky gorge of the river far below.

The Jingo-ji and Kozan-ji Temples are the two places of note in this region. Kozan-ji is a temple that seems to have become lost in

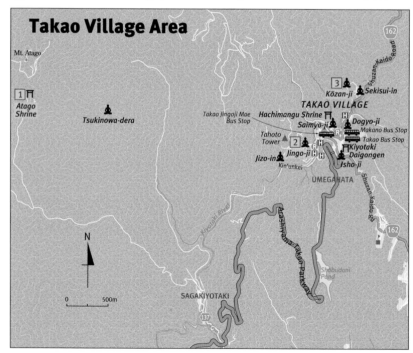

Takao Village Area

time. On three levels, its few buildings are not as important as those of Jingo-ji, nor is the scenery as spectacular, but it is remembered more for its association with some of its more colorful monastic members. Jingo-ji, on the other hand, is located at a far more interesting site. Coming from the Arashiyama Takano Parkway, you descend a long hill into the valley (the bus on the route from Ninna-ji stops in the valley) before undertaking another climb on the other side of the Kiyotaki River, which runs through the valley. The river valley itself is attractive, with its restaurants and their tables set out on the shingled riverside in season. A climb to Jingo-ji is worth the expenditure of energy, for its many buildings are of interest for their architecture and for their images as well as for the natural setting. After an exploration of the temple precinct and its stone stairways, it is a pleasure to sit in one of the outdoor restaurants back at the river edge for refreshments in this sylvan surrounding.

1 ATAGO SHRINE

The Atago Shrine is an interesting site in northwestern Kyoto, but the normal 2–3 hour pilgrimage route up the side of Mount Atago is only for the most hardy of visitors. Fortunately, a modern cable car, which serves skiers in season, can assist the less energetic at all times. The shrine and the traditional route to it are best seen, perhaps, at the time of the noted festival, which occurs on July 31st when the pass to the top is illuminated by lanterns.

Atago Shrine is located on top of Mount Atago, which lies to the west of Takao. It is about 3 miles (4.8 km) northwest of Arashiyama, above the hamlet of Kiyotaki.

Atago Mountain is 3,043 feet (913 m) above sea level and is noted for its Shinto shrine, which offers protection against fires. It is also known for skiing. The shrine is said to have been created in 781 by Wake-no-Kiyomaro (733–99), the founder of the nearby Jingo-ji Temple, when he became disillusioned with the political machinations of certain of the Nara temple priests. He thus abandoned Nara, as Emperor Kammu was to do just three years later. A vermilion *torii* gate in the village below the shrine marks the path that begins the 2–3 hour climb to the shrine. In Kiyotaki, a series of traditional thatched houses (primarily tea houses and pilgrim inns) are beside the path. Two ancient inns on either side of the road near the *torii* offer refreshments before the long climb. A bridge, the Toen-kyo, crosses the narrow gorge of the Kiyotaki River and then the 3 mile (4.8 km) climb commences.

On the path up the mountain to the Atago Shrine is the 50 foot (15 m) tall Kuya-daki waterfall, the place where priest Kuya performed the ascetic practice of repeating the Nembutsu while standing under the cold waters of the falls. Two-thirds of a mile (1 km) further on is the Tsuke-no-dera or Gatsurin-ji Temple, and then a little more than 1 mile (1.6 km) further and to the east is the Atago Shrine, a place sacred to Izanami and Izanagi, the godly progenitors of the Japanese islands and numerous Shinto gods. Their son Kogzuchi is the resident deity and is the protector against fire. The shrine, according to another account, was built in 701 by Yen-no-Shokoka. At a later time it came under Buddhist control as Buddhism and Shinto virtually merged (or as Shinto became submerged within the Japanese Buddhist world). In 1868, however, the new Meiji government caused the shrine to become solely a Shinto shrine once more. The festival date for the shrine is the 23rd of each month, and many people make the arduous climb to pray for protection against fire. Charms against fire are sold at the shrine. Then, on July 31st, the Senmichi Mairi Evening Fire Festival is celebrated. The mountain pass from Kiyotaki is lit by lanterns as thousands of people climb the mountain. Religious services begin at 9:00 p.m. and continue until 2:00 a.m. A visit to the shrine on this night is said to be equal to a thousand visits at any other time.

2 JINGO-JI TEMPLE

Not many visitors will reach the top of Mount Atago, but many will make their way to the Jingo-ji Temple in its more accessible and delightful setting in the hills. Jingo-ji is in the mountains to the northwest of Kyoto at Takao on the west bank of the Kiyotaki River, 8 miles (12.8 km) from Arashiyama.

HISTORY Jingo-ji was founded in 781, and it served as a private temple for Wake-no-Kiyomaro, who was buried here in 799. (In 1886, his spirit was brought from Jingo-ji to the newly created Go-O Shrine in Kyoto, and his former burial site was enclosed by a vermilion painted wood fence.)

The original temple had a Kondo (Golden or Main Hall) with a Yakushi Nyorai image of 802, a Kancho (Annointment Hall) and a Worship Hall. Saicho became the priest of the temple on his return from China in 805, and here he began to propound Tendai and esoteric Buddhist doctrines. He was teaching the tenets of the Womb Mandala at Jingo-ji by 805, but esoteric Buddhism was not fully realized until Priest Kukai added the Diamond World Mandala in 812. After the death of Saicho in 822, Kukai became the head priest of the temple and moved it from the Tendai to the Shingon approach to Buddhism. Here, he conducted the rites meant to protect the state, and here he began his form of esoteric (Shingon) Buddhism, which he later fully developed at To-ji in Kyoto. The location of his residence at the temple is marked by the Daishi-do (Founder's Hall) today. He added the Taho-to Pagoda to the temple with the five Godai Kokuzo images in it. The Taho-to Pagoda was erected in 845, but the present structure is a 1935 reconstruction.

The temple was destroyed by fire in the 10th century and again in the 12th century; it was then rebuilt in the 1100s by a strange savior named Endo Morito, better known as Priest Mongaku. When he was 18, Mongaku became enamored of his cousin, who was married to another man. He pursued her despite her refusal to give in to him. Finally, she seemed to succumb to his pursuit and set midnight for him to come into the house to kill her husband. As planned, he decapitated the sleeping husband, only to discover too late that she had misled him and had directed him to her own bedroom in order to save her husband. Becoming a priest, he made a pilgrimage to the Nachi Waterfall to stand under its icy waters, which are claimed to be able to absolve one of sins. There, the deity Fudo is said to have appeared to save him and to redirect his life.

Thereafter, Mongaku took as his purpose the rebuilding of Jingo-ji, which had been destroyed by fire in 1149. Forcing his way into an audience with the former Emperor Go-Shirakawa to ask for aid in rebuilding the temple, he was banished to the Izu Peninsula for his insolence in breaching Imperial decorum. In Izu, he fell in with Minamoto-no-Yoritomo and encouraged him to unseat the Taira government. Through connections at court, Mongaku obtained an Imperial decree from Emperor Go-Shirakawa authorizing

Yoritomo to overthrow the Taira and so free the Emperor from Taira-no-Kiyomari's control. The eventual defeat of the Taira by the Minamoto forces led to the support Mongaku desired for the reconstruction of Jingo-ji. Later in life, Mongaku became involved in political intrigue once more and was engaged in an attempt to overthrow the pleasure-loving Emperor Go-Toba. The attempt failed, and Mongaku was exiled to the island of Sado, where he died a miserable death at age 80. His remains were later buried at Jingo-ji, and the temple retains a portrait of him.

In the 1190s, the noted sculptor Unkei came to Jingo-ji to repair some of its images, and in 1196 he carved copies of two of the deities and the eight demons at the Gango-ji in Nara for Jingo-ji, all the figures of which have since been lost. Two years later, he was at Jingo-ji again, where he created the Dainichi Nyorai, the Fudo-Myo-o and the Kongo Satta for the Kodo (Lecture Hall), copies again, this time of statues he had repaired at the To-ji Kodo. These images too are no longer extant.

PRESENT STRUCTURES AND GROUNDS

As indicated above, it is a 20 minute or more uphill walk to the entry gate of Jingo-ji. A refreshment area midway along the path provides relief, if needed. After paying the entry fee, you enter the first of the two levels of the temple grounds through the Ro-mon (Tower Gate) or by its other name, the Sakura-mon (Cherry Tree Gate), with its Nio on guard in the niche on either side of the gate opening. Among the buildings still in existence at Jingo-ji are the Hondo (Main Hall), Kodo (Lecture Hall), Daishi-do (Founder's Hall), Myo-o-do, Jizo-do, Godai-do (Five Wrathful Gods Hall), Bishamon-do, and the vermilion and green and white Taho-to Pagoda. Beyond the entry gate, the Shoin (open to the public only from June 1 to June 5 when the temple treasures are shown within this structure) is on the right, and beyond it is the small Hozo (Treasury). A Shinto Shrine is next on the right, and then a memorial to Wake-no-Kiyomaro, the founder of the temple in the 8th century. Bypassing the path to the upper level for the moment, four more buildings lie on the flat area to the west. These include the Myo-do ahead, and then to the left the Go-dai, which houses the Five Great Wrathful Gods, the Bishamon-do, and then the Daishi-do (Founder's Hall).

In the Myo-o-do is a seated six-arm Aizen-Myo-o by Koen from 1275 of painted wood, 16 inches (40 cm) tall. The Go-dai-do is dedicated to the Five Wrathful Gods as well as a number of other images which are considered masterpieces of Heian (late 800s) sculpture. There is a central image of Dainichi along with the five Myo-o, the wrathful counterparts of the more merciful Godai Kokuzo images in the Taho-to Pagoda. The large Bishamon-do, to the west of the Go-dai-do, holds the image of Bishamon-ten, the guardian of the north, one of the four Shi-tenno, the guardian kings who protect the Buddhist world and law. In the Daishi-do (Founder's Hall) is an image of Kukai, abbot of the temple in the 9th century, a wood image in relief which was created by Jokei and later painted in 1302. The Daishi-do is located on the site of Kukai's original small living quarters.

The Hondo (Main Hall), whose interior was painted vermilion, is up a broad flight of steep steps to the second level of the temple grounds. It has the image of Yakushi Nyorai in wood, which is 5.5 feet (1.7 m) tall and was carved from a single block of cypress wood in 802. This unpainted image, with the jewel of healing in his left hand, is in the new fleshy style of portraiture that came from China at

about the time that Priest Saicho returned from that country. The image is reputed to have come from the family temple of Wake-no-Kiyomaro and was brought here some time after Kiyomaro's death. (Kiyomaro was buried up the hill to the right of the Hondo.) Additional images of Jizo, Amida, Daikaku-ten and other deities flank the Yakushi image.

The temple pagoda, on a level slightly above the Hondo to the west, is a 1930s reconstruction. It represents the Lotus Sutra in Shingon mysticism. Within (not open to the public) are the Godai Kokuzo Bodhisattva (Five Wise and Merciful Bodhisattvas), five identical images each seated on a lotus, and each with a rod in his left hand and wearing a large gilt crown on his head. Dated 847, they are 3 feet (1 m) tall. The central image is that of Hokai Kokuzo with his right hand raised in the sermon-giving *mudra* that signifies deliverance from all suffering. These richly colored images represent wisdom, mercy and the highest knowledge of the Buddha Dainichi, as pictured in the Womb Mandala. The images were all created under the influence of Kukai's esoteric teachings, and each has a symbolic color: Hokai is white, Kongo is yellow, Hoko is blue, Renge is red and Goyu is a dark purple.

The Main Hall at Jingo-ji Temple, which houses the central image of Yakushi Nyorai, the god of healing.

The Shoro (temple bell) is to the right (east) of the Hondo on a slight rise. The bell is dated from 875 with an inscription by the noted calligrapher Fujiwara-no-Toshiyaki. This bell is one of the three noted bells of Japan, known for their beauty, calligraphic inscription and sonorous tone. The other two are at the Mii-dera (Ono-ji) on Lake Biwa and at the Byodo-in in Uji. The Jingo-ji bell is famed as "The Bell of the Three Best Scholars" since the foremost scholars of the time took part in composing the inscription placed upon it. A path leads down to the Jizo-in, which sits above a precipice with the Kiyo-taki River far below. Traditionally, one would write a prayer on a plate and then sail the plate over the edge of the cliff so that it would fall into the river. What began as a religious rite has become a mirthful enter-tainment, and plates are sold for visitors to fling, Frisbee-like, over the edge of the preci-pice, the writing of a prayer on the plate no longer being of primary importance. The hill on which Jingo-ji sits is covered with pine and maple trees, and the Jizo-in area is noted for the beauty of its autumn foliage.

Among the temple treasures, other than the images in specific halls, are the Womb and Diamond Mandala in gold and silver on a patterned purple silk background, 13 by 11 feet (4 by 3.3 m), from Kukai's time (831), the oldest extant such mandala. The Womb Mandala centers on the Buddha Dainichi and shows the hierarchical order of the universe, while the Diamond Mandala represents the manifestations of the wisdom of Dainichi. There is a painting of Sakyamuni in a red robe from the 12th century, the portraits of Fujiwara-no-Mitsuyoshi, an advisor of Go-Shirokawa; Taira-no-Shigemori, the son of Taira-no-Kiyomori and the general who burned the temples of Nara in 1182, for which he was ultimately executed by the monks of Nara; and Minamoto-no-Yoritomo, all three by Fujiwara-no-Takanobu (1142–1201). These portraits are in color on silk and are 55 inch-es (1.4 m) in height by 44 inches (1.1 m) in width. In addition, there is a 12th century hanging scroll of priest Mongaku. A land-scape painting on a screen, which was used in the Kancho annointment service, presents a bird's eye view of mountains. (The trea-sures of the Jingo-ji are shown in the Shoin just beyond the entry gateway from June 1 through June 5 from 9:00 a.m. to 4:00 p.m. Entry fee to the Shoin to see the treasures.)

③ KOZAN-JI TEMPLE

The villages of Takao, Makino-o and Togano-o are close together, the temple of Jingo-ji (at Takao) and Kozan-ji (at Togano-o) being on the west bank of the Kiyotaki River. These three towns are noted for the brilliant color of their forests in the autumn. It was thought in past centuries that the river separated the human from the divine worlds both at Takao and Togano-o. At Takao, the red bridge across the Kiyotaki River symbolized the passage from the hell of this world to the world of paradise that the temple symbolized.

Kozan-ji, a Shingon temple, is the other temple worth visiting in this mountainous realm. It is upstream from Jingo-ji (in Takao) on the west side of the Kiyotaki River in Togano-o.

HISTORY Kozan-ji was founded in 774 by Imperial decree, but little is known of the temple until Myoe Shonin appears on the scene. In its earliest years it was known as the Shingan-ji Togano-bo, and then in 814 it was renamed Togano-o-jumujim-in. In 1206, Myoe Shonin refounded the temple as a Kegon sect monastery and became its abbot. Abbot Myoe (1173–1232) obtained the patronage of the cloistered Emperor Go-Toba (1180–1239), who gave him land as well as a building from his Detached Palace, which became the still extant Sekesui-in. Myoe also obtained the support of influential noble families such as the Konoe, Takatsukasa and Saionji, and thus he was able to recon-struct the temple which had fallen into ruins. The Fujiwara clan also favored the temple and treated it as though it were one of their clan temples; their patronage was of inesti-mable value to the monastery.

Myoe was opposed to the growing empha-sis on the Nembutsu prayer and its concomi-tant reliance on Amida as the only means of salvation, for he saw a need for human effort in the attempt to reach enlightenment. He tried to return to the old Nara schools of thought, and thus he made the temple a Kegon sect seminary as the Nara temples had been. Within the Zendo-in, the residential quarters of the monastery, was the Jibutsu-do, the per-sonal devotional chapel of Myoe. His influence among his disciples was such that for 21 years after his death his study lamp was lit and food was placed in the study by the monks in his honor. An outstanding poet, Myoe emphasized art as a legitimate expression of worship. He is known as well for the cultivation of tea plants from seeds given to him by Priest Eisai, who had brought such seeds back from China. As a result, Togano-o became a center for tea production, as did other sites where Myoe sponsored the growing of tea plants and of tea drinking, the towns of Uji and Sonbongi in Fukasa in particular being so encouraged. (In recent years, funds have been raised to restore the Togano Tea Plantation west of the Ike-an tea house at Kozan-ji so as to create a model tea plantation.)

In 1547, the temple burned down, and it was not until 1636 that Abbots Eiben and Shuyu revived it, but the temple declined after the 1868 Meiji Restoration with the anti-Buddhist attitudes of the government. The gate and monks' dwellings were lost to fire in 1881; the buildings that escaped destruction in that conflagration were the Konso, the Sekisui-in of Abbot Myoe, the Kaisan-do (Founder's Hall) and the Hoko-daihinko storehouse. Other buildings in the precincts

today are of post-1894 construction. In 1959, a large fireproof storehouse was built close to the Kaisan-do, and two years later, in 1961, a large Sei Kannon image was placed next to the Kaisan-do.

PRESENT STRUCTURES AND GROUNDS

From the Japan Rail bus stop on the highway or the tour bus parking lot, a rough stone stairway leads to the Kozan-ji entrance on the hillside above the Kiyotaki River. (A gentler and wider path leads up from the highway, but its entry is avoided by buses since it provides no stopping place to disgorge passengers.) The temple buildings are on three levels on the mountainside, the Sekisui-in being on the first level to the right of the top of the stone steps from the valley below. The Kaisan-do is on a higher level up further stone steps, and the Kondo (Golden or Main Hall) is higher up the hillside path and steps. The Kondo can also be reached directly from the highway by the gentler path mentioned

The small gateway leading to Sekesui-in, situated on the first level of the Kozan-ji Temple.

previously, but the path ends in a long, wide, steep set of steps just before the Kondo.

Of the original buildings, only the Sekisui-in of Abbot Myoe's time remains. According to tradition, this was the study hall of the Emperor Go-Toba when it was part of his Detached Palace in the Kamo area in northern Kyoto. It is also thought to have been the hermitage of Abbot Myoe when it was brought to the temple. In its original state it was east of the Kondo but was relocated in 1889.

The early 13th century Sekisui-in is entered through a small gateway to the right of the stone steps from the valley below. Beyond the small courtyard, the ticket counter is at the entry to a building that precedes the Sekisui-in. This first building has a large south-facing *tatami* room that overlooks the narrow pond and garden that separates it from Sekisui-in, to which it is connected by a roofed corridor bridge. A veranda/corridor runs from the bridge along the eastern side of a long room whose only object is a free-standing image of Prince Shotoku at two years of age, his hands clasped in his first Buddhist prayer.

At the end of the room, a turn to the left brings one to the main portion of Sekisui-in, a tripartite room which looks out over the mountains and the valley to the south, a view

noted for its lovely autumn colors. This room is divided into three sections, the first section having an image in its rear portion, a work attributed to Tankei (?1173–1256). It is a slender Byakko-shin of white painted wood 41.5 inches (104 cm) tall, with his hands formed in a *mudra*, an elaborate crown on his head and a large white halo behind him. (Byakko-shin was an indigenous Shinto deity who was adopted by Kozan-ji as one its deities.) An exhibit case with a scroll drawing is against the front left wall.

The second or middle section has a *toko-noma*, and in it hangs a scroll (or its copy) of a portrait of Priest Myoe painted in the early 13th century by Enichibo Jonin. It shows him seated in meditation alone in a pine forest in a tree. Myoe was opposed to the insistence by adherents of Zen that meditation had to take place within a room, and he often meditated in nature on a natural seat–a rock or a tree stump. In color on paper, the painting is 57 inches (143 cm) high by 23 inches (58 cm) wide. An additional work attributed to Tankei is a statue of Zemmyo-shin in painted wood from about 1223. The image wears an elaborate metal headdress with pendants, and it is holding a casket that it supports by both hands. The image may at times be represented by a picture in a *zushi* (image case) rather than

The ancient cedar and maple trees at Kozan-ji viewed from the Seksui-in study hall.

he original object. As with Byakko-shin, it was
n indigenous Shinto *kami* who has become
deity associated with this Buddhist temple.

The third portion of the main room has an
exhibit case with copies of the noted "animal"
scrolls (the originals are now in the Tokyo
National Museum). The scrolls are the Choju
imbutsu-gigag (Picture Scrolls of Frolicking
Birds and Animals) by Priest Kakuyu (Toba-
Sojo), who lived from 1043 to 1140. They are
he most important treasures of the more
han 1,600 items belonging to the temple
Treasury. These scrolls use animals to carica-
ure the times. Men and priests are parodied
n the shape of monkeys, frogs and rabbits,
making fun of men's pretenses or their dis-
orted forms of devotion. Four such scrolls
are owned by the temple. Created in the early
13th century, these *makimono* are done in ink
on paper. The scrolls are 12.5 inches (31 cm)
tall by 404 inches (1,010 cm) long. Of the four
such scrolls of Kozan-ji, the first two were
done in the Heian period (794–1185) and the
last two in the Kamakura period (1185–1333).

The path from the Sekisui-in climbs the
hillside and passes additional non-public
temple buildings before coming to a level
section on the right that includes the large
modern concrete treasure storage building
and the Kaisan-do. The Kaisan-do (Founder's
Hall), with a pyramidal roof with a ball at its
apex, has a statue from 1253 of Myoe Shonin,
the temple's founder. A seated painted image
of wood, 33 inches (81 cm) tall, this handsome and realistic image holds a rosary in
both hands. The top of his right ear is missing, as was true in life since Myoe had cut
off the top of his ear as an act of penance
during a period of austerity. A large statue
of the Sei Kannon (1961), with the mystic
jewel in his left hand and with his right hand
raised in blessing, stands out of doors to the
east of the Kaisan-do.

The path continues to mount the hill beyond the level area of the Kaisan-do. It eventually leads to the Kondo (Golden or Main
Hall) in a grove of exceedingly tall cryptomeria trees. Along the way, a small roofed
shrine covers a flat stone "Buddha's footprint." Then a small protective vermilion
Shinto shrine is east of the Kondo. The roof
of the Kondo is encased in modern copper
in the form of a traditional thatched roof.
Within the Kondo is the Yakushi Nyorai
image created in the early years of the temple.
The Kondo originally had a triad of images,

since the Yakushi was attended by a Gakko
and a Nikko. However, in the anti-Buddhist
campaign of the Meiji government in the late
19th century, the Nikko was given to the
Tokyo National Museum. The Gakko went to
the Tokyo University Fine Arts Collection.

Other than the images and scrolls mentioned above, the temple has six scrolls of
an illustrated history of the Kegon sect of
Buddhism by Fujiwara-no-Nobuzane (1176–
1265). The temple also has a 13th century
carved deer, 20.5 inches (51 cm) by 18.5
inches (46 cm), made for Kozan-ji since, as
a Fujiwara clan-supported temple, the deer
was considered to be a messenger of the
gods. Priest Koben (1173–1232) had ordered
a replica of the Kasuga Shrine built at Kozan-
ji, but this deer in the *yosegi* (woodblock construction) technique with crystal eyes is all
that remains of his intention.

GETTING THERE

Atago Shrine can be reach by taking Kyoto
bus 72 to Kiyotaki and then the cable car from
there—or the path followed by pilgrims. The
shrine is open during daylight hours without
charge.

To go to Jingo-ji Temple, take bus 104 or
9 or the Japan Rail bus from Kyoto Station to
Takao. You can also take a bus from the Takao-
guchi station of the Keifuku electric railway to
Takao (3 miles/4.8 km). The temple is high on
a cliff on Mount Takao in the rugged mountain
range overlooking the Kiyotaki River. If you
arrive by car along the Arashiyama-Takano
Parkway, there is a long hill to descend on foot
from the parking lot to the river before making
the climb to the temple from the red bridge
and then up a very long flight of steps (about a
20 minute climb). If you take the bus to Takao,
you arrive at the river and then cross the red
bridge to begin the climb to Jingo-ji. The
temple is open from 9:00 to 4:00. Entry fee.

To arrive at Kozan-ji from Kyoto, take the
Japan Rail bus from Kyoto Station to the
Togano-o bus stop. (The temple is about 1 mile
(1.6 km) north of Jingo-ji and the bus can be
taken between the two temples.) The Kozan-ji
is a five minute walk uphill opposite the
Togano-o bus stop, and it is open from 9:00
a.m. to 4:00 p.m. Entry fee.

A bus at the foot of the hill will return you
to Kyoto.

Walking Tour 24

OHARA VILLAGE AREA
A Rebirth in Paradise Hall and an Empress's Retreat

Once you pass the Takaraga-ike station of the Keifuku Eizan rail line, you are headed into the more rural area north of Kyoto. Yet, even here the city is beginning to intrude

Nowadays, women dressed in traditional Ohara-style costunes are seldom seen.

on what was formerly farm land and small villages. A modern sports center at Yase has helped the local economy, but is symptomatic of the slow spread of urbanization to the northeast of Kyoto. Changing times have stripped the village of Yase of many of its younger people, and old customs and former ways of life are gradually fading. It is not too often, other than at holiday times, that the traditional woman's Ohara style of dress is seen at Yase or even in Ohara.

Ohara is still the goal of many Kyoto folk on weekends and holidays. Its valley continues to maintain the flavor of country life, and old farmhouses with their steep thatched roofs can still be seen. Of course, people do not come to Ohara primarily for rural life. The beauty of the temple gardens is a major attraction, as is the Jakko-in Nunnery with its recollections of the tragic story of Kenrei-mon-in, the one-time Empress whose life was tragically altered in her 29th year with the collapse of the Taira rule in 1185. Ohara and its sites are best visited at times other than weekends or national holidays since you must come by bus, and this popular area makes for long lines at either terminal of the bus route and crowded vehicles. Buses or cars are the only means of travel to this most pleasant rural retreat. Within Ohara, the path to the Sanzen-in and the temples about it are crowded with souvenir stands, food stalls and small restaurants, and, as with the buses, these places can often be quite crowded. Fortunately, Japanese visitors to Ohara (as elsewhere) are always polite and accommodating.

1 YASE VILLAGE
The village of Yase is the first of the two communities in this tour. It lies in a valley to the northeast of Kyoto at the base of the Mount Hiei sector of the Higashiyama

mountain range. Yase is generally thought of in connection with the cable car to Mount Hiei, but it has a history in its own right.

According to local legend, in the 600s the future Emperor Temmu was badly wounded as a result of political intrigues while he happened to be in the Yase area. With a poisoned arrow in his back, he was carried to Yase, and his life was saved by the medicinal waters of the town's hot springs. In the 1300s, Yase hid another emperor from an attacking shogun and, in gratitude, the town's people were exempted from taxes thereafter by every emperor through to the Emperor Meiji. In return, Yase provided the Imperial court with coal, transportation and a steady stream of labor. When the Imperial court was moved from Kyoto to Tokyo on the accession of the Emperor Meiji in 1868, the men of Yase carried him there in his palanquin 320 miles (512 km) in two weeks.

The people of Yase still provide some services for the Imperial household and, in return, the Imperial Household Agency quietly refunds their tax payments—in a modern era no one can be truly exempt from government taxation, and thus the Imperial Household Agency provides a private subsidy to the town's people. For 650 years the men of Yase, sturdy woodcutters, have been pall-bearers at the funeral of their emperors, ever since the Emperor Go-Daigo was buried in 1339. In 1927, they provided the pallbearers at the funeral of Emperor Taisho, the father of Emperor Showa (Hirohito). The streets of Tokyo had been laid with sand for the event, and the pallbearers transferred the heavy coffin on to and off the ox cart that carried the body from the palace to the cemetery.

At Hirohito's death, there were still those in the village who had participated in the 1927 cortege and reminisced about it. Times change, however. In 1989, the police served as pallbearers at the funeral of Emperor Hirohito, and the coffin moved in a modern funeral limousine. Tradition did continue in part: some of the young men of Yase served as honorary pallbearers and marched next to the coffin as it was carried on the shoulders of others. With fewer than 1,600 people in Yase, and most of them elderly, there were not enough young men who could carry on the 650-year-old Imperial funeral tradition had they been asked to do so.

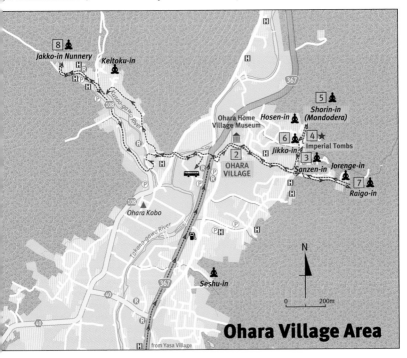

Ohara Village Area

Some of the old customs of the village remain, but some are gradually being lost. The women no longer carry heavy loads on their heads as was formerly their custom, nor is the traditional Ohara style of women's clothing regularly seen, where a narrow *obi* was worn, heads were covered with kerchiefs and white cotton cloth was worn over their arms and legs.

One traditional folk festival does continue. On October 10-11, the Shamemichi Odori, a traditional folk dance, is held in the evening at the Yase Akimoto Shrine. Then, men of the village dance in a circle in women's *kimono*, with lighted paper lanterns on their heads. Ten young women with flowered hats eventually join the men in these early folk dances. The paper lanterns themselves are delicate works of folk art. Since this is an outdoor affair, it is cancelled in the event of rain.

Today, Yase is thought of primarily as one of the locations from which one can reach Mount Hiei and the many temples of the Enryaku-ji complex (see Tour 21). On leaving the railway station at Yase Yuen, a left turn leads to the Sports Center while a right turn, over the bridge which crosses the river, and then left and up the driveway (steps and two ramps), brings you to the cable car station.

There is a magnificent view of the valley as the cable car rises above the maples and cryptomeria forest, with ridges and peaks, valleys and forests and distant villages below. The International Conference Center can be seen to the south and west. At the top of the mountain there is an amusement park, food and souvenir stands and a bus stop in the parking lot. The bus or path from this upper terminal can be taken (it is a good walk) to the temples of the Enryaku-ji on Mount Hiei.

2 OHARA VILLAGE

The bus to Yase continues on to its terminus in Ohara. A rural village beyond the urban reaches of Kyoto, Ohara has also been noted for its women and their characteristic attire as well as their custom of carrying heavy loads on their heads, all traditions that have virtually disappeared. The patterned *kimono* the women historically wore is said to have derived from that worn by the attendants to the former Empress Kenrei-mon-in (see Jakko-in) but this is an unlikely tale.

The village has a number of paths that lead to the attractive Sanzen-in, Raigo-in, Jikko-in, Shorin-in and Hosen-in Temples, as well as to the tombs of the Emperors Go-Toba (died 1239) and Juntoku (died 1242), all to the right

A traditional high-peaked thatched roof farmhouse in the rural village of Ohara.

of the main highway that runs through the village. The path to the Jakko-in and the tomb of the Empress Kenrei-mon-in is to the left of the main road. The area is most picturesque (and most crowded) in the autumn when the rice ricks are covered with their golden harvest, the persimmon trees have lost their leaves and their luscious fruit ripens on the branches, the shades of crimson and reds of the maples set the hillsides aglow, and the thatched roofed farmhouses and the drying rice straw on racks present a picture of "old" Japan. Ohara is at the end of the bus line from Kyoto. (Various buses can be taken to the village, but at the height of the autumn leaf color season it is well to start from the beginning of a line (such as at Kyoto Station or the Sanjo station terminal–a one hour ride) in order to get a seat. Be prepared for a long line and a wait for a very crowded bus back to Kyoto from Ohara. From Kyoto Station, take bus 17 or 18; from Sanjo-Keihan station bus depot, bus 5; from Kita-oji subway station, Kyoto bus 13, 14, or 15 or City bus 16.)

3 SANZEN-IN TEMPLE

The Sanzen-in Temple in Ohara is one of the primary sites that brings visitors to the area. A path to the right from the main highway (just follow the crowd) alongside a small stream takes you past rice fields and farmhouses, with their traditional high-peaked thatched roof (to the left off the main path) as well as a number of restaurants and souvenir shops–a path that is generally well trodden by visitors to the temple. (The Sanzen-in Temple is open from 8:30 a.m. to 4:00 p.m. from December through February and from 8:30 a.m. to 5:00 p.m. from March through November. Entry fee.)

For many centuries, the temples of Ohara were remote places, deep in a wooded valley, a good day's journey from Kyoto. Even today, despite the convenience of motor transport and the hordes of visitors attracted to this distant sector of Kyoto, Ohara and its temples still retain a quiet rural charm.

Among the many attractive temples in Kyoto that exert a strong appeal for worshippers and those who come for the beauty of buildings and gardens alone, the Sanzen-in remains a favorite. One of the finest of small temples created for the worship of Amida and the repetition of the Nembutsu ("Praise to Amida Buddha"), the most attractive time to visit it is in the fall (early November) when

its woodland setting becomes a kaleidoscope of colors. Sanzen-in, a Tendai sect temple, was founded by Saicho (Dengyo Daishi), in the early 800s. In 788, he had built a little temple on top of Mount Hiei with Yakushi Nyorai, the healing Buddha, as the main image. This was the beginning of what was in time to become the great Enryaku-ji Temple. Sent to China in 804 by order of the Emperor Kammu to study the Tendai branch of Buddhism, on his return Saicho brought these doctrines, based on the teachings of the Buddha in the Lotus Sutra, to form the Tendai sect of Buddhism in Japan. (Tendai doctrines derived from the sutras themselves as opposed to the previous Buddhism of Nara, which developed only from commentaries on the Lotus Sutra.)

Saicho is also said to have established Sanzen-in in the remote valley north of Kyoto and below Mount Hiei, and he is credited with carving the image of Yakushi Nyorai that is still in the temple. In 860, Priest Joun rebuilt the temple buildings at the order of Emperor Seiwa who, it is claimed, had the image of Yakushi Nyorai installed in the temple. In 985, at the request of Emperor Kazan, one of Saicho's successors at Enryaku-ji, Enchin (942–1017), created the Ojo-Gokuraku-in (Rebirth in Paradise Hall), which is the Honden (Main Hall) of Sanzen-in. Thus, the main image in the Hondo was Amida, carved by Enchin himself. From the 12th century, a prince of the Imperial family or a member of the aristocracy served as abbot of the temple until 1868, when the *monzek TAKAO i* tradition came to an end. Abbot Hoshin-no (1104–62), the second son of Emperor Horikawa, was the first Imperial abbot, and these well-to-do abbots brought many treasures to the temple, some of which are on display today.

The approach to Sanzen-in from the main road is via a long, slightly uphill path that follows a stream. Past the rice fields and traditional farmhouses, the restaurants and souvenir shops, the path eventually leads to a rather forbidding looking stone embankment reminiscent of the outer walls of a medieval Japanese castle. These 16 foot (4.8 m) high walls and the sturdy wooden doors of the gate mask the beauty that lies beyond them. The simile of a castle approach can be continued once inside the gate; the interior of the compound is hidden until the steps to the left are mounted and you finally clear the wall of greenery behind the stairway wall.

The Shinden of Sanzen-in Temple, viewed from the Yusei-en Garden with its carpet of moss.

KYAKU-DEN Within the walled grounds, proceed to the Kyaku-den (Reception Chamber or Guest Palace) after paying the entry fee. The Kyaku-den was built in 1587 from building materials of the old Imperial Palace, and it served as the residence for the abbot of the temple.

Beginning at the northwestern entrance, the first room that you will encounter is the Treasure Display Room. This six-mat room exhibits items of a royal nature that once belonged to the *monzeki* abbots. Many of the items formerly belonged to Abbot Hoshin-no (1104–62), the first princely abbot.

Second is a six-mat room with late 19th century painted *fusuma* of ducks by Michizuku Ryokusen. A late 16th century screen with an ornamental rim sits on a four-wheel lacquered cart. The screen has a gold ground, with flowers of red and purple against their green foliage in a huge vase. It is an example of the exuberance of art of the Momoyama period (1585–1615). The screen has a black lacquered frame with gold tassels hanging

on each side. The next room is really a hallway that leads from the west wing to the south wing of the Kyaku-den. A glass case on the west wall contains numerous *monzeki* articles, including letters of several emperors. The painted screens by Imao Keinen are of turtles in a pond filled with lotus plants.

Two eight-mat rooms face to the south and the Shuheki-en garden (Garden That Gathers Green) by Kanamori Sawa (1585–1656). Tall cryptomeria and maple trees shade the clipped azalea bushes and the moss-covered ground around the pond, which is composed in the form of the ideogram *shin* (heart). These is a Waiting Room and an adjacent Audience Chamber; the two rooms can be made into one chamber. The Waiting Room has painted *fusuma* by Suzuki Shonen, created at the beginning of the 20th century. The panels depict a worshipper praying to Shaka Nyorai, who is on top of a mountain, the large pine branches forming a dragon image from the manner in which they are shaped. The Audience Chamber contains a *konoma* with a painting of one of the Five ings of Light, the eight-arm Gundari Yashi yo-o. The *fusuma* depict a scene on the land Sea, the work of Kikuchi Hobun from e first decade of the 20th century.

A hallway in the southeast corner leads to n eight-mat room. It contains a portrait of riest Ennin of the Enryaku-ji Temple, *fusuma* y Takeuchi Seiko depicting a scene near akone on the three walls, and a *tokonoma* hich completes the rest of the north wall. he final hallway has a small altar and pic-ures of Priest Enshin, who built the Ojo-okuraku-in in 985, and Priest Ryogen 12–85), both of the Enryaku-ji. Past a public ilet, the walkway continues to the Shinden.

HINDEN The Shinden, together with the yaku-den, was originally constructed in 585 from materials from the Shishinden of e old Imperial Palace, but the present build-g is a 1926 reconstruction. It is basically three-room building with each of the end ooms subdivided in the middle.

This Butsu-den (Buddha Hall) has an mida Nyorai as its central image, with a uze Kannon from 1246 on the right and a

Fudo-myo-o on the left, the latter attributed to priest Enshin. The Kannon is dated from a letter that was found inside it (the sculpture comes apart at the neck). The central room has the Yakushi Nyorai image, which is said to have been created by Saicho in the early 800s. The altar enshrines the images of the first 58 abbots (including Saicho) of the tem-ple. A gilt Fudo is also held in this room, but it is not on view. The plaque above the altar reads Sanzen-in in the writing of Emperor Reigen (1654–1732). In this room the Empe-ror formerly held the Osen Boko ceremony on the 30th of May to honor all past emperors, to insure the safety of the realm, and to bring peace throughout the world. The end room is divided into two parts, the inner part having a raised platform (*jodan*) on which the Emperor sat while reading the sutras during the Osen Boko ceremony. The outer part has *fusuma* featuring a rainbow coursing across the pan-els, the work of Shimomura Kanzen commis-sioned by Sir Charles Eliot, a 19th century British ambassador to Japan and an authority on Japanese Buddhism.

YUSEI-EN The Yusei-en is the lovely garden on the left side as you proceed along the boardwalk between the Shinden and the Ojo Gokuraku-in. The garden has a carpet of moss under huge cryptomeria trees interspersed with maples, whose crimson colors in the autumn create an overwhelmingly beautiful scene. Clipped azaleas and stones border the Kudoko-ike (Charity Pond), alive with gold, yellow, red and white carp. The high branches of the trees form a canopy over this scene of calm beauty. The garden was first created in the 1100s by Shiba Hoshi and was named Pure Pleasure Garden: a more apt denomina-tion could not have been chosen. The present garden was redesigned by Kanamori Sawa in the 17th century. Between the Shinden and the Hondo are two Jizo images and a sprink-ling of stone lanterns of various shapes among the trees in the garden.

he glorious Yusei-en Garden in autumn colors.

HONDO The Hondo (Main Hall) was built by Eshin (Genshin) in 985 at the request of the Emperor Kazan, and was rebuilt in 1143 by priest Ryonin. In the 12th century, it was changed into the Ojo Gokuraku-in (Rebirth in Paradise Hall) by priest Shinnyobo, and later its outer shell was rebuilt in 1688. The three by four bay Hondo is 26 feet (8 m) in length by 30 feet (9 m) wide, and it is the oldest building in the Sanzen-in. The Hondo has an unusual ceiling in the shape of the bottom of a boat when seen from the interior, thereby providing the appropriate height for the Amida image and its aureole. The one-time sky blue ceiling was decorated with an Amida Raigo, a painting of the 25 Bodhisattvas who accompany Amida when he receives the soul of a recently dead person, as well as by *apsara* (heavenly maidens), to give the idea of Paradise. Mainly effaced by time, these paintings survive today only in framed fragments that hang about the hall. The walls were originally decorated with painted illustrations from the mandala of the Kongo-kai and the Taizo-kai (Diamond and Womb Mandalas) with some 3,000 figures, reputedly all done by Eshin. Traces of the many colored patterns of clouds and other designs still remain on the pillars of the hall.

The main images in the hall are unusual in that all three are seated or kneeling–normally the attendants of the Buddha are standing. The principal image is that of a gilded 7.5 foot (2.3 m) Amida, created by Eshin and made in the *yosegi-zukuri* technique (many fitted wood pieces). Behind the image is an aureole of golden clouds with 13 small Buddhas. To the right of Amida kneels Kannon, holding a lotus blossom on which to receive the souls of the newly deceased, while Seishi, on the left, also kneeling, has his hands raised in prayer for the newly received souls in Paradise. These two images are a little over 4 feet (1.2 m) tall and were created in 1148 (150 years after the Amida image); they are also in the *yosegi* (hollow block) technique. Before the images is black lacquered altar furniture, which was richly inlaid with mother-of-pearl.

TEMPLE GROUNDS Directly south of the Hondo is the original Main Gate, the Suzaku-mon, and the tiny Ro River. To the east are more of the temple gardens with a path to the east, which leads to a public toilet and a rest area. The image of the goddess Benten with her lute stands opposite, and to the north are the hydrangea gardens and eventually the small Ritsu River with a stone image of Amida. In the eastern portion of the grounds is an image of Avalokitesvara, the Buddha of Light, also called the Roshana Buddha (Birushana-butsu) or the Dainich Nyorai. The path to the south and west of the Hondo leads to a rest area and gift shop, and back to the Goten-mon

Gate through which the temple was originally entered. Two seasons of the year are noted for the variety the vegetation of the Sanzen-in can offer in heightening the attractiveness of the temple and its grounds. During June the hydrangeas in the eastern garden are in bloom, and then in November the leaves of the temple trees turn a golden yellow to orange to red. As a result, at these times the grounds are quite crowded with visitors.

④ IMPERIAL TOMBS

Four small temples and the tombs of two emperors are clustered about the Sanzen-in, three of the temples to the north and one to the east. (The temples are open from 9:00 a.m. to 5:00 p.m. Entry fee). From the exit of the Sanzen-in Temple, turn right and you will eventually reach the Imperial Tombs of the Emperors Go-Toba (1179–1239) and Juntoko (1197–1242), both of whom died in exile. The tombs are on the right side of the path, just before the Jikko-in on the left. They are typical of the "Imperial splendor" treatment given all such tombs at the end of the 19th century, the emperors buried there having been bureaucratically "identified" and the tombs having been "restored" in 1888 by the nationalistic Meiji period government.

⑤ SHORIN-IN TEMPLE AND SUBTEMPLES

The Shorin-in consists of the temple proper as well as several subtemples, notably the Jikko-in and the Hosen-in.

⑥ JIKKO-IN TEMPLE

The Jikko-in lies along the path to the right when you leave the Sanzen-in. Beyond the souvenir stands, the Imperial tombs lie on the right side of the main path while the Jikko-in is on the left. The temple can be recognized by the unusual trees in its garden, which are stripped of branches for most of their great height. Since the temple has a small staff, it may be necessary to strike the gong at the entrance to obtain the attention of the temple attendant. Beyond the small room with a *tokonoma* to the left of the entryway is a large room, open on two sides to permit a viewing of the garden. In this room, tea is served along with a Japanese sweet to all visitors, so that you may gladden both eye and palate. To the south of the room, a lovely hillside garden with a waterfall makes for a serene scene. To the west of the room, the rest of the temple garden can be viewed, a rivulet runing through the bushes, grasses about the temple's stroll garden, and the strangely trimmed trees rising from the garden like sentinels. In one corner of this quiet and delightful garden there is a small tea house. In the distance, beyond the garden, the hills on the other side of the valley can be seen.

SHORIN-IN Beyond the Jikko-in, continuing on the same path from the Sanzen-in, you come to the Shorin-in Temple at the end of the path. The Shorin-in, which backs to the narrow Ritsu River, has extensive grounds. It was here that Priest Honen debated the emphasis on the Nembutsu as the sole form of salvation with his opponents from the Tendai and other sects, and here he refuted the high-ranking priests of the other Buddhist schools of his day. On one occasion, during such a debate, the golden image of Amida in the temple was said to have begun to radiate a mysterious light to the surprise of the priests engaged in argument, thereby settling the issue over the doctrine in question.

The temple bell lies to the right of the path to the cypress bark roofed Hondo in the moss garden, and two large stone lanterns stand before the Hondo. Over the entry to the Hondo is a carved *ramma* (panel) with storks and trees and two people, a rather unusual decoration on the exterior of such a building. Within the main hall is a large golden Amida seated with his hands in the *mudra* of meditation; Tamon-ten (Bishamon-ten) stands on his left and Fudo to his right. Before the altar in front of the Amida is a Chinese raised lectern with steps leading up to its platform. To the right side of the altar is a life-sized Kannon in a case and a golden Monju on an elephant; a scroll depicting Honen is within a case behind the major image of the hall. To the left rear are three *zushi* with images as well.

HOSEN-IN The Hosen-in, also a subtemple of Shorin-in, is to the west of the path that ends at the Shorin-in. An additional small path leads downhill to the left, and the path to the Hosen-in leads off on the right to the temple. The entry fee includes a cup of *matcha* (thick green tea) and a bean cake. The Hosen-in has a noted 500-year-old pine tree, shaped like Mount Fuji, which is to the south of the temple building as you walk toward the entrance.

Hosen-in consists of a large room divided into three parts at its rear and with a veranda on its south and west sides. The three rear parts of this small temple are divided so that the left (west) portion is a *shoin*-style room with a *tokonoma*, *chigaidana* and desk. The middle portion has an altar with an Amida image, while the third section is used by the staff for the preparation of the tea that is offered to visitors on the building's veranda. The view from the veranda across the valley to the mountains on the far side is seen through a bamboo grove as well as through the branches of the huge Mount Fuji tree of which the temple is justifiably proud.

7 RAIGO-IN TEMPLE

Returning to the Sanzen-in, to the east and up the hillside path along the tiny Ro River is the Raigo-in temple. Raigo-in was begun by Priest Ryonin (1072–1132), the priest who rebuilt the Ojo Gokuraku-bo of Sanzen-in in 1143. After 23 years at Mount Hiei studying the doctrines of the Tendai sect, Ryonin moved to Ohara, where he started Raigo-in. Founder of the Yuzu-nembutsu-shu sect of Buddhism, he adopted the practice of repeating the Nembutsu 60,000 times a day. Under his guidance, the temple became a place to study the Buddhist chanting called *shomyo*.

The temple is entered through a small gate, and ahead lies a hall with the ticket booth before it. Built in June 1981 on the 850th anniversary of Ryonin's death, the hall holds a Buddhist scripture copying session each Sunday from 9:00 a.m. to noon. A set of short stairs on the right (rest rooms before the steps) leads to a higher level on which the main structures of the temple are located.

At the top of the steps, on the left, is the Shoro (Bell Tower) given by Fujiwara-no-Kokuketsu in the Muromachi period (1333–1568). The path beyond the Shoro leads to the Hondo (Main Hall), which was rebuilt in the late Muromachi period after its predecessor had been destroyed by fire. Three forms of the Buddha are reverenced in the Raigo-in Hondo: Yakushi Nyorai, Amida Nyorai and Shaka Nyorai. Over these images on the ceiling are Bodhisattvas; while lotuses decorate the area behind the three images. Scrolls to the right and left rear depict priests of importance to the sect and a Monju image seated on an elephant. In the front left side of the building is a painting of the Buddha at the moment he attained Nirvana.

Steps to the east of the Hondo lead to yet a higher level (since the temple is on a hillside), and here is the Chinju-do, the shrine to the Shinto god of the temple grounds. To the left (when facing the shrine) is the Jizo-do with 22 images of Jizo under a roof, these two structures being built during the Kamakura period (1185–1333). The path circles around the two buildings and leads to the Ritsu River where the Gobyo (Mausoleum), a small stone three-story pagoda was erected in Kamakura times. The path continues to the Nyorai-zo, constructed by Ryonin to hold the sutras. Finally, you come to the rear of the initial building, where the scriptures can be copied, and so to the exit though the gate by which you entered the grounds. To the east of the Raigo-in is the Waterfall of No Sound, a waterfall that is 164 feet (49 m) high but only 3.5 feet (1 m) wide.

8 JAKKO-IN NUNNERY

A return to the main highway, perhaps with a respite at one of the restaurants en route, will eventually bring you to the Jakko-in (Solitary Light) Nunnery, the most noted of the sites in this rural area. The small Jakko-in is about

The original Hondo of the Jakko-in, destroyed by fire in May 2000 but rebuilt in June 2005.

A long flight of stone steps leads to the Jakko-in.

a 20 minute walk to the west of the main road (to the left when facing away from Kyoto). You walk along a narrow path, past village houses to the temple, which is at the head of a stone stairway on the right. The temple is not difficult to find, since there is always a stream of visitors headed for the site. (The temple is open from 9:00 a.m. to 5:00 p.m. There is an entry fee that is collected at the head of the flight of stone steps to the temple.)

This Tendai Buddhist temple is said to have been created by Prince Shotoku in 594 and dedicated to his father, Emperor Yomei, the first emperor to become a Buddhist. These same sources also state that he appointed his nurse, Lady Tamatera (Shining Gem), as the first abbess. As with so many attributions to the founding of temples by Prince Shotoku, no verification can be offered. It is also claimed that the Prince carved the Jizo image in the temple and placed 60,000 small images of Jizo in the statue for the repose of his father's soul, another somewhat unlikely story. Even Kobo Daishi (Kukai), the 8th century Buddhist priest, is credited with the founding

Visitors are served tea at the Jakko-in.

of the temple some two centuries after Prince Shotoku.

The real importance of the temple, however, is connected with the tragedy of the Taira-Minamoto feud and war that ended in the sea battle off Dan-no-ura near Shimino-seki in 1185, in which the Taira were defeated. When it became obvious that the battle had been lost, the widow of Kiyomaro, the Taira leader, leaped into the sea with her 7-year-old grandson, Emperor Antoku, in her arms, preferring death for both of them over capture by the Minamoto. Her daughter, Tokoku-no-Taira (known as the Empress Kenrei-mon-in), the consort and widow of the Emperor Taka-kura, also preferring death to capture, jumped into the sea but was dragged by her hair back to safety by the Minamoto forces. Alone and abandoned, as the sole survivor of the Taira (who, if they had not previously been killed or drowned, were later executed), she took the tonsure at the Choraku-ji Temple in Kyoto and became a nun at 29. Destitute and forlorn, she finally found refuge in the Jakko-in in then faraway Ohara.

Kenrei-mon-in (1155–1213) spent the rest of her life, some 30 years, as a nun at the Jakko-in, praying before the image of Jizo in the temple for the souls of her family and of her son. Her living quarters next to the temple consisted of a cell, 10 feet (3 m) square with two small rooms. One was her sleeping room while the other held her shrine to the Buddha, and there she spent her time in prayer. Eventually, she became the head priestess of the Jakko-in, and on her death she was buried on the hillside to the east of the temple. The story of her tragic life is told in the *Heike Monogatari*–Heike being another name for the Taira.

The Jakko-in lies on a wooded hillside west of the village of Ohara, and it is reached by a long flight of stone steps. The present buildings were created in the Kamakura period (1185–1333) and have undergone restoration and alterations since that time. In 1603, Toyotomi Hideyori, the son of Hideyoshi, was responsible for one of the restorations at the request of his mother. The long flight of steps does not pass through the gateway at their top. Instead, a diversionary path to the left, near the head of the stairs, takes you past the

The garden of the Jakko-in features a pond in the shape of the character for "heart."

ticket booth and so into the grounds at a side gate near the temple bell.

The small Hondo (Main Hall), with its bark roof, looks like a miniature farmhouse. The building was burned down in May 2000 and reconstruction was completed in 2005. Its main image is a Jizo holding in his left hand the jewel which grants all wishes and his pilgrim's staff in his right hand. A new statue,

modeled after the original, was installed following the fire.

To the east (right) of the Hondo is the main garden of the temple. A waterfall descends in three stages from the hillside into a small pond in the form of the character *shin* (heart), a favorite design in Japanese gardens. About the pond are maples, pines, cherry trees, camellias and trimmed azaleas. A stream

by the 2000 fire and is slowly being restored.

Beyond the pond, toward the valley, is the four-room Shoin (Study) of a later time than that of the former Empress. Restored in the 19th century, the paintings on its sliding screens (*fusuma*) are painted by artists of that period. Among the treasures kept in the Shoin are a framed needlework design of the ideograms for the Nembutsu, ostensibly by Kenrei-mon-in using her hair as thread; the sandals worn by the former Emperor Go-Shirakawa on his visit to Kenrei-mon-in; and a piece of wood from one of the ships in the battle of Dan-no-ura. In the largest room of the Shoin (seven mats) is a *fusuma* painted with a view of the bay of Dan-no-ura. The original small hut in which Kenrei-mon-in lived stood on this site. On the hill below the Shoin is a tea house commissioned in 1929 by the Emperor Hirohito.

To the east of the stone steps leading up to the Jakko-in from the valley below is another series of such steps. These lead to the tomb of Kenrei-mon-in, a grave site that has been given the standard 19th century "Imperial tomb" treatment of stone *torii*, stone balustrades and austere simplicity. Kenrei-mon-in's life was filled with sorrow. The bitterness of her tragedy has fascinated the Japanese for almost 900 years, for in its essence it speaks of the transience of happiness and of life itself, a theme which suffuses Japanese life with its Buddhist undertones. Thus, it is little wonder that romantic tales have embroidered the accounts of her life and death. As with some saints of Japanese Buddhism, it is said that when Kenrei-mon-in died, music and a strange incense filled her deathbed room while purple clouds formed in the sky to the west—a certain sign that she was being received by Amida into his Western Paradise.

running from the pond through the garden and down the hillside creates an appropriately romantic and melancholy site in the shade of the overhanging trees. On the south side of the pond is a fenced area with the roots of a cherry tree, a tree about which former Emperor Go-Shirakawa composed a poem on his doleful visit to Kenrei-mon-in. Unfortunately, the garden was also damaged

GETTING THERE

Yase can be reached by train on the Yase line from the Demachi Yanagi rail terminal in northeast Kyoto to the Yase Yuen station (the last stop). Bus 17 or 18 from Kyoto Station or bus 5 from the Sanjo Keihan station bus depot will also bring you to Yase. To reach Ohara, take one of these same buses north to their northern terminus. At the end of a visit to Ohara, take one of the buses back to Kyoto from the bus stop at the main highway.

Walking Tour 25

CITY OF OTSU

Lake Biwa Sites: The Stone Mountain Temples, the Greatly Feared Mikoshi and an Art Museum in a Mountain Fastness

1 **Ishiyama-dera Temple** 石山寺
2 **Mii-dera Temple** 三井寺
3 **Hiyoshi Taisha Shrine** 日吉大社

Kyoto is bounded on its eastern side by the Higashiyama mountain range, which separates it from the city of Otsu and Lake Biwa to the east. According to tradition, Lake Biwa, the largest lake in Japan, was created in one night in 286 BC at the same time that Mount Fuji was born and rose to its present height. Geologists, however, believe that this large body of water was formed through land subsidence. The lake covers an area of 260 square miles (676 sq km) and is up to 315 feet (95 m) deep. It received its name from its shape, which resembles the form of a Chinese lute (*biwa.*) The Otsu area at the southern end of Lake Biwa was at times the home of the Imperial court from the 2nd to the 7th centuries, and it was an area of major importance since, after Kyoto became the capital, the Seta River, which flows south from Lake Biwa, was a primary defense line to protect the approaches to Kyoto in the various wars and uprisings that plagued Japan.

Above the shores of Lake Biwa and the Seta River, in the foothills of the mountain range, are a number of temples and shrines. Once the temples had to defend themselves against the monks of Mount Hiei, but that period of strife is long past, and today they pursue a more peaceful existence. At the Mii-dera (Onjo-ji) Temple, the buildings mount the side of the hills, as do the buildings of the Ishiyama-dera Temple to the south. Each of these temples is noted for a person whose fame remains, even though the individual was never a member of the temple

community–Lady Murasaki who is supposed to have written a portion of *The Tale of Genji* at the Ishiyama-dera Temple, and Ernest Fenellosa, the American art historian of Japan in the late 19th century, who is buried at the Homyo-in Temple just to the north of Mii-dera.

At the northern end of the Keihan Ishizaka railway line at Sakamoto (or from the Eizan station of the Japan Rail Kosei line) at the foot of the eastern side of Mount Hiei, the Hie (or Hiyoshi or Sanno) Shrine is also a place for quiet worship or visitation. It no longer is the scourge it once was when its deity was carried in its sacred *mikoshi* (palanquin) into Kyoto on the shoulders of armed monks from the Enryaku-ji Temple to force their demands on an unwilling emperor and court.

The Miho Museum, in its mountain fastness to the east of Lake Biwa, is the latest attraction to the area, and it is most easily reached by tour bus from Kyoto, as is described in the latter portion of this tour.

1 **ISHIYAMA-DERA TEMPLE**
We start with the Ishiyama-dera (Stony Mountain) Temple, a Shingon sect temple to the south of Otsu. It can be reached by the Keihan railway train from the east side of the Kamo River at Sanjo-dori in Kyoto to Hama Otsu, where you change to the Keihan Ishizaka line, which heads south to the Ishiyama-dera station, the last station of the line. The temple is 1.2 miles (2.3 km) beyond the station, a 10 minute walk south along the road that parallels the river. The entry to the temple grounds is to the right beyond a small park at the roadside. (The temple is open from 8:00 a.m. to 5:30 p.m. in summer and from 8:00 a.m. to 5:00 p.m. in winter. Entry fee. The Lady Murasaki mementos are shown

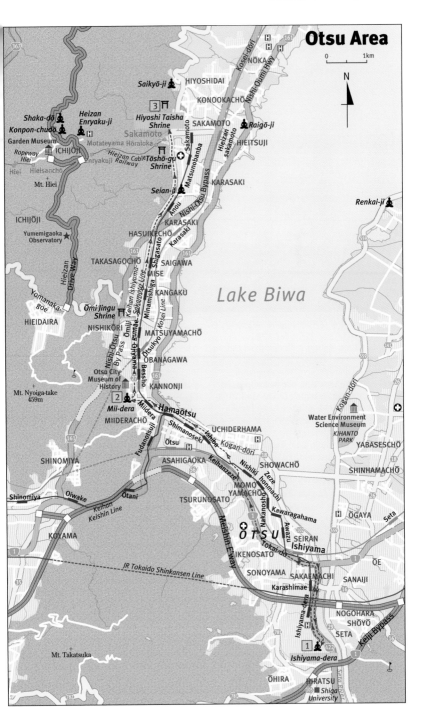

Otsu Area

0   1km

N

Lake Biwa

Saikyō-ji   HIYOSHIDAI

KONOOKACHŌ

3   Hiyoshi Taisha Shrine

Shaka-dō   Heizan Enryaku-ji

Konpon-chudō

Garden Museum

Ropeway Hiei   ICHIJŌJI

Motateyama Hōraika

Hieizan Cable

Enryakuji Railway

Hiei   Hieisanchō

Mt. Hiei

Sakamoto   SAKAMOTO

Tōshō-gū Shrine

Sakamoto   Matsunobanba

Raigō-ji

Hieizan sakamoto   HIEITSUJI

ICHIJŌJI

Yumemigaoka Observatory

Seian-ji

Anou

Nishi-Otsu Bypass

KARASAKI

Renkai-ji

HASUIKECHŌ

KARASAKI

TAKASAGOCHŌ

Shigasato

Karasaki

SAIGAWA

MISE

Hieizan Drive Way

Yomanaka-goe

Ōmi Jingu Shrine

HIEIDAIRA

NISHIKŌRI

Keihan Ishiyama-Sakamoto Line

Kōsei Line

Minamishiga

KANGAKU

MATSUYAMACHŌ

Ōtsukyo

OBANAGAWA

Ōmiji Ōhama

Nishi-Otsu By Pass

Otsu City Museum of History

Bessho

KANNONJI

Mt. Nyoiga-take 459m

2   Mii-dera

MIIDERACHŌ

Miidera

Fudanotsuji

Hamaōtsu

Shimanoseki

Ishiba

Kogan-dōri

UCHIDERHAMA

SHINOMIYA

Ōtsu

ASAHIGAOKA

Keihanzeze

Nishiki Kogan-dōri

Zeze honmachi

SHOWACHŌ

Water Environment Science Museum

KIHANTO PARK

YABASECHŌ

SHINHAMACHŌ

Shinomiya

Oiwake

Ōtani

Keihan Keishin Line

TSURUNOSATO

MOMO YAMACHŌ

Nakanoshō

Kawaragahama

ŌGAYA

Seta

KOYAMA

O T S U

SEIRAN

Ishiyama

ŌE

JR Tokaido Shinkansen Line

Tokai-dō

Meishin E-way

IKENOSATO

SONOYAMA

SAKAEMACHI

Karashimae

SANAIJI

Ishiyama-dera

NOGOHARA

SHŌYŌ

SETA

Keiji Bypass

Mt. Takatsuka

1   Ishiyama-dera

ŌHIRA   HIRATSU

Shiga University

A view of the city of Otsu, situated on the shores of Lake Biwa, by night.

from March 1st to June 30th and from August 1st to November 25th for an additional fee.)

Between Otsu and the Ishiyama-dera Temple, a few interesting places are passed en route. At Gichu-ji Temple, created in 1550, Matsuo Basho (1644–49), the famed *haiku* poet, is said to be buried. Gichu-ji is located in Zeze, 1.3 miles (2.1 km) from the Hama Otsu station, close to the Ishiba station. Near here, too, is the Baisen-kutzu Garden, which is noted for its miniature Japanese apricot trees, which are grown in pots and are trained in various shapes. After 3.7 miles (6 km) from Hama Otsu, the train passes the bridge at Seta.

The original bridge at Seta was famous in ancient Japanese history, for control of the bridge opened (or closed) the military route to Kyoto. An island in the river was connected with both banks by two bridges, and thus it has been the scene of numerous battles, and the bridges have been destroyed on various occasions to keep attacking troops from reaching Kyoto. At a later time, the Seta Bridge was memorialized as one of the classic views in Omi for the attractiveness of the "Evening Glow at Seta."

The Ishiyama-dera Temple was founded in 749 by priest Roben of the Todai-ji Temple in Nara at the command of the Emperor Shomu.

It was named for the Wollastonite rocks that crop up in the middle of the temple grounds. Roben had come to this spot and had built a small hermitage, and here he prayed to a Kannon image for a discovery of gold that would enable the Great Buddha image, which the Emperor had commissioned for Todai-ji, to be gilded. Miraculously, it seemed, gold was discovered in Mutsu Province, and thus the great bronze Buddha could be properly graced with a gilded coating. In gratitude to Kannon, Roben founded the present temple at the site of his tiny hermitage.

A later claim reports that Lady Murasaki wrote a portion of *The Tale of Genji* here one evening in 1004. This temple of the Toji school of Shingon Buddhism burned in 1078 and was rebuilt in 1096 by Minamoto-no-Yoritomo. Then, at the turn of the 17th century, part of the temple was rebuilt by Yodogimi, the wife of Toyotomi Hideyoshi.

Beyond the small park and the souvenir shops, the eastern gateway to Ishiyama-dera provides an entry to the temple grounds. The San-mon (Mountain Gate) or Todai-mon (Great East Gate) marks the entry to the temple precincts. It was built by order of Minamoto-no-Yoritomo in the 1200s, and its two Deva kings are the work of the noted sculptors Tankei and Unkei. The gate was repaired at the expense of Hideyoshi's wife at the beginning of the 17th century.

A row of maple trees, whose brilliant color is noted in the autumn, line the path that leads past subtemple buildings to the ticket booth. Ahead on the right, over a small stream, is the Purification Basin with its dragon, from whose mouth a stream of water issues. The natural stone of the hillside on which the temple is built creates a wall all along the north side of the stream.

At the end of the entry path, a long stairway on the right leads up to the levels on which the main buildings of the temple are situated. At the top of the steps is a courtyard with three small buildings on the right and a small service building on the left, and then the Hondo on a higher level on the left beyond the service building. Straight ahead are the impressive Wollastonite rocks, a metamorphosis of lime and granite which is quite rare and which gives the temple (Stony Temple) its name. Beyond the rocks, on a higher level, is the Taho-to Pagoda. At the head of the steps from the lower level, the first of the three small buildings on the right has a small golden Kannon at its center, with

two rows each of eight additional images on either side, for a total of 33 Kannon. (The Ishiyama-dera is the 13th of the 33 temples sacred to Kannon in the western provinces.)

The second building on the right is a memorial building capped with a pyramid-shaped roof with a flaming ball on its top, the Rennyo-do, built in honor of Rennyo Shonin, a descendent of Shinran Shonin, who was the founder of the Jodo Shinshu sect. Within the third building on the right, the Bishamon-do, is a life-sized image of Bishamon-ten with a small pagoda resting on the palm of his left hand.

HONDO Beyond the previously mentioned service building at the top of the steps from the lower level, a stairway leads up to the Hondo (Main Hall), which faces south, its veranda built on poles because of the drop in the ground. Created at the command of Minamoto-no-Yoritomo, it was later rebuilt by Yodogimi, Toyotomi Hideyoshi's wife. Thus, the exterior reflects the style of the Momoyama period of the late 16th century, while the interior bears the design of the Kamakura period (the 1300s) of Yoritomo's day.

The Hondo of Ishiyama-dera, its veranda supported by poles on the sloping stony ground.

The Hondo is a seven-bay building which holds a 16 foot (4.8 meter) tall Nyoirin Kannon image, said to have been created by Priest Roben in the 700s. Within the image is a smaller Kannon figure, 6 inches (15 cm) tall, which tradition claims belonged to Prince Shotoku in the early 600s. This smaller image is the true object of reverence, and it is said to be effective in bringing about good marriages, safe childbirth and good fortune. The image is only placed on view every 33 years. The case holding the larger Kannon image is in the center bay of the Hondo, while a scroll hangs on the rear wall on either side of the central bay. The many stickers that can be seen on the pillars of the Hondo are *senja fude*—"calling cards" which pilgrims have left as a reminder of their visit, a notice to the gods that they have been there.

GENJI-NO-MA To the rear and side of the Hondo (and attached to the Hondo) is the Genji-no-ma, the Hall of Genji, so-named since it was here that Murasaki Shikibu (975–1031) is said to have composed a portion of *The Tale of Genji* on the night of the full moon in August of the year 1004. A mannequin of the seated author with her scroll before her is in the room, and her ink slab and a sutra said to be in her handwriting are among the temple treasures. (A statue of Lady Murasaki has also been erected outside the temple at the riverside as another memorial to this famed author.)

TAHO-TO Up a flight of steps from the Hondo is the thatch-roofed two-story pagoda (Taho-to) in the shape of a stupa, one of the oldest of this type of pagoda in Japan. Its lower level is square in shape, while the upper level is round, a square roof covering each level. Within the pagoda is a painted Diamond and a Womb mandala and an image of the Dainichi Nyorai, indicative of the Shingon nature of worship here. The pagoda was built under Minamoto-no-Yoritomo in the early 1200s, and its pillar paintings of Buddhist deities enhance the interior of the pagoda. Adjacent is the Shoro, the temple bell tower.

TSUKIMI-TEI The Tsukimi-tei (Moon Viewing Pavilion), located on a level above the pagoda, is at a spot that has always been popular for the distant view of the lake, the river, the mountains and the moon. This

One of Mii-dera's two famous bells.

thatch-roofed pavilion sits at the edge of the cliff above the valley below, and it looks out over the Seta River and to Lake Biwa and Mount Hiei to the north. In the foreground of the view is the Seta Ohashi Bridge.

TREASURY The temple Treasury lies further up the hill, past a vermilion memorial building. The treasury is a modern ferro-concrete fireproof building, and its treasures include many images (Dainichi, Kannon, Miroku, Fudo, Jizo and small Shi-tenno) and scrolls as well as an *e-makemono* (scroll painting) that traces the history of the temple. In the center of the hall is a case with a picture scroll of *The Tale of Genji* screens decorated with scenes from the classic.

In a case, a seated Yuima image from the late 9th century, carved from a single block of wood, has an almost folk art quality to it. Yuima was a layman in the Buddha's time who was eloquent in debate and who argued theological points with the Bodhisattvas around Gautama. He pretended illness so as to mislead challengers into thinking they could best him in argument—thus the cap on his head such as was worn by invalids. On returning to the entry level of the temple, you pass the Daikoku-do hall at the foot of the last set of steps to the level of the lake; its central image case with its figure of Daikoku is not always open for viewing.

2 MII-DERA TEMPLE

Returning to the railway station to the north of Ishiyama-dera, take the train back to the Hama Otsu station, where a transfer to a train headed north will bring you to the Mii-dera (Onjo-ji), the Temple of Three Wells. Take the Keihan Ishizaka line train from Hama Otsu station to the north to the Mii-dera (Onjo-ji) station, the Mii-dera Temple being 1,600 feet (480 m) to the west of the station. Follow the path along the canal from Lake Biwa to the hillside, where a right turn will bring you to the temple's main gate; a left turn brings you to its southern entry. (The temple is open from 8:00 a.m. to 5:00 p.m. but is closed for the New Year holiday period. Entry fee.)

Mii-dera, a Tendai Jimon sect temple with strong ties to Shugendo (ascetic mountain priests), is the 14th of the 33 places sacred to Kannon. In ancient times, the area had a reputation as a spa, and it is claimed that the waters of its wells were used for bathing by Emperors Tenchi and Temmu as well as by Empress Jito in the mid to late 600s.

The temple was founded by Emperor Temmu in honor of Emperor Kobun in 674, and in the mid-800s, after it was restored by Chisho-Daishi (Enchin), it became a glorious temple that, at its height, could boast of 859 buildings. As the headquarters of the Tendai-Jimon sect of Buddhism, it was one of the most important Tendai temples in the Middle Ages. However, its rivalry with the original Tendai monastery of Enryaku-ji, from which it split, frequently led to attacks from the Enryaku-ji's monks, which led to the destruction of many edifices at Mii-dera. The worst time was the 12th century, when the temple was burned five to six times by its monastic opponents. Today, free from the fear of rampaging monks from Mount Hiei, the temple has 60 buildings dating from the 1690s.

The Mii-dera comprises three sections: the Hoku-in (north) numbers 12 buildings, as does the Chu-in (middle) group, while the Nan-in (southern) group has 19 buildings. The main gate is at the Hoku-in, in the northern section of the temple precincts. There is a Deva King on either side of the entryway, a gift from Tokugawa Ieyasu. Among the major buildings in the three sections of these northern grounds are the Kondo (Golden or Main Hall) and the Issaikyo-zo in the Hoku-in sector. The three-story pagoda in the Chu-in precinct and the Kannon-do in the Nan-in portion are also significant.

A woodblock print by Kuniyoshi of Bentei dragging the "Benkei Bell" to the top of Mount Hiei.

Fall foliage at Mii-dera Temple, a complex of 60 buildings at the foot of Mount Hiei in Otsu.

HOKU-IN The Kondo in the northern portion of the grounds is reached by a stairway up the hillside to the flat area on which the northern (Hoku-in) and middle (Chu-in) sections of the temple are situated. The Shoro (Belfry) with the temple bell is to the east of the Kondo. It was named one of "The "Eight Views of Omi," chosen by a prime minister in 1500 in imitation of the Chinese "Eight Views of Lake Tungting." The poet Basho memorialized the Shoro in his brief poem:

Though mists hide Omi's beauties seven,
Mii-dera's bell is heard in heaven.

The Kondo was rebuilt by Hideyoshi at the end of the 1500s in the then elaborate Momoyama style, and it holds a Miroku image attributed to Unkei. Next to the Kondo is the Akaiga, a roofed sacred spring-fed pool whose fame goes back to the 7th century (Mii-dera means Temple of Three Wells). In the adjacent Reisho-do, slightly to the west of the Kondo,

struck it, it would only tone "I want to return to Mii-dera." Thus, it is said, they threw it down the hill. It is thought that the two legends were a means of accounting for the scratches on the bell's surface.

To the north and west of the building housing the two bells is an enclosure in which peacocks are kept. Then, to the south of these is the Issaikyo-zo, the sutra repository building with its huge eight-sided revolving bookcase of many drawers which hold the sutras of the temple. The nearby Taishi Gobyo-sho has a hidden image of Shinran Zenshu, the founder of the temple.

CHU-IN Adjacent to the Issaikyo-zo to the south is the Chu-in or Middle Section of the temple, containing the three-story pagoda and two subtemples, the Kojo-in and the Kangeku-in, both noted for their handsome Shoin (Study). (These two subtemples are generally not open to the public, although application may be made to the temple office for permission to see them. The Kangeku-in Shoin has been reproduced in the Metropolitan Museum of Art in New York City.)

NAN-IN Continuing further to the south, a long stairway leads up the hill to the Nan-in, the southern part of Mii-dera. From the eminence of the Nan-in, there is a panoramic view over Lake Biwa to Otsu at the southern end of the lake, where the Seta River flows to the south to become the Uji River, as well as to the towns below the hillside and stretching to the north. The heights of the Mount Hiei range lie ahead, and the Biwako Ohashi, the 4,429 foot (1,329 m) long bridge across Lake Biwa between Katata, 11 miles (18 km) north of Otsu on the western shore, and Moriyama on the eastern shore, can be seen in the distance. Also in view is the island of Chikubu-shima and, on a clear day, the hills of Echizen in the far distance. Across the lake is the cone-shaped Mikami-yama, a reminder of the one-time volcanic nature of this region.

The most important building in the Nan-in is the Kannon-do (or Shoho-ji), dedicated to the Nyoirin Kannon and rebuilt in 1689. The Kannon image is a 10th century 1,000-arm Kannon in wood, which stands 6 feet (1.8 m) tall. There are many other images within the Kannon-do, including Fudo, the two-year-old Shotoku, Dainichi and the Emma King, among others. The Kannon-do is the 14th of the 33 sacred temples of the western

are the temple's two famous bells: the younger one of 1602 is noted for its sonorous tone, while the older is the Benkei Bell, famed for the legends of being removed to Mount Hiei. One account claims that Benkei carried the huge bell to the top of Mount Hiei, where he struck it all night long until the monks bribed him with a 5 foot (1.5 m) round pot of bean soup so he could eat his full and stop ringing the bell. Another legend states that the monks of Mount Hiei stole the bell and, when they provinces of Japan, and the charms obtained at this hall have made it a popular place for pilgrims. In front of the Kannon-do is a life-sized image of Jizo holding a baby, while two additional babies are at his feet. Many small images of Jizo have been left as offerings at the base of the statue by bereaved parents who have lost babies.

To the north of the Kannon-do is the Shoro (Belfry), which is to the west of the stairway to the Chu-in, and then a U-shaped building with many images of Kannon. Next to this latter building, to the east, is a stage-like structure. Across, on the southern side of the flat area on which these buildings are located, is a huge lotus fountain, and to its east is a covered structure holding *ema* (prayer plaques), a building to which a small refreshment stand is attached. A stairway on the southern end of this flat portion of the hill mounts further up the hillside for an even broader panoramic view of the lake and its attractive surroundings.

NEARBY SITES

In the Homyo-in, 1 mile (1.6 km) to the north of the Mii-dera Temple, is the tomb of Ernest Fenellosa (1853–1909), an American who came to Japan to teach at the Imperial University (now the University of Tokyo) in 1879. Fenellosa became interested in Japanese art at a time when the urge for Westernization was strong among the Japanese and when Japanese art was being ignored and even downgraded by many Japanese. He attempted successfully to get the Japanese to appreciate their artistic heritage, which otherwise could have been lost. (He and other Americans in Japan were responsible for many of the fine pieces of Japanese art that are at the Boston Museum of Fine Arts and elsewhere in Massachusetts.) In admiration of the teachings of the Buddha, Fenellosa became a Buddhist, and when he died in London his remains were brought to Japan for interment at Homyo-in.

Outside the Mii-dera Temple, examples of Otsu-e (Otsu pictures) are for sale. This folk art style was begun by Iwasa Matabei (1578–1650), a painter of the Tosa school, and additional examples can be seen in the Omi Local Crafts and Art Museum (Omi Kyofei Bijutsukan), which is on the grounds of Enman-in, a temple relocated here from Kyoto. It is to the right, 330 feet (100 m) north of the Nio-mon Gate to the Mii-dera

Temple. (The museum structure was once the kitchen of the Mii-dera. It is open from 9:00 a.m. to 5:00 p.m. and contains a number of Otsu-e folk paintings and local ceramics as well as a collection of paintings by Maruyama Okyo, 1733–95). The Enman-in Temple Shinden was a 1641 gift from the Imperial Palace and is an excellent example of the Momoyama style of architecture; its panels were painted by artists of the Kano school, including *fusuma* by Kano Eitoku (1543–90). The garden of the temple, supposedly by Soami (died 1525), is of particular note.

A minor recent shrine, the Omi Shrine, built in 1938, is 400 yards (365 m) west of the Omi-Jingumae station of the Keihan Ishizaka railway. It was built in memory of Emperor Tenchi (626–671), whose palace stood here in 667. A fine view of Lake Biwa

The Higashi Hon-gu is one of the two adjoining buildings at the Hiyoshi Taisha Shrine.

can be seen from the site, and the Rokokusai, or Water Clock Festival, is held here on June 10th each year.

To the north and east of the Omi Shrine (east of the Shiga station of the Kojoku rail line) by 1 mile (1.6 km) stood the noted Karasaki Pine made famous by Hiroshige Ando's (1797–1858) woodblock print, "Night Rain on Karasaki." The tree was the largest in Japan, standing over 90 feet (27 m) tall with a branch spread of 158 feet (32 m). Although dead, the tree has been retained. In its prime, it was said that the drops of rain falling on the lake through the branches of the tree made a sweet musical sound. A seedling of the original tree (New Pine Tree of Kara-saki) was planted 1.2 miles (2 km) north of Karasaki at Hie-tsuji along the lake, and itself is growing into a very large tree.

3 HIYOSHI TAISHA SHRINE

Further north along the lake is the Hiyoshi Taisha (Hie or Sanno Shrine), which was once one of the most feared shrines in Kyoto, even in temples and monasteries at a great distance from the ancient capital. Its warrior monks were some of the most ferocious and theologically unbending of opponents where Buddhist doctrine was concerned. Although those days of controversy and rampage are now over, the shrine itself is still of great interest.

The Hiyoshi Taisha Shrine is to the west of Lake Biwa at the foot of the eastern side of Mount Hiei at Sakamoto. The Keihan train can be taken to Hama Otsu from the Keihan-Sanjo rail terminal in Kyoto, and there transfer to the Keihan Ishizaka line headed north. Sakamoto is the terminus of the line. Walk west from the station toward the hills to the shrine, which is 1,000 feet (300 m) from the station. Alternatively, take a train from the Kyoto Station (the Japan Rail Kosei line) in 16 minutes to the Eizan station, and from there walk west to the shrine. This is the quickest approach, although it involves a little more of a walk from the station.

The shrine, which is open during daylight hours (entry fee), is older than the temples on Mount Hiei, and the original Hiyoshi Shrine held the seven spirits who protect Mount Hiei. The main deity is Oyamakui (Sanno or Mountain Kami), the Shinto deity whom Priest Saicho reverenced as protector of the Enryaku-ji Temple that he founded atop the mountain. Since, under Chinese geomancy, which formed the basis of aspects of Japanese beliefs, evil comes from the northeast (and Mount Hiei lay to the northeast of Kyoto), the court welcomed a temple on the heights of the mountain as a protection for the city. Thus, the Shinto deity who resided on the mountain naturally was regarded with the greatest of veneration, and Saicho, as the founder of the temple on the mountain, respected this deity highly. Although the Shinto deity was the spirit of the mountain, Saicho moved the shrine to the foot of the mountain at Sakamoto area where a series of shrines were built to Sanno and other Shinto spirits.

In time, the Chinese geomancy that the Japanese respected proved to be valid: evil did flow, as Chinese belief claimed, from the northeast. It flowed from the Enryaku-ji itself after the temple created a body of armed monks to fight for it. When the monks became involved in disputes with other Buddhist sects in Kyoto (and elsewhere), they would set out in a warlike manner. When they went on one of their periodic rampages, they would descend the mountain to Hiyoshi Shrine and carry one of the sacred *mikoshi* (palanquins), generally the one with the spirit of Sanno, into the city. Thus they could intimidate the city of Kyoto and even the Emperor and the court, since it was sacrilege to oppose the gods.

In one of their last great raids on Kyoto in 1536, the Enryaku-ji monks drove the Nichiren sect of Buddhism out of the city, destroying all 21 of their temples in Kyoto and killing 3,000 of their adherents. The days of the Enryaku-ji monks were soon to be numbered, however, for when Oda Nobunaga finally began to bring order to Japan after a hundred years of civil strife, he would brook

no opposition from *daimyo* or armed monks. In 1571, he determined to put an end to armed interference by the monks in Kyoto and elsewhere. His troops surrounded Mount Hiei and proceeded to destroy the 3,000 temple buildings on its heights, slaughtering the monks and anyone else on the mountain. Danger from the northeast was finally ended.

The Hiyoshi Taisha Shrine, which held the *mikoshi* used by the monks to intimidate the city, was also destroyed, its spirits no longer sacrosanct to a general who cared little for any religion. Thus, the present buildings date to no earlier than 1586, when Hideyoshi (Nobunaga's successor) permitted the rebuilding of some of the religious structures at the mountain. Built during the Momoyama period of the late 16th century, they reflect the ornate style of that era.

Hiyoshi Taisha Shrine is approached from the railway station up the main street and through a *torii* on the right at the shrine entrance, where the main street turns uphill to the south. The path from the *torii* leads to three stone bridges (Omiya Bridge, Hasi-rii Bridge and Ninomiya Bridge) over the small Omiya River, bridges donated by Toyotomi Hideyoshi. The shrine is in two parts: the Nishi Hon-gu (West Main Shrine) and the Higashi Hon-gu (East Main Shrine). The Nishi Hon-gu is approached up a slope and through a vermilion Sanno *torii* with a triangular top or gable peculiar to this shrine. A second gate, the two-story Ro-mon, is the entry to the vermilion-fenced main portion of the Western Shrine with its Heiden (Offertory/Stage), Haiden (Worship Hall) and Honden (Spirit Hall). Among the 21 *kami* (spirits) enshrined in this area, the most important shrines are the Usa and the Shirayama Shrines, along with their *mikoshi* (palanquins), which are stored here.

HIGASHI HON-GU AND NISHI HON-GU

The Higasghi Hon-gu (East Main Shrine) also has its Ro-mon, Heiden, Haiden and Honden, and among the most important shrines in this area are the Juga, San-no-miya and Ushino Shrines and their *mikoshi*. The layout of both the Nishi Hon-gu and the Higashi Hon-gu conform to the pattern of most Shinto shrines, and between them is a storage building, open to the public, which holds some of the more valuable *mikoshi*. Whereas the deer is the messenger of the gods at the Kasuga Shrine in Nara, the monkey is the messenger of the gods at Mount Hiei. Thus, caged monkeys can be found in the shrine area. In addition, the shrine has a white horse to please the gods.

TOSHU-GU SHRINE The Toshu-gu Shrine, founded in 1634 in honor of Shogun Tokugawa Ieyasu, lies a good distance to the south and west of the Nishi and Higashi Hon-gu. The main street from the railway station turns to the south (left) when it reaches the Hiyoshi Shrine. To reach the Toshu-gu Shrine, follow this street until you come on the right to a small stream with a path on its north bank, which leads up to the cable car to Mount Hiei. Crossing the stream to the left (south) just before the cable car station, the path leads to Tosho-gu, which was created in the ornate style of the main Tosho-gu Shrine in Nikko. No longer an important shrine, if time is limited, this memorial to Tokugawa Ieyasu can be omitted. One can continue this tour by taking the cable car up to the Enryaku-ji Temple (which is described in the next tour) or, if you have seen enough temples for one day, walk back to the rail station for a return trip to Kyoto.

MIHO MUSEUM In recent years the Miho Museum has been created in the Otsu area near Shigaraki-no-Sato in the mountain fastness where the Emperor Shomu built a palace in the early 700s and where the famed Shigaraki pottery has been made. The museum is but a portion of a complex that includes the religious headquarters of one of the "New Religions" of Japan which have developed in recent centuries. The Shinji Shumei-kai, a 1970 offshoot of Shinto, has offered the public a museum of note. Its major tenet is that spiritual fulfillment lies in an appreciation of nature and of art. To that end, it has not only created a public museum, but has its religious buildings (generally not open to the public) adjacent as the headquarters for its more than 300,000 adherents worldwide. The new religion was developed by Koyena Mihoko and is now under the charge of her daughter Hiroko. Koyena Mihoko is the heiress to the Toyobo textile firm, and having begun the Shinju Shumeikai movement in 1970 and having had its religious buildings built in the Shigaraki Mountains, in 1990 she commissioned the building of the Miho Museum which holds her personal art collection of over 2,000 objects, estimated to be in excess of up to a billion dollars in value.

The approach to the museum is through a stainless steel-lined tunnel that pierces the mountains of the area as it curves some 660 feet (200 m) within the roadway, bringing you to the exit on to a bridge which stretches 400 feet (120 m) over a gorge. At its end it leads to the museum's welcoming Moon Gate Entry. The building itself is clad in a beige-colored limestone from France. With its concern for nature, the religion has tried to create a heavenly retreat in the Shigaraki Mountains, and that concern is also evident in that the Miho Museum complex is 80 percent underground so as not to detract from the natural beauty of its environs. The museum, designed by I. M. Pei, is said to have cost $200 million, and its nearby religious buildings, with their Greek and Italian marble, are of inestimable value. The museum has two wings, one devoted to Japanese art as seen in its finest Buddhist images, its fine porcelain from local kilns, traditional screens and calligraphic and pictorial scrolls. The other wing is devoted to world art, which includes Assyrian reliefs carved in alabaster from the former palace at Nimrud in Persia, a Gandhara standing Buddha from Pakistan, frescoes from ancient Rome, a falcon-headed deity from Egypt in solid silver from c. 1290 BCE, a Syrian mosaic from the classical period, among other objects of note. (The museum can be reached most readily by the JTB Sunrise Tours, which pick up individuals from Kyoto hotels at 1:00 p.m., or by 13 minutes from the Japan Rail Kyoto station to the Ishiyama station and then a bus to the museum. The museum is generally closed from late December until March. There is a restaurant at the museum which serves vegetarian fare.)

GETTING THERE

Otsu and Lake Biwa are 17.5 miles (28 km) from Kyoto, and are reached by the Keihan railway from its street surface Sanjo Keihan terminal to Hama Otsu where trains can be changed to those of the Keihan Ishizaka line to Sakamoto in the north (for the Mii-dera Temple or for the Hie Shrine or the temples of Mount Hiei) and to Ishiyama-dera in the south. Alternatively, trains from Kyoto Central Station to the Eizan station can bring you to Sakamoto for the Hie Shrine or for Mount Hiei and the Enryaku-ji temples.

Walking Tour 26

ENRYAKU-JI TEMPLE COMPLEX

Enryaku-ji: The Temple at the Devil's Gate

1. **Monju-ro Gate** 文殊楼門
2. **Kompon-chu-do** 根本中堂
3. **Dai Kodo** 大講堂
4. **Kaidan-in** 戒壇院
5. **Shaka-do** 釈迦堂

While the Seta River, flowing out of Lake Biwa, could influence Kyoto history in times of combat, Mount Hiei to its northeast played a continuing part in the life of Kyoto in times of peace and of war. On its heights, Priest Saicho began a small monastery in the late 700s, a temple that was meant to protect the city and which brought the new Tendai form of Buddhist belief from China to Japan. As the highest of the peaks of the Higashi-yama range, 2,789 feet (930 m) to the north-east of the new capital, it served, under the doctrines of Chinese geomancy which the Japanese court observed, as a protector to the city against those forces of evil that flow from the northeast.

Unfortunately, in time the monasteries on the mountaintop became the forces of evil themselves, as armed monks raced down from their hill to kill their theological opponents and burn their temples. They even presumed to hold the city and court hostage to their demands when they swept into town

A view of Kyoto and the western mountains from Mount Hiei.

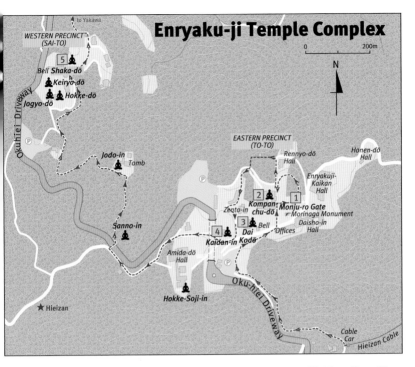

Enryaku-ji Temple Complex

WESTERN PRECINCT
(SAI-TO)

0   200m

N

to Yakawa

Bell Shaka-dō

Keiryo-dō

Hokke-dō

Jogyo-dō

Okuhiei Driveway

P

EASTERN PRECINCT
(TO-TO)

Jodo-in

Tomb

Rennyo-dō
Hall

Honen-dō
Hall

Enryakuji-
Kaikan
Hall

P

2

Kompan
chu-dō

1

Zento-in   Monju-ro Gate

Morinaga Monument

Sanno-in

3 Bell

Daisho-in
Hall

4   Dai

Kaidan-in Kodō   Offices

Amida-dō
Hall

P

Oku-hiei Driveway

Hokke-Soji-in

★ Hieizan

Cable
Car

Hieizan Cable

bearing the sacred palanquin of the Shinto Hiyoshi Shrine, which they controlled. Finally, in 1571, Oda Nobunaga, fed up with clerical intimidation, gave the temples and monks of Mount Hiei the *coup de grace*, destroying all 3,000 temple buildings and massacring all the monks, women and children on the mountain. Happily, the rebuilt temples of Mount Hiei today exist as a quiet and peaceful monastic complex, for the temples now concentrate on prayer and worship, their original purpose. Mount Hiei and its temples and shrines can now be enjoyed for their beauty, their solemnity and the peacefulness that their founder Saicho had as his goal when he established the monastery 1,200 years ago. A full day can be spent exploring the many temples of the Enryaku-ji, but a break from seeing so many temples is available opposite the Kompon-chu-do, just beyond the entrance to the Enryaku-ji grounds from the Sakamoto cable car that rises from the Lake Biwa side, where a light lunch may be obtained.

The temples of the Enryaku-ji complex on Mount Hiei are open from 8:30 a.m. to 4:30 p.m. from spring to autumn and from 9:00 a.m. to 4:00 p.m. in winter. It takes at least an hour to get to Mount Hiei from Kyoto. The various methods by which you can get there are described at the end of the tour. The temples in the Sai-to and Yokawa areas close at 4:00 p.m. during most of the year and at 3:30 in the winter. Once on the top of Mount Hiei, the temples are in three sectors, the third one some 3 miles (4.8 km) from the second.

Enryaku-ji, along with Koya-san, is one of the two most important monasteries in Japan. The Enryaku-ji represents the Tendai form of Buddhism of Priest Saicho, while Koya-san is of the Shingon sect that Kobo Daishi (Kukai) brought to Japan. The three major Buddhas revered at Enryaku-ji are Yakushi, Shaka and Amida, all manifestations of the eternal Buddha.

HISTORY Many of the most important priests of Japanese Buddhist history have studied and been ordained at Enryaku-ji: Enchin (814–91), founder of the Jimon sect of Tendai Buddhism; Kuya (903–72) of the Kuya school of Tendai Buddhism; Honen (1133–1212), founder of the Jodo (Pure Land) sect; Shinran (1174–1268), founder of the Jodo Shinshu (New Pure Land) sect; Eisai (1141–1215), founder of the Rinzai Zen sect; Dogen (1200–53), founder of the Soto Zen sect; Ippen (1239–89), founder of the Ji sect of Pure Land Buddhism; and Nichiren (1222–82), founder of the Nichiren (Hokke) sect. Thus, Enryaku-ji served as the mother temple to a variety of approaches to Buddhist truths. Here also at Enryaku-ji, Saicho, the founder of the temple and of the Tendai branch of Buddhism in Japan, is buried.

The first Buddhist temple atop Mount Hiei (Wisdom Mountain) was begun before Kyoto had been settled. Originally there was a small Shinto shrine on Mount Hiei to the *kami* (god) of the mountain, but, because of priest Saicho (767–822), the mountain eventually became the site of one of the most important and largest Buddhist temple complexes in Japan. Saicho had studied Buddhist doctrine in Nara and had been ordained there in the Kaidan-in of the Todai-ji Temple. Not totally happy with the exclusive nature of the teachings of the Buddhist sects in Nara, teachings which never reached out to the mass of the people, he retreated to a rustic hermitage on top of Mount Hiei in 785 when he was 18, and there he built a hut in which to study the Hosso, Kegon and Chinese Tendai doctrines and to meditate upon Buddhist teachings. Buddhism in Nara was concerned with and directed toward the ruling classes of the country, and it offered little to the rest of the people of Japan, who still primarily followed their Shinto beliefs. Saicho felt that Buddhism offered hope to all people, and his eventual study of Tendai doctrines in China was to confirm him in his new approach toward Buddhism.

In 788, with a few disciples, he began the construction of the first building of a new temple on Hiei, founding the Kompon-chu-do (Most Fundamental Central Hall) of what would in time become the Enryaku-ji. Here, he installed as the chief image a statue of Yakushi Nyorai, which he had carved from a fallen tree on the mountain top. His temple, as with those at Koya-san at the same time, was merely a collection of crude buildings for monks who led hermit-like lives of study and prayer, rather than majestic structures to awe worshippers such as might flock to lowland temples. He enjoined a life of cheerful poverty with his fellow monks.

Six years later, fortuitously for Saicho, Emperor Kammu decided to move his capital to a new location, and Heian-kyo (Kyoto) came into being below Mount Hiei to the southwest of the new temple. The city was laid out according to Chinese geomancy, with hills to the west, to the north and to the east. However, Chinese doctrine claimed that evil always came from the northeast, and thus the establishment of a new temple on top of Mount Hiei, northeast of Heian-kyo, offered a protection to the city against evil forces. On September 3, 794, the Emperor and the chief

Enryaku-ji Temple, spread over the ridges of Mount Hiei, is divided into three sections.

bbots of the Seven Great Temples of Nara came to a service at the new small Kompon-chu-do, a recognition by the Emperor (and by the reluctant priests of the Nara temples, who cared neither for new temples competing for royal favor nor for new religious ideas) of the importance of this fledgling temple.

The Emperor became a patron of Saicho, and in 804 he sent Saicho to China to further his studies of Buddhism at its source. At Mount T'ien-tai in China, Saicho studied Tendai and esoteric Buddhism and also became acquainted with a master of Zen meditation. On his return to Japan the following year, the Emperor, on January 26, 806, permitted Saicho to found the new (to Japan) Tendai sect of Buddhism on Mount Hiei. Here, Saicho established the system of a 12 year "learning and practice" program for priests of his sect. Saicho's desire to ordain priests at his temple might have been granted by the Emperor if Kammu had lived longer, but in the same year of 806 in which he gave Saicho permission to start the new Tendai sect, the Emperor died. On his death bed, Kammu was administered the new rite of Kancho by Saicho, a sprinkling of water on the head of the communicant normally given to monks as a form of ordination.

Saicho's wish to set up an ordination platform on Mount Hiei met with the firm opposition of the older sects in Nara, which had the only ordination platforms in Japan, and it was not until 828, six years after Saicho's death, that Emperor Saga finally granted the temple the right to ordain priests. With Imperial acceptance, the temple grew, and Gishin, the second head abbot (*zasu*), erected the Dai Kodo (Large Lecture Hall) where young monks could study. Then, with Imperial permission he created the Kaidan-in (Ordination Platform) where candidates for the priesthood could be ordained. The temple now officially became the Enryaku-ji, the official title of the era in which the name was granted. In 866, Emperor Seiwa named Saicho Dengyo Daishi (Great Teacher of the True Religion), the first priest to bear the title Daishi (Great Teacher), an appropriate title since he had instituted a course of study for Buddhist monks that took 12 years to complete.

No women were permitted on Mount Hiei, a prohibition to eliminate one form of temptation for celibate monks. Neither were constables permitted on the mountain, since the temples were considered a sanctuary of holiness. Unfortunately, this last prohibition encouraged the idle and fugitives from law to congregate on the mountain or to join the monasteries. The 36th bishop in the mid-11th century determined to clean house, and he organized his own force of military monks to bring order to Mount Hiei and to rid it of undesirables. Unfortunately, he had to recruit among the more aggressive elements in the temples for his warrior monks, and they in turn became a nucleus of monks who considered themselves above all law and order. Their combative nature came to the fore when a split within Enryaku-ji, which had occurred in the 10th century, led to the creation of a new Tendai monastery at the foot of the mountain at Mii-dera (Onjo-ji) near Otsu City (see Tour 20). Strife broke out between the armed monks of the two temples and, in a 250-year period, the monks of Mount Hiei burned down Mii-dera nine times.

For 500 years, the monks of the temple were the most powerful army in Japan. In addition, as an established sect, the monks of Tendai became as rigidly opposed to other new forms of Buddhism as had the established Nara temples been opposed to Tendai in Saicho's day. The warrior monks battled the temples in Nara and on Mount Koya as well as those in Kyoto, and, when they felt offended, they marched into Kyoto with the sacred palanquin of the Hiyoshi (Hie) Shrine to force compliance with their wishes, since it was sacrilegious to defy the deity of the Hie Shrine. They even threatened the Imperial Palace. Chinese geomancy had proved true in an unexpected way: evil did flow from the northeast into Kyoto, from Enryaku-ji. In desperation, Emperor Shirakawa (1056–1129) lamented that as Emperor there were three things he could not control: the waters of the Kamo River (which flooded the city), the fall of the dice in games of chance and the monks of Mount Hiei.

By 1571 Oda Nobunaga had brought to an end much of the military chaos that had afflicted the nation for over 100 years. A not very religious man, he would not brook the threat that the Enryaku-ji monks posed to the stability and order he was striving to bring to the country. Fed up with the monastic rampaging, he led his forces against Mount Hiei, leaving Enryaku-ji a devastated ruin. The temple of Mii-dera, naturally, sided with Nobunaga.

Nobunaga's assassination brought Toyotomi Hideyoshi to the fore as the civil ruler of Japan, and he permitted Enryaku-ji to be rebuilt, restricting its temple buildings to 125 in number, just a quarter of their previous number. Mii-dera felt his anger, and one of its buildings (the Hondo), which survived Hideyoshi's attack upon the armed monastic forces and the devastation of the temple, was given to the rebuilding of the Enryaku-ji. The days of warrior monks had come to an end, and the later rigid secular control over all aspects of society which ensued with the rule of the Tokugawa (after Hideyoshi's death) restricted Buddhist temples solely to religious purposes. A later Tokugawa Shogun, Iemitsu (Shogun from 1624 to 1643), gave new support to Enryaku-ji, and the rebuilding of the temple which began under his patronage resulted in many of the structures still extant. Today, there are some 130 or so buildings on Mount Hiei, a far smaller number than existed before Nobunaga's troops marched on Enryaku-ji in 1571.

SITE OVERVIEW Enryaku-ji is spread over the ridges of the Mount Hiei range and is divided into three sections: To-to (Eastern Pagoda), Sai-to (Western Pagoda) and the northern Yokawa group. The major buildings of the temple are in the Eastern Sector at an altitude of 2,230 feet (670 m). The most important buildings in these three areas are:
To-to (Eastern Pagoda Sector) The headquarters of the Tendai sect and the more important of the three sectors, comprising:
Enryaku-ji Kaikan (Administrative Offices)
Kompon-chu-do (Main worship hall)
Kaidan-in (Ordination Hall)
Dai Kodo (Lecture Hall for study and discussion by young monks)
Amida-do (Where masses for the dead are celebrated)
Hokke-Soji-in (Two-story pagoda)
Jodo-in (Amida Hall)
Sai-to (Western Pagoda Sector)
Shaka-do (Central Hall of the Sai-to)
Hokke-do (Lotus Sutra Hall)
Jogyo-do (Endless Walking Hall)
Yokawa (Northern Sector)
Yokawa-chu-do (Central Hall of Yokawa)
Shiki-do (Four Season Hall)
Enshin-in (Memorial Hall to Priest Enshin)
Hiho-kan (Treasury).

TO-TO (Eastern Sector)

If you come to Mount Hiei by either the Keihan or the Japan Rail train from Sakamoto, the path from the Eizanchudo station at the top of the cable car line leads to the eastern portion of the Enryaku-ji temples. Following the path, you first come to an image of Fudo on the left, and then, as the path widens into the plaza, there is the ticket booth for the entry fee to the grounds. A building for refreshments, modern rest rooms and the temple offices lie ahead on the right. Across from the offices is the Monju-ro. If one comes by bus, a path leads from the bus stop into the eastern section between the Amida-do and the Dai Kodo. The description here, for the sake of moving from east to west, starts at the upper terminal of the cable car from Sakamoto.

To the south of the Eizanchudo station, a path leads back down a portion of the mountain to the Mudo-ji-dani (Mudo-ji Valley or the Valley of the Motionless Temple), 1 mile (1.6 km) south of the station. There are a few buildings here, of which the most important is the Myo-o-do, with its life-sized image of Fudo-myo-o, which was carved by Soo Kasho (831–918). It was here that the Buddhist training practice of Sennichi-Kaihogy began under Soo Kasho, a practice which consists of walking the mountain and praying by repeating the mystical words of the sutras at each temple. The monks following this practice walk at least 20 miles (32 km) a day for 100 days. Those who wish to complete the full term do this walking prayer recitation for 1,000 days over a seven-year period, some 2,500 miles (4,000 km) through the mountains and the city of Kyoto. It is the most austere of the ascetic practices of Mount Hiei (The other temple buildings in this area include the Benten-do, Homan-in, Daijo-in and Gyo-kusho-in.)

⬚1 MONJU-RO GATE

Returning to the plaza at the end of the path from the Eizanchudo station to the To-to sector, the Monju-ro Gate is the first of the important units in this portion of the monastery. The Monju-ro was originally built in 866 by Ennin (Jikaku Daishi) in conjunction with holy stones he had brought from Mount Godai (Wu-t'ai) in China, stones which are under the Monju-ro. (Ennin was the third head abbot of the temple and a pupil of Saicho.) In former times, the Monju-ro served as the entry gate to Enryaku-ji and to all of its temples after visitors or pilgrims had climbed the 1.2 miles (2 km) from Sakamoto in the valley. Rebuilt in 1642 after a Chinese style, it was once one of four related buildings for separate "religious practices" of an austere nature, and it stands on a rise reached by a stone stairway on its east or west sides. The second floor of this gateway is ascended by a ladder on either side within the structure. In this upper level is an image of a golden Monju on a lion with a gold aureole behind the image. Monju is here protected by the four Shi-tenno guardians. At one point, prayers were said here in times of national emergency. (Down the path which pilgrims once climbed is the modern Enryaku-ji Kaikan, which serves as an administrative and religious center for the temple.)

2 KOMPON-CHU-DO

Perhaps the most important and historic building at the Enryaku-ji is the Kompon-chu-do (Fundamental Central Hall), which was originally named the Ichijo Shikan-in (One Vehicle Meditation Hall) by Saicho. It is below and to the west of the Monju-ro and across from the temple purification fountain, which is in the form of a dragon. When Saicho retreated to Mount Hiei and built his rustic hermitage on the mountaintop, his small hut for study and meditation stood where the monumental Kompon-chu-do now stands. In 788, he and a few disciples began the first Kompon-chu-do here, a 30 foot (9 m) by 15.5 foot (4.6 m) structure, and in its center he placed the image of Yakushi Nyorai that he had carved. This was the only building of the monastery at that time.

With the growth of the complex in the coming years, the original building proved inadequate, and through need or necessity (fire was a continuous plague), it was enlarged in 880 and 940 and again in 980. It was rebuilt in 1642 with the assistance of Tokugawa Iemitsu, almost 70 years after its destruction by Nobunaga, and this 123 foot (37 m) long by 78 foot (23 m) deep by 32 foot (10 meter) tall building still stands. The curved gable over the entry and the black and gold decoration under the eaves reflect the extravagant tastes of the century which followed the destruction of the simpler Kompon-chu-do of earlier times. In its more elegant reconstruction, it is a far cry from the rustic and simple retreat which Saicho created in the early 800s and where he enjoined "cheerful poverty" on his monks.

The temple is entered after traversing the corridor that surrounds the courtyard in front of the building itself, two huge bamboo planters and two tall bronze lanterns occupying the center of this forecourt. Tendai had an esoteric note to it from its beginnings, a factor which was enhanced by later abbots, and an air of the mystic infuses the present Kompon-chu-do.

Its interior is on three levels: the worshipper and the central altar area are at the same height, but between them is a sunken section for the priests. At the time of worship services, the worshippers and the altar, with its figures of divine beings, are illuminated. The priests in the lower portion are in a darkened area, symbolizing the gap between man and the Buddha and his paradise. Here, in the darkness of this life, the priests pray for mankind so as to bring the secular (worshippers) and the divine (Yakushi and his Eastern Paradise) together. Flowers on a gold ground decorate the squares of the coffered ceiling in the interior of the building, and a transom carved with golden *apsara* (heavenly angels) separates the inner area from the fore part of the interior of the hall. The altar, with its golden images against the blackness of the darkened building interior, represents the glories of the paradise to come. In the center is the image of Yakushi Nyorai, the Healing Buddha and the Buddha of the Eastern Paradise. (The image is a copy of Saicho's carved figure of Yakushi, which is kept within the altar.) On either side stand Nikko and Gakko, symbols of the sun and the moon, while images of Saicho, the young Prince Shotoku, and the 12 Divine Generals enhance the sides of the altar area. At the four corners are the Shi-tenno protecting Yakushi and the Buddha world against evil.

Before the altar hang three brass lanterns with the 16-petal chrysanthemum on their faces. These lanterns contain the everlasting Dharma light of Buddhist truth, and they burn as symbols of world peace and compassion, flames which Saicho lit in 788 and which will not be extinguished until Maitreya, the Buddha of the Future, appears. (According to temple tradition, the light of the original lamps was never extinguished in the 1571 destruction of the temple since the lamps were safely hidden away.) It is interesting to note that the 16-petal chrysanthemum on the lanterns and elsewhere has been the symbol of the Imperial house, but temple tradition claims that Emperor Kammu obtained this Imperial emblem from Saicho, who first used it as a symbol in his temple.

The Dai Kodo is a large lecture and discussion hall for both trainee and learned monks.

③ DAI KODO

The path to the south from the Kompon-chu-do leads to steps up to the previously mentioned plaza area and then to the west to the temple bell and then to the Dai Kodo (Great Lecture Hall), a structure originally built by the first head abbot after Saicho's death. The building serves as a place for study and doctrinal debate for young monks, for lectures on the sutras (Buddhist scriptures), and as a place where learned monks do research and discuss Buddhist studies. The ancient Hokke-daie rite has been held here since earliest times, the practice also being known as Toryu-mon or Gateway, as it is a rite through which all must pass who are admitted to the Buddhist priesthood.

The Dai Kodo was built in 1642, burned down in 1956, and was replaced in 1963 by the present structure, brought from Sakamoto where it served as the Sambutsu-do Hall. The main image of the Dai Kodo had always been a Dainichi Nyorai, and the image lost in the 1956 fire was replaced by a Dainichi Nyorai from the 1600s, taken from a Mujo-dani temple. To the right and left of the altar area are the Eight Masters of Tendai, which include life-sized statues of Saicho (Dengyo Daishi, 767–822), Ennin (Jikaku Daishi, 794–864),

Enchin (Chisho Daishi, 814–91), Kosho (Kuya Shonin, 903–72), Ryogen (Jie Daishi, 912–85), Genshin (Eshin, 942–1017), Honen Shonin (Enko Daishi, 1133–1212), Shinran Shonin (Kenshin Daishi, 1174–1268), Dogen (Shoyo Daishi, 1200–53) and Ippen Shonin (Ensho Daishi, 1239–89), while pictures of previous abbots are on the four walls of the interior of the building.

④ KAIDAN-IN

The temple bell stands to one side before the Dai Kodo while a small building (Zento-in) alongside of the Dai Kodo marks the location where Ennin lived. Beyond the Dai Kodo is the Kaidan-in, the important building in which priests are ordained.

The original ordination building of the temple was built by Gishin (Saicho's successor) in 828, six years after Saicho's death, after Emperor Saga had granted permission to the temple for its own ordination of priests, a permission which Saicho had been unable to obtain during his lifetime. Thus, Tendai as a form of the more liberal Chinese Mahayana Buddhism here declared its independence from Nara and its more conservative Hinayana form of Buddhism. In the Kaidan-in, candidates for the priesthood are ordained fter instruction in the Tendai Mahayana Perfect and Sudden Doctrines" and after aking a solemn vow to be a good priest. The Kaidan-in was rebuilt in 1604 in the Momoyama style, with its gabled roof and rched windows, all architectural details vhich had been absorbed from Zen architecture in the Momoyama period (1568–1603). The main image is that of Shaka.

OTHER TO-TO BUILDINGS Beyond the Kaidan-in and up a flight of steps is the brilliant vermilion painted Amida-do, which was rebuilt in 1937. Within, a 16 foot (4.8 m) image of Amida is the main object of reverence. The Buddhist masses for the dead are recited in this hall, and many *ihai* (ancestral tablets) line the walls. Behind is the charnel house. The Amida-do is connected with the Hokke Sojo-in To-to Pagoda by an overhead covered walkway. In order to bring peace and happiness to the nation, Dengyo Daishi (Saicho) built six pagodas at different locations in Japan, placing 1,000 copies of the Lotus Sutra in each one. The present Hokke Sojo-in of the Enryaku-ji unites all of the earlier six pagodas in one. The unified pagoda was destroyed by Nobunaga in 1571, and the present two-story pagoda of five by three bays was rebuilt in its resplendent vermilion in 1987. The golden images within are enhanced by the murals on the wall. Among the images n the worship area of the pagoda are Monju, Amida, Seish and Kannon.

Along the road to the western precinct is the Sanno-in, where the Shinto shrine to the god of the mountain once stood. When Saicho moved the shrine to the foot of Mount Hiei at Sakamoto and included the seven mountain gods in the relocated Hiyoshi (Hie) Shrine, he not only gave reverence to the native gods of the area but he reinterpreted them as incarnations of various Buddhas. This, in a sense, was the beginning of Ryobu Shinto, whereby the Shinto *kami* (spirits) of Japan became forms of the Buddhas and thus brought Shinto under Buddhist control, a situation which lasted until 1868. The Sanno-in was founded as the Senju-in by Enchin in 858 upon his return from studying in China. His temple held a Senju Kannon, the 1,000-arm Kannon, but its proximity to the original Sanno Shrine in time gave it the name of Sanno-in (Temple of the Mountain God). Destroyed in 1571, the present small temple holds an image of Kannon from the 1600s.

The path leading down to the western sector of the Enryaku-ji comes to the three-building Jodo-in (Paradise Temple) complex. Jodo-in was created by Saicho as an Amida temple, and it holds an Amida image that he carved. In 854, Ennin, the third abbot of Enryaku-ji, placed Saicho's ashes in a tomb behind the Jodo-in, an appropriate place for the founder's remains since Tendai reverences Amida and his Western Paradise, a paradise into which Saicho's soul had obviously been received. The Hondo (Main Hall) holds an image of Saicho, before which offerings of food are made daily. On the western side of this hall is the Amida-do (Amida Hall), which contains the Amida image which Saicho carved, a hidden image, a copy of which stands before the closed case that holds the original figure.

The building to the north of the Hondo contains the tomb where Saicho's ashes were deposited, and the many lanterns and small pagodas are offerings to Saicho by the faithful. In a symbolic gesture, a linden tree was placed to the left of the tomb, for this is the type of tree under which Gautama, the Buddha, taught. To the right is a sal tree, the type of tree under which Gautama died and attained Nirvana. These buildings represent a 1662 rebuilding. One of the ascetic practices, the "sweeping hell," takes place before the Jodo-in. Priests who stay at this temple must spend a period of three months in prayer and at least six hours a day sweeping the ground in front of the temple.

SAI-TO (Western Sector)
The path to the Sai-to area is by means of a steep downward hill, a path which you will later have to ascend on your return to the Eastern Precincts. The Sai-to (Western Sector) of the Enryaku-ji is entered under the elevated corridor which connects the 1595 Hokke-do (Lotus Sutra Hall) and the Jogyo-do (Endless Walking Hall). These two sparsely furnished buildings are the locus of two of the ascetic practices of the temple. The Jogyo-do (Endless Walking Hall) to the west of the connecting corridor is so-named from the practice of a walking repetition of the Nembutsu ("Praise to the Buddha Amida") in the hall, a hall whose only furnishing is an image of Amida. The Hokke-do (Lotus Sutra Hall) is also empty except for an image of Fugen seated on an elephant. The ascetic practice of Hokke Zammai (Half Walking Half Sitting

The Yokawa Chu-do (Central Hall) is one the major buildings of Enryaku-ji's northern sector.

Meditation) here requires the reading of the Lotus Sutra while walking, and then it calls for sitting in meditation upon the teachings of the sutra. Both buildings date from 1595, although the original structures were created in the 800s. They are also known by the nickname of Benkei-no-ninai-do from the old legend of Benkei, the 12th century legendary aide to Minamoto-no-Yoshitsune and reputed monk at Mount Hiei, having carried them on his shoulders.

5 SHAKA-DO

Steps lead up to the Shaka-do, the main building of the western area. Ironically, it is the oldest building on Mount Hiei. It dates from the early Kamakura period (1458), and the irony lies in the fact that it once belonged to Mii-dera (Onjo-ji) Temple, the rival Tendai temple that was established as a result of a theological splitting of Enryaku-ji in 858. The two temples became arch enemies, and the warrior monks of Enryaku-ji burned Mii-dera on numerous occasions. In 1571, Mii-dera sided with Oda Nobunaga when he destroyed Enryaku-ji and killed its monks. In turn, when Hideyoshi became the civil ruler of Japan in the 1580s on Nobunaga's death, he destroyed Mii-dera and brought to an end its army of warrior monks.

This building from Mii-dera (which was not destroyed) was granted to the rebuilding of Enryaku-ji by Hideyoshi in 1595. Within the Shaka-do, the main image is of Shaka (Sakyamuni), carved by Saicho, and protected by the four Shi-tenno about it. The original figure is a hidden image; the one on view is a copy. As with Kompon-chu-do, the building is in three parts: the worshippers' area and the image area are separated by a sunken section for the priests (see Kompon-chu-do above). Three lanterns hang before the image area here also. Once this hall saw important services, but today Kompon-chu-do is the more important building of Enryaku-ji.

OTHER SAI-TO BUILDINGS The Shoro belfry lies to the west of the Shaka-do. The Sorinto is to the northwest. The 33 foot (10 m) tall Sorinto was originally erected by Saicho in 820 and stood one-third taller than this later version. (A *sorinto* is the metal top to a pagoda, with its nine rings and flaming ball on its peak. It held mystic significance in esoteric Buddhism, standing for the mandalas of the Two Worlds, the Diamond and the Womb Mandalas.) This Sorinto sits above a vault which holds 23 different sutras. Behind the Shaka-do by 2,600 feet (800 m), a small 5 foot (1.5 m) tall pagoda from the Heian period (794–1185) was the only structure left unburned in 1571. It is the Pillar of the Devil's Gate, a talisman meant to protect Kyoto from the forces of evil flowing from the northeast.

OKAWA (Northern Sector)

The third sector of Enryaku-ji is 3 miles (4.8 km) beyond the western portion. Its two main buildings are the Yokawa Chu-do (Central Hall) and the Shiki-Kodo (Four Seasons Lecture Hall). Ennin (Jikaku Daishi) built the original Chu-do (Central Hall) in 848 to house an image of the Sho Kannon. The building was rebuilt between 1596 and 1615, burned when lightning hit it in 1941, and was re-established in 1971. A one-time large training hall, its training purpose is now centered at the To-to sector of the mountain complex.

As a center of Kannon worship, the Yokawa precincts contain stone Buddhas representing the 33 pilgrimage sites of western Japan. The Shiki Kodo (Four Season Lecture Hall) or Ganzan Saishi-do (the memorial hall to Priest Ryogen) gets its name from the fact that lectures on the Mahayana Buddhist sutras are given here four times a year. Originally constructed in 967, the present building dates from 1653. The building holds an image of its founder Ryogen, who lived from 912 to 985 and is credited with numerous miracles; many considered him to be a reincarnation of Saicho and the Bodhisattva Kannon.

The Enshin-in was created by Genshin (Enshin) when he retired from his administrative duties at Enryaku-ji in order to devote his life to study and worship in this more remote and isolated area of Mount Hiei. With a group of fellow monks, he began a ceremony using music and poetry to welcome the spirits of the individual worshippers who here met for group devotions. The image of a Dainichi Nyorai along with a Fudo-myo-o, an 11-headed Kannon, and a 1,000-arm Kannon were brought to the temple by Gishin and Ennin (both of whom were the successors to Saicho as head of the monastery) as they increased the esoteric nature of Tendai. These are kept in the Hiho-kan, the Hall of Secret Treasures. (Open spring and autumn only.)

A visit to the Yokawa portion of Enryaku-ji completes a tour of the monastery. A bus can occasionally be taken from the Yokawa area to Ogoto Onsen or Katada on the shores of Lake Biwa, and from there the train can be taken back to Kyoto. Given the limited bus service between the sections of the three major temple areas, it is best to confirm bus schedules at the Tourist Information Center in downtown Kyoto beforehand. (There is virtually no English spoken at Enryaku-ji, nor is there an information counter at the temple areas.)

Otherwise you must be prepared to walk between the To-to, the Sai-to and the Yokawa areas, a healthy task if you want to spend any time at each site. The alternative is to hire a taxi in Kyoto for at least half a day and drive from Kyoto to the Yokawa area first, then have the taxi bring you to the Sai-to sector, and thence to the To-to area, where you could always dismiss the taxi and eventually return by public transportation to Kyoto. The Yokawa area is otherwise difficult to reach, but it is the least important portion of Enryaku-ji complex and can be omitted if you are pressed for time.

GETTING THERE

There are four ways to reach Mount Hiei. One is by bus 101 from Kyoto Station or from the Keihan Sanjo bus terminal. There are magnificent views to Lake Biwa and Otsu and alternatively toward Kyoto as the bus snakes along the twisting toll road once it leaves Kyoto proper. An alternative is to take the Keihan railway from the Sanjo-Keihan terminal to Hama Otsu station, where you change for the train to Sakamoto. (Buy a ticket from Sanjo Keihan to Sakamoto.) At Sakamoto, walk to the left to a sign which points to the cable car to Eizanchu-do (the terminus atop Mount Hiei). From the top station of the cable car, follow the path to the Eastern Section (To-to) of Enryaku-ji. A third alternative is the JR train from Kyoto Station (Kosei line), 16 minutes to the Eizan station, and then walk to the left toward the hill and the cable car ride as above.

A fourth alternative is by train from the Demachi Yanagi station of the Keifuku railway (Yase branch) to Yase (the last stop), where you change to the cable car. This leaves you at the rotating restaurant building, about 1 mile (1.6 km) from the Eastern Sector (To-to) of the Enryaku-ji. A bus occasionally runs between the terminus and the temple, but you may have to walk. (This is the least satisfactory route to take.) The circular restaurant looks back on Kyoto, over the range of mountains and across to Lake Biwa. Near here are a botanical garden, a natural science museum and an amusement park. Finally, as noted in the Yokawa section, you might consider hiring a taxi if you wish to visit all three sectors. The return trip to Kyoto can be made by any of the above options.

Walking Tour 27

FUSHIMI AREA
A Torii-clad Mountain, Fushimi Castle and a Shrine of Fragrant Water

1. **Fushimi Inari Shrine** 伏見稲荷大社
2. **Fushimi Castle** 伏見城
3. **Goko-no-miya Shrine** 御香宮神社
4. **Meiji Tomb** 明治古墳墓
5. **Nogi Shrine** 乃木神社
6. **Terada-ya** 寺田屋
7. **Saké Brewery and Museum** 酒博物館
8. **Jonan-gu Shrine** 城南宮

The area south of Central Kyoto below Kujo-dori (Ninth Street) provides a spectrum of the continuing history of Kyoto. Ancient shrines dating back to the period before the founding of the capital of Heian-kyo are located here as are the sites of former Imperial palaces. Temples range from Amida temples of the early medieval era to Shingon and Zen temples, such as the To-ji and the Tofuku-ji which were covered in previous tours. The Momoyama period of the late 1500 is represented by Fushimi Castle, and the

The huge vermilion torii announcing the location of the major Shinto shrine, Fushimi Inari.

modern era is remembered with the Imperial tomb of the Emperor Meiji. Most important, perhaps, is the Inari Shrine which marks the descent of the Shinto goddess Inari to a mountain top where she is honored by the thousands of vermilion *torii* which climb the sides of the mountain named for this deity, thereby creating a spectacular tunnel of colorful Shinto gates.

In the 1590s, the area just south of the Inari Shrine became the political center of Japan, for here, on the hillside above the village of Fushimi, Toyotomi Hideyoshi built his castle, which gave him control over the approaches to Kyoto and thereby all of Japan. Used by Tokugawa Ieyasu, who succeeded Hideyoshi, the castle was later demolished by another Tokugawa Shogun, its ornate and fascinating halls and gateways being given to various temples and shrines to enrich them with some of the most glorious treasures of the Momoyama period. After an absence of more than 300 years, a castle again rose above Fushimi, a modern version of the original edifice, now part museum, part entertainment land. The site of Fushimi Castle has connections with the continuum of Kyoto history in other ways as well. Here is the reputed tomb of the Emperors Mommu (d. 707) and Kammu (d. 806) as well as the monumental mountainside tomb of the Emperor Meiji (1852–1912), preceded by the shrine to General Nogi and his wife who committed suicide on the Emperor Meiji's death and funeral, thereby embodying the old concept of *samurai* duty which the Shinto militarists of the early 20th century held up as a model.

Nearby is the Goko-no-miya Shrine, an elaborate Shinto shrine noted for its sweet-smelling spring (which still runs and continues to be used by local people, even though it has lost its fragrance). The shrine has huge, unusual porcelain lanterns at its Honden and a very fine *Noh* theater. A little further south is the Terada-ya, an inn in which the supporters of the Imperial house were attacked at a clandestine meeting by forces loyal to the Tokugawa Shogun in the mid-1800s. While still an inn, its first floor rooms were for a while almost a shrine to those who wished to overthrow the Tokugawa government, and the gashes in the woodwork created by the swords of the two sides can still be seen. Further to the west is the Jonan-gu Shrine, once the site of the palace of the Emperor Toba. The shrine is visited today primarily for

its gardens which surround the shrine buildings. Recreated in the style of their times, there is a Heian garden, a Tokugawa stroll garden and a 20th century garden, all quite lovely versions of landscaping styles through the centuries.

☐ FUSHIMI INARI SHRINE

This tour begins at one of the favorite shrines in the Kyoto area, the Fushimi Inari Shrine, with its hundreds of vermilion *torii* marching up the hillside above the shrine buildings.

HISTORY The Inari Shrine was begun on the First Horse Day of the lunar calendar in February 711 when Ukano-Mitama-no-Okami (Inari) manifested herself on the Mita-ga-mine peak of Mount Inari (764 feet/229 m high). She is the goddess of rice and food, the rural deity of growth and fertility and the daughter of Izanami and Izanagi, the ancestral deities of the land of Japan. Also enshrined on the peak of the mountain at Inari are Sado-Hiko-no-Okami and Omiya-no-mi-no-Okami. In 1266, Tanaka-no-Okami and Shi-no-Okami were also enshrined here.

These five *kami* are the fundamental ancestral deities who protect the necessities of human life such as clothing, food and housing. The shrine serves as the protector for business and merchants as well as for rice, *saké*, farmers and their crops. The fox is considered the sacred animal of the five deities of Inari and of Inari shrines in general. It is a symbolic animal in that its bushy tail represents fruitful years of rice harvests while the precious stone in the mouth of some of the shrine fox images represents the spirit of the deities. The key in the mouth of other such images stands for the key to rice granaries.

Historically, the shrine is associated with the Hata clan who first settled the Kyoto area in the 400s. In the 800s, Kukai chose the shrine to guard his temple of To-ji at the entrance to the new city of Heian-kyo, and at that time the shrine was moved from the hillside to its present location at the foot of Mount Inari. In the feudal period, the shrine was granted the First Grade of court rank. In 1871, under the Imperial restoration, when Buddhism was slighted and Shinto became virtually an arm of the state, the shrine was raised to the rank of Kampei Taisha, the highest status among national shrines and was then made the head of the nation's 40,000 Inari shrines.

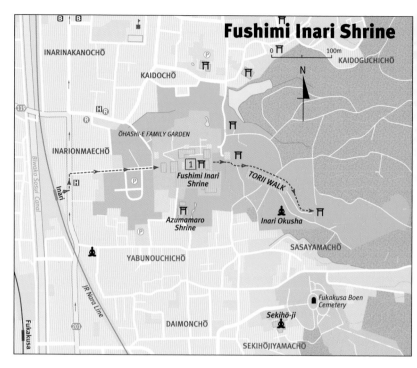

CURRENT STRUCTURES AND GROUNDS

A great vermilion *torii* at the main road announces the location of this major Shinto shrine—as do the many colorful shops on the streets leading to the shrine with their amulets, traditional candy, souvenirs, miniature shrines for home worship and various religious items for sale. (Vermilion has served as a symbol of peace and good harvests through the centuries, and its color is ubiquitous at the Inari Shrine.)

Up steps and through a large vermilion two-story gateway (restored in 1989) flanked by images of foxes, one enters the shrine precincts. The Haiden (Oratory) stands before the vermilion Honden (Spirit Hall) of 1499, with its protruding roof, a style peculiar to the Inari type of Shinto shrines. This inner worship hall of the main building of the shrine, with its cypress shingled roof, was rebuilt in 1961. To the right is a *Kagura* stage (sacred dance stage) where the shrine *miko* (unmarried female attendants) will perform a religious dance for a contribution to the shrine, while to the left is a structure for the placement of *ema* prayer plaques. The white storage building holds the shrine *mikoshi*

(palanquins for transporting the spirits during festivals), while the plain building at the extreme left is the Shamu-sho, the shrine offices. An Ochaya (tea house) south of the Honden was a gift from the Emperor Go-Mizuno-o in the 1600s, a structure which once stood in the Sento Palace in Kyoto.

As you walk further into the shrine grounds to the left of the main buildings, the main path leads to a flight of steps and to a series of minor shrines. A turn to the right and then to the left brings you to the continuous row of vermilion *torii* which virtually touch each other and create a red tunnel up the mountainside. This 2.5 mile (4 km) row of *torii* consists of gifts of these sacred portals from worshippers, and the *torii* line the 764 foot (230 m) Inari-san (Inari Mountain), a two hour climb. Each gift *torii* bears the name of the donor on its east (rear) side, such gifts being made to please the deities and to insure their protection of the donor. At one point, the row of *torii* splits into two parallel tunnels of *torii*. In addition, there are 20,000 Otsuka or sacred stones upon the mountainside as well as many images of the fox and numerous subshrines.

The shrine's popularity comes not only from the protection or the granting of prayers which the deities of the shrine offer but from the many colorful ceremonies which can be enjoyed throughout the year. The festivals of the Inari Shrine are primarily concerned with planting, harvesting, the coming-of-age by young people and prosperity in business as well as for the health and well-being of individual worshippers. (Ten million people annually visit the shrine, according to official shrine statistics.) Miniature *torii* are sold at the gate, and these are left as offerings at various shrines in the Inari complex. These offerings are then burned at the season's end as offerings to the deities and for the successful granting of the wishes made by the worshippers at the time of the offering.

In general, the festivals can have their solemn moments, but the overall approach to worship at such festivities is one of great gaiety and rejoicing. Shinto is a happy religion which celebrates the positive aspects of life. Thus, the Inari Shrine in Fushimi is one of the major shrines where religious belief and the joys of life can be celebrated together.

FUSHIMI INARI TEMPLE FESTIVALS

January 1—Hatsu Mode: The first visit to a shrine in the New Year to pray for good luck in the ensuing months.

January 15—Sejin-no-Hi (Adult's Day): A national holiday to celebrate the coming-of-age of those who have reached their 20th birthday. A religious service and festival from 2:00 to 4:00 p.m. with a four-part performance of customs of the Heian period (800–1200), Kamkaura period (1200–1333) and Edo period (1603–1868).

February 2—Setsubun: Young women from a Kyoto flower arranging school, dressed in lovely *kimono*, scatter beans to drive out evil at the end of winter. At 10:00, 11:30 and again at 1:00 and 2:00.

February 6—Hatsu-Uma Taishi (First Horse Day of the Lunar Calendar): In early February of 711, Inari Taijin, the deity of the Inari Shrine, is said to have arrived at the shrine. Since the date is calculated from the lunar calendar, the actual date varies from year to year. At 8:00 there are prayers for a prosperous year and each visitor is given a branch of cedar (Shirushi-no-sugi or Tome-no-ki/Tree of Wealth) as a talisman which will bring success in business. Effigies of foxes line the road since they are the messengers of the

A tunnel of vermilion torii going up the mountain.

gods. This ceremony began in the 800s.

April 1—Kenka-sai: A procession of young women from the Ikenobo School of Flower Arranging present flowers to the gods. Begins at 11:00 a.m. at the main gate.

April 10—Sagyo Matsuri: A ceremony for success for businesses held by the Trade Guilds. Traditional dance and music.

April 12—Minajuchi Hanshu: A planting of fir saplings to *gagku* music.

June 10—Taue: An agricultural festival celebrating the spring growing season. At 11:00 a.m. four young women in ancient costumes perform sacred rice dances to rice planting songs. At 2:00 p.m. the rice seedlings are placed in the shrine rice paddy by priests and laymen in traditional farm dress.

June 30—Nagishi-no-Harai: A service to purify people of sins they may have accumulated over the last six months. By walking through a miscanthus ring and eating *minazuki* (a rice pudding sweet) and red beans, one can face the torrid and humid summer months with equanimity.

July 22–23—Yoi Miya-sai and Moto Miya-sai: On the 22nd, 1,500 paper lanterns and 300 stone lanterns on the grounds are lit. Paper lanterns in the form of *torii* are set up on the hillside. Bon Odori dances are performed from 7:00 p.m. to 10:00 p.m.

October 10–11 Koin Tai-sai (Annual Grand Festival): Services at 1:00 p.m. for the safe-

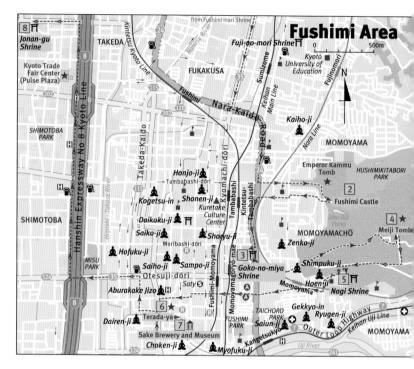

Fushimi Area

guarding of families and for the prosperity of businesses.

October 21–Yozo-sai: A *saké* festival from 11:00 a.m.

October 25–Nukiho Matsuri: A ritual harvesting of the rice crop. Dedicated to the fox god. At 11:00 a.m.

November 8–Ohitaki-sai: Wooden prayer sticks (*ema*), with the name and age of the donor and with a prayer, are ignited by Shinto priests at 2:00 p.m. in a ritual outdoor fire to make the prayers effective. At 8:00 p.m. dance (*Kagura*) and sacred music (*migura*) are performed by torchlight.

November 15–Shichi-Go-San Festival: Celebration for children of three (boys and girls), five (sons) and seven (daughters). Children are blessed and presented with "thousand year" candy to help to guarantee a long life.

NEARBY SITES

Kyoto and its environs are so covered with Shinto shrines, many of which are similar in layout and many others that are of a minor nature, that only a few of such shrines are worth recommending to visitors to the city.

The Fuji-no-mori Shrine, which dates back to the year 750, falls into the category of a minor shrine. However, its one festival is worth mentioning if one is at the Inari Shrine on June 5th, but on most other days it can be bypassed. On June 5th, there is a procession of armed warriors in ancient costumes and also a rural horse race in the fashion of earlier centuries. (The Fuji-no-mori Shrine is located to the south of the Fuji-no-mori station and north of the Sumizome station of the Keihan railway or one can take bus 16 from the Inari Shrine to the Fuji-no-mori Jinja-mae bus stop. The shrine is open without charge during daylight hours.)

② FUSHIMI CASTLE

The main highway and the railroads running south from the Inari Shrine area pass through Fushimi, a town which at one time had an importance far in excess of its size. Fushimi as a town developed around the villa of the wealthy Tachibana-no-Toshitsune (c. 1068), the fourth son of the founder of the Byodo-in in Uji (a temple covered in Tour 29). The town remained a quiet village for the next five centuries, but with the location by Toyotomi

Hideyoshi of his headquarters in the castle he built on the hill above the town, the area grew in size and importance.

HISTORY When Hideyoshi came to power in the 1580s, he had his headquarters in his castle in Osaka. In time, as de facto ruler of Japan, he needed a stronghold closer to Kyoto, the traditional seat of governance and the Emperor. Thus, after his first Korean expedition of 1592, he determined to build a castle/palace at Fushimi. The site was an appropriate one as it closed the military gap in front of Kyoto since the city was surrounded on its east, north and west sides by mountains but was open to the south. It was a logical spot commercially as well, since here the Uji River and a proposed canal from the Kamo River in Kyoto would meet to provide access to the Yodo River which flows to Osaka and the Inland Sea. Hideyoshi had the rivers dredged so that boats could sail from the Inland Sea to Fushimi along the cleared waterways.

The site Hideyoshi chose for the castle had historic connections, for here the Emperor Kammu, the founder of Kyoto, had been buried. (Did Hideyoshi move the tomb to make way for his castle? Archeological exploration of the original Fushimi Castle site is now impossible since the tomb of the Emperor Meiji covers a large portion of the original

castle compound.) The castle at Fushimi served a number of purposes. It offered protection to Kyoto from the south, it provided a residence for Hideyoshi, it taxed the *daimyo* for its construction thereby keeping them both occupied and financially strapped, and it was luxuriously and extravagantly furnished so as to overawe the Chinese embassy which was due to visit Hideyoshi in 1596. The castle was under construction from 1594 to 1596 (although work may have been begun as early as 1592), and an account from Hideyoshi states that as many as 250,000 men worked on it at one time. Each *daimyo* in Japan had not only to contribute funds and laborers, but he was responsible for a specific portion of the castle's construction. In 1595, Hideyoshi, having destroyed his luxurious Jurakudai Palace in Kyoto on suspicions of treachery by his adopted son to whom he had given the palace, had some of the structures of the Jurakudai moved to Fushimi.

By 1596 the castle was finished, and Hideyoshi removed villagers from his birthplace to Fushimi to create a city to serve the needs of the castle and its occupants. The local village of Fushimi therefore became a large city, rivaling Kyoto and Osaka in size, and it was, in a sense, the art capital of the nation since so many artists and artisans were in residence as a result of their work

The current Fushimi Castle is a 1964 replica in concrete of Hideyoshi's castle of 1596.

on the castle. The completed structure not only would awe the Chinese, but it would impress the *daimyo* of Japan as well—since they were all required to stop at Fushimi in order to obtain permission to continue on to Kyoto. Their trade helped to enrich the city of Fushimi beyond the wealth which was being engendered by the town as a port for the capital.

The year 1596 was to mark the visit of the Chinese embassy to Fushimi and to fulfill Hideyoshi's dream of having Japan reach parity with the Chinese empire as an equal power. His plans were extravagant and pretentious, designed to impress the Chinese with Japan's power and wealth as manifested in Hideyoshi's castle and equipage. The *daimyo* throughout Japan were ordered to supply mounted warriors in a ratio determined by their wealth (for example, Tokugawa Ieyasu had to send a levy of 5,000 warriors) so that the road to the castle would be lined for 7 miles (11.2 km) along the Chinese route by mounted warriors. Three days before the Chinese were to arrive, an earthquake created havoc in the area. Some 2,000 people died, perhaps 500 to 600 in the castle alone. Hideyoshi and his officers were safe since they had been quartered in thatch-covered buildings outside the castle.

Nonetheless, within 50 days the damage was repaired and the Chinese were received. The mission was a failure, however, and it ended with Hideyoshi destroying the message from the Chinese Emperor in a rage since the Emperor had offended him by offering to appoint him as Emperor of Japan—thereby implying that Japan was a vassal state of China, not an equal. Hideyoshi would, accordingly, launch a second attack on Korea and China within two years in the expectation that he would conquer China, a nation of whose size he had no knowledge.

In 1598, Hideyoshi unexpectedly died in the castle. Despite his plans to have a regency look after the nation until his five-year-old son Hideyori was old enough to rule, Tokugawa Ieyasu moved to take control of the land. In 1600, as Ieyasu fought elsewhere for total control of the country, the castle fell to Ieyasu's enemies through treachery from within. Of the 2,000 men defending the stronghold, only 384 were left alive as the battle ended, and they committed *seppuku* en masse rather than surrender. With his victory over his enemies at Sekigahara two

years later, Ieyasu took control of Fushimi Castle and made it his political headquarters for Kyoto. It was here that his appointment by the Emperor as Shogun was celebrated.

In 1607, a portion of the castle was removed, the main tower becoming a part of the Nijo Castle, which was later destroyed, in 1791, by lightning. After Ieyasu's death, probably beginning in the early 1620s, the serious dismantling of the castle began, and its parts were distributed among various temples, the Nishi Hongan-ji obtaining some of the prize chambers.

With the disappearance of the castle, the ground was plowed to remove any physical remembrance of Hideyoshi's connection with the site. Peach trees were planted over the next 100 years, thereby giving the hill its name of Momoyama (Peach Tree Mountain). The site saw fighting again in the 1865 period as the Tokugawa Shogun's government tottered and fell. In the 20th century, on the death of the Emperor Meiji in 1912, the Emperor's tomb was created on a portion of the castle grounds, land which is now off limits to the public and to archeologists.

CURRENT STRUCTURE AND GROUNDS

In 1931, Fushimi was annexed by its larger neighbor of Kyoto, 3.5 miles (5 km) to the north. Then, in 1964, a replica in concrete of Hideyoshi's Fushimi Castle was erected on the Momoyama Hill near the site of the original structure. A sevenfold tower of five stories (156 feet/46.8 m tall) and a smaller five-fold three-story tower (91 feet/27 m tall) were recreated in the flamboyant Momoyama style.

Roofed with 8,000 golden tiles in the Momoyama taste and surmounted by golden dolphins, the roofs of Fushimi Castle soar over the valley once more. The six floors of the castle serve as a museum for artifacts of the original castle, of materials from Hideyoshi's time, of items relating to the Emperor Meiji and his consort, the Empress Shoken, as well as historical dioramas of Fushimi's past. In general, the first two floors serve for seasonal and temporary exhibitions while floors three through five serve as the museum of Momoyama times. The top (sixth) floor is for viewing of the valley and hills. A playground (amusement park), a garden, a an open-air theater for light entertainment which can seat 3,000 people, a huge swimming pool, a tea room and a restaurant complete the complex.

A pair of stone Korean lion-dogs guard the entrance to the Honden (Spirit Hall) at Goko-no-miya.

3 GOKO-NO-MIYA SHRINE

Just a little to the southwest of Fushimi Castle is the Goko-no-miya Shrine (Palace of Noble Fragrance), a shrine on the site of a one-time Imperial palace. The Goko-no-miya Shrine is due east of the Momoyama Goryo-mae station of the Keihan railway and to the east and north of the Kintetsu railway Fushimi-Momoyama station. It is open during daylight hours without charge.

The Goko-no-miya is a Shinto shrine dedicated to and enshrining the Empress Jingu (170–269 according to tradition) as well as the god Hachiman. It was specially noted, however, for its spring which still flows today, a spring which once had a perfume to its flowing waters.

The entry gateway to Goko-no-miya is an historic one since it once was a fortified gateway to the nearby Fushimi Castle of the late 16th and early 17th centuries. A sturdy and simple gate, it has a tile roof topped with tile dolphins. A large stone *torii* stands behind the wooden gateway, and then a long pathway extends from the gate back toward the main shrine buildings, with stone lanterns lining the pathway. Along the way, on the left, is a fenced area with a hill which forms a base for a 15 foot (5 m) memorial stone. On the right side of the path is a subshrine with a Heiden (Offertory) and Honden (Spirit House) in dark wood.

The long path ends at a few steps which lead to the major shrine units, a *kura* (storage building) on the left and the visitor's water purification basin on the right. A large two-story wooden gate guarded by *koma-inu* (Korean lion-dogs) provides the entryway to the Honden (Spirit Hall) area, the path continuing under a roof from the gate to the Honden. On either side of the rear of the gate are huge wooden buckets, which are fed by the rainwater conducted from the roof of the gate by means of drain pipes to the buckets, thereby providing an ever-ready protection against fire. Small wooden pails atop the buckets can be used as fire pails in an emergency.

The Haidan (Oratory) to the shrine is a roofed area before and connected with the Honden. On either side of the entry to the Honden are two exceedingly tall lanterns with shafts of porcelain. The spring for which the shrine is named still flows from a bamboo pipe at the west side of the Honden enclosure, and local residents still come with buckets for the water for domestic use. To the east of the area before the Honden is a raised Ema-do, a building for display of the shrine's *ema*. To the west is the shrine's traditional *Noh* stage with its ramp and a large pine tree painted on the rear wall of the stage, a fine example of a classical *Noh* stage. Subshrines can be found on either side and behind the Honden area as well as a white horse in a shed in the northwest area of the grounds. The shrine also has a stone garden attributed to Kobori Enshu and a 300-year-old camellia tree, the Osoraku Tsubaki.

NEARBY SITES

The Fushimi-Momoyama area has three Imperial tombs and a memorial shrine. The oldest tomb is that of the Emperor Mommu (reigned 697–707) and then that of the Emperor Kammu (736–805), the founder of the city of Heian-kyo (Kyoto). Both are within the area devoted to the Emperor Meiji's tomb and are thus off-limits to the public. The other tomb is of the early 20th century, of the Emperor Meiji and his Empress Shoken. There is a sterile monumentality to the Meiji tomb, and for the foreign visitor the tomb is more a curiosity than a necessity to be visited. The memorial shrine mentioned here is to General Nogi. The Momoyama station of Japan Rail or the Momoyama Minami-guchi station of the Keihan railway are the closest to the Imperial mausolea area. The tombs are 3/4 mile (1 km) from the Japan Rail station and 2,000 feet (600 m) north of the Keihan station. The tombs may be visited during daylight hours.

4 MEIJI TOMB

The Emperor Meiji (1852–1912) came to the throne in 1867 as an adolescent on the death of his father. The momentous revolution in Japanese life began with the accession of this 15-year-old boy in 1868, although, of course, much of the change that was brought about in modernizing Japan during his reign was done in his name rather than by him, and he served primarily as a figurehead, as had emperors in the past. The so-called Imperial Restoration marked an end of the Shoguns' rule rather than (as was claimed by the military and Shinto nationalists who took over governmental rule) the true beginning of rule by the Emperor. Nonetheless, the Emperor was much acclaimed in his time, and on his death he was buried at a site which he had admired in the Momoyama area south of Kyoto, a city in which he was born but which he left on his accession to rule from the new capital in Tokyo. The site occupies a portion of the grounds of what had been Hideyoshi's Fushimi Castle, and to the north of the tomb is the place where the Emperor Kammu is said to have been buried.

The Tomb of the Emperor Meiji is best approached from the side path rather than up the 230 stone stairs which lead to the mound. The grave is inside a man-made mound 300 feet (90 m) wide by 330 feet (99 m) deep, while a 72 foot (21.6 meter) long ditch which is 16 feet (4.8 m) deep is before the mound. The tomb is covered with 300,000 overlapping pieces of granite in a fish-scale pattern. The mound is encircled by three granite fences, and the inner fence has a bronze gate with the Imperial chrysanthemum upon it.

Beyond the gate is a 90 foot (27 meter) wide by 60 foot (18 meter) deep Place of Worship, while outside the fence is a 120 foot (36 meter) square Ceremony Court, the ground of the two areas being covered with white sand. An adjacent grave for the Empress Shoken is of a smaller size. In all, the tomb site covers 300 acres (120 ha) of which 5 acres (2 ha) mark the site of the grave. The tomb was obviously part of the campaign to use the Emperor's purported return to rule over Japan as a political device by those who really ran the government of the era—little different from the previous centuries of Tokugawa rule, except that now the rule by the Emperor was proclaimed but still bypassed. In life and in death the Emperor thus served as a symbol for the nationalistic, militaristic and authoritarian goals of militant Shintoism which had been formed by the successors to the Tokugawa Shoguns into a state cult as well as retaining the tradiional native religious spirit of Japan.

5 NOGI SHRINE

In the environs of the grounds of the Meiji tomb is a shrine to General Maresuku Nogi (1849–1912), the victorious general of the Russo-Japanese War. On the evening of September 12, 1912, as the funeral cortege of the Emperor Meiji left the palace gates in Tokyo, the General and his wife committed *seppuku* to follow the Emperor into death. A stone *torii* at the turning from the highway below the Meiji tomb marks the entrance to the area of the Nogi Shrine. Partway down the street beyond the *torii*, on the left, is a large wooden gateway with a copper roof which marks the entrance to the shrine grounds, and a stone path leads back to the main shrine buildings. On the left side are two small structures; one is the stone building which served as General Nogi's headquarters at Port Arthur during the

Russo-Japanese War of 1905. At the end of the main path, a large stone lantern stands before two life-sized bronze horses on plinths on either side to the approach to the Honden (Spirit Hall). Racks for *ema* and then the *koma-inu* (lion-dogs) are next. Beyond the Heiden (Offertory) is a large raised Haiden (Oratory) with an area for guests to be seated during services. Beyond is the Honden holding the spirit of General Nogi.

6 TERADA-YA

Leaving the Meiji tomb and the General's shrine, a visit can be made to a site which predates the Meiji era which began in 1868. Just prior to the "restoration" of Emperor Meiji at the end of the Edo period (1603–1868), there were numerous plots to overthrow the Tokugawa Shogun in favor of the restoration of rule by the Emperor.

In 1866, a group of the Shogun's supporters made a surprise attack on some young revolutionaries who were meeting at the Terada-ya, an inn in the Fushimi-Momoyama area, to plot against the Tokugawas. Many were killed in the fight in the inn, but Sakamoto Ryoma, one of the heroes of the revolutionaries, escaped only to be assassinated a year later when he was 32. The cuts in the woodwork from this fight are still obvious, and there are items related to Sakamoto and the historic fight on display. The inn was a "shrine" to the heroes of the Restoration between the 1868 Restoration and World War II; now it is more of an historic relic although still of interest to students of modern Japanese history. (The Terada-ya, the inn which has these historic associations in the Fushimi area, can be reached from the Chushojima station of the Keihan Railway line. It lies a 10 minute walk from the station directly to the north to the Fushimi Canal and then a little to the west along the canal. The historic portion of the inn is open from 10:00 a.m. to 4:00 p.m.)

7 SAKE BREWERY AND MUSEUM

It may seem strange to list a brewery as a historic site after discussing the Terada-ya, but the Gekkeikan Brewery is a traditional brewery with a long history, and it maintains a museum of a past aspect of the trade of *saké* making. The Gekkeikan Brewery lies directly north of the Chusojima station of the Keihan railway on the edge of the Fushimi Canal where it bends from its east–west direction to head to the south. (Tours are offered from 8:30 a.m. to 5:00 p.m. English language tours can be provided if a reservation is made in advance.) Although the Gekkeikan brewery makes its *saké* in the most modern and efficient manner, it maintains the Okura Kinenkan (Okura Museum, named for the founder of the brewery) to demonstrate how *saké* was made 350 years ago when Rokurouemon Okura, the founder of the present company first began his brewery. Tours are offered daily. In addition, the streets about the brewery with the tile-roofed *saké kura* (storage buildings) provide an interesting area to explore.

8 JONAN-GU SHRINE

A return to Kyoto can be made by way of the Jonan-gu Shrine, another former Imperial palace which has become a shrine. This shrine is different from most former palace sites, however, since a series of lovely gardens of different periods have been developed around the main section of a typical Shinto shrine. (The Jonan-gu Shrine lies in the southern part of Kyoto. If coming from Kyoto one would take the City subway or the Kintetsu railway from the south side of the Kyoto Central Station to the Takeda station, and then follow the street on the south side of the Meishin expressway to the west to where it joins the major north–south highway (Route No. 1) just beyond the exits to the expressway. The Jonan-gu is just south of this intersection. (It is easiest to take a taxi from the east side of the station to the shrine. One can walk back to the station, but to try to find the shrine from the station can be difficult.) Alternatively, buses 19 and 20 go to the Jonan-gu bus stop on Route No. 1; the shrine is to the east of the bus stop. If coming from the Fushimi-Momoyama area, the Kintetsu train can be obtained at Momoyama-goryo-mae station and taken to the Takeda station. The shrine gardens (the reason for a visit) are open from 9:00 a.m. to 4:30 p.m. There is no fee to visit the shrine but there is a fee to visit the gardens.)

The Jonan-gu Shrine lies near the junction of the Kamo and Katsura Rivers, which are joined shortly thereafter by the Uji River to form the Yodo River which flows to Osaka and to the Inland Sea, and here was once the town of Toba which served as the port for Kyoto. The Emperor Shirakawa (reigned 1073–86) (whose grave is to the west of the Takeda station) first built a palace here, and

The Jonan-gu Shrine, a former Imperial palace, is surrounded by gardens of different historic periods.

later the former Emperor Toba (reigned 1108–23) created his retirement villa at this location. Here, Toba tried to recreate the ambience of Heian-kyo by building a palace and temples and pagodas.

All that remains today is the Anraku-in Temple where the emperor is buried and the Jonan-gu Shrine in the center of what at one time was the emperor's palace. The Jonan-gu enshrines the god of direction. When people build a new house, move into another house or plan to travel, it is at this shrine that they will pray. The shrine is said to predate the founding of Heian-kyo in 794.

The shrine is entered from the west through a small *torii*, the path leading to a Water Purification Basin and then to the left through a large vermilion *torii* beyond which lies the Heiden (Offertory) and then the Haiden (Oratory) and the Honden (Spirit Hall), the latter of which is preceded by two large stone lanterns, two *koma-inu* (lion-dog) images and two cones of sand (albeit these are permanent cement cones!). Shrine buildings to the east and west form a courtyard before the Haiden and Honden, while a huge tree stump on the right is encircled with a

rope and paper *gohei* to define this entity that is worthy of reverence. The Haiden has benches under a roof for participants in ceremonies, and the Honden is protected by two Shinto guardian images, the one on the left armed with a bow and arrows while the one on the right is armed with a pike. The area about the Honden is fenced, with four small shrines on the east and three on the west at which prayers can be offered.

The gardens encircling the main shrine grounds were recreated in the spirit of earlier gardens by Nakane Kinsaku after World War II. The entrance to the gardens is at the ticket booth to the left of the large *torii* just within the shrine grounds. The plants and shrubs throughout the garden are marked with wooden fan-like identification plaques which offer the Latin and the Japanese name of each specimen.

There are three main gardens at the Jonan-gu in the style of the Heian period (794–1185), the Tokugawa period (1615–1868) and the Showa period (1926–89). These gardens by Nakane Kinsaku may not be as historical as their names may imply, but each is attractive in its own right. From the entrance to

style green lawn rather than by raked sand. The exit from this last garden leaves you at the roadway which bisects the shrine grounds, and you can turn to the left to return to the shrine entrance/exit.

Among the shrine festivals, the most interesting one, the Kuyokusui-no-utage, occurs on April 29th and again on November 3rd. At 2:00 p.m. a re-enactment of a favorite pastime of Heian nobility is celebrated, and the gardens are open without charge. Individuals portraying Heian courtiers are seated along a stream and they have to compose a short poem (*tanka* in 31 syllables) in the time it takes for a small *saké* cup to float by on a saucer in the stream before them. This game is said to have originated in the Chinese court, and an ancient historical account, the *Nihon Shoki*, claims that on March 2, 485, the Emperor Kenso gathered his ministers in his garden and played this game. More likely, the game probably did not come into being until a few centuries later when knowledge of China had flowered in Japan and when Chinese literacy became more widespread among courtiers. It is known that the game was played during the Heian period (794–1185). The gardens are open without charge for this celebration, but the event is cancelled in the event of rain.

the gardens the path leads to the northwest section of the shrine grounds where a garden has a stream running through it. The path winds behind the fenced Honden and thence to the Heian Garden on the east. This garden is in the *shinden* style, that is, a garden which was meant to be viewed from a palace building. It involves a pond which has a stream leading into and out of it and a waterfall from a hill to the south. The path then crosses the roadway which bisects the shrine grounds, and on the southern side of the compound are the Tokugawa and Showa period gardens.

The Tokugawa Garden is in part an imitation of a stroll garden, and it contains a pond which is crossed in its center by a bridge, and then a second bridge crosses the outlet of the pond. A tea house sits to one side of the pond, and here, for a fee, a woman in *kimono* will serve *matcha*, thick green tea, to visitors who desire it. The path then wanders to the south side of the shrine's garden compound which is screened by shrubbery before it finally comes to the last section, the Modern Garden. This section offers a contemporary version of a dry garden in which the rocks of a green and a red tint are surrounded by a Western-

GETTING THERE

The Fushimi Inari Shrine is 2 miles (3 km) south of the Central Kyoto Station. It can be reached by means of the Japan Rail line to its Inari station, or the Keihan Railway to its Fushimi-Inari station, or by bus 16 or 83 to the Inari Taisha-mae bus stop. The shrine is to the east of these stations/bus stops, and it is open at all times without entry fee.

The modern rebuilt (1964) Fushimi Castle can be reached from the Momoyama Goryo-mae station of the Kintetsu Railway or the Fushimi Momoyama station of the Keihan Railway or the Momoyama station of Japan Rail. In each case, a bus goes from the station up the hill to the castle which is 2/3 of a mile (1 km) from the station. (The castle is open from 9:00 a.m. to 5:00 p.m. Entry fee.)

A return to Kyoto can be made from the Takeda station either on the Kintetsu line or by means of the City subway since they are both served from the platforms of the station.

YAMASHIMA RIVER VALLEY
A Luxurious Garden, an Ungracious Lover and a Near-naked Ceremony

1. **Daigo-ji Temple** 醍醐寺
2. **Sambo-in Temple** 三宝院
3. **Zuishin-in Temple** 随心院
4. **Kanshu-ji Temple** 勧修寺
5. **Hokai-ji Temple** 法界寺（日野薬師）

The valley in which Kyoto is centered and which leads south to Osaka and the Inland Sea is joined by two other valleys in the Momoyama area south of Fushimi. Coming from the northeast is the valley which begins at Yamashina, and from the southeast is the valley of the Uji River which flows from Lake Biwa. Both valleys are easily and quickly reached by subway, bus or rail from central Kyoto. The Yamashina valley, which is the concern of this tour, is home to the Daigo-ji and Sambo-in Temples, two important older temples in the Kyoto area. The Daigo-ji spreads from the valley floor to the heights of the mountain behind it, and thus it has two components, a lower temple area and an upper area whose buildings mount the hillside, both sectors tracing their history back to the early years of Kyoto. The Sambo-in at the valley level is adjacent to, if not a part of, the Daigo-ji, and in its present form it is an unusual temple, revived by Toyotomi Hideyoshi at the end of the 1500s to have one of the most luxurious of Momoyama gardens which Hideyoshi himself is credited with planning.

The upper reaches of the Yamashina valley include a number of minor temples, one of which once housed a famed poetess of Heian times whose beauty proved irresistible to her many admirers, including an emperor. Her wit, attractiveness and literary ability were only surpassed by her arrogance and her lack of feeling for others, and her unhappy end was one which moralists have enjoyed for a millennium since her death. On the other hand, a minor shrine and a minor temple honor a man who was responsible for the death of Lord Kira in the Shogun's capital of Edo in December of 1702. Oishi Kuranosuke was the leader of the famed 47 *ronin* who set out to avenge the disgrace and death of their master, Lord Asano. (*Ronin* were the followers of a *samurai* who were left without a master or employment when their lord was dishonored and had died.) Having succeeded in killing their former master's enemy, the 47 *ronin* were forced by the Shogun to commit *seppuku*, but their devotion to their master and to aspects of the *samurai* code have not been forgotten in the Yamashina territory where Oishi lived. Each December 14th, a festival is held at the Oishi Jinja (Shrine), south of the Yamashina rail station, in Oishi's memory to commemorate his observance of the *samurai* code of honor.

Where the Yamashina and Uji valleys meet is the location of the Hokai-ji Temple, now hidden away among the ever-growing suburban spread of the Kyoto metropolitan area. At one time the Uji valley reaching across to the town of Uji was the site of aristocratic villas, a place to escape the busy life of Heian-kyo at the turn of the 10th and 11th century. Here, the scions of the Fujiwara clan and the Imperial family could build their summer retreats, and since the period in which they lived marked the beginning of Mappo, the long predicted "Age of the Decline of Buddhism," many of the nobles gave concerned thought to their future existence. Thus they built small temples on their land in hopes that their newfound religious concern might assure a happy next life for them once their present existence came to an end. One such nobleman of the Hino family built a temple to Amida on his estate, and his Hokai-ji Temple continues to serve the worship of Amida.

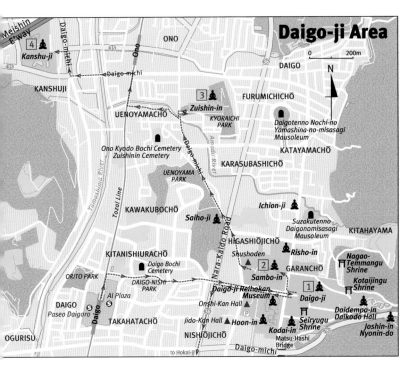

Of the sites of interest in the Yamashina valley, the most noted are the temples of the Daigo-ji, a Buddhist center which is also known by its other delightful name, "Temple of the Quintessence of Enlightenment." The Daigo-ji actually consists of three parts, the Lower Daigo-ji (Shimo Daigo-ji), the Upper Daigo-ji (Kami Daigo-ji) and the Sambo-in. The two Daigo-ji are described in this chapter while the Sambo-in is described under its own name.

1 DAIGO-JI TEMPLE

One of the older temples in the Kyoto area, the Daigo-ji has more than 70 buildings in its upper and lower sectors.

HISTORY Established in 874, it is one of the main temples of the Shingon sect, founded by Priest Shobo (Rigen Daishi, 832–909), the son of an Imperial prince, who took the tonsure at 16. Shobo had studied exoteric Buddhism in Nara as well as esoteric Buddhism under Priest Shinga. According to temple legend, in 874 Shobo noted a five-color cloud above a mountain in the Yamashina valley. He climbed toward the top of

the mountain where he encountered an old man who was drinking from a spring. The old man exclaimed, "This tastes like the finest milk." (Daigo means "finest milk," a Buddhist expression indicating the truest form of Buddhist teachings.) The old man, who was the god of the mountain, gave the mountain to Shobo as a place to practice his priestly austerities, and he then disappeared. Thus Shobo built a small hermitage atop the mountain and enshrined the Juntei Kannon and the Nyoirin Kannon as the objects of veneration.

With time, the hermitage developed into a center for the Shugendo (mountain priests) sect with its ascetic practices. Between 901 and 921, the Yakushi-do and Godai-do (Hall of the Five Great Kings of Light) were completed at the Upper Daigo-ji while at the Lower Daigo-ji the Shaka-do and Sammai-do (Hall for Study and Concentration) were created. When Shobo died on the mountain in 909, it is said that his body ascended to the heavens leaving only his shoes behind, items which his disciples then buried.

The Emperor Daigo (who reigned 898–903 and who took his name from the temple) named the Daigo-ji an Imperial temple in 907,

The small Benten-do Shrine is at the far side of a curved bridge over the pond of the Lower Daigo-Ji.

and he was responsible for its expansion. (When he died at age 46, he was buried to the north of the Sambo-in on temple ground.) He had ordered the Godai-do built as a place of prayer for the safety of the nation, and he expanded the temple from its original upper level mountain site by creating the Shimo (Lower) Daigo-ji as a place of worship to help his soul in the next life. By 904 the temple had become one of the principal Shingon temples. As with many other temples, it was decimated by fire on various occasions, burning down in 1260, 1295 and 1336 and was then destroyed in the Onin War in 1470.

The Emperor Suzaku (reigned 930–46, and buried near the Emperor Daigo on temple grounds) added the Hokke Sammai-do (Lotus Study Hall), now gone, and began the construction of the five-story pagoda which took 15 years to build and was completed in 951 under Emperor Murakami. (Both these Emperors were sons of Emperor Daigo. The pagoda was created by order of Daigo's widow for the repose of Daigo's soul, and his first son (Suzaku) began the pagoda while his second son (Murakami) completed it.) At the height of the temple's glory, there were 27 buildings atop the hill and 65 below. Of all the many buildings which once stood on the site, only the pagoda survived the Onin War in the late 15th century. In the 1590s,

Toyotomi Hideyoshi took an interest in the temple, and, after crushing the warlike monks of the Negoro-dera in the Kii Peninsula, he had some of that temple's buildings moved to the Daigo-ji to replace those lost in the Onin War.

SHIMO (LOWER) DAIGO-JI A cherry tree-lined path from the highway leads to the immense Nio-mon Gate with its two Deva Kings created in the style of the sculptors Unkei and Tankei. This Kamakura-style gate from the 13th or 14th century was brought to the temple from the Negoro-dera in the Kii Peninsula by order of Hideyoshi in the 1590s. (Hideyoshi had to fight the warrior monks of the Negoro-dera, and after defeating them, he distributed their buildings among several Kyoto temples.)

The path from the gateway leads through a forested area as one continues into the temple grounds. The single-story seven bay by five bay Kondo (Golden or Main Hall) with a steep tile roof is beyond the Nio-mon on the left. It too came from the Negoro-dera in 1598 along with its images. Originally, the Shaka-do, the first permanent building, stood here from 926 until its loss in 1295. The Kondo holds a Yakushi Nyorai triad from the 12th century with Nikko and Gakko as his attendants, all three decorated with delicate gold setting and guarded by the four Shi-tenno. In front of the Yakushi image are *ihai* (memorial tablets) to the Emperor Daigo, his consort Onji and their sons, the Emperors Suzaku and Murakami. The inner sanctuary with the images is three bays square with one bay sanctuaries to the left and right and with aisles on all four sides. The vermilion and white temple Shoro (Belfry) is in the northwest corner of the "plaza" before the Kondo.

To the south of the Nio-mon Gate and to the right of the path is the pagoda, which was built between 936 and 951. It is the oldest structure in the Kyoto area and one of the two five-story pagodas of Heian times still extant. The pagoda is 121 feet (36 m) tall and its metal *sorin* atop the pagoda is 39 feet (11.7 m) high. The interior of the pagoda (not open) is noted for its paintings of the Diamond and Womb Mandalas as well as representations of the Eight Founders (Patriarchs) of the Shingon sect. These are the oldest color paintings of their kind which still exist.

The central pillar of the pagoda is encased with wood, 8.5 feet (2.6 m) high by 40 inches (1 meter) wide in size, and is painted with the two mandala, the Taizo-kai mandala facing west and the Kongo-kai mandala facing east. The side walls of the pagoda are each 22 feet (6.6 m) across and have the pictures of the eight Shingon patriarchs, the portrait of Kukai among them being the oldest extant representation of the founder of Shingon in Japan. The other seven patriarchs of the sect are painted after the images in the To-ji in Kyoto. The four inner pillars of the pagoda have depictions of the Shi-tenno who guard these inner treasures; lotuses and imaginary flowers decorate the beams. The western wall has the Buddha Dainichi Nyorai richly bejeweled and flanked by two Bodhisattvas, and over him is a triangle, the symbol of absolute wisdom. The pagoda was restored in 1596 and again in 1961. (Shortly after the last restoration the pagoda was moved out of the perpendicular by a typhoon.)

West of the pagoda is the reconstructed small Shinto shrine of the Seiryu-gu (Clear Waterfall Shrine) which was founded in 1097 but burned in 1470; its Honden (Spirit Hall) was rebuilt in 1517 by Abbot Shoken. The Seiryu Gongen guardian is the tutelary Shinto deity who protects the Shimo (Lower) Daigo-ji. Uphill to the east of the Kondo is the Fudo-do, a small hall which holds an image of Fudo. A fenced graveled area before it has a stone with an image of Fudo on it and a *goma* stone (fire ritual stone) before the image. East of the Fudo-do are the Kuri, the private quarters for the priests.

The Dai Kodo (Great Lecture Hall) was built in 1930 on the west bank and just before the large pond uphill from the pagoda. It contains an image of Amida, and the building is in frequent use by the monks of the temple at prayer. As the terrain rises, the Benten-do, a small shrine to the Shinto goddess Benten, is at the far side of a curved bridge over the pond at the uphill portion of the Lower Daigo-ji. The vermilion bridge and shrine are reflected in the carp-filled pond which is surrounded by maple trees and bushes, and the combination makes for a most attractive scene. The last building in the Lower Daigo-ji is the Dai Denpo-in, a 1931 hall which was built on the 1,000th anniversary of the death of Emperor Daigo. It is a training hall for young monks, and it is set back in its own courtyard (it is generally not open to the public).

KAMI (UPPER) DAIGO-JI The Kami (Upper) Daigo-ji lies up Kasatori-yama (Kasatori Mountain) beyond and to the southeast of the Shimo (Lower) Daigo-ji buildings, and it is where the temple first began under Priest Shobo. The climb up the mountain is a steep 2.5 miles (4 km) for which sufficient time must be allowed for the exploration of this mountain top complex. About halfway to the top is Yari-yama where Hideyoshi held his famous cherry blossom viewing party in 1598, a party that is discussed when the Sambo-in is described.

A second cypress thatched Seiryu Shinto shrine from 1434, which like the lower shrine is dedicated to the Seiryu Gongen guardian who protects the Kami (Upper) Daigo-ji and its buildings, is the first structure encountered. Its deity is the dragon god of the Daigo-sui spring which is adjacent, the spring at which Rigen Daishi found the mountain god drinking of its waters. Pilgrims climbing the hill always stop here for a drink of the sacred waters and to pray to the dragon god. A Kannon-do (Hall), the Juntei-do, which is number 11 of the 33 western Kannon temple pilgrimage sites, sits above the steps at the Daigo-Sui and here pilgrims pray as part of their pilgrimage.

The original Yakushi-do was one of the first buildings erected on the mountainside, and this present 46 foot (13.8 m) building, up a path to the right of the Juntei-do, was rebuilt in 1211. It sits on a raised stone platform and has a low thatched roof; within it holds a primitive Yakushi Nyorai image from 907. A bronze statue of En-no-Gyoja, the 7th century founder of Shugendo, the *yamabushi* or mountain priest faith which combined native (Shinto) mountain worship with forms of Buddhism, stands before the Godai-do, the next structure further up the mountain.

Yamabushi were outlawed between the 1868 Meiji Restoration and 1945, during which years the Shinto militarists tried to expunge all aspects of Buddhism from Shinto. *Yamabushi* priests can be recognized by their dress of baggy trousers and a small box-like hat on their heads, the *yamabushi* movement having made a small comeback since World War II. These mountain priests can often be seen praying at the Daigo-ji because of its historical association with Shugendo. The Godai-do houses the five Myo-o whose fierce visages are meant to frighten away evil forces, and these deities were introduced to esoteric Buddhism by Kukai, whose faith Rigen Daishi followed. The Godai-do was rebuilt in 1938.

At the top of the hill is the Kaisan-do or Mie-do (Founder's Hall) which was rebuilt in 1608. It contains a 1261 image of Rigen Daishi (Priest Shobo), and adjacent is the 1608 Nyoirin-do (Kannon Hall) which contains a seated six-arm Kannon from 1089, two of its arms and hands supporting it while the other hands hold a jewel, a Wheel of the Law, a rosary and a lotus. The building burned in 1260 and was rebuilt in 1608. The other building to be noted is the Kyozo (Sutra Hall) which was built in 1198 and is in the Kamakura Indian style of architecture.

Returning to the Lower Daigo-ji, the temple Treasure House (Daigo-ji Hojuin Reiho-kan) is a 1935 building which is on the grounds of the Shimo Daigo-ji (Lower Daigo-ji) opposite the Sambo-in. A road to the right of the entrance to the temple grounds should be taken and then the second turning on the left to reach the Treasury. (It is open from 9:00 a.m. to 4:00 p.m. in April and May and again in October and November. Entry fee.)

The temple owns more esoteric paintings than any other temple in Japan as well as being rich in its holdings of calligraphy, temple documents, statuary, lacquer and metal work. The collections are too extensive to describe, and since the 60 or so objects on display (other than the large images) change with each semi-annual opening of the treasury, one has to rely on the checklist which is issued at the time of these openings. The manuscripts range from sutras (religious texts) in the hand of Kukai and the Emperor Go-Yozei (1593) to writings of Hideyoshi and others at the time of the Cherry Viewing Festival in 1598. In all, there are over 100,000 volumes of documents preserved. (The Treasure House is open from 9:00 a.m. to 4:00 p.m. daily from April 1st to May 30th and then from October 1st to November 24th. Entry fee.)

DAIGO-JI TEMPLE FESTIVALS

February 23–Godairiki: Godairiki, the deity who can prevent earthquakes, fires and other disasters is celebrated. A large sacred fire is lit to honor Godairiki, and visitors are given paper plaques to burn as a protection against personal disasters. On the lighter side, a contest is held to see who can lift two large cakes of rice (330 pounds/48.5 kg) and hold them the longest.

Second Sunday in April–Taiko Honami Gyoretsu Festival: In early April the cherry trees are in bloom and a commemoration of Toyotomi Hideyoshi's famous cherry viewing party at the Daigo-ji in 1598 is re-enacted. A long procession of individuals in costumes of the Momoyama period (1585–1615) takes place from 1:00 p.m. to 3:00 p.m. *Kyogen* and *Bugaku* are performed.

June 7–Sanboin Monzeki Nyubo Shugyo (Journey of the Mountain Ascetics): Monks and *yamabushi* set out on foot for Mount Omine in Kii at 5:30 a.m. (a three-day journey) as an austerity practice.

② SAMBO-IN TEMPLE

Adjacent to the lower Daigo-ji is the Sambo-in (Temple of the Three Treasures). It can be entered through its gateway not too far back from the highway. (The temple is open from 9:00 a.m. to 5:00 p.m. from March to October and from 9:00 a.m. to 4:00 p.m. from November to February. Entry fee. Photography is not permitted within the Sambo-in or its gardens.)

The Sambo-in was recreated by Hideyoshi at the end of the 1500s, and it was so changed that it is now seen as an excellent example of the *shoin* architectural style of the turn of the 1600s rather than as a religious unit. It is particularly lovely in early April when the cherry blossoms are in bloom. The name of the temple, the "Three Treasures Temple," refers to the three treasures of Buddhism: the Buddha, the Law and the Buddhist monastic community. The Sambo-in is one of the headquarters of the *yamabushi*, the itinerant mountain priests.

The Sambo-in was established in 1115 by Shokaku, the 14th abbot of the Daigo-ji, as a subtemple in its own enclosure outside the main gate to the Daigo-ji, and it was one of the five *monzeki* temples (its abbot being a member of the Imperial family) of the Daigo-ji. It was destroyed in the Onin War in 1470 and was not rebuilt until the very end of the 1500s, and then upon an audacious request by the abbot to Toyotomi Hideyoshi.

In March of 1598, Hideyoshi went with a large entourage from his Fushimi Castle, 2.5 miles (3.8 km) north of the Sambo-in, to enjoy the cherry blossoms at Hanami-yama (Flower Viewing Hill) on the site of the destroyed Daigo-ji Temple. At this time, Gien, the 16th abbot of the Daigo-ji, prevailed upon Hideyoshi to rebuild the Sambo-in Temple, and Hideyoshi not only undertook the project but he personally supervised the start to the construction of the temple and its remarkable gardens during the few short months left of his life. The project was not completed until 1615, 17 years after Hideyoshi's death (in August of 1598). One account relates that the buildings were completed within three years (by 1601) by Hideyori, Hideyoshi's son, a fairly unlikely event since Hideyori was still a child. Other stories relate that construction was finished within six weeks, in time for a second cherry blossom viewing party, an even more unlikely event.

The buildings are less temple buildings than structures that would have graced a villa of the Momoyama era. They consist of a Chokushi-mon (Imperial Messenger's Gate), the Genken (Entry Porch), the Omote Shinden (Front Residence) of three rooms, the Kuri (Priests' Quarters–not open to the public), the Shinden (Residence), the Junjo-kan (Temple of Purity) and the Miroku-do (Hall of Maitreya, the Buddha-to-be), all of which face to the south. The noted garden of the complex lies to the south of the Omote Shinden.

The walled Sambo-in is entered from the northwest through a secondary gateway. Its main gate, the Chokushi-mon (Imperial Messenger's Gate), is not used since it is a ceremonial gateway only, and it is reputed to have originally been one of the gates to Hideyoshi's Fushimi Castle or his Jurakudai Palace. On the other hand, some accounts suggest that it might have been built for Hideyoshi's cherry blossom viewing party, again an unlikely event. The gate is in the flat Chinese style with curved gables at its ends and a roof which curves slightly upward. Two of its doors bear the Imperial crest of the 16-petal chrysanthemum (*kiku*) while two other doors have Hideyoshi's paulownia (*kiri*) crest. The path from the Chokushi-mon leads to the First Building, and a stone on the left, the Koto Hike, is supposedly where one could sit to play the *koto*. A weeping cherry tree at the entryway is noted for its spring blossoms.

A gate in the west wall which surrounds the Sambo-in opens into a courtyard and then to the Dai Genkan (Great Porch) with its Kara-mon (Chinese gate) entry which leads to a corridor and thus into the First Building, the Shoin (Study) of three rooms built at the request of Hideyoshi in 1598. (A souvenir shop lies between the Genkan and the Aoi-no-ma, the first room.)

The 20-mat first room, the Aoi-no-ma (Hollyhock Room), is named from the *fusuma* paintings of 1760 by Ishida Yutei (1721–86) of the Aoi (Hollyhock) Procession to the Kamigamo Shrine which takes place in Kyoto each spring. The second room is the Akikusa-no-ma (Room of Autumn Grasses) whose *fusuma* on three sides of the room and under half of the *shoji* on the fourth (west) wall, are said to have been painted by Kano Sanraku (1559–1635) and which depict the seven grasses of autumn. This 15-mat room looks out to a weeping cherry tree. The third room is the Chokushi-no-ma (Imperial Messenger's Room), a 10-mat room whose *fusuma* of a landscape with flowers and birds are also said to have been painted by Kano Sanraku. This room has a *tokonoma* whose plain rear wall is a sliding panel. The closet to the right of the *tokonoma* and the outside wall both have *shoji* with paintings in their lower portion.

The corridor then leads to the second building, the Omote Shoin or the Omote Shinden. This building mixes the *shinden* tradition of the Heian period (794–1185) with the later *shoin* style of the Kamakura or Medieval period. Its three rooms are in the center of the building, surrounded by corridors or porches a portion of which are over water in the Heian style; the *tokonoma* and *chigai-dana* (staggered shelves) reflect the medieval architectural style.

The building, which looks out over the major garden of the Sambo-in, was probably completed just before Hideyoshi's death. The first room is the Agebutai (Stage Room) and it is lower than the other two rooms; it was used for *Noh* performances when the *tatami* mats were removed to expose the fine wooden floor. The veranda in front of the room on the garden side widens into a stage for theatrical presentations. The *fusuma* on two of the walls bear paintings of peacocks and palm trees by Ishida Yutai.

The second room, the Chudan-no-ma (Central Room), of 18 mats has *fusuma* painted by Kano Sanraku of flowers and pine and bamboo trees. The third and last room of this building is the 15-mat Yanagi-no-ma (Willow Room) or Jodan-no-ma (Platform Room). The room belies the latter name since there is no raised portion to it, the "platform" (*jodan*) probably being a small one that could be put in place as needed for distinguished guests. Sanraku has decorated these *fusuma* and the wall behind the *chigaidana* with willow trees in the four seasons of the year. The unusually large *tokonoma* has a painting of a large pine tree on its wall. The beams of the ceiling are at right angles to the *tatami* pattern, an unusual construction which has been suggested to have been done at Hideyoshi's request.

The extravagance of the Sambo-in Garden which the Omote Shoin looks out on makes it one of the more interesting gardens in Japan. Hideyoshi spared no money in the planning and execution of this garden which is said to have 700 to 800 stones of varying sizes within its confines. Its gardener spent 20 years bringing it to its final perfection, many years after the death of Hideyoshi who had planned it.

It is a Momoyama garden at the height of this luxurious style of decoration. Located on the south side of the Sambo-in First and Second Buildings, the garden is 180 feet (54 m) in length by 80 feet (24 m) deep. The background for the garden is a "hill" with both evergreen and deciduous trees so that a contrast in colors would occur throughout the year. Its pond is fed by two cascades, and the inevitable Crane, Tortoise and Horai (Blessed Isles) Islands are present and linked by two stone and one wooden bridge, the latter covered with earth and moss. For contrast there is a *karesansui* (dry garden), a raked gravel stream with stones as islands between the

pond and the Omote Shoin. Of the hundreds of stones in the garden, some came from Hideyoshi's own gardens (particularly from his Jurakudai Palace), some from his *daimyo* who were forced to make contributions of their finest stones, and some by outright removal from other gardens of items desired for this luxurious landscape.

The best known stone in the collection is the Fujito Stone which came from the Okayama region and is connected with a story of treachery and murder which became the basis for the *Noh* play called *Fujito*. This huge square pockmarked stone was eventually brought to Kyoto and at one time belonged to Nobunaga. Hideyoshi took possession of it and had it placed in the garden of his Jurakudai Palace. Given a choice of 5,000 bushels of rice (a truly princely sum at that time) or the stone, Abbot Gien chose the stone. Regarded as a representation of Amida by the abbot, it is accompanied by two other stones representing Seishi and Kannon. The stone was believed to have supernatural powers, and it was always wrapped in brocade and accompanied by music when it was moved. Additional small gardens exist between the buildings of the Sambo-in. One behind the Junjo-kan has designs in cedar moss against a gravel background representing gourds, a symbol associated with Hideyoshi and which also stood for good luck and longevity.

Up two short steps from the Omote Shoin, the third building, the Junjo-kan (Temple of Purity), is entered. It is a rustic thatched-roof structure which was meant for cherry viewing parties, and it is reputedly the one Hideyoshi had constructed for his 1598 cherry viewing party on the hillside above the Lower Daigo-ji. It contains two rooms of 20 and 15 mats, the latter with a *tokonoma* and *chigaidana*, and these rooms are set within a surrounding matted corridor. Its *fusuma* bear the paintings of pines and blossoming cherry trees by Domoto Insho and were painted in 1936 when the building was restored after damage from a typhoon of two years earlier. While Hideyoshi virtually turned the Sambo-in into a palatial villa and garden, the Sambo-in is still a religious unit of the Daigo-ji. Thus, the fourth building, just beyond the "villa" structures, the Gomado or Miroku-do, is devoted to Buddhism. This one-story seven by five bay building from the Kamakura period (1185–1333) holds a small mage of Miroku (Maitreya), the Buddha of the Future, created by Anami Kaikei in 1198. The gilded image of wood is seated on a lotus blossom and is 44 inches (112.5 cm) tall. It holds a stupa in one hand and an ornate necklace is upon its chest. The image comes from the Gakuto-in in the western valley of the Kami (Upper) Daigo-ji. On either side of Miroku are 17th century images of Kobo Daishi (Kukai) on the right and Priest Shobo (Reigen Daishi) on the left, the founders of Shingon Buddhism and of the Daigo-ji.

To the rear of the Omote Shoin is the Shinden of four rooms, two inner and two outer rooms, the inner rooms being the more important ones. A matted corridor encircles these rooms. The room with the small raised platform (Jodan-no-ma) would have been for use by important guests. This room has a *tokonoma* and a *chigaidana*, the latter being one of the three most noted shelf arrangements (along with the Katsura and Shugaku-in villa shelves) in Japan. The rear wall of the *chigaidana* is an independent wall whose contour can cast a shadow of its cut-out palm tree on the wall behind it. The *fusuma* in the Shinden are in black and white ink by pupils of the Kano school.

Two tea houses lie behind the major buildings of the Sambo-in. The Shogetsu-tei (Pines in the Moonlight Tea House) is attached to the rear of the Shinden, and it is a 15th century structure placed here in the 19th century, and it may have once been part of Hideyoshi's Fushimi Castle. This thatched-roof tea house is supported in part by one of its pillars which rests on a stone in the stream before the tea house. The stream continues through a garden and under the Junjo-kan into the main garden, and *saké* cups could have been floated between the two buildings during poetry reciting parties. The stone basin for ablutions stands in the water. The tea house has all the refinements of a fine *cha-no-yu* structure, including a round moon window in one wall and staggered planks across the stream to enable guests to reach the building.

The second tea house, the thatch-roofed Chenryu-tei (Pillow on the Stream Tea House), may have been part of Hideyoshi's Jurakudai Palace originally, and at the Sambo-in it lies on the garden side of the Junjo-kan. It has three rooms, one of two mats and two of three mats each. The three-mat central room is the entry room, and it has two hinged doors with a round window above them while the other

three-mat room is the tea room, and this room for special guests is slightly higher than the other two rooms and has a *tokonoma* as well as its own entry. The two-mat room is a pantry.

SAMBO-IN TEMPLE FESTIVAL

The Sambo-in has its own festivals, separate from those of the Daigo-ji although it partakes of the festivals of the Daigo-ji. On the second Sunday in April is the Taiko Hamai Gyoretsu, a re-enactment of the Daigo-no-Hanami (Cherry Blossom Viewing Party) which Hideyoshi held at the Daigo-ji in March of 1598. At 1:00 p.m. a procession in Momoyama period costumes moves from the Sambo-in Shikyoku Gate and through the Nio-mon Gate of the Daigo-ji to the Denpo-in. After a tea ceremony, there are performances of *Kyogen* and *Bugaku*.

③ ZUISHIN-IN TEMPLE

Some temples are noted for their architecture, some for their images, while others are noted for their gardens. In the case of the Zuishin-in, further up the Yamashina valley, it is a former occupant whose notoriety even after 1,000 years makes it a temple of interest. (The Zuishin-in is located to the north of the Daigo-ji/Sambo-in Temples. Take the Tozai subway to the Ono station. The temple is open from 9:00 a.m. to 4:00 p.m. Entry fee. Alternatively, it is approximately a 15 minute walk from the Daigo-ji/Sambo-in to the Zuishin-in and then another 15 minutes to the Kanshu-ji Temple).

The temple is known for its one-time resident, Ono-no-Komachi (834–900), who was a Heian poetess renowned for her beauty as well as for her writing, poetry which was so effective it could even be magical in bringing needed rain. Beauty and pride, and even cruelty, went hand in hand (one suitor, it is reported, delivered love poems to her door every day for 100 days in vain, dying of a broken heart on the last night). She is said to have led a miserable life in her old age, begging for food along the road. When she died, her body was eaten by dogs—a story which Buddhist moralists loved to recount.

A *Noh* play, *Sotoba Komachi*, has been built about her rebuttal of her suitor, recounting her existence in hell for her unkindness, a story which the theater provides with a happy ending when both she and her lover attain Buddhahood! A mound exists at the Zuishin-

The Hondo (Main Hall) at Zuishi-in Temple overlooks a peaceful garden.

in where, it is claimed, she buried her love letters and dressing case. The temple was created in 1018 by priest Ninkai, a Fujiwara descendent, as a prayer for the repose of his mother's soul. The Hondo was rebuilt in 1599, but its Amida image is from Heian times (794–1185). The style of the temple gate and Shoin (Study) is of this period also. The 13th century Kongo Satta image by Kaikei of wood is lacquered and gilded and it is a seated image 40 inches (100 cm) tall which holds a *vajra* (symbolic thunderbolt) in its right hand and a bell in its left hand. The adjacent Himuro Pond of the temple is noted for its springtime iris blossoms.

4 KANSHU-JI TEMPLE

A 15 minute walk from the Zuishin-in brings one to the Kanshu-ji Temple, a temple noted primarily for its garden. The Kanshu-ji is also to the north and east of the Daigo-ji/Sambo-

in. It is a 10 minute walk to the west of the Zuishin-in. (The temple is open from 9:00 a.m. to 4:00 p.m. Entry fee). The Kanshu-ji is said to have been built in the 900s by the Emperor Daigo at the site of his mother's family mansion as a religious act for the repose of his mother's soul, and from 942 an Imperial prince used the site as his residence. The temple buildings were reconstructed by the Tokugawa Shogun Tsunayoshi in 1682, but the Shoin (Study) and the Shinden (Residence) retain their Heian period (784–1185) style. The most important building is the Shoin with its 17th century painted *fusuma* by Tosa Mitsohi, while the Hondo has a 1,000-arm Kannon which was worshipped by Emperor Daigo. The temple's lovely gardens are centered on a pond, and there is a *kare-sansui* (dry garden) as well. The Kanshu-ji styled lantern is a noted feature in the garden since its roof resembles an open umbrella.

5 HOKAI-JI TEMPLE

If time is short, the previous two temples could be bypassed, but the Hokai-ji Temple at the base of the Yamashina valley is of greater importance. The Hokai-ji Temple was the family temple of the Hino family, a branch of the Fujiwaras. One of its members, Hino Sukenari, entered the priesthood and built the Hokai-ji in 1051 on the land of the family country estate, one of the many aristocratic country estates between the Momoyama and Uji area. In its Hondo (Main Hall) he established the Yakushi statue which his family had worshipped for generations. The image caught the attention of pilgrims, and it was particularly visited by those seeking the aid of the Buddha of Medicine (Yakushi) and especially by nursing mothers who considered it the "milk providing Buddha."

The separate Amida-do is its most famous building because of its Amida image which is attributed to the sculptor Jocho and is similar to the Amida of the Byodo-in in Uji. The Amida-do, which was created in 1098 (one of three such Amida halls which once stood at the Hokai-ji), is a five bay square hall, 61 square feet (5.5 sq m), with a pyramidal shingled roof. The veranda and overhanging intermediate roof were added in a 1226 renovation of the hall. The Amida image, seated on a lotus with its hands in the meditation *mudra*, is a gold leaf and lacquer wood image 9 feet (2.7 m) tall. It was made in the *yosegi* (assembled wood block) technique. A *mandorla* (aureole) with flaming filigree tips, enhanced by flying *apsara* (angelic figures) with flowing robes, is behind the image. The Amida sits in a one bay altar area surrounded by aisles with double eaves. The pillars of the hall are decorated with paintings of Buddhas and *apsara* which also appear on the narrow plaster band 18 inches (45 cm) tall by 36 inches (3.2 cm) wide from the late 12th or early 13th centuries. The wall paintings are of the Diamond and the Womb Mandalas, and the ceiling is decorated with flowers. Originally a Tendai sect temple, the Hokai-ji is now a Shingon temple. A modern temple unit has been built just above the original temple.

The temple is noted for its "near-naked" ceremony, the Hadaka Odori, on January 14. Originally a purifying ceremony at the start of a new year, it was interpreted in time as a ceremony for peace and a fruitful harvest. Young men clad only in a loin cloth are splashed with cold water in the cold night air.

GETTING THERE

There are various approaches to the temples. The best and fastest is the Tozai subway which can be taken at the Nijo Castle station in central Kyoto and which goes to the Daigo-ji station across from the Daigo-ji complex. In addition, the Keihan railway train to the Momoyama Minami-guchi station and then bus 26 from the main road takes one to the Daigo/Sambo-in-mae bus stop at the temple entry. Buses 39, 40 and 41 from Shijo-Karasuma-dori in Kyoto also go to the Daigo-ji and Sambo-in. Bus 21 from the Yamashina station of the Japan Railway also can take one to the temple bus stop. If using either of these alternative approaches other than the Tozai subway, it is easiest to take the train to either station and then a taxi from the station to the temple. The temple is open from 9:00 a.m. to 5:00 p.m. in summer and 9:00 a.m. to 4:00 p.m. in winter. Entry fee.

The Hokai-ji is a little more than 1 mile (1.6 km) south of the Daigo-ji and a bus or taxi goes between the two temples. When coming from Kyoto, the Keihan railway line can be taken to the Momoyama Minami-guchi station and then bus 26 to the Ishida bus stop followed by a walk 765 yards (688.5 m) northwest toward the mountain to the temple. (A taxi from the station is easier and quicker.) The temple is open from 8:30 a.m. to 5:00 p.m. in summer and from 9:00 a.m. to 4:00 p.m. in winter. Entry fee.

A return to Kyoto can be made from the temple (a bus line begins outside the modern temple unit) by bus and train or by returning to the main highway where buses 39 or 40 or 41 return to Kyoto to Shijo-dori and Karasuma-dori. Bus 26 from the highway goes to the Momoyama Minami-guchi railway station, while bus 21 goes to the Tozai subway stations as well as the Japan Rail station in Yamashina where a train can be taken back to Kyoto. If one is not too tired, and if time permits, this tour could be continued on to the Mampuku-ji Temple and to the Byodo-in in Uji. In this case, the train could be taken from the Momoyama Minami-guchi or the Rokujizo stations to Obaku station for the Mampku-ji or the Uji terminus for the Byodo-in. These sites are described in the next tour.

Walking Tour 29

UJI RIVER VALLEY

A Chinese Zen Temple and the Golden Buddha of Uji

1. **Mampuku-ji Temple** 萬福寺
2. **Uji City** 宇治
3. **Hojo-in Temple** 放生院
4. **Uji-Kami Shrine** 宇治上神社
5. **Kosho-ji Temple** 光照寺
6. **Byodo-in Temple** 平等院

The Hokai-ji, which was the last temple described in the previous tour, had at one time been the summer mansion of an aristocratic Fujiwara family member. Other aristocrats and members of the Imperial family had also built their summer mansions close to the Uji River from the 900s on, a river which has its beginnings in Lake Biwa and makes its way through a picturesque gorge just above the city of Uji on its way to the Yodo River and the Inland Sea. That the Uji valley was attractive to aristocrats was, in the long run, to be of benefit for temples as well, for as the Age of Mappo (Age of the Decline of Buddhist Law) drew near, many aristocrats gave thought to their future existence, and some even turned their mansions into temples for the sake of the future of their souls. The Heian period, which ran from the founding of Kyoto in 794 until the beginning of the rule by the Kamakura Shoguns in 1185, had for much of that time been a period of peace and prosperity. That glorious era gradually began to disintegrate about the time that Fujiwara-no-Michinaga died in 1127.

Michinaga had been the capable regent who had ruled Japan for the Imperial family (with or without their consent) in the late 900s and into the new century. In true Fujiwara style, he had married his daughters into the Imperial family, and thus, through his political skills, he became the father-in-law to two emperors, grandfather to a third, grandfather and great-grandfather to a fourth, and father-in-law to a fifth. While his death in one sense did not affect the body politic that greatly, in another sense it did mark the beginning of an end to an era. The interest in art, in literature, and the joyous expectancy which had filled the early Heian period was drawing to a close. The Buddhist doctrine of the Age of Mappo, that period when the Buddhist Law would decline, when an individual could no longer be responsible for his own salvation in the next existence, was at hand. The only solution was to turn to Amida for hope for a rebirth in Amida's Pure Land in the next world rather than expending too great a concern on this world and its cares.

This movement can, in a sense, be epitomized in the magnificent Byodo-in which Michinaga's son built in Uji at his mansion by the Uji River, and it is the Byodo-in Temple which is the primary reason today for a journey to this center of tea cultivation, for the Byodo-in in its restored condition offers an example of a Pure Land temple at its finest. Fujiwara-no-Yorimichi, Michinaga's son, as he approached his 60th birthday, created an Amida-do, an Amida Hall, on his estate, and from his mansion he could look across the small lake, beyond which lay a version of Amida's Western Paradise. The golden image of Amida, with his eyes half closed in contemplation, could be seen through an opening in the latticed screen gazing benignly on Yorimichi with a promise of the peace of paradise in the future. Today, that Amida image still sits in contemplation, albeit viewed not by Yorimichi but by Japanese and other visitors who come from afar to admire and perhaps to worship this excellent example of a gracious Buddha image in a medieval temple of the Pure Land faith.

The valley continued to have its appeal even when the concern for Mappo had passed

nd thus the valley remains richly endowed
vith temples and shrines. Long after the
Heian and Kamakura periods had come to
an end, the region attracted a 17th century
Buddhist sect from China, and the latest in
Buddhist thought was thus brought to the
Kohata region of the Uji River when the
Shogun permitted the establishment there
in the mid-1600s of a Chinese Zen temple,
the Mampuku-ji. Its Chinese flavor continues,
distinguishing this monastery with its attrac-
tive name of the "Temple of Abundant Good
Fortune" from traditional aspects of Japanese
Buddhism.

1 MAMPUKU-JI TEMPLE

Japan had always had a small Chinese population in Nagasaki due to that city serving as
the only official port of entry for ships from
China during Tokugawa rule (1615–1868).
In 1654, at the request of that Chinese community and of certain Zen priests who were
anxious to learn from Chinese Buddhism,
Priest Ingen (1592–1673), a high priest of
the Chinese Obaku sect of Zen Buddhism,
arrived in Japan (upon the fall of the Ming
dynasty to the Manchus) to establish the

Obaku sect of Buddhism, the newest form
of Buddhism from China. He brought with
him not only his religious disciples and cohorts but architects, artists, craftsmen, wood
carvers and other artisans from Ming China,
initiating new artistic ideas and forms in
Japan as well as new aspects in dry brush
calligraphy, diet and medicine.

Thus the Mampuku-ji is an interesting
temple since it represents the latest form of
Buddhism which came to Japan from China.
Ostensibly a Zen sect, it includes not only
Zen meditation, but Pure Land doctrines,
esoteric mysticism which came with Shingon,
and even aspects of Tibetan Lamaism. As a
late importation from China, it retains Ming
forms and styles in architecture, ceremony
and even monastic dress, and 350 years after
its arrival, it has over 500 branch temples in
Japan. The Mampuku-ji remains the headquarters of the Obaku sect, the smallest of
the Zen sects in Japan.

Ingen's arrival affected Japanese life in two
other ways as well: previously the drinking of
tea had been primarily a stimulant used by
Zen monks to keep them alert during extended religious services, and it had also become

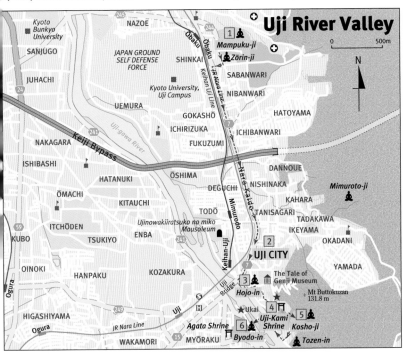

The Daiyuho-den (Main Hall), with its double tiled roof, is the center of the Mampuku-ji complex.

a pastime of the aristocracy with their interest in the formal tea ceremony. Ingen brought a new approach to tea making and tea imbibing when he introduced *sencha* (an infused leaf tea drink) as a different tea from *matcha* (powdered tea) which was used in the traditional tea ceremony. He thereby popularized tea drinking among the people at large. In the area of art he had an affect on painting also, for Western-style painting, with its use of perspective, had influenced Chinese art. Aspects of this Western style can be seen in some of the paintings at Mampuku-ji, an approach which the temple's art introduced to some Japanese artists, such as Ikeno Taiga.

In 1658, Ingen visited Tokugawa Shogun Ietsuna who, in 1661, gave Ingen 63 acres (25.2 ha) of land for a temple near Uji, land which had belonged to the aristocratic Konoye family. Thus, by 1678 a Chinese-style temple, the Mampuku-ji, and a monastery, the Obaku-san, arose, all crafted from teak wood imported from China and Thailand, the temple images indicating a Continental influence in as much as all the temple wood carving was done by a Chinese master sculptor. Shogun Ietsuna and the former Emperor Go-Mizuno-o embraced this new form of Buddhism, and support for the temple continued under Shogun Tsunayoshi and through to 1868 when the Shogun and government support for Buddhism ended. The new religious form brought a renewal of life to a Buddhism which was in decay in Tokugawa days since Neo-Confucianism had become the official doctrine of the Shogun's government. For the

next century the temple retained a distinctive Chinese flavor since the abbots of the temple continued to be Chinese priests. Although the abbots and priests thereafter have been Japanese, an attempt has been made to keep to the Chinese nature of the sect and the temple/monastery, and thus its priests wear a different outfit from other Zen priests, since they use Chinese-style shoes and a head covering which resembles a beret.

TEMPLE STRUCTURES AND GROUNDS

The temple's extensive grounds are entered through the So-mon (Entry or Outer Gate), a small two-story gate whose stepped roof was the first example of this Chinese style of roof design in Japan, and the fish on its roof are the mythical animals called *makara*. The calligraphic plaque over the entry reads "Dai Ichi-gi" (Fundamental Doctrine). To the east of the So-mon is a pond which is situated between the external temple wall and the inner San-mon Gate which can be reached by a pathway with diamond-shaped walking stones. A subtemple complex lies to the left of the So-mon behind a walled garden and pond, and a covered corridor, whose Chinese-style handrail is composed of Buddhist swastikas, leads from the subtemple past a multisided structure with round windows in the Chinese style. Along the corridor, en route to the San-mon Gate, is the Shoro with the temple bell. The Hozo-in is a subtemple north of the So-mon Gate, and it is in this building that copies of the Issaikyo sutra are pulled from the 60,000 woodblocks which

Priest Tetsugen created in the late 1600s and which are kept in the Hatto (Lecture Hall).

The San-mon, the Mountain or Main Gate, is a large two-story gate with 12 great red pillars and green latticed windows, and from its side stretch corridors, all the buildings being interconnected by the covered passageways. Beyond the San-mon is the Tenno-do (Hall of the Heavenly Kings) with four Shi-tenno guardians protecting Hotei, the main deity of this hall, the red and gold paint on their clothing being well preserved. Large Chinese-style lanterns hang from the ceiling, illuminating the image of Hotei, the laughing god of good fortune with his protruding belly, originally an image of a noted Chinese priest who was considered to be an incarnation of Miroku, the Buddha of the Future. The image was created by Fao Tan Sheng, a 17th century sculptor brought from China by Abbot Ingen.

Along the corridor on the left side of the Tenno-do as one walks to the Daiyuho-den are three buildings: the Koro, the Soshi-do, with an image of Dharma (Daruma) and *ihai* memorial tablets, and then the Zen-do meditation hall with a Kannon image. Walking clockwise about the complex along the corridors, the Daiyuho-den (Main Hall), with its double tiled roof, is in the center of the complex directly behind the Tenno-do. A raised mat for the priest is in the center of the floor with a wooden fish-shaped drum, a gong bowl and a drum on a stand to the rear and front of the mat on the right. On either side of this mid-section are 20 mats for other participants in the service. Large vermilion circular units hang from the two-story high ceiling, while before the large Chinese-style altar table there are gold metal lotus flowers in vases at each end of the table with offerings on a plate in the center of the table. The main image in this hall is a golden Shaka with Anan and Kosho, Shaka's most important disciples, at his side. The calligraphic tablet (*shinkyu*) over the altar is by the Emperor Meiji while to the sides of the hall are the 18 *rakan* (individuals who have achieved enlightenment in this existence), nine on either side of the room. The hall and the images were made from teak brought from Thailand. Services at 5:00 a.m. and 4:00 p.m. include the reading of Chinese sutras.

The corridor (still moving clockwise) from the Daiyuho-den to the Hatto passes a building at the point where the corridor turns to the right, and this colorful unit has an image

The wooden hollow fish "clock" at the dining hall.

on the altar which is virtually hidden by the bright orange and gold brocade about it. Vases with huge metal flowers in blue, white and pink are on either side of the altar table, while offerings are on shelves on either side of the altar. Chinese-style floor lamps stand beside the altar table, while *ihai* tablets line the side walls. The Sei Hojo (Western Priests' Quarters), just beyond the corridor turning, was one of the first buildings of the temple, and it contains the Itoku-den hall dedicated to Tokugawa Ieyasu. The Hatto (Lecture Hall) at the center of the rear corridor of the temple complex was a gift from Sakai Tadakiyo, a high Tokugawa official in the 17th century. A raised central platform (Shumiden) within the Hatto is one from which the abbot questions the monks to test their spiritual development, and it also serves as the Ordination Hall platform during the ordination of priests. The Hatto serves as well as a storehouse for the 60,000 woodblocks which were used in printing the previously mentioned Obaku edition of the Buddhist sutras in 7,334 volumes which were created by Priest Tetsugen (1630–82) with the aid of Ingen.

To the right of the Hatto, continuing in a clockwise direction along the corridor, at the corner are the buildings of the temple office and the Eastern Priests' Quarters (To Hojo). There is a reception room here in which the abbot can receive guests, and the famous 18th century set of Nanga screens by Ikeno Taiga (1723–76) were originally kept here before being placed in the Kyoto National Museum. A small stand for the sale of literature concerning the temple is just beyond this complex. The next building is the Sai-do, the dining hall, and before it hang two unusual objects: one is a wooden hollow fish (*kaipan*) with a ball (*hoju*) in its mouth; it is a "clock" which is struck to tell the hour of the day. Also hanging from the ceiling is an *umpan*, a cloud-shaped piece of metal which is struck to announce meal time. The dining hall has tables set up like a mess hall, and 300 individuals can be served at any one time. No conversation is permitted during the meal. Reservations one week in advance offer outsiders an opportunity to partake of *fucha ryori*, Chinese priests' food (vegetarian fare). (A very pleasant restaurant outside the temple also serves vegetarian meals in a building overlooking a lovely garden.) On the rear wall of the hall is enshrined the image of Kinnara, the guardian of meal times. Beyond, along the corridor, is a Chinese-style building with a gold Buddha in a gold patterned gown, while Chinese red lanterns with gold tassels hang from the ceiling. At the end of the corridor are modern rest rooms.

A walled tea garden beyond the corridor is next. Entry through its white walls is by means of the Haku-un-Haku, a white gateway with Chinese characters, which was typical of Chinese castles. This was the first example of this architectural style in Japan. Two buildings, the Maisa-do and the Yusei-kan, associated with the tea ceremony, lie within the walls. The Maisa-do enshrines the Zen priest Maisa ("Old Tea Seller"), the founder of the *sencha* style of tea ceremony which was derived from Chinese Ming usage; the *sencha* approach to tea making involves the steeping of tea leaves, a practice which the Mampuku-ji popularized in Japan. (The hall is opened on Sundays and the 16th of each month for tea ceremony.) The Yusei-kan was especially designed for the tea ceremony, and the headquarters of the Sencha League is located in this compound.

2 UJI CITY

Uji City is the ultimate destination for this trip, and it offers a variety of temples and shrines among which the Byodo-in is the glory of the city. Uji is 12 miles (19 km) south of Kyoto, and it can be reached either by the Japan Rail line to Nara from the Kyoto Central Station or by the Keihan electric railway. The latter is the more convenient in Uji since its terminal is close to the river and the places to be visited. Either line can be taken from Obaku and the Mampuku-ji to Uji City. The Uji River flows from Lake Biwa through the city of Uji as it makes its way to become part of the Yodo River which empties into the Inland Sea at Osaka. The major portion of the city and the Byodo-in are across the river from the Keihan railway station on the south side of the river, but there are a number of interesting sites on the north bank and these will be treated first.

When the Imperial court was resident in Kyoto (794 to 1868), Uji was the site of numerous country villas of the nobility and of the Imperial family as well as of the Buddhist temples they created. The site was settled not only for the beauty of its surroundings but for the convenience which the bridge across the river offered. The Uji Bridge that connects the two banks of the city was first erected in 646 by priest Docho, thereby unwittingly creating a strategic site which was fought over many times in Heian and Kamakura days (the 800s to the 1300s). There are more peaceful remembrances as well, for example, the small bay which juts out from the present-day bridge over the river, a reminder of the occasion when Hideyoshi dipped for water from the bridge for the making of his tea for a tea ceremony party.

To the east of the bridge is Tonoshima Island with a 13-tiered stone pagoda erected by Priest Eison (Kosho Bosatsu) in 1286 as a prayer to keep animals from being killed and to invoke the aid of the Dragon King in the reconstructing of the damaged Uji Bridge. In 1756, this pagoda was buried in the sands of a flood of that year, and it was not until 1908 that it was unearthed and rebuilt. At the north end of the island is an historical stone marking the site where Takatsuna Sasaki and Kagesue Kajiwara, warriors under Minamoto-no-Yoshitsune, in 1184 vied for the honor of being the first to cross the river on horseback to attack the forces of Yoshinaka Kiso which were camped on the opposite bank of the river. There are bridges to the island from both banks of the river, one of them being at the Uji-gami Shrine, and the island is a pleasant place for relaxation and perhaps a picnic lunch. Upstream is a suspension bridge, and around a bend in the hills is the Amagase Dam whose waters flow out of a diversionary stream from the electric generating turbines just before the Kosho-ji Temple. Cormorant fishing takes place in the river from mid-June to mid-August at night except at full moon and after heavy rains. Fishermen in boats with flaming torches to attract the fish release the cormorants into the water to capture the fish in their beaks but then disgorge them into the boats under the fishermen's control. (The fishing only lasts about 20–30 minutes, close to shore, but one can rent a boat for a closer view if one wishes.)

Uji has been one of the two great centers of tea plantations (along with Shizuoka) since Myoe Shonin (1173–1232) of the northwestern Kyoto Kozan-ji first came to Uji and planted tea seeds. Two types of tea are grown: *sencha*, which is a high quality green leaf tea, and *matcha*, where the tea leaves are ground to form a powdered green tea used in the formal tea ceremony. There are many shops selling tea in the city, and a number of festivals take place annually, some obviously concerned with tea. The Byodo-in is the main reason to come to Uji, but the following temples and shrines on the north bank of the river are of interest as well. The Hashi-dera (Bridge Temple) or Hojo-in is the first site. The Hashi-dera Temple can be most easily reached by the Keihan railway line to Uji since the temple is just upstream from the Keihan station and the Uji Bridge. The Japan Rail Nara line also stops in Uji, but then one has to walk down to the river and across the bridge to the temple. (The Hashi-dera is open from 9:00 a.m. to 4:00 p.m. No entry fee.)

3 HOJO-IN TEMPLE

The Hojo-in (Hashi-dera) is now a Shingon-Ritsu sect temple which was originally built by Hatano Kawakatsu, reputedly at the request of Prince Shotoku in 604, although most sources claim a founding date of 646. The temple was rebuilt in 1264 and called the Hojo-in because of a great compassionate Buddhist Hojo-e ceremony (setting birds free from cages) in connection with the dedication of the 13-story pagoda which was built on Tonoshima Island across the way. Since the temple was responsible for the care of the bridge which crosses the Uji River, it came to be known as the Hashi-dera (Bridge Temple). The temple holds the Uji-bashi Danpi, a stone inscribed with the account of how Priest Docho first built the Uji-bashi Bridge in the second year of Taika (646). It is one of the three oldest stone monuments in Japan. Stone steps lead up from the river road to this minor temple. In the open area at the top of the steps, the temple residence lies directly ahead while the temple's main building is to the left. The Uji-bashi Danpi stone (under its own protective roof) is to the left of the main

hall. To the right of the stairs from the street is a roofed structure with eight images, including a 1,000-arm Kannon, a Fudo and an Amida. On the far right are two Jizo images between memorial stones.

4 UJI-KAMI SHRINE

Further along the north side of the river is the Uji-Kami Shrine which is open during daylight hours without charge. The Uji-Kami Shrine is said to have been founded in 313 on the site of the residence of Prince Uji-no-Waka-iratsuko. Legend recounts that the Emperor Ojin had two sons, the future Emperor Nintoku and his younger brother, Prince Waka-iratsuko. The father named the younger son as Crown Prince, but on Ojin's death the younger brother refused to accept the throne since he felt it belonged to his elder brother. The older brother would not accept it either since he did not wish to negate his father's wishes. In the year 312, at the end of a three-year impasse when neither would mount the throne, the younger brother killed himself so that Nintoku could be Emperor. Thus, the Uji Shrine was dedicated to the Emperor Ojin and his two sons in 313.

The shrine is in two parts, the upper sector being the oldest (901–4). Unlike most Shinto shrines, the buildings were not replaced periodically, and thus the Kami (Upper) Uji Shrine has the oldest shrine building layout extant, and its Honden (Spirit Hall) is the oldest shrine building in Japan. This upper shrine is dedicated particularly to Waka-iratsuko. In the forecourt of the upper shrine is a spring noted for the clarity of its water, one of the "Seven Springs of Uji." The lower shrine was built in the Kamakura period (1185–1333) and its Haidan (Oratory) is regarded as an excellent example of architecture of that time. The main shrine building consists of three small shrines on raised piers; they are joined as one Honden by a surrounding structure. The painted figures of the two brothers are still faintly visible on the back of the doors of the shrine.

5 KOSHO-JI TEMPLE

The Kosho-ji is the next site along the river, being located beyond the Hashi-dera and the Uji Shrine on the slope of Asahi Hill just beyond the outlet of the hydroelectric station where the plant water runs into the Uji River. (The temple is open from 9:00 a.m. to 4:00 p.m.)

The Kosho-ji was founded by Priest Dogen (1200–53) in 1233 when he established the Soto sect of Zen in this temple on his return from China, and thus this temple is the pioneer temple of the Soto sect. The present structures were built from timber of the Fushimi Castle of Hideyoshi, given to the temple by the Tokugawa Shogun in 1649 in order to rebuild the temple which had fallen into ruins.

The temple's Chinese heritage is reflected in the architecture of the temple, particularly in its Chinese-style main gateway, which is at the end of a long tree-lined walk from the main road at the Uji River. Past the initial gateway, the path continues up a slight grade between sloping walls holding the hillside; the path is called the Koto Walk from the supposedly musical sound of the running water in the adjacent ditches. At the end of the walk, steps lead up to the temple wall and the Chinese-style white gateway with its rounded opening and with dolphins topping the edges of its tiled roof. The gate is said to resemble the style of gates used in Chinese castles. It is also known as a Dragon Palace type of gate.

Within the walls, beyond the gate, the temple Shoro (Bell Tower) is on the right and beyond it is the monastic Bath House. On the left is a small hexagonal building atop a stone base, and in front of the monks' living quarters building, which closes off the left side of this outer courtyard, is a small stone Fudo image and a stone lantern with a moveable Wheel of the Law in its shaft. At the side of the monks' quarters are an outdoor pump and a washing stand with faucets. Beyond, to its left, is a Memorial Hall.

The main portion of the temple has a corridor and buildings about its inner courtyard, a court which is entered up a few steps and through a gateway, and to the right, at the end of the corridor, is a gong in the shape of a fish. The unit behind it is the refectory and the kitchen for the temple. Directly ahead of the courtyard gate is the Hondo (Main Hall), with its altar colorfully decorated with orange and gold brocades above which hang golden chandeliers. The building on the left side of the court has at its end an image of Daikoku in red, green and gold, while behind the Hondo are other private temple buildings. The Kosho-ji is noted for its azaleas in the springtime and the rich color of its maple trees in the autumn.

6 BYODO-IN TEMPLE

The Byodo-in is, of course, the major attraction of Uji, and it is a site worth keeping until the end of this tour. It is on the south bank of the Uji River, across the Uji Bridge from the Keihan electric railway Uji station. On crossing the bridge, a sharp left turn leads one down the street to the temple. Originally a Tendai temple, the Byodo-in now belongs to the Jodo sect. (The large stone at the entrance to the temple grounds is an 1887 monument in honor of Uji's tea industry.) If coming by the Japan Rail train, walk down to the bridge and then into the street to the temple, a 10 minute walk from either station to the Byodo-in. (The temple is open from 8:30 a.m. to 5:30 p.m. from March to November and from 9:00 a.m. to 4:30 p.m. from December to February. Entry fee.)

HISTORY The history of the Byodo-in goes back to a series of country villas built by or for court nobles or members of the Imperial family after the capital was settled in Kyoto.

The splendid Phoenix Hall at Byodo-in Temple.

In the late 800s, the son of Emperor Saga, Minamoto-no-Toru (822–95), whom some think was the model for Genji, the hero of *The Tale of Genji*, built a villa in Uji. On his death, the Emperor Uda assumed its owner-ship, and eventually in 998 it became the villa of Fujiwara-no-Michinaga (966–1027), the Kampaku or advisor to the Emperor and the man who really controlled the state. In 1052, Michinaga's oldest son, Fujiwara-no-Yorimichi (992–1074), converted the villa into a temple on his 60th birthday, a temple which he named the Byodo-in. The date was signifi-cant as it marked the 2,001st year since the Buddha had entered Nirvana—and marked as well the first year of Mappo, the Age of the Decline of the Buddhist Law, the beginning of the degenerate "Latter Days of the Law."

The first building created was the Hondo (Main Hall) dedicated to the Dainichi Nyorai, attended by Shaka and Yakushi and two Deva Kings. In March of the following year (1053), the dedication services were held for the Amida-do or Hoo-do (Phoenix Hall) to house

the Amida Buddha by Jocho. In the next 20 years a number of other buildings were added to the temple: the Hokke-do (Hall for Medita-tion on the Lotus Sutra), the Taho-to (one-story pagoda), the Godai-do (Hall of the Five Wrathful Gods), the Kodo (Lecture Hall), the Kyozo (Sutra Storehouse) and the Hozo (Treasury).

In 1072, Yorimichi retired and became a monk at the Byodo-in, and when he died at 82, two years later, on February 2, 1074, the temple had 26 buildings and seven pagodas. The Byodo-in had its Imperial visitors: the Emperor Go-Reizei visited it in 1067 and Go-Daigo in 1330, the latter under adverse condi-tions since he hid and was captured here in his battles with Shogun Ashikaga Takauji. Battles also plagued the temple and its envi-rons, and in May 1180 Minamoto-no-Yorimasa committed *seppuku* on the temple grounds when his battle against the Taira turned against him. Again, in 1184, in the battle between the Sasaki and Kajiwara clans, and then in 1336 in the Ashikaga times, the temple found war swirling about it. A fire in 1483 left only the Hoo-do (the Amida-do) of the original buildings. Today what remains is the Hoo-do, the Kannon-do of the Kamakura period (1185–1336), the Shoro (Bell Tower) and the subsidiary temples of the Jodo-in and Saisgo-in. A new Treasury Building (Homotsukan) was built in 1965 to hold the remaining temple treasures.

TEMPLE STRUCTURES AND GROUNDS

The Hoo-do or Amida Hall is the most important building of the Byodo-in, and it is best to view it from across the pond in front of it—as Yorimichi would have seen it from his palace which once stood on this opposite shore. The path from the entrance to the grounds should thus be followed to the left and around the pond rather than toward the Hoo-do directly.

The Amida Hall, which was dedicated in March 1053, was Yorimichi's private chapel. For many years visitors had to worship Amida from across the Aji-ike Pond since they were not permitted to enter the Amida-do itself. From his villa on the opposite side of the pond, Yorimichi could look across the water to the face of Amida appearing through the opening of the trellis work before the image. Here was Amida in his Western Paradise, and here was Yorimichi, free of the world of politics and power, looking across the Lake of Paradise on to the Western Paradise as described in the Kammuryojukyo sutra, a paradise which, at his advanced age, he believed, would soon be his in reality.

Before the hall stands a stone lantern set in a bed of raked sand, and before that is the pond which once encircled the Amida Hall. When the doors to the Amida-do are open, the peaceful face of Amida can still be seen as Yorimichi saw it through the opening of the lattice work as Amida sits in quiet meditation. In the early 1600s, the vermilion Amida Hall was nicknamed the Phoenix Hall (Hoo-do) since its form was designed to resemble a bird landing after flight. To complement the imagery, two bronze phoenixes (male and female) adorn the roof of its central hall. (A phoenix was a mythical Chinese bird which had a front part like a Chinese unicorn (*kirin*), a rear part like a deer, a head like a snake, a tail like a fish, a back like a turtle, a chin like a swallow and a beak like a chicken.) The central hall represents the body of the bird while the side corridors are the wings and the rear corridor is the tail. The

"wings" and "tail" serve no other purpose than architectural symmetry.

The building is impressive both in its size and in its architectural balance. The central hall (the body) appears to be a two-story unit although it is only a one-story structure. It is a three bay by two bay unit 46.5 feet (14 m) long by 39 feet (8 m) deep, and it rises 33 feet (10 m) into the air. The two-story side corridors (the wings) of five bays each are 382 feet (115 m) long, while the rear corridor (tail) is 90 feet (27 m) long. This rear corridor originally connected the central hall with another building, which is now missing.

Within the hall, the almost 10 foot (3 m) tall Amida image, created by Jocho in 1083, is in the *yosegi* joined woodblock technique instead of being carved from a single block of wood. The image sits on a lotus of four layers of 16 petals each, the full pedestal itself being in nine layers. Amida sits crosslegged, his hands on his knees and joined in the *mudra* of meditation, symbolic of Amida's vow of redemption which embraces all beings in the nine stages of existence. Amida's eyes are cast down—so that when Yorimichi prayed before him privately, he could feel the eyes of the Buddha looking down at him in compassion.

Directly behind Amida is a lacy fretwork aureole with the Dainichi Nyorai of the Kongo-kai (Diamond World) Mandala in its center and 12 Bodhisattvas about the gilded background to Amida. Within the Amida is a lotus pedestal inscribed in ink with a mystic formula. The coved ceiling has bronze mirrors inset at 3 foot (1 m) intervals to reflect the light of the candles on the altar below. A lacy carved canopy of vegetation hangs above Amida's head, while on the white plaster walls float 52 flying *apsara* (heavenly beings) playing instruments, carrying flags, praying, practicing *mudra* or dancing on wisps of clouds. These cedar carved images range from 16 inches (40 cm) tall when seated to 34 inches (85 cm) in height when standing. Originally they were brilliantly colored, such brilliance now having faded.

On the wall behind the Amida is a painting of Amida's Pure Land, a vision which Yorimichi tried to duplicate in his temple complex. On the door to the rear wing (behind the Amida) is a painting of the "Contemplation of the Sunset," while the other doors had scenes of the Kubon Raigo on each door showing Amida descending with his Bodhisattvas, led by Seishi and Kannon, to welcome the souls of the dead into his Western Paradise. (Eight of the original doors can be seen in the Treasury; those in the Amida Hall are copies.) Atop the doors are sutra writings from the Kammuryoju-kyo sutra. These paintings were the work of Takuma Taminari, chief of the Picture Bureau of the Imperial court. The paintings are in the Yamato-e style, reflecting Japanese characteristics rather than Chinese art forms, and since the paintings in the Horyu-ji Kondo burned, these are among the oldest Japanese paintings extant. The altar was inlaid with mother-of-pearl and gold, now all virtually gone.

On the north side of the Hoo-do (Amidado), along the Uji River embankment, is the Kannon-do or Tsuridono (Fishing Hall). This latter nickname was once the popular name of the hall when the river flowed next to it and one could fish from the building. The building with its tiled hipped roof is seven bays by four bays (62 feet/18.6 m) by 33 feet/9.9 m).

Built in the Kamakura period (1185–1333), the Kannon-do is thought to have replaced the original Hondo (Main Hall) with its Dainichi Nyorai of Yorimichi's day. Within the Kannon-do is a cutaway model of the Hoo-do and of a phoenix, but its major image is a life-sized 11-headed Kannon 5.5 feet (1.7 m) tall, carved from a single block of cypress wood; the Kannon holds a vase with a lotus bud in it. On one side of Kannon stands Jizo, 5 feet (1.6 m) tall, carved from a single block of zelkova wood, the mystic jewel in his right hand and his staff held in his left hand. On the other side is an image of Fudo, 3 feet (1 m) tall carved from a single block of cypress wood; his traditional two small attendants are beside him. This standing image holds a rope in his left hand and a sword held up in his right hand, his pigtail flung over his left shoulder. Behind the image is a flaming *mandorla* (aureole).

A hundred years after Yorimichi died, on May 26, 1180, the 76-year-old Minamoto-no-Yorimasa (1104–80), together with the monks of the Mii-dera Temple, faced the forces of the Taira clan at the Uji Bridge. His forces numbered 300 men against the 28,000 mustered by his opponents. With the battle turning against his small army, he retreated to the Byodo-in, and behind the Kannon-do he spread his fan on the ground, composed his final poem, "How sad that the old buried tree should die without a single bloom," and

committed *seppuku*. (He is buried in the Saisho-in behind the Hoo-do.) A fan-shaped fence marks the site of his death.

The Shoro (temple bell tower) is on a rise to the south of the Hoo-do, and the bell in the belfry is a copy of the original, which is in the Treasure House. The original bell is considered one of the three most famous bells of Japan and is said to be the most beautiful of all. It is divided into squares which frame dragons and phoenixes, a flower and vine motif separating the units. *Apsara* (flying angels) and lions fill the spaces above and below the main squares. The bell is 6.5 feet (2 m) tall, has a diameter of 4.5 feet (1.4 m) and weighs 3 tons.

Two small temples lie behind the Hoo-do, the Jodo-in and the Saisho-in. The Saisho-in is where Minamoto-no-Yorimasa was buried, and it retains some of his personal effects. This temple also has an early prototype of the Japanese flag. The Homotsu-kan (Treasure House) of the temple is open in April and May and again in October and November. (Entry fee.) Among its numerous objects, the original temple bell and the painted doors from the Hoo-do are the most important.

The Agata Shrine which is close to the south gate of the Byodo-in is a minor shine which is dedicated to a Shinto goddess, Konohana-Sakuya-hime-no-mikoto, the spouse of Ninigi-no-mikoto (Amaterasu's grandson). (The goddess is also enshrined in the Sengen Shrine at the foot of Mount Fuji.) The shine conforms to the standard Shinto layout, and its one mark of distinction lies in its annual festival which occurs on June 5th each year at midnight in darkness when the goddess's spirit is taken in procession for placement in the inner shrine. Paper bits scattered during the procession are considered to be talismans of good luck.

GETTING THERE

The Mampuku-ji can be reached from Kyoto on either the Japan Rail Nara line or the Keihan electric railway Uji line to their separate Obaku stations. The temple is to the east of the stations, and it is open from 9:00 to 4:00 p.m. Entry fee.

A return to Kyoto can be made either on the Japan Rail or the Keihan rail line. The latter probably offers more frequent service.

General Information

Each of the sites described within this guide-book lists the hours at which the site is open and whether there is an entry fee. In general, most temples charge a small entry fee to cover the upkeep of buildings and grounds. Shrines, on the other hand, usually do not charge for entrance. Entry fees have not been indicated since they vary. Imperial palaces and villas (the Old Imperial Palace, the Shugaku-in Villa and the Katsura Villa) do not charge a fee, but you must register in advance for permission to visit these sites— see below. Virtually all museums, private villas and gardens charge an entry fee.

THE OLD IMPERIAL PALACE, THE SHUGAKU-IN AND KATSURA VILLA

These three imperial sites require registration in advance for entry to their grounds. Registration takes place at the Imperial Household Agency office on the grounds of the Old Imperial Palace just south of Imadegawa-dori to the east of Karasuma-dori. You should bring along your passport for identification purposes. The office is closed on Saturday afternoons, all day Sunday, on national holidays and from December 25 through January 5.

Permission for the tour of the palace grounds can frequently take place the same day, such tours being offered at 9:00, 11:00, 13:30 and 15:00. The grounds of the palace can be visited, but not the interior of the buildings. A separate reservation must be made for the Sento Gosho (the retired emperor's palace), where the lovely grounds and stroll garden remain, even though the original palace structures have been destroyed by fire. This tour is at 11:00 and 13:30 and is in Japanese only.

WEEKENDS AND HOLIDAYS IN KYOTO

Kyoto is a popular venue for the Japanese as well as for tourists. Thus, on weekends and national holidays, all sites can be very crowded. Food facilities can be strained at meal times, and therefore it might be well to purchase a boxed lunch such as those sold in the Central Railway Station.

National holidays occur on 13 occasions throughout the year, and on these days banks and public offices are closed. If a national holiday falls on a Sunday, the next day is marked as the holiday. Golden Week (April 29 to May 5) is a period when all Japan seems to be traveling, and advance reservations for hotels, trains and public events are essential during this week.

The national holidays occur on:
January 1, January 15, February 11, March 21, April 29, May 3, May 5, September 15, September 23, October 10, November 3, November 23 and December 23.

The Obon period of August 13 to 16 also sees heavy travel. Many public venues (museums, etc.) are closed from approximately December 25 through January 5.

KYOTO TOURIST INFORMATION

The Japan National Tourist Office in the Kyoto Tower Building to the north of the Central Station Plaza on Karasuma-dori can answer questions as to any of the sites in the Kyoto area. Maps, brochures and other information can be readily and cheerfully obtained without charge.

The Japan Travel Bureau, as well as other travel agencies in the buildings around the Central Railway Plaza, can assist with reservations.

MONEY EXCHANGE

Travelers' checks and foreign currency are most easily exchanged at banks. As a courtesy, some of the major department stores, such as Hankyu and Takashimaya, will also exchange travelers' checks for ¥, and most tourist hotels are able to cash travelers' checks as well.

Getting to Kyoto

RAIL LINES

The Japan Rail Pass is valid on the Japan Rail Line but not on the other private lines mentioned below. Most rail lines have automatic ticket machines and these tickets must be placed in the turnstile, reclaimed and then finally deposited in the turnstile at the exit. Tickets are also available at ticket offices in the stations if you do not have the correct change for the ticket machine. Long journeys usually require a regular rather than a machine ticket.

Japan Rail Japan Rail trains from Kyoto Station run in all directions to the north, south, east and west. Various lines emanate from the station, including local and regular express trains as well as the Shinkansen line.

Tickets can be purchased from machines or from the ticket office in the station (language can sometimes be a problem at such offices).

Kintetsu (Kinki Nippon) Line The Kintetsu Line to Nara has its main entrance on the southwest side of Kyoto Station. Here, trains can be taken to areas in the southern part of Kyoto as well as on to Nara or further south to the Asuka region and to Yoshino. Tickets can be purchased from machines at each station or from the ticket office.

Hankyu Rail Line The Hankyu Rail Line begins as a subway under Shijo-dori in Kyoto at Kawaramachi-dori. It runs to Katsura (change for Matsuo and Arashiyama) and on to Osaka. For stations within the general Kyoto area, be certain to take a local and not an express train as you may miss stops.

Keihan Rail Line The Keihan Rail Line, in a sense, connects three rail lines:
1 The main line operates from its underground (subway) Imade-gawa-dori station terminal on the east side of the Kamogawa River and goes south to Uji or Osaka.
2 The Eizan Railway operates from the Demachi Yanagi station at Imadegawa-dori (just above the Keihan subway station of its Osaka or Uji line) to Kurama or to Yase.

The Keihan Rail Line runs on the east side of the Kamo-gawa River, becoming a subway north from Tofuku-ji station to the terminus at Imadegawa-dori just below the Demachi Yanagi surface station to Yase or Kurama to the north. To the south, the Keihan Rail Line serves stations in south Kyoto and Uji as well as providing access to Osaka and stations in between.

Keifuku Rail Line The Keifuku Rail Line serves the western part of Kyoto. One terminal is at the Shijo Omiya-dori intersection from where it departs for Arashiyama. Another terminal for its Kitario Line is at the Nishioji Imadegawa-dori intersection. The Kitano Line runs west to its junction with the Arashiyama Line where one is able to change to an Arishiyama train. These two lines run along the surface, sometimes on city streets.
Kyoto Subway The efficient subway system runs due north–south through Kyoto from the Kokusai Kaikan station at the Kyoto International Conference Hall in the north to the Takeda station in the south. Some trains run through to Nara via the subway system and these trains continue on beyond Takeda station. The Tozai subway line runs from the Nijo Station on west Oike-dori to the Keage station on eastern Sanjo-dori to the south and to the Daigo-ji Temple complex. Tickets are purchased from vending machines at subway entrances, and these tickets are placed in the turnstile at the entrance and then at the exit at one's destination, as described above.

BUS LINES

Kyoto is well served by efficient bus lines that cover all of the major areas of the city as well as locations beyond the city itself. Most lines begin from the bus plaza in front of Kyoto Station, while some begin at the Keihan Sanjo station on the east side of the Kamo-gawa River. One enters a bus from the rear and, within the city, pays the set fare that is listed at the front of the bus. Buses are exited from the front where the fare is paid to the driver. A machine behind the driver makes change.

For buses going beyond the city center, one takes a ticket from the machine at the rear entry to the bus. An electric board above the driver indicates the number on the ticket (the point at which one entered the bus) and the fare at the point at which the bus arrived. One exits through the door at the front, paying the driver the appropriate fare on leaving.

Long-distance buses also leave from the terminal in front of Kyoto Station.

Buses are numbered with one or two digits. Three-digit number buses are loop buses within the city of Kyoto, while two-digit buses start at either Kyoto Station or Keihan Sanjo station.

Bus stops are marked by a sign with a half circle for City (green) buses while Kyoto (pale brown) bus stops are marked by a full circle. Such signs indicate the number of the bus route and the times at which buses stop at that position. (Kyoto buses offer longer runs.)

A one-day pass for the buses and the subway may be obtained from the Kyoto City Visitors Information Center located in the plaza across from the Kyoto Tower Building.

A map of the bus lines may be obtained at the Japan National Tourist office and is included as an insert on many maps of the city.

AIRPORT BUS

The bus to Osaka Airport can be taken from its starting point in front of the Avanti Department Store across the street from the south side of the Kyoto Central Station.

TAXIS

Taxis may be found at taxi stands throughout the city, but they can be hailed on the street as well. Taxis are metered for fares, and tips are not expected by the drivers. Your hotel can provide you with a card with your destination written in Japanese that you can show the driver–if you are concerned about your pronunciation of Japanese place and street names. A card listing the hotel's name and address can be acquired at the front desk and given to the driver, who will wait and return you to your hotel if you so wish.

Kyoto Festivals

The major festivals or ceremonies occurring at central Kyoto sites are listed below. These events may occur on a date other than as stated since some events take place according to the traditional lunar calendar. Since other events may now be scheduled for weekends for the convenience of attendees, you should check with the Tourist Information Bureau and the events calendars which are issued monthly as to the exact date of the following ceremonies or festivals. Such calendars are available at most hotels and at the Japan National Tourist Office in the Kyoto Tower Building on Karasuma-dori. The information below was obtained from shrine and temple publications, from the Kyoto Monthly Calendar, and from Bauer and Carlquist's *Japanese Festivals*.

Asterisks (*) indicate monthly events that are not listed with each month's festivals.

January

1 Okera-mairi, Yasaka Shrine. Devotees attend the shrine to bring home a portion of the sacred fire on which the first meal of the year will be cooked. The action is thought to ward off illness during the new year.

1–3 Hatsumode. The year's first visit to Shinto shrines to pray for good luck during the ensuing year. Women often wear their best *kimono* at this time. Among the shrines that are most popular for this visit are Yasaka Shrine, the Heian Shrine, and the Kitano Tenman-gu, among other locations.

1–3 Obukucha, Rokuharamitsu-ji. Green tea is presented to visitors to ward off illness in the new year.

2–4 Shinzen Kakizome, Kitano Tenman-gu. The year's first calligraphy. Children do their first writing of the new year at this shrine in honor of Sugawara-no-Michizane, the patron of writing, of scholarship and of scholars, who is enshrined here.

2 Religious service at 9:30 a.m.

2–4 New Year's writing from 10:30 a.m. to 3:00 p.m.

3 *Kyogen* performances and calligraphy demonstrations from 1:00 p.m. to 2:30 p.m.

8–12 Kanchu Takuhatsu, Shogo-in. A hundred monks start on their first begging walk of the year.

8–12 Toka Ebisu, Gion Ebisu and all Ebisu shrines. Ebisu is the patron of business and good luck. (He is one of the Seven Gods of Good Fortune, and thus he is very popular with merchants and businessmen.) Stalls are set up for the sale of various items. The following are some of the main events of Toka Ebisu held at the Gion Ebisu Shrine:

8 Shofukusai (Festival for Happiness): A Shinto service is held from 2:00 p.m. to 3:00 p.m. and then the festival begins. *Bugaku* is offered as well as *kagura* (sacred dance to traditional music) performed by the *miko* (female shrine attendants), and *mochi* (rice cakes) are made–all to please the gods.

9 Yoi-Ebisu Bugaku. Performances are offered throughout the evening.

10 Hon-Ebisu (Main Festival of Ebisu). A service is held at 2:00 p.m. in honor of Ebisu's first taking up residence in this shrine on this date.

11 Nokori Fuku (Remaining Luck). From 2:00 p.m. to 4:00 p.m. and again from 8:00 p.m. to 10:00 p.m. *Miko* distribute to those present the sacred *mochi* which were made on January 8.

9 Ho-onko, Nishi Hongan-y. Annual service in honor of Shinran, founder of the Jodo Shinshu sect of Buddhism.

11 Shobo Dezome-shiki (Fire Brigade Parade), Okazaki Park. Over 2,000 firemen and 100 fire vehicles (including helicopters) perform fire drills and rescues using ladder trucks and helicopters. Antique fire vehicles form part of the parade.

15 Seijin-no-hi (Adults' Day, a national holiday). A coming-of-age celebration for those who have reached their 20th birthday. Celebrated by municipalities and individual families as well as at certain shrines and temples.

15 Toshiya (Archery Contest), Sanjusangen-do. A traditional archery contest under the eaves of the rear platform of the temple from 8:30 a.m. to 4:00 p.m. No charge to temple visitors who have paid their entrance fee.

21 (monthly) *Hatsukobo, To-ji temple. First service of the year in honor of Kobo Daishi. Monthly fair held on the temple grounds.

25 (monthly) *Tenjin Matsuri, Kitano Tenman-gu. First service of the year in honor of Sugawara-no-Michizane. Monthly fair on the temple grounds and precinct.

February

2–4 Setsubun. The day of the celebration varies according to the lunar calendar. This festival marks the final day of winter. It is celebrated by driving demons away by throwing beans (*mamemaki*) throughout the house and about the temple. "Oni wa soto, fuku wa uchi!" (Out with evil, in with good fortune,) is the cry which accompanies the scattering of the beans. The festival is celebrated at most temples and shrines among which are the following ceremonies:

2–3 Mibu-dera. On February 2 at 1:00 p.m., *yamabushi* (itinerant "mountain" priests) and *chigo* (a boy who serves the gods) hold a religious procession about the temple grounds. At 2:00 p.m. thousands of pieces of wood that have been donated by devotees are set aflame to protect the people from illness or misfortune. On February 3, *Kyogen* is performed eight times from 1:00 p.m. to 8:00 p.m. by members of the temple district to exorcise demons.

2 Tsuinashiki (Ceremony to Chase Devils), Yoshida Shrine. A very popular festival in which Hossoshi, in a strange costume and wearing a golden mask, appears with a halberd and sword. He and his associates, carrying torches, chase away a pair of red and green devils. An evening bonfire and stalls selling charms and food make this evening into a partial fair at which some attendees wear masks and colorful costumes. From 6:00 p.m.

3 Okame Setsubun, Senbon Shaka-do. Okame is the round, cheerful-faced deity whose mask is very popular. She is considered the patron of business and prosperity and, as a one-time living person, she was associated with this temple. At 3:00 p.m. well-known citizens of Kyoto wear an Okame mask as they scatter beans from the temple Hondo.

3 Setsubun, Shogo-in. The itinerant mountain priests (*yamabushi*) gather at their headquarters for a ceremony in which a large log is burned as an invocation.

3 Oni Horaku (Devils' Dance), Rozan-ji. 3:00 p.m. to 4:00 p.m. In a ceremony with a 1,000-year heritage, three devils (a red one representing greed, a green one representing jealousy and a black one representing complaints) dance to the accompaniment of drums and conch shells. After a lengthy dance, they are chased away by the scattering of beans. A fire is lit as an invocation.

3 Setsubun, Kitano Tenman-gu. At 1:30 p.m. *Kyogen* is presented at the Kagura-den (Hall for Sacred Dances) of the shrine. Afterwards, a group of *geisha* offer dances and then conclude their performance by scattering beans to ward off evil.

March

1 to April 3 Doll Display, Hokyo-ji. A display of dolls from the 14th to the 19th century and costumed mannequins. From 9:00 a.m. to 4:00 p.m. Fee.

3 Hina Matsuri. The traditional Girls' Festival when dolls were displayed on five- or seven-tiered stands, particularly dolls representing the emperor and empress and their court. The day was also known as "Peach Blossom Day" since a bloom of the peach tree often decorated the display.

14–16 Nehan-e (Commemoration of Buddha's Death and Attainment of Nirvana). This important Buddhist celebration is held at many temples.

20–May 24 Treasury Opening, To-ji. The temple treasures are on view. 9:00 a.m. to 4:00 p.m. Fee.

21 Shunbun-no-hi (Vernal Equinox Day, a national holiday). A holiday reputedly begun under Prince Shotoku in the 600s. Today, it marks respect for growing things in nature and, as a portion of the *higan* Buddhist ceremony, families often visit their family graves.

21 Izumi Shikibu-ki, Seishin-in. A memorial service for Izumi Shikibu, a famous Heian era poet. A 9 foot (2.8 m) tall tower is erected as a memorial in this small temple in the Shin Kyogoku shopping area.

April

1–18 Kano Chakai (Cherry Viewing Tea Ceremony), Heian Shrine. Daily from 9:00 a.m. to 4:00 p.m. Fee. At noon on April 16, court and other traditional dances are presented on a stage in front of the Daigoku-den in order to please the gods.

1–30 Miyako Odori, Gion Kaburenjo Theater. The annual spring "Capital Dances" by *geisha*. Fee. Tea ceremony may be enjoyed for an additional fee. Performances daily at 12:30, 2:00, 3:30 and 4:50 p.m.

4 Go-o Taisai, Go-o Shrine. Karate and the recitation of Chinese poetry to please the deities.

8 Hana Matsuri (Flower Festival). Birthday services in honor of the birth of the Buddha featuring a baptizing ceremony called *kanbutsue*. In all temples.

10 Hirano Jinja Sakura Matsuri, Hirano Shrine. A festival celebrating the cherry blossoms and featuring a parade of costumes said to go back to Heian times.

14 Shunki Taisai, Shiramine Shrine. Heian-period football (*kemari*) is played in Heian costume after religious services.

15 Heian Shrine Festival. *Kagura* dance is performed to *gagaku* music.

15–28 Kyo-odori, Minami-za Theater. Springtime *geisha* dance performances. Fee.

17 Yoshida Matsuri, Yoshida Shrine. Court dances in early costumes to please the gods. 9:30 a.m.

21–29 Mibu Kyogen, Mibu-dera. A very popular performance of *Kyogen* skits by devotees of the temple is given from 1:00 p.m. to 5:30 p.m.; five performances daily and then until 10:00 p.m. on the last day.

29–May 5 Golden Week: A series of national holidays when the Japanese travel to popular resort areas and tourist-oriented cities and towns.

29 Conservation Day, a national holiday. A holiday which replaces the former Emperor Hirohito's birthday holiday.

May

1–4 Nenbutsu Kyogen, Senbon Emma-do, Inno-ji. *Kyogen* performances have taken place at this temple since the 14th century. Performances at 7:00 p.m. the first two days and from 2:00 p.m. to 6:00 p.m. on the last two days. Admission free.

1–4 Shinsen-en Kyogen, Shinsen-en. *Kyogen* as performed by devotees of the Shinsen-en Temple. Performances from 1:30 p.m. to 6:00 p.m. the first two days and from 1:30 p.m. to 10:00 p.m. the last two days. No charge.

1–24 Kamogawa Odori, Pontocho Kaburenjo Theater. Springtime *geisha* dance performances. Fee. Tea ceremony available for an extra fee.

2 Ochatsubo Dochu (Parade of Tea Jars).

From Kennin-ji to Yasaka Shrine. Each spring the Shogun required the tea dealers of Uji to present him with the first tea leaves of the season. The leaves were packed in large ceramic jars, and on this occasion, such jars are paraded from the Kennin-ji to Shijo-dori and on to the Yasaka Shrine in remembrance of this past event.

3 Constitution Day, a national holiday. *Yabusame* horseback archery performed at Shimogamo Jinja from 1:00 p.m.

5 Jishu Matsuri, Jishu Jinja. Noon. Procession of 100 children in *samurai* costumes leaves Kiyomizu-dera at 2:30 p.m. *Rei-taisai* prayer ceremony.

5 Kodomo-no-hi (Children's Day, a national holiday). Formerly known as "Boys' Day." Cloth carp are flown from poles and various martial arts displays take place, particularly at the Budo Center in Okazaki Park.

15 Aoi Matsuri (Hollyhock Festival), Shimogamo and Kamigamo shrines. An Imperial messenger in an ox cart, his suite and some 300 courtiers start from Kyoto Gosho at 10:00 a.m. and arrive at the Shimogamo Shrine at 11:40 for ceremonies. They leave there at 2:00 p.m. and arrive at the Kamigamo Shrine at 3:30. During the Heian period, hollyhocks were thought to ward off thunderstorms and earthquakes; thus, these leaves are worn on headgear, decorate the carts and are offered to the gods as well. Reserved seats can be obtained at the Imperial Palace, the starting point of the procession.

18 Yoshida Reisai, Yoshida Shrine. Yamato-mai traditional dances are offered to the gods at the shrine on this date.

21 Gotan-e, Nishi Hongan-ji. Memorial services for Shinran Shonin, founder of the Shinshu Jodo sect of Buddhism.

June

1 Kaminari-yoke Taisai, Kitano Tenman-gu. A festival to honor the god of thunder. Protective talismans are distributed. From 4:00 p.m.

1–2 Kyoto Takigi Noh, Heian Shrine. In the light of burning torches, *Noh* performances begin at 5:30 p.m. (Postponed in the event of rain.) Fee.

5–6 Oda Nobunaga Service, Honno-ji. Services for the assassinated 15th century civil head of state. Ninja show and flamenco guitar. Temple treasures are on view at 2:00 p.m.

5 Eisai-ki, Kennin-ji. A memorial service in honor of Priest Eisai who brought tea seeds from China and popularized tea drinking in Japan.

8 Iris viewing, Heian Shrine.

9–12 Toki-ichi (Pottery Fair), Senbon Shakado. A service in appreciation of used pottery held at 2:00 p.m. on June 10. Pottery sold at reduced prices.

12 Yatsuhashi Ki Matsuri, Honen-in. *Koto* music in honor of Yatsuhashi Ki and his contribution to the *koto*.

15 Aoba Matsuri (Green Tea Festival), Chishaku-in. A group of *yamabushi* (itinerant mountain priests) hold a religious service in honor of Kobo Daishi on the anniversary of his birth. 9:00 a.m. to 4:00 p.m.

15 Yasaka Matsuri, Yasaka Shrine. Performances of the *azuma asobi* shrine dance. 10:30 a.m.

25 Gotanshin-sai, Kitano Tenman-gu. The monthly celebration and fair held in honor of Sugawara-no-Michizane. On this occasion, a large ring of miscanthus (Japanese plume grass) is installed around the main gate with anyone passing through it guaranteed freedom from any summer epidemic. The shrine art treasures are on view. About 1,500 festival stalls. From 9:00 a.m.

30 Nagoshi-no-harai, various temples. A service to purify people of the sins that they may have accrued during the first six months of the year. If one passes through the miscanthus ring which is set up on the shrine grounds and eats *minazuki* (rice pudding) and red beans, one can then face the torrid and humid summer months with equanimity. Ebisu Shrine, 6:00 p.m./Heian Shrine, 4:00 p.m./Kamigamo Shrine, 6:00 p.m.

July

7 Seitai-Myojin Reisai, Shiramine Shrine. The Tanabata celebration when the Princess Weaver Star and the Cowherd Star cross paths. The story was taken from a Chinese fairy tale of the separation of two lovers. At this shrine, a traditional folk dance (*komachi odori*) is performed by young girls in 16th century costumes. The festival begins at 3:00 p.m. while the dances begin at 4:30.

7 Tanabata Matsuri, Yasaka Shrine, Kiyomizu-dera and Jishu Shrine. Same as above. At the Jishu Shrine, *kokeshi* dolls are blessed in hopes of a good marriage.

7 Mitarashi Matsuri, Kitano Tenman-gu. Prayers for improvement of artistic skills.

10 Omukae Chochin (Welcoming Lanterns: the beginning of the Gion Festival). Traditionally, costumed celebrants carrying lanterns on long poles to welcome the three sacred *mikoshi* (portable shrines) of the Yasaka Shrine and accompany them on a procession through the center of the city. Three traditional dance groups perform when the procession stops at City Hall on Oike-dori at 6:10 p.m. and then back at the Yasaka Shrine on the return at 8:40 p.m. The procession moves from the Yasaka Shrine along Shijo-dori to Kawaramachi-dori to Oike-dori to Teramachi-dori, and then back along Shijo-dori to the shrine.

10 Mikoshi-arai (Cleansing of the Main Mikoshi), Yasaka Shrine. The main *mikoshi* for the chief deity of the Yasaka Shrine is carried on the shoulders of young men to the Shijo Bridge over the Kamo-gawa River. Here, the chief priest of the shrine purifies the *mikoshi*, after which it is returned to the shrine by the young men. 7:00 p.m. to 8:30 p.m.

13–16 Gion Bayashi. The Gion floats are parked in their respective neighborhoods. Traditional music is performed on each float in the evening. On June 15 and 16, many homes traditionally display their family treasures.

13–15 Obon, many temples. The welcoming home of the spirits of the deceased for their annual visit.

16–17 Yamaboko Junko (Procession of Floats), Gion procession. Leaves Karasuma-shijo at 9:00 a.m. and passes through Shijo-dori, Karasuma-dori, Oike-dori, and Shinmachi-dori ending at around 3:00 p.m.

17 Shinkosai (procession of *mikoshi*), Yasaka Shrine. At 6:00, 6:30 and 6:40 p.m. the three sacred *mikoshi* carried on the shoulders of young men, each following a different route, arrive at Shijo Teramachi where the *mikoshi* remain until July 24.

24 Hanagasa Gyoretsu (Procession of Flowered Sunshades), Yasaka Shrine. A colorful procession of many *geisha*, traditional dancing groups and children, all in ancient costume featuring flowers. Various dances are performed in the Yasaka precincts. The procession starts at Teramachi-Oike at 10:15 a.m., reaches Teramachi-Shijo by 11:00 a.m. and arrives at the Yasaka Shrine by 11:25 a.m.

August

1 Rokusai Nenbutsu Odori (Nenbutsu Prayer Dance), various temples at various dates. This traditional religious dance, attributed to Kuya, dates back more than a millennium. It can be observed at Mibu-dera on the second Sunday of the month at 8:00 p.m., and on the following day at 8:30 p.m. On the third Sunday, it can be seen at 8:30 p.m.

1 Gion Hassaku, Gion Hanamachi. A ceremony in which *maiko* (apprentice *geisha*) and *geisha* show gratitude to their seniors. 11:00 a.m.

4 Kanosai, Kitano Tenman-gu. A memorial service in memory of Emperor Ichijo. 9:00 a.m.

7–10 Manto-e (candle lighting), Rokuharamitsu-ji. Lighting of human-shaped lanterns and religious service to welcome back the souls of the dead during the Obon period. From 8:00 p.m.

7–10 Rokudo-mairi (Pilgrimage to Rokudo), Rokudo Chinno-ji. A part of the Obon ceremonies. According to tradition, the entrance to the Six Regions (Rokudo) of the nether world is located in the area of the Chinno-ji Temple. Legend relates that the temple bell resounds some 10 billion miles, as far as the other world. Thus, thousands crowd into this area to ring the temple bell to call the souls of their dead back to earth for Obon. Obon continues until August 16 when the fires on the five hills about Kyoto light the souls back to the nether world.

8 Rokudo-mairi, Senbon Shaka-do. Welcoming services for ancestral spirits. The Shaka image in the main shrine is shown on this occasion.

8–9 Kamo-gawa Noryo (night stalls along the Kamo-gawa River). Along the western side of the Kamo-gawa River between Oike-dori and Shijo-dori, some 200 stalls are set up for sales from 6:00 p.m. to 11:00 p.m. A folk song concert and stage events take place.

8–10 Toki Matsuri (Pottery Fair), Gojo-dori. Stalls selling ceramics at a discount line both sides of the street to honor the deity of pottery who is enshrined in the Wakamiya Hachiman Shrine on Gojo-dori. The fair runs from early morning until night.

Second Sunday Yuzen Washing, west bank, Kamo-gawa River. A once a year event held at Sanjo-mon when the final process of washing excess dye from Yuzen fabrics takes place as a reminder of a practice used before pollution laws forbade use of the river for this purpose.

9–16 Manto Kuyo (ceremony of lantern lighting), Mibu-dera. Some 800 lanterns are lit in the corridor to the Hondo (Main Hall) to welcome back ancestral souls. Nenbutsu Odori on August 9 at 8:00 p.m. and on August 10 and 16 at 8:30 p.m.

9 and 16 Rokusai Nenbutsu Odori, Mibu-dera. Teaching Buddhist doctrine through a 1,000-year-old ceremony in which a dance in colorful

costumes teaches by means of entertainment. *Kyogen* is also performed. Free.

14–16 Manto-e (candle lighting), Higashi Otani Cemetery. Beginning at 6:00 p.m., each of the thousands of graves in the cemetery are lit with a candle to welcome back the souls of the dead.

15 Manto-e, To-ji. Service to welcome back the souls of the dead.

16 Daimonji Gosan Okuribi (the lighting of fires on the five hills surrounding Kyoto to help guide the souls of the dead back to the nether world). At 8:00 p.m. the fire in the shape of the character for *dai* (great) is lit on the eastern hill, Nyoigatake. The fires on four other mountains to the west and north (Myoho, Funagata, Hidari Daimonji and Torii) are also lit at this time.

20 Rei-taisai, Goryo Shrine. Obon dances.

23–30 Jizo-bon A children's festival in local residential areas (i.e. Nishijin, among others) when lanterns are lit, games are played and parties are held all in honor of Jizo, the patron deity of children.

September

14 Mantosai, Hirano Shrine. Hundreds of paper lanterns illuminate the inner precincts of the shrine from 6:30 p.m.

15 Respect for the Aged Day, a national holiday.

15 Konpira Kushi Matsuri (Comb Festival), Yasui Konpira-gu. An exhibition of old combs is held, and women in costumes of the past parade at 1:00 p.m. Religious services are held for old, used combs brought to the shrine and a "Black Hair Dance" (Kurokami Odori) is held.

15–November 24 (Showing of the Treasures of To-ji). The temple Treasure House is open from 9:00 a.m. to 4:00 p.m. Fee.

Third Sunday Hagi Matsuri (Bush Clover Festival), Nashinoki Shrine. A two-day festival in which a *haiku* contest is held on the first day from noon to 3:30 p.m. Fine paper tablets with *tanzaku* poems inscribed upon them are hung on the bush clover, all dedicated to and for the pleasure of the shrine deities. On the second day there are religious services in the morning. This is followed, after 1:00 p.m., by traditional dances, flower arrangements and *Kyogen* plays. An open-air tea ceremony is also held.

22 or 23 Higan (Autumn Equinox, a national holiday). On this day, the sun sets in the due west, the location of the Buddhist Western

Paradise. Thus, temples hold services for the dead during this period and families tend the graves of their deceased. (*Higan* means "other shore" in reference to the land of the dead.)

21 Rei-taisai, Shiramine Shrine. *Noh* plays by firelight at 3:45 p.m. and 6:00 p.m. Free.

22–23 Shinkosai, Seimei Shrine. Abe-no-Seimei (921–1005), the noted Heian era scholar of astrology, is enshrined here. On September 23, the *mikoshi* holding his spirit is taken through the streets around the shrine by girls in traditional attire, a boys' band and decorated horses. The procession lasts from 1:00 p.m. to 5:00 p.m.

October

1–5 Zuiki Matsuri, Kitano Tenman-gu. A harvest festival to please the gods so that the harvest will be plentiful. A 1,000-year-old festival begun by the emperor Murakami (reigned 946–67). The roof and other portions of the shrine *mikoshi* are decorated with *zuiki* (taro), pumpkin and other vegetables. The *mikoshi* is placed in a temporary shrine at Nishioji-Shimodachiuri. On October 1 at 1:00 p.m. there is a procession of young men carrying three ordinary *mikoshi* on their shoulders around the shrine and then to the *otabishi* (temporary location) where they will remain until October 4.

2 Kenchasai, tea ceremony at the *otabishi* at 10:00 a.m. with explanations by a noted tea master.

4 Kankosai, a procession to return the *mikoshi* to the shrine held from 1:00 p.m. to 5:00 p.m. The *zuiki mikoshi*, covered with vegetables, also returns.

5 Goensai (Last Festival). Eight young women in ancient costumes perform religious dances at the shrine from 3:30 p.m.

All month Treasure viewing, To-ji. The Treasure House is open from 9:00 a.m. to 4:00 p.m. daily.

1–15 Treasure viewing, Ninna-ji. The Ninna-ji Treasure House is open from 9:00 a.m. to 4:00 p.m. daily. Fee.

5–December 20 Autumn treasure viewing, Jotenkaku Museum of the Shokoku-ji. Open from 9:00 a.m. to 4:00 p.m. Fee.

8–November 15 Autumn Exhibition, Ryozen Rekishi-kan. Exhibit of Meiji era personalities and activities. 10:00 a.m. to 4:30 p.m. daily. Fee.

9–13 Treasure viewing, Toji-in.

10 Sports Day, a national holiday.

10 Shuki Konpira Taisai, Yasui Konpira-gu.

Konpira, a half dragon half fish demon, is the patron saint of travelers. At 1:00 p.m. a parade of children in *samurai* outfits accompany the demon.

Mid-month to early November Kamogawa Odori, Pontocho Kaburenjo Theater. *Geisha* dances weekdays at 12:30, 2:20 and 4:10. On Sundays and national holidays at 12:00, 1:40, 3:20 and 5:10. Fee. Additional fee for tea ceremony. All seats reserved.

16 Inzei Amida Kyo-e, Shinnyodo Temple. An annual recitation of a rare sutra which was brought from China by the monk Jikaku Taishi Enju (Ennin). From 9:00 a.m. to 10:30 a.m. A rare mandala, the *jodohensozu*, is on display.

19–21 HatsukaEbisuTaisai, Ebisu Shrine. An annual festival in which a dancer portrays Ebisu and performs a joyous traditional dance on a temporary stage in the shrine grounds. Many stalls on the evenings of October 19 through October 21 enliven the scene.

19 Funaoka Matsuri, Kenkun Shrine. A parade of boys in medieval armor portraying Oda Nobunaga's soldiers as they marched into Kyoto to take control of the government in the 500s. Exhibition of cultural assets from Nobunaga's household. From 11:00 a.m.

22 Jidai Matsuri (Festival of the Ages), Heian Shrine. A procession which illustrates the costumes of residents of Kyoto from the earliest days (794) to the Meiji period of the late 19th century. Reserved seats available on Oike-dori. One of the three great processions in Kyoto each year. There are thousands in the parade, all in costume. Starts from the Imperial Palace at noon and reaches Heian Shrine by 2:20 p.m.

26 Unagi Hojo-e, Mishima Shrine. Autumn prayers for eels eaten during the year and a release of eels into the shrine pond. 2:00 p.m.

29 Yokosai (Ceremony of Poem Recitation), Kitano Tenman-gu. A recitation of the 20 best poems selected from all over Japan. Read by eight descendants of Sugawara-no-Michizane dressed in costumes of Michizane's time. The event recalls the occasion when Michizane wrote a poem to the emperor while in exile. 3:00 p.m.

November

Early November A period when the color of the autumn leaves are at their height. Some of the more attractive areas at this time of year are Kiyomizu-dera, Shinnyo-do, Zenrin-ji/Eikan-do and Nanzen-ji.

1 and 3 Tea Ceremony, Nijo Castle. From

9:30 a.m. to 3:00 p.m., tea ceremony is conducted for the public in the Seiryu-en Garden of Nijo Castle. Fee.

1–10 Gion Odori, Gion Kaikan Theater. Reservations needed for the dance performance by *geisha*. 1:00 and 3:30 p.m.

1–15 Meiji Era Exhibition, Ryozen Rekishi-kan. The museum is open from 10:00 a.m. to 4:30 p.m. Fee.

1–24 Viewing of temple treasures, To-ji. Treasure House open daily from 9:00 a.m. to 4:00 p.m. Fee.

1–30 Viewing of temple treasures, Zenrin-ji/Eikan-do. Treasure House open from 9:00 a.m. to 4:00 p.m.

1–30 Shichi-go-san (Festival for seven, five, and three-year-old children). November 15 is the date for the celebration for children of three (boys and girls), five (boys) and seven (girls). Parents take them to the shrine for blessing, the children often dressed in traditional costumes. The following shrines are particular sites for parents and children: Yasaka Shrine, Kitano Shrine, Ebisu Shrine and Heian Shrine.

1 to December 20 Viewing of temple treasures, Shokoku-ji. Autumn exhibition at the Jotenkaku Art Museum. 9:00 a.m. to 4:00 p.m. Fee.

3 Culture Day, a national holiday.

5–15 Ojuya, Shinnyo-do Temple. A 10 day recitation of the *nenbutsu* in remembrance of the 10 day recitation by Ise-no-kami Tadetani. Nenbutsu service 5:00 p.m. to 7:00 p.m. from November 5 through November 14. On **November 5**, the service runs from 9:00 a.m. to 5:00 p.m. On **November 11**, a tea ceremony is held at 9:00 a.m. Procession at 2:00 p.m. on **November 15**. The Inner Hall is open from 9:00 a.m. to 5:00 p.m. Fee. **Second Sunday** Kuya-do Kaizanki, Kuya-do Temple. Dancing Nenbutsu service in honor of Kuya.

21–22 Opening of the Honmaru Goten (castle keep), Nijo Castle. Special opening of the Honmaru Goten of Nijo Castle from 9:30 to 3:30. The one time a year this palace is open to the public.

21–28 Ho-onko, Higashi Hongan-ji. Memorial services all week for Shinran Shonin, founder of the Jodo Shinshu sect of Buddhism.

23 Labor Thanksgiving Day, a national holiday.

26 Ochatsubo Hokensai (Annual Grand Tea Ceremony), Kitano Tenman-gu. Tea ceremony by major tea masters in memory of Hideyoshi's great tea party held at the Kitano Shrine in 1587. At 11:00 a.m. a service in which the new tea is dedicated and tea containers from famous collections are placed before the gods to please them. Tea ceremony by four major tea houses follow all day long. A display of many kinds of traditional confections from 10:00 a.m. to 3:00 p.m.

December

1–25 Kaomise (Kabuki dramas), Minami-za. The climax of the *kabuki* year. The most famous and capable *kabuki* actors offer samples of their best performances in the traditional grand style.

2–13 Gion Odori, Gion Kaikan Theater. Dance performances by *geisha*.

10 Shimai Konpira (Last Service of the Year), Yasui Konpira-gu. Konpira is the patron of voyages. One can have one's name inscribed on a votive stick which is then placed in a "treasure ship" as protection in future travels and for "sailing" into the new year. The shrine's collection of *ema* (votive tablets) are also shown this day.

13 Ofuku Ume, Kitano Tenman-gu. *Mochi* (rice cakes) made from plums (Japanese apricots) taken from the shrine trees. The sale continues through December 20, and if these *mochi* are eaten on New Year's Day, health and happiness will be ensured throughout the new year.

Third weekend Shimabara Sumiya, Shimabara Kaburenjo Theater. *Mochi* pounding for the making of rice cakes for the New Year festivities takes place in the demonstration hall. Singing and dancing by *geisha* and *maiko*. 10:30 a.m. and 1:30 p.m.

21 Shimai Kobo (Last Service of the Year), To-ji. A special service at the end of the year for Kobo Daishi and the monthly fair are held.

25 Shimai Tenjin (Last Service of the Year), Kitano Tenman-gu. Last service of the year for Sugawara-no-Michizane and the monthly fair are held.

25 Ominugui-shiki, Chion-in. The abbot of the Chion-in polishes the image of Honen with a pure white silk cloth during the service. The prayers offered on this day are meant to eradicate the sins of the past year. 1:00 p.m.

31 Omisoka (Grand Last Day), Chion-in, To-ji, Myoshin-ji, Kiyomizu-dera, Shinnyodo, etc. All old debts are paid and the business and house put in order for the end of the year. At midnight, the temple bells toll 108 times to symbolize the 108 failings of mankind.

Index

All maps are listed in bold type.

Photo Credits

All photographs that appear in this book are by H. Martin and Phyllis G. Martin, except for those on the pages listed below:

Japan Photo Library (JNTO): front cover and pages 14, 20-1, 26, 28, 180, 226-7 (above)

Akira Okado/ JNTO: pages 94, 168, 322

Japan Convention Services, Inc./JNTO: page 102

Kyoto Convention Bureau/JNTO: pages 5 (middle), 16, 115, 211, 332

Kyoto Prefecture/JNTO: page 90-1

Mr. Colin Sinclair/JNTO: pages 146, 147

Q. Sawami/JNTO: pages 4 (middle), 67, 135, 139, 174

Soryofo/JNTO: pages 316-17

Y.Shimizu/JNTO: pages 71, 73 (above)

Yasufumi Nishi/JNTO: pages 241, 306 (bottom)

Kyoto Design (kyoto-design.jp): pages 1, 59, 64, 82, 86, 88, 117, 171, 172, 184-5, 237, 285, 287, 293, 328, 360

Kyoto Photo Collections: pages 4 (left 1), 7, 38, 46, 53, 68, 69, 72, 73 (bottom), 74, 100, 125, 156, 178, 197, 198, 199, 289, 302, 335

Kyoto Photo Library: pages 31, 41, 43, 57, 87, 105, 107, 110, 112, 143, 144, 145, 160, 170, 173, 190, 192, 206, 254, 263, 283, 295, 296, 330, 339, 342-3, 352, 356

Kyoto City Tourism Office: pages 55, 60-1, 62, 92

Kyoto Bunkashimin-kyoku (Kyoto Culture and Public Bureau): page 83

About Tuttle
"Books to Span the East and West"

Our core mission at Tuttle Publishing is to create books which bring people together one page at a time. Tuttle was founded in 1832 in the small New England town of Rutland, Vermont (USA). Our fundamental values remain as strong today as they were then—to publish best-in-class books informing the English-speaking world about the countries and peoples of Asia. The world has become a smaller place today and Asia's economic, cultural and political influence has expanded, yet the need for meaningful dialogue and information about this diverse region has never been greater. Since 1948, Tuttle has been a leader in publishing books on the cultures, arts, cuisines, languages and literatures of Asia. Our authors and photographers have won numerous awards and Tuttle has published thousands of books on subjects ranging from martial arts to paper crafts. We welcome you to explore the wealth of information available on Asia at **www.tuttlepublishing.com**.

Also available from Tuttle Publishing

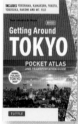

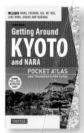

ISBN 978-4-8053-1474-6   ISBN 978-4-8053-0917-9   ISBN 978-4-8053-1066-3   ISBN 978-4-8053-096

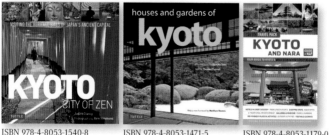

ISBN 978-4-8053-1540-8   ISBN 978-4-8053-1471-5   ISBN 978-4-8053-1179-0   ISBN 978-4-8053-096

Notes